WITHDRAWN
HARVARD LIBRARY
WITHDRAWN

What 1.3 Billion Muslims Really Think: An Answer to a Recent Gallup Study, Based on the World Values Survey

What 1.3 Billion Muslims Really Think: An Answer to a Recent Gallup Study, Based on the World Values Survey

Arno Tausch

Nova Science Publishers, Inc.
New York

Copyright © 2009 by Nova Science Publishers, Inc.

All rights reserved. No part of this book may be reproduced, stored in a retrieval system or transmitted in any form or by any means: electronic, electrostatic, magnetic, tape, mechanical photocopying, recording or otherwise without the written permission of the Publisher.

For permission to use material from this book please contact us:
Telephone 631-231-7269; Fax 631-231-8175
Website: http://www.novapublishers.com

NOTICE TO THE READER

The Publisher has taken reasonable care in the preparation of this book, but makes no expressed or implied warranty of any kind and assumes no responsibility for any errors or omissions. No liability is assumed for incidental or consequential damages in connection with or arising out of information contained in this book. The Publisher shall not be liable for any special, consequential, or exemplary damages resulting, in whole or in part, from the readers' use of, or reliance upon, this material.

Independent verification should be sought for any data, advice or recommendations contained in this book. In addition, no responsibility is assumed by the publisher for any injury and/or damage to persons or property arising from any methods, products, instructions, ideas or otherwise contained in this publication.

This publication is designed to provide accurate and authoritative information with regard to the subject matter covered herein. It is sold with the clear understanding that the Publisher is not engaged in rendering legal or any other professional services. If legal or any other expert assistance is required, the services of a competent person should be sought. FROM A DECLARATION OF PARTICIPANTS JOINTLY ADOPTED BY A COMMITTEE OF THE AMERICAN BAR ASSOCIATION AND A COMMITTEE OF PUBLISHERS.

LIBRARY OF CONGRESS CATALOGING-IN-PUBLICATION DATA

Tausch, Arno, 1951-
  What 1.3 billion Muslims really think : an answer to a recent Gallup study, based on the "World Values Survey" / Arno Tausch.
       p. cm.
  Includes index.
  ISBN 978-1-60692-731-1 (hbk.)
  1. Muslims--Attitudes. 2. Islam--21st century. I. Title.
  DS35.6.T33 2009
  305.6'97--dc22
                        2009002413

Published by Nova Science Publishers, Inc. ✦ New York

The Church regards with esteem also the Moslems. They adore the one God, living and subsisting in Himself; merciful and all- powerful, the Creator of heaven and earth, who has spoken to men; they take pains to submit wholeheartedly to even His inscrutable decrees, just as Abraham, with whom the faith of Islam takes pleasure in linking itself, submitted to God. Though they do not acknowledge Jesus as God, they revere Him as a prophet. They also honor Mary, His virgin Mother; at times they even call on her with devotion. In addition, they await the day of judgment when God will render their deserts to all those who have been raised up from the dead. Finally, they value the moral life and worship God especially through prayer, almsgiving and fasting.

Since in the course of centuries not a few quarrels and hostilities have arisen between Christians and Moslems, this sacred synod urges all to forget the past and to work sincerely for mutual understanding and to preserve as well as to promote together for the benefit of all mankind social justice and moral welfare, as well as peace and freedom.

DECLARATION ON
THE RELATION OF THE CHURCH TO NON-CHRISTIAN RELIGIONS
NOSTRA AETATE
PROCLAIMED BY HIS HOLINESS
POPE PAUL VI
ON OCTOBER 28, 1965

http://www.vatican.va/archive/hist_councils/ii_vatican_council/documents/vat-ii_decl_19651028_nostra-aetate_en.html

CONTENTS

Forward		ix
	Mansoor Moaddel	
Foreword		xiii
	Arno Tausch	
Preface		xvii
Abstract		1
Amitai Etzioni on Islam		3
Anti-Enlightenment Prejudice in a Nutshell: The Covenant of the Islamic Resistance Movement—Hamas		5
Executive Summary and Synopsis of This Study		7
Chapter 1	Introduction	53
Chapter 2	Inglehart and the Consequences: Islam on the Map of Global Value Changes—A First Assessment	69
Chapter 3	Euro-Islam and Europe's Leading Culture: 6.6 Million Homophobes among 229 Million Tax Evaders?	97
Chapter 4	The Global Protest Potential against the "Washington Consexus" (= Liberal Market Economy + Liberal Democracy + Sexual Permissiveness + Secularization)	111
Chapter 5	Another Look at *Asabiyya*: The Social Cohesion of Society	127
Chapter 6	The Northward Migration of Global Intolerance and the Global Tolerance Index	147
Chapter 7	Simon Kuznets Revisited: The U-Shaped Tradeoff between Tolerance and Development	173
Chapter 8	Active Society, Tolerance and Development: The Cross-National Evidence	183

Chapter 9	"Who Are We"?: A Factor Analysis of Global Value Differences	203
Chapter 10	By Way of Conclusion: How Much Secularization Is Necessary, and How Much Secularization Is Recommendable?	241
Appendix I	Analysis of WVS Data: Methodological Notes on Sample Size, Error Probability, Sample Composition, Et Cetera	259
Appendix II	What the Gallup Booklet Unfortunately Does Not Tell You: What Muslims Really Think – The Data from the World Values Survey, with a Full Documentation and the Original SPSS XIV/XV Tables, and the Most Important Survey Results for the Muslim Global Sample from the World Values Survey	303
Appendix III	IBN Khaldoun Revisited: A Factor Analytical Model of Central World Values Survey Indicators	379
Appendix IV	The Active Society Index	393
Appendix V	Islam and Enlightenment: The Possible Way Ahead— A Quantitative View; the Cross-National Determinants of Economic Growth, the Active Society, Global Tolerance, Traditional Values, the Intransparent Society and *Asabiyya*	405
Appendix VI	Mapping the World Civilizations: Is Islam Compatible with Enlightenment? A Factor Analytical Model	411
Appendix VII	Secularization—How Much? Some Further Materials on the Scylla and Charybdis on the Path to Modernization and the Governance of Value Change	485
Appendix VIII	Muslims Are No Security Risk in a Multicultural Europe: A World Values Survey Comparison of European Union, EEA and EFTA Country Opinions on Major Issues and Social Realities by the Major Religious Groups in Europe	509
About the Author		581
Index		583

FOREWORD

Mansoor Moaddel

Muslim attitudes toward modernity have become a subject of an unrelenting controversy in Western media. The issues are whether the Islamic publics value democracy, are tolerant of other faiths, support gender equality, and, for the Muslims living in Europe, whether they are willing to assimilate into the continent's democratic culture. The background to this controversy is more than fifty years of religious extremism, political violence, and revolutionary upheavals in Islamic countries that have taken the form of either revolutionary Shi'ism spearheaded by the ruling clerics in Iran or Sunni extremism led by al-Qaeda. The horrific act of violence by Muslim terrorists on the American soil on September 11, 2001; the Madrid commuter train bombing on March 11, 2004; the London public transportation bombing on July 7, 2005; and the gruesome beheadings by fanatical groups in Afghanistan, Iraq, and Pakistan have all given rise to prejudicial and stereotypical thinking about Muslims, and about Euro-Muslims in particular. Essentially, many Westerners have come to question whether Islamic culture is at odds with a modern multicultural, democratic society. And worst, some simply view Islam as the source of Muslim extremism and terrorism.

The history of Islam, however, reveals the development of a much more open and moderate society -- one that stands in remarkable contrast to the behavior and doctrine of the Muslim extremists who make current headlines. Historians have found that, compared to historical Christianity, classical Islamic shari'a took a more egalitarian orientation toward women, was more accepting of the rights of religious minorities living under its rule (including Jews), and was less tolerant of slavery. Moreover, in historical Islam the utility of secular politics was recognized, and in the debates over the construction of the modern political order, Muslim theologians-cum-political theorists used their distinctive religious reasoning in support of a constitutional government. As a result, the Islamic movements of the late 19th and early 20th centuries favored democratic rule-making. For example, Muslim modernists in late 19th-century Egypt argued that Islam was thoroughly capable of adapting itself to the changing conditions of every age, the hallmark of the perfect Muslim community being law and reason; Islamic theologians in Iran supported the Fundamental Law in the Iranian Constitutional Revolution of 1905 that called for democratic legislation; and leading Muslim thinkers and activists in early 20th-century Algeria went as far as demanding the separation of religion and politics.

The rise of religious extremism over the past five decades is thus anomalous to the historical tradition of Islamic countries. This fact, however, may bring little comfort to today's Westerners, many of whom feel disdain for the social restrictions imposed by some forms of Islamic fundamentalism and threatened by the deadly hostilities of Muslim extremism. Moreover, the past Muslim glory and associated achievements in the arts, scholarship, science, and technology seem remote from the serious problems in contemporary Muslim societies that have given rise to terrorism. After all, the death and social devastation caused by the rise of Nazism in Germany and fascism in Italy during the 1930s are not easier to bear or comprehend when considered in light of the vast historical contributions of Germany and Italy to human civilization and the making of the modern world. Indeed, these authoritarian ideologies seem to thrive in opposition to the democratic societies that preceded them. Thus, scholars looking for answers to why Nazism and fascism took root in Europe have often studied the attitudes and perceptions of the Italian and German publics who supported these extreme ideologies. The same fruitful approach serves well when we consider the rise in Muslim extremism and its relationship to values in the larger Muslim society. We want to know: Do most of today's Muslims eschew violence and religious extremism? Do they favor social modernism over traditionalism? How knowledgeable are they about sociopolitical issues in their nations and elsewhere? Do they support their leaders? What are their outlooks on religion, family, work, national identity? More specifically, how do they feel about democracy, gender equality, homosexuality, religious freedom? How do they make sense of the structures, issues, and events they encounter? And do Muslims the world over share values that distinguish them from non-Muslims?

Using findings from the World Values Survey -- which gathers data from more than 80 countries on the political and social values of the world's Muslim communities -- Arno Tausch tackles these questions. His objective is ambitious, as he tries to settle the debate on how Muslim sociopolitical values across the globe align with modern ideologies. He systematically assesses Muslim attitudes toward democracy, gender equality, family, and other major social institutions. He operationalizes the concept of *assabyyat,* or the tradition of tribal Arab social solidarity, to assess the degree of values cohesion among European Muslim communities. He also assesses Muslim and non-Muslim involvement in voluntary organizations, or the extent of their active social engagement. He views volitional participation in religious or secular activities that promote social good as essential to maintaining a multicultural society. Tausch concludes that, overall, Muslims are value-conservative, family-oriented, and supportive of democracy.

One can only applaud Tausch's impressive work. He has demonstrated that such an important social issue as Muslim attitudes toward modernity may be resolved, and the debate on interfaith relations settled, by means of objective facts—the data collected by scientific methods. Nonetheless, one crucial question remains. If the great majority of the Islamic publics eschew political violence, why haven't they responded forcefully against this terrorism? After all, innocent men, women, and children are slaughtered by misguided suicide bombers; powerless captives and political opponents are hideously beheaded in front of the camera; and billions of dollars worth of property are destroyed—all in the name of Islam and God's handsome rewards for the perpetrators in the paradise. Where is the Muslim outrage against these horrors?

We certainly have seen concerted opposition among contemporary Islamic communities to Western activities deemed offensive. When the U.S. president used the word "crusade" in an ill-prepared speech, when a Danish cartoonist drew an unflattering caricature of Muhammad, and when British author Salmon Rushdie published his novel *Satanic Verses*, Islamic communities in different parts of the globe were mobilized in indignation against the West. The American flag and effigies of the U.S. president were burned publicly, the Imams and Western-educated politicians alike in certain Arab countries called for the boycott of Danish products, and Ayatollah Khomeini issued a fatwa calling for the execution of Salmon Rushdie. In regard to the last, did these indignant Muslims fail to notice that this was the same ayatollah who had just ordered the execution of several thousand political prisoners in Iran?

Muslim ownership of the problems of political violence and terrorism that have grown in their midst is not just the right thing to do in order to calm the anxiety of their non-Muslim neighbors. It is also crucial in their efforts to establish a better—more democratic, empowering, and humane—society. When Muslims act in unison against violence, as they have done on numerous occasions in the past, other changes will follow. For example, following the massacre of Christians in Syria in 1860, Syrian citizens collectively condemned the violence and instigated discussions of the moral stagnation and ignorance that promoted sectarian hatred -- a dialectic that intensified efforts to reform and rebuild the country's educational system. This recognition of the domestic roots of backwardness and political violence, we may argue, acted as a buffer against the repetition of religious violence in the country for another one hundred years.

For scholars of Islam, it is certainly important to analyze Muslim political attitudes and Muslim perspectives on Western influences in particular. A perplexing problem, however, is to understand the cognitive and emotional factors that have thus far hindered the Islamic publics from recognizing and confronting the religious extremism and accompanying violence that plague their societies. Without this recognition, alas, the problem of violence may continue.

—Mansoor Moaddel
Eastern Michigan University

FOREWORD

Arno Tausch

This quantitative study on global cultures, which in a way expands, contradicts and puts the recent data, presented by the in many ways controversial Gallup Institute (Esposito/ Mogahed, 2008) into a more global perspective, now appears for the first time.

A word about locations: this book was written in Vienna, Austria, which in various ways enters the intellectual itinerary of the empirical research, presented here.

1) As early as 1674, Vienna University already began to teach oriental languages, and in 1754, the "Oriental Academy", a kind of state think-tank on "oriental questions", was founded. Further milestones of a peaceful coexistence of the world religions in Europe, emanating from Austria, were the Austrian "Toleranzpatent" *(Edict of Tolerance)* of 1781/82 and the "Staatsgrundgesetz" *(Basic law on the general rights of citizens)* of 1867. In *1912*, the *"Law dated 15th July, 1912, referring to the recognition of the adherents of Islam according to the Hanafite rite as [a] religious community"*[1], was a further milestone of Western tolerance vis-à-vis Islam, for it was the first time that a major Western country recognized Islam as an official religious group[2].

---

[1] http://www.univie.ac.at/veil/Home3/index.php?id=22,0,0,1,0,0. For further references, see also Schmidinger/ Larisse, 2008

[2] Let us quote here from the United States Department of State Religious Freedom Report 2007, released on September 14, 2007: The status of religious organizations is governed by the 1874 Law on Recognition of Churches and by the 1998 Law on the Status of Religious Confessional Communities, which establishes the status of "confessional communities." Religious organizations are divided into three legal categories (listed in descending order of status): Officially recognized religious societies, religious confessional communities, and associations. Each category of organizations possesses a distinct set of rights, privileges, and responsibilities. Recognition as a religious society under the 1874 law has wide-ranging implications, such as the authority to participate in the mandatory church contributions program, to provide religious instruction in public schools, and to bring religious workers into the country to act as ministers, missionaries, or teachers. Under the 1874 law, religious societies have "public corporation" status. This status permits religious societies to engage in a number of public or quasi-public activities that are denied to confessional communities and associations. The Government provides financial support for religious teachers at both public and private schools to religious societies but not to other religious organizations. The Government provides financial support to private schools run by any of the 13 officially recognized religious societies: the Roman Catholic Church, the Protestant churches (Lutheran and Presbyterian, called "Augsburger" and "Helvetic" confessions), Islamic

2) But Vienna has also been the place, where one of the first path-breaking studies of empirical sociology, *"Die Arbeitslosen von Marienthal. Ein soziographischer Versuch über die Wirkungen langandauernder Arbeitslosigkeit. (Paul F. Lazarsfeld, Hans Zeisel) Hirzel, Leipzig 1933, later: Suhrkamp, Frankfurt a.M. 1975, ISBN 3-518-10769-0, latest English language edition: Marienthal: the sociology of an unemployed community by Marie Jahoda; Paul Felix Lazarsfeld; Hans Zeisel. New Brunswick, N.J.; London: Transaction, 2002"* was written by Paul Lazarsfeld, who emigrated during the darkest times of Europe in 1933 to the United States of America. Actually, Lazarsfeld's "Marienthal" is just 16.7 kilometers by car from my present home in Lower Austria. Thus, nothing would look more logical than to apply methods of empirical social research to questions of the social realities of the Muslim communities in Europe and in the world.

3) Vienna before the Shoa and the Anschluss was also the city of the global humanist and Muslim convert Dr. Baron Omar Rolf von Ehrenfels (28 April 1901–1980, conversion in 1927), who was an Austrian anthropologist and orientalist, and who became a Muslim refugee from the Nazi terror in 1938. During the second part of his life, which he spent in his country of asylum, India from 1938 onwards, he became a leading researcher on Islam and an early champion of Muslim feminism around the globe. Only now, the importance of his theories becomes fully appreciated.

4) Last, but not least, Vienna before 1938 had its own Sephardic synagogue, which was called "Turkish Temple", built in 1887, and destroyed during the November Pogrom of 1938 by the Nazi mob. The Vienna Sephardic community was founded in 1736. The descendants of the expulsions and persecutions in Spain 1492, which found their asylum in Turkey under Sultan Bāyezīd II "Veli" (the Holy), kept their customs and their language ("Djudeo-Espanyol"), and the pleasant memories of Turkish tolerance and Turkish hospitality during all these decades and centuries. Their story, which ended in the *Shoa* in Auschwitz, Bergen-Belsen … is a stark reminder of the fact, that "Europe" not always can claim to be associated with "tolerance" and hold up the claim that "Islam" is associated with "intolerance" … At this juncture, it is also worthwhile to recall Behiç Erkin (1876 to 1961) Turkish army officer, first director of the Turkish State Railways, Minister of Public Works, Turkish diplomat and co-founder of the Turkish intelligence service *Milli Emniyet Hizmeti* (MAH), the National Security Service, which became after 1965 the *Milli Istihbarat Teskilati* (MİT), National Intelligence Organization, who saved during his tenure as Turkish Ambassador to Paris from 1939 to 1943 20,000 Jewish lives from the Holocaust by providing them with Turkish passports and organizing 20 exit trains to freedom in Turkey across Europe at times of war.

The author would like to thank his family for all support that he received. His wife Krystyna, as always, presented him with insightful and often challenging questions and perspectives of his interpretation of the facts.

---

community, Old Catholic Church, Jewish community, Eastern Orthodox Church (Russian, Greek, Serbian, Romanian, and Bulgarian), Church of Jesus Christ of Latter-day Saints (Mormons), New Apostolic Church, Syrian Orthodox Church, Armenian Apostolic Church, Methodist Church of Austria, Buddhist community, and Coptic Orthodox Church. http://www.state.gov/g/drl/rls/irf/2007/90163.htm.

My thanks also go to my colleagues from the Departments of Political Science at Innsbruck and Vienna University, and especially also to the Department of European Union Coordination (V/1) and the Directorate-General for European, International and Social Policies at the Federal Ministry of Social Affairs and Consumer Protection of the Republic of Austria in Vienna. Thinking about and working on the "Grundsatzfragen" ("basic issues") of European Integration these days becomes a highly complex and multicultural task, and data collection and analysis is part of the process to analyze European social realities and the mechanisms of social exclusion.

Upholding a perspective of Enlightenment, Rationalism and Dialogue of the major global civilizations will be an important task in Europe in the years ahead.

Let us quote here Ehrenfels:

> "The essential features of Islam, which impressed me most and attracted me to this great religion are as follows:-
>
> 1) The Islamic teaching of successive revelation implies in my opinion the following: The source from, which all the great world religions sprang is one. The founders of these great paths, prepared for peace-seeking mankind, gave witness to one and the same basic divine teaching. Acceptance of one of these paths means search for Truth in Love;
> 2) Islam, in essence, means peace in submission to the Eternal Law.
> 3) Islam is, historically speaking, the last founded among the great world religions on this planet.
> 4) Prophet Muhammad is the messenger of Islam and is thus the last in the sequence of great religious world-prophets.
> 5) The acceptance of Islam and the path of the Muslims by a member of an older religion thus means as little rejection of his former religion, as for instance the acceptance of Buddha's teachings meant the rejection of Hinduism to the Indian co-nationals of Buddha. It was only later that schools of thought within Hinduism rejected the Buddhist way as heretical. The differences of religions are man-made. The unity is divine. The teachings of the Holy Qur'an stress this basic unity. To witness it, means acceptance of a spiritual fact, which is common to all men and women.
> 6) The spirit of human brotherhood under the all-encompassing divine fatherhood is much stressed in Islam and not hampered by concepts of racialism or sectarianism, be it of linguistic, historic-traditionalistic, or even dogmatic nature.
> 7) This concept of divine fatherly love, however, includes also the motherly aspect of Divine love, as the two principal epithets of God indicate" Al-Rahman - Al-Rahim, both being derived from the Arabic root rhm. The symbolic meaning of this root equals Goethe's Das Ewing-Weibliche Zieht uns hinan, whilst its primary meaning is womb.
> 8) [...] In this spirit the prophet gave these unforgettable words to his followers: "Paradise lies at the feet of the Mother." http://www.geocities.com/embracing_islam/ehrenfels.html

Arno Tausch, September 2008
Vienna and Leopoldsdorf near Vienna

PREFACE

This book is based on the quantitative, multivariate analysis of the World Values Survey data from more than 80 countries around the globe on the political and social values of the world's Muslim communities by international comparison. Global Muslims and the Muslim communities in Western democracies are value-conservative, family-oriented, but supportive of democracy. This study takes up the idea of "Asabiyya" ("social cohesion"), inherent in classic Arab historiography, first described by Ibn Chaldun (1332 to 1406) in his important work "Muqaddimah". Is "modernization" without "spiritual values" possible in the long run? As a way out from the modernization trap of societies, characterized by large-scale social anomaly, the "active society" of volunteer organization work is the best societal medicine against this kind of value decay, which is so common in countries like France, Brazil, or most of East Central Europe and the former USSR. An active form of religious or non-religious humanism, which provides a noble motivation for such activities as volunteer social services, is a very necessary precondition for social cohesion in the twenty-first century.

ABSTRACT

This book is based on the quantitative, multivariate analysis of the World Values Survey data from more than 80 countries around the globe on the political and social values of the world's Muslim communities by international comparison.

For the first time, a fully documented and comprehensive world-wide representative analysis of

- Global Muslim perceptions of life
- Global Muslim perceptions on problems of the environment
- Global Muslim attitudes to work
- Global Muslim attitudes on the family
- Global Muslim opinions on politics and society
- Global Muslim opinions on religion and morale
- Global Muslim opinions on national identity
- Global Muslim Sociodemographics

is thus available to the public. By and large, the study comes to the conclusion that global Muslims and also the Muslim communities in Western democracies are value-conservative, family-oriented, but supportive of democracy.

Which perspectives then are available to analyze the facts? The study takes up the idea of *Asabiyya* ("social cohesion"), inherent in classic Arab historiography, first described by Ibn Chaldun (1332 to 1406) in his important work *Muqaddimah*.

Is "modernization" without "spiritual values" possible in the long run? Starting from the sophisticated multivariate analysis of the World Values Survey data (factor analysis), it is shown that two factors are decisive in understanding global value change: a continuum of "traditional versus secular", and a continuum "cheating versus active society". *Asabiyya* is defined then empirically by the residuals from the factor scores of "traditional versus secular", and "cheating versus active society". *Asabiyya* in the twenty-first century, as a way out from the modernization trap of societies, characterized by large-scale social anomaly, is a high secularism combined with a high active society score, thus avoiding the "modernization trap" of an increasingly secular society, which accepts cheating on taxes; accepts government benefits fraud and taking bribes.

According to the empirical analysis of this book, the "active society" of volunteer organization work is the best societal medicine against this kind of value decay, which is so common in countries like France, Brazil, or most of East Central Europe and the former USSR. An active form of religious or non-religious humanism, which provides a noble motivation for such activities as volunteer social services, is a very necessary precondition for social cohesion in the twenty-first century.

Our study also constructs various indices of global value change and also performs a factor analysis of global value differences. Without active society, multicultural societies will fail. The study also quantitatively compares European values and paths of secularization, and cautiously argues in favor of the rediscovery of the classic democratic workers' parties agenda of Europe during the pre-war and post-World-War II period in large sections of the Muslim world.

JEL-class.: *C43, F15, F5, Z12*

Keywords: *C43* - Index Numbers and Aggregation; *F15* - Economic Integration; *F5* - International Relations and International Political Economy; *Z12* - Religion

AMITAI ETZIONI ON ISLAM

Islam is no different than the other major religions. For every Muslim who favors a religious war, there are many who see jihad as a spiritual journey of self-improvement. For every Muslim who blindly accepts the rulings of the mullahs, there are many more who favor communal consultation—the notion of shura. Hence, rather than vainly trying to replace religious education with secular teaching, the issue should be what kind of religious education is made available.

Teaching Western, secular ethics, such as the moral theories of Immanuel Kant and John Rawls, will not get one much traction in large parts of the devout Muslim world. Instead, the best remedy to extremist, violence-prone interpretations of Islam is a moderate, albeit religious, one. Muslims accept that while there is the text of the Quran, there are also records of the words and deeds of the prophet known as hadith. These different texts open the door to varying interpretations of Islam rather than simply going "by the book," tolerating only one strict and rigid interpretation. This is especially true about the status of women, which is much less restricted in some texts than in others. Also, moderates hold that although there are three major "Abrahamic" religions, in, which respectively Muhammed, Christ and Moses play a key role, all are to be respected, as those of "people of the book."

In the United States we hear a largely liberal chorus arguing that value education should take place only at home. However, given the beleaguered state of the family in much of the modern world—and the cacophony of commercial and sexual voices that youngsters are increasingly exposed to—schools should play a role in the proper upbringing of the next generation. Religion is the major source of such education, especially in large parts of the Muslim world. It follows that the choice the United States and its allies often face—to the extent that they are involved in reforming Muslims schools in the first place—is not between Islamic or secular education, but rather between Islamist and moderate religious education.
http://www.huffingtonpost.com/amitai-etzioni/is-secularism-the-best-an_b_44911.html

Anti-Enlightenment Prejudice in a Nutshell: The Covenant of the Islamic Resistance Movement—Hamas

"The enemies have been planning expertly and thoroughly for a long time in order to achieve what they have achieved, employing those means, which affect the course of events. They strove to accumulate huge financial resources, which they used to realize their dream.

With money they have taken control of the world media—news agencies, the press, publishing houses, broadcasting services, et cetera. With money they sparked revolutions in various countries around the world in order to serve their interests and to reap profits. They were behind the French Revolution and the Communist Revolution and [they are behind] most of the revolutions about which we hear from time to time here and there. With money they have formed secret organizations, all over the world, in order to destroy [those countries'] societies and to serve the Zionists' interests, such as the Freemasons, the Rotary Clubs, the Lions, the Sons of the Covenant [i.e., B'nei B'rith], et cetera. All of these are organizations of espionage and sabotage. With money they were able to take control of the colonialist countries, and [they] urged them to colonize many countries so that they could exploit their resources and spread moral corruption there.

There is no end to what can be said about [their involvement in] local wars and world wars. They were behind World War I, through, which they achieved the destruction of the Islamic Caliphate, reaped material profits, took control of numerous resources, obtained the Balfour Declaration, and established the League of the United Nations [sic] so as to rule the world through this organization. They were [also] behind World War II, through, which they reaped enormous profits from commerce in war materials and paved the way for the establishment of their state. They [also] suggested the formation of the United Nations and the Security Council to replace the League of the United Nations [sic] and to rule the world through this [new organization]. Wherever there is war in the world, it is they who are pulling the strings behind the scenes. "Whenever they ignite the fire of war, Allah extinguishes it. They strive to spread evil in the land, but Allah does not love those who do evil." (*Koran*, 5:64) http://www.memri.de/uebersetzungen_analysen/2006_01_JFM/hamas_charta_17_02_06.html

EXECUTIVE SUMMARY AND SYNOPSIS OF THIS STUDY

Only a quick glance at the international media will already convince everybody that intercultural questions are THE issue of global politics in the early twenty-first century.

Here are the three most important results about global Muslim opinions and living conditions for global decision makers:

MAIN RESULT

- Muslims are value-conservative, but supportive of democracy.
- They want more state action.
- Radical minorities are only minorities, and there are various groups of discontent, not just the radical Islamists.

Our analysis yielded the following global results:

The Muslim silent majority

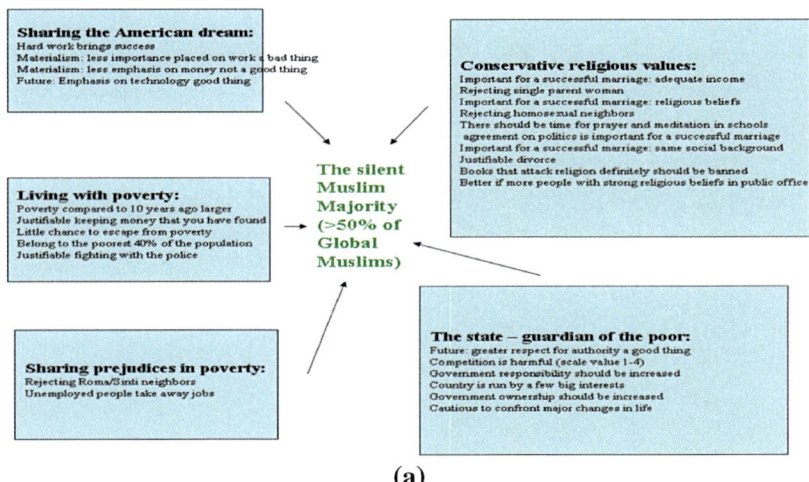

(a)

The noisy minorities:

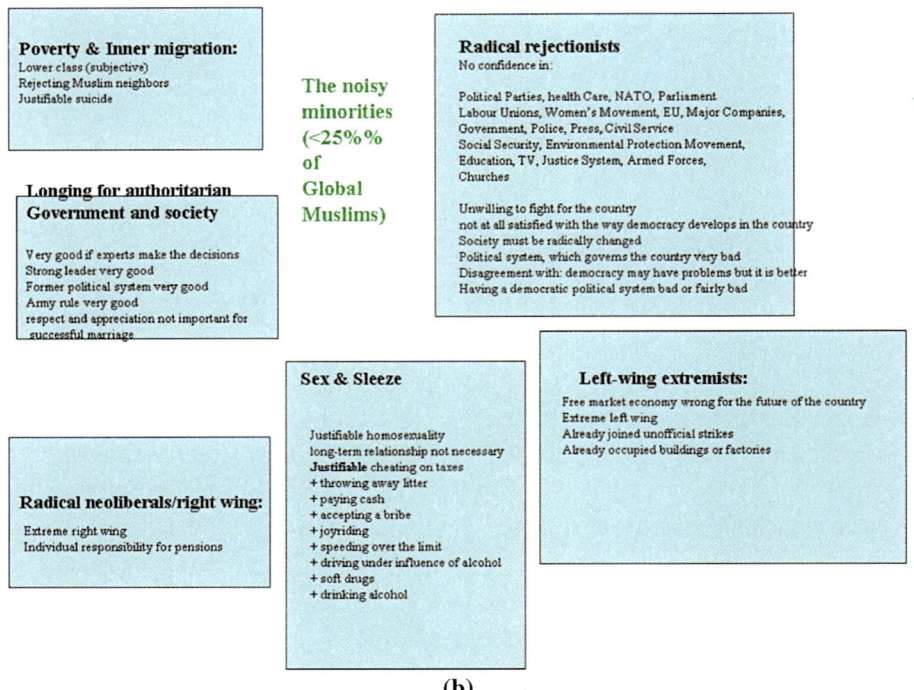

(b)

Source (a) and (b): Our own compilations, based on the official Website of the *World Values Survey (WVS)* Project, http://www.worldvaluessurvey.org./. Our calculations are based on the WVS data (Download survey data files) and the SPSS XIV statistics program, Innsbruck University. All waves of the WVS surveys are integrated into the data file. To weight for country population size, we used the WVS routine: weights 1000. The sample comprised 204303 representative interview partners with available data on religious confession, gender and age of the respondent.

EUROPEAN ISLAM

- There were some important success stories in integration policy, but also a lot went wrong: the European 15 Million Muslims are certainly value-conservative, and six million are openly homophobic and thus would not support EU-policies against discrimination on the grounds of sexual orientation.
- Three million hold the view of the priority of God's laws over man-made laws.
- One million already joined in some form of radical action.
- The violent Islamist focus is to be estimated at around 100,000 to 200,000 persons.

Executive Summary and Synopsis of This Study 9

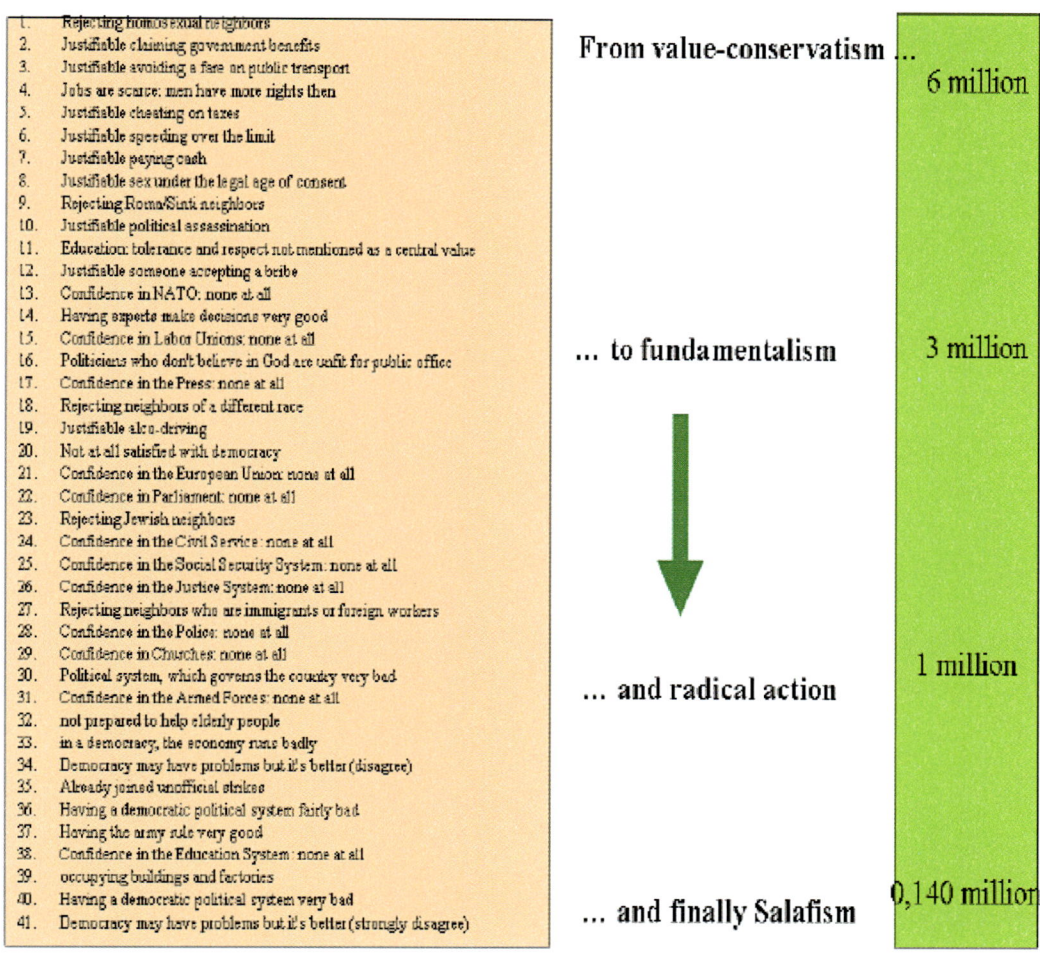

Source: Our own compilations, based on the official Website of the *World Values Survey*, http://www.worldvaluessurvey.org/

EUROPEAN YEAR OF INTERCULTURAL DIALOGUE

In Europe, which for historical reasons already has very long common borders with the Muslim world, the existence of a minority of some 15 million Muslims makes the question of "Intercultural Dialogue" all important. Europe only slowly seems to come to terms with this challenge. Among the positive measures, one has to single out the "European Year of Intercultural Dialogue". Slowly, but surely, the statistical and bureaucratic apparatus of the European institutions begins to react to the new challenges and starts to collect statistics on "multiculturalism".

RESEARCH DESIGN

This study uses an array of quantitative methods to come to terms with global values, global value change, and the position of Muslims in these changing global value maps. So finally, one might argue, the *behavioral revolution* is beginning to be firmly established in the debate about "global Islam" and the future of the European continent. Ronald T. Inglehart, Jytte Klausen, Dalia Mogahed, Mansoor Moaddel, Pippa Norris, and Thorleif Pettersson introduced the necessary empirical elements into a value-laden debate, otherwise characterized by such terms as "leading culture" or "guiding culture".

Absurd, as it may seem at first sight, there are hardly any international comparative data on values across cultures – if it were not for the World Values Survey. A generation of political scientists, headed by Michigan University's Ronald T. Inglehart, studied global and Muslim values for more than two decades now and even made their data freely available on the Internet (http://www.worldvaluessurvey.org/). Their gigantic project, analyzing global values and global value change in now over 80 countries is based on advanced social survey methodology, and uses a questionnaire and sampling methods, which are unparalleled in the social science profession.

To begin with, the almost 30,000 interviews with representative Muslims in 80 countries are not faring badly with the 50,000 Muslim interview partners, surveyed by Gallup in their in many ways highly controversial survey in 35 countries. The World Values Survey, in addition, neatly portrays the opinions, anxieties and the social situation of the Muslim minorities in western countries, although small sample sizes caution against too rapid conclusions.

INGLEHART AND BEYOND

Our *re-analysis* re-iterates the basic optimism inherent in the writings by Inglehart (2003), Inglehart and Baker (2000), and Inglehart and Norris (2003). *Global Muslims might be "conservative" in their attitudes on family, gender and sexuality, but certainly "Islam" cannot be blamed as such for a rejection of democracy or for a tendency to generally support political violence.* The World Values Survey data, re-analyzed here, are in fact a dire warning to those who think that Europe is THE home of democratic stability and non-violence *per se*, and that European values are uniform, democratic and non-violent. The percentage of those people who disagree or strongly disagree with the statement that democracy may have problems, but it's better, is 12.2% for the global Muslim population, and thus comparable to the percentages among global Protestants (13.4%), Sikhs (12.3%), Jews (11.8%), Buddhists (11.7%), Roman Catholics (10.6%) or Hindus (8.4%). It is true that some Muslim countries, like Iran, Indonesia, Saudi Arabia and Kyrgyzstan figure prominently among those nations, whose population is basically skeptical about democracy, but one should not forget that also the EU-27 member countries UK, Romania, Bulgaria and Hungary are placed worse than Pakistan, Iraq, and Turkey on this scale.

When people are asked whether they (strongly) agree or disagree with the sentence that using violence to pursue political goals is never justified, only 5.2% of global Muslims strongly disagreed with the statement and another 7.4% of global Muslims disagreed. It is really stunning to observe that global Roman Catholics, Orthodox and Protestants are much more prepared to concede that using violence to pursue political goals is justified. Thus it is then no surprise that among the most violence-condoning nations on earth we find the Dominican Republic, Peru, the EU-member Spain, Venezuela, and the EU-newcomers

Romania and Lithuania, and not just the Islamic Conference member with a religiously mixed population, Nigeria.

The population in the Muslim EU-candidate country Turkey is far less inclined towards condoning the use of violence for political ends than in the EU-27-core country Sweden, and Bangladesh and Azerbaijan are two shining examples of majority Muslim political cultures, almost totally rejecting the use of violence for political purposes.

Putting things further into perspectives, it also emerges from the WVS data that yes; indeed, many Muslims believe that it is better for society that immigrants do maintain their customs and traditions. 67.5% of global Muslims think in such a way. But global Hindus (68.1%) and global Jewry (67.5%) thinks likewise, just as Buddhists (61.1%) and the Orthodox (58.4%) do. By contrast, only a minority of Catholics (41.6%) and Protestants (29.9%) hold such a belief.

One of the hardest tasks in the fight against global terrorism will be to convince global Muslims, worldwide that not Jews, but dictatorships are their enemy, and that in comparison with the unprecedented religious freedom Muslims enjoy in Western countries, it would be worthwhile to start a real debate on Muslim religious freedom in countries like China, Myanmar and others, where there are indeed just grievances to be observed about the repression of Muslim religious freedoms.

The global existence of "Muslim Calvinist attitudes", as reflected in the data of this publication, is a sign of hope; and data like the ones, reproduced in this book, will contribute to focus the Muslim debate on what should be the real center of the debate: not the "evil West", and not the "evil Jews", are the enemy, and the culture of Enlightenment, Democracy and Social Market economy are the true allies of Muslim humanism.

In his Palgrave/Macmillan essay in 2007, Inglehart (2007) even ventured for the first time into the tricky and politically highly charged and – many people will assume – even politically incorrect field of the quantitative comparison of the worldviews of Islamic publics in a global perspective. Inglehart for one shows with his empirical data and methods, which we will discuss at length in our "*Asabiyya*" chapter, that there is a strong distinction between mainstream Muslim societies on the one hand and post-Communist Muslim societies on the other hand. Inglehart's preferred method of factor analyzing the WVS data and interpreting the outcomes as representing the *dimensions self-expression* (combining acceptance of postmaterial values, female leaders, women in the work-sphere, accomplishment as the prime aim of work, homosexuality justifiable, no xenophobia, happiness, and favoring environmental protection) and *rational values* (no great importance given to religion, obedience no value any more in education, weak national pride, not parent's but my own pride is important, acceptance of divorce, abortion, free trade, and no importance for the respect of authority) again was applied, with self-expression on the x-axis and rational values on the y-axis. Zimbabwe, Morocco and Jordan are in the lowest, left-hand-corner of such scales, because these countries are presumed to be combining low self expression values and low rational, secular values, while countries like Sweden, Norway, Denmark and the Netherlands are the "superstars" of modernization, i.e., combining self-expression and rationality. But on the path of modernization, there are several contradictions to be solved – the United States, for example, is highly placed on the self-expression dimension, but relatively low on the rational dimension (about the same level as India (!)). The Muslim ex-Communist countries are highly rational/secular, about as equal as France and the United Kingdom, but they are still far behind in the development of their self-expression.

Inglehart then calculates the mean results of his surveys for 11 Protestant European, four Confucian, 13 Orthodox, 14 Catholic, seven English-speaking, three South Asian, 14 Islamic, 11 Latin American and six African surveys and looks at the differences in the mean responses to the following questions (abridged formulations)

- Is God important
- Proud of nationality
- Respect for authority
- Autonomy index
- Is abortion never justifiable
- Mean score secular/traditional scale

He also looks into

- Differences in percentages per population, postmaterialists minus materialists
- Very happy
- Tolerance for homosexuals
- Signed petitions
- Trust people
- Disagree: men make better politicians
- Self-expression versus survival scale

While Inglehart admits that there are predominantly "conservative" traditional family values prevalent in the Muslim world, these countries are not alone. In terms of self-expression, more economically advanced Muslim countries are well on their way towards modernity. Inglehart also looked into the acceptance rates of democracy and gender equality. While Muslim countries are now very strongly favoring democracy, their acceptance of "modern" gender roles is predictably lower.

In our work, the focus is on the construction of indices of an

- Active society index
- Global opinion structures, both at the level of aggregate national results as well as at the level of global citizens and the global *Umma* of Muslim believers
- Global tolerance
- Sexual permissiveness index

EURO-ISLAM: MYTH AND REALITY

Main results on Euro-Islam

- Poor
- Pro-European
- Value-conservative

- Needed: integration into the EU's anti-discrimination policy vis-à-vis "other" multi-cultural and discriminated groups

Educational attainment

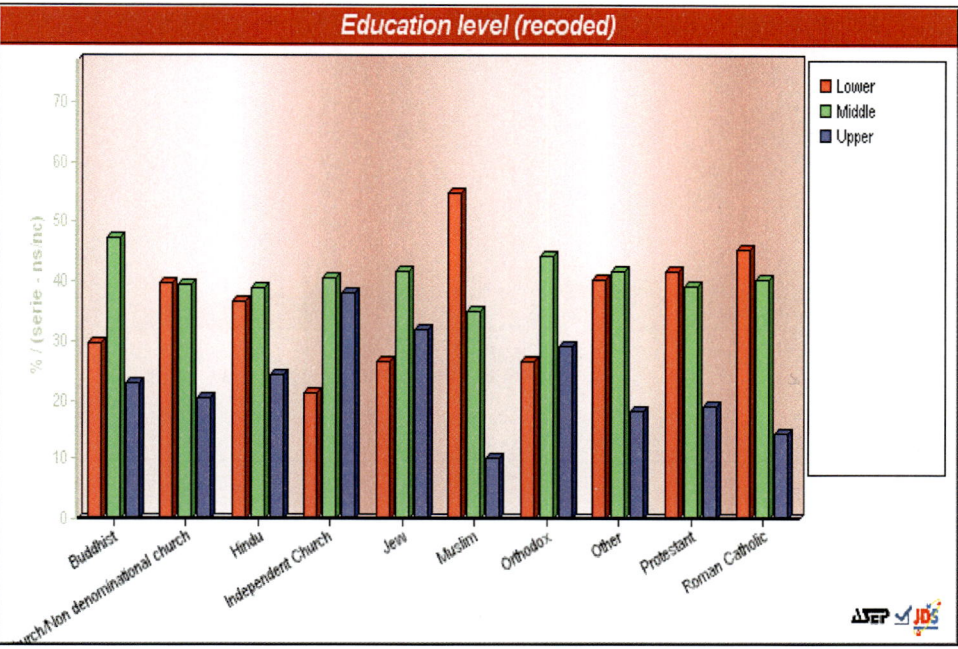

Socio-economic status

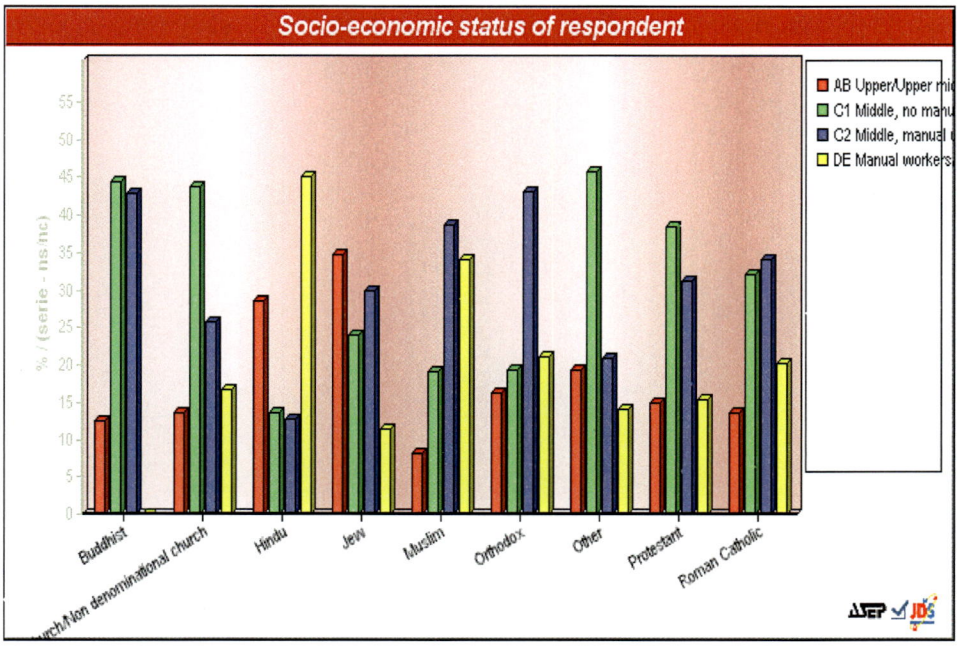

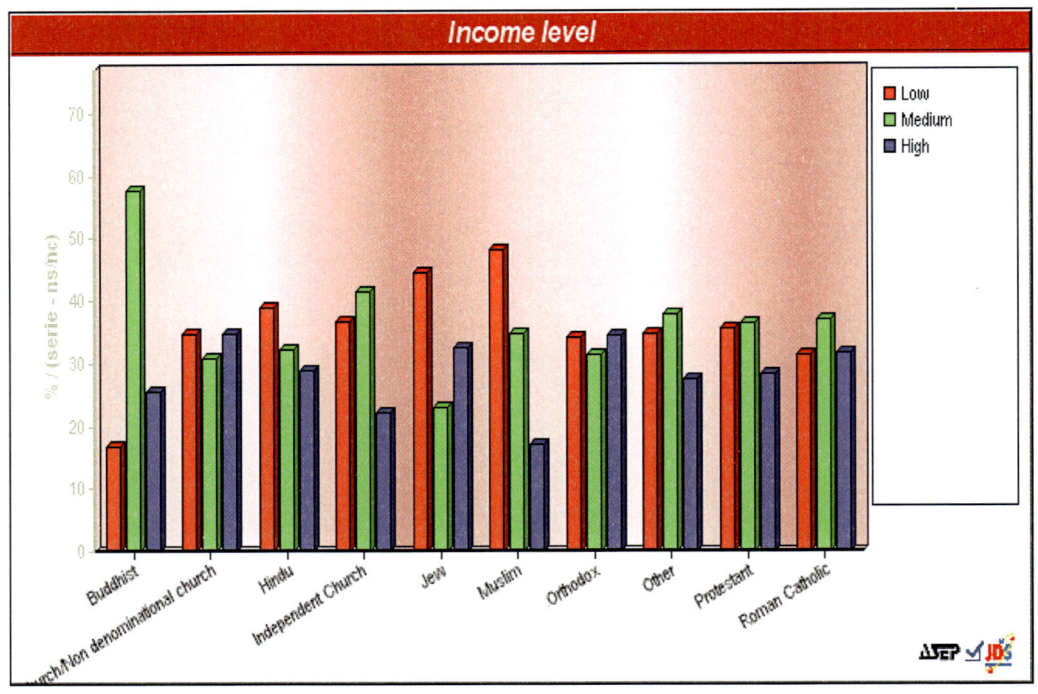

Political positions

Democracy

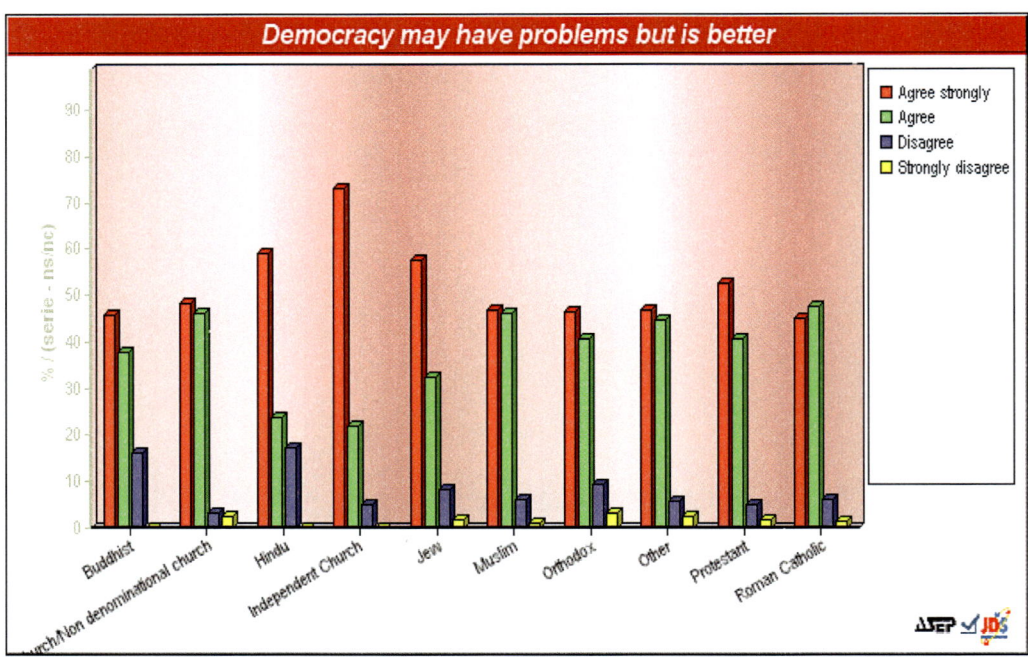

Left-right-scale

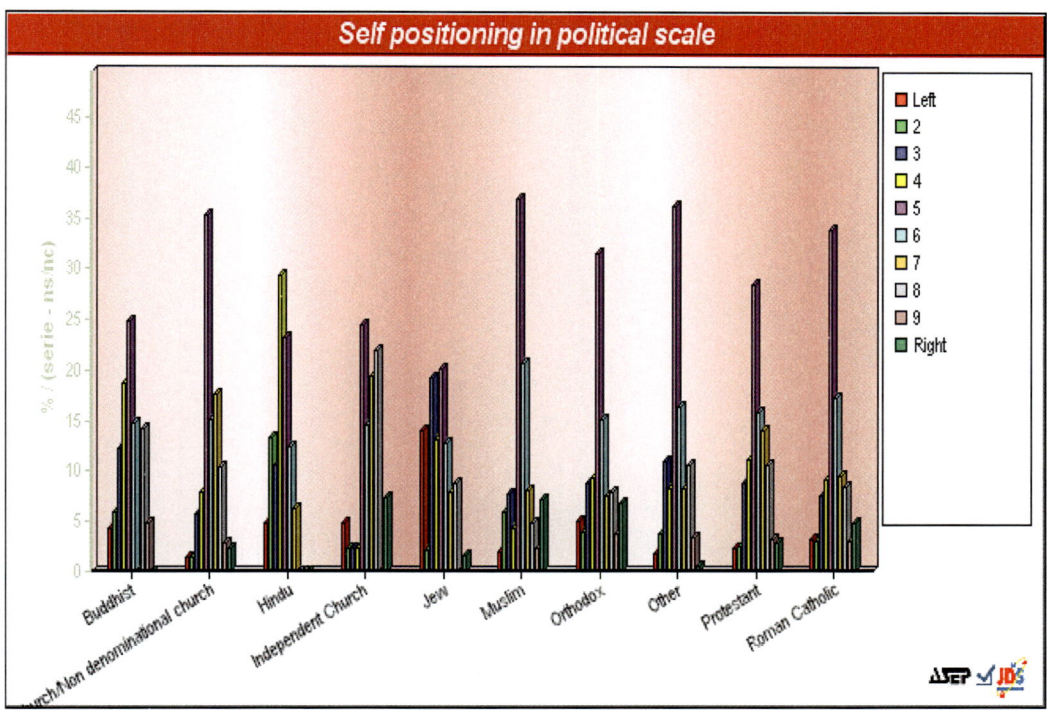

Politicians who don't believe in God are unfit for public office

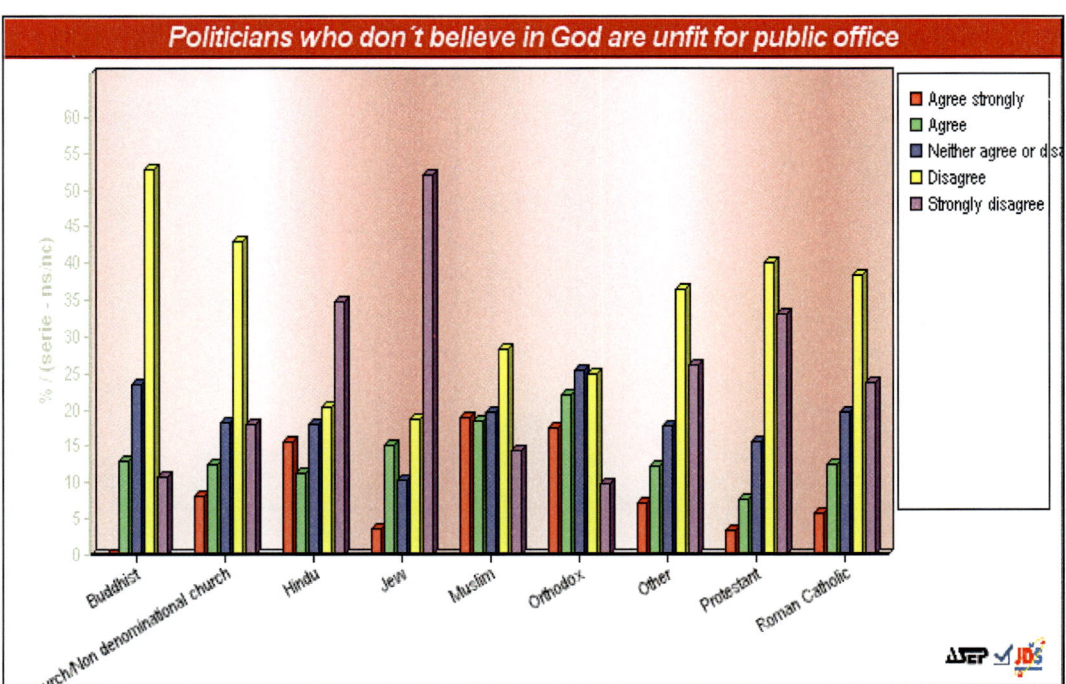

Prejudice

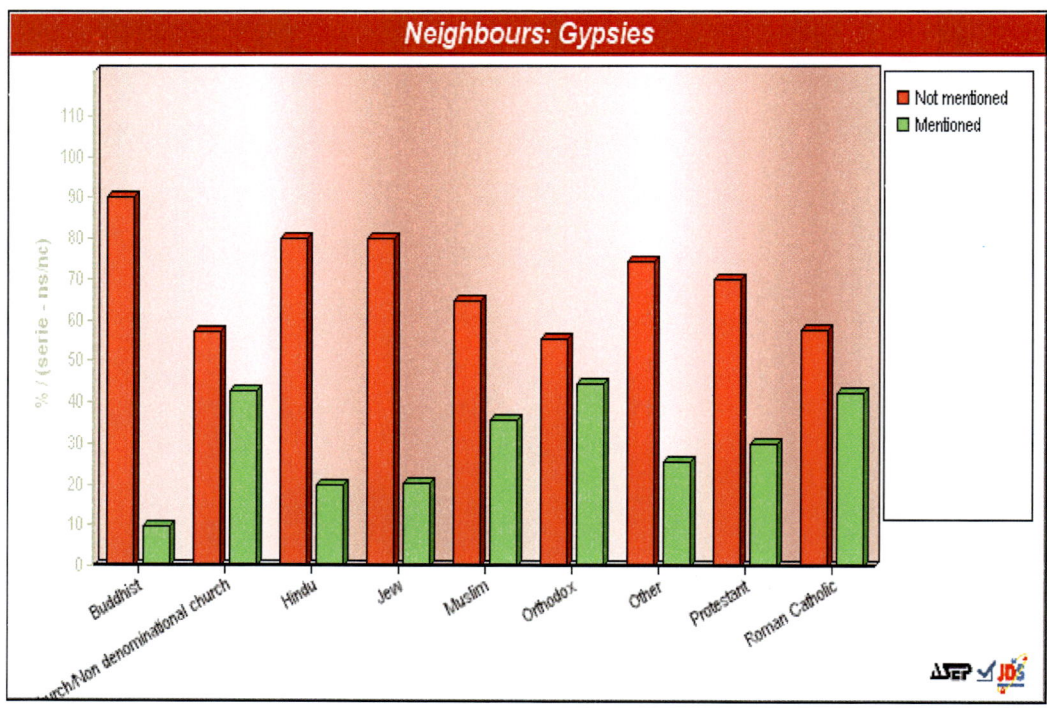

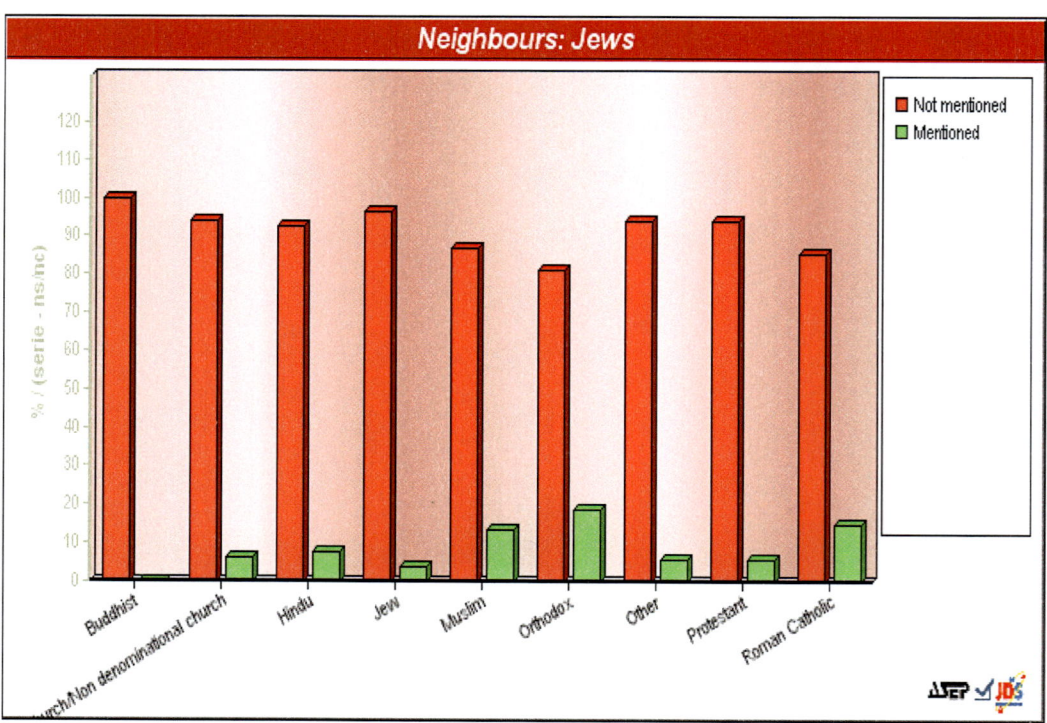

Executive Summary and Synopsis of This Study 17

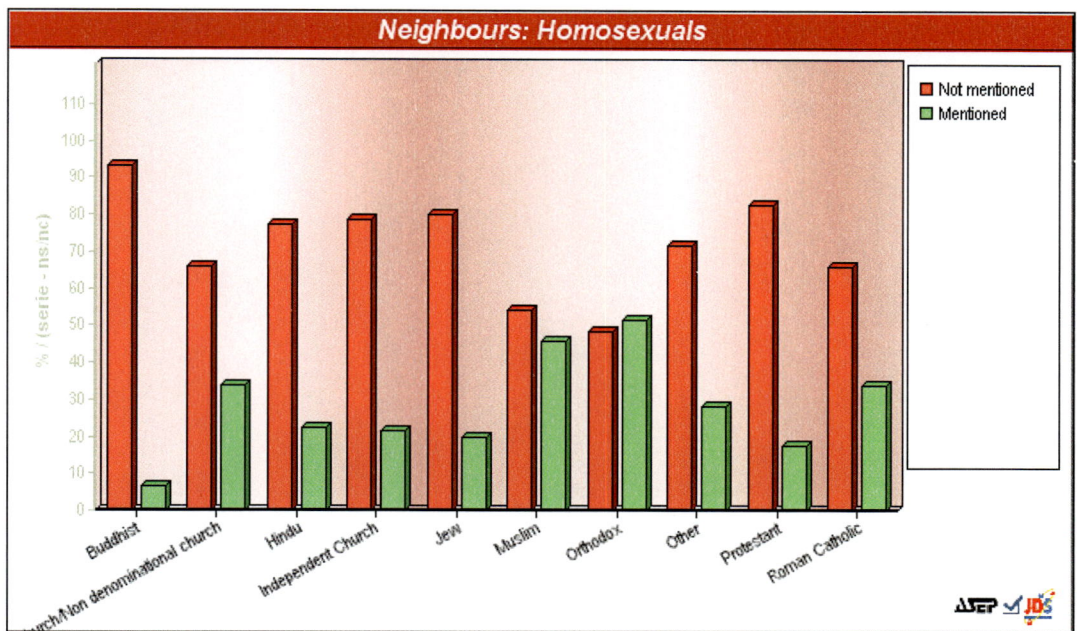

Confidence in major social institutions

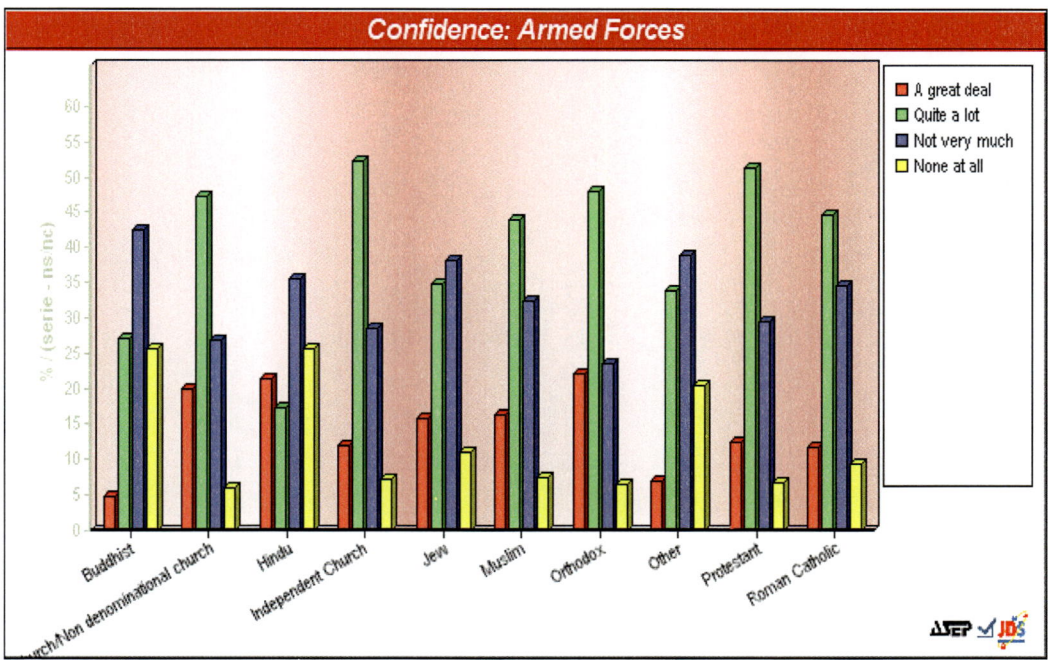

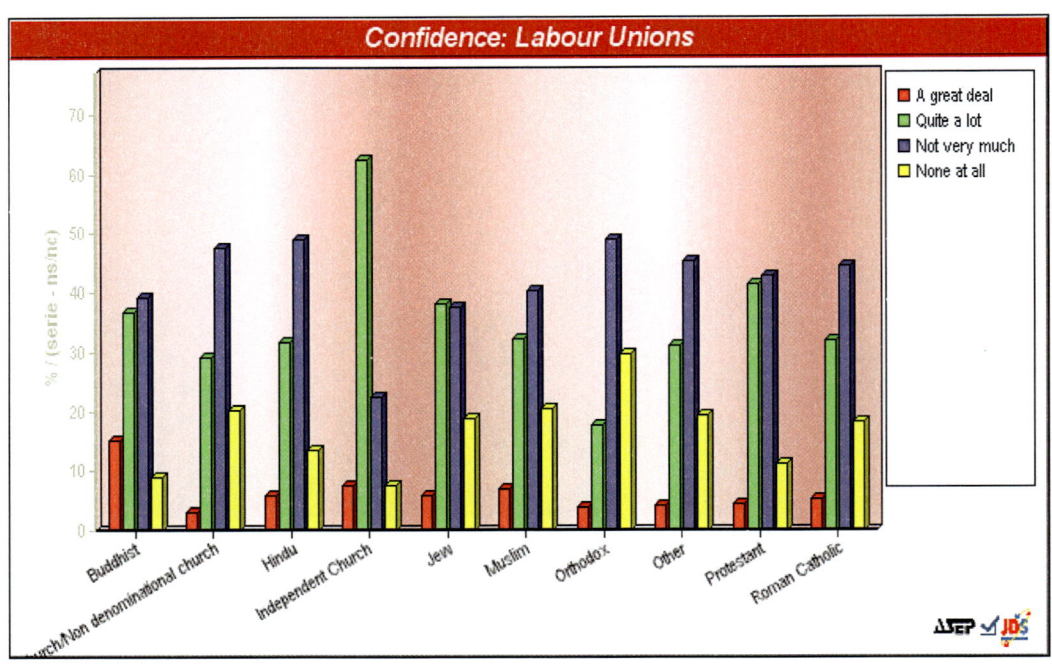

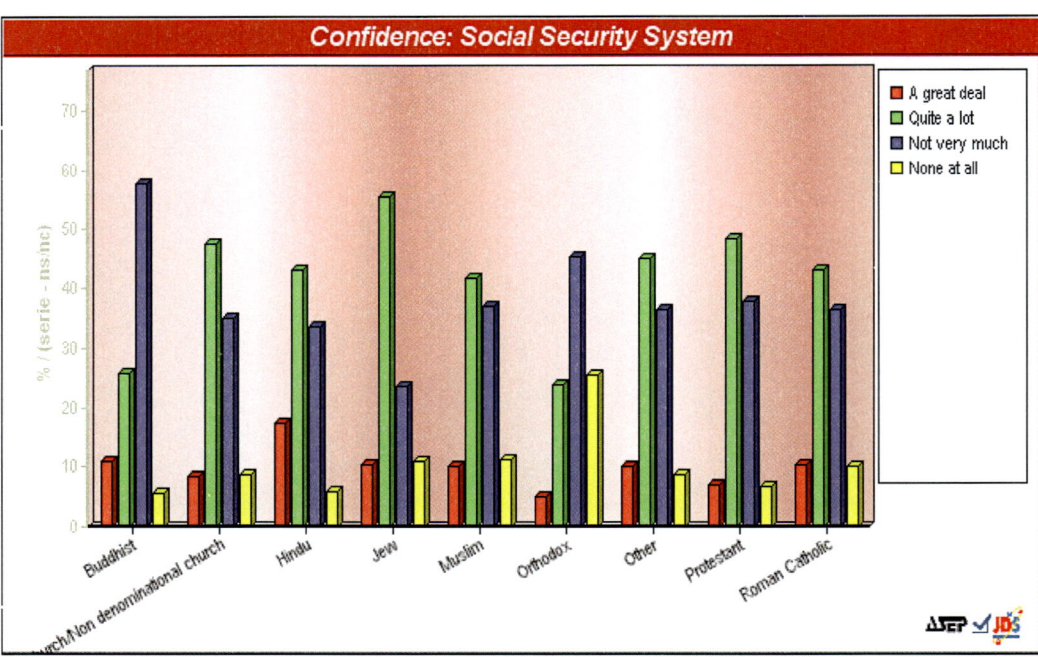

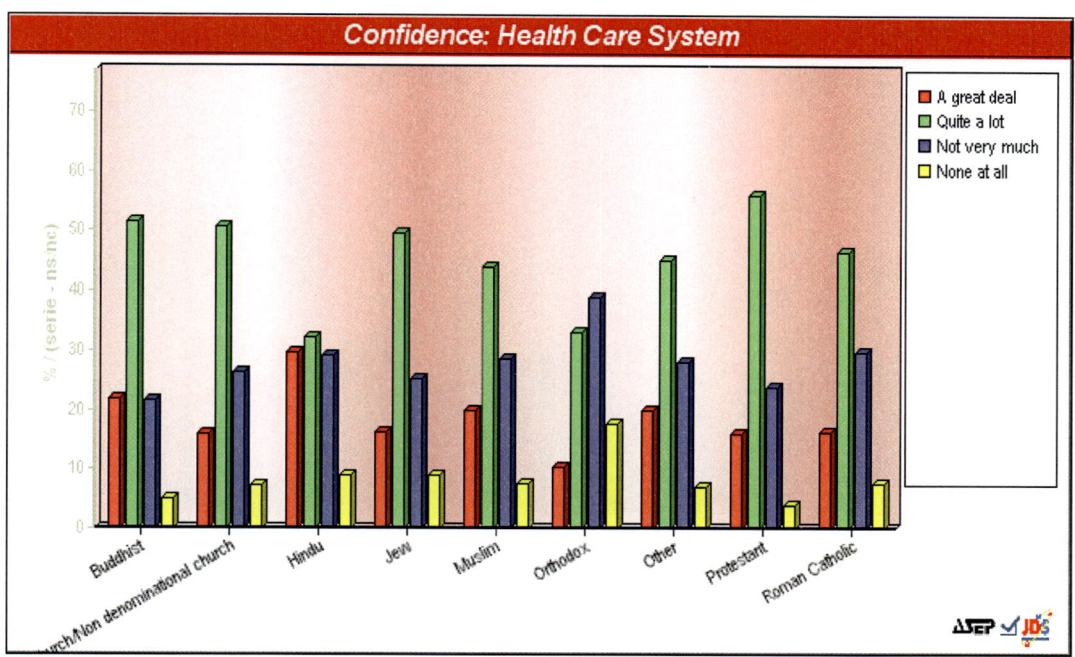

Law and order

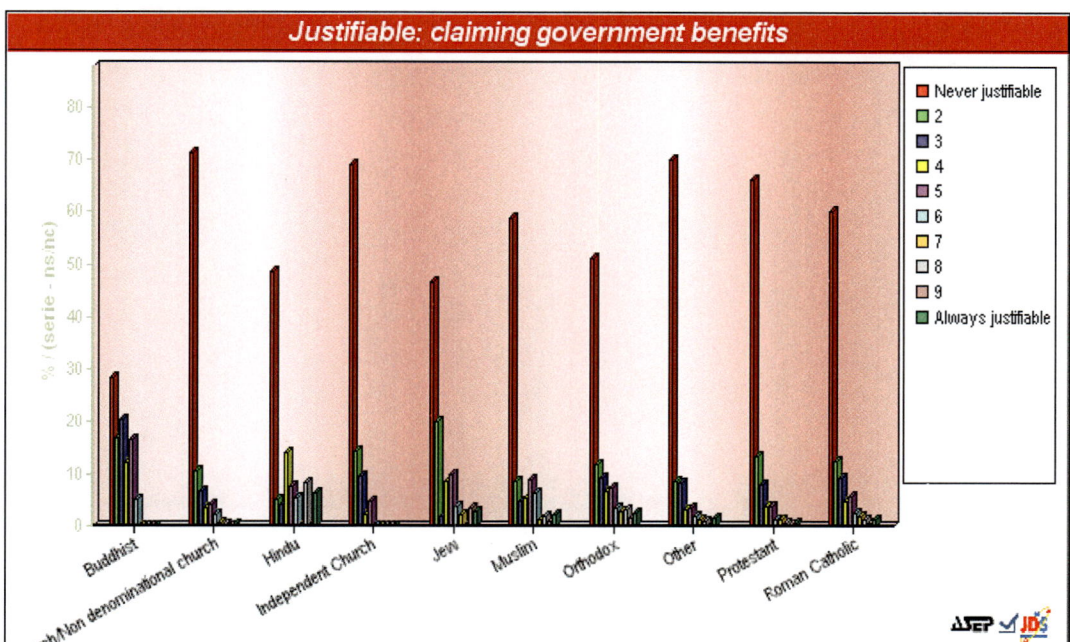

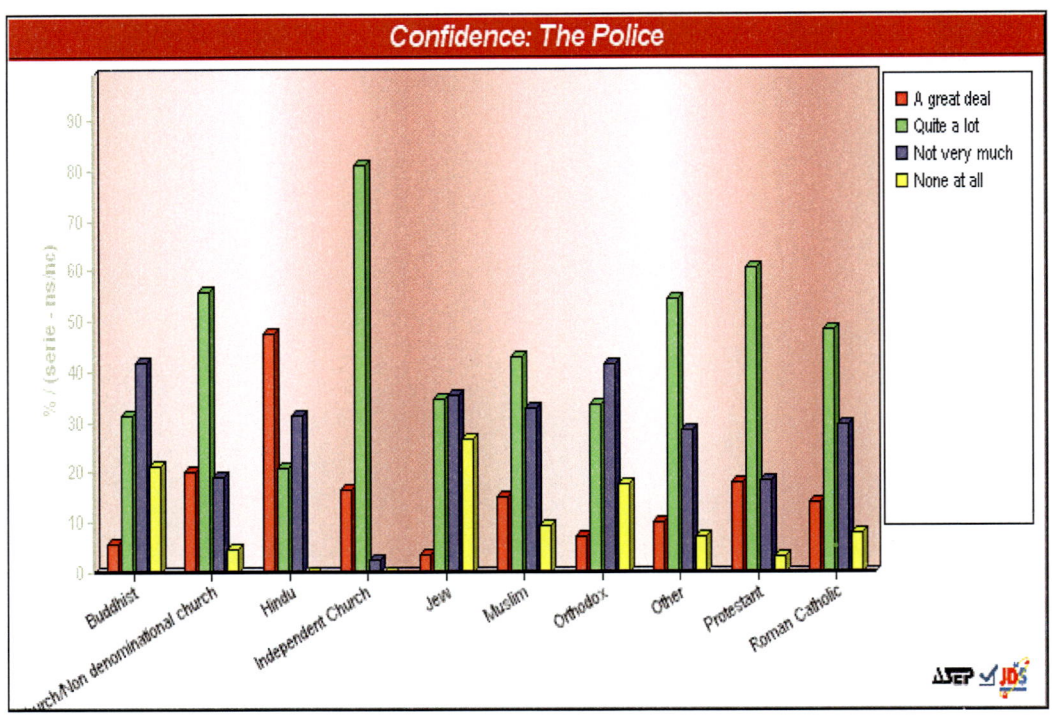

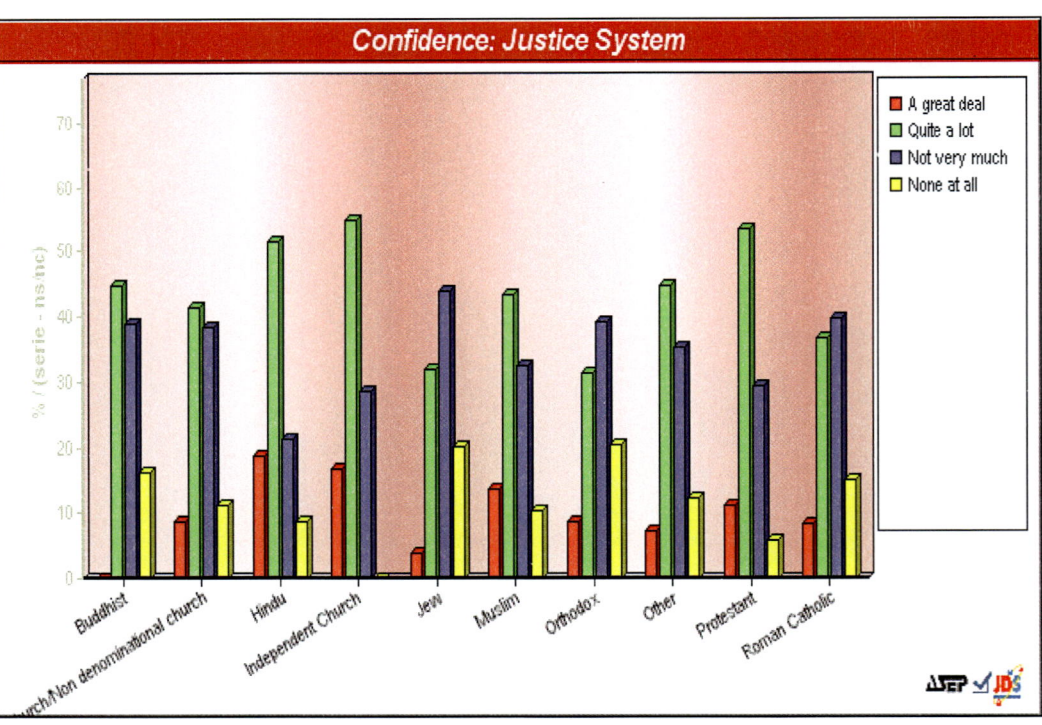

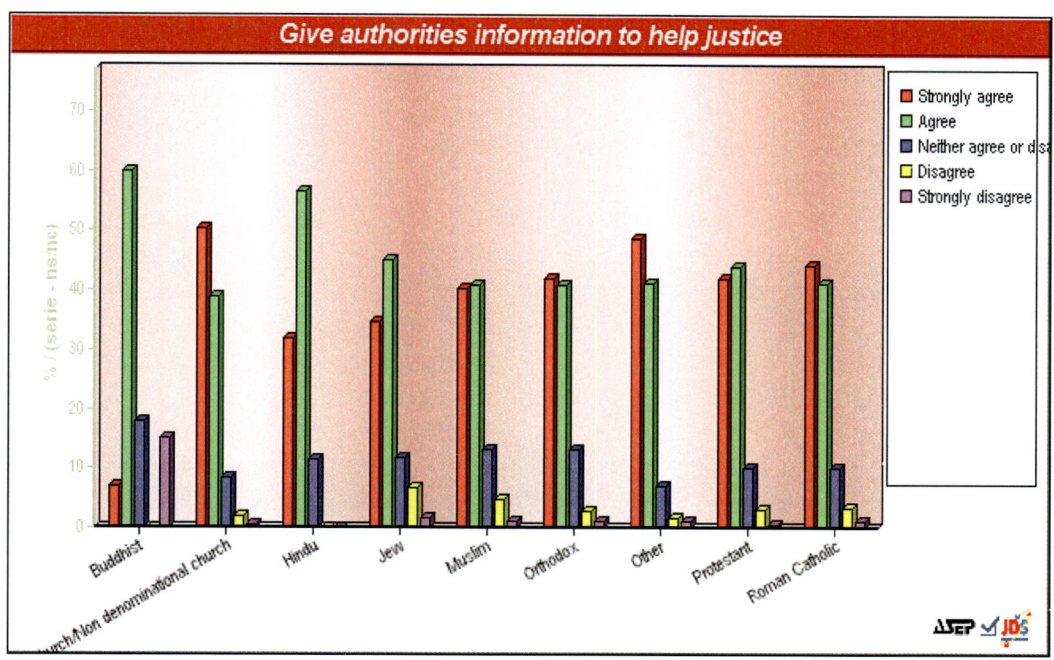

European integration

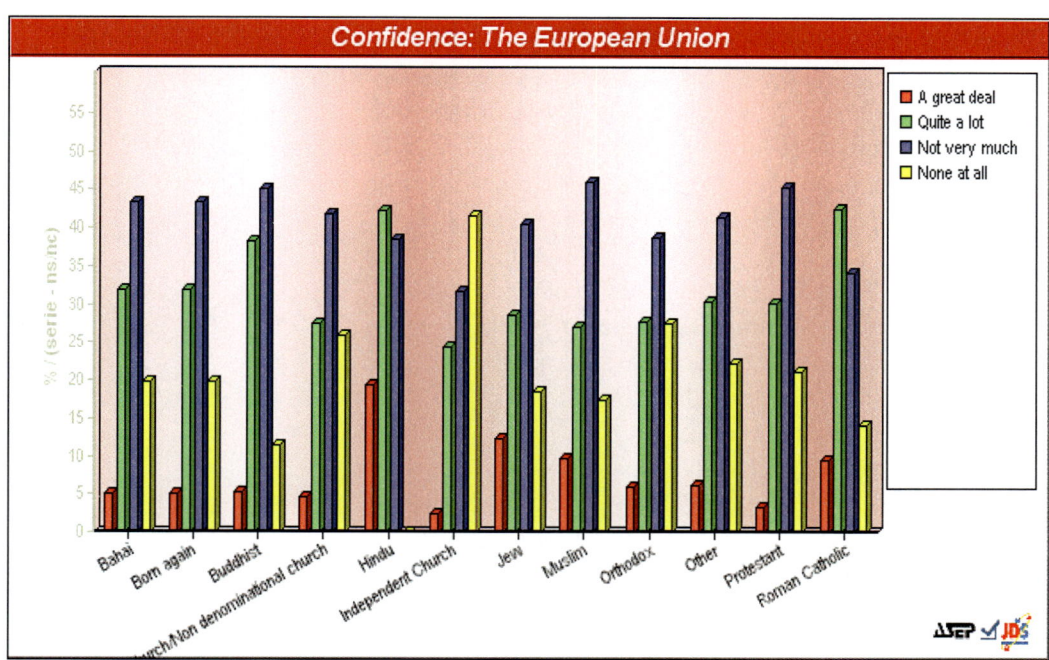

Selected WVS samples: Austria [1999], Belgium [1999], Bulgaria [1999], Czech Republic [1999], Denmark [1999], Estonia [1999], Finland [2000], France [1999], Germany East [1999], Germany West [1999], Great Britain [1999], Greece [1999], Hungary [1999], Iceland [1999], Ireland [1999], Italy [1999], Latvia [1999], Lithuania [1999], Luxembourg [1999], Malta [1999], Netherlands [1999], Northern Ireland [1999], Norway [1996], Poland [1999], Portugal [1999], Romania [1999], Slovakia [1999], Slovenia [1999], Spain [2000], Sweden [1999], Switzerland [1996]

GLOBAL ISLAM

Our appendix for the first time in the literature presents a real panorama of global Muslim opinion and social conditions.

Our analysis of the opinions of global Muslims starts with the assertion that in the contemporary period of the 1990s and the early 2000s, 13.2% of Muslims—in comparison to 12.7% of the global citizenry—disagree or strongly disagree with the opinion that "Democracy may have problems but is better". Seen in such a perspective, the Gallup Institute is probably right with its figure of 8 percent Muslims extremists world-wide.

But what Gallup does NOT tell us for example is the value gap between Muslims and the Orthodox world on the one side and the rest of European society on the other side regarding the acceptability and or necessity of societal integration of immigrants.

The WVS dimensions on family, gender, sexuality and religious values show by contrast that Muslim conservative personal values are to be reckoned with especially in Europe, a continent, which has gone a much further way on its path to secularization and the decay of traditional family values than the United States of America.

Our summary of our results thus re-iterates the findings, already reported by Inglehart (2003), Inglehart and Baker (2000), and Inglehart and Norris (2003). Islam is basically democratic and non-violent, but value-conservative.

Arguing from an Enlightenment perspective, Muslim societies, like other societies especially in the global East and South of the world system, must become more inclusive in their approach to minorities.

It is this "center" of Muslim global opinion, which believes in technology, competition, gradual reform and hard work as the basis of success, which must be termed as the "silent Muslim Calvinist majority" and, which is the basis of our optimistic projections.

The 5 real core tenets of the real existing Muslim identity around the globe, shared by an estimated 900 million Muslims or more, are indeed a combination of conservative family values, a belief in government and a belief in technology:

- Future: Emphasis on technology good thing
- Competition is harmful (scale value 1-4)
- Important for a successful marriage: adequate income
- Government responsibility should be increased (value 5–10 on people responsibility versus government scale)
- Rejecting a single parent woman

By contrast, around 200 million Muslims or even less share the opinion that:

- Society must be radically changed
- Confidence in the civil service: none at all
- Confidence in the social security system: none at all
- Political system, which governs the country very bad
- Extreme right wing
- Strong leader very good
- Former political system very good

- Army rule very good
- Confidence in the education system: none at all
- Confidence in television: none at all
- Disagreement or strong disagreement with: democracy may have problems but it is better
- Confidence in the justice system: none at all
- Percent not agreeing: respect and appreciation important for successful marriage
- Confidence in the armed forces: none at all
- Confidence in churches: none at all
- Extreme left wing
- Having a democratic political system bad or fairly bad
- Already joined unofficial strikes
- Already occupied buildings or factories

In fact, World Values Survey data also support the hypothesis that today central values of democracy and the market economy are widely shared throughout the Muslim world.

A very large percentage of global Muslims belongs to the political center, and although we can observe a somewhat larger percentage of people belonging to the very extreme right and the very extreme left in the Muslim world than in global society, the shape of the political distribution according to the self-positioning on the ideological map in global Islam and in global society is about the same.

Large majorities of people both among global Muslims as among the global citizenry support a gradual transition of society and they reject radical changes, quite in accordance with the logic proposed by Sir Karl Raimund Popper decades ago, and they do not want a total change of society. This result is especially optimistic – whatever the direction of results, the transition has to be a gradual one and a radical overthrow of the existing order is rejected.

But in this context, we also should point to a paradoxon, which should be immediately followed up by Western political action. Although 923.000 Websites are listed by "Google advanced search" as explicitly referring to "Karl Popper" by June 19, 2008, only 844 such Websites were in Arabic language (traditional and simplified Chinese Websites, mentioning "Karl Popper", are above 10,000 each, and Russian language Websites 1320. In the other major languages of the Muslim world, we find 2200 Websites on Popper in Indonesian, 31200 Websites in Turkish, 2190 in Farsi). The Arab masses in particular and the Muslim masses around the globe would be absolutely eager to follow the path of gradual reform, but they do not even have proper access to the writings of the visionary of gradual societal reform.

The struggle for democracy in the Muslim world might be presented in optimistic terms, as suggested by Esposito and Mogahed (2008). There is a very vast area of societal change necessary to assure future opinion structures, which are compatible with truly democratic enlightened societies with peaceful methods of conflict settlement and conflict resolution:

The Struggle for Democracy: How to Convince up to 100 Million Muslims

- Already occupied buildings or factories
- Already joined unofficial strikes

- Having a democratic political system bad or fairly bad
- Extreme left wing
- Confidence in churches: none at all

The Struggle for Democracy: How to Convince 100 to 200 Million Muslims

- Confidence in the armed forces: none at all
- Perent not agreeing: respect and appreciation important for successful marriage
- Disagree or strongly disagree: long-term relationship is necessary to be happy
- Confidence in the justice system: none at all
- Disagreement or strong disagreement with: democracy may have problems but it is better
- Confidence in television: none at all
- Confidence in the education system: none at all
- Army rule is very good
- Former political system: very good
- Strong leader: very good
- Confidence in the Environmental Protection Movement: none at all
- Justifiable taking soft drugs (sometimes or always, scale value 2–10)
- Justifiable driving under influence of alcohol (sometimes or always, scale value 2–10)
- Political system that governs the country: very bad
- Extreme right wing
- Confidence in the social security system: none at all
- Justifiable speeding over the limit (sometimes or always, scale value 2–10)
- Confidence in the civil service: none at all
- Society must be radically changed

The Struggle for Democracy: How to Convince 200 to 300 Million Muslims

- Satisfaction with the way democracy develops in the country: not at all satisfied
- Confidence in the press: none at all
- Confidence in the police: none at all
- Confidence in the government: none at all
- Justifiable joyriding (sometimes or always, scale value 2–10)
- Justifiable someone accepting a bribe (sometimes or always, scale value 2–10)
- Justifiable paying cash (sometimes or always, scale value 2–10)
- Confidence in the European Union: none at all
- Confidence in major companies: none at all
- Confidence in the women's movement: none at all
- Confidence in labor unions: none at all
- Confidence in Parliament: none at all
- Confidence in NATO: none at all
- Justifiable throwing away litter (sometimes or always, scale value 2–10)

- Confidence in the health care system: none at all

To demand from Europe's Muslims that they should "adapt" or assimilate themselves to the "lead culture" would deserve the cynical answer from the empirical social science community that this "lead culture", by the turn of the Millennium, was a culture of over 200 million tax evaders, 200 million Roma-phobes, 155 million homophobes and 67 million open anti-Semites, and in between these "lead culture values" more than 100 million people who think that somehow political assassinations are justified and that taking bribes is somehow acceptable. So what is Europe's "lead culture"? The conviction, shared by more than 193 million Europeans that sex under the legal age of consent is sometimes or always justifiable? The more than 60 million Europeans, who openly reject a neighbor of a different race? To which "Europe" "the Muslims" should adapt in the end?

According to the WVS, in Europe we are confronted with a considerable potential of mistrust in democracy, distance to and mistrust in basic societal institutions, and we are also confronted with a very large group of people holding xenophobic and anti-Semitic world views on the part of the total population.

EURO-ISLAM

To successfully integrate the 15 million Muslims in Europe, above all means to convince the following number of people (in millions) of the central European values of the Enlightenment, the values of tolerance, democracy and respect for the law:

Rejecting homosexual neighbors	6.57
Justifiable claiming government benefits (sometimes or always)	5.90
Justifiable avoiding a fare on public transport (sometimes or always)	5.82
Jobs are scarce: men have more rights then	5.79
Justifiable cheating on taxes (sometimes or always)	5.70
Justifiable speeding over the limit (sometimes or always)	5.47
Justifiable paying cash (sometimes or always)	5.44
Justifiable sex under the legal age of consent (sometimes or always)	5.36
Rejecting Roma/Sinti neighbors	5.11
Justifiable political assassination (sometimes or always)	4.61
Education: tolerance and respect not mentioned as a central value	4.29
Justifiable someone accepting a bribe (sometimes or always)	3.72
Confidence in NATO: none at all	3.41
Having experts make decisions very good	3.07
Confidence in labor unions: none at all	2.95
Politicians who don't believe in God are unfit for public office (strongly agree)	2.74
Confidence in the Press: none at all	2.71
Rejecting neighbors of a different race	2.62
Justifiable alco-driving (sometimes or always)	2.59
Not at all satisfied with democracy	2.45

Confidence in the European Union: none at all	2.19
Confidence in Parliament: none at all	2.06
Rejecting Jewish neighbors	1.92
Confidence in the civil service: none at all	1.83
Confidence in the social security system: none at all	1.63
Confidence in the justice system: none at all	1.51
Rejecting neighbors who are immigrants or foreign workers	1.37
Confidence in the police: none at all	1.34
Confidence in churches: none at all	1.28
Political system, which governs the country very bad	1.20
Confidence in the armed forces: none at all	1.07
not prepared to help elderly people	0.98
in a democracy, the economy runs badly	0.96
Democracy may have problems but it's better (disagree)	0.89
Already joined unofficial strikes	0.85
Having a democratic political system fairly bad	0.81
Having the army rule very good	0.49
Confidence in the education system: none at all	0.48
occupying buildings and factories	0.43
Having a democratic political system very bad	0.23
Democracy may have problems but it's better (strongly disagree)	0.14

So, are Muslims really that "dangerous" as Islamophobic circles in the non-Muslim world pretend to think? Or aren't Muslims and non-Muslims alike sharing a culture of protest against many aspects of globalization? We again would like to let the facts speak for themselves. And the facts are clear—hundreds of millions of people on earth, Muslims and non-Muslims alike, share traditional family values, share values of protest against the secular globalized culture, and even would consider more radical and violent forms of protest. We above all would like to emphasize that global value transformation is an intricate process, with optimistic and pessimistic aspects in all societies around the world at the same time.

But let us for a minute imagine that "we" are "policy planners" in a western transnational corporation, in a western international government bureaucracy, and we would like to figure out how many millions of people are "against" the well-known neo-liberal "Washington Consensus" or against "liberal democracy and the market economy" as such, or do not share the values of secularism and the kind of permissive sexual morality, which seems to be a consensus in many Western countries nowadays. A Muslim fundamentalist would perhaps combine these phenomena under the heading "Washington Consexus" (= liberal market economy + liberal democracy + sexual permissiveness + secularization).

So we compare the total world "protest potential" with the Muslim "protest potential" and calculate the share of the global *Umma* in the total world "protest potential" and anti-Enlightenment consensus.

The World Values Survey data permit us to state exactly, in which "issue area" of "discontent" with the neo-liberal "Washington Consexus" of neo-liberalism, competitive party democracy and the market economy, and permissive sexuality the Muslim global protest potential is largest, and where the Muslim global protest potential share is smallest.

COMPARISONS

Global Muslims represent more than 50% of all people on Earth, who hold the following opinions:

- Former political system is very good
- Books that attack religion definitely should be banned
- Important for a successful marriage: religious beliefs
- Important for a successful marriage: same ethnic background
- Confidence in the education system: none at all

Global Muslims are more than 40% of all people on earth, who hold the following opinions:

- Confidence in the health care system: none at all
- Army rule is very good
- Politicians who don't believe in God are unfit for public office (strongly agree)
- Rejecting Jewish neighbors

Equally, global Muslims are more than 30% of all people on Earth who hold the following beliefs:

- Identification with the extreme right wing
- Rejecting neighbors of a different race
- Important for a successful marriage: adequate income
- Justify political assassination (sometimes or always, scale value 2–10)
- Reject neighbors who are immigrants or foreign workers
- Reject single parent women
- Percent saying that agreement on politics is important or very important for a successful marriage
- Justify threatening workers who refuse to join a strike (sometimes or always, scale value 2–10)

By contrast, global Islam represents less than 10% of all global citizens who think that:

- It is justifiable to smoke in public places (sometimes or always, scale value 2–10)
- Free market economy is wrong for the future of the country
- Disagree or strongly disagree: long-term relationship is necessary to be happy
- Justifiable euthanasia (sometimes or always, scale value 2–10)
- Justifiable prostitution (sometimes or always, scale value 2–10)
- Justifiable speeding over the limit (sometimes or always, scale value 2–10)
- Justifiable paying cash (sometimes or always, scale value 2–10)

ASABIYYA: UNDERSTANDING GLOBAL VALUE CHANGE

Of course, politicians and journalists all over the globe can engage in a never-ending debate about values, culture, and the "leading Western/European culture". The classic Arab historian and philosopher Ibn Khaldun, who died in 1405, explained in his most important book *Muqaddimah (Introduction to History)* [see also Tibi (1996) and (Darling (2007)] that historical change and the succession of dynasties are a function of the interactions between nomadic culture and urban civilization.

His major contribution in this context then consisted in the analysis of the correlation between *Asabiyya,* the social cohesion of a society, and political power. This sociological perspective on *Asabiyya* should not be confounded with the religious, theological debate about the *Asabiyya* as the pre-Islamic kinship or identity feeling among the inhabitants of Arabic countries, severely criticized by the *Prophet Mohammed (Peace be upon him)* in *Hadiths*.

Our understanding of *Asabiyya* is only a sociological one in the tradition of Ibn Khaldoun, referring to the "social cohesion" of a societal system.

In terms of modern social science theory, the following Khaldounian scheme can be proposed. Societies do not generally experience a smooth transformation from a traditional and survival oriented value set towards a secular and self-expression oriented value set. The "*Asabiyya*" counter-model to Inglehart, relies on a factor analytical evaluation of the following variables in the world values survey, and combines theoretical insights of the Inglehart School with those by Columbia University sociologist Amitai Etzioni.

At the very beginning of the modernization process, societies are traditional, religious, and pre-modern; but at the same time they are also "active" societies with functioning neighborhood structures, and very clear perceptions of what are "good" and "evil", and a high respect of the law. As the modernization process proceeds, traditional religious values seem to be on the losing side of the societal equation. The uneasiness of the "religious right" in the United States, of the Islamist camp in many countries of the Muslim world, and the religious right in many developing countries is best understood by the process, whereby traditional values get lost at the same time with dimensions of the active society and respect of the law in such vital areas as tax morale, non-acceptability of bribery and government benefits fraud.

Islamists are of course wrong in assuming that countries of the Muslim world are the only ones to suffer the downward trend in public morale. The worst global performers, it seems, are Belarus, Brazil, Slovakia, and the Ukraine. As churches are emptying, so do the volunteer organizations; and since "God" does not "exist", everything becomes feasible, acceptable, and even becomes practice: cheating taxes, taking bribes, receiving government benefits even if you are not entitled for them.

The residuals from our function now can be called a modern, factor analytical and regression analytical definition of *Asabiyya*. It is also interesting to note that Muslim societies approximately adhere to the same process of secularization, but that their chances to recover from the "trough" of the modernization crisis are better than for the global average.

Thus, a modern vision of Islam in the twenty-first century would exactly presuppose to provide an answer to the "trough" of the "modernization crisis" around the world—to stimulate an active law-abiding society, and giving an answer to the secularization of values by networks of volunteers.

The Inglehart school is famous for its world maps; however, our explanatory factor analysis with the main WVS country indicators "always respect parents; belief in hell; cheating taxes; education for tolerance and respect important; jobs scarce men have rights; mean acceptability homosexuality; mean acceptance government benefits fraud; never praying; not satisfied with democracy; only God-believing politicians; openly racist; rejecting foreign workers; rejecting homosexual neighbor, belong voluntary welfare elderly; taking bribes; unpaid social welfare work" yields just two factors—traditional versus secular; and cheating versus active society. We specified that *Asabiyya* is a high residual along this pathway of modernization; societies, which are active and transparent along the course of the secularization process, are characterized by *Asabiyya*.

The global logic of *Asabiyya* has the following basic characteristics. First we look at the continuum traditional versus secular.

The factor "traditional societies versus secular societies" has positive factor loadings above 0.500 with

- always respect parents
- belief in hell
- jobs are scarce and men have rights
- rejecting foreign workers
- openly racist
- rejecting homosexual neighbor
- only God-believing politicians

The factor "traditional societies versus secular societies" has negative factor loadings of minus 0.500 or more with the variables:

- mean acceptability homosexuality
- education for tolerance and respect important
- never praying

The map of this traditional universe is characterized as follows: the traditionalist cultural gap in San Diego, California, USA, is far less pronounced as the traditionalist versus secular gap, which separates Europe from its Muslim neighbors; and in general, the Muslim countries are presenting the most traditional "landscape". The 10 most traditional societies in the world are all Muslim societies:

- Bangladesh [2002]
- Egypt [2000]
- Turkey [2001]
- Algeria [2002]
- Indonesia [2001]
- Tanzania, United Republic of [2001]
- Jordan [2001]
- Pakistan [2001]
- Zimbabwe [2001]
- Morocco [2001]

The 10 most secular countries on earth are:

- Netherlands [1999]
- Denmark [1999]
- Sweden [1999]
- Iceland [1999]
- France [1999]
- Norway [1996]
- Germany West [1999]
- Finland [2000]
- Switzerland [1996]
- Luxembourg [1999]

In a way, Etzioni's "active society" paradigm shows the way how a society can steer the pathways of modernization and secularization. If you want to avoid having a society, where cheating taxes, taking bribes, dissatisfaction with democracy and acceptance of government benefits frauds becomes the rule, you have to mobilize society in volunteer organizations, all the more so in a multicultural society. This is a most welcome form of "djihad"; the "djihad" of caring for the elderly and sick, the "djihad" of unpaid social welfare work. It is no coincidence that some European societies are among the most crisis-ridden countries along this scale:

- Republic of Moldova [2002]
- Belarus [2000]
- Lithuania [1999]
- Ukraine [1999]
- Russian Federation [1999]
- Armenia [1997]
- Brazil [1997]
- Azerbaijan [1997]
- Estonia [1999]
- Greece [1999]

But also developments in

- Slovakia [1999]
- Georgia [1996]
- Macedonia, Republic of [2001]
- Hungary [1999]
- France [1999]
- Philippines [2001]
- Romania [1999]
- Kyrgyzstan [2003]
- Slovenia [1999]
- Latvia [1999]

are far from satisfactory. The real stars along this scale are:

- Bangladesh [2002]
- Tanzania, United Republic of [2001]
- Viet Nam [2001]
- Egypt [2000]
- United States [1999]
- China [2001]
- Sweden [1999]
- Iceland [1999]
- Netherlands [1999]
- Canada [2000]

These are the societies, where a "civic culture" (Almond/Verba, 1963) is fairly developed and where resistance against the darker sides of modernity—the kind of moral decay, which you associate with cheating taxes, taking bribes, dissatisfaction with democracy, and acceptance of government benefits fraud, is greatest.

MEASURING GLOBAL TOLERANCE

The data from the World Values Survey can also be used to project a *scale of global tolerance*. This is all the more relevant because the European Commission now officially embraces a policy according to which Islamophobia has no place within the European Union, which is now always understood as a community of values. To develop a statistical "yardstick" of discrimination and exclusion is absolutely important in Europe. The World Values Survey data provide the international public with a unique opportunity to measure the existence of prejudice and discrimination "on the ground".

Without question, *Anti-Semitism* is the most alarming of the phobias to be observed in Europe. Our materials show the extent of global Anti-Semitism according to the WVS data base for the different religious denominations of the world. We only used the results for those denominations, which were represented in more than two countries of the world, and in with more than 50 respondents in the WVS sample. The extent of Anti-Semitism in Asia is striking and has already been commented on by many observers. Open Anti-Semitism is professed by more than 25% of global Buddhists, Muslims and Hindus.

In Belarus, Russia and Spain there was a noticeable increase of Anti-Semitism over time, while in Argentina and Chile Anti-Semitism decreased. The extent of open Anti-Semitism in Iraq, Turkey, Korea, Spain, Mexico, Bosnia, Venezuela, Poland and Moldova is astonishing and is being shared by more than 25% of the respective population, while the least anti-Semitic nations today are *[anti-Semitic prejudice (< 5%)]*

Canada [2000]; Czech Republic [1999]; Denmark [1999]; Germany West [1999]; Iceland [1999]; Netherlands [1999]; Sweden [1999]

where open Anti-Semitism according to the WVS was expressed by the less than 10% of the total population.

Islamophobia with justification is targeted by European policy makers as one of the other major dangers on the European horizon. Our materials show the extent of global Islamophobia according to the WVS data base for the different religious denominations of the world. *Some Muslim leaders around the globe best perhaps should start wondering whether or not "the West" is the arch-enemy.* The facts of global opinion surveys are simple and striking at the same time: *The extent of Islamophobia in non-Christian Asia is alarming.* And in general, Protestants tend to be more Islamophobic than Catholics, and the Muslim communities world-wide would do well to reflect on the fact that *Jews, in accordance with their tradition of tolerance and the Enlightenment, are more tolerant of Muslim neighbors than even the global Muslims themselves, and only 1/6 of global Jews openly stated that they do NOT want a Muslim neighbor.*

The spirit of tolerance, so prevalent during much of the history of Muslim *al –Andalus* (Bossong, 2007) has to be contrasted with the spirit of *salafist anti-Enlightenment,* which is summarized in such a condensed fashion in the *Charta of the Palestinian group Hamas,* reproduced in this work. The present author can only refer here to the excellent background analysis by the Spanish diplomat Juan José Escobar Stemmann, which appeared under the title "MIDDLE EAST SALAFISM'S INFLUENCE AND THE RADICALIZATION OF MUSLIM COMMUNITIES IN EUROPE" at Israel's "Gloria Institute" in Herzliya (http://meria.idc.ac.il/journal/2006/issue3/jv10no3a1.html).

MORE THAN 25% OF GLOBAL BUDDHISTS, HINDUS AND ANCESTRAL WORSHIPPERS OPENLY HOLD ISLAMOPHOBIC ATTITUDES

Islamophobia decreased over time in Finland, the Philippines, Sweden and the United States, but it increased in Spain. The extent of open Islamophobia in Albania [2002]; Belarus [2000]; Croatia [1999]; India [1995]; Lithuania [1999]; Macedonia, Republic of [2001]; Malta [1999]; Philippines [2001]; Republic of Korea [2001]; Republic of Moldova [2002]; Romania [1999]; and Viet Nam [2001] is again astonishing and is being shared by more than 25% of the population. The least openly Islamophobic nations of the world are [Islamophobia (< 10%)]

Argentina [1999]; Canada [2000]; Chile [2000]; Portugal [1999]; Sweden [1999]

Romaphobia, also with justification, is targeted by European policy makers, together with Anti-Semitism and Islamophobia, as one of the other major xenophobic threats on the European horizon. Our materials show the extent of global Romaphobia according to the WVS data base for the different religious denominations of the world. The extent of Romaphobia among Muslims is striking and alarming. In general, Catholics tend to be more Romaphobic than Protestants, and again it turns out that Jews, in accordance with their tradition of tolerance and the Enlightenment, are very tolerant of Roma neighbors, and only slightly less than 1/5 of global Jews openly stated that they do NOT want a Roma neighbor. More than 25% of global Muslims, Catholics, Free Church members, Orthodox, Protestants and adherents of other faiths openly profess an anti-Roma prejudice:

The Czech Republic, Montenegro and Serbia must be praised for their decreasing Roma-phobia over time, while the Slovak Republic should be singled out as the country, where an appalling rate of Romaphobia still increased over time. The battle against Romaphobia is an uphill one, and Romaphobia is being shared by more than 25% of the total population in the following countries *[Roma-phobia (< 25%)]* are:

> Austria [1999]; Denmark [1999]; Iceland [1999]; Montenegro [2001]; Netherlands [1999]; Serbia [2001]; Sweden [1999]

The worst offenders are

- Slovakia [1999]
- Turkey [2001]
- Lithuania [1999]
- Northern Ireland [1999]
- Italy [1999]
- Bulgaria [1999]
- Ukraine [1999]
- Romania [1999]
- Belarus [2000]

To assess the totality of tolerance in Europe and in the world by global comparison, we now propose to construct a non-parametric index of "global tolerance", which combines the following WVS data with sufficient availability on the percentages per total population overcoming xenophobia and racism:

- People that respondent would like to have as neighbors: People of a different race (WVS A125)
- Qualities that children can be encouraged to learn at home - Important child qualities: tolerance and respect for other people (WVS A035)
- Not saying: Jobs scarce: Men should have more right to a job than women (WVS C001)
- People that respondent would like to have as neighbors: Immigrants/foreign workers (WVS A129)
- People that respondent would like to have as neighbors: Neighbors: Homosexuals (WVS A132)

Global tolerance then was most pronounced in the following political cultures:

- Sweden [1999]
- Netherlands [1999]
- Iceland [1999]
- Denmark [1999]
- Canada [2000]
- France [1999]

- United States [1999]
- Australia [1995]
- Finland [2000]
- New Zealand [1998]
- Luxembourg [1999]

The worst offenders, lacking a climate of tolerance, as operationalized by our Index, were:

- Turkey [2001]
- Bangladesh [2002]
- Republic of Korea [2001]
- Jordan [2001]
- Algeria [2002]
- Egypt [2000]
- Armenia [1997]
- Nigeria [2000]
- Indonesia [2001]
- Azerbaijan [1997]
- India [2001]

Among the 72 surveyed nations, the countries of the EU-27 had the following world ranks of global tolerance:

1 Sweden [1999]
2 Netherlands [1999]
3 Denmark [1999]
4 France [1999]
5 Finland [2000]
6 Luxembourg [1999]
7 Spain [2000]
8 Great Britain [1999]
9 Germany West [1999]
10 Belgium [1999]
11 Ireland [1999]
12 Portugal [1999]
13 Austria [1999]
14 Latvia [1999]
15 Italy [1999]
16 Czech Republic [1999]
17 Slovenia [1999]
18 Estonia [1999]
19 Greece [1999]
20 Poland [1999]
21 Malta [1999]
22 Slovakia [1999]

23 Lithuania [1999]
24 Bulgaria [1999]
25 Romania [1999]

The World Values Survey also permits the calculation of global tolerance world ranks for the surveyed populations in the following predominantly Muslim countries:

1   Iran (Islamic Republic of) [2000]
2   Bosnia and Herzegovina [2001]
3   Pakistan [2001]
4   Kyrgyzstan [2003]
5   Albania [2002]
6   Morocco [2001]
7   Azerbaijan [1997]
8   Indonesia [2001]
9   Nigeria [2000]
10 Egypt [2000]
11 Algeria [2002]
12 Jordan [2001]
13 Bangladesh [2002]
14 Turkey [2001]

Among the great social scientists of our time, Yale economics Professor and Nobel laureate Simon Kuznets (April 30, 1901–July 8, 1985) was the pioneer of the thought *that the development process is characterized by an inverted U-shaped relation between income inequality and economic growth.*

The Enlightenment perspective of this work raises the question of such an interrelationship between development and global tolerance. Is there a similar process as the one observed by Kuznets, with income inequality and thus the worst contradictions peaking at middle income stages, and with inequalities leveling off later on at higher stages of development?

If tolerance is low at low levels of socio-economic development, and if it decreases first with economic progress, is there at least a hope that tolerance increases with mature development levels?

Systematic research into the trajectory of global tolerance across nations reveals indeed that global tolerance corresponds pretty much to the U-shaped relationship between development level on the one hand and economic equality on the other hand. The non-linear function explains 62% of global tolerance. Very poor societies, as measured by the UNDP's Human Development Index, are relatively tolerant, and with rising income levels, as societal polarization increases, intolerance increases and tolerance decreases. But with rising levels of development, tolerance increases. With almost 2/3 of explained variance, our interrelationship is fairly strong and lets one predict that richer and more developed nations tend to be much more tolerant towards people of a different race, that people tend to regard tolerance and respect for other people as an important target of education, that society accepts job perspectives for women, more people tend to accept immigrants/foreign workers, and homosexual neighbors.

The income inequality Kuznets hypothesis would well explain why intolerance increases with development, and would even provide a kind of "materialist" explanation for the phenomenon. As societies are traditional, multi-culturanism, different gender roles *et cetera* pose no problem. *With inequality increasing with development, differentiations set in, which make the Buddhists, the Christians, the Confucians, the Hindus, the Jews, the Muslims, and the Sikhs the "enemies". With the leveling off of inequalities at later stages of development, people start to discover again that it is not "religion" or "culture", but socio-economics and education, which distribute the life chances in a society. Further research would be well advised to focus on this relationship, and to work with a Kuznets-style explanation of the development -> inequality -> intolerance trade-off.*

The next important question in this context is whether or not some countries are performing well at low levels of development, while other nations perform badly at high levels of development. To this end, we calculated residuals to show the positive and negative outlayers.

The 10 countries with the most unsatisfactory performance in the development of global tolerance, duly considering their development level, are:

- Republic of Korea
- Turkey
- Jordan
- Bangladesh
- Nigeria
- Armenia
- Algeria
- Egypt
- Singapore
- Greece
- Bulgaria

Among the EU-27 countries, the negative record holders are:

- Greece
- Bulgaria
- Lithuania
- Italy
- Slovakia

The 10 best global performers are:

- Peru
- Sweden
- Netherlands
- South Africa
- Argentina
- Denmark
- Dominican Republic

- Venezuela (Bolivarian Republic of)
- Republic of Moldova
- Iceland
- Zimbabwe

The world maps of the development -> global tolerance trade-off defy a simplistic reasoning. Catholic Italy is one of the worst performing countries in Europe; as well as the Asian country Korea, the predominantly Muslim nations Turkey, Jordan, and Bangladesh as well as Orthodox Armenia, Greece and Bulgaria. Catholic Peru and Argentina, as well as Protestant Sweden and the Netherlands are among the world leaders in the development->tolerance trade-off. There are good and bad performers in ALL cultural regions of the world. Compared to its development level, the populations of Iran, Pakistan and Russia all perform surprisingly well – surprisingly and in terms of the current standing of their governments in the global press, while EU-decision makers should take a closer look at the development of tolerance in at least 10 EU member countries - Greece, Bulgaria, Lithuania, Italy, Malta, Slovakia, Romania, Austria, Slovenia, and Ireland.

Our statistics also show that Turkey, Jordan and Bangladesh are the three Muslim countries with the most problematic trade-off between development and tolerance, while the populations in Iran (Islamic Republic of), Pakistan, and Kyrgyzstan have, compared to the development level of their countries, achieved the highest levels tolerance.

Anti-Semitism and Islamophobia have 46% of common variance; Anti-Semitism and Romaphobia 44% of common variance, and Islamophobia and Romaphobia 38% of common variance.

Above, we already said that societies do not generally experience a smooth transformation from a traditional and survival oriented value set towards a secular and self-expression oriented value set. The *Asabiyya* counter-model to Inglehart, which we proposed above, relies on a factor analytical evaluation of the variables in the world values survey, and combines theoretical insights of the Inglehart School with those by Columbia University sociologist Amitai Etzioni. At the very beginning of the modernization process, societies are traditional, religious, and pre-modern; but at the same time they are also "active" societies with functioning neighborhood structures, and very clear perceptions of what is "good" and "evil", and a high respect of the law. We stated that as the modernization process proceeds, traditional religious values seem to be on the losing side of the societal equation. The uneasiness of the "religious right" in the United States, of the Islamist camp in many countries of the Muslim world, and the religious right in many developing countries is best understood by the process, whereby traditional values get lost at the same time with dimensions of the active society and respect of the law in such vital areas as tax morale, non-acceptability of bribery and government benefits fraud. The worst global performers, on this account, it seems, are Belarus, Brazil, Slovakia, and the Ukraine. As churches are emptying, so do the volunteer organizations; and since "God" is said to be not "existing", everything becomes feasible, acceptable, and even becomes practice: cheating taxes, taking bribes, receiving government benefits even if you are not entitled for them.

THE ACTIVE SOCIETY PERSPECTIVE

Our new "active society index" is a non-parametric standard UNDP-type index of the World Values Survey country results (wave 3+4) for the voluntary work variables:

1. social welfare service for elderly, handicapped or deprived people
2. religious or church organization
3. education, arts, music or cultural activities
4. labor unions
5. political parties or groups
6. local political action groups
7. human rights
8. environment, conservation, animal rights
9. professional associations
10. youth work
11. sports or recreation
12. women's group
13. peace movement
14. organization concerned with health

The 10 superstars of the active society according to this investigation are:

- Tanzania, United Republic of [2001]
- Bangladesh [2002]
- Viet Nam [2001]
- China [2001]
- United States [1999]
- Uganda [2001]
- Algeria [2002]
- Albania [2002]
- Philippines [2001]
- Sweden [1999]
- India [2001]

The 10 worst performers are:

- Turkey [2001]
- Russian Federation [1999]
- Lithuania [1999]
- Serbia [2001]
- Portugal [1999]
- Ukraine [1999]
- Poland [1999]
- Romania [1999]

- Spain [2000]
- Hungary [1999]
- Latvia [1999]

THE CROSS-NATIONAL DETERMINANTS OF GROWTH, TOLERANCE, THE ACTIVE SOCIETY, AND GLOBAL VALUES

The all-important question now is: does an active society propel economic growth? And what are the cross-national determinants of global tolerance, the active society; traditional values; the intransparent, inactive society, and, finally, of social cohesion ("*Asabiyya*")?

Today, a truly massive cross-national research literature exists on the determinants of global development, whose results are often diametrically opposed to one another. The novel idea that an active society is the catalyst of global development has at least several contenders. Our chosen 12 predictors measure the already achieved development level as an important control variable for possibly diminishing returns on capital, three important processes of economic history and geography (the transition process from Communism, access to the sea versus landlocked countries, urbanization) as well as four dimensions of globalization, economic freedom versus state interventions and two variables, which measure possible counter-identities to the otherwise now "unified house of capitalism" – the percentage of Muslims per total population or membership in the European Union (EU-15).

The choice of a country to be included in the final analysis was determined by the availability of a complete data series for these independent variables (if not mentioned otherwise, UNDP data):

- development level ln (GDP PPP pc)
- development level, square (maturity effects) ln (GDP PPP pc)^2
- Dummy: landlocked country
- Dummy: transition country
- Foreign saving (I-S)/GNP (calculated from UNDP 2000)
- MNC PEN 1995 (UNCTAD)
- Percentage of Muslims per total population (Nationmaster)
- state interventionism (absence of economic freedom; Heritage Foundation and Wall Street Journal Website for economic freedom, 2000)
- unequal transfer (calculated from UNDP, concept: ERDI, reciprocal value of comparative "price levels" (developed on the basis of the ERD-Index Yotopoulos et al.) (the Commission maintaining that a low value is good result)
- Urbanization
- World Bank pension reform

Thus, we use the following regression equation:

(Equation 1) dependent variable = a1 +- b1*first part curvilinear function of development level +- b2*second part curvilinear function of development level +- b3.. . *stock of transnational investment per GDP (UNCTAD) mid 1990s +- b4.. . * comparative price levels

(ERDI) +- b5.. . * foreign saving +- b6.. . * dummy transition economy +-b7 * percentage of the population adhering to the Muslim faith +- b8 * European Union membership +- b9 * state interventionism +- b10 * urbanization +- b11 * dummy landlocked country+- b12 * dummy World Bank pension reform

Our results largely confirm the theoretical reasoning, put forward in this publication, and almost half of the variations in economic growth rates are being determined by our chosen variables.

The *active society accelerates economic growth*, and also there are good conditions for economic convergence in the former communist countries nowadays. *Ceteris paribus* it also holds that premature urbanization, high foreign savings and a low comparative price level are a blockade against economic growth, as predicted by dependency theory.

There is a very strong "Kuznets" effect of global tolerance, with modernizing societies becoming more intolerant, before tolerance can spread. A fascinating theme for further research could be the trade-off between the well-known "Kuznets"-effect of international income inequalities and global (in)tolerance. Unfortunately, Muslim population shares – *ceteris paribus* – are a significant international predictor of intolerance.

There is also a Kuznets-type of effect on active society rates. Only rich and mature societies, as a rule, gain what they initially lost in terms of voluntary social organizations, and landlocked and urbanized societies are significantly less involved in voluntary social work as non-urbanized societies and nations with a maritime tradition.

An inverse Kuznets-type of relationship also holds for the determination of traditional values: poor societies are traditional and rich societies non-traditional, while *Muslim population shares, irrespective of development levels, are closely bound to traditional* **values**. EU membership and World Bank pension reforms both shatter the prevalence of traditional values. EU membership has such effects, because in the long run the Union indeed is unthinkable as not being a community of modern, enlightened values. And pension reform, because traditional patterns of social security, based on the pay-as-you-go principle of Bismarckian pensions are very much related to non-market, traditionalist thinking of late 19th Century Europe. Not without coincidence, the staunchest resistance against World Bank inspired pension reforms is to be encountered in the West European Catholic nations.

The intransparent, inactive, cheating society is, just as the phenomenon of inequality and intolerance, a by-product of the modernization process, and decreases at high stages of achieved economic growth. As to be expected by non-secular Muslims throughout the globe, *Islam indeed is a blockade against these phenomena of decay, underlying the strict consequences of the religious belief system for everyday life* (in difference to many lamentable aspects of Catholicism, which is, as we shall analyze below, much more "Sunday" oriented than Islam and Judaism). Landlocked and transition societies all suffer from higher rates of inactiveness and lack of transparency, and all the sleaze and corruption that go with it. Urbanized societies are more prone to these phenomena than rural societies; and EU membership is, lamentably enough, not a blockade against it, but – *ceteris paribus* – even an incentive for such phenomena. Just figure out recent press reports that around 12% of the EU's 308 billion Euro cohesion funds end up in dark channels, while Europe desperately would need more social cohesion among its many different regions. Finally, World Bank pension reforms were usually implemented in countries, which are good disciples of the two Bretton Woods financial institutions, which decidedly fight corruption:

Our final analysis looks at the cross-national determinants of *Asabiyya*. What happens is that again there is a Kuznets-type of relationship, with *Asabiyya* diminishing at middle stages of development, and only later again increasing. Urbanized, landlocked, and transition countries all show much lower kinds of *Asabiyya* as their rural, maritime and non-ex-Warsaw-Pact counterparts. *Very bad for the European Union, their member countries are characterized by a lower degree of Asabiyya than their non-EU counterparts.*

The consequences of this are pretty dire: Especially in East Central Europe, the degree of social *Asabiyya* will be very low by international comparison, and national identity crises and questions about national identity will prop up, the longer European Union membership is already established.

The hard and sometimes bitter medicine against all this can only be a policy and a spirit of Enlightenment and tolerance of an open society in the sense of Sir Karl Popper.

While globalization and dependency play a pivotal role in the determination of economic growth rates, as predicted by dependency theory, the effects of dependency and globalization on

- Global tolerance
- The active society
- Traditional values
- The inactive, intransparent society
- *Asabiyya*

are rather to be neglected.

MEASURING HUNTINGTON: HOW DIFFERENT ARE GLOBAL CULTURES REALLY, AND HOW SIMILAR ARE THEY?

With his works on global cultures and the identity of the leading rich Western democracy nowadays, Huntington (1996 and 2004) has set the trend for current writing and thinking about global cultures.

In view of the huge qualitative international debate on intercultural dialogue, world religions and global tolerance, we decided to start a first truly comparative research into the differences between the major global civilizations on the basis of the World Values Survey data. In all, the SPSS format data, as downloaded from the University of Michigan Website, list 975 variables.

We introduced the proper SPSS weights for country size (1000-weights) into the analysis.

After long deliberations and explorative trials, and keeping in mind that many of the variables of the WVS data set do not render themselves at all for multivariate analysis (see our appendix), we finally included 291 variables with sufficient observations for the major global religious civilizations into our final analysis of the percentage differences of the means of each of the 291 variables from the global mean. The global means and the global means for all the religious groups are documented as well in the appendix. Any member of a religious denomination is considered as "practicing" if she or he attends religious services of his or her denomination at least once a month or more often. The religious groups of our analysis are:

- Buddhism
- Catholicism
- Hinduism
- Judaism
- Muslims
- Orthodoxy
- Practicing Catholicism
- Practicing Islam
- Practicing Orthodoxy
- Practicing Protestantism
- Protestantism

Our results again show the overwhelming importance of the concepts and analyses of Amitai Etzioni for understanding the true underlying dimensions of global value change. The *active society factor* explains *36.6% of total variance,* while the *phobia factor explains 24.4% of total variance*, and the *"homo Catholicus" factor 19.7%.* In all, the three factors *explain 80.7% of the total variance of value systems in the world, as measured by 291 WVS indicators.*

Practicing Islam, Judaism, and practicing Protestantism are the superstars of the "Etzioni paradigm", while Orthodoxy, Catholicism, and practicing Orthodoxy are the cultures, presently least inclined towards an "active society".

The next factor, which combines pretty alarming phenomena of *xenophobia and racism* with a kind of proto-socialist communautarianism and trade-unionism, and, which we call "communautarianism and phobias", is strongest among *practicing Orthodox, Orthodox and Muslims* (less so among the practicing ones), while *Protestantism, practicing Protestantism and Judaism are very far from such a value set.* Typically, these results can also be interpreted as a scale on how de facto values of the active society, market economy, democracy and the Enlightenment are present or absent among the different publics of the different denominations around the globe.

The next and last factor is *the "homo Catholicus"*. Indeed, the factor combines all the characteristics of what is commonly associated with a "good Catholic" – belonging to the Church structures, *celebrating Sunday, educating children to be good believers, but not educating children to be independent. Good Catholics will believe in devil and heaven, but they will be comparatively less participating in human rights organizations.*

In the light of our quantitative analysis of the World Values Survey data, the following consequences for research on global political culture can be drawn. All denominations are being described - not by what they aim to be, but what the sociological WVS data show their members currently believing:

- Buddhism has a higher degree of commitment towards the active society, and a small, but also existent element of phobia and communautarianism
- Catholicism is characterized by a relatively high degree of the "fiesta" factor, by a somewhat higher degree of phobias and by a somewhat lower degree of the active society
- Hinduism is characterized by a high degree of commitment towards an active society, but unfortunately did not overcome as yet the phobias and the

communautarianism, so characteristic also of the countries of the Orthodox political culture. The fiesta factor is not present in this political culture
- Real existing Islam in the world currently characterized, like Hinduism, by a combination of high commitments towards the active society, but unfortunately also many of the phobias and the communautarianism, present also in global Hinduism.
- Judaism is characterized by a very high degree of commitment towards the active society, and by the notable absence of phobia + communautarianism and also by the absence of the "fiesta" factor. The data of the WVS suggest that Judaism is indeed the religion of the active society, of global tolerance and liberal values, often also regarding marriage and family matters
- Orthodox political cultures in many ways combine the politically most unstable mix of all global political/religious cultures: a very high degree of phobias and communautarianism, and a very low degree of commitment towards an active society.
- Protestantism is characterized by a strong rejection of phobias and communautarianism, by a higher commitment to the active society and somewhat also by the "fiesta" factor

We analyzed the performances of the numerically biggest global practicing religious communities i.e., practicing Catholics, practicing Muslims, practicing Orthodox and practicing Protestants.

In all four denominations, the practicing component is more active in organizations of the "active society" than the total, i.e. practicing believers are more involved in organizations of the active society than the passive members of each denomination. But there is an alarming phenomenon of Orthodox phobia and communautarianism: while all other denominations show a phobia and communautarianism reducing aspect of regular religious service attendance, in accordance with the fact that all religions of the "book" demand from their members tolerance and respect of humankind, it is the religiously active segment of the Orthodox denomination, which is more xenophobic and more longing towards communautarianism forms of order than the Orthodox average, and, hence, the secular Orthodox population. Needless to say that not only the Catholic regular practitioners, but also the practicing segment of the other Christian denominations share with the Catholics a good part of the "fiesta" factor, while practically there are no differences between practicing Muslims and secular Muslims in this respect.

The results of this analysis are fairly radical – Islam cannot be portrayed as the most intolerant political culture of the world, and it is the revival of xenophobic and often anti-Semitic attitudes in Orthodox Europe and in the Buddhist and the Hindu world, which should cause the greatest alarm among policy planners and policy makers. Islam and Judaism are religions, which strictly affect everyday life, and it is not prayer-day alone, but everyday life, which decides over your "assets" in "heaven" "above". Christianity, especially Catholic Christianity, runs the danger of merely sticking towards a tradition, and not really translating itself into activities from "Monday" to "Friday". In addition, it is shown that – especially in our multicultural Europe – the active society has a great chance of becoming the glue, which brings all these different traditions and believes together in a positive and future-oriented competition.

Having analyzed the structures of the opinions of the adherents of the major world religions in comparison to the global sample, we have come to the conclusion that in reality

- active society,
- phobias and the
- "fiesta" of the "homo Catholicus"

are the determining underlying currents, explaining 4/5 of the variance of the percentage differences from the global means along more than 290 variables of the World Values Survey. Our results are partially optimistic about the possibilities to overcome phobias in the Muslim world, and especially the active society component of the real existing belief structures of the Muslim *Umma* permit us to say that in globally secularizing societies, Islam is rather an asset and not a burden on development.

In a separate Chapter, we contrasted these images with the images of three of the most famous nineteenth-century European artists, whose works featured "the Orient" in a very "orientalist" way (Jean Léone Gérôme; Jean Auguste Dominique Ingres; Eugène Delacroix). At the height of French colonialism and the brutal conquest of Algeria, and the still existing rigid moral conduct structures of post-revolutionary France in the nineteenth century, these artists depicted the "Orient" as the lustful, lascivious and brute "other" to be conquered by the banner of French-inspired Enlightenment. The globally available images of Islam and Muslims on the Internet, as evidenced by the Google search engine, today, are a different story. *While sexual repressive Europe imagined the world of the Orient as the sexually permissive and brute "other", which has to be civilized, the twenty-first century presents Islam and Muslims as "the headscarf" and the "veil",* which has to be *"liberated",* and Muslim "political and religious violence", which is "threatening" and has to be "repressed".

WHAT THE EUROPEAN YEAR OF INTERCULTURAL DIALOGUE PERHAPS DID NOT DARE TO DISCUSS: CULTURAL DIFFERENCES IN ANTI-SEMITISM AND GLOBAL PHOBIAS

The research design for the following analysis on the individual level of the *tens of thousands of pooled global citizens from all World Values Survey waves and of the tens of thousands of pooled global Muslim respondents from all World Values Survey waves* is completely different from the earlier investigations. This time, we look into the determinants of the global phobias on a global scale (pooled results of all WVS surveys, all times, all countries) and on the level of the Muslim respondents in the WVS (all times, all countries), with listwise deletion of missing values.

The variables for our analysis are:

- Anti-egalitarian position on „Income equality" scale
- Believe in: God
- Child qualities: tolerance and respect for other people
- Competition harmful (Competition good or harmful)
- For state ownership of business

- Highest educational level attained
- Income level
- Never attend religious services (How often do you attend religious services?)
- No family savings during past year (Family savings during past year)
- Rejecting neighbors: Homosexuals
- Rejecting neighbors: Immigrants/foreign workers
- Rejecting neighbors: Jews
- Rejecting neighbors: People of a different race
- Right wing (self positioning in political scale)

What interrelations exist between these variables on the level of global society, and on the level of the Muslim global sample? Short of a confirmatory factor analytical design, which might be the subject of future research, we opted for a standard orthogonal factor analytical research design, which looks into the way, in, which the following indicators of tolerance and phobias

- Child qualities: tolerance and respect for other people
- Rejecting neighbors: Homosexuals
- Rejecting neighbors: Immigrants/foreign workers
- Rejecting neighbors: Jews
- Rejecting neighbors: People of a different race

are being determined by the "classical" political science variables:

- Educational level
- Income levels and savings
- Left-right scale
- Position on competition policy
- Position on state ownership
- Religious dimension

Contradicting hypotheses about these phenomena abound around the globe. *Are religious people more tolerant or less tolerant than secular people? Is the rejection of homosexuals the same stereotype or a different stereotype, than, say, phobia of immigrants, racism or Anti-Semitism? Is the global right wing less tolerant than the global left-wing?*

Our 6 extracted factors with *Eigenvalues* above or equal to one in our standard-type SPSS XIV/XV factor analysis, based on more than 200.000 representative respondents around the globe in more than 80 countries since the 1980s shows that among the 6 extracted factors, which together explain almost 60% of total variance of all the variables used in this analysis, the most important factor is indeed the "phobia of the other", or *"phobia of multiculturalism"* be it the foreign worker, the Jew, the person of a different race, while homophobia is a different factor, which must not be confounded with the typical "xenophobia/racism" dimension.

It should be also emphasized that the "political" or "social" background-variables show relatively weak loadings with this dimension. As squared factor loadings correspond to explained percentages of variance, it can be said that secularism, for example (never attending religious services) is far less strongly and negatively connected with the phobia factor than expected by many. The phobia factor explains some 15% of total variance.

The next important factor, upper strata, reflects the life perspectives and the dimensions of thinking of the well-to-do on this Earth. But interestingly enough, the connections of the richer people around the globe with the hard-core values of economic liberalism such as competition policy, income redistribution, and private ownership are far weaker than most would expect. Interestingly enough, also the political affiliation of the upper strata with the political right is far weaker than expected, and in fact explains far less than 10% of the variance of the political left-right-scale.

The next factor is *secularism*. But while secular people are in their majority politically at home on the left and not on the right-wing, and tend to be somewhat richer and more educated than their religious counterparts, and are also in favor of state interventions rather than a pure market economy, the great hope of followers of secularism around the globe that with secularism comes tolerance is rather decidedly to be rejected. Nowadays, there is also a marked positive relationship between secularism and Anti-Semitism, i.e. we are confronted in the 21st Century by a phenomenon of "pagan Anti-Semitism".

Our results about the *contemporary etatist mentality* present also some surprising and interesting aspects. It is not so much the political left, but the political right nowadays, which feels attracted to this kind of perspective. Competition is seen as harmful, one is in favor of state-owned businesses, and one accumulated some family savings over the life cycle, and one believes somewhat in God but one rejects tolerance as a value in education. The conservative etatist mentality also accepts homosexual neighbors, while the profile *vis-à-vis* the other "multicultural groups" is unclear.

The next factor, *anti-egalitarianism*, is an interesting and also frightening combination of anti-egalitarianism, savings poverty, a decided yes to state ownership of the means of production, homophobia and – interestingly enough – the theoretical support for the thesis that tolerance and respect for other people are important qualities of a child. The adherents of this model tend to identify themselves rather with the political right, and not with the political left; they in some way represent the "socialism of the desperate".

The last factor, which achieved an *Eigenvalue* greater or equal to 1, is *homophobia*. Homophobes rather tend to disregard tolerance in education; they will be – *ceteris paribus* – rather in favor of state ownership of the means of production and they will be interestingly enough rather left-wing and not right-wing. Homophobia is a phenomenon of the educated and the rather well-to-do, but interestingly, homophobes will be also rather anti-Semites, but not xenophobes.

The all important question now is of course, whether the "Umma" – the community of Muslim believers – as reflected in the World Values Survey – shares these value structures, or whether there are other forces at work, which sharply distinguish the Umma from the non-believers. It should be emphasized at the outset that the present study deals with the real existing people around the globe and not with an imagined and idealized *Umma*.

Are religious Muslims more tolerant or less tolerant than secular Muslims? Is the rejection of homosexuals the same stereotype or a different stereotype, than, say, phobia of immigrants, racism or Anti-Semitism also in the world of the *Umma*? Is the Muslim right wing less tolerant or more tolerant than the Muslim left-wing? To make a long story short, we have come to the surprising conclusion here that the contemporary ideological landscape, as analyzed by our global factor analysis with almost 30.000 Muslim representative respondents, is far nearer to the political causal mechanisms, so well-known to European sociology from the 1930s to the days of the first appearance of the "guest workers" in Europe during the 1960s. In theoretical terms, our analysis would suggest far more classical answers to the contemporary crisis of the Muslim world than many would suggest—i.e., to concentrate on the "bread and butter issues" of a decent worker's and trade union movement, to try to integrate migrants and nationals in the Muslim countries themselves, et cetera.

Our again 6 extracted factors with *Eigenvalues* above or equal to one in our standard-type SPSS XIV/XV factor analysis, based on around 30.000 representative Muslim respondents around the globe in more than 60 countries since the 1980s shows that among the 6 extracted factors, which together explain again almost 60% of total variance of all the variables used in this analysis, the most important factor is indeed—just as in the case of global society—the "phobia of the other", or "phobia of multiculturalism" or "Muslim racism" against foreign workers, and persons of a different race. Muslim racists, in contrast to non-Muslim racists (see above) tend to be decidedly tolerant of homosexuals, but they tend to be somewhat anti-Semitic, be of upper class origin, and they will be decidedly politically right-wing and they will hold anti-egalitarian positions on income inequality. So in a way, their mindset will rather better reflect the *classical picture of racism and xenophobia, which sociology had from the days of the 1930s through to the days of the "guest worker economy" in the 1960s.* Muslim xenophobes will also be – *ceteris paribus* – more often to be seen at prayer services than their non-xenophobic Muslim counterparts. It should be emphasized that the "social" background-variables show medium loadings with this dimension. As squared factor loadings correspond to explained percentages of variance, it can be said that Muslim racists are not secularists. The racism factor explains again some 15% of total variance. The existence of such a strong, xenophobic phenomenon in the Muslim world and also among the Muslims in the developed, Western democracies raises the question about the political strategies of the right and left in Western democracies, including Turkey, to balance such tendencies.

The next important factor, Muslim poverty, reflects the life perspectives and the dimensions of thinking of the *Muslim poor*. Interestingly enough, the connections of the Muslim poor around the globe with the hard-core values of left wing ideology are still in force, such as their rejection of competition policy, their favoring income redistribution, their rejection of private ownership. But these identities tend to be weaker than most would expect, Interestingly enough, also the political affiliation of the lower strata with the political left are far weaker than expected, and in fact explain far less than 10% of the variance of the political left-right-scale. *The Muslim poor share the common phobias—rejecting immigrants, Jews, people of a different race, but not homosexuals.*

The next factor is *Muslim secularism*. But while secular Muslims also—like their global counterparts—are in their majority more left than right-wing, and tend to be somewhat richer and more educated than their religious counterparts, they will be very much in favor of state interventions and will also think that competition is harmful. Their mindset corresponds neatly to the mindset of "Arab socialism", "Kemalism", "Third Worldism", *and there is only a weak and lamentably enough positive relationship between secularism and phobias.*

The next three factors are in total difference to the global sample. *Muslim Anti-Semitism* rather reminds us of the typical *petite bourgeoisie* Anti-Semitism sociology is so familiar with in the *Europe of the 1930s—anti-Semites will be strongly in favor of competition, they will reject state ownership, but in contrast to the Europe of the 1930s they will be somewhat sympathizing with the Left, and they will be rather secular. They will share several other phobias, most notably against homosexuals.*

Finally, there will be two strings of tolerance at work among the global *Umma* – a kind of decided *secular tolerance movement, rejecting Anti-Semitism, and interestingly enough combining anti-egalitarian positions with a relatively low socio-economic status*. Together with their religious counterpart, they will be strongly of the opinion that tolerance is an important factor in education.

The *religiously tolerant current* received a somewhat higher education and enjoys a higher income, is *politically rather on the left and is also in favor of state ownership, but does not transpose its theoretical commitment towards tolerance and respect in education into the daily practice of not rejecting Jews* and/or homosexuals, and is at best indifferent *vis-à-vis* immigrants and people of a different race.

Needless to say, the political conclusions from our analysis this time are only partially optimistic. To be sure, factors 1–3 of our analysis are pretty similar in their structure for both global society and the *Umma*.

Racism, poverty and petite bourgeoisie thinking prolong and deepen such phenomena as Muslim Anti-Semitism, and the religiously tolerant currents "exclude" Jews from their discourse. Only the current of "secular tolerance" inspires some hope here, but in many ways, it will be not strong enough to influence several Muslim societies from the fatal projections of their real existing problems onto scapegoats. The task of building up true workers movements and workers parties, social democracies in the classical sense of the European word of the 1930s through to the mid 1970s would be very high on the agenda. From the viewpoint of liberal Western democracy, including secular Turkey, the quantitative and qualitative leap of the religious current of tolerance into a religious democratic mass movement with a social and economic agenda comparable to parties like the CDU/CSU in the 1950s, 1960s and early 1970s would be (and in the case of the Turkish AKP was) a highly welcome. Last but not least, the secularist but upper-class current, which is the fruit of "Arab socialism", "secular Kemalism", et cetera, at least would have the potential to become a true socio-liberal movement. Compared to the tendencies of Muslim racism and Muslim poverty/global racism and global upper class identities, it is clear how important it would be to act politically to save the Muslim world from the siren calls of religious fanatism and secular anti-imperialist anti-Zionism, which brought the region to nowhere during the last 60 years, and to save the globe from the siren calls of etatism and anti-egalitarianism as the unifying characteristics of the populist movements around the globe in the early twenty-first cetnury.

One of the surprising conclusions of this work is that the sophisticated analysis of the World Values Survey shows that the dimension of the active society is absolutely necessary for advanced and also for the transformation and the developing democracies. The dimension of the active society and the religious or post-religious humanistic convictions, which are necessary to fuel such a system of an active society, become all the more important as societies transform themselves from the "traditional" to the "modern" spectrum in the sense of Inglehart's theory.

LAÏCITÉ AND ITS LIMITS

Religious conservatives in many countries, in Latin America, in the Middle East and North Africa, in India, in Eastern Europe and the former USSR, fearing a dwindling role of religion around the globe, observe the dwindling global role of religion, but they get it all wrong in their analysis. They will blame female emancipation as the arch-enemy, responsible for what they perceive as the destruction of religious values, the family and what have you. Enlightened liberals of all sorts, inside and outside the European Union, will by contrast push relentlessly for what they term "anti-discrimination policy", and they will underline the role of gender policy in the evolving democratic systems. Note at this point, perhaps, that EURLEX, the data archive for the existing *"Acquis Communautaire"*, i.e., the European Union law, which has to be implemented by all acceding countries, lists "discrimination" 1292 times, "gender" 109 times, "sexual orientation" 18 times, homosexual" 12 times, "lesbian" two times, while the term "Muslim" appears only 18 times, "Christianity" only six times, and "religion" in general only 39 times! The European Union, seen in such a way, is "top-less", and all the former talk of the EU as a "Christian Club" to the contrary, it is a "Club" of the (ultra)liberal market economy plus – well plus some anti-discrimination policy. A critic at this point might also remark that the word "wage" appears throughout the "Acquis" only 66 times, while the term "market" appears 14,221 times!

For the empirical political scientist, sharing humanistic and liberal values, neither the vision of the religious conservatives nor the vision of the ultraliberal anti-discriminationists is correct.

Nowadays, the word "family" appears only 461 times in the *"Acquis"*, and most of these references are to such combined terms as "family members", "family allowances", "family benefits" … The fact is that in most European countries, and in many other countries around the globe, a growing number of people regard the institution of marriage as outdated. A still larger number of people is not willing anymore even to consider a religious ceremony in the context of marriage; and this kind of thinking made heavy inroads in Catholic Latin America, in Protestant South Africa and interestingly enough also in Muslim Kyrgyzstan and in Muslim Iran, as well as in Muslim Bangladesh and in Orthodox Russia.

The countries still regarding "marriage" not as being outdated are quickly named here – above all the Protestant and increasingly plural United States of America, but also Japan, Protestant Iceland, Catholic Croatia and Poland, the Catholic Dominican Republic and religiously plural Tanzania, and Muslim Morocco, Egypt, Turkey, Pakistan and Indonesia.

One now could argue that all this is a matter of individual choice, and that no societal consequences are connected with such patterns. And here, the match between the religious conservatives around the globe and the "progressives" in such divergent countries as France or Iran could be tilted in favor of the religious conservatives, insofar as our empirical analyses clearly show that there are certain societal limits to such a state of affairs.

One very clear consequence of the erosion of the model of marriage (and mind you, the WVS question was NOT about religious marriage, but marriage IN GENERAL) is sexual permissiveness, which in the UNDP-type of index developed here is understood to be the combination of three syndromes:

- The rejection of the model of marriage as such
- Adultery is permissible
- Casual sex is acceptable

France and Slovenia lead the field here, with a large chunk of the European continent – the UK, the BENELUX countries, Germany, Spain, Greece, Sweden and Estonia as well as Belarus following behind in a group. The third group of medium permissiveness is constituted by Portugal, Ireland, Italy, the Central European countries, the Ukraine, Russia, the rest of the Baltic States, and Finland, while Croatia, Romania, and Poland are the least sexually permissive European societies.

The provocative question in this context then is: which trade-off exists between the erosion of the institution of civil heterosexual marriage and societal decay? For this reason, we calculated again a UNDP type of index, this time called the clean hands index, composed of the acceptance of bribery, cheating on taxes, and acceptance of government benefits fraud.

Clean Hands Index

- Mean acceptance level: bribery
- Mean acceptance level: cheating on taxes
- Mean acceptance level: government benefits fraud

The most lamentable results are to be observed in ultra-permissive societies like France, Belarus, Belgium et cetera, while the countries most immune against the combination of bribery, cheating on taxes and government benefits fraud are the family-value oriented countries like Morocco, Egypt, and Turkey.

Being an empirical political scientist, we now can also estimate the *"trigger levels" of sexual permissiveness, beyond which a society will increasingly face the danger of a social implosion, constituted by bribery, tax evasion and government benefits fraud.* Our estimate, well usable for policy planners and religious and civil society leaders around the globe is that a society must under any circumstances avoid a situation where more than *one third of the adult population assumes that marriage is outdated.*

Our next empirical test deals with the hotly contested question—how much secularization is necessary, or for that matter, even possible? Or do we really need a stronger religious consciousness throughout the globe? Does frequent religious service attendance make people more tolerant, less accepting corruption, more optimistic or less optimistic about the market economy, does it drive them politically to the right or to the left, and what are the effects on such policy areas as economic inequality?

Are empty churches, mosques, synagogues and temples really in the interest of enlightened humanity? Our empirical analysis tests the effects of falling religious service attendance rates on societal attitudes and behavior, using a partial correlation analyses between religious service non-attendance rates with 77 key World Values Survey indicators for the four separate global religious groups: Catholics, Muslims, Orthodox and Protestants. A sophisticated research design, looking at the correlations of religious service non-attendance versus attendance rates (high numerical values: no attendance, low numerical values: daily attendance) in the global Catholic, Muslim *et cetera* sample with the 77 variables, has to exclude the obvious intervening effects of poverty and education in the game. Religious sociology around the globe fairly reasonably assumes that religious service attendance rates among the poor are higher than among the rich, and they also assume that the same holds for the trade-off with education. Thus we did not run bi-variate correlations, but partial SPSS XIV and XV correlations, keeping constant the WVS variables: Highest educational level attained and Income level.

The most notable increases in the process of secularization among the global Muslims are to be observed for:

- Lack of confidence: churches
- Hard work brings success
- Lack of confidence: justice system
- Justifiable: abortion
- Justifiable: manipulation of food

The most notable decreases along the process of secularization are to be observed for the following variables:

- Justifiable: keeping money that you have found
- Justifiable: joyriding
- Self positioning in political left-right scale on the right
- Rejecting neighbors: gypsies
- Justifiable: lying

It has to be noted that the observed effects in all religious groups around the world are rather small.

In general, it can be safely assumed that secularization does NOT have the general and beneficial effects, which secularists around the globe assume to have. Although the tendency to justify political assassinations decreases among secular Muslims and secular Protestants, and increases among secular Catholics and secular Orthodox, the effects explain a rather small percentage of total variance (squared partial correlations). *The direct comparison between the "secularization paths" of the four large global denominations however yields quite interesting results: Muslims are the religious denomination, whose "yes" to the "American dream" ("hard work brings success") is strongly secularization-driven.*

Let us thus sum up in a few sentences: Muslims generally are more value-conservative than the main other European denominations. But their commitment to democracy is clear, and their trust in the European Union is greater than the trust, the followers of many other denominations have in the European Union. Generally, it can be said: in order to further strengthen the alliance of Enlightenment, there is no need for Muslims to give up their spirituality. This is the positive and optimistic message of this work. For Europe it would be foolish to alienate a good part of its future human capital.

Integration agenda for European policy makers: where Muslim integration failed in Europe (European Muslims + 20% or higher values than European population in general)

- Politicians who don't believe in God are unfit for public office (strongly agree)
- Having the army rule very good
- Not at all satisfied with democracy
- Jobs are scarce: men have more rights then
- Justifiable political assassination (sometimes or always)
- Rejecting neighbors of a different race
- Rejecting homosexual neighbors
- Having experts make decisions very good
- Confidence in the Press: none at all
- in a democracy, the economy runs badly
- Political system, which governs the country very bad
- Confidence in the Police: none at all
- Already joined unofficial strikes

Where the integration agenda for European policy makers went well and where Muslim integration succeeded in Europe (European Muslims - 20% or lower values than European population in general):

- Having a democratic political system very bad
- Rejecting neighbors who are immigrants or foreign workers
- Justifiable paying cash (sometimes or always)
- Democracy may have problems but it's better (strongly disagree)

Chapter 1

INTRODUCTION

Only a quick glance at the international media will already convince everybody that intercultural questions are THE issue of global politics in the early twenty-first century[3].

In Europe, which for historical reasons already had the longest common borders with the Muslim world, the existence of a minority of some 15 million Muslims makes the question of "Intercultural Dialogue" all important. Europe only slowly seems to come to terms with this challenge. Among the positive measures, one has to single out the "European Year of Intercultural Dialogue". The European Year of Intercultural Dialogue (2008) was established, as it is well-known, by Decision N° 1983/2006/EC of the European Parliament and of the Council (18 December 2006):

> "Europe is becoming more culturally diverse. The enlargement of the European Union, deregulation of employment laws and globalisation have increased the multicultural character of many countries, adding to the number of languages, religions, ethnic and cultural backgrounds found on the continent. As a result, intercultural dialogue has an increasingly important role to play in fostering European identity and citizenship." (http://www.interculturaldialogue2008.eu/406.0.html?andredirect_url=my-startpage-eyid.html)

About the term *religion,* the official Website of the European Year states:

> Religious beliefs, philosophies and convictions are an integral part of cultural diversity which, through dialogue, enriches our societies and contributes to individual fulfilment. But in our increasingly multicultural societies, the diversity of faiths, beliefs and convictions can lead to misconceptions and fears. A people-to-people dialogue based on respect can overcome these fears by fostering mutual knowledge and openness. (http://www.interculturaldialogue 2008.eu/414.0.html).

Slowly, but surely, the statistical and bureaucratic apparatus of the European institutions begins to react to the new challenges and starts to collect statistics on *multiculturalism.*

Eurobarometer, the official opinion survey data collection body of the European Union, presents the following data series on the issues – one is a survey on the percentage of people saying that in their countries of residence there is something like "religious discrimination", the other survey, published only as recently as November 2007, directly asked the residents of the EU-27 about "intercultural dialogue". But beyond that, comparative and hard facts about multicultural social and opinion realities in Europe are very hard to come by, to say the least, and are even impossible to collect in France[4], nota bene, the country with the largest Muslim minority in Europe. France prohibits nowadays the collection of religion-based statistical data, so that no complete data set on such phenomena as, say, Muslim poverty as compared to Catholic, Protestant or agnostic poverty, or Muslim rejection of democracy as compared to Catholic, Protestant or agnostic rejection of democracy can be collected for the EU-27 as a whole.

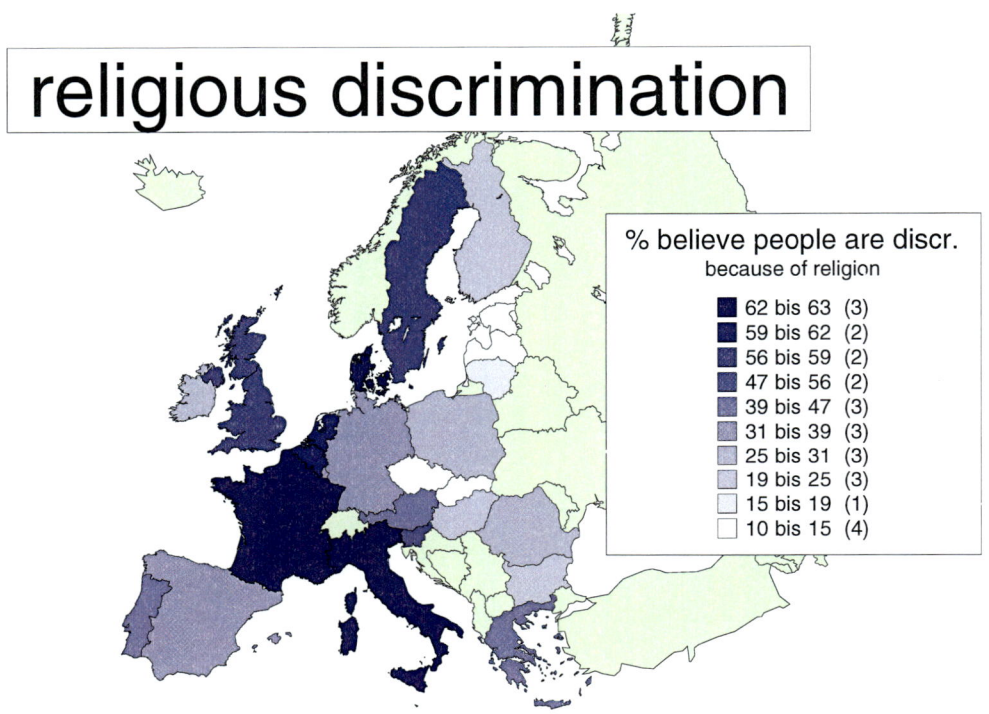

Map 1. Discrimination because of religion or religious confession in Europe – Eurobarometer data on the percentage of the total European population saying that such discrimination exists in their countries.

Source: Eurobarometer 263 EB65.4, http://ec.europa.eu/public_opinion /archives/ eb_special_en.htm. Our own compilations, based on Microsoft EXCEL 2000 map system. Only data for the EU-27 are available.

Explanatory note: "bis" is shorthand for "ranging from … to"; countries with missing values are marked in green color

---

[3] For a quantitative content analysis of global media, see below.
[4] Giry St. (2006), "France and Its Muslims" *Foreign Affairs,* September/October 2006

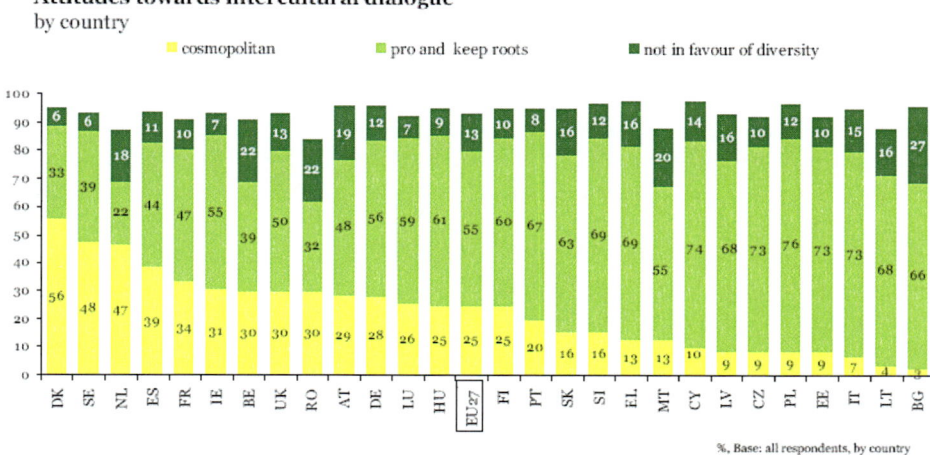

Source: Eurobarometer, November 2007, available from: http://www.interculturaldialogue2008.eu/407.0.html?andredirect_url=my-startpage-eyid.html

Graph 1. European attitudes towards intercultural dialogue.

But nonetheless, social scientists try very hard to get the data they need at least by relying on international data collections like the World Values Survey or the European Social Survey.

ON THE QUANTITATIVE METHODOLOGY OF THIS WORK

This study uses an array of quantitative methods to come to terms with global values, global value change, and the position of Muslims in these changing global value maps.

Europe, confronted with a plurality of values, tries to come to terms with it. So finally, one might argue, the behavioral revolution is beginning to be firmly established in the debate about "global Islam" and the future of the European continent. *Robert Barro[5], Ronald T. Inglehart[6], Jytte Klausen[7], Dalia Mogahed[8], Mansoor Moaddel[9], Marcus Noland[10], Pippa*

---

[5] *Religion and economic growth /* (together Rachel M McCleary), Cambridge, Mass.: National Bureau of Economic Research, 2003.
[6] *Islam, gender, culture, and democracy: findings from the World Values Survey and the European Values Survey /* Willowdale, ON: De Sitter Publications, 2002, and *Islam and the West: testing the clash of civilizations thesis /* (gemeinsam mit Pippa Norris), Cambridge, Mass.: Research Programs, John F. Kennedy School of Government, Harvard University, 2002.
[7] *The Islamic challenge: politics and religion in Western Europe /* New York, N.Y.: Oxford University Press, 2005; *Continuity and change in contemporary capitalism /* Cambridge, UK; New York, NY: Cambridge University Press, 1999; *War and welfare: Europe and the United States, 1945 to the present /* New York: St. Martin's Press, 1998; *European integration in social and historical perspective: 1850 to the present /* Lanham, Md.: Rowman and Littlefield Publishers, 1997; *Has liberalism failed women?: assuring equal representation in Europe and the United States /* New York, N.Y.: PALGRAVE, 2001
[8] *Who Speaks for Islam?: What a Billion Muslims Really Think.* By John L. Esposito, Dalia Mogahed, March 2008, New York: Gallup Press.
[9] Class, politics, and ideology in the Iranian revolution / Columbia University Press, 1993; The Oxford handbook of global religions / (with Juergensmeyer, Mark) Oxford; New York: Oxford University Press, 2006; Modernist and fundamentalist debates in Islam: a reader / New York: Palgrave Macmillan, 2002, 2000; Islamic modernism, nationalism, and fundamentalism: episode and discourse / Chicago: University of Chicago Press, 2005; Jordanian exceptionalism: a comparative analysis of state-religion relationships in Egypt, Iran, Jordan,

Norris[11], *and Thorleif Pettersson*[12] introduced the necessary empirical elements into a value-laden debate, otherwise characterized by such terms as "leading culture" or "guiding culture". Professor *Bassam Tibi* said in an interview with *Der Spiegel:*

> "I have always emphasized how dangerous it is to talk about a specifically German Leitkultur. [...] The important thing is: the line doesn't run between Europe and Islam, but between all open societies and their enemies. I myself am Muslim and I stand on the side of an open society. Democratic Muslims like myself can push for a European Leitkultur and against its enemies. [...]My idea of a European Leitkultur is based on the foundation of a democratic community whose members are bound together through a collective identity as citizens of that community. Such a collective identity—in the sense of the French Citoyenite (citizenship)—stands above religious identity. Religion may, of course, be practiced privately, but in public only citizenship counts. Such a concept would unite Muslims with non-Muslims. [...] In my understanding [...] multiculturalism means "anything goes." [...] The better concept would be cultural pluralism. Unlike multiculturalism, cultural pluralism doesn't just mean diversity but also togetherness—primarily the understanding of the rules of the game—the European values structure. (*http://www.spiegel.de/international/0,1518,329784,00.html*)

Absurd, as it may seem at first sight, there are hardly any international comparative data on values across cultures—if it were not for the World Values Survey. A generation of political scientists, headed by Michigan University's Ronald T. Inglehart, studied global and Muslim values for more than two decades now and even made their data freely available on the Internet (http://www.worldvaluessurvey.org/). Their gigantic project, analyzing global values and global value change in now over 80 countries is based on advanced social survey methodology, and uses a questionnaire and sampling methods, which are unparalleled in the social science profession. The sociological and political science approach, underlying the project, asks global respondents the same kind of questions, like:

Qualities That Children Can Be Encouraged to Learn at Home

Important child qualities: good manners (A027)
Important child qualities: independence (A029)
Important child qualities: hard work (A030)
Important child qualities: feeling of responsibility (A032)
Important child qualities: imagination (A034)

---

and Syria / Houndmills, Basingstoke, Hampshire; New York: Palgrave, 2002; Values and perceptions of the Islamic and Middle Eastern publics / New York: Palgrave Macmillan, 2007

[10] The Arab economies in a changing world / (with Howard Pack), Washington, DC: Peterson Institute for International Economics, 2007.

[11] Sacred and secular: religion and politics worldwide / Pippa Norris; Ronald Inglehart; Cambridge, UK; New York: Cambridge University Press, 2004.

[12] Measuring and mapping cultures: 25 years of comparative value surveys / Leiden; Boston: Brill, 2007; The retention of religious experiences / Uppsala: [Univ.]; Stockholm: distr., Almqvist and Wiksell international, 1975 und Scandinavian values: religion and morality in the Nordic countries / Uppsala: S. Academiae Ubsaliensis; Stockholm: Distributor, Almqvist and Wiksell International, 1994. Also, his path-breaking article "The Religious Factor in Contemporary Society: The Differential Impact of Religion on the Private and Public Sphere in Comparative Perspective" (together with Halman, Loek; und Verweij, Johan) in International journal of comparative sociology. 40, no. 1, (1999): 141ff. has to be duly mentioned here.

Important child qualities: tolerance and respect for other people (A035)
Important child qualities: thrift saving money and things (A038)
Important child qualities: determination perseverance (A039)
Important child qualities: religious faith (A040)
Important child qualities: unselfishness (A041)
Important child qualities: obedience (A042)

The hundreds of questions, available to users of the WVS Website, are grouped into the following categories and are available for the time periods 1981–1984, 1989–1993, 1994–1999, and 1999–2004 (the so-called "waves" of the World Values Survey):

1 Structure
2 Perceptions of life
3 Environment
4 Work
5 Family
6 Politics and Society
7 Religion and Morale
8 National Identity
9 Sociodemographics

The importance of these data cannot be overestimated. Jim Clifton, the chairman and chief executive officer of The Gallup Organization, spoke about a reporter's question after 9/11 to then-US-Defense Secretary Donald H. Rumsfeld. The reporter wanted to know whether Muslims supported the attacks (http://www.mcclatchydc.com/ homepage /story /20236.html). Rumsfeld said the story goes:

> "No one knew", according to Clifton, "because you can't do a Gallup Poll of Muslim opinion." (http://www.mcclatchydc.com/homepage/story/20236.html).

No one in Washington seemed to have any idea what 1.4 billion Muslims in the world were thinking.

Gallup's answer today, according to which 8 percent of Muslims are "extremists", and 35 percent "love us" may sound straightforward, but overlooks the available data from the World Values Survey, which draw a clear distinction between outright support for political violence, conservative value scales, and values, which are conservative, and reject central egalitarian values of democracy (http://www.gallup.com/press/104209/Who-Speaks-Islam-What-Billion-Muslims-Really-Think.aspx).

Systematic use of the WVS to study the fathoms of Muslim global opinion are emerging in the social science profession, but up to today the almost 30.000 interviews with global Muslim respondents were not as yet used to study the totality of the challenge, posed by Islamist radicalism and global terrorism.

These materials will be important in the current debate about Professor John Esposito's and Dalia Mogahed's *Who Speaks for Islam?: What a Billion Muslims Really Think* (Esposito/Mogahed, 2008).

John L. Esposito is Professor of Religion and International Affairs at Georgetown University. (Photo credit: http://news-service.stanford.edu/news/2003/november19/gifs/Esposito-034.jpg)

Dalia Mogahed is Senior Analyst and Executive Director of the Gallup Center for Muslim Studies. (Photo credit: http://www.allamericanspeakers.com/speakers/Dalia-Mogahed/9240.)

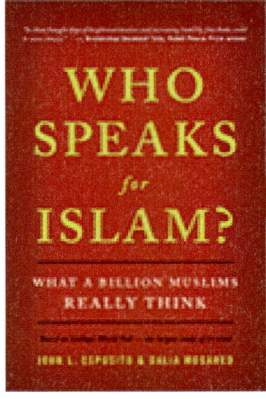

(Photo credit: http://media.gallup.com/dataviz/WWW/WhoSpeaksForIslam-C.gif.)

Who Speaks for Islam?: What a Billion Muslims Really Think (John L Esposito and Dalia Mogahed, 2007, 204 pp. New York, N.Y.: Gallup Press) aroused many controversies. A recent reviewer remarked: *"It provides a very small and partial account of the responses to some questions, but fails to include even one table or chart of data. It does not even provide a clear list of the questions that were asked. The appendix, where one might expect to find questionnaires, charts, and tables, provides only a short narrative discussion of Gallup's sampling techniques and general mode of operation."* Hillel Fradkin, Director, Center for Islam, Democracy and the Future of the Muslim World, Senior Fellow, Hudson Institute, Washington, D.C. Headquarters, available at: http://blogs.law.harvard.edu/mesh/2008/04/who_does_speak_for_islam/

To begin with, the almost 30,000 interviews with representative Muslims in 80 countries are not faring badly with the 50,000 Muslim interview partners, surveyed by Gallup in 35 countries. The World Values Survey, in addition, neatly portrays the opinions, anxieties and the social situation of the Muslim minorities in western countries, although small sample sizes caution against too rapid conclusions. Nevertheless: do you know me any better comparative data, on, say, income and trust in democracy among Muslims in Western Europe or the traditional countries of "immigration" in the OECD? And even if some of our conclusions might be wrong, they would be at least a worthwhile starting point to run survey research projects with the WVS questionnaire among the 15 million people of the Muslim minorities in the European Union, the European Free Trade Area (EFTA, Switzerland) and the countries of the European Economic Area (EEA), Iceland, and Norway. Or to compare the integration patterns of Muslims in the US, Canada, or Australia with those in Western Europe.

Thanks to the University of Michigan Professor Ronald T. Inglehart, global scholarship has free data available on the opinions, values and life trajectories of thousands of representative Muslims since the 1990s, among them the representative surveys in Albania [1998], Albania [2002], Algeria [2002], Azerbaijan [1997], Bangladesh [1996], Bangladesh

[2002], Bosnia and Herzegovina [1998], Bosnia and Herzegovina [2001], Egypt [2000], Indonesia [2001], Iran (Islamic Republic of) [2000], Iraq [2004], Jordan [2001], Kyrgyzstan [2003], Morocco [2001], Morocco [2001], Nigeria [1990], Nigeria [1995], Nigeria [2000], Pakistan [1997], Pakistan [2001], Saudi Arabia [2003], Turkey [1990], Turkey [1996], Turkey [2001], and Turkey [2001].

Photo credit: http://word.world-citizenship.org/wp-content/uploads/2007/08 /Ronald%20Inglehart%20-USA.jpg

Mansoor Moaddel, professor of sociology at Eastern Michigan University, was the principal investigator for values surveys in Egypt, Iran, Jordan, Morocco and Saudi Arabia. (Photo credit: http://www.decadeofbehavior.org/policyseminars/Terrorism/moaddel.jpg)

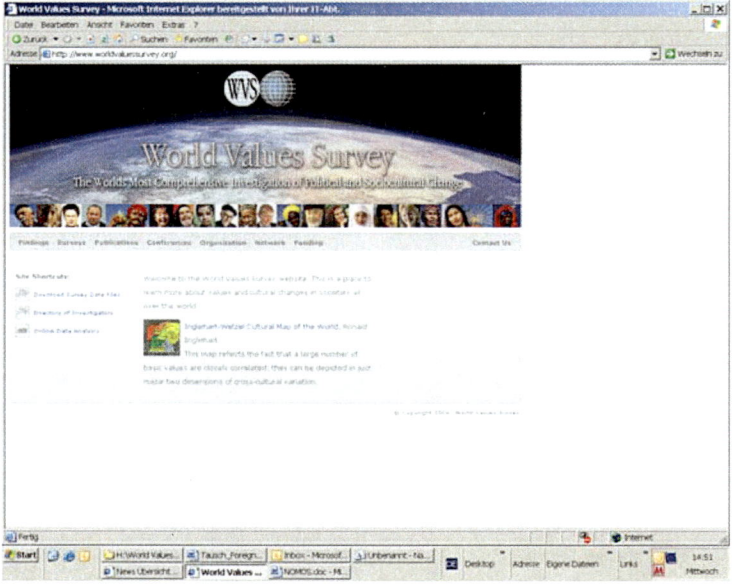

13.2% of Muslims – in comparison to 12.7% of the global citizenry – disagree or strongly disagree with the opinion that *"Democracy may have problems but is better"*.

Our re-analysis re-iterates the *basic optimism* inherent in the writings by Inglehart (2003), Inglehart and Baker (2000), and Inglehart and Norris (2003). Global Muslims might be *"conservative"* in their attitudes on *family, gender and sexuality*, but certainly *"Islam" cannot be blamed* as such for a *rejection of democracy* or for a tendency to generally support *political violence*. The World Values Survey data, re-analyzed here, are in fact a dire warning to those who think that Europe is THE home of democratic stability and non-violence *per se*, and that European values are uniform, democratic and non-violent. The percentage of those people who disagree or strongly disagree with the statement that democracy may have problems, but it's better, is 12.2% for the global Muslim population, and thus comparable to the percentages among global Protestants (13.4%), Sikhs (12.3%), Jews (11.8%), Buddhists (11.7%), Roman Catholics (10.6%) or Hindus (8.4%). It is true that some Muslim countries, like Iran, Indonesia, Saudi Arabia and Kyrgyzstan figure prominently among those nations, whose population is basically skeptical about democracy, but one should not forget that also the EU-27 member countries UK, Romania, Bulgaria and Hungary are placed worse than Pakistan, Iraq, and Turkey on this scale.

When people are asked whether they (strongly) agree or disagree with the sentence that using violence to pursue political goals is never justified, only 5.2% of global Muslims strongly disagreed with the statement and another 7.4% of global Muslims disagreed. It is really stunning to observe that global Roman Catholics, Orthodox and Protestants are much more prepared to concede that using violence to pursue political goals is justified. Thus it is then no surprise that among the most violence-condoning nations on earth we find the Dominican Republic, Peru, the EU-member Spain, Venezuela, and the EU-newcomers Romania and Lithuania, and not just the Islamic Conference member with a religiously mixed population, Nigeria.

The population the Muslim EU-candidate country Turkey is far less inclined towards condoning the use of violence for political ends than in the EU-27-core country Sweden, and Bangladesh and Azerbaijan are two shining examples of majority Muslim political cultures, almost totally rejecting the use of violence for political purposes.

Putting things further into perspectives, it also emerges from the WVS data that yes; indeed, many Muslims believe that it is better for society that immigrants do maintain their customs and traditions. 67.5% of global Muslims think in such a way. But global Hindus (68.1%) and global Jewry (67.5%) thinks likewise, just as Buddhists (61.1%) and the Orthodox (58.4%) do. By contrast, only a minority of Catholics (41.6% and Protestants (29.9) hold such a belief.

The limited number of countries, which permit conclusions from the WVS in this direction, can be neatly ranked into the 8 leading pro-assimilation countries (East Germany, Austria, Denmark, Belgium, West Germany, France, Iceland and the Netherlands), and the 8 separate customs and traditions nations (Greece, Romania, Bulgaria, Italy, Luxembourg, Ireland, Croatia, and Malta). Among the *European* "assimilationist" religious denominations, the Protestants are leading (69.6% of EU-27 + EEA + EFTA Protestants being in favor of assimilation), while only 24.3% of Euro-Islam wants to be assimilated, while 75.7% of Euro-Islam wants to remain distinct. But again, it would be wrong to assume that Muslims are alone in this their belief – in fact, Euro-Orthodoxy is about the same as resentful against "assimilation" as Euro-Islam.

One of the hardest tasks in the fight against global terrorism will be to convince global Muslims, worldwide that not *Jews*, but *dictatorships* are their enemy, and that in comparison with the *unprecedented religious freedom Muslims enjoy in Western countries, it would be worthwhile* to start a real debate on *Muslim religious freedom in countries like China, Myanmar* and others, where there are indeed just grievances to be observed about the repression of Muslim religious freedoms.

The global existence of *"Muslim Calvinist attitudes"*, as reflected in the data of this publication, is a sign of hope; and data like the ones, reproduced in this book, will contribute to focus the Muslim debate on what should be the real center of the debate: *not the „evil West", and not the „evil Jews", are the enemy, and the culture of Enlightenment, Democracy and Social Market economy are the true allies of Muslim humanism.*

Only 7% radicals? Yet another terrorist attack in Israel. (Photo credit: http://berlin.mfa.gov.il/mfm/Data/36834.jpg.)

The bombing outrages in Madrid and London, just to name a few, pose a vital question: how big is the percentage of terror sympathizers and conditional sympathizers, and how big is the percentage of absolute opponents of terrorism in the global Muslim world? (Photo credit: http://varifrank.com/images/madrid-bombing-large-01.jpg)

So, thanks to the University of Michigan Professor Ronald T. Inglehart, global scholarship has free data available on the opinions, values and life trajectories of thousands of representative Muslims since the 1990s, among them the representative surveys in Albania [1998], Albania [2002], Algeria [2002], Azerbaijan [1997], Bangladesh [1996], Bangladesh [2002], Bosnia and Herzegovina [1998], Bosnia and Herzegovina [2001], Egypt [2000], Indonesia [2001], Iran (Islamic Republic of) [2000], Iraq [2004], Jordan [2001], Kyrgyzstan [2003], Morocco [2001], Morocco [2001], Nigeria [1990], Nigeria [1995], Nigeria [2000], Pakistan [1997], Pakistan [2001], Saudi Arabia [2003], Turkey [1990], Turkey [1996], Turkey [2001], and Turkey [2001].

In his Palgrave/Macmillan essay in 2007, Inglehart (2007) ventured for the first time into the tricky and politically highly charged and – many people will assume – even politically incorrect field of the quantitative comparison of the worldviews of Islamic publics in a global perspective. Inglehart for one shows with his empirical data and methods, which we will discuss at length in our "Asabiyya"-Chapter that there is a strong distinction between mainstream Muslim societies on the one hand and post-Communist Muslim societies on the other hand. Inglehart's preferred method of factor analyzing the WVS data and interpreting the outcomes as representing the dimensions self-expression (combining acceptance of postmaterial values, female leaders, women in the work-sphere, accomplishment as the prime aim of work, homosexuality justifiable[13], no xenophobia, happiness, and favoring

---

[13] One thing is our own own choice of family values, another thing is our rejection and even phobia vis-à-vis people who do not share these values. As we show in this work, the implosion of traditional family values centered around the family, as envisaged by the three Abrahamic religions, empirically indeed will lead to a social value implosion, when more than 1/3 of the population start to think that "marriage is outdated". In this sense, religious conservatives all around the globe, from the United States to Israel and Turkey, got a valid point. However, liberal democracy very certainly excludes the perspective of socially rejecting or even discriminating against people whose sexual orientation is gay or lesbian. Currently there are 18 texts now in the "Acquis", the cumulated European Union law, referring to the term "sexual orientation". For further reference, see: http://eur-lex.europa.eu/RECH_mot.do. Predictably, the implementation of these laws into national law raises many

environmental protection) and rational values (no great importance given to religion, obedience no value any more in education, weak national pride, not parent's but my own pride is important, acceptance of divorce, abortion, free trade, and no importance for the respect of authority) again was applied, with self-expression on the x-axis and rational values on the y-axis. Zimbabwe, Morocco and Jordan are in the lowest, left-hand-corner of such scales, because these countries are presumed to be combining low self expression values and low rational, secular values, while countries like Sweden, Norway, Denmark and the Netherlands are the "superstars" of modernization, i.e. combining self-expression and rationality. But on the path of modernization, there are several contradictions to be solved – the United States, for example, is highly placed on the self-expression dimension, but relatively low on the rational dimension (about the same level as India (!)). The Muslim ex-Communist countries are highly rational/secular, about as equal as France and the United Kingdom, but they are still far behind in the development of their self-expression.

Inglehart then calculates the mean results of his surveys for 11 Protestant European, four Confucian, 13 Orthodox, 14 Catholic, seven English-speaking, three South Asian, 14 Islamic, 11 Latin American and six African surveys and looks at the differences in the mean responses to the following questions (abridged formulations)

- God is important
- Proud of nationality
- Respect for authority
- Autonomy Index
- Abortion never justifiable
- Mean score secular/traditional scale

He also looks into

- Differences percentages per population postmaterialists minus materialists
- Very happy
- Tolerance for homosexuals
- Signed petitions
- Trust people
- Disagree: men make better politicians
- Self-Expression versus survival scale

While Inglehart admits that there are predominantly "conservative" traditional family values prevalent in the Muslim world, these countries are not alone. In terms of self-expression, more economically advanced Muslim countries are well on their way towards modernity. Inglehart also looked into the acceptance rates of democracy and gender equality. While Muslim countries are now very strongly favoring democracy, their acceptance of "modern" gender roles is predictably lower.

---

controversies in EU-accession countries, but the experience from the countries, which joined in 2004 tells us that at the end of the day, the voices of reason prevail.

STARTING THE HARD TASK OF GLOBAL CULTURAL COMPARISONS: THE METHODOLOGIES

There is a literature developed to quantitatively measure previously not measurable outcomes and opinion structures. Outcomes and opinion structures are often multidimensional and represented by several indicators with both positive and negative effects. However, here the objective is not to evaluate the effects of certain policy programs, rather to quantify the state of the outcome or opinion structures. The multidimensionality of the outcome or opinion structures requires creation of *composite indices* to have a single measure and also to *aggregate the indicators*. Here the focus is on the *construction of indices* of

- Active society
- Global opinion structures, both at the level of aggregate national results as well as at the level of global citizens and the global *Umma* of Muslim believers
- Global tolerance
- Sexual permissiveness

The indices on the basis of the World Values Survey are multidimensional and decomposable. Such indices will be useful tools in quantification of the state of global opinion and values and the evaluation of their impacts on development. In this section, we introduce two approaches—non-parametric and parametric indices—frequently used in the construction of such indices[14].

INDEX CONSTRUCTION: NON-PARAMETRIC INDICES

A non-parametric index is a composite index constructed such as to aggregate a number of indicators of a certain process, opinion structure or outcome. Such indices are used in the social science literature for the measurement of globalization (Heshmati, 2006; Heshmati and Tausch, 2007; Andersen and Herbertsson, 2003; Dreher, 2005; Kearney, 2002 and 2003; Lockwood, 2004; Lockwood and Redoano, 2005; Mahler, 2001), environment (Kang, 2002), human development (Noorbakhsh, 1998), development strategy, technology and research (Heshmati and Oh, 2007; Archibugi and Coco, 2004; Grupp and Mogee, 2004), or other types of indices (Inglehart and associates). For instance, the globalization index is a simple combination of forces driving the integration of ideas, people, and economies, worldwide. It is composed of four major components: economic integration, personal contact, Internet technology, and political engagement, each being generated from a number of determinant variables. Such an index can serve as a model for the computation of a volunteer index or a sexual permissiveness index.

In the much debated case of child well-being, the index following Innocenti (2007) is composed of six components: material well-being, health and safety, educational well-being, peers and family relationships, behaviors and risk, and social well-being. The CWI was then estimated parametrically or computed non-parametrically based on the normalization of the

---

[14] The author is grateful to Professor Almas Heshmati for the following materials

child well-being indicators and their subsequent aggregation, using an ad hoc weighting system as follows:

$$CWI_t = \sum_{j=1}^{J}\sum_{m=1}^{M} \omega_{jm}\{(X_{jmi} - X_{jm}^{\min})/(X_{jm}^{\max} - X_{jm}^{\min})\} \quad (1)$$

where i and indicate country; m and j are within and between component variables; ω_{jm} are the weights attached to each contributing X-variable within a component and weights attached to each of the six components; and min and max are minimum and maximum values of respective variables across countries in a given year. Such an index is similar to the commonly-used index, the United Nations Human Development Index (HDI), which is based on educational attainment, life expectancy and real GDP per capita.[15]

An index of type (1) is suitable for indicators with an expected positive effect on volunteer work *et cetera*. In cases where the indicators are expected to have a negative impact on volunteer work, the corresponding index is written as:

$$CWI_i = \sum_{j=1}^{J}\sum_{m=1}^{M} \omega_{jm}\{(X_{jm}^{\max} - X_{jmi})/(X_{jm}^{\max} - X_{jm}^{\min})\} \quad (2)$$

where the two indices differ only by the nominator of the ratio. Alternatively, prior to the normalization in (1) and aggregation, the negative indicators are transformed to inverses, ($1/X$) reversing their expected impact from negative to positive.

The index component's weights in equations (1) and (2) are chosen on an ad hoc basis and are constant across countries. However, this non-parametric index can be used as a benchmark index. Lockwood (2001), in computation of a globalization index, finds the ranking of countries to be sensitive to the way the indicators are measured, normalized and weighted. Here we choose the weighting approach similar to the commonly used human development index, where all indicators are given equal weight (see Noorbakhsh, 1998). Ideally the weights should differ by indicators, countries as well as over time.

Parametric Indices

The literature on index numbers is diverse and volumes. There are at least two other alternative but parametric approaches to the non-parametric index above for computing opinion indices or behavior indices; using the principal component (PC) or factor analysis approach (for recent applications see Heshmati, 2003; and Andersen and Herbertsson, 2003).[16] In this study we adopt the PC approach. Since the two methods in normalized form

---

[15] For a review of the HDI, its components, criticisms on the index, alternative measures and suggestions for some improvements of the index, see Noorbakhsh (1998).
[16] For recent surveys on the literature on the use of composite indices in different development research context, see also Archibugi and Coco (2004) and Grupp and Mogee (2004).

give PC scores with unit variance, we use only the PC results in the analysis of child well-being.

Principal component analysis is a multivariate technique for examining relationships within a set of interrelated quantitative variables. Given a dataset with J numeric indicators, at most P principal components can be computed; each is a linear combination of the original indicators with coefficients equal to the eigenvectors of the correlation of the covariance matrix. The principal components are sorted according to the descending order of the *Eigenvalues*, which are equal to the variance of the components. In short, PC analysis can be viewed as a way to uncover approximate linear dependencies among variables. This method gives a least square solution to the following model:

$$Y = XB + E \qquad (3)$$

where Y is a $n \times p$ matrix of the centered observed variables, X is the $n \times j$ matrix of scores of the first j principal components, B is a $j \times p$ matrix of eigenvectors or factor patterns, E is a $n \times p$ matrix of residuals, n is the number of observations, p the number of partial variables, and j the number of variables or indicators of strategy. Unlike in a traditional least squares estimation method case, where the vertical distance to the fitted line is minimized, here the sum of the squared residuals measured as distances from the point to the first principal axis.

PC analysis was originated by Pearson (1901) and further developed by Hotelling (1933). The method has been employed in many areas including the computation of an environmental index (Kang, 2002) and in computation of a simple globalization index using trade and financial openness by Agénor (2003). Heshmati and Oh (2007) used the method for computation of a Lisbon Development Strategy Index.

Each of the parametric and non-parametric indices and weighted or un-weighted indices has their own advantages and disadvantages. In this study they are used to measure global values and attribute it to the possible underlying sources of global values.

Chapter 2

INGLEHART AND THE CONSEQUENCES: ISLAM ON THE MAP OF GLOBAL VALUE CHANGES—A FIRST ASSESSMENT

Our analysis of the opinions of global Muslims starts with the assertion that in the contemporary period of the 1990s and the early 2000s, 13.2% of Muslims—in comparison to 12.7% of the global citizenry—disagree or strongly disagree with the opinion that "Democracy may have problems but it is better". Seen in such a perspective, the Gallup Institute is probably right with its figure of eight percent Muslims extremists world-wide. But what Gallup does NOT tell us is the value gap between Muslims and the Orthodox world on the one side and the rest of European society on the other side regarding the acceptability and or necessity of societal integration of immigrants:

Table 1a. Putting things into a perspective: global disagreement with democracy as such

E123. I'm going to read off some things that people sometimes say about a democratic political system. Could you please tell me if you agree strongly, agree, disagree or disagree strongly, after I read each one of them?

Democracy may have problems but it's better than any other form of government

1. Agree strongly
2. Agree
3. Disagree
4. Strongly disagree

Table 1a.

BASE=179850	Disagree or strongly disagree: Democracy may have problems but is better	Agree strongly	Agree	Disagree	Strongly disagree	Total
Ancestral worshipping	44.5	10.1	45.4	41.1	3.4	207
Armenian Apostolic Church	27.3	15.1	57.6	23.9	3.4	1385
Jehovah witnesses	24.7	31.4	43.8	20.9	3.8	121
Al-Hadis	20	35.3	44.7	16	4	150
Orthodox	18.2	33.8	48	14.7	3.5	14576
Evangelical	18.1	32	49.9	16.4	1.7	1150
Independent African Church (e.g. ZCC. Shembe. *et cetera*)	14.5	43.5	42.1	10.1	4.4	565
Iglesia ni Cristo (INC)	13.6	10	76.3	12.5	1.1	80
Shia	13.5	52.1	34.4	6.9	6.6	666
Protestant	13.4	43.1	43.5	10.4	3	17532
Tac	13.3	57.8	28.9	11.1	2.2	61
Total	12.8	41.3	46	10	2.8	114576
Other	12.4	39.7	48	9.9	2.5	1886
Sikh	12.3	33.6	54.2	9.2	3.1	66
Muslim	12.2	46.4	41.5	8.8	3.4	24486
Pentecostal	11.9	57.9	30.2	9.5	2.4	547
Jew	11.8	46.3	41.9	9.7	2.1	395
Buddhist	11.7	23.2	65.2	10.4	1.3	1665
Roman Catholic	10.6	40.8	48.6	8.6	2	42204
Hindu	8.4	48.4	43.3	6.6	1.8	2596
The Church of Sweden	6.4	68	25.5	5.7	0.7	807
Free church/Non denominational church	6.1	49.1	44.8	3.7	2.4	676
C and S Celestial	5.5	63	31.5	3	2.5	59
Seven Day Adventist	5.5	32.3	62.1	5.5	0	57
Jain	3.9	46.8	49.3	0	3.9	51

Source: our own calculations from World Values Survey, 3rd and 4th wave, http://www.worldvaluessurvey.org/

Table 1b. The most democracy-skeptical political cultures and the least democracy-skeptical political cultures of the world

BASE=179850	Disagree or strongly disagree: Democracy may have problems but is better	Agree strongly	Agree	Disagree	Strongly disagree	Total
Nigeria [2000]	54.6	15.5	29.9	40	14.6	1971
Russian Federation [1995]	41.1	9.8	49.1	35.4	5.7	1486
Russian Federation [1999]	36.9	12	51.1	31.3	5.6	1893
Iran (Islamic Republic of) [2000]	30.7	32.7	36.5	17.4	13.3	1527
Indonesia [2001]	28.7	13.6	57.7	21.5	7.2	869
Viet Nam [2001]	27.7	19.7	52.6	25.5	2.2	783
Republic of Moldova [1996]	27.5	17.8	54.8	25.8	1.7	900
Armenia [1997]	26.8	14.9	58.3	23.3	3.5	1673
Saudi Arabia [2003]	25.8	33.7	40.5	16.5	9.3	1244
Macedonia, Republic of [1998]	25.2	26.4	48.4	21.3	3.9	830
Ukraine [1996]	23.5	16.4	60.1	18.8	4.7	1908
Philippines [1996]	23.1	16.5	60.4	20	3.1	1164
Kyrgyzstan [2003]	22.5	19	58.5	18.4	4.1	1001
Mexico [1996]	22.4	22.4	55.2	19.9	2.5	2018
Great Britain [1999]	22.1	47.3	30.6	5.3	16.8	949
Republic of Moldova [2002]	22.1	15.6	62.3	17.4	4.7	744
Romania [1999]	21.8	33.9	44.3	14.9	6.9	973
Mexico [2000]	20.3	26.8	52.9	15	5.3	1199
Philippines [2001]	20.2	21.9	57.9	18.3	1.9	1181
Bulgaria [1997]	19.4	36.9	43.7	14.8	4.6	871
Belarus [1996]	19.3	23.5	57.3	17.2	2.1	1696
Hungary [1999]	18.8	26.3	55	15.7	3.1	863
Macedonia, Republic of [2001]	18.7	32.2	49	13.8	4.9	929
Chile [2000]	18.5	42	39.5	14.6	3.9	1133
Chile [1996]	18.1	28.9	52.9	16.1	2	943
Pakistan [2001]	17.8	42.6	39.6	9.3	8.5	1950
Ukraine [1999]	17.5	23.7	58.8	15.4	2.1	928
Brazil [1997]	16.6	50.1	33.3	8.1	8.5	1091
Latvia [1996]	16.6	18.7	64.7	14.5	2.1	1069
Taiwan [1994]	16.5	10.9	72.6	15.8	0.7	697
Bulgaria [1999]	16.4	43.3	40.3	12.8	3.6	804
South Africa [2001]	15.9	36	48.1	13.3	2.6	2729
Slovakia [1999]	15.7	31.9	52.4	12.7	3	1212
Iraq [2004]	15.1	51.2	33.8	9.7	5.4	1869

Table 1b. (Continued)

BASE=179850	Disagree or strongly disagree: Democracy may have problems but is better	Agree strongly	Agree	Disagree	Strongly disagree	Total
Hungary [1998]	15.1	47.3	37.6	9.8	5.3	564
Finland [1996]	14.8	44.1	41.1	11.3	3.5	892
Nigeria [1995]	14.7	57.3	27.9	11.4	3.3	1881
Georgia [1996]	14.4	27.7	58	12.9	1.5	1832
Venezuela [1996]	13.7	48.2	38.1	9.5	4.2	1162
Peru [1996]	13.7	30.4	56	11.3	2.4	1047
Australia [1995]	13.3	32.5	54.2	12.3	1	1939
Belarus [2000]	13.3	33.5	53.2	11.3	2	755
Canada [2000]	13.1	39.1	47.9	11.5	1.6	1782
Romania [1998]	13.1	63.8	23.1	9.9	3.2	1078
TOTAL	13	40	47	10.3	2.7	146031
United States [1999]	12.6	41.3	46.1	10.8	1.8	1165
New Zealand [1998]	12.6	31.8	55.6	11.7	0.9	972
Zimbabwe [2001]	12.4	33.3	54.3	10.2	2.2	854
Turkey [2001]	12.1	41.8	46.1	9.3	2.8	1072
Slovenia [1995]	11.9	24	64.2	9.8	2.1	901
Lithuania [1999]	11.9	23.3	64.7	9.3	2.6	748
Tanzania. United Republic Of [2001]	11.6	66.2	22.2	7.1	4.5	1122
Algeria [2002]	11.6	48.5	39.9	7.7	3.9	1080
Poland [1997]	11.6	29.7	58.7	10.1	1.5	888
Turkey [2001]	11.5	42.5	45.9	9.5	2	3025
Puerto Rico [1995]	11.5	49.9	38.6	9.9	1.6	1112
Serbia [1996]	11.3	39.5	49.2	9.5	1.8	1112
Slovakia [1998]	11.2	33.9	55	8.6	2.6	1019
Latvia [1999]	11.1	22.3	66.6	10.2	0.9	886
Peru [2001]	10.9	30.3	58.7	9.1	1.8	1411
Serbia [2001]	10.9	39.7	49.4	9.5	1.4	1006
Bosnia and Herzegovina [1998]	10.6	48.6	40.7	6.3	4.3	1127
Jordan [2001]	10.6	38.2	51.2	7.2	3.4	1032
South Africa [1996]	10.4	45.2	44.4	8.4	2	2383
Poland [1999]	10.2	24	65.8	9.1	1.1	954
Estonia [1996]	10.2	41.9	47.9	8.6	1.6	917
China [2001]	10.1	9.3	80.6	9.8	0.3	653
Slovenia [1999]	9.9	25.4	64.8	8.7	1.2	942
India [1995]	9.8	45.9	44.4	8.1	1.7	1474
Lithuania [1997]	9.7	22	68.3	8.6	1.1	804
Estonia [1999]	9.6	19.9	70.5	8.8	0.8	834
Finland [2000]	9.3	36.7	53.9	8.8	0.5	982
Czech Republic [1998]	9.1	34.8	56.2	7.4	1.7	1070

Inglehart and the Consequences: Islam on the Map of Global Value Changes 73

BASE=179850	Disagree or strongly disagree: Democracy may have problems but is better	Agree strongly	Agree	Disagree	Strongly disagree	Total
Republic of Korea [2001]	9.1	20.5	70.5	6.7	2.4	1061
United States [1995]	8.9	49.3	41.7	7.8	1.1	1463
Puerto Rico [2001]	8.8	63.5	27.8	7.5	1.3	695
Argentina [1999]	8.7	46	45.3	6.5	2.2	1196
Switzerland [1996]	8.7	42.7	48.6	7.8	0.9	1107
Turkey [1996]	8.5	48.9	42.7	7.2	1.3	1645
Republic of Korea [1996]	8.5	32.3	59.3	7	1.5	1237
Belgium [1999]	8.3	54.8	37	6.6	1.7	1786
India [2001]	8.3	46.3	45.3	6	2.3	1422
Montenegro [2001]	8.2	51.4	40.4	5.8	2.4	930
Ireland [1999]	8.2	38.1	53.7	6.6	1.6	920
Uganda [2001]	8.2	42.9	48.9	4.5	3.7	916
Japan [2000]	8.1	16.9	75	6.9	1.2	973
Bosnia and Herzegovina [2001]	8	37.9	54.1	5.1	2.9	1095
Spain [2000]	7.7	47.8	44.5	5.6	2.1	1127
Argentina [1995]	7.6	48.4	44	6.4	1.2	1022
Germany East [1997]	7.6	25.2	67.1	6.6	1	967
Venezuela [2000]	7.5	69.6	23	4.6	2.9	1180
Czech Republic [1999]	7.4	39.9	52.7	6.8	0.6	1825
Portugal [1999]	7.2	40.5	52.4	6.3	0.9	919
Dominican Republic [1996]	7.2	58.6	34.2	5	2.2	403
Spain [1995]	7	40.4	52.6	6.1	0.9	1110
Germany East [1999]	7	34.9	58.1	6.1	0.9	893
Japan [1995]	6.9	19.4	73.7	6.2	0.7	815
Northern Ireland [1999]	6.6	45.6	47.8	5.5	1.1	873
France [1999]	6.5	61.6	31.8	5.2	1.3	1501
Montenegro [1996]	6.5	46.8	46.8	5.6	0.9	216
Spain [1999]	6.3	41.7	52.1	5.1	1.2	1089
Sweden [1996]	6.2	69.1	24.6	5.4	0.8	958
Germany West [1997]	6.1	49.1	44.8	5.3	0.8	996
Malta [1999]	6	46.3	47.7	5.7	0.3	951
Sweden [1999]	5.9	50.5	43.6	5.1	0.8	997
Italy [1999]	5.7	43.7	50.6	4.8	0.9	1898
Croatia [1996]	5.7	64	30.3	3.4	2.3	1141
Albania [2002]	5.3	55.5	39.2	4.7	0.6	939
Norway [1996]	5.1	72.9	22.1	3	2.1	1111
Luxembourg [1999]	4.3	64	31.7	2.9	1.4	1052
Croatia [1999]	4.3	41.8	54	4	0.3	929
Azerbaijan [1997]	3.9	22.5	73.7	3	0.9	1732
Morocco [2001]	3.9	79.6	16.6	2.3	1.6	721

Table 1b. (Continued)

BASE=179850	Disagree or strongly disagree: Democracy may have problems but is better	Agree strongly	Agree	Disagree	Strongly disagree	Total
Netherlands [1999]	3.7	47.8	48.6	3.3	0.4	988
Uruguay [1996]	3.7	41.5	54.8	3.1	0.6	944
Morocco [2001]	3.7	75.3	21	2.1	1.6	632
Greece [1999]	3.3	65.8	30.9	2.8	0.5	1130
Albania [1998]	3.2	67.4	29.4	2.5	0.7	915
Austria [1999]	2.7	60.4	36.8	2.4	0.3	1473
Bangladesh [1996]	2.5	73.6	23.9	1.8	0.7	1411
Germany West [1999]	2.5	66.8	30.6	2.1	0.4	1012
Iceland [1999]	2.5	52.8	44.7	2.3	0.2	940
Egypt [2000]	2.3	63.6	34.1	1.9	0.4	2779
Bangladesh [2002]	1.8	69.1	29.1	1.5	0.3	1442
Denmark [1999]	1.4	71.8	26.8	1.1	0.3	983

Source: our own calculations from World Values Survey, 3rd and 4th wave, http://www.worldvaluessurvey.org/

Selected samples: Albania [1998], Albania [2002], Algeria [2002], Argentina [1995], Argentina [1999], Armenia [1997], Australia [1995], Austria [1999], Azerbaijan [1997], Bangladesh [1996], Bangladesh [2002], Belarus [1996], Belarus [2000], Belgium [1999], Bosnia and Herzegovina [1998], Bosnia and Herzegovina [2001], Brazil [1997], Bulgaria [1997], Bulgaria [1999], Canada [2000], Chile [1996], Chile [2000], China [1995], China [2001], Colombia [1997], Colombia [1998], Croatia [1996], Croatia [1999], Czech Republic [1998], Czech Republic [1999], Denmark [1999], Dominican Republic [1996], Egypt [2000], El Salvador [1999], Estonia [1996], Estonia [1999], Finland [1996], Finland [2000], France [1999], Georgia [1996], Germany East [1997], Germany East [1999], Germany West [1997], Germany West [1999], Great Britain [1998], Great Britain [1999], Greece [1999], Hungary [1998], Hungary [1999], Iceland [1999], India [1995], India [2001], Indonesia [2001], Iran (Islamic Republic of) [2000], Iraq [2004], Ireland [1999], Israel [2001], Italy [1999], Japan [1995], Japan [2000], Jordan [2001], Kyrgyzstan [2003], Latvia [1996], Latvia [1999], Lithuania [1997], Lithuania [1999], Luxembourg [1999], Macedonia, Republic of [1998], Macedonia, Republic of [2001], Malta [1999], Mexico [1996], Mexico [2000], Montenegro [1996], Montenegro [2001], Morocco [2001], Morocco [2001], Netherlands [1999], New Zealand [1998], Nigeria [1995], Nigeria [2000], Northern Ireland [1999], Norway [1996], Pakistan [1997], Pakistan [2001], Peru [1996], Peru [2001], Philippines [1996], Philippines [2001], Poland [1997], Poland [1999], Portugal [1999], Puerto Rico [1995], Puerto Rico [2001], Republic of Korea [1996], Republic of Korea [2001], Republic of Moldova [1996], Republic of Moldova [2002], Romania [1998], Romania [1999], Russian Federation [1995], Russian Federation [1999], Saudi Arabia [2003], Serbia [1996], Serbia [2001], Singapore [2002], Slovakia [1998], Slovakia [1999], Slovenia [1995], Slovenia [1999], South Africa [1996], South Africa [2001], Spain [1995], Spain [1999], Spain [2000], Sweden [1996], Sweden [1999], Switzerland [1996], Taiwan [1994], Tanzania, United Republic Of [2001], Turkey [1996], Turkey [2001], Turkey [2001], Uganda [2001], Ukraine [1996], Ukraine [1999], United States [1995], United States [1999], Uruguay [1996], Venezuela [1996], Venezuela [2000], Viet Nam [2001], Zimbabwe [2001]

As we already stated above, the results for "political violence" are as clear-cut as before:

Table 1c. Putting things into a perspective: Agreement/Disagreement with political violence

E198. Here's one more statement. How strongly do you agree or disagree with it?

"Using violence to pursue political goals is never justified."

1. Strongly agree
2. Agree
3. Disagree
4. Strongly disagree

BASE=179850	Using violence for political goals not justified (strongly agree+agree)	Strongly agree	Agree	Disagree	Strongly disagree	Total
Muslim	87.5	57.7	29.8	7.4	5.2	6586
Protestant	84.7	62.3	22.4	8	7.3	7912
Buddhist	83.1	43.1	40	12.8	4.1	600
Hindu	82.1	63.8	18.3	12.6	5.3	1522
Total	79.6	52.3	27.3	11.9	8.5	51700
Jew	78.9	55.7	23.2	17.9	3.2	183
Armenian Apostolic Church	78.3	39.8	38.5	17.6	4.1	1565
Orthodox	78	45.5	32.5	14.3	7.7	7789
Roman Catholic	76.2	49.7	26.5	13.1	10.7	21005
Pentecostal	71	47.6	23.4	16.5	12.4	514
Evangelical	69.4	38.5	30.9	18.9	11.7	712
Jehovah witnesses	55.8	35.8	20	22.1	22.1	95

Source: our own calculations from World Values Survey, 3rd and 4th wave, http://www.worldvaluessurvey.org/.

Table 1d. The most violent political cultures and the least violent political cultures of the world

BASE=179850	Using violence for political goals not justified	Strongly agree	Agree	Disagree	Strongly disagree	Total
Dominican Republic [1996]	xx	43.6	6.8	6	43.6	399
Peru [1996]	xx	28.6	14.9	14.3	42.3	1136
Spain [1995]	xx	66	9.9	4.1	20	1177
Nigeria [1995]	xx	41.8	24.5	17.6	16.1	1767
Venezuela [1996]	xx	38.2	35.2	14.1	12.5	1153
Romania [1998]	xx	45.7	31.3	10.5	12.5	1123
Lithuania [1997]	xx	54.1	22.3	11.3	12.3	886
Bosnia and Herzegovina [1998]	xx	44.7	27.3	16.4	11.6	1133
Republic of Moldova [1996]	xx	32.9	32.7	22.9	11.4	902
Argentina [1995]	xx	63.5	15.4	10.3	10.8	1057
Colombia [1998]	xx	43.1	25	21.3	10.6	2963
Philippines [1996]	xx	22.2	40.8	26.6	10.5	1195
Hungary [1998]	xx	65.4	14.1	10.7	9.9	619
Slovakia [1998]	xx	41.6	31.6	17.4	9.4	1023
Slovenia [1995]	xx	41.5	28.6	20.5	9.4	956
Sweden [1996]	xx	82.9	5.4	2.4	9.3	1000
South Africa [1996]	xx	55.3	25.6	10.2	8.9	2655
Macedonia, Republic of [1998]	xx	62.7	16.5	12.3	8.6	930
TOTAL	xx	51.5	28.2	12	8.3	65054
Ukraine [1996]	xx	35.5	42.2	14.2	8.1	2159
Uruguay [1996]	xx	51.3	27.9	12.9	7.9	957
Serbia [1996]	xx	43.5	29.5	19.5	7.4	1198
Turkey [1996]	xx	50.1	32.9	9.7	7.3	1751
United States [1995]	xx	57.9	25.2	9.6	7.3	1494
Estonia [1996]	xx	53.5	29.3	9.8	7.3	955
Australia [1995]	xx	59.2	25.4	8.2	7.2	2012
Czech Republic [1998]	xx	49.8	30.5	12.6	7.1	1079
New Zealand [1998]	xx	60.3	26.5	6.1	7	1074

BASE=179850	Using violence for political goals not justified	Strongly agree	Agree	Disagree	Strongly disagree	Total
Croatia [1996]	xx	67.8	19.1	6.3	6.8	1170
Mexico [1996]	xx	47.1	32.6	13.6	6.7	2281
Puerto Rico [1995]	xx	59.6	22.1	11.9	6.4	1140
Bulgaria [1997]	xx	47.4	30.9	15.3	6.4	935
Georgia [1996]	xx	45.3	36.8	11.8	6.1	1888
Brazil [1997]	xx	81.3	9.6	3.1	6	1142
India [1995]	xx	59.6	19.3	15.4	5.6	1628
Norway [1996]	xx	86.2	4.8	3.4	5.5	1119
Montenegro [1996]	xx	48.7	28.8	16.9	5.5	236
Latvia [1996]	xx	41.5	41.2	11.9	5.4	1137
Belarus [1996]	xx	49.9	33.3	11.8	5.1	1913
El Salvador [1999]	xx	33.4	41.7	19.8	5.1	1151
Albania [1998]	xx	71.4	21.1	2.4	5.1	910
Taiwan [1994]	xx	24.7	48.9	21.3	5.1	745
Germany East [1997]	xx	45.6	39.6	9.9	4.9	994
Chile [1996]	xx	43.4	35.9	15.9	4.8	972
Germany West [1997]	xx	49	36.3	10	4.7	998
Armenia [1997]	xx	40.6	38.1	17.1	4.1	1875
Japan [1995]	xx	56.5	37.1	2.2	4.1	927
Russian Federation [1995]	xx	44.2	37.3	15.1	3.4	1791
Finland [1996]	xx	78.4	12.3	6	3.3	934
Switzerland [1996]	xx	66.2	26.1	5.2	2.6	1166
Bangladesh [1996]	xx	91.2	6.1	1.1	1.7	1323
Azerbaijan [1997]	xx	48.8	50	1	0.2	1926

Source: our own calculations from World Values Survey, 3rd and 4th wave, http://www.worldvaluessurvey.org/ Selected samples: see before.

The WVS dimensions on family, gender, sexuality and religious values show by contrast that Muslim conservative personal values are to be reckoned with especially in Europe, a continent, which has gone a much further way on its path to secularization and the decay of traditional family values than the United States of America:

Table 1e. Putting things into a perspective: disagreement with "integration" in the world

E145. Which of these statements is the nearest to your opinion?

A. For the greater good of society it is better if immigrants maintain their distinct customs and traditions.

B. For the greater good of society it is better if immigrants do not maintain their distinct customs and traditions but take over the customs of the country.

1. Maintain distinct customs and traditions.
2. Take over the customs of the country.

BASE=179850	Immigrants and their customs and traditions	Maintain distinct customs and traditions	Take over the customs of the country	Total
Hindu	xx	68.1	31.9	14
Jew	xx	67.5	32.5	47
Muslim	xx	67.5	32.5	224
Buddhist	xx	61.1	38.9	19
Orthodox	xx	58.4	41.6	4070
Other	xx	49.7	50.3	382
Total	xx	42.4	57.6	24012
Roman Catholic	xx	41.6	58.4	13697
Free church/Non denominational church	xx	40.7	59.3	579
Protestant	xx	29.9	70.1	4980

Source: our own calculations from World Values Survey, 3rd and 4th wave, http://www.worldvaluessurvey.org/

Table 1f. Acceptance and rejection of the cultural distinctness of immigrants in the political cultures of the world

BASE=179850	Immigrants and their customs and traditions	Maintain distinct customs and traditions	Take over the customs of the country	Total
Greece [1999]	xx	77.3	22.7	1031
Romania [1999]	xx	61.8	38.2	1002
Bulgaria [1999]	xx	60.4	39.6	661
Italy [1999]	xx	59.7	40.3	1763
Luxembourg [1999]	xx	57.5	42.5	1006
Ireland [1999]	xx	57.3	42.7	867
Croatia [1999]	xx	56.2	43.8	900
Malta [1999]	xx	55.7	44.3	927

BASE=179850	Immigrants and their customs and traditions	Maintain distinct customs and traditions	Take over the customs of the country	Total
Northern Ireland [1999]	xx	53.9	46.1	835
Estonia [1999]	xx	52.5	47.5	806
Spain [1999]	xx	52	48	950
Portugal [1999]	xx	48.9	51.1	837
Belarus [2000]	xx	48.4	51.6	702
Poland [1999]	xx	47.5	52.5	903
Latvia [1999]	xx	47.1	52.9	853
Ukraine [1999]	xx	46.5	53.5	850
Great Britain [1999]	xx	44.7	55.3	832
Russian Federation [1999]	xx	43.1	56.9	1928
TOTAL	xx	41.7	58.3	33590
Slovakia [1999]	xx	39.9	60.1	949
Lithuania [1999]	xx	36.5	63.5	639
Sweden [1999]	xx	36	64	814
Hungary [1999]	xx	33.5	66.5	876
Finland [2000]	xx	32	68	924
Czech Republic [1999]	xx	31	69	1710
Slovenia [1999]	xx	30.8	69.2	923
Netherlands [1999]	xx	30.1	69.9	913
Iceland [1999]	xx	27.2	72.8	896
France [1999]	xx	26.8	73.2	1437
Germany West [1999]	xx	25.3	74.7	974
Belgium [1999]	xx	25	75	1742
Denmark [1999]	xx	23.4	76.6	837
Austria [1999]	xx	18.4	81.6	1404
Germany East [1999]	xx	17.3	82.7	899

Source: our own calculations from World Values Survey, 3rd and 4th wave, http://www.worldvaluessurvey.org/
Selected samples: see before

As we already emphasized, the confrontation of conservative and liberalized family, gender and sexual values is far greater in Europe than in North America:

Table 1g. Putting things into a perspective: disagreement with "integration" in Europe (EU-27 + EEA + EFTA)

Which of these statements is the nearest to your opinion?
a. For the greater good of society it is better if immigrants maintain their distinct customs and traditions
b. For the greater good of society it is better if immigrants do not maintain their distinct customs and traditions but take over the customs of the country

1. Maintain distinct customs and traditions
2. Take over the customs of the country

BASE=51102	Immigrants and their customs and traditions	Maintain distinct customs and traditions	Take over the customs of the country	Total n
Muslim		75.7	24.3	156
Orthodox		66.7	33.3	2538
Total		43.5	56.5	19350
Roman Catholic		42.3	57.7	11872
Protestant		30.4	69.6	4027

Source: our own calculations from World Values Survey, 3rd and 4th wave, http://www.worldvaluessurvey.org/

Selected sample: Austria [1999], Belgium [1999], Bulgaria [1997], Bulgaria [1999], Czech Republic [1998], Czech Republic [1999], Denmark [1999], Estonia [1996], Estonia [1999], Finland [1996], Finland [2000], Germany East [1997], Germany East [1999], Germany West [1997], Germany West [1999], Great Britain [1998], Great Britain [1999], Greece [1999], Hungary [1998], Hungary [1999], Ireland [1999], Italy [1999], Latvia [1996], Latvia [1999], Lithuania [1997], Lithuania [1999], Luxembourg [1999], Malta [1999], Northern Ireland [1999], Norway [1996], Poland [1997], Poland [1999], Portugal [1999], Romania [1998], Romania [1999], Slovakia [1998], Slovakia [1999], Slovenia [1995], Slovenia [1999], Spain [1995], Spain [1999], Spain [2000], Sweden [1996], Sweden [1999], Switzerland [1996]. Source: our own compilations from http://www.worldvaluessurvey.org/, wave 3+4

Our summary of the results thus re-iterates the findings, already reported by Inglehart (2003), Inglehart and Baker (2000), and Inglehart and Norris (2003). Islam is basically democratic and non-violent, but value-conservative. Our maps re-iterate the conclusions, already drawn from our Tables before:

Biggest Skepticism against Democracy:

1. Nigeria [2000]
2. Russian Federation [1999]
3. Iran (Islamic Republic of) [2000]
4. Indonesia [2001]
5. Viet Nam [2001]

6. Armenia [1997]
7. Saudi Arabia [2003]
8. Kyrgyzstan [2003]
9. Great Britain [1999]
10. Republic of Moldova [2002]
11. Romania [1999]
12. Mexico [2000]
13. Philippines [2001]
14. Hungary [1999]
15. Macedonia, Republic of [2001]

Biggest Optimism about Democracy:

1. Denmark [1999]
2. Bangladesh [2002]
3. Egypt [2000]
4. Germany West [1999]
5. Iceland [1999]
6. Austria [1999]
7. Greece [1999]
8. Netherlands [1999]
9. Uruguay [1996]
10. Azerbaijan [1997]
11. Morocco [2001]
12. Croatia [1999]
13. Luxembourg [1999]
14. Norway [1996]
15. Albania [2002]

So, a global opinion barometer of the opinions of Muslims around the globe would reveal above all that the overwhelming majority of the 1.3 billion Muslims might be conservative in their family values (in many ways similar to practicing Roman Catholics), but that they very strongly believe in core values of the *market economy, modern technology, and democracy*. Is this a major problem?

Arguing from an *Enlightenment perspective,* Muslim societies, like other societies especially in the global East and South of the world system, must become more inclusive in their approach to minorities. It is this "center" of Muslim global opinion, which believes in *technology, competition, gradual reform* and *hard work* as the basis of success, which must be termed as the *silent Muslim Calvinist majority* and, which is the basis of our optimistic projections. Our materials show the entire scale of the projected strength of Muslim opinions around the globe.

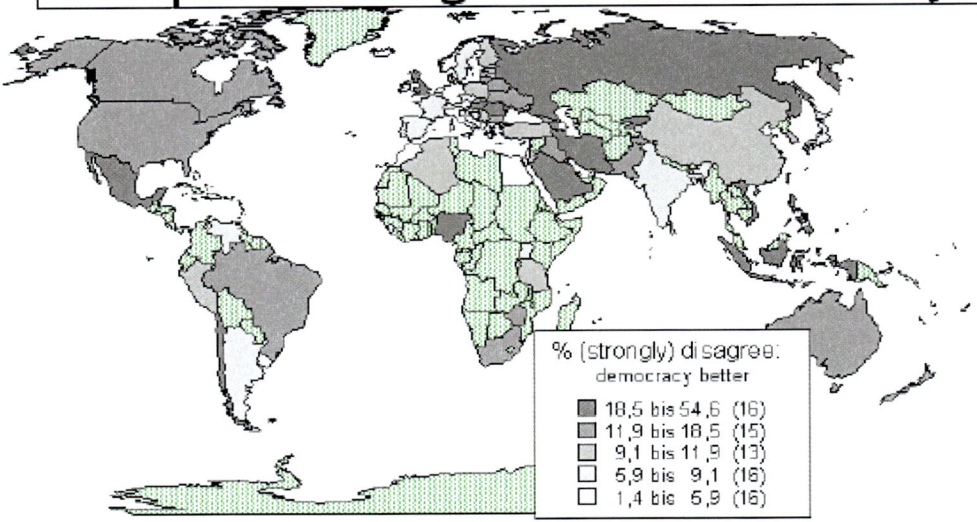

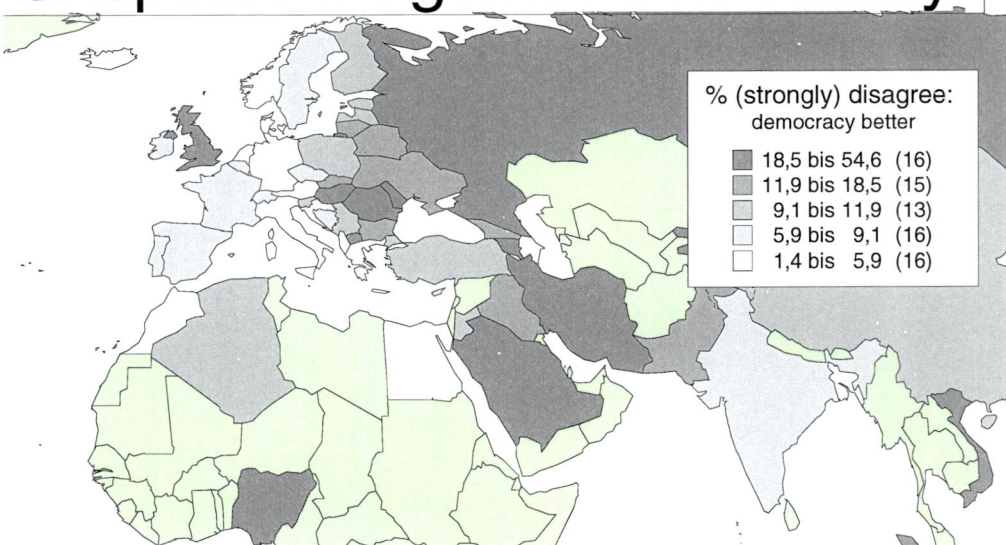

Map 2. Disagreement with: democracy is better...

Source: our own calculations from World Values Survey, 3rd and 4th wave, http://www.worldvaluessurvey.org/

Note: "bis" is shorthand for "ranging from ... to"

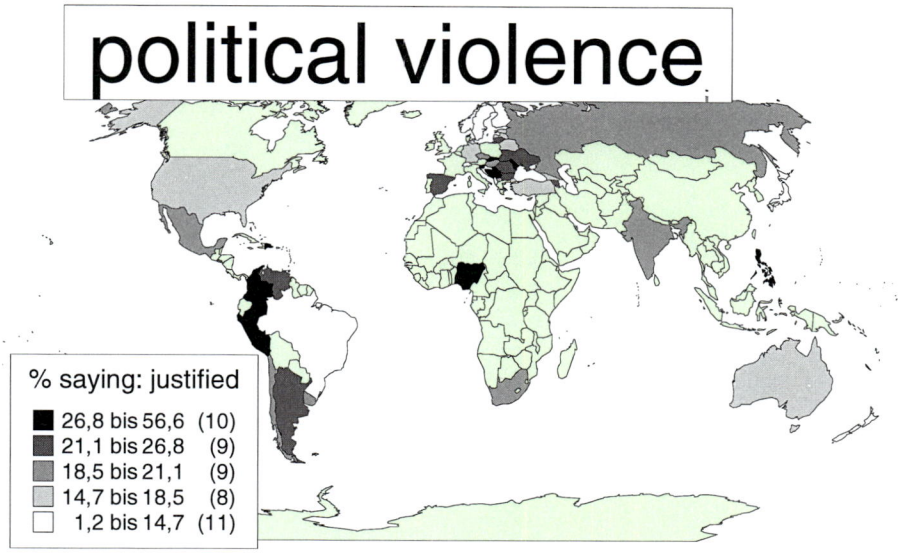

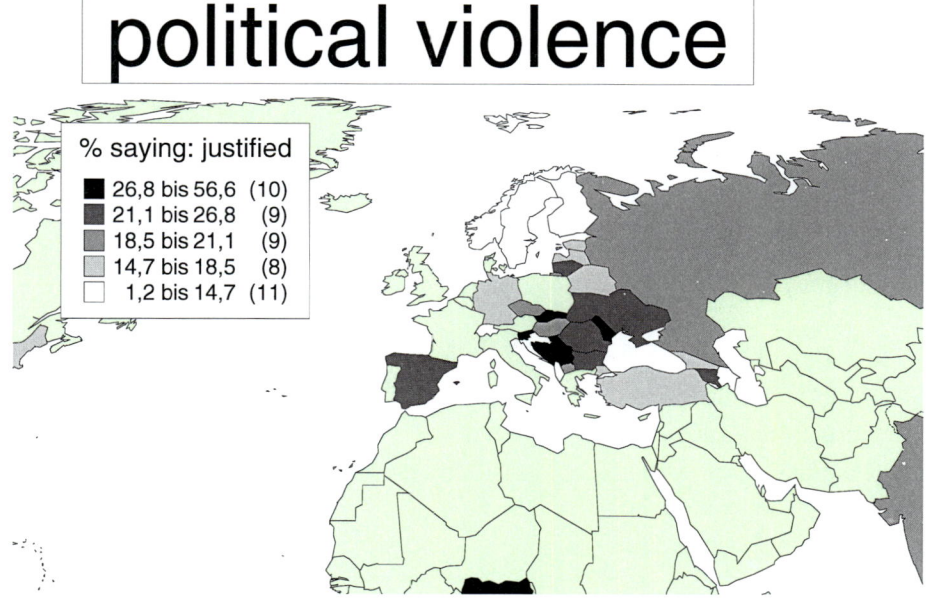

Map 3. People saying: political violence is justified …

Source: our own calculations from World Values Survey, 3rd and 4th wave, http://www.worldvaluessurvey.org/

Note: "bis" is shorthand for "ranging from … to"

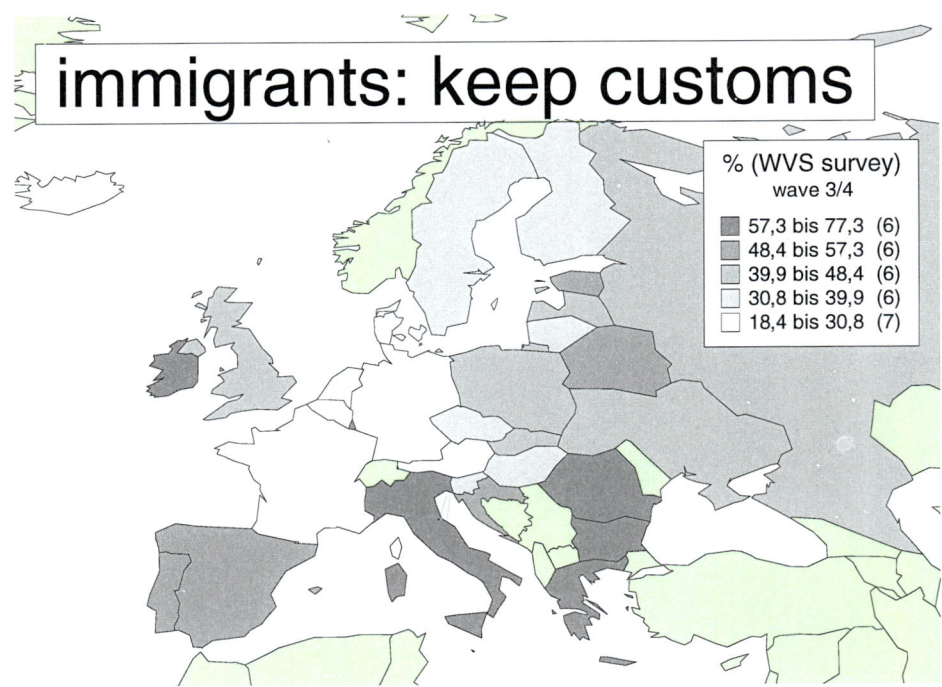

Map 4. Acceptance of the keeping of customs by immigrants.

Source: our own calculations from World Values Survey, 3rd and 4th wave, http://www.worldvaluessurvey.org/
Note: "bis" is shorthand for "ranging from … to"

The five real core tenets of the real existing Muslim identity around the globe, shared by an estimated *900 million Muslims* or more, are:

- Future: Emphasis on technology good thing
- Competition is harmful (scale value 1–4)
- Important for a successful marriage: adequate income
- Government responsibility should be increased (value 5–10 on people responsibility versus government scale)
- Rejecting a single parent woman

By contrast, around *200 million Muslims* or even less share the opinion that:

- Society must be radically changed
- Confidence in the Civil Service: none at all
- Confidence in the Social Security System: none at all
- Political system, which governs the country very bad
- Extreme right wing
- Strong leader very good
- Former political system very good
- Army rule very good

- Confidence in the Education System: none at all
- Confidence in Television: none at all
- Disagreement or strong disagreement with: democracy may have problems but it is better
- Confidence in the Justice System: none at all
- % not agreeing: respect and appreciation important for successful marriage
- Confidence in the Armed Forces: none at all
- Confidence in Churches: none at all
- Extreme left wing
- Having a democratic political system bad or fairly bad
- Already joined unofficial strikes
- Already occupied buildings or factories

Our voyage into the real of Muslim opinions shows the following proportions of the quantitative strengths of believes and opinions:

Table 1h. What do global Muslims really think?

Projections from the WVS data on 30.000 representative Muslims	Estimated Millions of Muslims, world-wide, expressing this opinion
Future: Emphasis on technology good thing	1053.0
Competition is harmful (scale value 1-4)	943.8
Important for a successful marriage: adequate income	939.9
Government responsibility should be increased (value 5-10 on people responsibility versus government scale)	932.1
Rejecting single parent woman	915.2
Important for a successful marriage: religious beliefs	894.4
Poverty compared to 10 years ago larger	893.1
Country is run by a few big interests	887.9
Future: greater respect for authority a good thing	865.8
Rejecting homosexual neighbors	864.5
Hard work brings success (scale value 1-4)	863.2
Materialism: future changes - less importance placed on work a bad thing	843.7
There should be time for prayer and meditation in schools (agree + strongly agree)	826.8
% saying that agreement on politics is important or very important for a successful marriage	804.7
Justifiable keeping money that you have found (sometimes or always, scale value 2-10)	774.8
Little chance to escape from poverty	767.0
Justifiable divorce (sometimes or always, scale value 2-10)	764.4
Government ownership should be increased (value 5-10 on private ownership versus government ownership scale)	759.2
Income class 1-4 (=belong to the poorest 40% of the population)	743.6

Table 1h. (Continued)

Projections from the WVS data on 30.000 representative Muslims	Estimated Millions of Muslims, world-wide, expressing this opinion
Books that attack religion definitely should be banned	739.7
Rejecting Roma/Sinti neighbors	711.1
Better if more people with strong religious beliefs in public office (strongly agree + agree)	708.5
Important for a successful marriage: same social background	707.2
Unemployed people take away jobs (scale value 1-4)	692.9
Justifiable fighting with the police (sometimes or always, scale value 2-10)	648.7
Materialism: future changes - less emphasis on money not a good thing	629.2
Cautious to confront major changes in life (one should be cautious about major changes in life, scale values 1-4)	629.2
Justifiable failing to report damage you've done accidentally to a parked vehicle (sometimes or always, scale value 2-10)	604.5
Justifiable sex under the legal age of consent (sometimes or always, scale value 2-10)	573.3
Justifiable threatening workers who refuse to join a strike (sometimes or always, scale value 2-10)	565.5
Politicians who don't believe in God are unfit for public office (strongly agree)[17]	564.2
Important for a successful marriage: same ethnic background	525.2
Justifiable adultery (sometimes or always, scale value 2-10)	514.8
Justifiable abortion (sometimes or always, scale value 2-10)	492.7
Low income level	483.6
If only one child were to be allowed: preference for a boy	483.6
Justifiable political assassination (sometimes or always, scale value 2-10)	469.3
Rejecting Jewish neighbors	445.9
Justifiable claiming government benefits (sometimes or always, scale value 2-10)	436.8
Rejecting neighbors with a different religion	430.3
Justifiable lying (sometimes or always, scale value 2-10)	405.6
Justifiable smoking in public places (sometimes or always, scale value 2-10)	404.3
Incomes should be made more equal (value 1-4 on egalitarian versus anti-egalitarian scale)	399.1
Rejecting neighbors who are immigrants or foreign workers	390.0
Justifiable avoiding a fare on public transport (sometimes or always, scale value 2-10)	375.7

---

[17] It is not only important, but very important to state here that this variable, due to the distribution of the highest and the lowest numerical values in the World Values Survey, has to be interpreted in the multivariate analysis as "Politicians who don´t believe in God are fit for public office". However, the present analysis of value patterns took properly care of the distribution of the highest and the lowest numerical values, and correctly measures the percentages of those who think that „Politicians who don´t believe in God are unfit for public office". The WVS wording of the F102 WVS question is: „.- How much do you agree or disagree with each of the following statement: Politicians who do not believe in God are unfit for public office
    1 Agree strongly
    2 Agree
    3 Neither agree or disagree
    4 Disagree
    5 Strongly disagree"

Inglehart and the Consequences: Islam on the Map of Global Value Changes

Projections from the WVS data on 30.000 representative Muslims	Estimated Millions of Muslims, world-wide, expressing this opinion
Rejecting neighbors of a different race	367.9
Justifiable euthanasia (sometimes or always, scale value 2-10)	358.8
State should give more freedom to firms (scale value 1-4)	353.6
People can only get rich at the expense of others (scale value 1-4)	352.3
Confidence in the United Nations: none at all	338.0
Justifiable buy stolen goods (sometimes or always, scale value 2-10)	331.5
Free market economy wrong for the future of the country	325.0
Justifiable having casual sex (sometimes or always, scale value 2-10)	321.1
Justifiable cheating on taxes (sometimes or always, scale value 2-10)	317.2
Confidence in the Political Parties: none at all	315.9
Very good if experts make the decisions	313.3
Individual responsibility for pensions (scale value 1-4)	300.3
Confidence in the Health Care System: none at all	282.1
Justifiable throwing away litter (sometimes or always, scale value 2-10)	267.8
Confidence in NATO: none at all	263.9
Confidence in Parliament: none at all	257.4
Confidence in Labor Unions: none at all	249.6
Enjoy sexual freedom	241.8
Confidence in the Women's Movement: none at all	241.8
Confidence in the European Union: none at all	237.9
Confidence in Major Companies: none at all	237.9
Justifiable paying cash (sometimes or always, scale value 2-10)	232.7
Justifiable someone accepting a bribe (sometimes or always, scale value 2-10)	228.8
Justifiable joyriding (sometimes or always, scale value 2-10)	226.2
Unwilling to fight for the country	215.8
Confidence in the Government: none at all	211.9
Rejecting Muslim neighbors	210.6
Confidence in the Police: none at all	205.4
Confidence in the Press: none at all	202.8
Saying marriage is an outdated institution	201.5
satisfaction with the way democracy develops in the country: not at all satisfied	200.2
Society must be radically changed	195.0
Justifiable speeding over the limit (sometimes or always, scale value 2-10)	192.4
Justifiable prostitution (sometimes or always, scale value 2-10)	192.4
Confidence in the Civil Service: none at all	192.4
Confidence in the Social Security System: none at all	191.1
Political system, which governs the country very bad	189.8
Extreme right wing	189.8
Justifiable driving under influence of alcohol (sometimes or always, scale value 2-10)	188.5
Justifiable taking soft drugs (sometimes or always, scale value 2-10)	185.9

Table 1h. (Continued)

Projections from the WVS data on 30.000 representative Muslims	Estimated Millions of Muslims, world-wide, expressing this opinion
Lower class (subjective)	184.6
Confidence in the Environmental Protection Movement: none at all	184.6
Strong leader very good	180.7
Former political system very good	174.2
Justifiable suicide (sometimes or always, scale value 2-10)	167.7
Army rule very good	167.7
Justifiable homosexuality (sometimes or always, scale value 2-10)	163.8
Confidence in the Education System: none at all	163.8
Confidence in Television: none at all	162.5
Justifiable drinking alcohol (sometimes or always, scale value 2-10)	159.9
Disagreement or strong disagreement with: democracy may have problems but it is better	153.4
Confidence in the Justice System: none at all	150.8
Disagree or strongly disagree: long-term relationship is necessary to be happy	148.2
% not agreeing: respect and appreciation important for successful marriage	133.9
Confidence in the Armed Forces: none at all	122.2
Confidence in Churches: none at all	97.5
Extreme left wing	93.6
Having a democratic political system bad or fairly bad	83.2
Already joined unofficial strikes	45.5
Already occupied buildings or factories	16.9

Source: Our own compilations, based on the official Website of the World Values Survey (WVS) Project, http://www.worldvaluessurvey.org./. Our calculations are based on the WVS data (Download survey data files) and the SPSS XIV statistics program, Innsbruck University. All waves of the WVS surveys are integrated into the data file. To weight for country population size, we used the WVS routine: weights 1000. The sample comprised 204303 representative interview partners with available data on religious confession, gender and age of the respondent.

In fact, World Values Survey data also support the hypothesis that today central values of democracy and the market economy are widely shared throughout the Muslim world.

A very large percentage of global Muslims belongs to the political center, and although we can observe a somewhat larger percentage of people belonging to the very extreme right and the very extreme left in the Muslim world than in global society, the shape of the political distribution according to the self-positioning on the ideological map in global Islam and in global society is about the same.

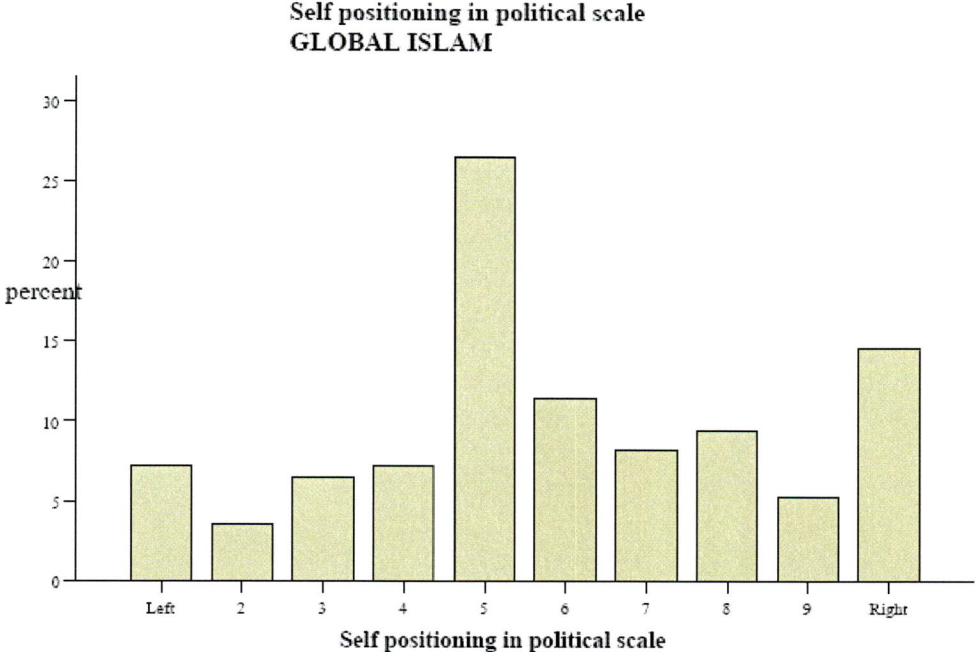

Diagram 1. Left and right in the global "Umma" and in global society.

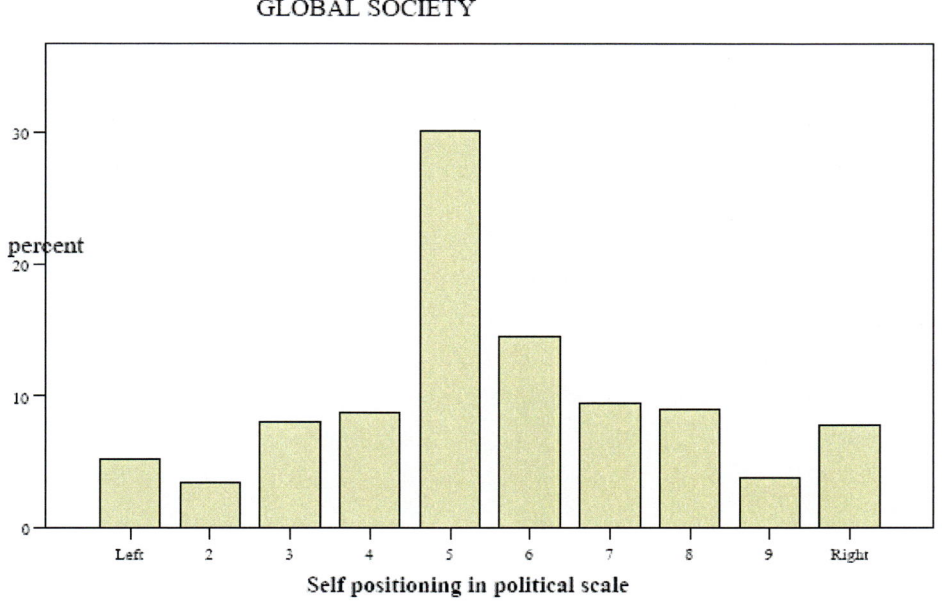

Source: our own calculations from World Values, all waves, SPSS download http://www.worldvaluessurvey.org/. Country weights 1000.

Cases are weighted with equilibrated weights 1000 (with split-ups), WVS all waves

Large majorities of people both among global Muslims as among the global citizenry support a *gradual transition of society and they reject radical changes,* quite in accordance with the logic proposed by *Sir Karl Raimund Popper* decades ago, and they do not want a total change of society. This result is especially optimistic – whatever the direction of results, the transition has to be a gradual one and a radical overthrow of the existing order is rejected. But in this context, we also should point to a paradoxon, which should be immediately followed up by democratic political action. Although 923,000 Websites are listed by "Google advanced search" as explicitly referring to "Karl Popper" by June 19, 2008, only 844 such Websites were in Arabic language (traditional and simplified Chinese Websites, mentioning "Karl Popper", are above 10.000 each, and Russian language Websites 1320. In the other major languages of the Muslim world, we find 2200 Websites on Popper in Indonesian, 31,200 Websites in Turkish, 2190 in Farsi). The Arab masses in particular and the Muslim masses around the globe would be absolutely eager to follow the path of gradual reform, but they do not even have proper access to the writings of *the* visionary of gradual societal reform[18].

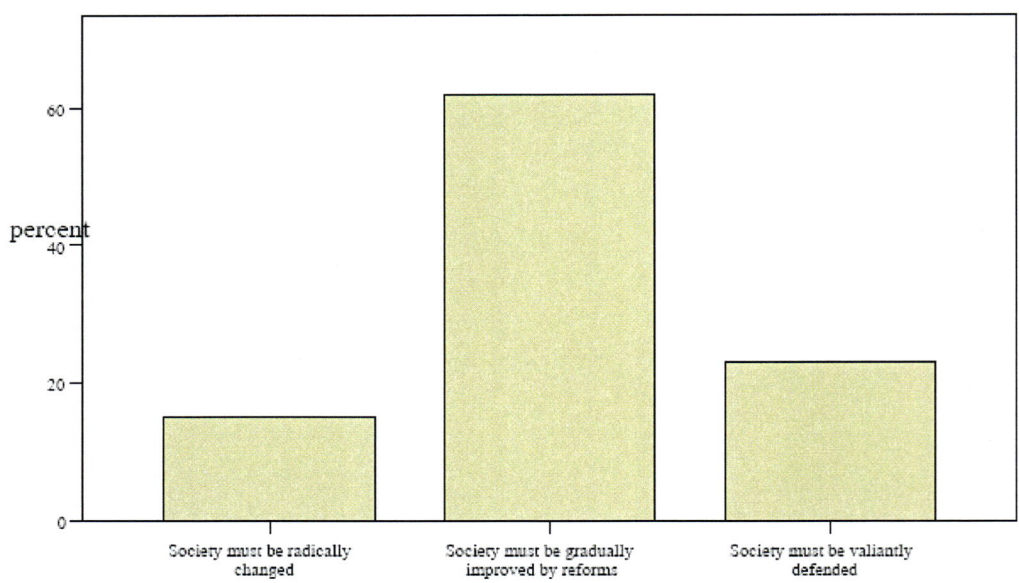

Diagram 2. gradual reforms – their acceptance/rejection in the global "Umma" and in global society.

Source: our own calculations from World Values, all waves, SPSS download http://www.worldvaluessurvey.org/. Country weights 1000.

---

[18] The OCLC World Catalogue of academic and research library holdings around the globe lists by June 19, 2008, 943 original and or translated works authored by "Karl Popper", while only one text in Arabic language by Popper is available – the 1959 and the 1992 translation of the "Poverty of Historicism". As to the availability of the Popper works in other major languages of the Muslim world, 12 works are available in Turkish, 5 works in Farsi, and 1 in Indonesian, while 23 works were translated into Chinese and 4 into Russian.

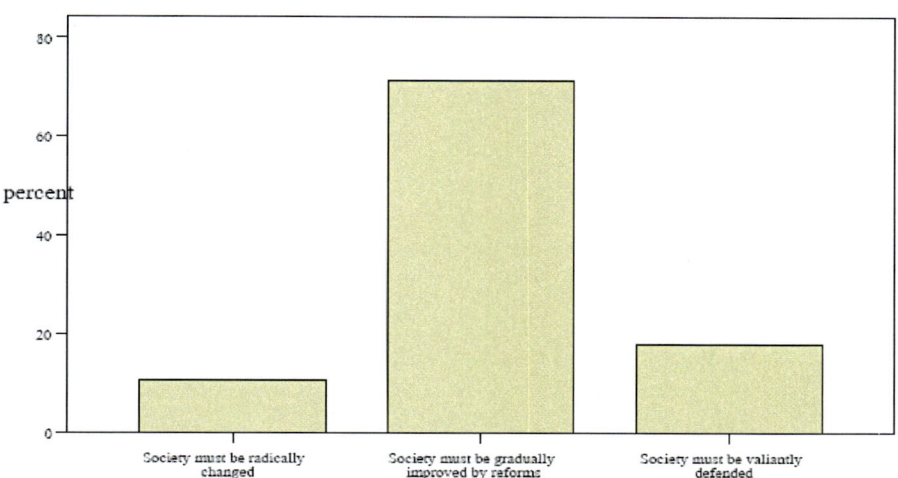

Source: our own calculations from World Values, all waves, SPSS download http://www.worldvaluessurvey.org/. Country weights 1000.

Cases are weighted with equilibrated weights 1000 (with split-ups), WVS all waves

Even more stunning is the fact that global Muslims share the American dream of "hard work bringing success" in an even more convinced way than global citizens:

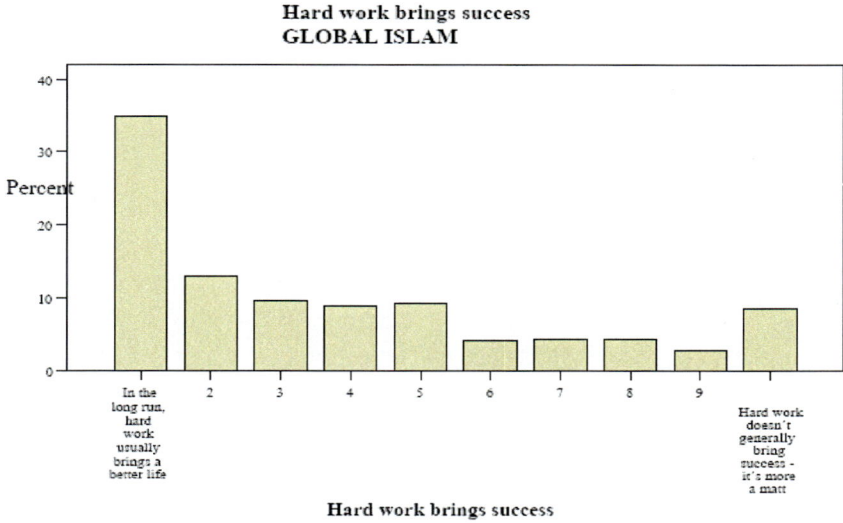

Diagram 3. the American dream: hard work brings success—its sharing in the global "Umma" and in global society.

Source: our own calculations from World Values, all waves, SPSS download http://www.worldvaluessurvey.org/. Country weights 1000.

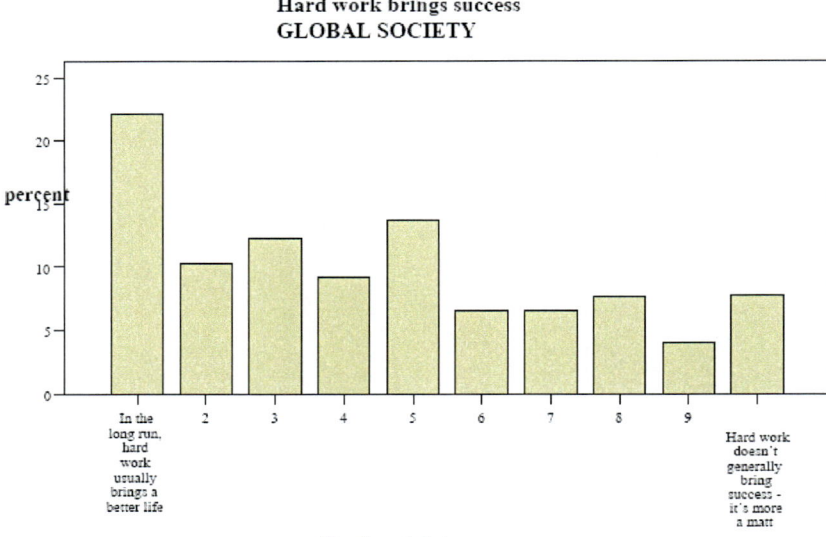

Source: our own calculations from World Values, all waves, SPSS download http://www.woridvaluessurvey.org/. Country weights 1000.

Cases are weighted with equilibrated weights 1000 (with split-ups), WVS all waves

However, we think that the *totality of Muslim values and non-Muslim values* along the paths of modernization are underrepresented by these dimensions alone. The Inglehart-school is absolutely right in insisting that all cultures are undergoing changes in their values across countries, across birth cohorts and over time, and that on the map of global values, there are striking similarities between societies in, say, parts of Latin America, Africa and the Muslim world.

The entire opinion spectrum in the Muslim world, as well as the estimated absolute number of global Muslim citizens, which would correspond to the social milieu, as evidenced by the World Values Survey data, is reproduced in our Tables and in the materials directly below. The *struggle for democracy* in the Muslim world might be presented in optimistic terms, as suggested by Esposito and Mogahed (2008), but there is a very vast area of societal change necessary to assure future opinion structures, which are compatible with truly *democratic enlightened societies with peaceful methods of conflict settlement and conflict resolution:*

The Struggle for Democracy: How to Convince up to 100 Million Muslims

- Already occupied buildings or factories
- Already joined unofficial strikes
- Having a democratic political system bad or fairly bad
- Extreme left wing
- Confidence in churches: none at all

The Struggle for Democracy: How to Convince 100 to 200 Million Muslims

- Confidence in the armed forces: none at all
- Percent not agreeing: respect and appreciation important for successful marriage
- Disagree or strongly disagree: long-term relationship is necessary to be happy
- Confidence in the Justice System: none at all
- Disagreement or strong disagreement with: democracy may have problems but it is better
- Confidence in television: none at all
- Confidence in the education system: none at all
- Army rule very good
- Former political system very good
- Strong leader very good
- Confidence in the environmental protection movement: none at all
- Justifiable taking soft drugs (sometimes or always, scale value 2–10)
- Justifiable driving under influence of alcohol (sometimes or always, scale value 2–10)
- Political system, which governs the country very bad
- Extreme right wing
- Confidence in the social security system: none at all
- Justifiable speeding over the limit (sometimes or always, scale value 2–10)
- Confidence in the civil service: none at all
- Society must be radically changed

The Struggle for Democracy: How to Convince 200 to 300 Million Muslims

- satisfaction with the way democracy develops in the country: not at all satisfied
- Confidence in the press: none at all
- Confidence in the police: none at all
- Confidence in the government: none at all
- Justifiable joyriding (sometimes or always, scale value 2–10)
- Justifiable someone accepting a bribe (sometimes or always, scale value 2–10)
- Justifiable paying cash (sometimes or always, scale value 2–10)
- Confidence in the European Union: none at all
- Confidence in major companies: none at all
- Confidence in the women's movement: none at all
- Confidence in labor unions: none at all
- Confidence in Parliament: none at all
- Confidence in NATO: none at all
- Justifiable throwing away litter (sometimes or always, scale value 2–10)
- Confidence in the health care system: none at all

The Struggle for Democracy: How to Convince 300 to 400 Million Muslims

- Very good if experts make the decisions
- Confidence in the Political Parties: none at all
- Justifiable cheating on taxes (sometimes or always, scale value 2–10)
- Free market economy wrong for the future of the country
- Justifiable buy stolen goods (sometimes or always, scale value 2–10)
- Confidence in the United Nations: none at all
- Rejecting neighbors of a different race
- Justifiable avoiding a fare on public transport (sometimes or always, scale value 2–10)
- Rejecting neighbors who are immigrants or foreign workers

The Struggle for Democracy: How to Convince 400 to 500 Million Muslims

- Justifiable smoking in public places (sometimes or always, scale value 2–10)
- Justifiable lying (sometimes or always, scale value 2–10)
- Rejecting neighbors with a different religion
- Justifiable claiming government benefits (sometimes or always, scale value 2–10)
- Rejecting Jewish neighbors
- Justifiable political assassination (sometimes or always, scale value 2–10)
- If only one child were to be allowed: preference for a boy

The Struggle for Democracy: How to Convince 500 to 600 Million Muslims

- Important for a successful marriage: same ethnic background
- Politicians who don't believe in God are unfit for public office (strongly agree)
- Justifiable sex under the legal age of consent (sometimes or always, scale value 2–10)

The Struggle for Democracy: How to Convince 600 to 700 Million Muslims

- Justifiable failing to report damage you've done accidentally to a parked vehicle (sometimes or always, scale value 2–10)
- Justifiable fighting with the police (sometimes or always, scale value 2–10)
- Unemployed people take away jobs (scale value 1–4)

The Struggle for Democracy: How to Convince 700 to 800 Million Muslims

- Important for a successful marriage: same social background
- Better if more people with strong religious beliefs in public office (strongly agree + agree)

- Rejecting Roma/Sinti neighbors
- Justifiable keeping money that you have found (sometimes or always, scale value 2–10)

The Struggle for Democracy: How to Convince More Than 800 Million Muslims

- Rejecting homosexual neighbors
- Rejecting single parent woman

The above data are first roadmaps to what is really at issue, and they suggest that there is hope, but that the struggle for global enlightenment and global democracy will be a hard one.

Chapter 3

EURO-ISLAM AND EUROPE'S LEADING CULTURE: 6.6 MILLION HOMOPHOBES AMONG 229 MILLION TAX EVADERS?

To demand from Europe's Muslims that they should "adapt" or assimilate themselves to the *"lead culture"* would deserve the cynical answer from the empirical social science community that this "lead culture", by the turn of the Millennium, was a culture of over 200 million tax evaders, 200 million Roma-phobes, 155 million homophobes and 67 million open anti-Semites, and in between these "lead culture values" more than 100 million people who think that somehow political assassinations are justified and that taking bribes is somehow acceptable. *So what is Europe's "lead culture"?* The conviction, shared by more than 193 million Europeans that sex under the legal age of consent is sometimes or always justifiable? The more than 60 million Europeans, who openly reject a neighbor of a different race? To which "Europe" "the Muslims" should adapt in the end?

According to the WVS, in Europe we are confronted with a considerable potential of mistrust in democracy, distance to and mistrust in basic societal institutions, and we are also confronted with a very large group of people holding xenophobic and anti-Semitic world views on the part of the total population.[19] The *total number of Europeans* in the EU-27, the EEA and EFTA, which would fall under this category, are given in our Table in millions. To successfully continue the European project, above all means to convince the following number of people (in millions) of the central European values of tolerance, democracy and respect for the law:

Justifiable paying cash (sometimes or always)	301.46
Justifiable speeding over the limit (sometimes or always)	229.51
Justifiable cheating on taxes (sometimes or always)	228.99
Justifiable avoiding a fare on public transport (sometimes or always)	226.89
Rejecting Roma/Sinti neighbors	206.40
Justifiable claiming government benefits (sometimes or always)	203.78
Justifiable sex under the legal age of consent (sometimes or always)	193.27
Rejecting homosexual neighbors	155.46
Education: tolerance and respect not mentioned as a central value	142.85

---

[19] Total population figure for he EU-27 + EEA + EFTA 525,188 million people (CIA World Factbook).

Justifiable someone accepting a bribe (sometimes or always)	132.35
Jobs are scarce: men have more rights then	125.52
Justifiable alco-driving (sometimes or always)	110.29
Confidence in NATO: none at all	109.24
Justifiable political assassination (sometimes or always)	103.99
Confidence in the European Union: none at all	99.26
Confidence in Labor Unions: none at all	92.44
Confidence in Parliament: none at all	83.51
Having experts make decisions very good	75.63
Rejecting neighbors who are immigrants or foreign workers	74.05
Confidence in the Press: none at all	72.48
Confidence in the Justice System: none at all	68.28
Rejecting Jewish neighbors	67.23
Confidence in the Civil Service: none at all	65.12
Rejecting neighbors of a different race	61.97
Confidence in the Social Security System: none at all	57.77
Not at all satisfied with democracy	51.47
Confidence in the Armed Forces: none at all	44.12
Confidence in the Police: none at all	40.44
Confidence in Churches: none at all	39.92
Political system, which governs the country very bad	35.19
Politicians who don't believe in God are unfit for public office (strongly agree)	35.19
Democracy may have problems but it's better (disagree)	32.04
Having a democratic political system fairly bad	31.51
not prepared to help elderly people	30.99
in a democracy, the economy runs badly	26.79
Already joined unofficial strikes	25.73
Confidence in the Education System: none at all	20.48
occupying buildings and factories	15.23
Having a democratic political system very bad	10.50
Democracy may have problems but it's better (strongly disagree)	9.45
Having the army rule very good	6.83

To successfully integrate the *15 million Muslims in Europe*, above all means to convince the following number of people (in millions) of the central European values of the Enlightenment, the values of tolerance, democracy and respect for the law:

Rejecting homosexual neighbors	6.57
Justifiable claiming government benefits (sometimes or always)	5.90
Justifiable avoiding a fare on public transport (sometimes or always)	5.82
Jobs are scarce: men have more rights then	5.79
Justifiable cheating on taxes (sometimes or always)	5.70
Justifiable speeding over the limit (sometimes or always)	5.47

Justifiable paying cash (sometimes or always)	5.44
Justifiable sex under the legal age of consent (sometimes or always)	5.36
Rejecting Roma/Sinti neighbors	5.11
Justifiable political assassination (sometimes or always)	4.61
Education: tolerance and respect not mentioned as a central value	4.29
Justifiable someone accepting a bribe (sometimes or always)	3.72
Confidence in NATO: none at all	3.41
Having experts make decisions very good	3.07
Confidence in Labor Unions: none at all	2.95
Politicians who don't believe in God are unfit for public office (strongly agree)	2.74
Confidence in the Press: none at all	2.71
Rejecting neighbors of a different race	2.62
Justifiable alco-driving (sometimes or always)	2.59
Not at all satisfied with democracy	2.45
Confidence in the European Union: none at all	2.19
Confidence in Parliament: none at all	2.06
Rejecting Jewish neighbors	1.92
Confidence in the Civil Service: none at all	1.83
Confidence in the Social Security System: none at all	1.63
Confidence in the Justice System: none at all	1.51
Rejecting neighbors who are immigrants or foreign workers	1.37
Confidence in the Police: none at all	1.34
Confidence in Churches: none at all	1.28
Political system, which governs the country very bad	1.20
Confidence in the Armed Forces: none at all	1.07
not prepared to help elderly people	0.98
in a democracy, the economy runs badly	0.96
Democracy may have problems but it's better (disagree)	0.89
Already joined unofficial strikes	0.85
Having a democratic political system fairly bad	0.81
Having the army rule very good	0.49
Confidence in the Education System: none at all	0.48
Occupying buildings and factories	0.43
Having a democratic political system very bad	0.23
Democracy may have problems but it's better (strongly disagree)	0.14

As the international value debate, initiated by the ***World Values Survey*** research, with justification shows, values do not fall from heaven, but are developing both in "traditional" and in "modern" societies, across birth cohorts, educational levels and over time, according to very clear societal patterns.

This essay takes up this issue and tries to show the differences and similarities between the major global cultures, and tries to project the major tendencies for Europe. Our first respective comparative Table starts out with a picture, mostly in descending order of the numerical strength of believes held, among the European "*Umma*" in comparison to the entire European population by the turn of the Millennium:

Table 2. The opinions of Euro-Islam (EU-27+EEA+EFTA) compared with the opinions of the European total population (EU-27+EEA+EFTA)—percentages per total population by the turn of the Millennium

	% EU-27+EEA+EFTA "*Umma*"	% EU-27+EEA+EFTA total population	Percentage deviation of the Muslim population from the total population in Europe (EU-27+EEA+EFTA) (B2-C2)*100/C2)	*n* representative Muslims in the WVS sample for Europe	Error margin +- (in %) at the 10% error probability level
Believe in God	91.4	89.4	2.24	233	5.37
Justifiable alco-driving (never)	82	79	3.8	217	5.57
Justifiable someone accepting a bribe (never)	74.2	74.8	-0.8	226	5.45
Justifiable political assassination (never)	68	80.2	-15.21	47	11.96
Justifiable homosexuality (never)	66.2	36.7	80.38	217	5.57
Justifiable sex under the legal age of consent (never)	62.8	63.2	-0.63	58	10.77
Justifiable paying cash (never)	62.2	42.6	46.01	202	5.77
Justifiable speeding over the limit (never)	62	56.3	10.12	207	5.7
Justifiable prostitution (never)	61.5	49	25.51	73	9.6
Justifiable cheating on taxes (never)	60.4	56.4	7.09	225	5.47
Justifiable avoiding a fare on public transport (never)	59.6	56.8	4.93	112	7.75
Justifiable claiming government benefits (never)	59	61.2	-3.59	229	5.42
Never joining a boycott	57.7	55	4.91	138	6.98
very important to eliminate big inequalities	50.6	38	33.16	215	5.59
low income level	48.1	33.3	44.44	191	5.93
Rejecting homosexual neighbors	45.6	29.6	54.05	236	5.34
Never joining an unlawful demonstration	44.5	38.6	15.28	209	5.67
Jobs are scarce: men have more rights then	40.2	23.9	68.2	227	5.44
Never signing petitions	40.1	22.7	76.65	204	5.74
Rejecting Roma/Sinti neighbors	35.5	39.3	-9.67	222	5.5

	% EU-27+EEA+EFTA "*Umma*"	% EU-27+EEA+EFTA total population	Percentage deviation of the Muslim population from the total population in Europe (EU-27+EEA+EFTA) (B2-C2)*100/C2	*n* representative Muslims in the WVS sample for Europe	Error margin +- (in %) at the 10% error probability level
Justifiable divorce (never)	33.3	17	95.88	225	5.47
Education: tolerance and respect not mentioned as a central value	29.8	27.2	9.56	238	5.32
Confidence in NATO: none at all	23.7	20.8	13.94	102	8.12
Having experts make decisions very good	21.3	14.4	47.92	164	6.4
Confidence in Labor Unions: none at all	20.5	17.6	16.48	176	6.18
Politicians who don't believe in God are unfit for public office (strongly agree)	19	6.7	183.58	185	6.03
Confidence in the Press: none at all	18.8	13.8	36.23	191	5.93
Rejecting neighbors of a different race	18.2	11.8	54.24	236	5.34
Not at all satisfied with democracy	17	9.8	73.47	207	5.7
Confidence in the European Union: none at all	15.2	18.9	-19.58	149	6.72
Confidence in Parliament: none at all	14.3	15.9	-10.06	203	5.76
Rejecting Jewish neighbors	13.3	12.8	3.91	236	5.34
Confidence in the Civil Service: none at all	12.7	12.4	2.42	198	5.83
Religious service attendance = once a week	12.7	21.1	-39.81	237	5.33
Confidence in the Social Security System: none at all	11.3	11	2.73	194	5.89
Confidence in the Justice System: none at all	10.5	13	-19.23	208	5.69
Rejecting neighbors who are immigrants or foreign workers	9.5	14.1	-32.62	236	5.34
Confidence in the Police: none at all	9.3	7.7	20.78	229	5.42
Confidence in Churches: none at all	8.9	7.6	17.11	211	5.65

Table 2. (Continued)

	% EU-27+EEA+EFTA "Umma"	% EU-27+EEA+EFTA total population	Percentage deviation of the Muslim population from the total population in Europe (EU-27+EEA+EFTA) (B2-C2)*100/C2)	n representative Muslims in the WVS sample for Europe	Error margin +- (in %) at the 10% error probability level
Political system, which governs the country very bad	8.3	6.7	23.88	220	5.53
Religious service attendance > once a week	7.7	6.8	13.24	237	5.33
Confidence in the Armed Forces: none at all	7.4	8.4	-11.9	216	5.58
not prepared to help elderly people	6.8	5.9	15.25	208	5.69
in a democracy, the economy runs badly	6.7	5.1	31.37	185	6.03
Democracy may have problems but it's better (disagree)	6.2	6.1	1.64	197	5.84
Already joined unofficial strikes	5.9	4.9	20.41	202	5.77
Having a democratic political system fairly bad	5.6	6	-6.67	192	5.92
mean left-right-scale (10 right wing)	5.52	5.53	-0.18	138	6.98
mean government responsibility acceptance	5.04	5.34	-5.62	230	5.41
mean state ownership acceptance	4.33	4.87	-11.09	59	10.68
with University degree	4.1	8.4	-51.19	236	5.34
Rejecting Muslim neighbors	3.9	18.7	-79.14	236	5.34
Having the army rule very good	3.4	1.3	161.54	186	6.01
Confidence in the Education System: none at all	3.3	3.9	-15.38	214	5.61
occupying buildings and factories	3	2.9	3.45	201	5.78
Active in social welfare services	2.9	4.8	-39.58	228	5.43
Having a democratic political system very bad	1.6	2	-20	192	5.92
Democracy may have problems but it's better (strongly disagree)	1	1.8	-44.44	197	5.84

Source: Our own compilations, based on the official Website of the World Values Survey, http://www.worldvaluessurvey.org/.

It would be absolutely erroneous to assume that the European majority population is free from authoritarian opinions Thus Table 3 lists the comparison of the values of Muslims and non-Muslims in Europe. This time, we order the WVS variables by the strength of the difference between Euro-Islam and the European total population. Put in other terms – the probability is far greater that a European Muslim will have theocratic world views, prefers army rule and is totally dissatisfied with democracy than the average European, but at the same time, the probability is very small – compared to the average European – that a European Muslim generally rejects democracy or proposes to pay in cash (to the detriment of the tax collectors), or rejects immigrants or foreign workers. Our table also shows that the probability is about the same, for European Muslims and non-Muslims alike, to be anti-Semitic or to mistrust the Social Security system or to illegally claim government social benefits. Thus again, our investigation shows that Muslims are value-conservative, but that they respect the law.

Table 3. The political algebra of Muslim integration in Europe (EU-27, EEA and EFTA)[20] in comparison to the total European population by the turn of the Millennium

European social reality according to the WVS	% of Muslims saying (1)	% Europeans saying (2)	This corresponds to the following number of millions of Muslims in Europe saying (3)	This corresponds to the following number of millions of Europeans saying (4)	Where Muslim integration failed (> 100) or succeeded (<100) (total population 100) (5)
Politicians who don't believe in God are unfit for public office (strongly agree)	19.00	6.70	2.74	35.19	283.58
Having the army rule very good	3.40	1.30	0.49	6.83	261.54
Not at all satisfied with democracy	17.00	9.80	2.45	51.47	173.47
Jobs are scarce: men have more rights then	40.20	23.90	5.79	125.52	168.20

---

[20] Conservative estimates based on EUMC, CIA Factbook (https://www.cia.gov/library/publications/the-world-factbook/) Nationmaster.com and Wikipedia. For the EU-2,5 we used the EUMC-Data: http://eumc.europa.eu/eumc/material/pub/muslim/Manifestations_EN.pdf, which put the number of Muslims in the EU-25 (conservative estimate) at 13 Million people. For the 2 new EU-27 member countries, which joined the EU after 2004, we used the following figures: Bulgaria: Nationmaster http://www.nationmaster.com/index.php 890.000 Muslims (CIA: 893 000); Rumania: Nationmaster: http://www.nationmaster.com/index.php 0.3% of population. Rumania's population was estimated at 22,276,056 (CIA Factbook July 2007 https://www.cia.gov/library/publications/the-world-factbook/geos/ro.html#People), thus we can safely assume the number of Muslims in Rumania to be 66 800 persons. For the EEA country Iceland we used the Wikipedia figure of 341 Muslims in 2006 (http://en.wikipedia.org/wiki/Islam_in_Iceland). For Norway, we used the following figures: CIA Factbook: 4,627,926 inhabitants and 1.8% Muslims, which would imply a Muslim community of 83300 persons. EFTA country Switzerland: CIA Factbook figure of 7554661 inhabitants and a percentage of 4.8% Muslims, yielding a figure of 363.000 persons for the size of the Muslim community in Switzerland. We thus can assume the number of Muslims in Europe (EU-27+EEA+EFTA) to be at least 14.4 million people. Most probably, the true figure is somewhere around 15 million.

Table 3. (Continued)

European social reality according to the WVS	% of Muslims saying (1)	% Europeans saying (2)	This corresponds to the following number of millions of Muslims in Europe saying (3)	This corresponds to the following number of millions of Europeans saying (4)	Where Muslim integration failed (> 100) or succeeded (<100) (total population 100) (5)
Justifiable political assassination (sometimes or always)	32.00	19.80	4.61	103.99	161.62
Rejecting neighbors of a different race	18.20	11.80	2.62	61.97	154.24
Rejecting homosexual neighbors	45.60	29.60	6.57	155.46	154.05
Having experts make decisions very good	21.30	14.40	3.07	75.63	147.92
Confidence in the press: none at all	18.80	13.80	2.71	72.48	136.23
in a democracy, the economy runs badly	6.70	5.10	0.96	26.79	131.37
Political system, which governs the country very bad	8.30	6.70	1.20	35.19	123.88
Confidence in the police: none at all	9.30	7.70	1.34	40.44	120.78
Already joined unofficial strikes	5.90	4.90	0.85	25.73	120.41
Confidence in churches: none at all	8.90	7.60	1.28	39.92	117.11
Confidence in labor unions: none at all	20.50	17.60	2.95	92.44	116.48
not prepared to help elderly people	6.80	5.90	0.98	30.99	115.25
Confidence in NATO: none at all	23.70	20.80	3.41	109.24	113.94
Education: tolerance and respect not mentioned as a central value	29.80	27.20	4.29	142.85	109.56
Justifiable claiming government benefits (sometimes or always)	41.00	38.80	5.90	203.78	105.67
Rejecting Jewish neighbors	13.30	12.80	1.92	67.23	103.91
occupying buildings and factories	3.00	2.90	0.43	15.23	103.45
Confidence in the Social Security System: none at all	11.30	11.00	1.63	57.77	102.73
Confidence in the Civil Service: none at all	12.70	12.40	1.83	65.12	102.42
Justifiable someone accepting a bribe (sometimes or always)	25.80	25.20	3.72	132.35	102.38
Democracy may have problems but it's better (disagree)	6.20	6.10	0.89	32.04	101.64

European social reality according to the WVS	% of Muslims saying (1)	% Europeans saying (2)	This corresponds to the following number of millions of Muslims in Europe saying (3)	This corresponds to the following number of millions of Europeans saying (4)	Where Muslim integration failed (> 100) or succeeded (<100) (total population 100) (5)
Democracy may have problems but it's better (disagree)	6.20	6.10	0.89	32.04	101.64
Justifiable sex under the legal age of consent (sometimes or always)	37.20	36.80	5.36	193.27	101.09
Justifiable avoiding a fare on public transport (sometimes or always)	40.40	43.20	5.82	226.89	93.52
Having a democratic political system fairly bad	5.60	6.00	0.81	31.51	93.33
Justifiable cheating on taxes (sometimes or always)	39.60	43.60	5.70	228.99	90.83
Rejecting Roma/Sinti neighbors	35.50	39.30	5.11	206.40	90.33
Confidence in Parliament: none at all	14.30	15.90	2.06	83.51	89.94
Confidence in the armed forces: none at all	7.40	8.40	1.07	44.12	88.10
Justifiable speeding over the limit (sometimes or always)	38.00	43.70	5.47	229.51	86.96
Justifiable alco-driving (sometimes or always)	18.00	21.00	2.59	110.29	85.71
Confidence in the education system: none at all	3.30	3.90	0.48	20.48	84.62
Confidence in the justice system: none at all	10.50	13.00	1.51	68.28	80.77
Confidence in the European Union: none at all	15.20	18.90	2.19	99.26	80.42
Having a democratic political system very bad	1.60	2.00	0.23	10.50	80.00
Rejecting neighbors who are immigrants or foreign workers	9.50	14.10	1.37	74.05	67.38
Justifiable paying cash (sometimes or always)	37.80	57.40	5.44	301.46	65.85
Democracy may have problems but it's better (strongly disagree)	1.00	1.80	0.14	9.45	55.56

The World Value Surveys also permit a comparative analysis of the values of the *global Umma* (the totality of the believers in the Muslim religion) *with global society* as a whole. This analysis is presented in Table 4. The ordering principle this time is numerical strength of opinions among the global citizenry. The global results in terms of anti-globalization protest potential, distrust and even open-non-compliance with the law are stunning. A quarter of the global citizenry has nothing against the buying of stolen goods, for example, and 6.4% of the global citizens think that having a democratic political system is bad or fairly bad:

Table 4. The *"Umma"* of 1.3 billion people and global society according to the World Values Survey

WVS questionnaire (A)	% of the global Umma (B)	% of global society (C)	% points higher or lower in the global Umma than in global society - formula (B2-C2)*100/C2)	Size of the global Muslim sample in the WVS	Error margin +- (in %) at 10% error probability
Future: emphasis on technology a good thing	81	70.7	14.57	17578	0.62
Competition is harmful (scale value 1-4)	72.6	68.1	6.61	10386	0.8
Important for a successful marriage: adequate income	72.3	39.2	84.44	1665	2.01
Government responsibility should be increased (value 5-10 on people responsibility versus government scale)	71.7	64.7	10.82	17995	0.61
Rejecting single parent women	70.4	40.4	74.26	16639	0.64
Important for a successful marriage: religious beliefs	68.8	25.7	167.7	1658	2.01
Poverty compared to 10 years ago larger	68.7	70.5	-2.55	4669	1.2
Country is run by a few big interests	68.3	68.7	-0.58	14602	0.68
Future: greater respect for authority a good thing	66.6	58.7	13.46	17536	0.62
Rejecting homosexual neighbors	66.5	47.4	40.3	16940	0.63
Hard work brings success (scale value 1-4)	66.4	53.8	23.42	5252	1.13
Materialism: future changes—less importance placed on work a bad thing	64.9	58.3	11.32	17646	0.62
There should be time for prayer and meditation in schools (agree + strongly agree)	63.6	44.7	42.28	1038	2.55
% saying that agreement on politics is important or very important for a successful marriage	61.9	36.1	71.47	1626	2.03
Justifiable keeping money that you have found (sometimes or always, scale value 2-10)	59.6	49.6	20.16	446	3.88
Little chance to escape from poverty	59	60.4	-2.32	4447	1.23
Justifiable divorce (sometimes or always, scale value 2-10)	58.8	75.9	-22.53	16644	0.64
Government ownership should be increased (value 5-10 on private ownership versus government ownership scale)	58.4	55.4	5.42	17006	0.63
Income class 1-4 (=belong to the poorest 40% of the population)	57.2	50.4	13.49	16916	0.63
Books that attack religion definitely should be banned	56.9	21	170.95	1017	2.57
Rejecting Roma/Sinti neighbors	54.7	38.7	41.34	1735	1.97

WVS questionnaire (A)	% of the global Umma (B)	% of global society (C)	% points higher or lower in the global Umma than in global society - formula (B2-C2)*100/C2)	Size of the global Muslim sample in the WVS	Error margin +- (in %) at 10% error probability
Better if more people with strong religious beliefs in public office (strongly agree + agree)	54.5	36.4	49.73	8498	0.89
Important for a successful marriage: same social background	54.4	20	172	1628	2.03
Unemployed people take away jobs (scale value 1-4)	53.3	47.5	12.21	652	3.21
Justifiable fighting with the police (sometimes or always, scale value 2-10)	49.9	44	13.41	565	3.45
Cautious to confront major changes in life (one should be cautious about major changes in life, scale values 1-4)	48.4	38	27.37	5173	1.14
Materialism: future changes - less emphasis on money not a good thing	48.4	42.8	13.08	17502	0.62
Justifiable failing to report damage you've done accidentally to a parked vehicle (sometimes or always, scale value 2-10)	46.5	34	36.76	445	3.89
Justifiable sex under the legal age of consent (sometimes or always, scale value 2-10)	44.1	35.2	25.28	645	3.23
Justifiable threatening workers who refuse to join a strike (sometimes or always, scale value 2-10)	43.5	26	67.31	559	3.47
Politicians who don't believe in God are unfit for public office (strongly agree)	43.4	18.8	130.85	10471	0.8
Important for a successful marriage: same ethnic background	40.4	15.4	162.34	175	6.2
Justifiable adultery (sometimes or always, scale value 2-10)	39.6	43.5	-8.97	804	2.89
Justifiable abortion (sometimes or always, scale value 2-10)	37.9	61.8	-38.67	15727	0.65
If only one child were to be allowed: preference for a boy	37.2	31	20	4761	1.19
Low income level	37.2	33.8	10.06	16435	0.64
Justifiable political assassination (sometimes or always, scale value 2-10)	36.1	20.3	77.83	615	3.31
Rejecting Jewish neighbors	34.3	15.8	117.09	6336	1.03
Justifiable claiming government benefits (sometimes or always, scale value 2-10)	33.6	38.1	-11.81	15601	0.66
Rejecting neighbors with a different religion	33.1	26	27.31	9883	0.82
Justifiable lying (sometimes or always, scale value 2-10)	31.2	51.7	-39.65	1773	1.95
Justifiable smoking in public places (sometimes or always, scale value 2-10)	31.1	60.3	-48.42	1188	2.38
Incomes should be made more equal (value 1-4 on egalitarian versus anti-egalitarian scale)	30.7	31.5	-2.54	17804	0.61
Rejecting neighbors who are immigrants or foreign workers	30	17	76.47	17950	0.61

Table 4. (Continued)

WVS questionnaire (A)	% of the global Umma (B)	% of global society (C)	% points higher or lower in the global Umma than in global society - formula (B2-C2)*100/C2	Size of the global Muslim sample in the WVS	Error margin +- (in %) at 10% error probability
Justifiable avoiding a fare on public transport (sometimes or always, scale value 2-10)	28.9	40	-27.75	14778	0.67
Rejecting neighbors of a different race	28.3	15.1	87.42	17950	0.61
Justifiable euthanasia (sometimes or always, scale value 2-10)	27.6	57.9	-52.33	15411	0.66
State should give more freedom to firms (scale value 1-4)	27.2	38.3	-28.98	1101	2.47
People can only get rich at the expense of others (scale value 1-4)	27.1	23.6	14.83	5069	1.15
Confidence in the United Nations: none at all	26	17	52.94	14848	0.67
Justifiable buy stolen goods (sometimes or always, scale value 2-10)	25.5	24.9	2.41	4583	1.21
Free market economy wrong for the future of the country	25	48.7	-48.67	541	3.53
Justifiable having casual sex (sometimes or always, scale value 2-10)	24.7	52.9	-53.31	1191	2.38
Justifiable cheating on taxes (sometimes or always, scale value 2-10)	24.4	39.2	-37.76	14896	0.67
Confidence in the political parties: none at all	24.3	27.9	-12.9	13902	0.7
Very good if experts make the decisions	24.1	18.5	30.27	14130	0.69
Individual responsibility for pensions (scale value 1-4)	23.1	21.8	5.96	1015	2.57
Confidence in the health care system: none at all	21.7	8.9	143.82	1181	2.39
Justifiable throwing away litter (sometimes or always, scale value 2-10)	20.6	30.1	-31.56	1632	2.03
Confidence in NATO: none at all	20.3	24.3	-16.46	4493	1.22
Confidence in Parliament: none at all	19.8	19	4.21	15655	0.66
Confidence in Labor Unions: none at all	19.2	20.3	-5.42	14022	0.69
Confidence in the women's movement: none at all	18.6	16.8	10.71	13421	0.71
Enjoy sexual freedom	18.6	23.9	-22.18	4062	1.29
Confidence in major companies: none at all	18.3	15.1	21.19	14297	0.69
Confidence in the European Union: none at all	18.3	17.5	4.57	6396	1.03

WVS questionnaire (A)	% of the global Umma (B)	% of global society (C)	% points higher or lower in the global Umma than in global society - formula (B2-C2)*100/C2)	Size of the global Muslim sample in the WVS	Error margin +- (in %) at 10% error probability
Justifiable paying cash (sometimes or always, scale value 2-10)	17.9	57	-68.6	1178	2.39
Justifiable someone accepting a bribe (sometimes or always, scale value 2-10)	17.6	25	-29.6	16729	0.63
Justifiable joyriding (sometimes or always, scale value 2-10)	17.4	14.8	17.57	1646	2.02
Unwilling to fight for the country	16.6	25.9	-35.91	10050	0.82
Confidence in the Government: none at all	16.3	18.6	-12.37	15077	0.67
Rejecting Muslim neighbors	16.2	20	-19	4243	1.26
Confidence in the police: none at all	15.8	13.6	16.18	16289	0.64
Confidence in the press: none at all	15.6	13.4	16.42	16827	0.63
Saying marriage is an outdated institution	15.5	16.6	-6.63	17402	0.62
Satisfaction with the way democracy develops in the country: not at all satisfied	15.4	14.5	6.21	10410	0.8
Society must be radically changed	15	10.7	40.19	14379	0.68
Confidence in the civil service: none at all	14.8	14.4	2.78	16170	0.64
Justifiable prostitution (sometimes or always, scale value 2-10)	14.8	39.3	-62.34	13190	0.71
Justifiable speeding over the limit (sometimes or always, scale value 2-10)	14.8	43.7	-66.13	1192	2.38
Confidence in the social security system: none at all	14.7	12	22.5	1679	2
Extreme right wing	14.6	7.7	89.61	11922	0.75
Political system that governs the country is very bad	14.6	12.7	14.96	12287	0.74
Justifiable driving under influence of alcohol (sometimes or always, scale value 2-10)	14.5	21.2	-31.6	1763	1.95
Political system that governs the country is very bad	14.6	12.7	14.96	12287	0.74
Justifiable driving under influence of alcohol (sometimes or always, scale value 2-10)	14.5	21.2	-31.6	1763	1.95
Justifiable taking soft drugs (sometimes or always, scale value 2-10)	14.3	19.4	-26.29	1766	1.95

Table 4. (Continued)

WVS questionnaire (A)	% of the global Umma (B)	% of global society (C)	% points higher or lower in the global Umma than in global society - formula (B2-C2)*100/C2	Size of the global Muslim sample in the WVS	Error margin +- (in %) at 10% error probability
Confidence in the Environmental Protection Movement: none at all	14.2	11.2	26.79	13391	0.71
Lower class (subjective)	14.2	13.5	5.19	16264	0.64
Strong leader very good	13.9	12.5	11.2	14715	0.68
Former political system very good	13.4	3.2	318.75	10484	0.8
Army rule very good	12.9	5.4	138.89	14169	0.69
Justifiable suicide (sometimes or always, scale value 2-10)	12.9	40.7	-68.3	15928	0.65
Confidence in the education system: none at all	12.6	4.9	157.14	1768	1.95
Justifiable homosexuality (sometimes or always, scale value 2-10)	12.6	44.1	-71.43	14029	0.69
Confidence in television: none at all	12.5	11.8	5.93	16189	0.64
Justifiable drinking alcohol (sometimes or always, scale value 2-10)	12.3	16	-23.13	6593	1.01
Disagreement or strong disagreement with: democracy may have problems but it is better	11.8	12.3	-4.07	15365	0.66
Confidence in the justice system: none at all	11.6	12.1	-4.13	6438	1.02
Disagree or strongly disagree: long-term relationship is necessary to be happy	11.4	22.7	-49.78	1171	2.4
% not agreeing: respect and appreciation important for successful marriage	10.3	16.1	-36.02	1669	2.01
Confidence in the armed forces: none at all	9.4	11.6	-18.97	15927	0.65
Confidence in churches: none at all	7.5	12.9	-41.86	17993	0.61
Extreme left wing	7.2	5.2	38.46	11922	0.75
Having a democratic political system bad or fairly bad	6.4	9.9	-35.35	15063	0.67
Already joined unofficial strikes	3.5	5.1	-31.37	14692	0.68
Already occupied buildings or factories	1.3	2.1	-38.1	14723	0.68

Source: Source: Our own compilations, based on the official Website of the World Values Survey (WVS) Project, http://www.worldvaluessurvey.org./. Our calculations are based on the WVS data (Download survey data files) and the SPSS XIV statistics program, Innsbruck University. All waves of the WVS surveys are integrated into the data file. To weight for country population size, we used the WVS routine: weights 1000. The sample comprised 204303 representative interview partners with available data on religious confession, gender and age of the respondent.

Chapter 4

THE GLOBAL PROTEST POTENTIAL AGAINST THE "WASHINGTON CONSEXUS" (= LIBERAL MARKET ECONOMY + LIBERAL DEMOCRACY + SEXUAL PERMISSIVENESS + SECULARIZATION)

So, are Muslims really that "dangerous" as Islamophobic circles in the non-Muslim world pretend to think? *Or aren't Muslims and non-Muslims alike sharing a culture of protest against many aspects of globalization?* We again would like to let the facts speak for themselves. And the facts are clear—hundreds of millions of people on earth, Muslims and non-Muslims alike, share traditional family values, share values of protest against the secular globalized culture, and even would consider more radical and violent forms of protest. We above all would like to emphasize that *global value transformation is an intricate process, with optimistic and pessimistic aspects in all societies around the world at the same time.*

But let us for a minute imagine that "we" are "policy planners" in a western transnational corporation, in a western international government bureaucracy, and we would like to figure out how many millions of people are "against" the well-known neo-liberal "Washington Consensus" or against "liberal democracy and the market economy" as such, or do not share the values of secularism and the kind of permissive sexual morality, which seems to be a consensus in many Western countries nowadays. A Muslim fundamentalist would perhaps combine these phenomena under the heading "Washington Consexus" (= liberal market economy + liberal democracy + sexual permissiveness + secularization).

So we compare the total *world protest potential* with the *Muslim protest potential* and calculate the share of the global *Umma* in the total world protest potential and anti-Enlightenment consensus (data for global population, April 2008, from World POPClock Projection According to the International Programs Center, U.S. Census Bureau, the total population of the World, projected to 04/16/08 at 20:58 *GMT (EST+5) is 6,661,757,863* (http://www.census.gov/ipc/www/popclockworld.html).

Table 5. Total world "protest potential", global Muslim "protest potential" and the "anti-Enlightenment consensus"—ranked by the percentage of global society, falling under this WVS category

WVS category according to WVS questionnaire	% of global society	Millions of global citizens	% of the global Umma	Millions of Muslims	Muslims as a percentage of the total global social or political spectrum, described by the WVS category
Total	100	6662	100	1300	19.5
Poverty compared to 10 years ago larger	70.5	4697	68.7	893.1	19
Country is run by a few big interests	68.7	4577	68.3	887.9	19.4
Competition is harmful (scale value 1-4)	68.1	4537	72.6	943.8	20.8
Government responsibility should be increased (value 5-10 on people responsibility versus government scale)	64.7	4310	71.7	932.1	21.6
Justifiable abortion (sometimes or always, scale value 2-10)	61.8	4117	37.9	492.7	12
Little chance to escape from poverty	60.4	4024	59	767	19.1
Justifiable smoking in public places (sometimes or always, scale value 2-10)	60.3	4017	31.1	404.3	10.1
Future: greater respect for authority a good thing	58.7	3910	66.6	865.8	22.1
Materialism: future changes - less importance placed on work a bad thing	58.3	3884	64.9	843.7	21.7
Justifiable euthanasia (sometimes or always, scale value 2-10)	57.9	3857	27.6	358.8	9.3
Justifiable paying cash (sometimes or always, scale value 2-10)	57	3797	17.9	232.7	6.1
Government ownership should be increased (value 5-10 on private ownership versus government ownership scale)	55.4	3691	58.4	759.2	20.6
Hard work brings success (scale value 1-4)	53.8	3584	66.4	863.2	24.1
Justifiable lying (sometimes or always, scale value 2-10)	51.7	3444	31.2	405.6	11.8
Income class 1-4 (=belong to the poorest 40% of the population)	50.4	3358	57.2	743.6	22.1
Justifiable keeping money that you have found (sometimes or always, scale value 2-10)	49.6	3304	59.6	774.8	23.5
Free market economy wrong for the future of the country	48.7	3244	25	325	10
Unemployed people take away jobs (scale value 1-4)	47.5	3164	53.3	692.9	21.9

WVS category according to WVS questionnaire	% of global society	Millions of global citizens	% of the global Umma	Millions of Muslims	Muslims as a percentage of the total global social or political spectrum, described by the WVS category
Rejecting homosexual neighbors	47.4	3158	66.5	864.5	27.4
There should be time for prayer and meditation in schools (agree + strongly agree)	44.7	2978	63.6	826.8	27.8
Justifiable fighting with the police (sometimes or always, scale value 2-10)	44	2931	49.9	648.7	22.1
Justifiable speeding over the limit (sometimes or always, scale value 2-10)	43.7	2911	14.8	192.4	6.6
Justifiable adultery (sometimes or always, scale value 2-10)	43.5	2898	39.6	514.8	17.8
Materialism: future changes - less emphasis on money not a good thing	42.8	2851	48.4	629.2	22.1
Rejecting single parent woman	40.4	2691	70.4	915.2	34
Justifiable avoiding a fare on public transport (sometimes or always, scale value 2-10)	40	2665	28.9	375.7	14.1
Justifiable prostitution (sometimes or always, scale value 2-10)	39.3	2618	14.8	192.4	7.3
Important for a successful marriage: adequate income	39.2	2611	72.3	939.9	36
Justifiable cheating on taxes (sometimes or always, scale value 2-10)	39.2	2611	24.4	317.2	12.1
Rejecting Roma/Sinti neighbors	38.7	2578	54.7	711.1	27.6
State should give more freedom to firms (scale value 1-4)	38.3	2551	27.2	353.6	13.9
Justifiable claiming government benefits (sometimes or always, scale value 2-10)	38.1	2538	33.6	436.8	17.2
Cautious to confront major changes in life (one should be cautious about major changes in life, scale values 1-4)	38	2531	48.4	629.2	24.9
Better if more people with strong religious beliefs in public office (strongly agree + agree)	36.4	2425	54.5	708.5	29.2
% saying that agreement on politics is important or very important for a successful marriage	36.1	2405	61.9	804.7	33.5
Justifiable sex under the legal age of consent (sometimes or always, scale value 2-10)	35.2	2345	44.1	573.3	24.4

Table 5. (Continued)

WVS category according to WVS questionnaire	% of global society	Millions of global citizens	% of the global Umma	Millions of Muslims	Muslims as a percentage of the total global social or political spectrum, described by the WVS category
Justifiable failing to report damage you've done accidentally to a parked vehicle (sometimes or always, scale value 2-10)	34	2265	46.5	604.5	26.7
Low income level	33.8	2252	37.2	483.6	21.5
Incomes should be made more equal (value 1-4 on egalitarian versus anti-egalitarian scale)	31.5	2098	30.7	399.1	19
If only one child were to be allowed: preference for a boy	31	2065	37.2	483.6	23.4
Justifiable throwing away litter (sometimes or always, scale value 2-10)	30.1	2005	20.6	267.8	13.4
Confidence in the political parties: none at all	27.9	1859	24.3	315.9	17
Justifiable threatening workers who refuse to join a strike (sometimes or always, scale value 2-10)	26	1732	43.5	565.5	32.7
Rejecting neighbors with a different religion	26	1732	33.1	430.3	24.8
Unwilling to fight for the country	25.9	1725	16.6	215.8	12.5
Important for a successful marriage: religious beliefs	25.7	1712	68.8	894.4	52.2
Justifiable someone accepting a bribe (sometimes or always, scale value 2-10)	25	1665	17.6	228.8	13.7
Justifiable buy stolen goods (sometimes or always, scale value 2-10)	24.9	1659	25.5	331.5	20
Confidence in NATO: none at all	24.3	1619	20.3	263.9	16.3
People can only get rich at the expense of others (scale value 1-4)	23.6	1572	27.1	352.3	22.4
Disagree or strongly disagree: long-term relationship is necessary to be happy	22.7	1512	11.4	148.2	9.8
Justifiable driving under influence of alcohol (sometimes or always, scale value 2-10)	21.2	1412	14.5	188.5	13.3
Books that attack religion definitely should be banned	21	1399	56.9	739.7	52.9
Justifiable political assassination (sometimes or always, scale value 2-10)	20.3	1352	36.1	469.3	34.7

WVS category according to WVS questionnaire	% of global society	Millions of global citizens	% of the global Umma	Millions of Muslims	Muslims as a percentage of the total global social or political spectrum, described by the WVS category
Confidence in Labor Unions: none at all	20.3	1352	19.2	249.6	18.5
Justifiable taking soft drugs (sometimes or always, scale value 2-10)	19.4	1292	14.3	185.9	14.4
Confidence in Parliament: none at all	19	1266	19.8	257.4	20.3
Politicians who don't believe in God are unfit for public office (strongly agree)	18.8	1252	43.4	564.2	45.1
Confidence in the government: none at all	18.6	1239	16.3	211.9	17.1
Very good if experts make the decisions	18.5	1232	24.1	313.3	25.4
Confidence in the European Union: none at all	17.5	1166	18.3	237.9	20.4
Rejecting neighbors who are immigrants or foreign workers	17	1132	30	390	34.5
Confidence in the United Nations: none at all	17	1132	26	338	29.9
Confidence in the women's movement: none at all	16.8	1119	18.6	241.8	21.6
Saying marriage is an outdated institution	16.6	1106	15.5	201.5	18.2
% not agreeing: respect and appreciation important for successful marriage	16.1	1073	10.3	133.9	12.5
Rejecting Jewish neighbors	15.8	1053	34.3	445.9	42.3
Important for a successful marriage: same ethnic background	15.4	1026	40.4	525.2	51.2
Rejecting neighbors of a different race	15.1	1006	28.3	367.9	36.6
Confidence in major companies: none at all	15.1	1006	18.3	237.9	23.6
Justifiable joyriding (sometimes or always, scale value 2-10)	14.8	986	17.4	226.2	22.9
Satisfaction with the way democracy develops in the country: not at all satisfied	14.5	966	15.4	200.2	20.7
Confidence in the civil service: none at all	14.4	959	14.8	192.4	20.1
Confidence in the police: none at all	13.6	906	15.8	205.4	22.7
Lower class (subjective)	13.5	899	14.2	184.6	20.5
Confidence in the press: none at all	13.4	893	15.6	202.8	22.7
Confidence in churches: none at all	12.9	859	7.5	97.5	11.4

Table 5. (Continued)

WVS category according to WVS questionnaire	% of global society	Millions of global citizens	% of the global Umma	Millions of Muslims	Muslims as a percentage of the total global social or political spectrum, described by the WVS category
Political system, which governs the country very bad	12.7	846	14.6	189.8	22.4
Strong leader very good	12.5	833	13.9	180.7	21.7
Disagreement or strong disagreement with: democracy may have problems but it is better	12.3	819	11.8	153.4	18.7
Confidence in the Justice System: none at all	12.1	806	11.6	150.8	18.7
Confidence in the social security system: none at all	12	799	14.7	191.1	23.9
Confidence in television: none at all	11.8	786	12.5	162.5	20.7
Confidence in the armed forces: none at all	11.6	773	9.4	122.2	15.8
Confidence in the environmental protection movement: none at all	11.2	746	14.2	184.6	24.7
Society must be radically changed	10.7	713	15	195	27.3
Having a democratic political system bad or fairly bad	9.9	660	6.4	83.2	12.6
Confidence in the health care system: none at all	8.9	593	21.7	282.1	47.6
Extreme right wing	7.7	513	14.6	189.8	37
Army rule very good	5.4	360	12.9	167.7	46.6
Extreme left wing	5.2	346	7.2	93.6	27.1
Already joined unofficial strikes	5.1	340	3.5	45.5	13.4
Confidence in the education system: none at all	4.9	326	12.6	163.8	50.2
Former political system very good	3.2	213	13.4	174.2	81.8
Already occupied buildings or factories	2.1	140	1.3	16.9	12.1

Source: Source: Our own compilations, based on the official Website of the *World Values Survey (WVS)* Project, *http://www.worldvaluessurvey.org./*. Our calculations are based on the WVS data (Download survey data files) and the SPSS XIV statistics program, Innsbruck University. All waves of the WVS surveys are integrated into the data file. To weight for country population size, we used the WVS routine: weights 1000. The sample comprised 204303 representative interview partners with available data on religious confession, gender and age of the respondent.

The World Values Survey data permit us to state exactly, in, which "issue area" of "discontent" with the neo-liberal "Washington Consexus" of neo-liberalism, competitive party democracy and the market economy, and permissive sexuality the Muslim global protest potential is largest, and where the Muslim global protest potential share is smallest:

Table 6. Total world "protest potential", global Muslim "protest potential" and the "anti-Enlightenment consensus"—the size of the Muslim share in the total "anti-Enlightenment consensus"—ranked by the Muslim share

WVS categories according to the WVS questionnaire	% of global society	Millions of global citizens	% of the global Umma	Millions of Muslims	Muslims as a percentage of this total global social or political spectrum
Former political system very good	3.2	213	13.4	174.2	81.8
Books that attack religion definitely should be banned	21	1399	56.9	739.7	52.9
Important for a successful marriage: religious beliefs	25.7	1712	68.8	894.4	52.2
Important for a successful marriage: same ethnic background	15.4	1026	40.4	525.2	51.2
Confidence in the education system: none at all	4.9	326	12.6	163.8	50.2
Confidence in the health care system: none at all	8.9	593	21.7	282.1	47.6
Army rule is very good	5.4	360	12.9	167.7	46.6
Politicians who don't believe in God are unfit for public office (strongly agree)	18.8	1252	43.4	564.2	45.1
Rejecting Jewish neighbors	15.8	1053	34.3	445.9	42.3
Extreme right wing	7.7	513	14.6	189.8	37
Rejecting neighbors of a different race	15.1	1006	28.3	367.9	36.6
Important for a successful marriage: adequate income	39.2	2611	72.3	939.9	36
Justifiable political assassination (sometimes or always, scale value 2-10)	20.3	1352	36.1	469.3	34.7
Rejecting neighbors who are immigrants or foreign workers	17	1132	30	390	34.5
Rejecting single parent woman	40.4	2691	70.4	915.2	34
% saying that agreement on politics is important or very important for a successful marriage	36.1	2405	61.9	804.7	33.5
Justifiable threatening workers who refuse to join a strike (sometimes or always, scale value 2-10)	26	1732	43.5	565.5	32.7
Confidence in the United Nations: none at all	17	1132	26	338	29.9

Table 6. (Continued)

WVS categories according to the WVS questionnaire	% of global society	Millions of global citizens	% of the global Umma	Millions of Muslims	Muslims as a percentage of this total global social or political spectrum
Better if more people with strong religious beliefs in public office (strongly agree + agree)	36.4	2425	54.5	708.5	29.2
There should be time for prayer and meditation in schools (agree + strongly agree)	44.7	2978	63.6	826.8	27.8
Rejecting Roma/Sinti neighbors	38.7	2578	54.7	711.1	27.6
Rejecting homosexual neighbors	47.4	3158	66.5	864.5	27.4
Society must be radically changed	10.7	713	15	195	27.3
Extreme left wing	5.2	346	7.2	93.6	27.1
Justifiable failing to report damage you've done accidentally to a parked vehicle (sometimes or always, scale value 2-10)	34	2265	46.5	604.5	26.7
Very good if experts make the decisions	18.5	1232	24.1	313.3	25.4
Cautious to confront major changes in life (one should be cautious about major changes in life, scale values 1-4)	38	2531	48.4	629.2	24.9
Rejecting neighbors with a different religion	26	1732	33.1	430.3	24.8
Confidence in the environmental protection movement: none at all	11.2	746	14.2	184.6	24.7
Justifiable sex under the legal age of consent (sometimes or always, scale value 2-10)	35.2	2345	44.1	573.3	24.4
Hard work brings success (scale value 1-4)	53.8	3584	66.4	863.2	24.1
Confidence in the social security system: none at all	12	799	14.7	191.1	23.9
Confidence in major companies: none at all	15.1	1006	18.3	237.9	23.6
Justifiable keeping money that you have found (sometimes or always, scale value 2-10)	49.6	3304	59.6	774.8	23.5
If only one child were to be allowed: preference for a boy	31	2065	37.2	483.6	23.4
Justifiable joyriding	14.8	986	17.4	226.2	22.9

WVS categories according to the WVS questionnaire	% of global society	Millions of global citizens	% of the global Umma	Millions of Muslims	Muslims as a percentage of this total global social or political spectrum
(sometimes or always, scale value 2-10)					
Confidence in the police: none at all	13.6	906	15.8	205.4	22.7
Confidence in the press: none at all	13.4	893	15.6	202.8	22.7
People can only get rich at the expense of others (scale value 1-4)	23.6	1572	27.1	352.3	22.4
Political system, which governs the country very bad	12.7	846	14.6	189.8	22.4
Future: greater respect for authority a good thing	58.7	3910	66.6	865.8	22.1
Income class 1-4 (=belong to the poorest 40% of the population)	50.4	3358	57.2	743.6	22.1
Justifiable fighting with the police (sometimes or always, scale value 2-10)	44	2931	49.9	648.7	22.1
Materialism: future changes —less emphasis on money not a good thing	42.8	2851	48.4	629.2	22.1
Unemployed people take away jobs (scale value 1-4)	47.5	3164	53.3	692.9	21.9
Materialism: future changes —less importance placed on work a bad thing	58.3	3884	64.9	843.7	21.7
Strong leader very good	12.5	833	13.9	180.7	21.7
Government responsibility should be increased (value 5-10 on people responsibility versus government scale)	64.7	4310	71.7	932.1	21.6
Confidence in the women's movement: none at all	16.8	1119	18.6	241.8	21.6
Low income level	33.8	2252	37.2	483.6	21.5
Competition is harmful (scale value 1-4)	68.1	4537	72.6	943.8	20.8
satisfaction with the way democracy develops in the country: not at all satisfied	14.5	966	15.4	200.2	20.7
Confidence in television: none at all	11.8	786	12.5	162.5	20.7
Government ownership should be increased (value 5-10 on private ownership versus government ownership scale)	55.4	3691	58.4	759.2	20.6
Lower class (subjective)	13.5	899	14.2	184.6	20.5
Confidence in the European Union: none at all	17.5	1166	18.3	237.9	20.4

Table 6. (Continued)

WVS categories according to the WVS questionnaire	% of global society	Millions of global citizens	% of the global Umma	Millions of Muslims	Muslims as a percentage of this total global social or political spectrum
Confidence in Parliament: none at all	19	1266	19.8	257.4	20.3
Confidence in the civil service: none at all	14.4	959	14.8	192.4	20.1
Justifiable buy stolen goods (sometimes or always, scale value 2-10)	24.9	1659	25.5	331.5	20
Total	100	6662	100	1300	19.5
Country is run by a few big interests	68.7	4577	68.3	887.9	19.4
Little chance to escape from poverty	60.4	4024	59	767	19.1
Poverty compared to 10 years ago larger	70.5	4697	68.7	893.1	19
Incomes should be made more equal (value 1-4 on egalitarian versus anti-egalitarian scale)	31.5	2098	30.7	399.1	19
Disagreement or strong disagreement with: democracy may have problems but it is better	12.3	819	11.8	153.4	18.7
Confidence in the justice system: none at all	12.1	806	11.6	150.8	18.7
Confidence in labor unions: none at all	20.3	1352	19.2	249.6	18.5
Saying marriage is an outdated institution	16.6	1106	15.5	201.5	18.2
Justifiable adultery (sometimes or always, scale value 2-10)	43.5	2898	39.6	514.8	17.8
Justifiable claiming government benefits (sometimes or always, scale value 2-10)	38.1	2538	33.6	436.8	17.2
Confidence in the Government: none at all	18.6	1239	16.3	211.9	17.1
Confidence in the political parties: none at all	27.9	1859	24.3	315.9	17
Confidence in NATO: none at all	24.3	1619	20.3	263.9	16.3
Confidence in the armed forces: none at all	11.6	773	9.4	122.2	15.8
Justifiable taking soft drugs (sometimes or always, scale value 2-10)	19.4	1292	14.3	185.9	14.4
Justifiable avoiding a fare on public transport (sometimes or always, scale value 2-10)	40	2665	28.9	375.7	14.1

WVS categories according to the WVS questionnaire	% of global society	Millions of global citizens	% of the global Umma	Millions of Muslims	Muslims as a percentage of this total global social or political spectrum
State should give more freedom to firms (scale value 1-4)	38.3	2551	27.2	353.6	13.9
Justifiable someone accepting a bribe (sometimes or always, scale value 2-10)	25	1665	17.6	228.8	13.7
Justifiable throwing away litter (sometimes or always, scale value 2-10)	30.1	2005	20.6	267.8	13.4
Already joined unofficial strikes	5.1	340	3.5	45.5	13.4
Justifiable driving under influence of alcohol (sometimes or always, scale value 2-10)	21.2	1412	14.5	188.5	13.3
Having a democratic political system bad or fairly bad	9.9	660	6.4	83.2	12.6
Unwilling to fight for the country	25.9	1725	16.6	215.8	12.5
% not agreeing: respect and appreciation important for successful marriage	16.1	1073	10.3	133.9	12.5
Justifiable cheating on taxes (sometimes or always, scale value 2-10)	39.2	2611	24.4	317.2	12.1
Already occupied buildings or factories	2.1	140	1.3	16.9	12.1
Justifiable abortion (sometimes or always, scale value 2-10)	61.8	4117	37.9	492.7	12
Justifiable lying (sometimes or always, scale value 2-10)	51.7	3444	31.2	405.6	11.8
Confidence in churches: none at all	12.9	859	7.5	97.5	11.4
Justifiable smoking in public places (sometimes or always, scale value 2-10)	60.3	4017	31.1	404.3	10.1
Free market economy wrong for the future of the country	48.7	3244	25	325	10
Disagree or strongly disagree: long-term relationship is necessary to be happy	22.7	1512	11.4	148.2	9.8
Justifiable euthanasia (sometimes or always, scale value 2-10)	57.9	3857	27.6	358.8	9.3
Justifiable prostitution (sometimes or always, scale value 2-10)	39.3	2618	14.8	192.4	7.3

Table 6. (Continued)

WVS categories according to the WVS questionnaire	% of global society	Millions of global citizens	% of the global Umma	Millions of Muslims	Muslims as a percentage of this total global social or political spectrum
Justifiable speeding over the limit (sometimes or always, scale value 2-10)	43.7	2911	14.8	192.4	6.6
Justifiable paying cash (sometimes or always, scale value 2-10)	57	3797	17.9	232.7	6.1

Source: Source: Our own compilations, based on the official Website of the World Values Survey (WVS) Project, http://www.worldvaluessurvey.org/. Our calculations are based on the WVS data (Download survey data files) and the SPSS XIV statistics program, Innsbruck University. All waves of the WVS surveys are integrated into the data file. To weight for country population size, we used the WVS routine: weights 1000. The sample comprised 204303 representative interview partners with available data on religious confession, gender and age of the respondent.

Global Muslims represent more than 50% of all people on Earth, who hold the following opinions:

- Former political system is very good
- Books that attack religion definitely should be banned
- Important for a successful marriage: religious beliefs
- Important for a successful marriage: same ethnic background
- Confidence in the education system: none at all

Global Muslims total more than 40% of all people on Earth, who hold the following opinions:

- Confidence in the health care system: none at all
- Army rule is very good
- Politicians who don't believe in God are unfit for public office (strongly agree)
- Rejecting Jewish neighbors

Equally, global Muslims are more than 30% of all people on earth who think that

- Extreme right wing
- Rejecting neighbors of a different race
- Important for a successful marriage: adequate income
- Justifiable political assassination (sometimes or always, scale value 2–10)
- Rejecting neighbors who are immigrants or foreign workers
- Rejecting single parent woman
- Percent saying that agreement on politics is important or very important for a successful marriage

- Justifiable threatening workers who refuse to join a strike (sometimes or always, scale value 2–10)

By contrast, global Islam represents less than 10% of all global citizens who think that:

- Justifiable smoking in public places (sometimes or always, scale value 2–10)
- Free market economy wrong for the future of the country
- Disagree or strongly disagree: long-term relationship is necessary to be happy
- Justifiable euthanasia (sometimes or always, scale value 2–10)
- Justifiable prostitution (sometimes or always, scale value 2–10)
- Justifiable speeding over the limit (sometimes or always, scale value 2–10)
- Justifiable paying cash (sometimes or always, scale value 2–10)

Another question in this context is whether *Euro-Islam* is any different from global Islam in this context. Euro-Islam, it seems, learnt rapidly the lessons of partial lawlessness and corruption, existing to some extent in many European countries and interestingly enough, distinguishes itself to +20% or more from global Islam by the following attitudes:

- Justifiable prostitution (sometimes or always, scale value 2–10)
- Justifiable speeding over the limit (sometimes or always, scale value 2–10)
- occupying buildings and factories
- Justifiable paying cash (sometimes or always, scale value 2–10)
- Already joined unofficial strikes
- Justifiable cheating on taxes (sometimes or always, scale value 2–10)
- Justifiable someone accepting a bribe (sometimes or always, scale value 2–10)
- Justifiable avoiding a fare on public transport (sometimes or always, scale value 2–10)
- low income level
- Justifiable claiming government benefits (sometimes or always, scale value 2–10)
- Confidence in the Press: none at all

Compared to total Islam, there is a 20% or more negative *numerical* difference in Euro-Islam for following attitudes.

- Confidence in the armed forces: none at all
- Confidence in the social security system: none at all
- Confidence in Parliament: none at all
- Rejecting homosexual neighbors
- Rejecting Roma/Sinti neighbors
- Rejecting neighbors of a different race
- Confidence in the police: none at all
- Political system, which governs the country very bad
- Democracy may have problems but it's better (disagree+strongly disagree)
- Politicians who don't believe in God are unfit for public office (strongly agree)

- Rejecting Jewish neighbors
- Rejecting neighbors who are immigrants or foreign workers
- Having the army rule is very good
- Confidence in the Education System: none at all
- Rejecting Muslim neighbors

The conclusions from this can be partially optimistic: Euro-Islam has a better confidence in the Army than global Islam, a better confidence in the Social Security System, in Parliament, in the police, in the political system, in democracy, in the education system than global Islam; and Euro-Islam tends to be less anti-Semitic, homophobe, Romaphobe and racist and anti-immigrant than global Islam, and also less self-hating, and tends to be less fascinated by army rule than global Islam. Sure, that's a good point for European decision makers. Euro-Islam, in a way lost its "innocence" by partially having learnt the lessons of partial lawlessness and corruption, existing in Europe, but it also became less rigid in other aspects – in terms of Confidence in the army, the institutions of the state of residence, and it became more respectful of the many other minorities around it.

Table 7. Euro-Islam in comparison with global Islam: total global Muslim "protest potential", European Muslim "protest potential" and the numerical difference between Euro-Islam and global Islam (ranked by the difference between Euro-Islam and global Islam)

Myth and reality of Euro-Islam according to the WVS	% EU-27+EEA+EFTA "Umma"	% of the global Umma	Global Umma = 100
Justifiable prostitution (sometimes or always, scale value 2-10)	38.5	14.8	260.1
Justifiable speeding over the limit (sometimes or always, scale value 2-10)	38	14.8	256.8
occupying buildings and factories	3	1.3	230.8
Justifiable paying cash (sometimes or always, scale value 2-10)	37.8	17.9	211.2
Already joined unofficial strikes	5.9	3.5	168.6
Justifiable cheating on taxes (sometimes or always, scale value 2-10)	39.6	24.4	162.3
Justifiable someone accepting a bribe (sometimes or always, scale value 2-10)	25.8	17.6	146.6
Justifiable avoiding a fare on public transport (sometimes or always, scale value 2-10)	40.4	28.9	139.8
low income level	48.1	37.2	129.3
Justifiable claiming government benefits (sometimes or always, scale value 2-10)	41	33.6	122
Confidence in the press: none at all	18.8	15.6	120.5
Confidence in churches: none at all	8.9	7.5	118.7
Confidence in NATO: none at all	23.7	20.3	116.7
Having a democratic political system fairly bad or very bad	7.2	6.4	112.5
Not at all satisfied with democracy	17	15.4	110.4
Confidence in labor unions: none at all	20.5	19.2	106.8

Myth and reality of Euro-Islam according to the WVS	% EU-27+EEA+EFTA "Umma"	% of the global Umma	Global Umma = 100
Confidence in the justice system: none at all	10.5	11.6	90.5
Justifiable political assassination (sometimes or always, scale value 2-10)	32	36.1	88.6
Confidence in the civil service: none at all	12.7	14.8	85.8
Justifiable sex under the legal age of consent (sometimes or always, scale value 2-10)	37.2	44.1	84.4
Confidence in the European Union: none at all	15.2	18.3	83.1
Confidence in the armed forces: none at all	7.4	9.4	78.7
Confidence in the social security system: none at all	11.3	14.7	76.9
Confidence in Parliament: none at all	14.3	19.8	72.2
Rejecting homosexual neighbors	45.6	66.5	68.6
Rejecting Roma/Sinti neighbors	35.5	54.7	64.9
Rejecting neighbors of a different race	18.2	28.3	64.3
Confidence in the police: none at all	9.3	15.8	58.9
Political system, which governs the country very bad	8.3	14.6	56.8
Democracy may have problems but it's better (disagree+strongly disagree)	7.2	13.2	54.5
Politicians who don't believe in God are unfit for public office (strongly agree)	19	43.4	43.8
Rejecting Jewish neighbors	13.3	34.3	38.8
Rejecting neighbors who are immigrants or foreign workers	9.5	30	31.7
Having the army rule is very good	3.4	12.9	26.4
Confidence in the education system: none at all	3.3	12.6	26.2
Rejecting Muslim neighbors	3.9	16.2	24.1

Source: our own compilations from the WVS based Tables, reported above.

Our next table neatly lists in descending order the main WVS-characteristics of the Muslim communities in Europe:

Table 8. The myth of Euro-Islam? A WVS comparison

Myth and reality of Euro-Islam according to the WVS	% EU-27+EEA+EFTA "Umma"	% of the global Umma	Global Umma = 100
low income level	48.1	37.2	129.3
Rejecting homosexual neighbors	45.6	66.5	68.6
Justifiable claiming government benefits (sometimes or always, scale value 2-10)	41	33.6	122
Justifiable avoiding a fare on public transport (sometimes or always, scale value 2-10)	40.4	28.9	139.8
Justifiable cheating on taxes (sometimes or always, scale value 2-10)	39.6	24.4	162.3
Justifiable prostitution (sometimes or always, scale value 2-10)	38.5	14.8	260.1

Table 8. (Continued)

Myth and reality of Euro-Islam according to the WVS	% EU-27+EEA+EFTA "Umma"	% of the global Umma	Global Umma = 100
Justifiable speeding over the limit (sometimes or always, scale value 2-10)	38	14.8	256.8
Justifiable paying cash (sometimes or always, scale value 2-10)	37.8	17.9	211.2
Justifiable sex under the legal age of consent (sometimes or always, scale value 2-10)	37.2	44.1	84.4
Rejecting Roma/Sinti neighbors	35.5	54.7	64.9
Justifiable political assassination (sometimes or always, scale value 2-10)	32	36.1	88.6
Justifiable someone accepting a bribe (sometimes or always, scale value 2-10)	25.8	17.6	146.6
Confidence in NATO: none at all	23.7	20.3	116.7
Confidence in Labor Unions: none at all	20.5	19.2	106.8
Politicians who don't believe in God are unfit for public office (strongly agree)	19	43.4	43.8
Confidence in the Press: none at all	18.8	15.6	120.5
Rejecting neighbors of a different race	18.2	28.3	64.3
Not at all satisfied with democracy	17	15.4	110.4
Confidence in the European Union: none at all	15.2	18.3	83.1
Confidence in Parliament: none at all	14.3	19.8	72.2
Rejecting Jewish neighbors	13.3	34.3	38.8
Confidence in the civil service: none at all	12.7	14.8	85.8
Confidence in the social security system: none at all	11.3	14.7	76.9
Confidence in the justice system: none at all	10.5	11.6	90.5
Rejecting neighbors who are immigrants or foreign workers	9.5	30	31.7
Confidence in the Police: none at all	9.3	15.8	58.9
Confidence in Churches: none at all	8.9	7.5	118.7
Political system, which governs the country very bad	8.3	14.6	56.8
Confidence in the Armed Forces: none at all	7.4	9.4	78.7
Having a democratic political system fairly bad or very bad	7.2	6.4	112.5
Democracy may have problems but it's better (disagree+strongly disagree)	7.2	13.2	54.5
Already joined unofficial strikes	5.9	3.5	168.6
Rejecting Muslim neighbors	3.9	16.2	24.1
Having the army rule very good	3.4	12.9	26.4
Confidence in the education system: none at all	3.3	12.6	26.2
occupying buildings and factories	3	1.3	230.8

Source: our own compilations from the WVS based Tables, reported above.

Thus having learned the lessons of "sin and tolerance", what other guiding experiences are available to conjecture the future trajectory of Islam in Europe?

Chapter 5

ANOTHER LOOK AT *ASABIYYA*: THE SOCIAL COHESION OF SOCIETY

Of course, politicians and journalists all over the globe can engage in a never-ending debate about values, culture, and the "leading Western/European culture". Inglehart and his sociological school came up with the most plausible and also empirically well-founded scheme of global value development and measurement:

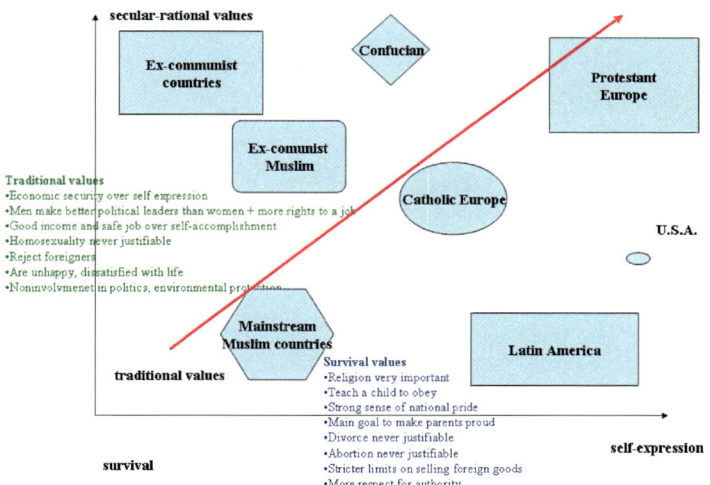

Graph 2. The transition from traditional to modern societies, according to Inglehart.

Note: Inglehart factor-analyzed the WVS-country results for the variables: Abortion never justifiable; Divorce never justifiable; Main goal to make parents proud; More respect for authority; Religion very important; Stricter limits on selling foreign goods; Strong sense of national pride; Teach a child to obey and drew the conclusion that the resulting principal component represents *survival versus self expression*. Likewise, he factor-analyzed the country results for the WVS variables: Are unhappy, dissatisfied with life; Economic security over self expression; Good income and safe job over self-accomplishment; Homosexuality never justifiable; Men make better political leaders than women + more rights to a job; Noninvolvement in politics, environmental protection; Reject foreigners and drew the conclusion that this dimension represents *"traditional versus secular"*.

One of the most famous pieces of Inglehart's research tradition is the world map of human values, which depicts the trajectory of all the countries of the world both over space and time. Starting from the left-hand lower corner, a society, as a rule, will move to the upper right hand corner of Graph 3. This sociological "law", which was obtained by the statistical mathematical model of factor analysis, based on the WVS data, must be regarded as one of the most solidly based observations of sociological theory today.

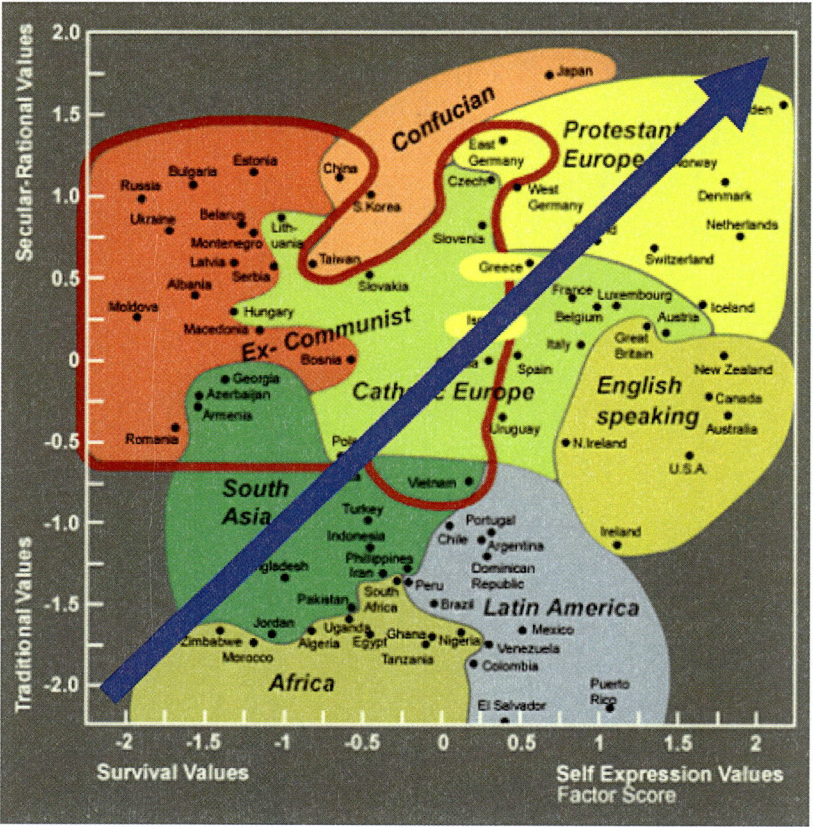

Graph 3. The Inglehart-Welzel map of global values.

Source: http://www.worldvaluessurvey.org/

Note: Inglehart would assume that societies do move along the global path, symbolized by the arrow, from a traditional and survival oriented value set towards a secular and self-expression oriented value set.

But what can we say about the outlayers? The classic Arab historian and philosopher Ibn Khaldun, who died in 1405, explained in his most important book, *Muqaddimah (Introduction to History)* [see also Tibi (1996) and (Darling (2007)], that historical change and the succession of dynasties are a function of the interactions between nomadic culture and urban civilization.

Another Look at *Asabiyya*: The Social Cohesion of Society

Ibn Khaldūn or Ibn Khaldoun (May 27, 1332 AD/732 AH – March 19, 1406 AD/808 AH).

This sociological perspective on *"Asabiyya"* should not be confounded with the religious, theological debate about the *"Asabiyya"* as the pre-Islamic kinship or identity feeling among the inhabitants of Arabic countries, severely criticized by the *Prophet Mohammed* (Peace be upon him) in *Hadiths*. This debate would amount in modern sociological terms to the very necessary debate about "nationalism" and racism, and in this respect the

> "patronizing or defending one's kindred or those with whom one has some kind of affinity or relation, whether it be creed and religious ideology, soil or home, language or

colour. This affinity may also be due to similarity of profession or the relationship of teacher and pupil, or something else . . ."

and indeed would be

". . . a moral vice that appears to take the form of defence of truth or religion, but in reality it is aimed at extending one's own influence or that of one's coreligionist(s), relative(s), friend(s), or member(s) of group" [http://www.al-emaan.org/prejudice.htm].

Muslim theologians would be quick to point out that

"One who calls towards Asabiyyah is not from us, one who fights for Asabiyyah is not from us and the one who dies on Asabiyyah is not from us." [Mizan al Hikmah, Hadith # 13035]

Our extensive data, documented in this work, say, on the extent of anti-Roma prejudice, and Anti-Semitism in many parts of the world, including in Muslim countries, precisely underline the eternal correctness and the humanistic well-reasoned criticism inherent in *Hadith* 13035.

Our understanding of *Asabiyya* is only a *sociological one* in the tradition of Ibn Khaldoun, referring to the "social cohesion" of a *societal system*.

For the social cohesion of society, tolerance *vis-à-vis* foreigners and immigrants are absolutely necessary. That is the eternal truth of *Hadith* 13035.

In terms of modern *social science theory,* the following Khaldounian scheme can be proposed. Societies do not generally experience a smooth transformation from a traditional and survival oriented value set towards a secular and self-expression oriented value set. The *"Asabiyya"* counter-model to Inglehart, relies on a factor analytical evaluation of the following variables in the world values survey, and combines theoretical insights of the *Inglehart School* with those by Columbia University sociologist *Amitai Etzioni.*

At the very beginning of the modernization process, societies are *traditional, religious*, and *pre-modern*; but at the same time they are also "active" societies with functioning neighborhood structures, and very clear perceptions of what are "good" and "evil", and a high respect of the law. As the *modernization process* proceeds, traditional religious values seem to be on the losing side of the societal equation. The uneasiness of the "religious right" in the United States, of the Islamist camp in many countries of the Muslim world, and the religious right in many developing countries is best understood by the process, whereby traditional values get lost at the same time with dimensions of the active society and respect of the law in such vital areas as tax morale, non-acceptance of bribery and government benefits fraud.

Islamists are of course wrong in assuming that countries of the Muslim world are the only ones to suffer the downward trend in public morale. The worst global performers, it seems, are Belarus, Brazil, Slovakia, and the Ukraine. As churches are emptying, so do the volunteer organizations; and since "God" does not "exist", everything becomes feasible, acceptable, and even becomes practice: cheating taxes, taking bribes, receiving government benefits even if you are not entitled for them:

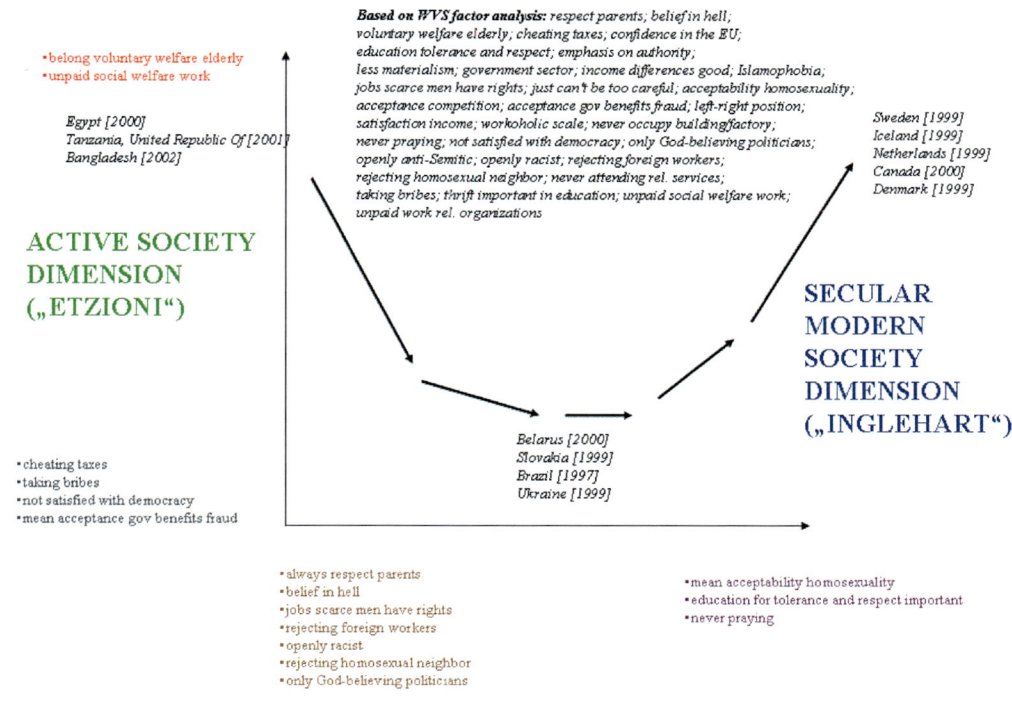

Graph 4. The Inglehart/Etzioni synthesis.

Note: the following WVS country values were submitted to an explorative factor analysis: always respect parents; belief in hell; cheating taxes; education for tolerance and respect important; jobs scarce men have rights; mean acceptability homosexuality; mean acceptance government benefits fraud; never praying; not satisfied with democracy; only God-believing politicians; openly racist; rejecting foreign workers; rejecting homosexual neighbor, belong voluntary welfare elderly; taking bribes; unpaid social welfare work. Our analysis yielded two factors: a continuum of *traditional versus secular,* and a continuum *cheating versus active society.*

Our factor analysis of the country values from the WVS surveys in the 3rd and 4th wave yields the following results:

- Political values are often similar, but personal values on morality, gender and family often are differing dramatically across the globe.

First Lady, NATO member country, Western democracy: Turkey. (Photo credit: http://affordablehousinginstitute.org/blogs/us/wp-content/uploads/2007/09/imagesabdullah-hayrunisa-gul-small.jpg)

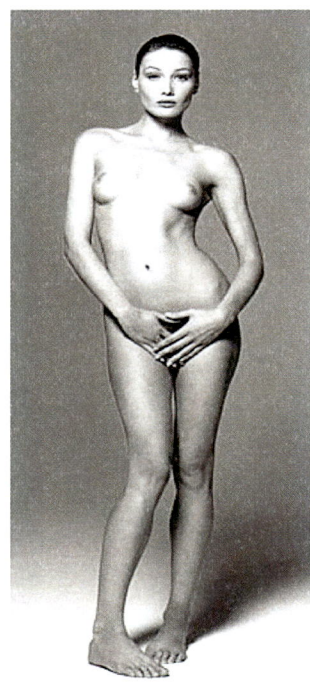

First Lady, NATO member country, Western democracy: France. Photo credit: http://images.mirror.co.uk/upl/m3/mar2008/0/0/EA6FBDD6-9D03-DB87-EC5B99D78CFC7278.jpg.

Table 9. The logic of global value change – results from a factor analysis of the WVS data

	Traditional versus secular attitudes	Cheating versus active society
Albania [2002]	0.9823	0.4326
Algeria [2002]	1.45209	-0.49094
Argentina [1999]	-0.44307	-0.05472
Armenia [1997]	0.7798	1.66401
Australia [1995]	-0.93678	-0.76537
Austria [1999]	-0.97091	-0.07798
Azerbaijan [1997]	0.61006	1.19167
Bangladesh [2002]	2.1835	-2.9929
Belarus [2000]	-0.21767	1.97288
Belgium [1999]	-1.2322	0.493
Bosnia and Herzegovina [2001]	0.31595	0.42056
Brazil [1997]	0.07281	1.59396
Bulgaria [1999]	0.14131	0.55246
Canada [2000]	-1.17932	-1.15722
Chile [2000]	-0.42296	0.39903
China [2001]	0.45827	-1.50132
Colombia [1998]	0.13339	-0.3286
Croatia [1999]	-0.07525	0.58302
Czech Republic [1999]	-0.99273	0.2238
Denmark [1999]	-2.15271	-1.02601
Dominican Republic [1996]	0.23134	-0.37255
Egypt [2000]	1.55878	-1.80361
El Salvador [1999]	0.86786	0.06298
Estonia [1999]	-0.62562	1.18742
Finland [2000]	-1.3551	-0.61301
France [1999]	-1.60311	0.7987
Georgia [1996]	0.90504	0.8305
Germany West [1999]	-1.38045	-0.11204
Great Britain [1999]	-1.20566	-0.26451
Greece [1999]	-0.75721	1.02687
Hungary [1999]	-0.15168	0.82649
Iceland [1999]	-1.64298	-1.34893
India [2001]	0.79819	-0.16288
Indonesia [2001]	1.32012	-0.45486
Iran (Islamic Republic of) [2000]	0.54234	-0.72874
Iraq [2004]	0.95986	-0.5991
Ireland [1999]	-0.60975	-0.41524
Israel [2001]	-0.49082	-0.0905
Italy [1999]	-0.55784	-0.07662
Japan [2000]	-0.56309	-0.13872
Jordan [2001]	1.25786	-0.94243
Kyrgyzstan [2003]	0.5641	0.69381

Table 9. (Continued)

	Traditional versus secular attitudes	Cheating versus active society
Latvia [1999]	-0.39771	0.59187
Lithuania [1999]	0.0978	1.81607
Luxembourg [1999]	-1.2328	0.22259
Macedonia, Republic of [2001]	0.54884	0.82797
Malta [1999]	0.73998	-0.34532
Mexico [2000]	0.38685	0.40264
Morocco [2001]	1.18597	-0.85225
Netherlands [1999]	-2.37923	-1.33596
New Zealand [1998]	-1.12324	-0.577
Nigeria [2000]	0.96989	-0.53043
Norway [1996]	-1.405	-0.67692
Pakistan [2001]	1.2233	-0.16422
Peru [2001]	0.49801	0.25632
Philippines [2001]	1.06083	0.74534
Poland [1999]	0.25855	0.4905
Portugal [1999]	-0.5729	0.50291
Republic of Korea [2001]	1.06552	0.2993
Republic of Moldova [2002]	0.90879	2.44318
Romania [1999]	0.73986	0.73428
Russian Federation [1999]	-0.25748	1.74323
Saudi Arabia [2003]	0.94484	-0.42943
Serbia [2001]	-0.21779	0.51637
Singapore [2002]	0.39791	-0.09253
Slovakia [1999]	-0.06542	1.00414
Slovenia [1999]	-0.66117	0.6279
South Africa [2001]	0.74342	0.21813
Spain [2000]	-1.01087	0.22768
Sweden [1999]	-2.1202	-1.371
Switzerland [1996]	-1.31573	-0.41449
Tanzania, United Republic Of [2001]	1.28572	-2.24675
Uganda [2001]	0.85649	-0.42537
Ukraine [1999]	0.08443	1.75682
United States [1999]	-0.66609	-1.55408
Uruguay [1996]	-0.84206	-0.30694
Venezuela [2000]	0.57608	-0.18172
Viet Nam [2001]	0.4508	-2.21551
Zimbabwe [2001]	1.21187	-0.66514

Source: our own calculations from World Values Survey, 3rd and 4th wave, http://www.worldvaluessurvey.org/.

Our model has the following mathematical properties:

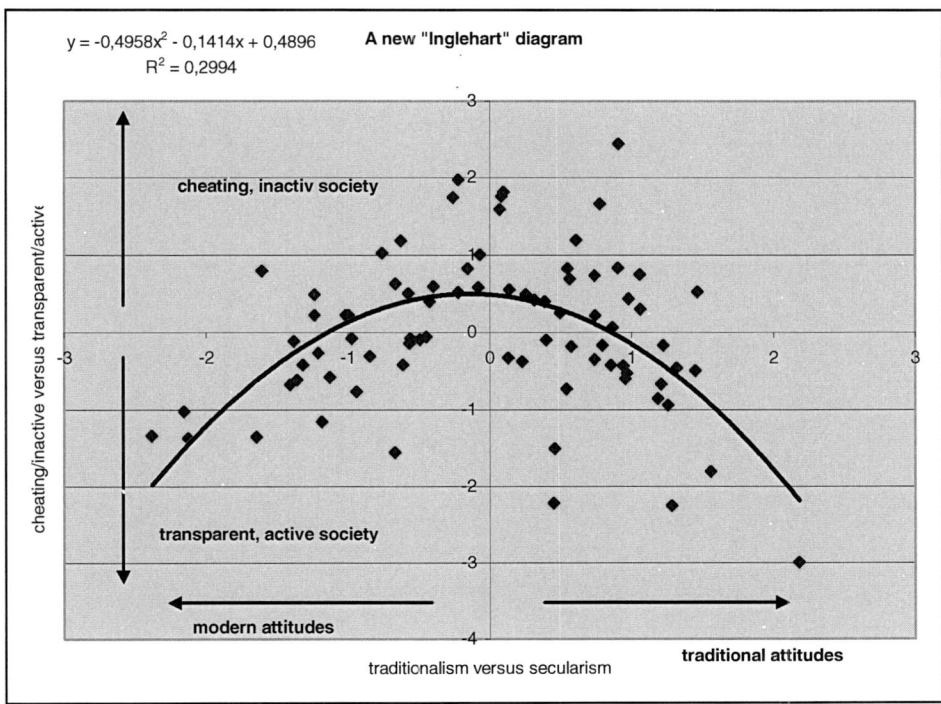

Graph 5. Residuals from the Inglehart/Etzioni path of transformation from tradition to modernity.

Note: the following WVS country values were submitted to an explorative factor analysis: always respect parents; belief in hell; cheating taxes; education for tolerance and respect important; jobs scarce men have rights; mean acceptability homosexuality; mean acceptance government benefits fraud; never praying; not satisfied with democracy; only God-believing politicians; openly racist; rejecting foreign workers; rejecting homosexual neighbor, belong voluntary welfare elderly; taking bribes; unpaid social welfare work. Our analysis yielded two factors: a continuum of *traditional versus secular,* and a continuum *cheating versus active society. Asabiyya* is defined then empirically by the residuals from the factor scores of *"traditional versus secular,* and *cheating versus active society. Asabiyya* means high secularism and a high active society score, thus avoiding the *modernization trap* of an increasingly secular society, which accepts cheating on taxes; accepts government benefits fraud and taking bribes. According to the empirical analysis of this essay, the "active society" of volunteer organization work is the best societal medicine against this kind of value decay, which is so common in countries like France, Brazil, or most of East Central Europe and the former USSR.

The residuals from the above function now can be called a modern, factor analytical and regression analytical definition of *Asabiyya*. It is also interesting to note that Muslim societies approximately adhere to the same process of secularization, but that their chances to recover from the "trough" of the modernization crisis are better than for the global average.

Thus, a modern vision of Islam in the twenty-first century would exactly presuppose to provide an answer to the "trough" of the "modernization crisis" around the world—to stimulate an active law-abiding society, and giving an answer to the secularization of values by networks of volunteers.

Table 10. How Islam could overcome the modernization crisis

	secular society	active society	trend global active society	trend Muslim active society
Albania [2002]	-0.9823	-0.4326	0.12772691	0.08530043
Algeria [2002]	-1.45209	0.49094	0.76124692	0.85197953
Azerbaijan [1997]	-0.61006	-1.19167	-0.2188279	-0.23519324
Bangladesh [2002]	-2.1835	2.9929	2.18320337	2.85004324
Bosnia and Herzegovina [2001]	-0.31595	-0.42056	-0.39546735	-0.30897578
Egypt [2000]	-1.55878	1.80361	0.93561723	1.08240801
Indonesia [2001]	-1.32012	0.45486	0.56117711	0.59578959
Iran (Islamic Republic of) [2000]	-0.54234	0.72874	-0.26710175	-0.26621937
Iraq [2004]	-0.95986	0.5991	0.10294314	0.05879277
Jordan [2001]	-1.25786	0.94243	0.47278557	0.48599817
Kyrgyzstan [2003]	-0.5641	-0.69381	-0.25208614	-0.25716565
Morocco [2001]	-1.18597	0.85225	0.37550415	0.3680551
Nigeria [2000]	-0.96989	0.53043	0.11395901	0.07052692
Pakistan [2001]	-1.2233	0.16422	0.42537934	0.42811761
Saudi Arabia [2003]	-0.94484	0.42943	0.08663335	0.04156528
Turkey [2001]	-1.46386	-0.52287	0.77992942	0.87637738

Source: our own calculations from World Values Survey, 3rd and 4th wave, http://www.worldvaluessurvey.org/ .

Note: the following WVS country values were submitted to an explorative factor analysis: always respect parents; belief in hell; cheating taxes; education for tolerance and respect important; jobs scarce men have rights; mean acceptability homosexuality; mean acceptance government benefits fraud; never praying; not satisfied with democracy; only God-believing politicians; openly racist; rejecting foreign workers; rejecting homosexual neighbor, belong voluntary welfare elderly; taking bribes; unpaid social welfare work. Our analysis yielded two factors: a continuum of *traditional versus secular,* and a continuum *cheating versus active society. Asabiyya* is defined then empirically by the residuals from the factor scores of *traditional versus secular,* and *cheating versus active society. Asabiyya* means high secularism and a high active society score, thus avoiding the *modernization trap* of an increasingly secular society, which accepts cheating on taxes; accepts government benefits fraud and taking bribes. According to the empirical analysis of this essay, the "active society" of volunteer organization work is the best societal medicine against this kind of value decay, which is so common in countries like France, Brazil, or most of East Central Europe and the former USSR.

The trend line graphs are the following:

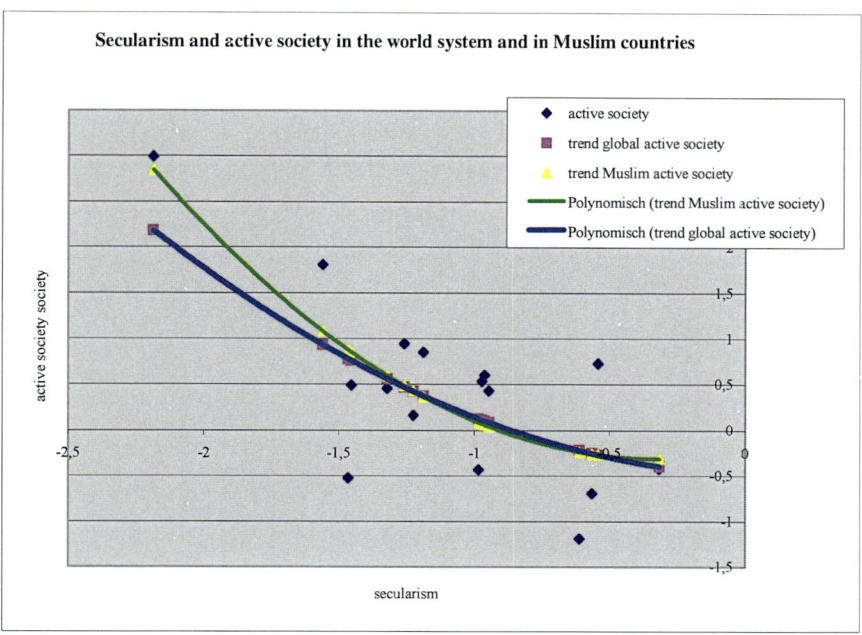

Graph 6. Muslim nations have more "*Asabiyya*" (social cohesion) in the process of modernization.

Note: the following WVS country values were submitted to an explorative factor analysis: always respect parents; belief in hell; cheating taxes; education for tolerance and respect important; jobs scarce men have rights; mean acceptability homosexuality; mean acceptance government benefits fraud; never praying; not satisfied with democracy; only God-believing politicians; openly racist; rejecting foreign workers; rejecting homosexual neighbor, belong voluntary welfare elderly; taking bribes; unpaid social welfare work. Our analysis yielded two factors: a continuum of *traditional versus secular,* and a continuum *cheating versus active society. Asabiyya* is defined then empirically by the residuals from the factor scores of *traditional versus secular,* and *cheating versus active society. Asabiyya* means high secularism and a high active society score, thus avoiding the *modernization trap* of an increasingly secular society, which accepts cheating on taxes; accepts government benefits fraud and taking bribes. According to the empirical analysis of this essay, the "active society" of volunteer organization work is the best societal medicine against this kind of value decay, which is so common in countries like France, Brazil, or most of East Central Europe and the former USSR It turns out that Muslim societies undergo the same type of "modernization crisis trap" as non-Muslim societies, but that their capacity to recover from this crisis in the long run would be greater.

THE COUNTRY MAPS OF GLOBAL VALUE CHANGE

In the following, we will try to map the main results of our analysis on a global scale. The Inglehart school is famous for its world maps; however, our explanatory factor analysis with the main WVS country indicators "always respect parents; belief in hell; cheating taxes; education for tolerance and respect important; jobs scarce men have rights; mean acceptability homosexuality; mean acceptance government benefits fraud; never praying; not satisfied with democracy; only God-believing politicians; openly racist; rejecting foreign workers; rejecting homosexual neighbor, belong voluntary welfare elderly; taking bribes;

unpaid social welfare work" yields just two factors – traditional versus secular; and cheating versus active society. We specified that *Asabiyya* is a high residual along this pathway of modernization; societies, which are active and transparent along the course of the secularization process, are characterized by *Asabiyya*.

The global logic of *Asabiyya* has the following basic characteristics. First we look at the continuum traditional versus secular.

The factor *traditional societies versus secular societies* has *positive factor loadings* above 0.500 with

- always respect parents
- belief in hell
- jobs scarce men have rights
- rejecting foreign workers
- openly racist
- rejecting homosexual neighbor
- only God-believing politicians

The factor *traditional societies versus secular societies* has *negative factor loadings* of minus 0.500 or more with the variables:

- mean acceptability homosexuality
- education for tolerance and respect important
- never praying

The map of this traditional universe is characterized as follows: *the traditionalist cultural gap in San Diego, California, USA, is far less pronounced as the traditionalist versus secular gap, which separates Europe from its Muslim neighbors;* and in general, the Muslim countries are presenting the most traditional "landscape". The 10 most traditional societies in the world are all Muslim societies:

- Bangladesh [2002]
- Egypt [2000]
- Turkey [2001]
- Algeria [2002]
- Indonesia [2001]
- Tanzania, United Republic of [2001]
- Jordan [2001]
- Pakistan [2001]
- Zimbabwe [2001]
- Morocco [2001]

The 10 most secular countries on earth are:
- Netherlands [1999]
- Denmark [1999]
- Sweden [1999]
- Iceland [1999]

- France [1999]
- Norway [1996]
- Germany West [1999]
- Finland [2000]
- Switzerland [1996]
- Luxembourg [1999]

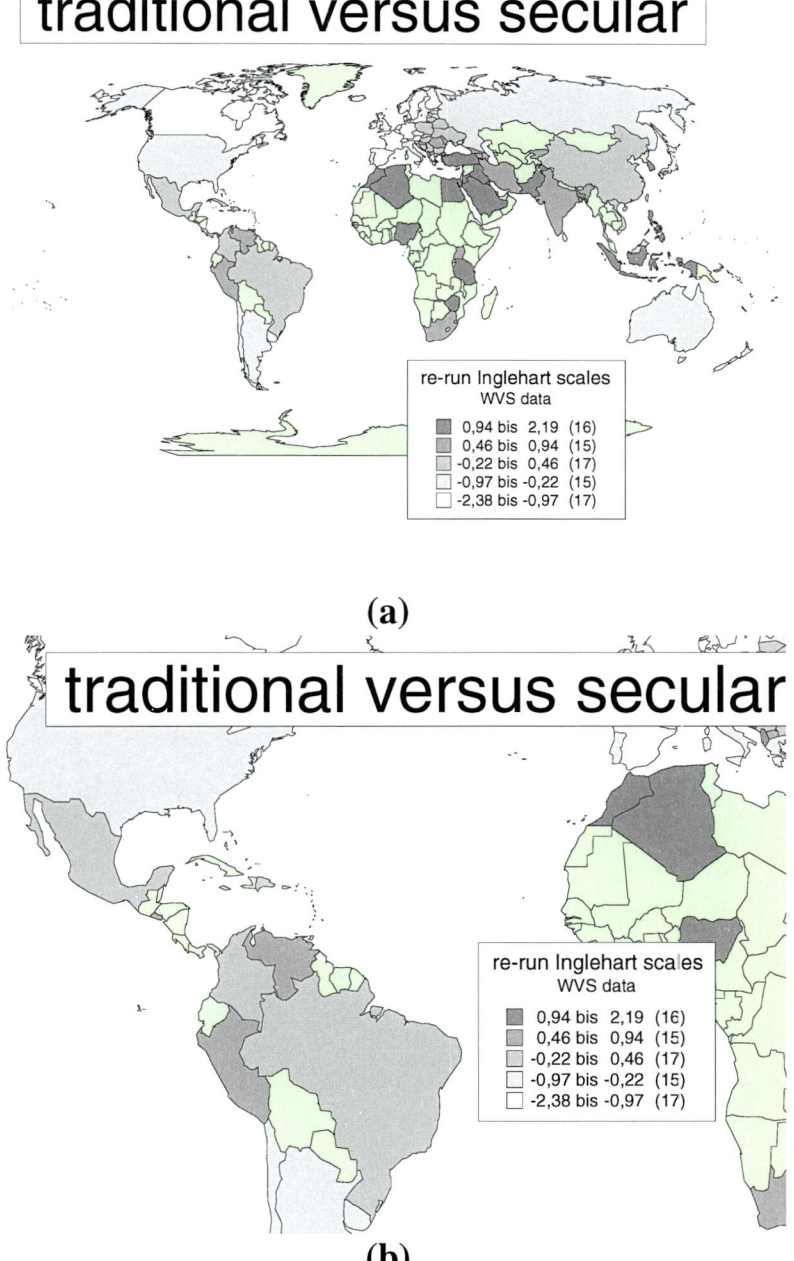

(a)

(b)

Map 5. Traditional versus secular values in the global system (continues)

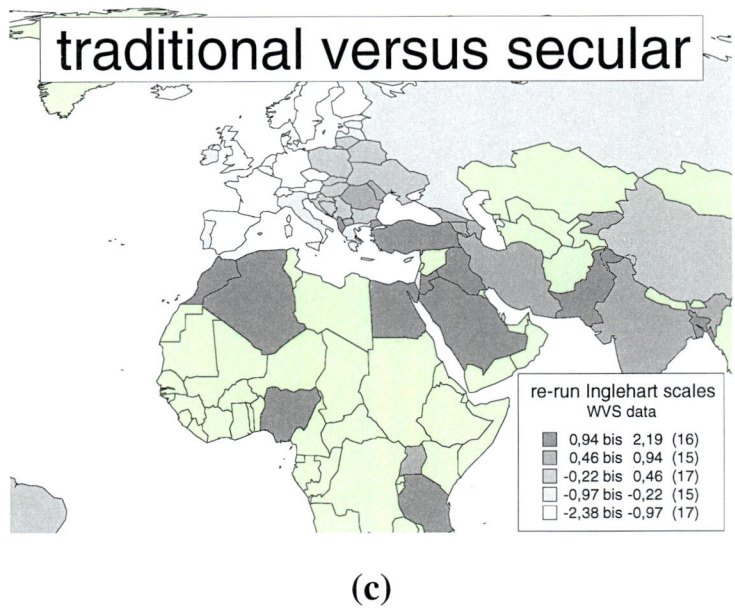

(c)

Map 5 a-c. Traditional versus secular values in the global system.

Note: the following WVS country values were submitted to an explorative factor analysis: always respect parents; belief in hell; cheating taxes; education for tolerance and respect important; jobs scarce men have rights; mean acceptability homosexuality; mean acceptance government benefits fraud; never praying; not satisfied with democracy; only God-believing politicians; openly racist; rejecting foreign workers; rejecting homosexual neighbor, belong voluntary welfare elderly; taking bribes; unpaid social welfare work. Our analysis yielded two factors: a continuum of *traditional versus secular*, and a continuum *cheating versus active society*.

Explanatory note: "bis" is shorthand for "ranging from ... to"; countries with missing values are marked in green color.

The *intransparent, inactive society,* which emerges on Factor 2 of our model, is characterized by loadings of more than .500 with the following variables:

- cheating taxes
- taking bribes
- not satisfied with democracy
- mean acceptance government benefits fraud

The *highest negative loadings* (i.e. *signs of a transparent, active society*) of minus 0.5000 or more are achieved on this factor by the variables:

- belong voluntary welfare elderly
- unpaid social welfare work

In a way, Etzioni's "active society" paradigm shows the way how a society can steer the pathways of modernization and secularization. If you want to avoid having a society, where cheating taxes, taking bribes, dissatisfaction with democracy and acceptance of government benefits frauds becomes the rule, you have to mobilize society in volunteer organizations, all the more so in a multicultural society. This is a most welcome form of *"djihad"*; the *"djihad"* of caring for the elderly and sick, the *"djihad"* of unpaid social welfare work. It is no coincidence that some European societies are among the most crisis-ridden countries along this scale:

- Republic of Moldova [2002]
- Belarus [2000]
- Lithuania [1999]
- Ukraine [1999]
- Russian Federation [1999]
- Armenia [1997]
- Brazil [1997]
- Azerbaijan [1997]
- Estonia [1999]
- Greece [1999]

But also developments in

- Slovakia [1999]
- Georgia [1996]
- Macedonia, Republic of [2001]
- Hungary [1999]
- France [1999]
- Philippines [2001]
- Romania [1999]
- Kyrgyzstan [2003]
- Slovenia [1999]
- Latvia [1999]

are far from satisfactory. The real stars along this scale are:

- Bangladesh [2002]
- Tanzania, United Republic Of [2001]
- Viet Nam [2001]
- Egypt [2000]
- United States [1999]
- China [2001]
- Sweden [1999]
- Iceland [1999]
- Netherlands [1999]
- Canada [2000]

These are the societies, where a "civic culture" (Almond/Verba, 1963) is fairly developed and where resistance against the darker sides of modernity—the kind of moral decay, which you associate with cheating taxes, taking bribes, dissatisfaction with democracy, and acceptance of government benefits fraud, is greatest.

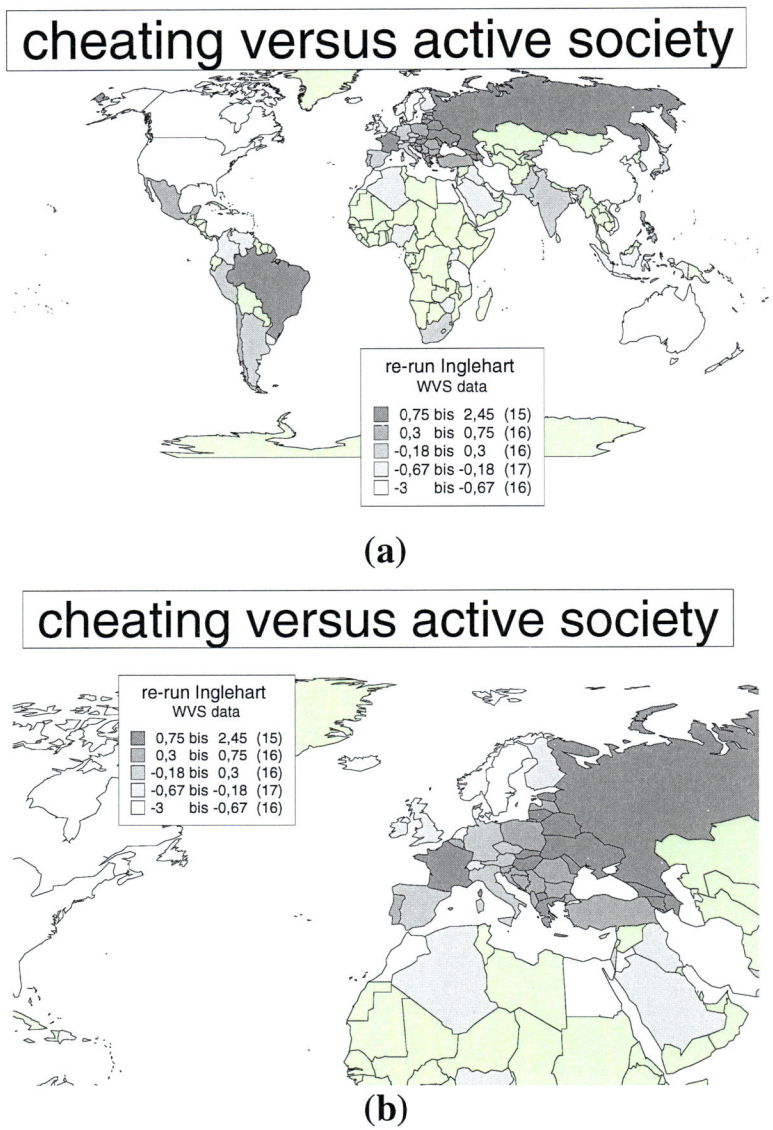

Map 6 a-b. The cheating versus the active society – global values in the global system (cont.)

Note: the following WVS country values were submitted to an explorative factor analysis: always respect parents; belief in hell; cheating taxes; education for tolerance and respect important; jobs scarce men have rights; mean acceptability homosexuality; mean acceptance government benefits fraud; never praying; not satisfied with democracy; only God-believing politicians; openly racist; rejecting foreign workers; rejecting homosexual neighbor, belong voluntary welfare elderly; taking bribes; unpaid social welfare work. Our analysis yielded two factors: a continuum of *traditional versus secular*, and a continuum *cheating versus active society*.

Explanatory note: "bis" is shorthand for "ranging from ... to"; countries with missing values are marked in green color.

"Asabiyya" is nothing else, we already stated, but the ability of a society to perform well along the path of Graph 5. All upward residuals (good transparency standards, good volunteer services, the process of modernization, i.e. secularization notwithstanding) are societies possessing *"Asabiyya"*, while societies, which are intransparent and do not care for the social needy in voluntary services, do not possess *"Asabiyya"*.

The 20 leading countries along this scale are:

- Viet Nam [2001]
- United States [1999]
- China [2001]
- Tanzania, United Republic of [2001]
- Canada [2000]
- Iran (Islamic Republic of) [2000]
- Australia [1995]
- Egypt [2000]
- Bangladesh [2002]
- Ireland [1999]
- Dominican Republic [1996]
- Colombia [1998]
- Iceland [1999]
- New Zealand [1998]
- Uruguay [1996]
- Japan [2000]
- Israel [2001]
- Argentina [1999]
- Iraq [2004]
- Italy [1999]

The 20 most problematic cases are:

- Republic of Moldova [2002]
- Armenia [1997]
- Belarus [2000]
- France [1999]
- Lithuania [1999]
- Turkey [2001]
- Ukraine [1999]
- Russian Federation [1999]
- Brazil [1997]
- Azerbaijan [1997]
- Philippines [2001]
- Georgia [1996]
- Estonia [1999]
- Greece [1999]
- Netherlands [1999]
- Romania [1999]

- Belgium [1999]
- Macedonia, Republic of [2001]
- Albania [2002]
- Republic of Korea [2001]

In a way, their social cohesion is severely threatened, and they are very much in need of the positive role models, which are so characteristic of Amitai Etzioni's "active society". It is interesting to note that there are two categories of Muslim societies along this scale—the high *"Asabiyya"* Muslim countries, like Iran, Egypt, Bangladesh, and the post-communist or post secularism Muslim countries, like Turkey, Azerbaijan and Albania, characterized by low values of "social cohesion".

The world map of *Asabiyya* is the following:

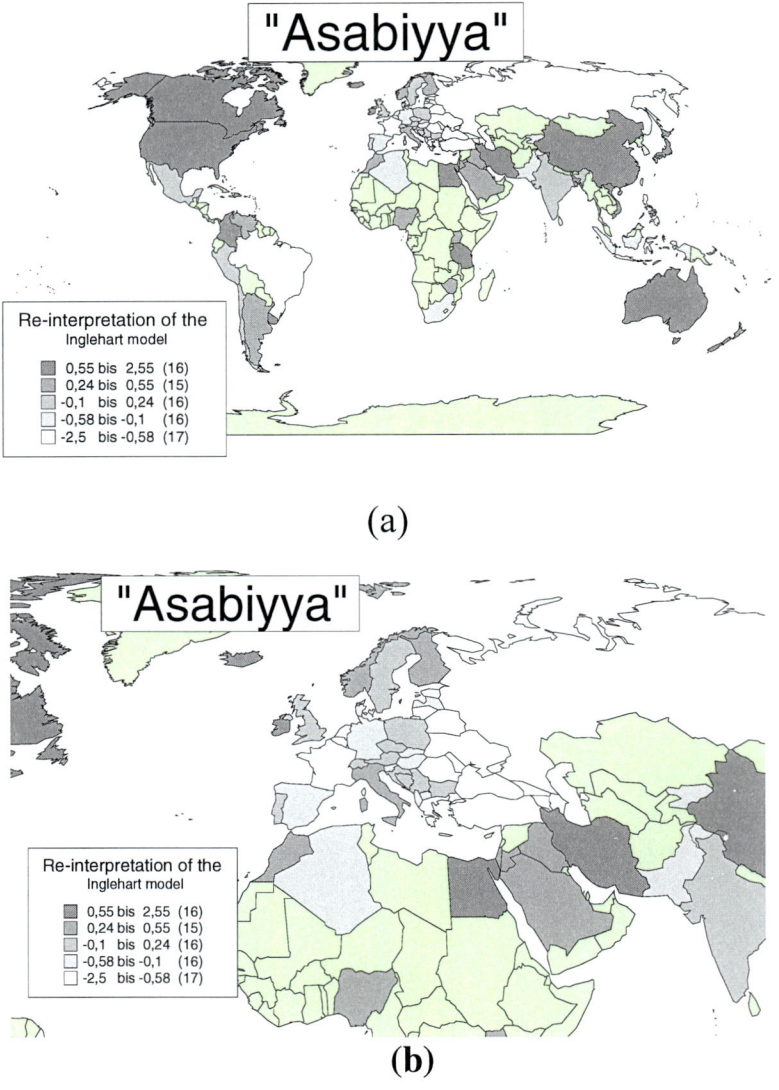

(a)

(b)

Map 7. (continues.).

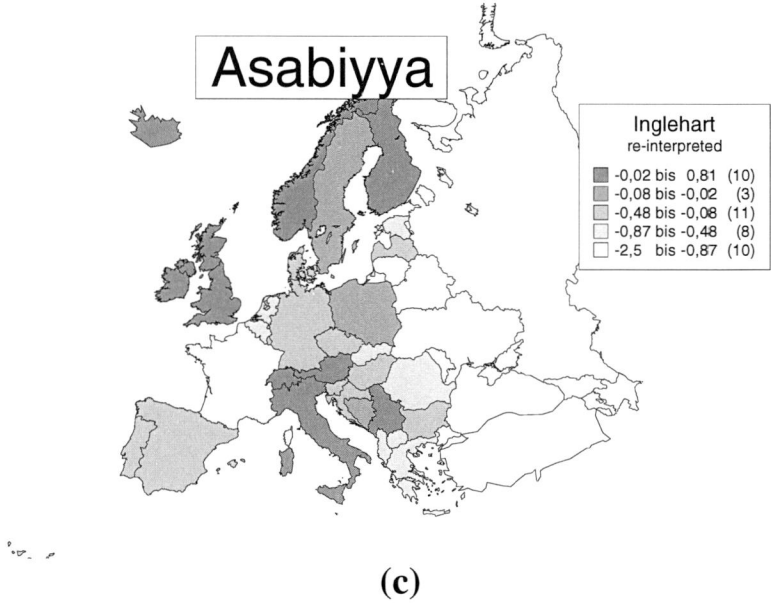

(c)

Map 7. Global *Asabiyya* – countries with a high capacity to avoid the modernization trap of high secularism + loss of civic values, absolutely needed for the functioning of a democracy and the market economy.

Note: the following WVS country values were submitted to an explorative factor analysis: always respect parents; belief in hell; cheating taxes; education for tolerance and respect important; jobs scarce men have rights; mean acceptability homosexuality; mean acceptance government benefits fraud; never praying; not satisfied with democracy; only God-believing politicians; openly racist; rejecting foreign workers; rejecting homosexual neighbor, belong voluntary welfare elderly; taking bribes; unpaid social welfare work. Our analysis yielded two factors: a continuum of *traditional versus secular,* and a continuum *cheating versus active society. Asabiyya* is defined then empirically by the residuals from the factor scores of *traditional versus secular,* and *cheating versus active society. Asabiyya* means the capacity to combine secularism and a high active society score, thus avoiding the *modernization trap* of an increasingly secular society, which nevertheless accepts cheating on taxes; accepts government benefits fraud and taking bribes. According to the empirical analysis of this essay, the "active society" of volunteer organization work is the best societal medicine against this kind of value decay, which is so common in countries like France, Brazil, or most of East Central Europe and the former USSR.

Explanatory note: "bis" is shorthand for "ranging from … to"; countries with missing values are marked in green color.

Chapter 6

THE NORTHWARD MIGRATION OF GLOBAL INTOLERANCE AND THE GLOBAL TOLERANCE INDEX

This chapter starts from the perhaps politically absolutely incorrect assumption that the future of tolerance in the world – and especially the recipient countries of immigration – also has to do with the systematic fostering of a climate of the Enlightenment among the immigrant populations in the North themselves, and not just among the mainstream political cultures of the immigration receiving countries. The idea that the immigrant communities in the North must participate also actively in the climate of tolerance of overall society, and that they in turn must leave behind the often virulent racism, Anti-Semitism, Romaphobia and homophobia of their countries and or cultures of origin, is a clear consequence of our quantitative data and as such cannot be denied.

The data from the World Values Survey can also be used to project a scale of global tolerance. This is all the more relevant because the European Commission now officially embraces a policy according to which Islamophobia[21] has no place within the European Union, which is now always understood as a community of values. On May 5, 2008, the President of the European Commission, Jose Manuel Barroso, underlined accordingly that Islam as such is part and parcel of Europe and he also condemned the concept of clash of civilizations:

> "Islam today is part of Europe. It is important to understand this. One should not see Islam as outside Europe. We already have an important presence of Islam and Muslims among our citizens" "We can be a European citizen being a Christian, being Jewish or Muslim or having no religion."

---

21 The author of this work is well aware of the many controversies surrounding this term (see also: http://en.wikipedia.org/wiki/Anti-Muslim). But for many years now, it has become part of the official European Union law, the "Acquis", as any can be neatly shown by a search term analysis in the EURO-LEX data file at: http://eur-lex.europa.eu/RECH_mot.do.
As of August 26, 2008, there are 22 texts of European Union law, referring to this subject. Here it is understood as "measurable prejudices against Muslims" in terms of the World Values Survey, or simply "Xenophobia against Muslims". We measure Islamophobia in Table 12a and 12b of this work.

President Barroso also said that the inter-faith dialogue proved that "preachers of clash of civilisations are wrong" (http://www.kuna.net.kw/NewsAgenciesPublicSite/ArticleDetails.aspx?id=1905408andLanguage=en).

To develop a statistical "yardstick" of discrimination and exclusion is absolutely important in Europe. For many years the focus of EU action in the field of non-discrimination was on preventing discrimination on the grounds of nationality and gender (http://ec.europa.eu/employment_social/fundamental_rights/legis/lgdirect_en.htm).

In 1997, the Member States approved unanimously the Treaty of Amsterdam. Article 13 of this Treaty granted the Community new powers to combat discrimination on the grounds of gender, racial or ethnic origin, religion or belief, disability, age or sexual orientation. Since the Treaty of Amsterdam came into force in 1999, *new EC laws*, or Directives that have been enacted in the area of anti-discrimination are the *Racial Equality Directive,* 2000/43/EC, and the *Employment Equality Directive*, 2000/78/EC. The Council Directive 2000/43/EC implements the principle of equal treatment between persons irrespective of racial or ethnic origin, and Council Directive 2000/78/EC establishes a general framework for equal treatment in employment and occupation.

The World Values Survey data provide the international public with a unique opportunity to measure the existence of prejudice and discrimination "on the ground". The World Values Survey data series includes the following items for the following countries and samples:

People that respondent would not like to have as neighbors

- Neighbors: People with a criminal record (A124)
- Neighbors: People of a different race (A125)
- Neighbors: Heavy drinkers (A126)
- Neighbors: Emotionally unstable people (A127)
- Neighbors: Muslims (A128)
- Neighbors: Immigrants/foreign workers (A129)
- Neighbors: People who have AIDS (A130)
- Neighbors: Drug addicts (A131)
- Neighbors: Homosexuals (A132)
- Neighbors: Jews (A133)
- Neighbors: Evangelists (A134)
- Neighbors: People of a different religion (A135)
- Neighbors: People of the same religion (A136)
- Neighbors: Militant minority (A137)
- Neighbors: Zoroastrians (A138)
- Neighbors: People not from country of origin (A139)
- Neighbors: Gypsies (A140)
- Neighbors: Political Extremists (A141)
- Neighbors: Traficant's (A142)
- Neighbors: Indians or Lebanese (A143)
- Neighbors: Chinese or Philippino Chinese (A144)
- Neighbors: Spiritists (A145)
- Neighbors: Protestants (A146)
- Neighbors: Christians (A147)
- Neighbors: Witchdoctors and related labels (A148)
- Neighbors: Left wing extremists (A149)
- Neighbors: Right wing extremists (A150)

- Neighbors: People with large families (A151)
- Neighbors: Hindus (A152)
- Neighbors: North-American persons (A153)
- Neighbors: Haitians (A154)
- Neighbors: Members of new religious movements (A155)
- Neighbors: Jews, Arabs, Asians, gypsies, etc (A156)
- Neighbors: Black people (A157)
- Neighbors: White people (A158)
- Neighbors: Colored people (A159)
- Neighbors: Indians (A160)
- Neighbors: Kurds, Esids (A161)
- Neighbors: Sunnis (A178)
- Neighbors: Shia (A180)
- Neighbors: French (A182)
- Neighbors: British (A183)
- Neighbors: Iranian (A184)
- Neighbors: Kuwaiti (A185)
- Neighbors: Turkish (A186)
- Neighbors: Jordanian (A187)
- Neighbors: Kildani (A188)

Countries of the Analysis

Albania [1998], Albania [2002], Algeria [2002], Argentina [1995], Argentina [1999], Armenia [1997], Australia [1995], Austria [1999], Azerbaijan [1997], Bangladesh [1996], Bangladesh [2002], Belarus [1996], Belarus [2000], Belgium [1999], Bosnia and Herzegovina [1998], Bosnia and Herzegovina [2001], Brazil [1997], Bulgaria [1997], Bulgaria [1999], Canada [2000], Chile [1996], Chile [2000], China [1995], China [2001], Colombia [1997], Colombia [1998], Croatia [1996], Croatia [1999], Czech Republic [1998], Czech Republic [1999], Denmark [1999], Dominican Republic [1996], Egypt [2000], El Salvador [1999], Estonia [1996], Estonia [1999], Finland [1996], Finland [2000], France [1999], Georgia [1996], Germany East [1997], Germany East [1999], Germany West [1997], Germany West [1999], Great Britain [1998], Great Britain [1999], Greece [1999], Hungary [1998], Hungary [1999], Iceland [1999], India [1995], India [2001], Indonesia [2001], Iran (Islamic Republic of) [2000], Iraq [2004], Ireland [1999], Israel [2001], Italy [1999], Japan [1995], Japan [2000], Jordan [2001], Kyrgyzstan [2003], Latvia [1996], Latvia [1999], Lithuania [1997], Lithuania [1999], Luxembourg [1999], Macedonia, Republic of [1998], Macedonia, Republic of [2001], Malta [1999], Mexico [1996], Mexico [2000], Montenegro [1996], Montenegro [2001], Morocco [2001], Morocco [2001], Netherlands [1999], New Zealand [1998], Nigeria [1995], Nigeria [2000], Northern Ireland [1999], Norway [1996], Pakistan [1997], Pakistan [2001], Peru [1996], Peru [2001], Philippines [1996], Philippines [2001], Poland [1997], Poland [1999], Portugal [1999], Puerto Rico [1995], Puerto Rico [2001], Republic of Korea [1996], Republic of Korea [2001], Republic of Moldova [1996], Republic of Moldova [2002], Romania [1998], Romania [1999], Russian Federation [1995], Russian Federation [1999], Saudi Arabia [2003], Serbia [1996], Serbia [2001], Singapore [2002], Slovakia [1998], Slovakia [1999], Slovenia [1995], Slovenia [1999], South Africa [1996], South Africa [2001], Spain [1995], Spain [1999], Spain [2000], Sweden [1996], Sweden [1999], Switzerland

[1996], Taiwan [1994], Tanzania, United Republic Of [2001], Turkey [1996], Turkey [2001], Turkey [2001], Uganda [2001], Ukraine [1996], Ukraine [1999], United States [1995], United States [1999], Uruguay [1996], Venezuela [1996], Venezuela [2000],Viet Nam [2001], Zimbabwe [2001]

Without question, Anti-Semitism is the most alarming of the phobias to be observed in Europe. The reason for this obvious: the Shoah, in, which more than 6 million Jews in Europe were murdered in the time between 1939 and 1945, is part and parcel not only of Nazi Germany, but is part and parcel of European history. Our following Table shows the extent of global Anti-Semitism according to the WVS data base for the different religious denominations of the world. We only used the results for those denominations, which were represented in more than two countries of the world, and in with more than 50 respondents in the WVS sample. The extent of Anti-Semitism in Asia is striking and has already been commented on by many observers. Open Anti-Semitism is professed by more than 25% of global Buddhists, Muslims and Hindus.

Table 11a. Anti-Semitism, worldwide, by religion

BASE=179850 (WVS, waves 3 + 4 combined) – Religious denomination	People that respondent would not like to have as neighbors: Jews	n (number of observations, sample size)
Buddhist	38.0	308
Muslim	34.7	8869
Hindu	28.9	194
Independent African Church (e.g., ZCC, Shembe, et cetera)	22.8	652
Evangelical	22.0	1007
Total	19.1	57162
Orthodox	15.9	9313
Roman Catholic	15.4	25034
Other	12.6	1208
Jew[22]	12.0	173
Protestant	10.7	8543
Free church/Non denominational church	6.2	665

Source: our own calculations from World Values Survey, all countries of wave 3+4

The question of rising Anti-Semitism among Islamist groups in Europe received proper attention by the Stephen Roth Institute for the Study of Contemporary Anti-Semitism and Racism in Israel (http://www.tau.ac.il/Anti-Semitism/CR.htm) and by the United States Department of State (http://www.state.gov/g/drl/rls/40258.htm). We can only refer here to their in-depth country-to-country reporting on the issue, which has also aroused an intensive controversy between the EU Agency for Fundamental Rights and the Anti-Defamation

---

[22] As we will also observe for the case of the Muslim minorities around the globe, there is the well-known phenomenon of Jewish self-hatred to be observed, affecting 12% of Jewish respondents, who said according to the WVS that they do not want a Jewish neighbour.

League of the Jewish organization B'nai B'rith. Without question, it is worthwhile to statistically document the incidence of Anti-Semitism and Xenophobia among the various religious and cultural groups in Europe. Open Anti-Semitism among the predominantly "Southern" cultural and religious communities of Buddhists, Muslims and Hindus is about double or even triple the size of openly confessed rejection of Jewish neighbors by global Roman Catholics or global Protestants. Anti-Semitism, though widespread in the Muslim world, cannot be blamed on all Muslims, and in fact, Anti-Semitism rates are highest among the very secular Muslims

In Belarus, Russia and Spain there was a noticeable increase of Anti-Semitism over time, while in Argentina and Chile Anti-Semitism decreased. The extent of open Anti-Semitism in Iraq, Turkey, Korea, Spain, Mexico, Bosnia, Venezuela, Poland and Moldova is astonishing and is being shared by more than 25% of the respective population, while the least anti-Semitic nations today are where open Anti-Semitism according to the WVS was expressed by the less than 10% of the total population.

The best practice countries in overcoming anti-Semitic prejudice (< 5%) Canada [2000]; Czech Republic [1999]; Denmark [1999]; Germany West [1999]; Iceland [1999]; Netherlands [1999]; Sweden [1999]

Table 11b. Anti-Semitism, worldwide, by country

BASE=179850 - Country	People that respondent would not like to have as neighbors: Jews	n (number of observations, sample size)
Iraq [2004]	83.4	2325
Turkey [2001]	61.9	1206
Republic of Korea [2001]	40.9	1200
Spain [2000]	34.2	1209
Mexico [1996]	30.7	2364
Bosnia and Herzegovina [2001]	28	1200
Venezuela [1996]	26	1200
Poland [1999]	25.1	1095
Republic of Moldova [2002]	25	1008
South Africa [2001]	24.4	3000
Romania [1999]	23.2	1146
Lithuania [1999]	23	1018
Uganda [2001]	22.2	1002
Malta [1999]	20.8	1002
Bangladesh [2002]	20.4	1500
Kyrgyzstan [2003]	20.4	1043

Table 11b. (Continued)

BASE=179850 - Country	People that respondent would not like to have as neighbors: Jews	n (number of observations, sample size)
Macedonia, Republic of [2001]	20	1055
Zimbabwe [2001]	19.3	1002
Greece [1999]	18.7	1142
Croatia [1999]	18.2	1002
Bulgaria [1999]	18.1	1000
TOTAL	17.3	75063
Albania [2002]	17	1000
Slovenia [1999]	16.8	1006
Egypt [2000]	16.5	2230
Belarus [2000]	14.8	1000
Chile [1996]	13.5	1000
Belgium [1999]	13	1912
Italy [1999]	12.9	2000
Northern Ireland [1999]	11.7	1000
Russian Federation [1999]	11.4	2500
Ireland [1999]	11.2	1007
Estonia [1999]	11.2	1005
Portugal [1999]	10.8	1000
Ukraine [1999]	10.4	1195
Uruguay [1996]	10.4	1000
Slovakia [1999]	9.9	1331
Russian Federation [1995]	9.6	2040
Spain [1999]	9.2	1200
United States [1999]	9.1	1200
Chile [2000]	8.8	1200
Finland [2000]	8.6	1038
Austria [1999]	8.3	1522
Luxembourg [1999]	8.3	1211
Germany East [1999]	8.2	899
Argentina [1995]	7.1	1079
Belarus [1996]	6.9	2092
Argentina [1999]	6.4	1280
Great Britain [1999]	6.2	1000

BASE=179850 - Country	People that respondent would not like to have as neighbors: Jews	n (number of observations, sample size)
France [1999]	5.9	1615
Latvia [1999]	5.2	1013
Germany West [1999]	4.5	925
Czech Republic [1999]	4.4	1908
Iceland [1999]	4.1	967
Canada [2000]	3.8	1931
Denmark [1999]	2.5	1019
Sweden [1999]	2.1	1015
Netherlands [1999]	1.6	1003

Source: our own calculations from World Values Survey, all countries of wave 3+4

In many Arab and Muslim countries, some of the most unbridled anti-Semitic literature goes on sale unpunished even today, more than 60 years after the end of Nazism (Source: http://www.terrorism-info.org.il/malam_multimedia/html/final/eng/eng_n/pro_10_05_e.htm)

The Protocols of the Elders of Zion and their Biblical and Talmudic Origins. Authors: Dr. Ahmad Hijazi al-Saqa; Hisham Khadr First edition: 2003, S/N: 2003/3584; All rights reserved; Publisher: Maktabat al-Nafidha, Giza: 2 Al-Shahid Ahmed Hamdi (al-Thalathini) – Faisal St., Tel.: 7233935

Islamophobia with justification is targeted by European policy makers as one of the other major dangers on the European horizon. Our following Table shows the extent of global Islamophobia according to the WVS data base for the different religious denominations of the world. We again only used the results for those denominations, which were represented in more than two countries of the world, and with more than 50 respondents in the WVS sample. As we also observe for the case of the Jewish minorities around the globe, there is also a phenomenon of Muslim self-hatred to be observed, affecting 16.1% of Muslim respondents, who said according to the WVS that they do not want a Muslim neighbor. But Muslim leaders around the globe should start wondering whether or not "the West" is the arch-enemy. The facts of global opinion surveys are simple and striking at the same time: *The extent of Islamophobia in non-Christian Asia is alarming.* And in general, Protestants tend to be more Islamophobic than Catholics, and the Muslim communities world-wide would do well to reflect on the fact that Jews, in accordance with their tradition of tolerance and the Enlightenment, are more tolerant of Muslim neighbors than even the global Muslims themselves, and only 1/6 of global Jews openly stated that they do NOT want a Muslim neighbor.

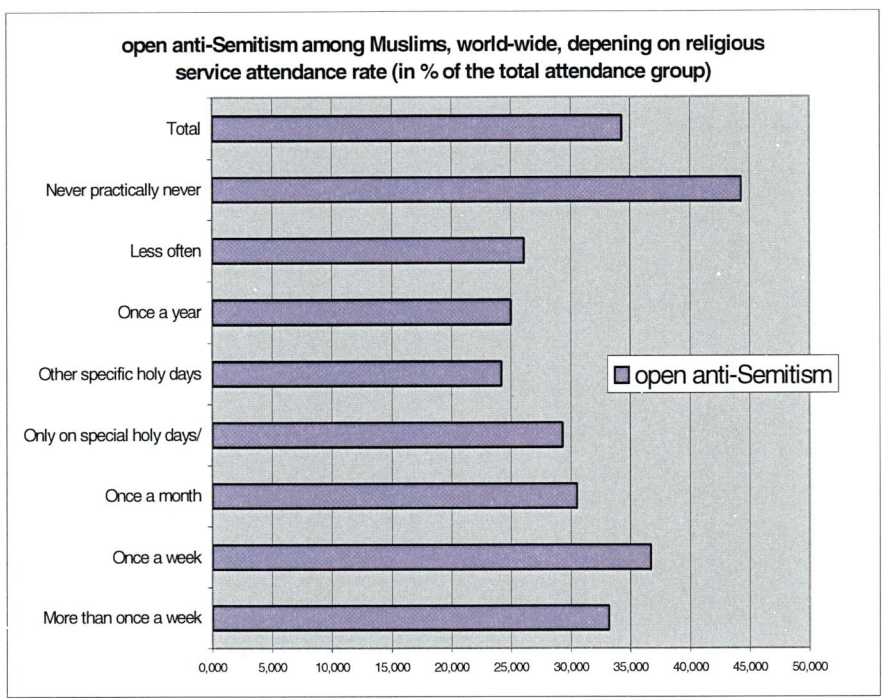

Graph 6. Anti-Semitism, though widespread in the Muslim world, cannot be blamed on all Muslims, and in fact, Anti-Semitism rates are highest among the very secular Muslims.

Source: our own calculations from World Values Survey, all countries of wave 3+4.

An image of good days past – the synagogue in Cordoba, Spain as a sign of the coexistence of the three major monotheistic world religions.

Photo credit: http://www.bluffton.edu/~sullivanm/spain/cordoba/synagogue/0115.jpg.

The spirit of tolerance, so prevalent during much of the history of Muslim *al –Andalus* (Bossong, 2007) has to be contrasted with the spirit of salafist anti-Enlightenment, which is summarized in such a condensed fashion in the Charta of the Palestinian group Hamas. The present author can only refer here to the excellent background analysis by the Spanish diplomat Juan José Escobar Stemmann, which appeared under the title *"MIDDLE EAST SALAFISM'S INFLUENCE AND THE RADICALIZATION OF MUSLIM COMMUNITIES IN EUROPE"* at Israel's "Gloria Institute" in Herzliya (http://meria.idc.ac.il/journal/2006/issue3/jv10no3a1.html).

"World Zionism and the colonialist powers attempt, by clever maneuvering and meticulous planning, to pull the Arab states, one by one, out of the circle of the conflict with Zionism, so as to ultimately isolate the Palestinian people. It has already taken Egypt out of the circle of conflict to a large extent through the treacherous Camp David Accords [of September 1978], and it is trying to pull additional [Arab] countries into similar agreements so that they leave the circle of conflict.

The Islamic Resistance Movement calls upon all the Arab and Muslim peoples to strive seriously and diligently to prevent this horrible scheme, and to alert the masses to the danger inherent in leaving the circle of the conflict with Zionism. Today it is Palestine, and tomorrow some other country or countries, for the Zionist plan has no limits, and after Palestine they want to expand [their territory] from the Nile to the Euphrates, and when they finish devouring one area, they hunger for further expansion and so on, indefinitely. Their plan is expounded in The Protocols of the Elders of Zion, and their present [behavior] is the best proof for what we are saying."

"The role of the Muslim woman in the war of liberation is no less important than that of the man, for she is the maker of men. Her role in guiding and educating the next generation is very important. The enemies have realized [the significance of] her role, and they believe that if they can educate her according to their wishes, guiding her away from Islam, they will have won the war. You find, therefore, that they continually make great efforts [to do this] by means of the media, the cinema and school curricula, through their agents who are incorporated in Zionist organizations that assume various names and forms such as the Freemasons, Rotary Clubs, espionage groups, et cetera - all of, which are dens of sabotage and saboteurs. These Zionist organizations have an enormous abundance of material resources, which enable them to play their game in [various] societies with the aim of realizing their purpose while Islam is absent from the scene and the Muslims are estranged [from their faith]. The followers of the Islamic movements [10] should fulfill their role in countering the schemes of these saboteurs. When Islam is at the helm, it will totally eradicate these organizations, which are hostile to humanity and to Islam." http://www.memri.de/uebersetzungen_analysen/2006_01_JFM/hamas_charta_17_02_06.html

More than 25% of global Buddhists, Hindus and ancestral worshippers openly hold Islamophobic attitudes:

Table 12a. Islamophobia, worldwide, by religion

BASE=179850 – Religious denomination	People that respondent would not like to have as neighbors: Muslims	n (number of observations, sample size)
Buddhist	36.6	711
Hindu	33.5	1669
Ancestral worshipping	25	304
Orthodox	23.2	8970
Independent African Church (e.g. ZCC, Shembe, et cetera)	21.3	652
Protestant	19.6	11840
Total	19.5	61723
Pentecostal	19.5	465
Roman Catholic	18.2	27704
Evangelical	17	911
Muslim	16.1	4306
Jew	15.2	245
Other	14.8	1392
Free church/Non denominational church	13.6	705
Jehovah witnesses	13.5	65

Source: our own calculations from World Values Survey, all countries of wave 3+4

Islamophobia *decreased* over time in Finland, the Philippines, Sweden and the *United States*, but it increased in Spain. The extent of open Islamophobia in Albania [2002]; Belarus [2000]; Croatia [1999]; India [1995]; Lithuania [1999]; Macedonia, Republic of [2001]; Malta [1999]; Philippines [2001]; Republic of Korea [2001]; Republic of Moldova [2002]; Romania [1999]; and Viet Nam [2001] is again astonishing and is being shared by more than 25% of the population. The least openly Islamophobic nations of the world are:

The best practice countries in overcoming Islamophobia (< 10%):

Argentina [1999]; Canada [2000]; Chile [2000]; Portugal [1999]; Sweden [1999]

Table 12b. Islamophobia, worldwide, by country

BASE=179850 - Country	People that respondent would not like to have as neighbors: Muslims	n (number of observations, sample size)
Republic of Korea [2001]	57.3	1200
Republic of Moldova [2002]	44.4	1008
Finland [1996]	39.6	987
Lithuania [1999]	33.1	1018
India [1995]	32.8	2040

BASE=179850 - Country	People that respondent would not like to have as neighbors: Muslims	n (number of observations, sample size)
Romania [1999]	31.4	1146
Albania [2002]	30.4	1000
Philippines [1996]	29.1	1200
Malta [1999]	27.8	1002
Viet Nam [2001]	27	1000
Belarus [2000]	26.6	1000
Croatia [1999]	26.5	1002
Philippines [2001]	26.4	1200
Macedonia, Republic of [2001]	26.2	1055
Slovakia [1999]	24.5	1331
Ukraine [1999]	24	1195
South Africa [2001]	23.9	3000
Poland [1999]	23.8	1095
Slovenia [1999]	22.6	1006
Estonia [1999]	22.2	1005
Belgium [1999]	22	1912
Bulgaria [1999]	21.2	1000
Greece [1999]	20.9	1142
Montenegro [2001]	20.2	1060
Norway [1996]	19.3	1127
Finland [2000]	19.3	1038
TOTAL	19.1	78797
Taiwan [1994]	19.1	780
Switzerland [1996]	18.5	1212
Zimbabwe [2001]	17.7	1002
Italy [1999]	17.2	2000
Mexico [2000]	17	1535
Nigeria [1995]	16.8	1996
Denmark [1999]	16.3	1019
France [1999]	16	1615
Northern Ireland [1999]	15.5	1000
Austria [1999]	15.4	1522
Spain [2000]	15.4	1209
Czech Republic [1999]	15.2	1908
Germany East [1999]	14.7	899

Table 12b. (Continued)

BASE=179850 - Country	People that respondent would not like to have as neighbors: Muslims	*n* (number of observations, sample size)
Kyrgyzstan [2003]	14.6	1043
Latvia [1999]	14.5	1013
Luxembourg [1999]	14.2	1211
Uganda [2001]	14.2	1002
Russian Federation [1999]	13.7	2500
Serbia [2001]	13.6	1200
Ireland [1999]	13.6	1007
Great Britain [1999]	13.6	1000
Peru [2001]	13.5	1501
Sweden [1996]	13	1009
Bosnia and Herzegovina [2001]	12.8	1200
Tanzania, United Republic Of [2001]	12.6	1171
United States [1995]	12.3	1542
Netherlands [1999]	11.9	1003
Iceland [1999]	11.6	966
Spain [1995]	11.5	1211
Spain [1999]	10.8	1200
United States [1999]	10.7	1200
Germany West [1999]	10.2	925
Sweden [1999]	9	1015
Portugal [1999]	7.9	1000
Chile [2000]	7.4	1200
Canada [2000]	6.5	1931
Argentina [1999]	6.2	1280

Source: our own calculations from World Values Survey, all countries of wave 3+4.

Islamophobia, Anti-Semitism and Romaphobia often, but not always have the same roots.

Romaphobia, also with justification, is targeted by European policy makers, together with Anti-Semitism and Islamophobia, as one of the other major xenophobic threats on the European horizon. Our following Table shows the extent of global Romaphobia according to the WVS data base for the different religious denominations of the world. We again only used the results for those denominations, which were represented in more than two countries of the world, and in with more than 50 respondents in the WVS sample. *The extent of Romaphobia among Muslims is striking and alarming.* In general, Catholics tend to be more Romaphobic than Protestants, and again it turns out that Jews, in accordance with their tradition of tolerance and the Enlightenment, are very tolerant of Roma neighbors, and only slightly less than 1/5 of global Jews openly stated that they do NOT want a Roma neighbor. More than 25% of global Muslims, Catholics, Free Church members, Orthodox, Protestants and adherents of other faiths openly profess an anti-Roma prejudice:

Protest gathering against the building of a Mosque in Germany. (Photo credit: http://www.taz.de/uploads/hp_taz_img/full/gegenmoschee_f.jpg)

Arson attack against Muslims in Germany. (Photo credit: http://media.de.indymedia.org/images/2008/01/204193.jpg)

"At home instead of Islam". Right wing politicians in all over Europe try to gather support by spreading anti-Muslim sentiments and Islamophobia. Targeting Muslims as scapegoats for the ills of European neoliberal capitalism has become a common practice nowadays. (Photo credit: http://www.wiedenmeier.ch/wordpress/wp-content/uploads/2006/09/daham1.jpg)

Table 13a. Romaphobia, all European countries, by religion

BASE=179850	People that respondent would not like to have as neighbors: "Gypsies"	n (number of observations, sample size)
Muslim	56.9	1877
Roman Catholic	42.7	17368
Free church/Non denominational church	42.2	661
Total	40.2	34136
Orthodox	38.1	7798
Protestant	31.2	5791
Other	29.6	503
Jew	19.8	62

Source: our own calculations from World Values Survey, all countries of wave 3+4

The Czech Republic, Montenegro and Serbia must be praised for their decreasing Romaphobia over time, while the *Slovak Republic* should be singled out as the country, where an *appalling rate of Romaphobia still increased over time.* The battle against Romaphobia is an uphill one, and Romaphobia is being shared by more than 25% of the total population in the following countries:

The best pratice countries of overcoming Roma-phobia (< 25%) are:

Austria [1999]; Denmark [1999]; Iceland [1999]; Montenegro [2001]; Netherlands [1999]; Serbia [2001]; Sweden [1999]

The worst offenders are

Slovakia [1999]
Turkey [2001]
Lithuania [1999]
Northern Ireland [1999]
Italy [1999]
Bulgaria [1999]
Ukraine [1999]
Romania [1999]
Belarus [2000]

where more than half of the total population rejects a Roma neighbor.

Roma and Sinti – persecuted by the Nazis, discriminated against in the EU-27

French Roma and Sinti in a Nazi camp, 1942. (Photo credit: http://isurvived.org/TOC-I.html.)

Photo credit: http://www.datum.at/0104/static/0104datum/images/roma2.jpg

Photo credit: http://incentraleurope.radio.cz/pictures/romove/jarovnice3.jpg

Table 13b. Romaphobia, all European countries, by country

BASE=179850	People that respondent would not like to have as neighbors: "Gypsies"	n (number of observations, sample size)
Slovakia [1999]	77.2	1331
Turkey [2001]	72	1206
Slovakia [1998]	68.4	1095
Lithuania [1999]	63.3	1018
Northern Ireland [1999]	58.3	1000
Italy [1999]	55.6	2000
Bulgaria [1999]	53.7	1000
Ukraine [1999]	52.7	1195
Romania [1999]	51.5	1146
Belarus [2000]	51.1	1000
Estonia [1999]	49.7	1005
Russian Federation [1999]	45.6	2500

BASE=179850	People that respondent would not like to have as neighbors: "Gypsies"	n (number of observations, sample size)
Czech Republic [1998]	45.5	1147
Finland [2000]	44.3	1038
Hungary [1998]	42.5	650
Czech Republic [1999]	39.9	1908
France [1999]	39.8	1615
TOTAL	39.5	46575
Croatia [1999]	38.7	1002
Poland [1999]	38.7	1095
Great Britain [1999]	36.9	1000
Slovenia [1999]	36.6	1006
Portugal [1999]	36.5	1000
Belgium [1999]	35.1	1912
Greece [1999]	32.7	1142
Germany West [1999]	32.5	925
Germany East [1999]	31.5	899
Malta [1999]	30.3	1002
Montenegro [1996]	28.7	240
Spain [1999]	28	1200
Serbia [1996]	27.5	1280
Latvia [1999]	27.2	1013
Ireland [1999]	25.4	1007
Luxembourg [1999]	25.2	1211
Austria [1999]	24.9	1522
Montenegro [2001]	23.6	1060
Sweden [1999]	19.9	1015
Netherlands [1999]	19.4	1003
Denmark [1999]	15.3	1019
Serbia [2001]	12.4	1200
Iceland [1999]	9.3	967

Source: our own calculations from World Values Survey, all countries of wave 3+4

The following maps further underline the urgency of the tasks of combating Anti-Semitism, and Islamophobia in Europe and in the world:

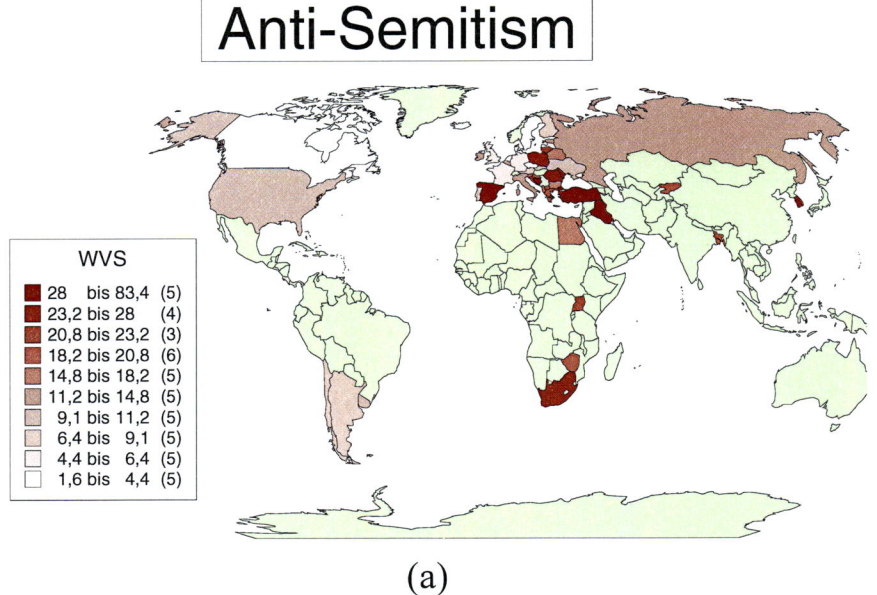

(a)

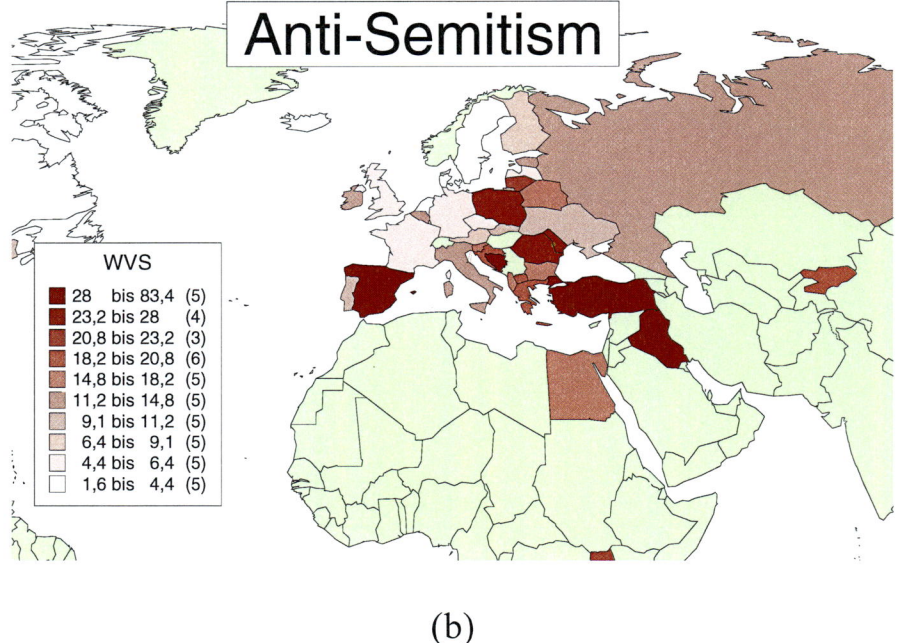

(b)

Map 8 a-b. Anti-Semitism

Note: our own compilations from World Values Survey, waves 3 + 4, openly available at http://www.worldvaluessurvey.org/.

Explanatory note: "bis" is shorthand for "ranging from ... to"; countries with missing values are marked in green color.

The Northward Migration of Global Intolerance and the "Global Tolerance Index" 165

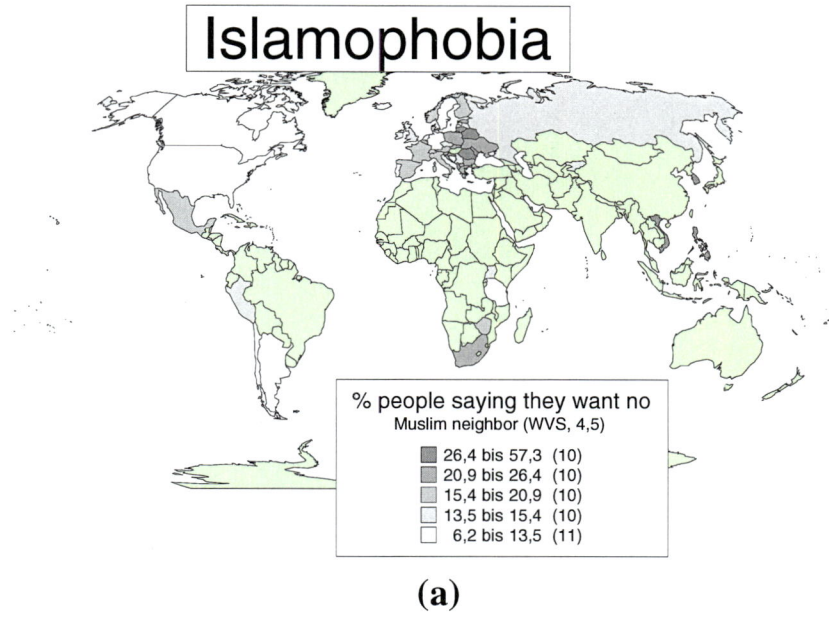

(a)

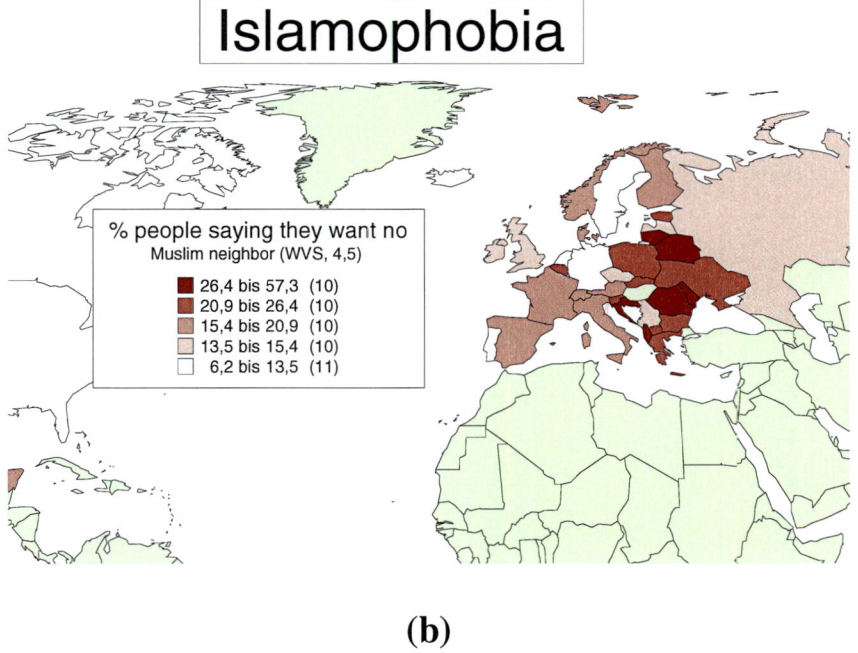

(b)

Map 9 a-b. Islamophobia

Note: our own compilations from World Values Survey, waves 3 + 4, openly available at http://www.worldvaluessurvey.org/

Explanatory note: "bis" is shorthand for "ranging from … to"; countries with missing values are marked in green color

To assess the totality of tolerance in Europe and in the world by global comparison, we now propose to construct a non-parametric *index of "global tolerance"*, which combines the following WVS data with sufficient availability on the percentages per total population overcoming xenophobia and racism:

- People that respondent would like to have as neighbors: People of a different race (WVS A125)
- Qualities that children can be encouraged to learn at home - Important child qualities: tolerance and respect for other people (WVS A035)
- Not saying: Jobs scarce: Men should have more right to a job than women (WVS C001)
- People that respondent would like to have as neighbors: Immigrants/foreign workers (WVS A129)
- People that respondent would like to have as neighbors: Neighbors: Homosexuals (**WVS** A132)

The results of this exercise are given in Table 14:

Table 14. Global Tolerance Index – the four different components and the final index

	Overcoming racism	education for tolerance and respect	accepting gender empowerment	accepting foreign workers	accepting homosexual neighbors	Global tolerance index
Albania [2002]	0.597	0.717	0.331	0.783	0.161	0.518
Algeria [2002]	0.632	0.127	0.208	0.675	0.180	0.364
Argentina [1999]	0.971	0.499	0.645	0.947	0.775	0.768
Armenia [1997]	0.759	0.000	0.329	0.704	0.153	0.389
Australia [1995]	0.967	0.732	0.721	0.967	0.749	0.827
Austria [1999]	0.939	0.522	0.575	0.850	0.742	0.726
Azerbaijan [1997]	0.860	0.243	0.293	0.731	0.078	0.441
Bangladesh [2002]	0.000	0.510	0.171	0.000	0.950	0.326
Belarus [2000]	0.798	0.540	0.675	0.774	0.357	0.629
Belgium [1999]	0.798	0.785	0.737	0.757	0.823	0.780
Bosnia and Herzegovina [2001]	0.845	0.528	0.504	0.655	0.348	0.576
Brazil [1997]	0.996	0.249	0.014	0.983	0.733	0.595
Bulgaria [1999]	0.630	0.247	0.476	0.658	0.452	0.493
Canada [2000]	0.987	0.730	0.832	0.974	0.828	0.870
Chile [2000]	0.906	0.626	0.545	0.873	0.667	0.723
China [2001]	0.825	0.549	0.454	0.791	0.256	0.575
Czech Republic [1999]	0.895	0.331	0.698	0.738	0.800	0.692
Denmark [1999]	0.929	0.882	0.948	0.875	0.919	0.910

	Overcoming racism	education for tolerance and respect	accepting gender empowerment	accepting foreign workers	accepting homosexual neighbors	Global tolerance index
Dominican Republic [1996]	0.769	0.442	0.705	0.768	0.505	0.638
Egypt [2000]	0.085	0.367	0.000	0.384	0.996	0.366
Estonia [1999]	0.816	0.519	0.800	0.715	0.530	0.676
Finland [2000]	0.857	0.778	0.881	0.837	0.784	0.827
France [1999]	0.908	0.834	0.723	0.853	0.841	0.832
Georgia [1996]	0.899	0.129	0.269	0.870	0.217	0.477
Germany West [1999]	0.974	0.571	0.589	0.924	0.866	0.785
Great Britain [1999]	0.912	0.796	0.674	0.799	0.753	0.787
Greece [1999]	0.828	0.093	0.769	0.827	0.728	0.649
Iceland [1999]	0.991	0.814	1.000	0.992	0.920	0.943
India [2001]	0.432	0.336	0.329	0.447	0.707	0.450
Indonesia [2001]	0.535	0.322	0.424	0.416	0.445	0.428
Iran (Islamic Republic of) [2000]	0.686	0.240	0.237	0.890	0.991	0.609
Ireland [1999]	0.857	0.603	0.816	0.851	0.722	0.770
Italy [1999]	0.811	0.603	0.601	0.783	0.708	0.701
Jordan [2001]	0.747	0.429	0.126	0.421	0.000	0.344
Kyrgyzstan [2003]	0.770	0.388	0.415	0.732	0.329	0.527
Latvia [1999]	0.967	0.478	0.736	0.887	0.538	0.721
Lithuania [1999]	0.895	0.209	0.670	0.673	0.314	0.552
Luxembourg [1999]	0.945	0.673	0.677	0.909	0.811	0.803
Macedonia, Republic of [2001]	0.762	0.610	0.371	0.751	0.456	0.590
Malta [1999]	0.767	0.286	0.466	0.802	0.598	0.584
Mexico [2000]	0.816	0.503	0.590	0.817	0.547	0.655
Morocco [2001]	0.838	0.587	0.080	0.743	0.055	0.461
Netherlands [1999]	0.964	0.968	0.887	0.961	0.937	0.944
New Zealand [1998]	0.993	0.669	0.676	0.955	0.773	0.813
Nigeria [2000]	0.597	0.243	0.314	0.605	0.252	0.402
Norway [1996]	0.918	0.397	0.845	0.887	0.855	0.780
Pakistan [2001]	0.942	0.104	0.186	0.588	1.000	0.564
Peru [2001]	0.874	0.549	0.710	0.870	0.500	0.701
Philippines [2001]	0.728	0.265	0.161	0.802	0.760	0.543
Poland [1999]	0.788	0.719	0.505	0.675	0.439	0.625
Portugal [1999]	0.926	0.385	0.624	1.000	0.744	0.736
Republic of Korea [2001]	0.535	0.370	0.284	0.314	0.163	0.333

Table 14. (Continued)

	overcoming racism	education for tolerance and respect	accepting gender empowerment	accepting foreign workers	accepting homosexual neighbors	Global tolerance index
Republic of Moldova [2002]	0.877	0.669	0.410	0.748	0.213	0.583
Romania [1999]	0.686	0.224	0.501	0.712	0.337	0.492
Russian Federation [1999]	0.919	0.424	0.554	0.867	0.412	0.635
Serbia [2001]	0.948	0.365	0.606	0.918	0.501	0.668
Singapore [2002]	0.968	0.485	0.565	0.638	0.536	0.638
Slovakia [1999]	0.790	0.195	0.575	0.684	0.553	0.560
Slovenia [1999]	0.863	0.492	0.718	0.791	0.550	0.683
South Africa [2001]	0.695	0.583	0.595	0.565	0.530	0.594
Spain [2000]	0.870	0.649	0.720	0.872	0.850	0.792
Sweden [1999]	1.000	1.000	0.990	0.995	0.938	0.985
Switzerland [1996]	0.910	0.701	0.589	0.884	0.812	0.779
Tanzania, United Republic Of [2001]	0.795	0.798	0.596	0.768	0.247	0.641
Turkey [2001]	0.546	0.206	0.362	0.336	0.085	0.307
Uganda [2001]	0.773	0.190	0.504	0.837	0.227	0.506
Ukraine [1999]	0.884	0.388	0.635	0.808	0.332	0.609
United States [1999]	0.921	0.705	0.868	0.882	0.763	0.828
Uruguay [1996]	0.938	0.483	0.018	0.929	0.676	0.609
Venezuela [2000]	0.812	0.707	0.556	0.762	0.417	0.651
Viet Nam [2001]	0.571	0.442	0.477	0.529	0.608	0.525
Zimbabwe [2001]	0.750	0.676	0.578	0.721	0.324	0.610

Note: our own compilations from World Values Survey, waves 3 + 4, openly available at http://www.worldvaluessurvey.org/.

In the following chapter, we will analyze the trade-off between development level and the development of tolerance. As we will see, in many ways countries in the world center tend to be characterized by more tolerance than countries in the periphery. Leaving that important trade-off at the side for a while, we first concentrate on the global rank scale of tolerance. Now, if we assume that tolerance can be adequately measured by a non-parametric index of

- People that respondent would like to have as neighbors: People of a different race (WVS A125)
- Qualities that children can be encouraged to learn at home - Important child qualities: tolerance and respect for other people (WVS A035)
- Not saying: Jobs scarce: Men should have more right to a job than women (WVS C001)

- People that respondent would like to have as neighbors: Immigrants/foreign workers (WVS A129)
- People that respondent would like to have as neighbors: Neighbors: Homosexuals (WVS A132)

then the assumption is correct that global tolerance was most pronounced in the following political cultures:

- Sweden [1999]
- Netherlands [1999]
- Iceland [1999]
- Denmark [1999]
- Canada [2000]
- France [1999]
- United States [1999]
- Australia [1995]
- Finland [2000]
- New Zealand [1998]
- Luxembourg [1999]

The worst offenders, lacking a climate of tolerance, as operationalized by our Index, were:

- Turkey [2001]
- Bangladesh [2002]
- Republic of Korea [2001]
- Jordan [2001]
- Algeria [2002]
- Egypt [2000]
- Armenia [1997]
- Nigeria [2000]
- Indonesia [2001]
- Azerbaijan [1997]
- India [2001]

Among the 72 surveyed nations, the countries of the EU-27 had the following world ranks of global tolerance:

1 Sweden [1999]
2 Netherlands [1999]
3 Denmark [1999]
4 France [1999]
5 Finland [2000]
6 Luxembourg [1999]
7 Spain [2000]
8 Great Britain [1999]

9   Germany West [1999]
10   Belgium [1999]
11   Ireland [1999]
12   Portugal [1999]
13   Austria [1999]
14   Latvia [1999]
15   Italy [1999]
16   Czech Republic [1999]
17   Slovenia [1999]
18   Estonia [1999]
19   Greece [1999]
20   Poland [1999]
21   Malta [1999]
22   Slovakia [1999]
23   Lithuania [1999]
24   Bulgaria [1999]
25   Romania [1999]

The World Values Survey also permits the calculation of global tolerance world ranks for the surveyed populations in the following predominantly Muslim countries:

1   Iran (Islamic Republic of) [2000]
2   Bosnia and Herzegovina [2001]
3   Pakistan [2001]
4   Kyrgyzstan [2003]
5   Albania [2002]
6   Morocco [2001]
7   Azerbaijan [1997]
8   Indonesia [2001]
9   Nigeria [2000]
10   Egypt [2000]
11   Algeria [2002]
12   Jordan [2001]
13   Bangladesh [2002]
14   Turkey [2001]

Our world maps further document these results:

The Northward Migration of Global Intolerance and the "Global Tolerance Index" 171

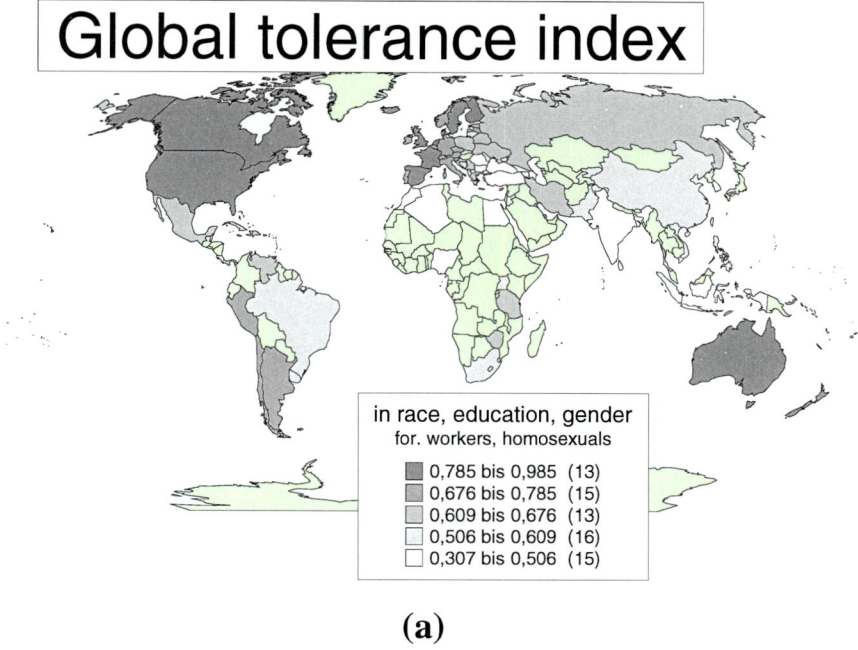

(a)

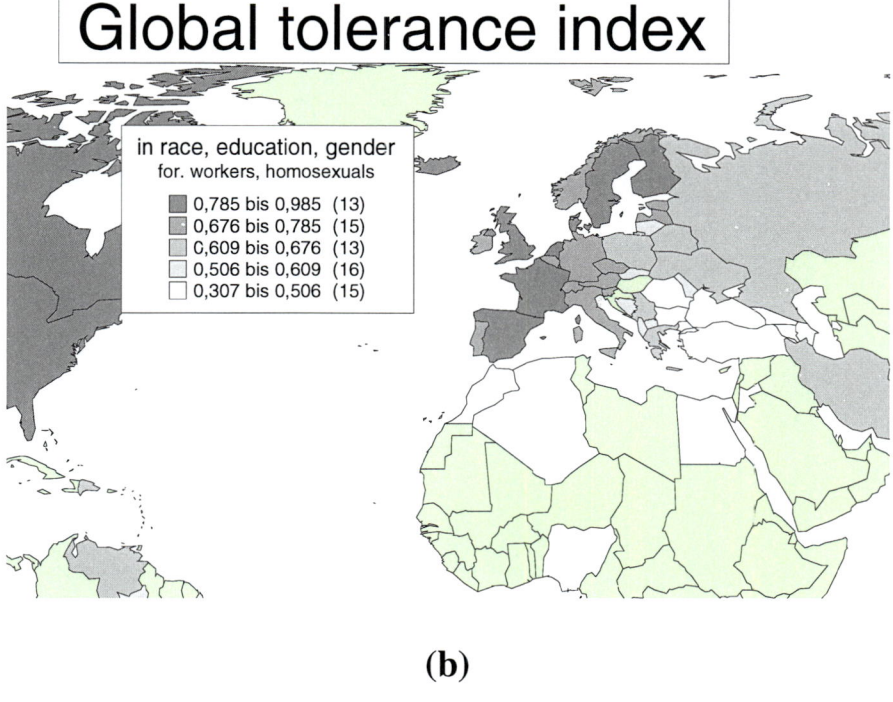

(b)

Map 10. Global tolerance (continues)

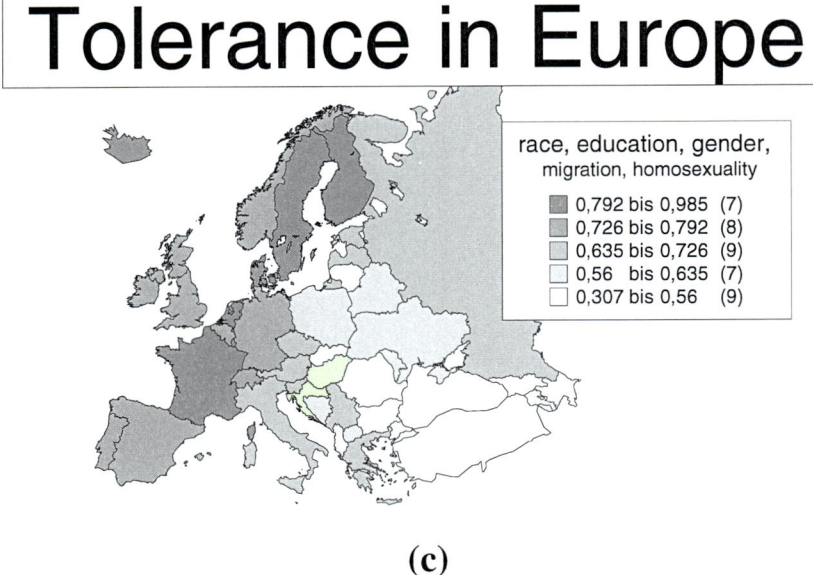

(c)

Map 10 a-c. Global tolerance

Note: best combined World Values Survey country results for: People that respondent would like to have as neighbors: People of a different race (WVS A125); Qualities that children can be encouraged to learn at home - Important child qualities: tolerance and respect for other people (WVS A035); Not saying: Jobs scarce: Men should have more right to a job than women (WVS C001); People that respondent would like to have as neighbors: Immigrants/foreign workers (WVS A129); People that respondent would like to have as neighbors: Neighbors: Homosexuals (WVS A132). The indicators were combined according to the standard *UNDP non-parametric index technique.*

Explanatory note: "bis" is shorthand for "ranging from ... to"; countries with missing values are marked in green color.

Chapter 7

SIMON KUZNETS REVISITED: THE U-SHAPED TRADEOFF BETWEEN TOLERANCE AND DEVELOPMENT

Among the great social scientists of our time, Yale economics professor and Nobel laureate Simon Kuznets (April 30, 1901–July 8, 1985) was the pioneer of the thought that the development process is characterized by an inverted U-shaped relation between income inequality and economic growth.

The Enlightenment perspective of this work raises the question of such an interrelationship between development and global tolerance. Is there a similar process as the one observed by Kuznets, with income inequality and thus the worst contradictions peaking at middle income stages, and with inequalities leveling off later on at higher stages of development?

If tolerance is low at low levels of socio-economic development, and if it decreases first with economic progress, is there at least a hope that tolerance increases with mature development levels?

Systematic research into the trajectory of global tolerance across nations reveals indeed that global tolerance corresponds pretty much to the U-shaped relationship between development level on the one hand and economic equality on the other hand. The non-linear function explains 62% of global tolerance. Very poor societies, as measured by the UNDP's Human Development Index, are relatively tolerant, and with rising income levels, as societal polarization increases, intolerance increases and tolerance decreases. But with rising levels of development, tolerance increases. With almost 2/3 of explained variance, our interrelationship is fairly strong and lets one predict that richer and more developed nations tend to be much more tolerant towards people of a different race, that people tend to regard tolerance and respect for other people as an important target of education, that society accepts job perspectives for women, more people tend to accept immigrants/foreign workers, and homosexual neighbors.

The income inequality Kuznets hypothesis would well explain why intolerance increases with development, and would even provide a kind of "materialist" explanation for the phenomenon. As societies are traditional, multi-culturanism, different gender roles et cetera pose no problem. With inequality increasing with development, differentiations set in, which make the Buddhists, the Christians, the Confucians, the Hindus, the Jews, the Muslims, and the Sikhs the "enemies". With the leveling off of inequalities at later stages of development, people start to discover again that it is not "religion" or "culture", but socio-economics and education, which distribute the life chances in a society. Further research would be well advised to focus on this relationship, and to work with a Kuznets-style explanation of the development -> inequality -> intolerance trade-off.

For the time being, it suffices to mention here the bi-variate relationship:

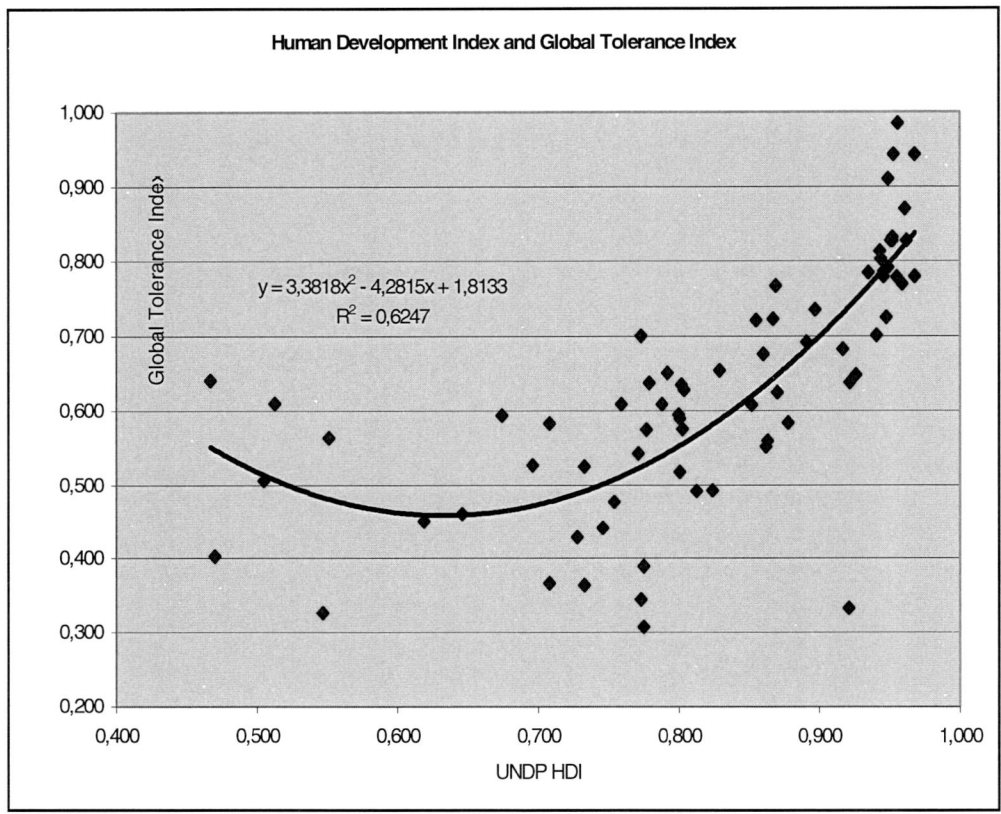

Graph 7. Global development and global tolerance.

Source: our own calculations from World Values Survey, 3rd and 4th wave, http://www.worldvaluessurvey.org/ and UNDP HDR http://hdr.undp.org/en/statistics/. Notes: x-axis: UNDP Human Development Index; y-axis: global tolerance index. Note: best combined World Values Survey country results for: People that respondent would like to have as neighbors: People of a different race (WVS A125); Qualities that children can be encouraged to learn at home - Important child qualities: tolerance and respect for other people (WVS A035); Not saying: Jobs scarce: Men should have more right to a job than women (WVS C001); People that respondent would like to have as neighbors: Immigrants/foreign workers (WVS A129); People that respondent would like to have as neighbors: Neighbors: Homosexuals (WVS A132). The indicators were combined according to the standard UNDP non-parametric index technique. The global tolerance index (y-scale) is explained here by the level of the achieved human development index. The curve-linear function explains 2/3 of global tolerance. At very low levels of human development, tolerance decreases along the paths of development, while tolerance increases from approximately from the level of the HDI of 0.800 onwards.

The next important question in this context is whether or not some countries are performing well at low levels of development, while other nations perform badly at high levels of development. To this end, we calculated the residuals from Graph 7 to show the positive and negative outlayers:

Table 15. Human development and global tolerance, and the residuals from the general function (high tolerance even at comparatively lower levels of development)

Country	HDI	HDI^2	Global tolerance index	Predicted GTI	Residual
Peru	0.773	0.598	0.701	0.524	0.177
Sweden	0.956	0.914	0.985	0.811	0.174
Netherlands	0.953	0.908	0.944	0.804	0.140
South Africa	0.674	0.454	0.594	0.464	0.130
Argentina	0.869	0.755	0.768	0.647	0.121
Denmark	0.949	0.901	0.910	0.796	0.114
Dominican Republic	0.779	0.607	0.638	0.530	0.108
Venezuela (Bolivarian Republic of)	0.792	0.627	0.651	0.544	0.107
Republic of Moldova	0.708	0.501	0.583	0.477	0.106
Iceland	0.968	0.937	0.943	0.838	0.105
Zimbabwe	0.513	0.263	0.610	0.507	0.103
Iran (Islamic Republic of)	0.759	0.576	0.609	0.512	0.097
Latvia	0.855	0.731	0.721	0.625	0.096
Tanzania (United Republic of)	0.467	0.218	0.641	0.551	0.090
Pakistan	0.551	0.304	0.564	0.481	0.083
Russian Federation	0.802	0.643	0.635	0.555	0.080
Chile	0.867	0.752	0.723	0.643	0.080
Belarus	0.804	0.646	0.629	0.557	0.072
Ukraine	0.788	0.621	0.609	0.539	0.070
Mexico	0.829	0.687	0.655	0.588	0.067
Kyrgyzstan	0.696	0.484	0.527	0.472	0.055
Canada	0.961	0.924	0.870	0.822	0.048
China	0.777	0.604	0.575	0.528	0.047
Estonia	0.860	0.740	0.676	0.632	0.044
Brazil	0.800	0.640	0.595	0.552	0.043
Portugal	0.897	0.805	0.736	0.694	0.042
Macedonia (TFYR)	0.801	0.642	0.590	0.554	0.036
Viet Nam	0.733	0.537	0.525	0.492	0.033
New Zealand	0.943	0.889	0.813	0.783	0.030
France	0.952	0.906	0.832	0.802	0.030
United States	0.951	0.904	0.828	0.800	0.028
Finland	0.952	0.906	0.827	0.802	0.025
Philippines	0.771	0.594	0.543	0.523	0.020

Table 15. (Continued)

Country	HDI	HDI^2	Global tolerance index	Predicted GTI	Residual
Bosnia and Herzegovina	0.803	0.645	0.576	0.556	0.020
Germany	0.935	0.874	0.785	0.767	0.018
Luxembourg	0.944	0.891	0.803	0.785	0.018
Czech Republic	0.891	0.794	0.692	0.683	0.009
Australia	0.962	0.925	0.827	0.824	0.003
Morocco	0.646	0.417	0.461	0.459	0.002
Great Britain United Kingdom	0.946	0.895	0.787	0.789	-0.002
Spain	0.949	0.901	0.792	0.796	-0.004
Uganda	0.505	0.255	0.506	0.513	-0.007
India	0.619	0.383	0.450	0.459	-0.009
Belgium	0.946	0.895	0.780	0.789	-0.009
Uruguay	0.852	0.726	0.609	0.620	-0.011
Poland	0.870	0.757	0.625	0.648	-0.023
Switzerland	0.955	0.912	0.779	0.809	-0.030
Georgia	0.754	0.569	0.477	0.508	-0.031
Albania	0.801	0.642	0.518	0.554	-0.036
Ireland	0.959	0.920	0.770	0.818	-0.048
Slovenia	0.917	0.841	0.683	0.731	-0.048
Norway	0.968	0.937	0.780	0.838	-0.058
Azerbaijan	0.746	0.557	0.441	0.501	-0.060
Indonesia	0.728	0.530	0.428	0.489	-0.061
Austria	0.948	0.899	0.726	0.794	-0.068
Romania	0.813	0.661	0.492	0.568	-0.076
Slovakia	0.863	0.745	0.560	0.637	-0.077
Malta	0.878	0.771	0.584	0.661	-0.077
Italy	0.941	0.885	0.701	0.779	-0.078
Lithuania	0.862	0.743	0.552	0.635	-0.083
Bulgaria	0.824	0.679	0.493	0.582	-0.089
Greece	0.926	0.857	0.649	0.748	-0.099
Singapore	0.922	0.850	0.638	0.741	-0.103
Egypt	0.708	0.501	0.366	0.477	-0.111
Algeria	0.733	0.537	0.364	0.492	-0.128
Armenia	0.775	0.601	0.389	0.526	-0.137
Nigeria	0.470	0.221	0.402	0.548	-0.146
Bangladesh	0.547	0.299	0.326	0.483	-0.157
Jordan	0.773	0.598	0.344	0.524	-0.180
Turkey	0.775	0.601	0.307	0.526	-0.219
Republic of Korea	0.921	0.848	0.333	0.739	-0.406

Source: our own calculations from World Values Survey, 3rd and 4th wave, http://www.worldvaluessurvey.org/ and UNDP HDR http://hdr.undp.org/en/statistics/ .

The 10 countries with the most unsatisfactory performance in the development of global tolerance, duly considering their development level, are:

- Republic of Korea
- Turkey
- Jordan
- Bangladesh
- Nigeria
- Armenia
- Algeria
- Egypt
- Singapore
- Greece
- Bulgaria

Among the EU-27 countries, the negative record holders are:

- Greece
- Bulgaria
- Lithuania
- Italy
- Slovakia

The 10 best global performers are:

- Peru
- Sweden
- Netherlands
- South Africa
- Argentina
- Denmark
- Dominican Republic
- Venezuela (Bolivarian Republic of)
- Republic of Moldova
- Iceland
- Zimbabwe

The world maps of the development -> global tolerance trade-off defy a simplistic reasoning. Catholic Italy is one of the worst performing countries in Europe; as well as the Asian country Korea, the predominantly Muslim nations Turkey, Jordan, and Bangladesh as well as Orthodox Armenia, Greece and Bulgaria. Catholic Peru and Argentina, as well as Protestant Sweden and the Netherlands are among the world leaders in the development->tolerance trade-off. There are good and bad performers in ALL cultural regions of the world. Compared to its development level, the populations of Iran, Pakistan and Russia all perform surprisingly well – surprisingly and in terms of the current standing of their governments in the global press, while EU-decision makers should take a closer look at the development of tolerance in at least 10 EU member countries—Greece, Bulgaria, Lithuania, Italy, Malta, Slovakia, Romania, Austria, Slovenia, and Ireland.

Our statistics also show that Turkey, Jordan and Bangladesh are the three Muslim countries with the most problematic trade-off between development and tolerance, while the populations in Iran (Islamic Republic of), Pakistan, and Kyrgyzstan have, compared to the development level of their countries, achieved the highest levels tolerance.

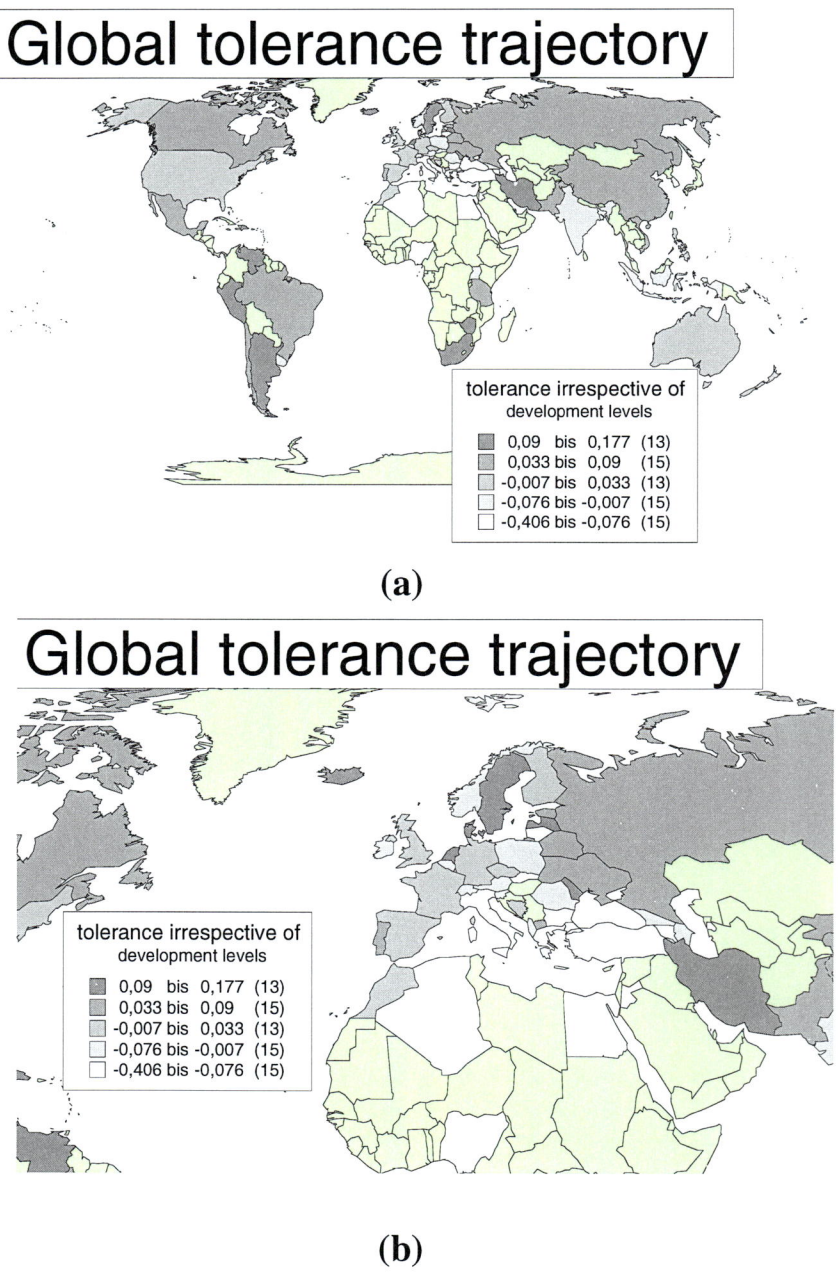

Map 10 (continues).

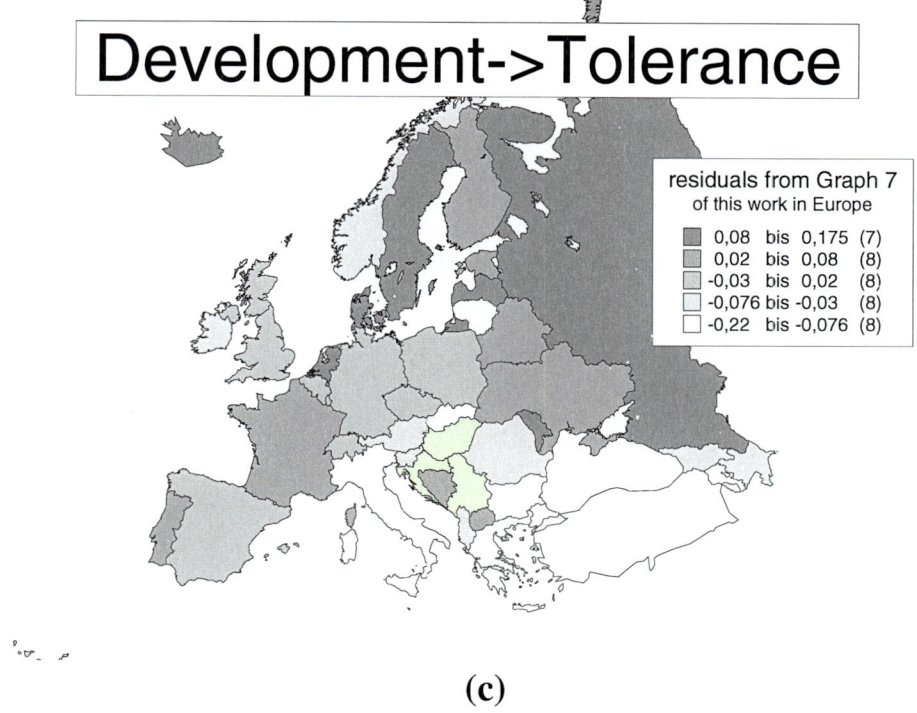

(c)

Map 10 a-c. Global tolerance, properly considering the development level-tolerance trade-off. Residuals from Graph 7 of this work.

Source: our own calculations from World Values Survey, 3rd and 4th wave, http://www.worldvaluessurvey.org/ and UNDP HDR http://hdr.undp.org/en/statistics/

Explanatory note: "bis" is shorthand for "ranging from … to"; countries with missing values are marked in green color. *Dark color:* good development of societal tolerance, compared to the attained development level. *Light color: insufficient development of structures of tolerance,* compared to the development level.

A basic assumption of this work is that global tolerance and the active society – as the practical political guiding principles to be deduced from all this value analysis – are very strongly inter-linked with success or failure of a society to fulfill what has been called in Europe as the "Lisbon agenda" or "Lisbon process" or "Lisbon strategy". As it is well-known, the Lisbon process/agenda/strategy aims to make the EU *"the most dynamic and competitive knowledge-based economy in the world capable of sustainable economic growth with more and better jobs and greater social cohesion, and respect for the environment by 2010".* It was decided upon by the European Council in Lisbon in March 2000 (http://europa.eu /scadplus/glossary/lisbon_strategy_en.htm).

Limited, as it may be, the evidence is clear: almost ¾ of the "Lisbon process" success or failure of the EU-27 nations can be statistically explained by "global tolerance":

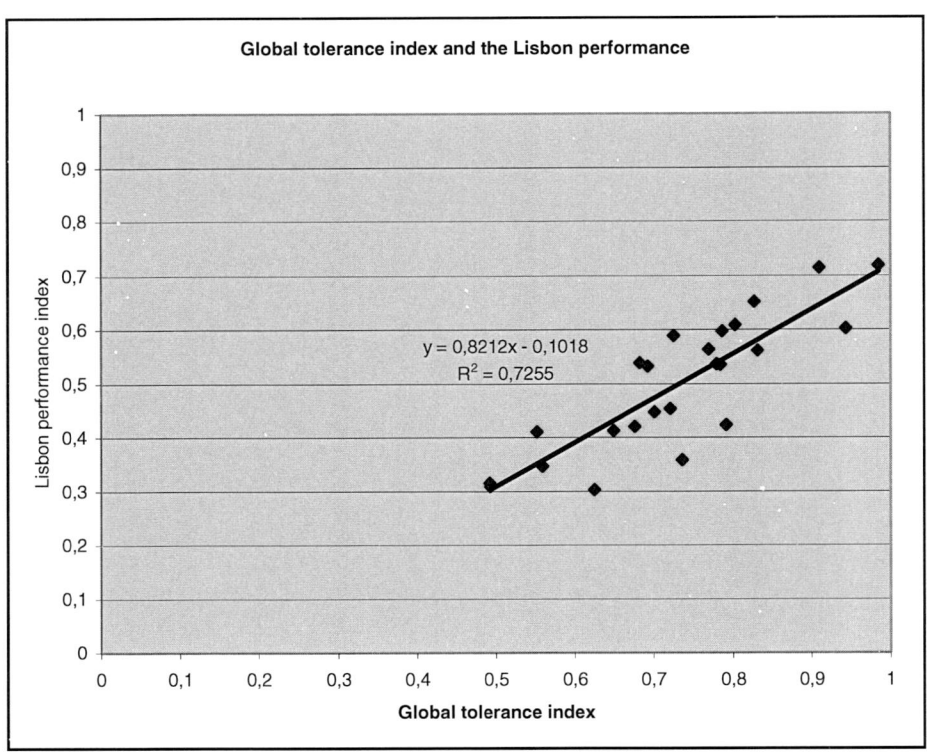

Graph 8. Global tolerance and the aggregate Lisbon performance in the EU-27.

Source: our own calculations from World Values Survey, 3rd and 4th wave, http://www.worldvaluessurvey.org/ and UNDP HDR http://hdr.undp.org/en/statistics/ as well as Tausch A. (2006), 'On heroes, villains and statisticians'. The Vienna Institute for International Economic Studies Monthly Report, No. 7, July 2006: 20 - 23. Vienna: The Vienna Institute for International Economic Studies (wiiw)

Anti-Semitism and Islamophobia have 46% of common variance; Anti-Semitism and Romaphobia 44% of common variance, and Islamophobia and Romaphobia 38% of common variance. As Table 18 will show, there is indeed one common factor of *"phobias"* in the world, which explains 1/6 of all the variance of all the responses of the more than 250.000 respondents in all the waves of the "world values survey". *Phobias* are lamentably enough the strongest underlying dimension of all the social and political opinions in our world today, and as we will see, the factor loadings are very high indeed:

Rejecting neighbors: Immigrants/foreign workers	0,782
Rejecting neighbors: Jews	0,717
Rejecting neighbors: People of a different race	0,769

In the present analysis, the simple bi-variate correlations and scatterplots should suffice:

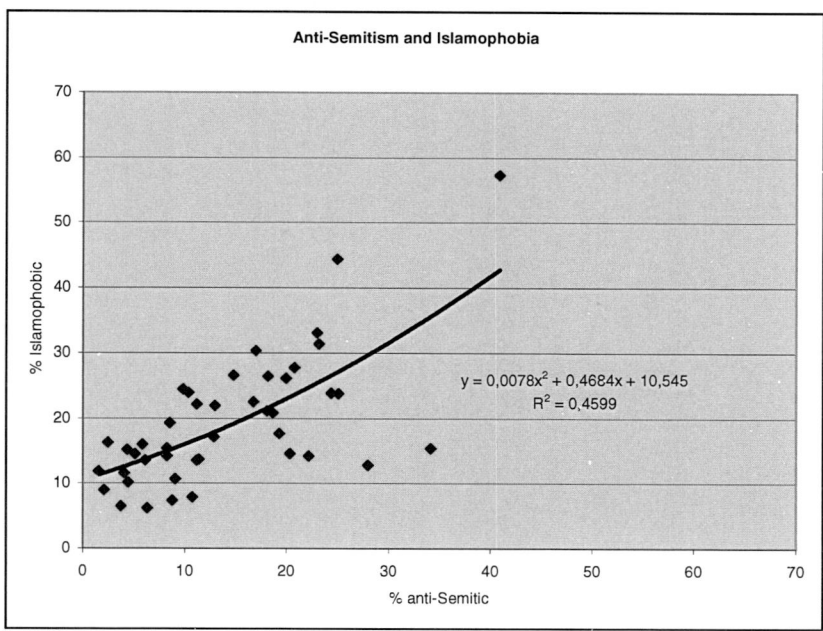

Graph 9. Anti-Semitism and Islamophobia.

Source: our own calculations from World Values Survey, 3rd and 4th wave, http://www.worldvaluessurvey.org/ and UNDP HDR http://hdr.undp.org/en/statistics/

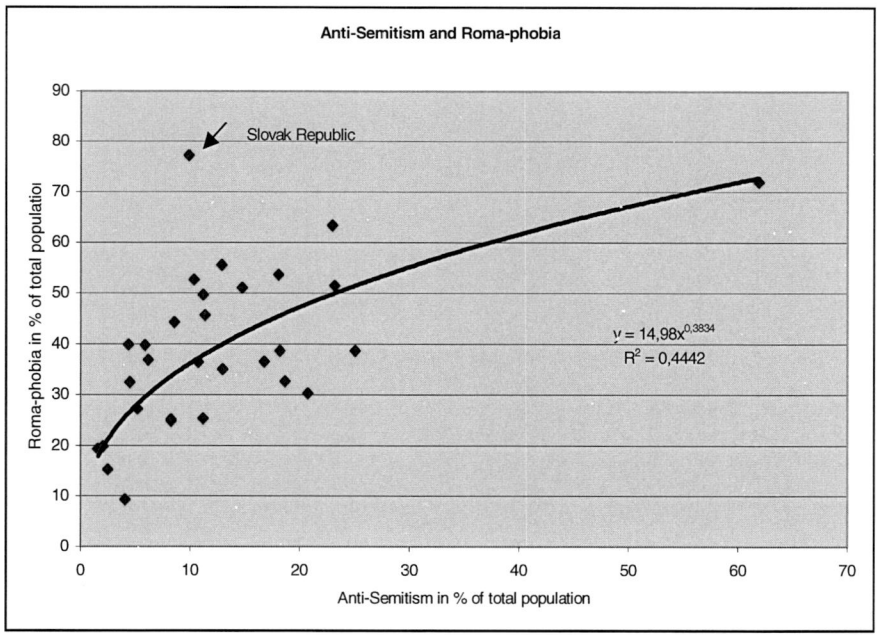

Graph 10. Anti-Semitism and Roma-phobia.

Source: our own calculations from World Values Survey, 3rd and 4th wave, http://www. World valuessurvey.org/ .

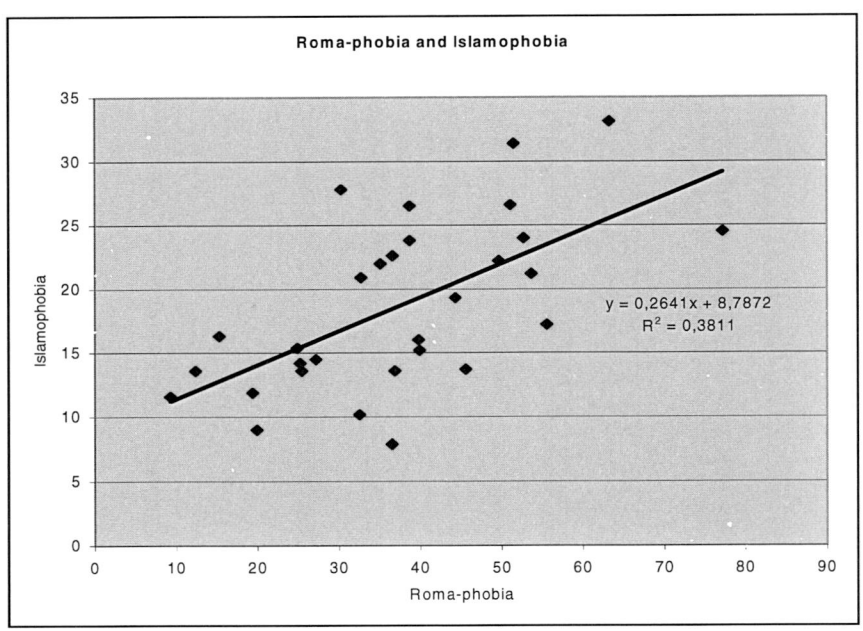

Graph 11. Roma-phobia and Islamophobia.

Source: our own calculations from World Values Survey, 3rd and 4th wave, http://www. World valuessurvey.org/

Chapter 8

ACTIVE SOCIETY, TOLERANCE AND DEVELOPMENT: THE CROSS-NATIONAL EVIDENCE

In the present chapter, we would like to weigh the determinants and the effects of global tolerance, the active society, and traditional society on development. Above, we already said that societies do not generally experience a smooth transformation from a traditional and survival oriented value set towards a secular and self-expression oriented value set. The *Asabiyya* counter-model to Inglehart, which we proposed above, relies on a factor analytical evaluation of the variables in the world values survey, and combines theoretical insights of the Inglehart School with those by Columbia University sociologist Amitai Etzioni. At the very beginning of the modernization process, societies are traditional, religious, and pre-modern; but at the same time they are also "active" societies with functioning neighborhood structures, and very clear perceptions of what is "good" and "evil", and a high respect of the law. We stated that as the modernization process proceeds, traditional religious values seem to be on the losing side of the societal equation. The uneasiness of the "religious right" in the United States, of the Islamist camp in many countries of the Muslim world, and the religious right in many developing countries is best understood by the process, whereby traditional values get lost at the same time with dimensions of the active society and respect of the law in such vital areas as tax morale, non-acceptability of bribery and government benefits fraud. The worst global performers, on this account, it seems, are Belarus, Brazil, Slovakia, and the Ukraine. As churches are emptying, so do the volunteer organizations; and since "God" is said to be not "existing", everything becomes feasible, acceptable, and even becomes practice: cheating taxes, taking bribes, receiving government benefits even if you are not entitled for them.

Our new "active society index" is a non-parametric standard UNDP-type index of the World Values Survey country results (wave 3+4) for the voluntary work variables:

1. social welfare service for elderly, handicapped or deprived people
2. religious or church organization
3. education, arts, music or cultural activities
4. labor unions
5. political parties or groups
6. local political action groups

7   human rights
8   environment, conservation, animal rights
9   professional associations
10 youth work
11 sports or recreation
12 women's group
13 peace movement
14 organization concerned with health

The 10 superstars of the active society according to this investigation are:

- Tanzania, United Republic Of [2001]
- Bangladesh [2002]
- Viet Nam [2001]
- China [2001]
- United States [1999]
- Uganda [2001]
- Algeria [2002]
- Albania [2002]
- Philippines [2001]
- Sweden [1999]
- India [2001]

The 10 worst performers are:

- Turkey [2001]
- Russian Federation [1999]
- Lithuania [1999]
- Serbia [2001]
- Portugal [1999]
- Ukraine [1999]
- Poland [1999]
- Romania [1999]
- Spain [2000]
- Hungary [1999]
- Latvia [1999]

The world map of voluntary organization around the globe is thus the following:

Active Society, Tolerance and Development: The Cross-National Evidence 185

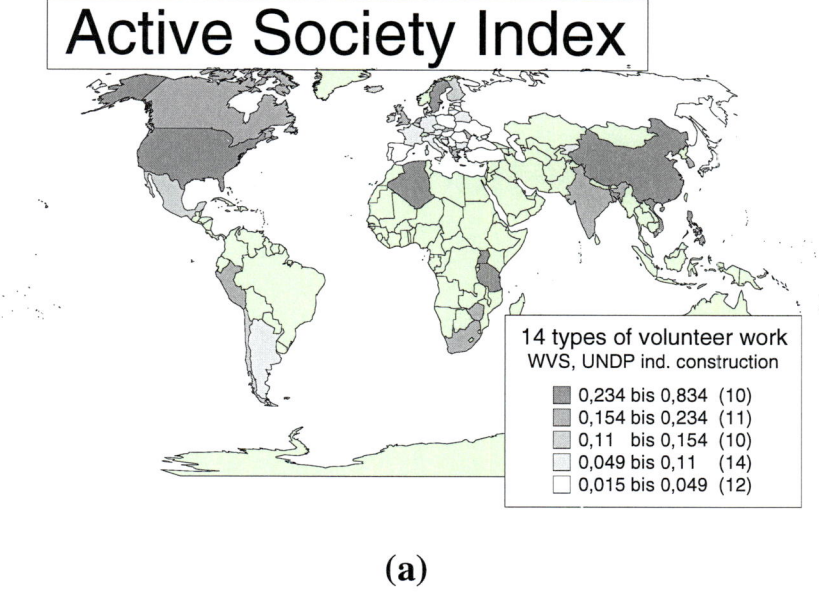

(a)

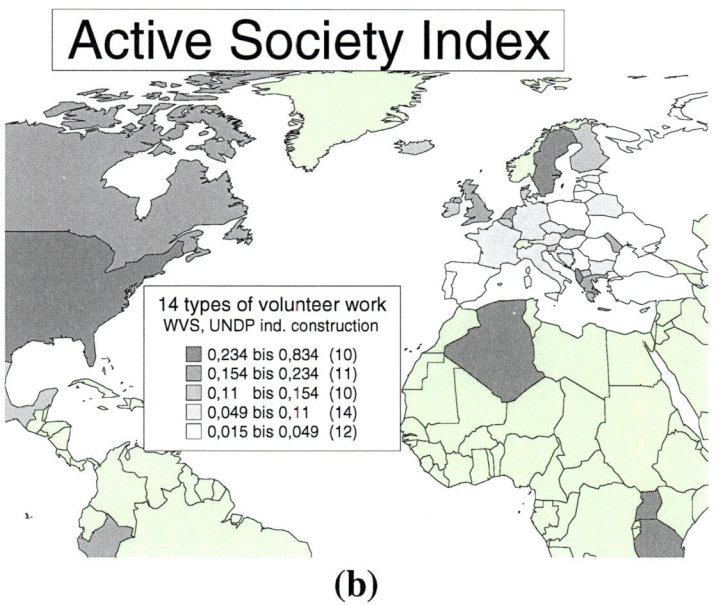

(b)

Map 11 a-b. The active society index.

Note: non-parametric standard UNDP-type index of the World Values Survey country results (wave 3+4) for the voluntary work variables: social welfare service for elderly, handicapped or deprived people; religious or church organization; education, arts, music or cultural activities; labor unions; political parties or groups; local political action groups; human rights; environment, conservation, animal rights; professional associations; youth work; sports or recreation; women's group; peace movement; organization concerned with health; other groups.

Explanatory note: "bis" is shorthand for "ranging from … to"; countries with missing values are marked in green color.

The all-important question now is: does an active society propel economic growth? And what are the cross-national determinants of global tolerance, the active society; traditional values; the intransparent, inactive society, and, finally, of social cohesion *("Asabiyya")?*

TOWARDS AN EMPIRICAL RESEARCH DESIGN

Today, a truly massive cross-national research literature exists on the determinants of global development, whose results are often diametrically opposed to one another. The novel idea that an active society is the catalyst of global development has at least several contenders. Our survey will be brief and readers, interested in the further debates about the issues, are being referred to Tausch/Ghymers (2007).

Indeed, if a factor is to be held responsible for global economic growth, it *must* hold that in cross-national research such a factor is highly associated statistically with subsequent economic growth, irrespective of the development levels reached. For example, if it should be the case that secondary school enrollment is the key factor; it would have to be the case that secondary school enrollment rates significantly, positively and persistently affect growth.

Without question one of the issues dominating the social scientific debate over recent years has been *globalization*. A very thorough liberal globalist flagship synopsis of the quantitative peace- and development research evidence by de Soysa and Gleditsch (2002) maintains that globalization, especially openness to trade and foreign direct investment, lead towards

a) increased democracy
b) development
c) less inequality
d) a better environment
e) peace.

So, following the advice of de Soysa and Gleditsch, European governments should continue their path towards globalization and open markets in order to better integrate Muslim minorities. De Soysa and Gleditsch would say: the *banlieues* in France remained so poor because France did not sufficiently open up to the world economy, while countries like Sweden did. This school implies: world market open capitalism is compatible with economic growth, indeed it would be one of its main preconditions.

The "Washington Consensus", whose key empirical indicator would be "economic freedom", has been summarized by Raffer (pp. 305-323 in Tausch, 2003) as to represent the following policy priorities:

1. Fiscal discipline: a primary budget surplus of several percent of GDP
2. Public expenditure priorities: defined as re-directions of public expenditures towards fields with high economic returns such as primary health and education
3. Tax reform: cutting marginal tax rates

4   Financial liberalization: moderately positive real interest rates and the abolition of preferential interest rates (such as for developmentally useful or socially demanded projects)
5   Exchange rates: unified and competitive
6   Trade liberalization: abolishing quotas (replacing them by tariffs) and reducing tariffs to a uniform low level within three to ten years.
7   Foreign direct investment: equal treatment with domestic firms. The World Bank calls this the elimination of barriers. This principle is also enshrined in the WTO treaties.
8   Privatization
9   Deregulation: abolishing regulations aiming at achieving developmental or social aims
10 Property rights: must be guaranteed.

Literature, supporting the "Washington Consensus" now abounds, highlighting pro-market policies and world economic openness as strategies for economic growth.

For neoliberal authors, foreign investments are a solid pre-condition of growth. A reliance on foreign savings would not necessarily exclude rapid economic growth in a world of liberalized financial markets (for an overview of these debates, see Kendall P., 2000; see furthermore Shaw (1973) and McKinnon (1973), as well as the studies by Roubini and Sala-i-Martin (1992) and Barro (1991). Contradicting the neo-Marxist dependency theories, neo-liberals also would argue that the leveling of world price levels is beneficial for world system and country economic growth rates. Comparative price levels are part and parcel of the 14 Lisbon structural indicators, accepted by the EU-member governments, and regularly updated by the Eurostat statistical office.

Dependency and world system theory, which dominated the quantitative political science and sociological writing for many years on the subject and, which we can present here only briefly, generally held that poverty and backwardness are caused by the peripheral position that nations/regions/social systems have in the international division of labor. It seems to be important at this point to emphasize that our three indicators of dependency measure three different types of "dependent development" at the aggregate, national level:

- MNC penetration measures the different weight that foreign capital investments have in the host countries
- Unequal exchange/low comparative price levels (ERDI) measures the degree to which globalization has contributed to lowering the international price level of a country; i.e. it is an indicator about the openness of the price system *vis-à-vis* the pressures of globalization. The result of this is, dependency theory says, an unequal transfer from the peripheries to the centers, which used to be high-price countries
- For dependency authors, foreign savings show the weight that foreign savings, mostly from the centers and richer semi-peripheries, have in the accumulation process of the host countries in the periphery and semi-periphery.

Dependency authors generally explain backwardness and stagnation by the ever-growing dependent insertion of these countries into the world economy. Starting with the writings of Perroux, Prebisch and Rothschild in the 1930s, their leading spokespersons all would stress the unequal and socially imbalanced nature of development in regions that are highly dependent on investment from the highly developed countries. Short-term spurts of growth notwithstanding, long-term growth will be imbalanced and unequal, and will tend towards high negative current account balances.

Later world system analyses—that started with the writings of the Austro-Hungarian socialist Karl Polanyi after the First World War—tended to confirm and expand this dependency argument. Capitalism in the periphery, like in the center, is characterized by strong cyclical fluctuations, and there are centers, semi-peripheries and peripheries. The rise of one group of semi-peripheries tends to be at the cost of another group, but the unequal structure of the world economy based on unequal transfer tends to remain stable. Authors from the world system approach tended to discard the "culturalist" explanations, offered by Huntington, and rather would support the argument that world economic position and not culture, determine growth or stagnation. The massive world systems literature continues to be a stream of the scientific debate subsisting at the major Universities, publishing houses and scholarly journals around the world, the near complete global triumph of the neo-liberal theory notwithstanding.

Macroquantitative analyses modeled around the dependency/world system school generally claimed to have confirmed dependency arguments. According to these quantitative data analyses, there are powerful influences at work, which cause external imbalances in the periphery. Flagship essays and book publications of this school include nowadays over 50 studies, published internationally, dealing with economic and social development and dependency.

By comparison, MNC penetration received a vast attention in the published titles of the comparative research literature of the last three decades.

While different authors disagree on the direction of the influence of MNC penetration on the human condition, they'd all underline the strong influence of MNC penetration on employment, economic growth, income distribution and overall development.

As to the causality of the dependency/underdevelopment connection, perhaps one of the clearest paragraphs to be found in the current literature is to be encountered in the essay written by L. Beer in 1999:

> "As opposed to Modernization theory's emphasis on the internal dynamics of economic growth, World-System and Dependency theories are neo-Marxist perspectives that focus on the global structure of the capitalist world economy.
>
> (…) This approach argues that national economic growth, inequality and sociopolitical change can only be understood through the analysis of a nation's relative position in the spacioeconomic hierarchy of the world system. That is, the relationship between economic growth and income inequality within any single nation is dependent on that society's relational position in the world division of labor and global power structure. It is asserted that the dynamics of capitalist accumulation in developing countries are different than the processes observable in core nations.
>
> (…) The issue that World-System/Dependency analyses point our attention to is not the lack of economic growth in developing nations, but the type of growth their dependent status affords them and it's consequences.
>
> (…) In the World-System/Dependency perspective, capitalist development is dependent on social and material inequality and this inequality is in turn a result of incorporation into the world system. National economic growth and income distribution are in large part determined

by growth potentials of productive activities in the larger global structure. Therefore, this approach hypothesizes that stratification of income will correspond with the world division of labor and position in the world economy.

(…) . First, foreign investment in developing countries generates large sectoral disparities in the national economy, creates labor aristocracies and results in the underutilization of indigenous labor. Second, transnational corporations operating in developing nations accrue a disproportionate share of local sources of credit and repatriate profits rather than reinvesting them in the local economy. Finally, the governments of these nations, motivated by the necessity (generated by their incorporation into the capitalist world economy) of attracting and maintaining foreign investment, implement policies and strategies that decrease the power of labor and inhibit vertical mobility. These include tax concessions, guarantees of profit repatriation, and labor laws unfavorable to workers.

(…) Scholars in the World-System/Dependency tradition argue that the relationship between foreign investment and internal income inequality has different effects on various sectors of the economy, but in all segments it creates and sustains income inequality in the national population.

(…) Foreign capital investment in the agricultural sector destroys traditional production processes and leads to unemployment and overurbanization through its capital intensive means of organization (i.e. labor shedding, land enclosure). In the extractive sector of the economy, foreign investment benefits only a small portion of the national population and thereby increases income inequality. This is because TNC penetration in this sector creates only a small well-paid labor force and because ownership of natural resources is typically concentrated.

(…) World-System theorists argue that foreign investment in the manufacturing sector has the most harmful effect on national income distribution. National economies in non-core nations with large manufacturing sectors have high levels of income inequality because profits in this sector are increased by the maintenance of a large, surplus low-wage labor force. Therefore, high rates of income inequality are in the interest of transnational corporations and national elites who benefit from foreign investment; they have little incentive to take action to distribute income more equitably. Contrary to the hypotheses of Modernization theorists, the World-System perspective argues that the uneven development of highly penetrated developing economies benefits transnational corporations in that the only segment of the population, which can afford to buy these manufactured goods is the wealthy elite.

(…) Domestic demand for these goods depends on the concentration of wealth and high levels of income inequality. Although redistribution of wealth and the resultant expansion of markets may be in the long term interest of foreign corporations, they are driven primarily by the short-term profit logic of capitalism.

(…) Furthermore, there is a convergence of interests between transnational corporations and the wealthy elite segments of the national population in maintaining income inequality, which creates barriers to the "trickle-down" effect of industrialization predicted by Modernization theories. In addition to the incentives for inequity for foreign investors discussed above, the national elite strive to maintain their power and higher income so as to maintain privileged consumption patterns and access to status symbols. A common international class interest in the persistence of high levels of inequality thus link foreign investors and indigenous elites, leading these powerful groups to support (and in some cases attempt to increase) the existing unequal income distribution and to coopt and repress opposition from other segments of the population (…) (Beer, 1999: 4-7)

Cultural theories of development tend to stress that at present development perspectives for the large Muslim region between Morocco in the West and Iran in the East are not good.

Their principal spokesperson today is Huntington, but also such diverse sources as the UNDP's *Arab Human Development Report* (2002) or the World Bank's *MENA Report* (2002) tend to highlight the various development constraints in that region. While the UNDP stresses lack of democracy, human resource development and gender equality as the main development blocks, the World Bank highlights the negative heritage of "Arab Socialism" or past state sector influence. Several authors, among them Noland[23] and Tausch, explicitly contradicted Huntington with empirical, cross-national evidence, however. With all the global interest being expressed nowadays on Islam after the 9/11 terrorist attacks, the negligence of the issue of Muslim culture as a variable in cross-national comparative social science is surprising. For an informed debate, *inter alia* the following cross-national-research-relevant literature is available.

On a global economy level, neo-liberal authors like Barro; Barro and associates; Crafts; Dadush and Brahmbatt; Dollar and Kraay and Weede generally tended to think that with the establishment of "economic freedom" positive patterns of development will prevail in practically all countries of the globe, irrespective of their development level. Especially the painful experience of the neo-liberal transformation process in Eastern Europe after the end of Communism is however a warning sign to decision-makers and scholars alike that "economic freedom" plus "world economic openness" alone cannot be for themselves the only necessary, let alone the sufficient condition for a successful capitalist.

Thus, selective intervention by the state seemed for many to be the development lesson of East and South-East Asia as well as Scandinavia during the last decades. "Industrial policy", and "active adoption to the changing structures of the international division of labor", and not pure economic freedom seemed to be the catchword of the day.

In addition, the "Keynesian" legacy should not be under-estimated. "Keynesians" would expect positive trade-offs to hold between "government intervention" and the human condition, and not the other way around.

Our theoretical survey should be concluded by three processes, being of great importance especially to the European continent. One is the obvious argument about the European Union as a determining factor of European development patterns, for good or for bad. There are very diverse views nowadays on the European Union. As a research paper, published in the journal *Parameters* of the US Army, maintains (Wilkie, 2003):

"Still, there are those on both sides of the Atlantic who believe that the European Union, as an old-fashioned socialist bureaucracy, is "fundamentally unreformable" and also culturally hostile to the United States" (Wilkie, 2003: 46)[24]

There is a wide range of literature now available that highlights also the negative effects of European integration in a globalized world economy [for a survey of the literature and politometric evidence, see Tausch and Herrmann, 2001].

---

[23] See especially: Marcus Noland and associates: http://www.iie.com/publications/pb/pb04-4.pdf and http://www.iie.com/publications/wp/2003/03-8.pdf. Arno Tausch: (2005) 'Is Islam really a development blockade? 12 predictors of development, including membership in the Organization of Islamic Conference, and their influence on 14 indicators of development in 109 countries of the world with completely available data'. Ankara Center for Turkish Policy Studies, ANKAM, Insight Turkey, 7, 1, 2005: 124 - 135. Full PDF version available at http://www.insightturkey.com/tausch2005_multivariate_analysis_world_dev.pdf

[24] http://carlisle-www. army. mil/usawc/Parameters/02winter/wilkie. htm

The voice of "euro-optimists" is small, but influential, including later works by Volker Bornschier, and the writings by economics Nobel laureate Robert Mundell and Stanford Professor emeritus Pan Yotopoulos. [Bornschier V. (1992), Bornschier V. (1999), Mundell R. A. and Clesse A. (Eds.)(2000), Mundell R. A. et al. (Eds.)(2005), and Yotopoulos P. A. (2004)].

The well-known acceleration and maturity effects of development have to be qualified in an important way. Ever since the days of Simon Kuznets, development researchers have applied curve-linear formulations in order to capture these effects. The curve-linear function of growth, being regressed on the natural logarithm of development level and its square, is sometimes called the "Matthew's effect" following Matthew's (13, 12):

> "For whosoever hath, to him shall be given, and he shall have more abundance: but whosoever hath not, for him shall be taken away even that he hath."

Social scientists interpreted this effect mainly in view of an acceleration of economic growth in middle-income countries vis-à-vis the poor countries and in view of the still widening gap between the poorest periphery nations ("have-nots") and the "haves" among the semi-periphery countries (Jackman, 1982).

We also should mention the variable "pension reform", which was included into our research design. Proponents and critics of fully funded, three-pillar pension models alike agree on the fact that pension reform policy is one of the biggest challenges that especially advanced democracies with their age structure are facing in world society. To neglect pension funds in investigations about the capitalist world economy would be misleading. Private pension funds already amount to 44 % of current world GDP, with countries like the United States; Japan; United Kingdom; Netherlands; Canada; Switzerland; Australia; Sweden; Ireland; Finland; and Denmark taking the lead in fund development either via the introduction of a "World Bank" three pillar pension model or simply via a strong element of private pensions ("the third pillar") besides the first, traditional PAYGO pillar (like presently in the United States of America). Slow pension fund development in most countries of the €-zone determines that the overall share of private pension funds from the €-zone is just over 2 % of world GDP. If Europe wants to fulfill its Lisbon agenda of catching up with the United States, it must, the argument runs, overhaul its pension systems and introduce some form or other of private pension funds, which are a major force in financing technological advance in the capitalist world economy today. Tausch (2004) showed that World Bank pension reforms are associated in a positive way with the rates of change of a country's performance to the better. Persistent non-reform, as the German example especially dramatically shows, can lead to a circulus viciosus of stagnation and unemployment under the conditions of globalization [see also Tausch A. (2004), Tausch A. (Ed.) (2003)].

The present publication is well within these traditions of cross-national, macro-political and macro-sociological research. The fundamental literature on the subject and recent highlights in the relevant methodological debate are assumed to be known here.

Our chosen 12 predictors measure the already achieved development level as an important control variable for possibly diminishing returns on capital, three important processes of economic history and geography (the transition process from Communism, access to the sea versus landlocked countries, urbanisation) as well as four dimensions of globalization, economic freedom versus state interventions and two variables, which measure possible counter-identities to the otherwise now "unified house of capitalism" – the percentage of Muslims per total population or membership in the European Union (EU-15).

The choice of a country to be included in the final analysis was determined by the availability of a complete data series for these independent variables (if not mentioned otherwise, UNDP data):

- development level ln (GDP PPP pc)
- development level, square (maturity effects) ln (GDP PPP pc)^2
- Dummy: landlocked country[25]
- Dummy: transition country[26]
- EU-15-membership (EU member by the year 2000, dummy variable)
- Foreign saving (I-S)/GNP (calculated from UNDP 2000)
- MNC PEN 1995 (UNCTAD)
- Percentage of Muslims per total population (Nationmaster[27])
- state interventionism (absence of economic freedom; Heritage Foundation and Wall Street Journal Website for economic freedom[28], 2000)
- unequal transfer (calculated from UNDP, concept: ERDI, reciprocal value of comparative "price levels" (developed on the basis of the ERD-Index Yotopoulos et al.)[29] (the Commission maintaining that a low value is good result)
- Urbanisation[30]
- World Bank pension reform[31]

These variables correspond to the following dimensions:

World economic openness and globalization

foreign saving [(I-S)/GNP]
low comparative international price level [ERD]
state interventionism (absence of economic. freedom)
transnational capital penetration [MNC PEN 1995]

---

[25] Taken from William Easterly, EXCEL data file freely available at http://www.cgdev.org/content/expert/detail/2699/
[26] Taken from William Easterly, EXCEL data file freely available at http://www.cgdev.org/content/expert/detail/2699/
[27] See nationmaster.com at http://www.nationmaster.com/graph/rel_isl_per_mus-religion-islam-percentage-muslim
[28] These data are contained in http://www.freetheworld.com/; also: http://www.heritage.org/research/features/index/. We used the latter website as the source of our data. It has to be kept in mind that the "worst" countries on the economic freedom scale have the numerically highest values, while the best countries have the numerically lowest values. Lao People's Dem. Rep. – the economically "unfreest" country in our sample, has the numerical value 4.6, while the economically freest country, Singapore, scores 1.45. We thus decided to call our indicator "state interventionism"
[29] It can be shown that the Eurostat data series GDP PPP per capita/GDP exchange rate per capita (EU-25=100), used for the "price level", in reality measure GDP exchange rate per capita/GDP PPP per capita (EU-25=100).
[30] Taken from William Easterly, EXCEL data file freely available at http://www.cgdev.org/content/expert/detail/2699/
[31] Argentina; Australia; Bolivia; Chile; Colombia; Croatia; Denmark; El Salvador; Hungary; Kazakhstan; Mexico; Netherlands; Peru; Poland; Sweden; Switzerland; United Kingdom; Uruguay

Percentage of the population adhering to the Muslim faith

Membership in the European Union

Geography

Dummy for being landlocked
Urbanization ratio, 1990

Recent world economic history

Dummy for transition economy
Development level and development level squared [ln(GDP PPP pc) and ln (GDP PPP pc)^2]

Pension Reform efforts

World Bank pension reform

Our list of the dependent variables corresponds to the new WVS indicators, presented in this work.

economic growth

global tolerance

active society

tradional values

inactive society

Asabiyya

Thus, we use the following regression equation:

(Equation 1) dependent variable = a_1 +- b_1*first part curvilinear function of development level +- b_2*second part curvilinear function of development level +- b_3 *stock of transnational investment per GDP (UNCTAD) $_{mid\ 1990s}$ +- b_4 * comparative price levels (ERDI) +- b_5 * foreign saving +- b_6 * dummy transition economy +- b_7 * percentage of the population adhering to the Muslim faith +- b_8 * European Union membership +- b_9 * state interventionism +- b_{10} * urbanisation +- b_{11} * dummy landlocked country +- b_{12} * dummy World Bank pension reform

To begin with, the active society paradigm indeed must be regarded as a serious contender for the explanation of differences in international economic growth rates. Urbanized and very mature economies have slower economic growth rates, while there is a considerable effect of income convergence in poorer countries. Dependency (foreign saving and low comparative price levels) are detrimental for economic growth, as foreseen by dependency theory, and in addition, an active society is good for global economic growth.

Table 16. The active society and World economic growth

Coefficients (a)						
Model		Unstandardized coefficients		Standardized coefficients	T	Error probability
		B	Standard error	Beta		
1	(Constant)	-1.573	1.313		-1.198	0.238
Dummy for being landlocked	VAR00002	-0.069	0.046	-0.189	-1.48	0.147
Dummy for transition economy	VAR00003	0.088	0.051	0.278	1.709	0.096
Urbanization ratio, 1990	VAR00004	-0.006	0.001	-0.852	-3.772	0.001
(I-S)/GNP	VAR00005	-0.006	0.003	-0.367	-2.294	0.027
state interventionism (absence of ec. freedom)	VAR00006	-0.051	0.046	-0.242	-1.107	0.275
MNC PEN 1995	VAR00007	0.002	0.002	0.217	1.63	0.111
low comparative international price level (ERD)	VAR00008	-0.057	0.028	-0.542	-2.047	0.048
EU-membership (EU-15)	VAR00009	-0.018	0.047	-0.056	-0.377	0.708
Muslims as % of total population	VAR00010	0	0.001	-0.052	-0.451	0.655
ln(GDP PPP pc)	VAR00011	0.617	0.332	4.22	1.858	0.071
ln (GDP PPP pc)^2	VAR00012	-0.035	0.02	-4.175	-1.721	0.093
world bank pension reform	VAR00013	0.031	0.044	0.088	0.699	0.489
unpaid social work	VAR00053	0.007	0.002	0.422	2.955	0.005
a	Dependent variable: VAR00023					

SPSS XIV and XV calculations, University Computing Center, Innsbruck University, based on the data of this work and our own calculations from World Values Survey, 3rd and 4th wave, http://www.worldvaluessurvey.org/. Adj R^2 = 0,458; F = 4,322, error p = .000; df = 51.

As we already stated, in the present study, we analyze

- economic growth
- global tolerance
- active society
- traditional values
- inactive society
- *Asabiyya*

as being determined by

World Economic Openness and Globalization

- foreign saving [(I-S)/GNP]
- low comparative international price level [ERD]
- state interventionism (absence of economic. freedom)
- transnational capital penetration [MNC PEN 1995]

Percentage of the Population Adhering to the Muslim Faith

Membership in the European Union

Geography

- Dummy for being landlocked
- Urbanization ratio, 1990

Recent World Economic History

- Dummy for transition economy
- Development level and development level squared [ln(GDP PPP pc) and ln (GDP PPP pc)^2]

Pension Reform Efforts

Our results largely confirm the theoretical reasoning, put forward in this publication, and almost half of the variations in economic growth rates are being determined by our chosen variables.

The active society accelerates economic growth, and also there are good conditions for economic convergence in the former communist countries nowadays. *Ceteris paribus* it also holds that premature urbanization, high foreign savings and a low comparative price level are a blockade against economic growth, as predicted by dependency theory.

There is a very strong "Kuznets" effect of global tolerance, with modernizing societies becoming more intolerant, before tolerance can spread. A fascinating theme for further research could be the trade-off between the well-known "Kuznets"-effect of international income inequalities and global (in)tolerance.

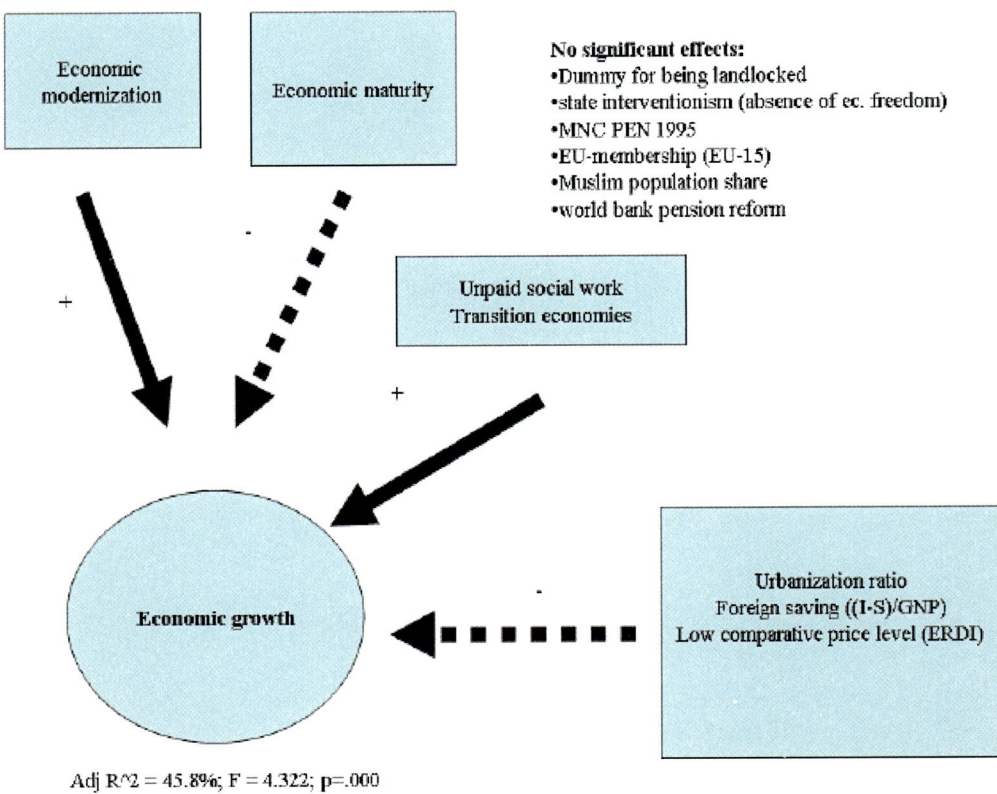

Graph 12. the determinants of economic growth.

SPSS XIV and XV calculations, University Computing Center, Innsbruck University, based on the data of this work and our own calculations from World Values Survey, 3rd and 4th wave, http://www.worldvaluessurvey.org/

Unfortunately, Muslim population shares–*ceteris paribus*–are a significant international predictor of intolerance; i.e., the tolerance-enhancing aspects of Islamic religion vis-à-vis such population groups and/or tolerance phenomena as

- People of a different race (WVS A125)
- Important child qualities: tolerance and respect for other people (WVS A035)
- Not saying: Jobs scarce: Men should have more right to a job than women (WVS C001
- Neighbors: Immigrants/foreign workers (WVS A129)
- Neighbors: Homosexuals (WVS A132)

could well be underlined in future political action by the political forces, committed to the aims of tolerance and Enlightenment. What obviously happens is that important segments of the Muslim global population practice *"Asabiyya number 2"*, about, which the famous *Hadith* 13035 states:

"One who calls towards Asabiyyah is not from us, one who fights for Asabiyyah is not from us and the one who dies on Asabiyyah is not from us." [Mizan al Hikmah, Hadith # 13035].

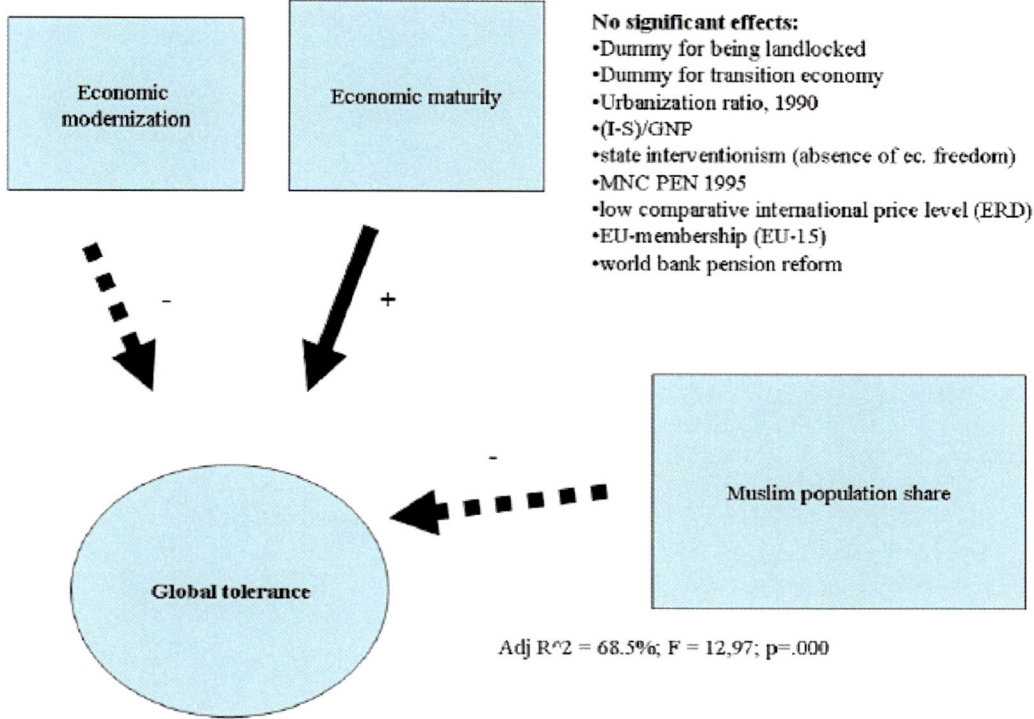

Graph 13. the cross-national determinants of global tolerance.

SPSS XIV and XV calculations, University Computing Center, Innsbruck University, based on the data of this work and our own calculations from World Values Survey, 3rd and 4th wave, http://www.worldvaluessurvey.org/

There is also a Kuznets-type of effect on active society rates. Only rich and mature societies, as a rule, gain what they initially lost in terms of voluntary social organizations, and landlocked and urbanized societies are significantly less involved in voluntary social work as non-urbanized societies and nations with a maritime tradition.

An inverse Kuznets-type of relationship also holds for the determination of traditional values: poor societies are traditional and rich societies non-traditional, while Muslim population shares, irrespective of development levels, are closely bound to traditional values. EU membership and World Bank pension reforms both shatter the prevalence of traditional values. EU membership has such effects, because in the long run the Union indeed is unthinkable as not being a community of modern, enlightened values. And pension reform, because traditional patterns of social security, based on the pay-as-you-go principle of Bismarckian pensions are very much related to non-market, traditionalist thinking of late 19th Century Europe. Not without coincidence, the staunchest resistance against World Bank inspired pension reforms is to be encountered in the West European Catholic nations.

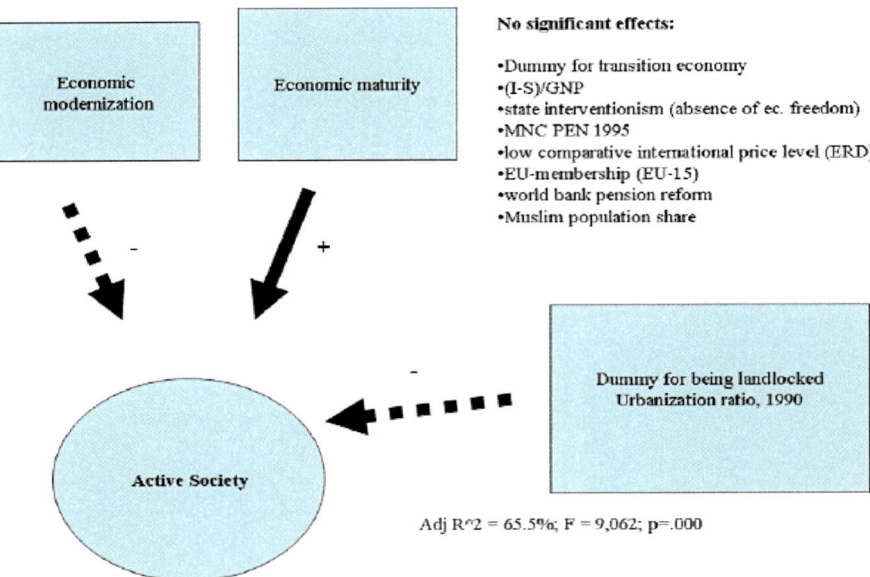

Graph 14. the cross-national determinants of the active society.

SPSS XIV and XV calculations, University Computing Center, Innsbruck University, based on the data of this work and our own calculations from World Values Survey, 3rd and 4th wave, http://www.worldvaluessurvey.org/

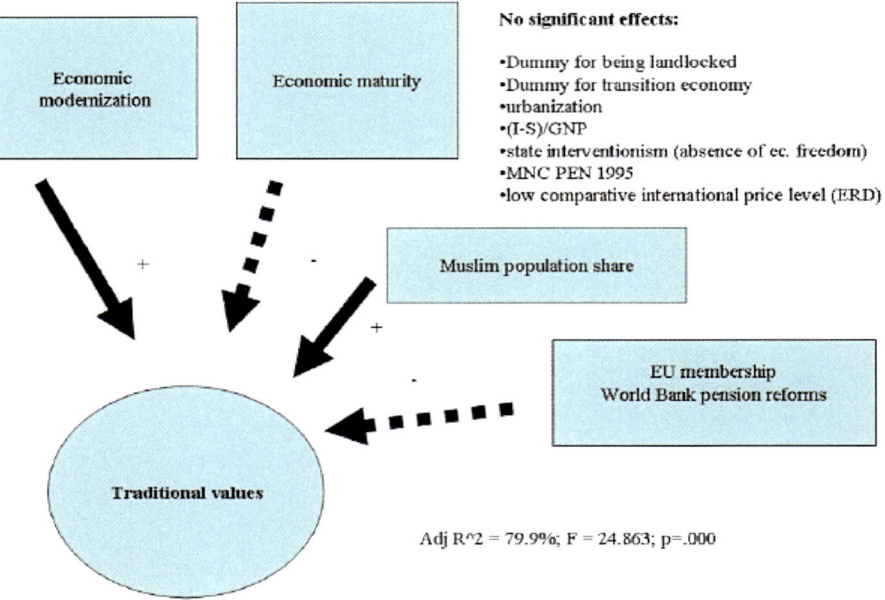

Graph 15. the cross-national determinants of traditional values.

SPSS XIV and XV calculations, University Computing Center, Innsbruck University, based on the data of this work and our own calculations from World Values Survey, 3rd and 4th wave, http://www.worldvaluessurvey.org/

The intransparent, inactive, cheating society is, just as the phenomenon of inequality and intolerance, a by-product of the modernization process, and decreases at high stages of achieved economic growth. As to be expected by non-secular Muslims throughout the globe, Islam indeed is a blockade against these phenomena of decay, underlying the strict consequences of the religious belief system for everyday life (in difference to many lamentable aspects of Catholicism, which is, as we shall analyze below, much more "Sunday" oriented than Islam and Judaism). Landlocked and transition societies all suffer from higher rates of inactiveness and lack of transparency, and all the sleaze and corruption that go with it. Urbanized societies are more prone to these phenomena than rural societies; and EU membership is, lamentably enough, not a blockade against it, but – *ceteris paribus* – even an incentive for such phenomena. Just figure out recent press reports that around 12% of the EU's 308 billion Euro cohesion funds end up in dark channels, while Europe desperately would need more social cohesion among its many different regions. Finally, World Bank pension reforms were usually implemented in countries, which are good disciples of the two Bretton Woods financial institutions, which decidedly fight corruption:

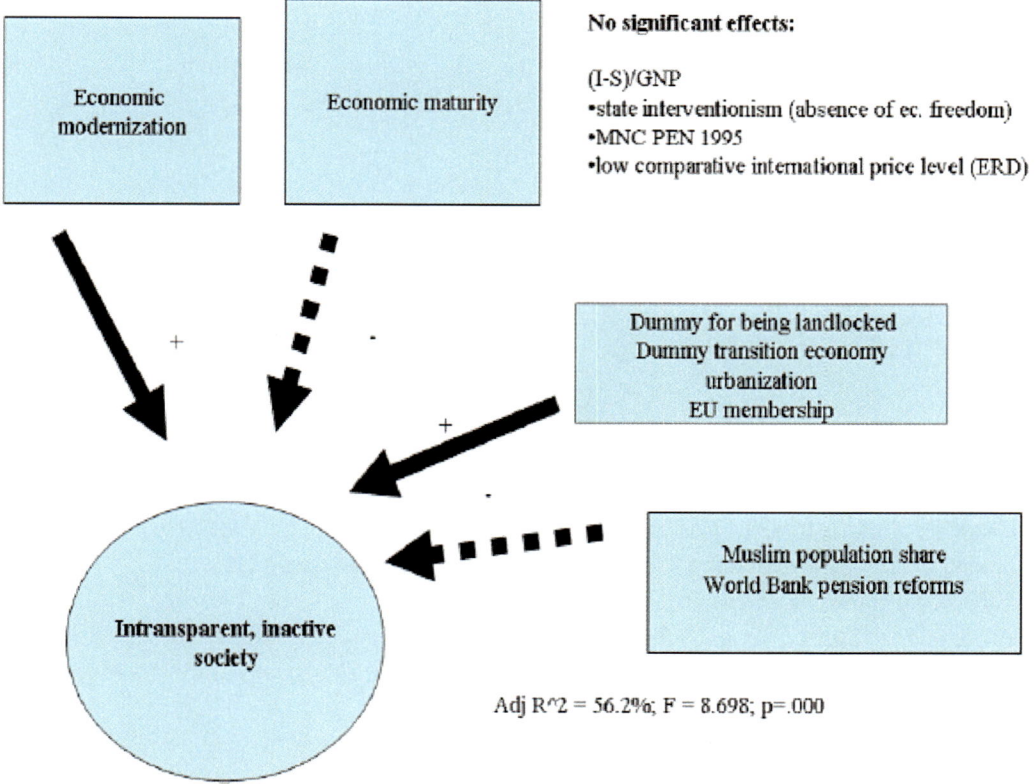

Graph 16. the cross-national determinants of the intransparent, inactive society.

SPSS XIV and XV calculations, University Computing Center, Innsbruck University, based on the data of this work and our own calculations from World Values Survey, 3rd and 4th wave, http://www.worldvaluessurvey.org/

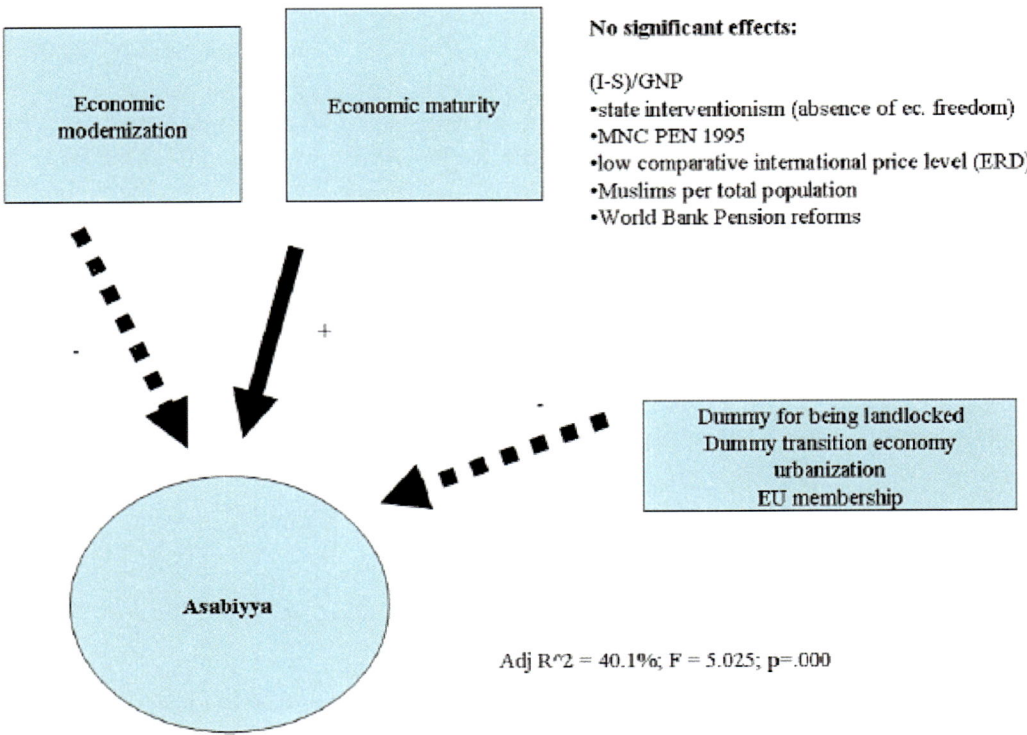

Graph 17. the cross-national determinants of *"Asabiyya"*.

SPSS XIV and XV calculations, University Computing Center, Innsbruck University, based on the data of this work and our own calculations from World Values Survey, 3rd and 4th wave, http://www.worldvaluessurvey.org/

Our final analysis looks at the cross-national determinants of *Asabiyya*. What happens is that again there is a Kuznets-type of relationship, with *Asabiyya* diminishing at middle stages of development, and only later again increasing. Urbanized, landlocked, and transition countries all show much lower kinds of *Asabiyya* as their rural, maritime and non-ex-Warsaw-Pact counterparts. Very bad for the European Union, their member countries are characterized by a lower degree of *Asabiyya* than their non-EU counterparts.

The consequences of this are pretty dire: Especially in East Central Europe, the degree of social *Asabiyya* will be very low by international comparison, and national identity crises and questions about national identity will prop up, the longer European Union membership is already established.

The hard and sometimes bitter medicine against all this can only be a policy and a spirit of Enlightenment and tolerance of an open society in the sense of Sir Karl Popper.

While globalization and dependency play a pivotal role in the determination of economic growth rates, as predicted by dependency theory, the effects of dependency and globalization on

- Global tolerance
- The active society
- Traditional values

- The inactive, intransparent society
- *Asabiyya*

are rather to be neglected.

In the next chapter of this work, we systematically look at identities, phobias and the way these are connected with religious denominations.

Chapter 9

"WHO ARE WE"?: A FACTOR ANALYSIS OF GLOBAL VALUE DIFFERENCES

With his works on global cultures and the identity of the leading rich Western democracy nowadays, Huntington (1996 and 2004) has set the trend for current writing and thinking about global cultures.

In view of the huge qualitative international debate on intercultural dialogue, world religions and global tolerance, we decided to start a first truly comparative research into the differences between the major global civilizations on the basis of the World Values Survey data. In all, the SPSS format data, as downloaded from the University of Michigan Website, list 975 variables.

We introduced the proper SPSS weights for country size (1000-weights) into the analysis.

After long deliberations and explorative trials, and keeping in mind that many of the variables of the WVS data set do not render themselves at all for multivariate analysis (see our appendix), we finally included 291 variables with sufficient observations for the major global religious civilizations into our final analysis of the percentage differences of the means of each of the 291 variables from the global mean. The global means and the global means for all the religious groups are documented as well in the appendix. Any member of a religious denomination is considered as "practicing" if she or he attends religious services of his or her denomination at least once a month or more often. The religious groups of our analysis are:

- Buddhism
- Catholicism
- Hinduism
- Judaism
- Muslims
- Orthodoxy
- Practicing Catholicism
- Practicing Islam
- Practicing Orthodoxy
- Practicing Protestantism
- Protestantism

	N Muslim sample	Minimum	Maximum	Global Islam mean	Global Protestantism - mean	Global Catholicism - mean	Global Judaism - mean	Global Orthodoxy - mean	Global Hinduism - mean	Global Buddhism - mean	Global practicing Catholicism - mean	Global citizens - mean
A woman has to have children to be fulfilled	18138	0	1	0.830	0.440	0.580	0.600	0.800	0.860	0.710	0.580	0.610
How important is God in your life	18604	1	10	9.190	6.350	7.850	7.270	7.000	8.150	5.880	8.880	6.930

SPSS XIV and XV calculations as well as Microsoft EXCEL 2000 and 2003 calculations, University Computing Center, Innsbruck University, based on the data of this work and our own calculations from World Values Survey, 3rd and 4th wave, http://www.worldvaluessurvey.org/

From such data we now deduced the following *291 percentage differences* from the global means, which included all the respondents of the World Values Surveys, believers and non-believers, adherents of religious denominations and people without religion, alike:

	Muslims	Judaism	Hinduism	Orthodoxy	Buddhism	Protestantism	Catholicism	Practicing Orthodoxy	Practicing Islam	Practicing Catholicism	Practicing Protestantism
A woman has to have children to be fulfilled	36.1	-1.6	41.0	31.1	16.4	-27.9	-4.9	34.4	41.0	-4.9	-16.4
God important in your life	32.6	4.9	17.6	1.0	-15.2	-8.4	13.3	22.5	38.7	27.1	27.0

SPSS XIV and XV calculations as well as Microsoft EXCEL 2000 and 2003 calculations, University Computing Center, Innsbruck University, based on the data of this work and our own calculations from World Values Survey, 3rd and 4th wave, http://www.worldvaluessurvey.org/

To further explain our *omnibus* research design, never attempted before in global social research to check the perceived or the real differences between the global civilizations we show here the global means for two of the 291 variable results (all documented in the appendix) – the global mean responses to two WVS questions on gender issues *(a woman has to have children to be fulfilled)* and religious identity *(how important is God in your life)*. More than 18.000 global Muslims gave an answer to these two WVS questions. On global average, it turns out that global Hindus agreed strongest and global Protestants weakest with the sentence that *"a woman has to have children to be fulfilled"*. Predictably, Muslims and practicing Catholics gave the highest importance to God in their life, while Buddhists gave the weakest importance to God in their life.

The usual social science research answer to such a type of given data situation would be to draw a Graph, showing the differences between the various denominations on just two scales – gender and importance of God to personal life:

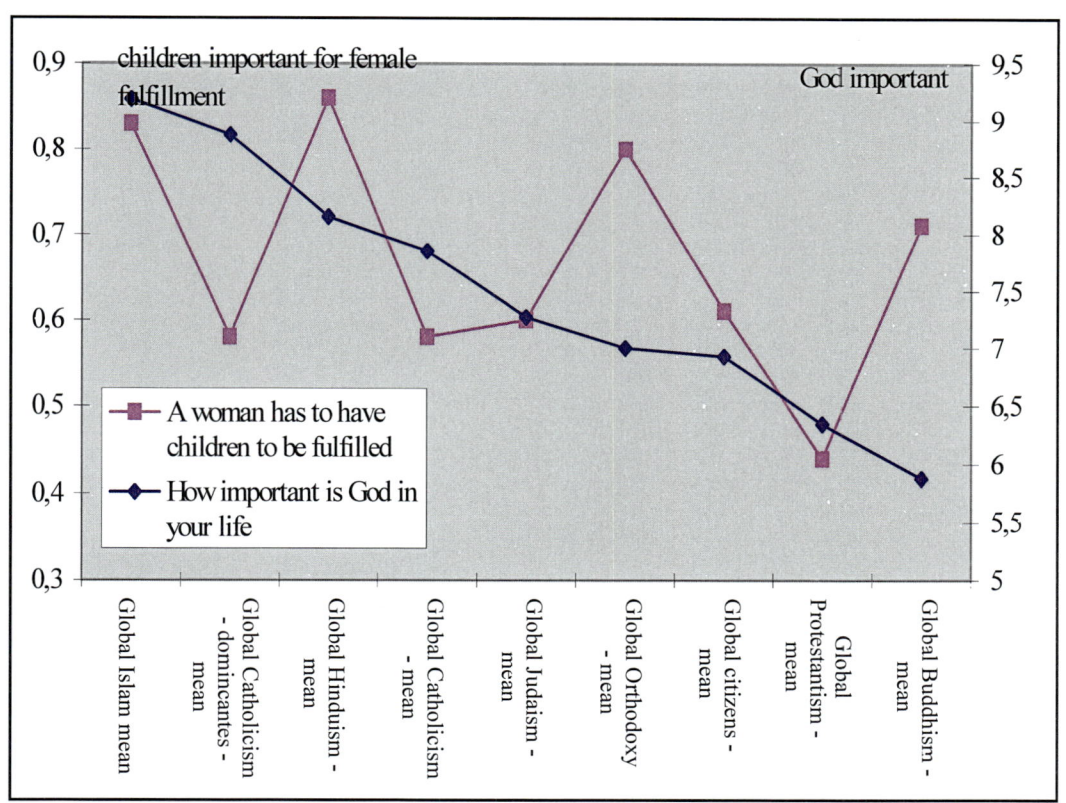

Graph 18. Differences between the global civilizations – the usual standard approach.

SPSS XIV and XV calculations as well as Microsoft EXCEL 2000 and 2003 calculations, University Computing Center, Innsbruck University, based on the data of this work and our own calculations from World Values Survey, 3rd and 4th wave, http://www.worldvaluessurvey.org/.

Although this Graph already tells us a lot about the daily practice-relevant belief and value systems of adherents of major world religions, a two or even ten or twenty variable comparisons will not be sufficient in the long run to catch the major underlying dimensions. Practicing Catholics, for example, will be far less inclined to say that a woman has to have children in order to be fulfilled as originally suggested by their "traditional" mindset of giving importance to God in their life originally suggests. Orthodox and Buddhists, on the other hand, are far more traditional in their gender attitude than in their religious belief in God. In Graph 19 we now show our research design, which tries to integrate all the dimensions of the World Values Survey at once[32]:

---

[32] It is important to check for sample sizes, sample compositions et cetera to carefully evaluate the results. Let us mention here, for example, the dimension of "lying" and its supposed admissibility. Using the sample: Selected samples: Albania [1998], Albania [2002], Algeria [2002], Argentina [1984], Argentina [1991], Argentina [1995], Argentina [1999], Armenia [1997], Australia [1981], Australia [1995], Austria [1990], Austria [1999], Azerbaijan [1997], Bangladesh [1996], Bangladesh [2002], Belarus [1990], Belarus [1996], Belarus [2000], Belgium [1981], Belgium [1990], Belgium [1999], Bosnia and Herzegovina [1998], Bosnia and Herzegovina [2001], Brazil [1991], Brazil [1997], Bulgaria [1990], Bulgaria [1997], Bulgaria [1999], Canada [1982], Canada [1990], Canada [2000], Chile [1990], Chile [1996], Chile [2000], China [1990], China [1995], China [2001], Colombia [1997], Colombia [1998], Croatia [1996], Croatia [1999], Czech Republic [1990], Czech Republic [1991], Czech Republic [1998], Czech Republic [1999], Denmark [1981], Denmark [1990], Denmark [1999], Dominican Republic [1996], Egypt [2000], El Salvador [1999], Estonia [1990], Estonia [1996], Estonia [1999], Finland [1990], Finland [1996], Finland [2000], France [1981], France [1990], France [1999], Georgia [1996], Germany East [1990], Germany East [1997], Germany East [1999], Germany West [1981], Germany West [1990], Germany West [1997], Germany West [1999], Great Britain [1981], Great Britain [1990], Great Britain [1998], Great Britain [1999], Greece [1999], Hungary [1982], Hungary [1991], Hungary [1998], Hungary [1999], Iceland [1984], Iceland [1990], Iceland [1999], India [1990], India [1995], India [2001], Indonesia [2001], Iran (Islamic Republic of) [2000], Iraq [2004], Ireland [1981], Ireland [1990], Ireland [1999], Israel [2001], Italy [1981], Italy [1990], Italy [1999], Japan [1981], Japan [1990], Japan [1995], Japan [2000], Jordan [2001], Kyrgyzstan [2003], Latvia [1990], Latvia [1996], Latvia [1999], Lithuania [1990], Lithuania [1997], Lithuania [1999], Luxembourg [1999], Macedonia, Republic of [1998], Macedonia, Republic of [2001], Malta [1983], Malta [1991], Malta [1999], Mexico [1990], Mexico [1996], Mexico [2000], Montenegro [1996], Montenegro [2001], Morocco [2001], Morocco [2001], Netherlands [1981], Netherlands [1990], Netherlands [1999], New Zealand [1998], Nigeria [1990], Nigeria [1995], Nigeria [2000], Northern Ireland [1981], Northern Ireland [1990], Northern Ireland [1999], Norway [1982], Norway [1990], Norway [1996], Pakistan [1997], Pakistan [2001], Peru [1996], Peru [2001], Philippines [1996], Philippines [2001], Poland [1989], Poland [1990], Poland [1997], Poland [1999], Portugal [1990], Portugal [1999], Puerto Rico [1995], Puerto Rico [2001], Republic of Korea [1982], Republic of Korea [1990], Republic of Korea [1996], Republic of Korea [2001], Republic of Moldova [1996], Republic of Moldova [2002], Romania [1993], Romania [1998], Romania [1999], Russian Federation [1990], Russian Federation [1995], Russian Federation [1999], Saudi Arabia [2003], Serbia [1996], Serbia [2001], Singapore [2002], Slovakia [1990], Slovakia [1991], Slovakia [1998], Slovakia [1999], Slovenia [1992], Slovenia [1995], Slovenia [1999], South Africa [1990], South Africa [1996], South Africa [2001], Spain [1981], Spain [1990], Spain [1990], Spain [1995], Spain [1999], Spain [2000], Sweden [1982], Sweden [1990], Sweden [1996], Sweden [1999], Switzerland [1989], Switzerland [1996], Taiwan [1994], Tanzania, United Republic Of [2001], Turkey [1990], Turkey [1996], Turkey [2001], Turkey [2001], Uganda [2001], Ukraine [1996], Ukraine [1999], United States [1982], United States [1990], United States [1995], United States [1999], Uruguay [1996], Venezuela [1996], Venezuela [2000], Viet Nam [2001], Zimbabwe [2001] we first have to make sure what the question is. It is formulated like this: F127. Please tell me for each of the following statements whether you think it can always be justified, never be justified, or something in between, using this card. (Read out statements. Code one answer for each statement). Lying in your own interest (The list ranges from 1 Never justifiable to 10 – always justifiable). We then arrive at the following denomination-specific global means: 88223 global citizens – mean 2.65 et cetera. For Anglicans and Jews, for example, the sample size is below 300, so that the error margin even at a 10% significance level is quite high (almost +-5%). For this reason, results for smaller religious communities, like Anglicans and Jews, have to be treated with utmost statistical care in any WVS analysis.

"Who Are We"?: A Factor Analysis of Global Value Differences

		1	2	3	4	5	6	7	8	9	10	11
		Musl im	Juda ism	Hind uism	Orth odox y	Bud dhis m	Prot estan tism	Cath olici sm	Pract icing Orth odox y	Pract icing Isla m	Pract icing Cath olici sm	Pract icing Prot estan tism
1	A woman has to have children to be fulfilled											
2	Abortion if not wanting more children											
3	Abortion when child physically handicapped											
4	Abortion when the mother's health is at risk											
5	Abortion when woman not married											

$v = 11$

$n = 291$

Graph 19. The factor analytical research design – the data matrix for the analysis.

The identification of the factors in such a design will rest on a close inspection of the factor scores (see appendix, and Tables 17b and following). Contrary to standard factor analysis, where the variables of the World Values Survey would be "variables" of a factor analysis, and the world religious groups the "individuals", our analysis thus had to invert a classical data matrix. With 291 types of responses to the World Values Survey questionnaire, given by the aggregates of the 11 religious groups chosen for comparison here, we had no other choice but to invert the matrix. Three factors in our orthogonal standard SPSS XIV and XV research design have an Eigenvalue of greater or equal to 1.0.

Our results again show the overwhelming importance of the concepts and analyses of Amitai Etzioni for understanding the true underlying dimensions of global value change. The active society factor explains 36.6% of total variance, while the phobia factor explains 24.4% of total variance, and the "homo Catholicus" factor 19.7%. In all, the three factors explain 80.7% of the total variance of value systems in the world, as measured by 291 WVS indicators.

Table 17a now shows the factor scores of factor 1 (active society) greater or equal to +- 1. The table clearly explains what is to be understood by an "active society"

Table 17a. a factor analytical model of global civilizations
factor loadings of the new extracted factors for the 11 variables of the model
(the 11 main global religious civilizations)

	Factor 1 Active society	Factor 2 communautarianism, phobia	Factor 3 homo Catholicus
Muslims	0.742	0.596	-0.084
Judaism	0.821	-0.219	-0.122
Hinduism	0.731	0.523	-0.206
Orthodoxy	-0.650	0.637	-0.162
Buddhism	0.484	0.254	-0.264
Protestantism	0.433	-0.757	0.198
Catholicism	-0.242	0.209	0.850
Practicing Orthodoxy	-0.234	0.806	0.355
Practicing Islam	0.830	0.436	-0.061
Practicing Catholicism	0.231	0.144	0.934
Practicing Protestantism	0.754	-0.243	0.496

SPSS XIV and XV calculations, University Computing Center, Innsbruck University, based on the data of this work and our own calculations from World Values Survey, 3rd and 4th wave, http://www.worldvaluessurvey.org/.

Explained total variance

Component	Initial Eigenvalues			Sums of squared factor loadings for extraction		
	Total	% of variance	cumulated %	Total	% of variance	cumulated %
1	4.026	36.604	36.604	4.026	36.604	36.604
2	2.684	24.396	60.999	2.684	24.396	60.999
3	2.169	19.717	80.716	2.169	19.717	80.716
4	.836	7.598	88.314			
5	.480	4.363	92.677			
6	.278	2.530	95.207			
7	.244	2.215	97.422			
8	.157	1.423	98.846			
9	.062	.566	99.412			
10	.048	.432	99.844			
11	.017	.156	100.000			

Extraction method: principal components

SPSS XIV and XV calculations, University Computing Center, Innsbruck University, based on the data of this work and our own calculations from World Values Survey, 3rd and 4th wave, http://www.worldvaluessurvey.org/.

Table 17b. Factor scores for the factor "active society"

	Factor 1 Active society
Unpaid work peace movement	7.352
Belong to peace movement	4.029
Belong to women's group	3.398
Unpaid work women's group	3.374
Unpaid work organization concerned with health	3.347
Belong to religious organization	3.251
Unpaid work religious or church organization	3.233
Belong to local political actions	3.134
Unpaid work local political action groups	2.815
Unpaid work youth work	2.564
Belong to organization concerned with health	2.461
Belong to youth work	2.439
Belong to social welfare service for elderly	2.353
Unpaid work human rights	2.169
Rejecting neighbors: People with large families	2.119
Belong to human rights	2.081
Unpaid work other groups	2.079
Unpaid work social welfare service for elderly, handicapped or deprived people	2.059
Unpaid work professional associations	2.057
Unpaid work environment, conservation, animal rights	1.993
Unpaid work political parties or groups	1.972
Belong to professional associations	1.888
Belong to education, arts, music or cultural activities	1.885
Unpaid work education, arts, music or cultural activities	1.854
Belong to conservation, the environment, ecology, animal rights	1.694
Belong to political parties	1.533
Belong to other groups	1.351
Active/Inactive membership of charitable/humanitarian organization	1.307
Unpaid work sports or recreation	1.167
Active/Inactive membership of any other organization	1.156
Active/Inactive membership of church or religious organization	1.046
Belong to sports or recreation	1.046
Justifiable: avoiding a fare on public transport	-1.003
Ever felt very excited or interested	-1.107
Ever felt that things were going your way	-1.194
Ever felt proud because someone complimented you	-1.357
Ever felt restless	-1.447
Ever felt on top of the world	-1.478
Ever felt bored	-1.481
Ever felt depressed or very unhappy	-1.494
Ever felt very lonely or remote from other people	-1.579
Ever felt upset because somebody criticized you	-1.591
Sharing with parents: no sharing attitudes	-1.799

SPSS XIV and XV calculations, University Computing Center, Innsbruck University, based on the data of this work and our own calculations from World Values Survey, 3rd and 4th wave, http://www.worldvaluessurvey.org/.

Practicing Islam, Judaism, and practicing Protestantism are the superstars of the "Etzioni paradigm", while Orthodoxy, Catholicism, and practicing Orthodoxy are the cultures, presently least inclined towards an "active society".

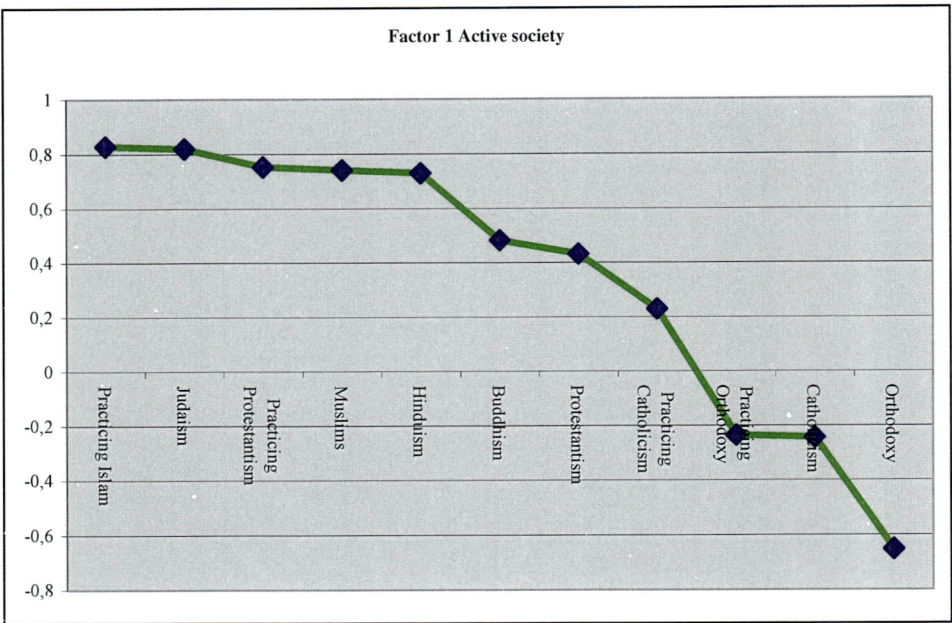

Graph 20. Factor 1 – the active society.

Note: based on a factor analysis of the percentage differences of ALL *World Values Survey* variables, all waves, from the global mean, working with the subsamples of the following religious groups: Muslims; Judaism; Hinduism; Orthodoxy; Buddhism; Protestantism; Catholicism; Practicing Orthodoxy; Practicing Islam; Practicing Catholicism; Practicing Protestantism. "Practicing" was understood to comprise all those religious denomination members, whose regular religious service attendance rate was once greater or equal to once a month or more frequent. Only those WVS variables, which rendered themselves for a multivariate analysis due to their scales, were included in the final analysis. As a further rule, we included only those variables with more than 50 global observations even for the smallest religious groups in question. The list of variables, the global means, and the percentage differences from the global means are all documented in the appendix to this work. Our results are based on SPSS XIV calculations, Innsbruck University, 2008. We used standard orthogonal factor rotation, and the *Eigenvalue* criterion *Eigenvalues* greater or equal to 1. The free data download in SPSS format is available from the WVS Website (data downloads).

The next factor, which combines pretty alarming phenomena of xenophobia and racism with a kind of proto-socialist communautarianism and trade-unionism, and, which we call "communautarianism and phobias", is described in the following way by the factor scores higher or equal than +-1:

Table 17c. Factor scores for the factor "communautarianism and phobia"

	Factor 2 communautarianism, phobia
Unpaid work peace movement	5.445
Rejecting neighbors: People with large families	4.163
Rejecting neighbors: Jews	3.761
Unpaid work labor unions	2.727
Rejecting neighbors: People of a different race	2.635
Believe in: re-incarnation	2.297
Rejecting neighbors: People who have AIDS	2.116
Important child qualities: hard work	2.034
Rejecting neighbors: Immigrants/foreign workers	1.903
Believe in: devil	1.856
Believe in: hell	1.839
Important child qualities: religious faith	1.806
A woman has to have children to be fulfilled	1.799
Rejecting neighbors: Homosexuals	1.793
Rejecting neighbors: Left wing extremists	1.767
Rejecting neighbors: Emotionally unstable people	1.716
Important in a job: a useful job for society	1.626
Important in a job: good chances for promotion	1.606
Get comfort and strength from religion	1.435
Unpaid work local political action groups	1.418
Rejecting neighbors: Right wing extremists	1.407
Important in a job: a respected job	1.376
Rejecting neighbors: Muslims	1.347
Rejecting neighbors: People with a criminal record	1.336
Moments of prayer, meditation...	1.311
Important child qualities: thrift saving money and things	1.17
Believe in: sin	1.162
Churches give answers: moral problems	1.069
Sharing with parents: attitudes towards religion	1.041
Belong to organization concerned with health	-1.009
Belong to education, arts, music or cultural activities	-1.027
Environmental action: attend meeting, signed petition	-1.048
Belong to women's group	-1.085
Justifiable: suicide	-1.086

Table 17c. (Continued)

	Factor 2 communautarianism, phobia
Environmental action: contributed to environmental organization	-1.087
Unpaid work social welfare service for elderly, handicapped or deprived people	-1.168
Justifiable: prostitution	-1.223
Active/Inactive membership of church or religious organization	-1.297
Environmental action: chosen products that are better for environment	-1.327
Never attend religious services	-1.365
Sharing with parents: no sharing attitudes	-1.388
Active/Inactive membership of environmental organization	-1.424
Unpaid work professional associations	-1.496
Unpaid work sports or recreation	-1.504
Environmental action: recycle	-1.605
Belong to youth work	-1.647
Unpaid work youth work	-1.747
Belong to human rights	-1.824
Active/Inactive membership of professional organization	-1.87
Belong to professional associations	-1.932
Justifiable: homosexuality	-1.933
Active/Inactive membership of art, music, educational	-2.033
Belong to social welfare service for elderly	-2.142
Unpaid work other groups	-2.164
Active/Inactive membership of charitable/humanitarian organization	-2.252
Belong to religious organization	-2.338
Active/Inactive membership of sport or recreation	-2.659
Belong to labor unions	-2.782
Belong to sports or recreation	-2.815
Belong to other groups	-2.949
Active/Inactive membership of any other organization	-2.975

SPSS XIV and XV calculations, University Computing Center, Innsbruck University, based on the data of this work and our own calculations from World Values Survey, 3rd and 4th wave, http://www.worldvaluessurvey.org/.

This value structure is strongest among practicing Orthodox, Orthodox and Muslims (less so among the practicing ones), while Protestantism, practicing Protestantism and Judaism are very far from such a value set. Typically, these results can also be interpreted as a scale on how *de facto* values of the active society, market economy, democracy and the Enlightenment are present or absent among the different publics of the different denominations around the globe.

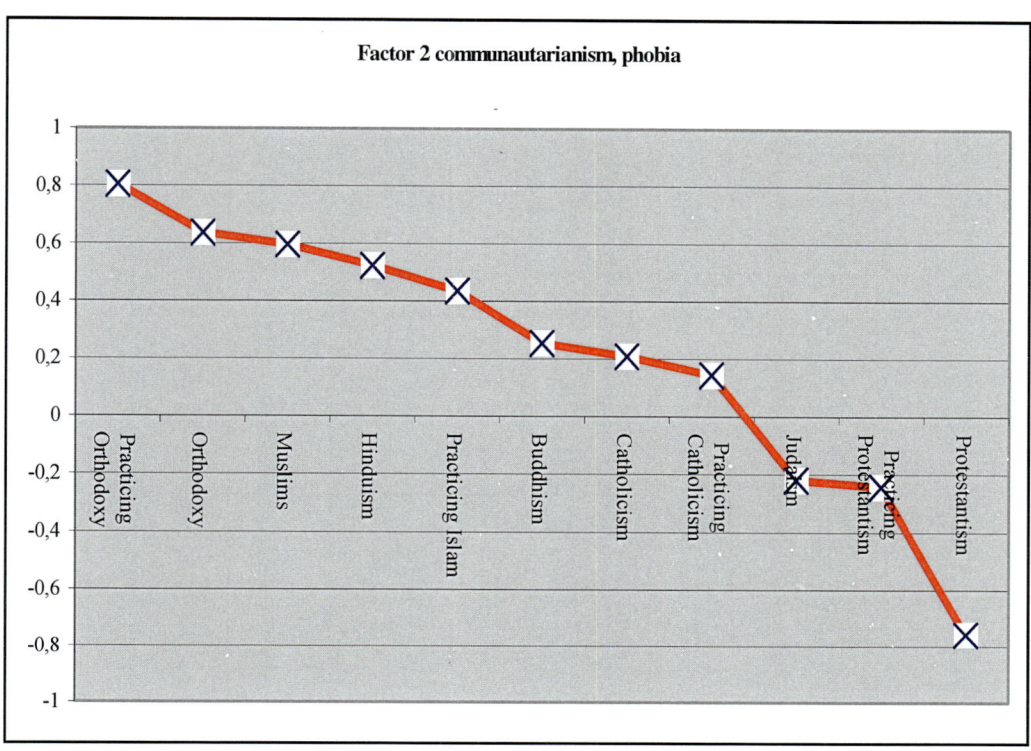

Graph 21. Factor 2: communautarianism and phobias.

Note: based on a factor analysis of the percentage differences of ALL *World Values Survey* variables, all waves, from the global mean, working with the subsamples of the following religious groups: Muslims; Judaism; Hinduism; Orthodoxy; Buddhism; Protestantism; Catholicism; Practicing Orthodoxy; Practicing Islam; Practicing Catholicism; Practicing Protestantism. "Practicing" was understood to comprise all those religious denomination members, whose regular religious service attendance rate was once greater or equal to once a month or more frequent. Only those WVS variables, which rendered themselves for a multivariate analysis due to their scales, were included in the final analysis. As a further rule, we included only those variables with more than 50 global observations even for the smallest religious groups in question. The list of variables, the global means, and the percentage differences from the global means are all documented in the appendix to this work. Our results are based on SPSS XIV calculations, Innsbruck University, 2008. We used standard orthogonal factor rotation, and the *Eigenvalue* criterion *Eigenvalues* greater or equal to 1. The free data download in SPSS format is available from the WVS Website (data downloads).

Table 17d now explains the factor loadings of the next and last factor, which we are calling the **"homo Catholicus"**.

Indeed, the factor combines all the characteristics of what is commonly associated with a "good Catholic" – belonging to the Church structures, celebrating Sunday, educating children to be good believers, but not educating children to be independent. Good Catholics will believe in devil and heaven, but they will be comparatively less participating in human rights organizations.

Table 17d. Factor scores for the factor "homo Catholicus"

	homo Catholicus
Active/Inactive membership of church or religious organization	5.117
Unpaid work religious or church organization	3.573
Important child qualities: religious faith	3.478
Belong to religious organization	3.407
Raised religiously	2.745
Believe in: devil	2.649
Believe in: heaven	2.287
Churches give answers: the social problems	2.213
Churches give answers: the problems of family life	2.119
Moments of prayer, meditation...	2.11
Important: Religious service birth	2.078
Get comfort and strength from religion	2.053
Believe in: sin	1.993
Believe in: life after death	1.992
Environmental action: contributed to environmental organization	1.982
Environmental action: attend meeting, signed petition	1.938
Important: Religious service marriage	1.936
Active/Inactive membership of charitable/humanitarian organization	1.832
Believe in: hell	1.809
Churches give answers: moral problems	1.588
Sharing with parents: attitudes towards religion	1.516
God important in your life	1.473
Sharing with parents: sexual attitudes	1.451
Churches give answers: people's spiritual needs	1.323
Believe in: God	1.29
Belong to youth work	1.236
Important: Religious service death	1.205
Belong to women's group	1.203
Believe in: people have a soul	1.177
Active/Inactive membership of environmental organization	1.078
Rejecting neighbors: Emotionally unstable people	-1.029
not spend time with people at your church, mosque or synagogue	-1.037
Rejecting neighbors: Right wing extremists	-1.038

	homo Catholicus
Justifiable: adultery	-1.06
Justifiable: euthanasia	-1.063
Unpaid work women's group	-1.186
Belong to conservation, the environment, ecology, animal rights	-1.193
Rejecting neighbors: Political Extremists	-1.246
Important child qualities: imagination	-1.249
no religious person	-1.255
Active/Inactive membership of labor unions	-1.266
Unpaid work education, arts, music or cultural activities	-1.278
Important child qualities: independence	-1.31
Important child qualities: determination perseverance	-1.311
No confidence: Churches	-1.317
Abortion when child physically handicapped	-1.368
Justifiable: abortion	-1.374
Belong to political parties	-1.379
Religion not important in life	-1.406
Rejecting neighbors: Immigrants/foreign workers	-1.42
Unpaid work peace movement	-1.549
Rejecting neighbors: People with large families	-2.014
Belong to labor unions	-2.139
Unpaid work human rights	-2.175
Unpaid work professional associations	-2.195
Never pray to God outside of religious services (I)	-2.262
Unpaid work environment, conservation, animal rights	-2.303
Sharing with parents: no sharing attitudes	-2.339
Unpaid work political parties or groups	-2.624
Never attend religious services	-2.655
Belong to peace movement	-2.695
Abortion when woman not married	-3.182
Abortion if not wanting more children	-3.278

SPSS XIV and XV calculations, University Computing Center, Innsbruck University, based on the data of this work and our own calculations from World Values Survey, 3rd and 4th wave, http://www.worldvaluessurvey.org/.

Apart from the practicing Catholics, and the global Catholics in general, practicing Protestants and practicing Orthodox still share some of the characteristics of the "Catholic" mindset. Buddhism and Hinduism are the real counter-models to this type of tradition.

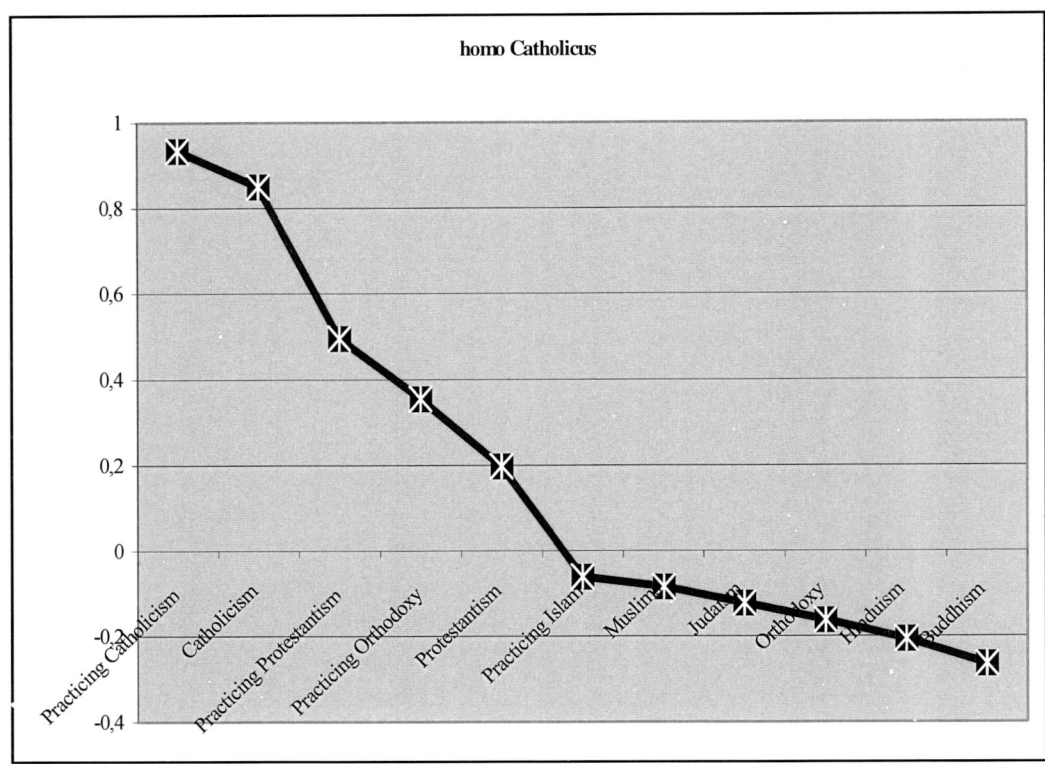

Graph 22. The "fiesta" is the message – the *homo Catolicus*.

Note: based on a factor analysis of the percentage differences of ALL *World Values Survey* variables, all waves, from the global mean, working with the subsamples of the following religious groups: Muslims; Judaism; Hinduism; Orthodoxy; Buddhism; Protestantism; Catholicism; Practicing Orthodoxy; Practicing Islam; Practicing Catholicism; Practicing Protestantism. "Practicing" was understood to comprise all those religious denomination members, whose regular religious service attendance rate was once greater or equal to once a month or more frequent. Only those WVS variables, which rendered themselves for a multivariate analysis due to their scales, were included in the final analysis. As a further rule, we included only those variables with more than 50 global observations even for the smallest religious groups in question. The list of variables, the global means, and the percentage differences from the global means are all documented in the appendix to this work. Our results are based on SPSS XIV calculations, Innsbruck University, 2008. We used standard orthogonal factor rotation, and the *Eigenvalue* criterion *Eigenvalues* greater or equal to 1. The free data download in SPSS format is available from the WVS Website (data downloads).

Where are then the real differences? In the following, we will now map the value differences from the global mean for all the major religious civilizations under consideration here. We concentrate our investigations only on the numerically very large religious groups, in order to avoid errors due to small sample sizes:

Global Buddhists are 25% or more above the global average for the following indicators:

- Rejecting neighbors: People with large families
- Believe in: re-incarnation
- Unpaid work peace movement

- Rejecting neighbors: Jews
- Belong to local political actions
- Poverty compared to 10 years ago decreased
- Unpaid work social welfare service for elderly, handicapped or deprived people
- Unpaid work other groups
- Unpaid work local political action groups
- Unpaid work women's group
- Environmental action: recycle
- Rejecting neighbors: Right wing extremists
- Belong to organization concerned with health
- Belong to women's group
- Belong to peace movement
- Important in a job: generous holidays
- Environmental action: chosen products that are better for environment
- Rejecting neighbors: Immigrants/foreign workers
- Not important for successful marriage: Apart from in-laws
- Environmental action: reduce water consumption
- Rejecting neighbors: Muslims
- bad future changes: Greater respect for authority
- Abortion when woman not married
- Rejecting neighbors: Left wing extremists
- Important child qualities: independence
- Important child qualities: thrift saving money and things
- Important in a job: not too much pressure
- Rejecting neighbors: People of a different race
- Unpaid work organization concerned with health
- Justifiable: fighting with the police
- Belong to religious organization
- Belong to social welfare service for elderly
- Service to others not important in life

Global Buddhists are 25% or more below the global average for the following indicators:

- Ever felt very lonely or remote from other people
- Ever felt upset because somebody criticized you
- Ever felt bored
- Ever felt depressed or very unhappy
- Ever felt restless
- Ever felt on top of the world
- Ever felt that things were going your way
- Ever felt proud because someone complimented you
- Ever felt very excited or interested
- Important child qualities: religious faith
- Important in a job: good chances for promotion
- Belong to labor unions
- Unpaid work human rights

- Churches give answers: the social problems
- Ever felt pleased about having accomplished something
- Important child qualities: obedience
- Sharing with parents: no sharing attitudes
- Sharing with parents: political views
- Active/Inactive membership of labor unions
- Active/Inactive membership of political party
- Active/Inactive membership of art, music, educational
- Sharing with parents: sexual attitudes
- Churches give answers: the problems of family life
- Belong to human rights
- Unpaid work labor unions
- Important: Religious service birth
- Justifiable: cheating on taxes
- Believe in: sin
- Important in a job: pleasant people to work with
- Active/Inactive membership of environmental organization
- Belong to political parties
- Justifiable: keeping money that you have found
- Sharing with parents: social attitudes
- Active/Inactive membership of church or religious organization
- Unpaid work political parties or groups

Global Catholics are 25% or more above the global average for the following indicators:

- Raised religiously
- Active/Inactive membership of church or religious organization
- Environmental action: attend meeting, signed petition

Global Catholics are 25% or more below the global average for the following indicators:

- Unpaid work human rights
- Unpaid work political parties or groups
- Belong to peace movement
- Belong to labor unions
- Abortion if not wanting more children
- Belong to human rights
- Unpaid work professional associations
- Unpaid work environment, conservation, animal rights
- Unpaid work women's group
- Abortion when woman not married
- Active/Inactive membership of labor unions
- Belong to political parties
- Belong to professional associations

Global Hindus distinguish themselves from the world mean by 25% or more on the following indicators:

- Unpaid work peace movement
- Believe in: re-incarnation
- Rejecting neighbors: People with large families
- Rejecting neighbors: Jews
- Belong to peace movement
- Unpaid work organization concerned with health
- Rejecting neighbors: People of a different race
- Unpaid work education, arts, music or cultural activities
- Rejecting neighbors: Left wing extremists
- Rejecting neighbors: Immigrants/foreign workers
- Unpaid work environment, conservation, animal rights
- Unpaid work labor unions
- Unpaid work local political action groups
- Unpaid work political parties or groups
- Unpaid work women's group
- Rejecting neighbors: Right wing extremists
- Important in a job: good chances for promotion
- Belong to organization concerned with health
- Belong to local political actions
- Belong to women's group
- Abortion when woman not married
- Unpaid work other groups
- Unpaid work professional associations
- Important child qualities: obedience
- Belong to conservation, the environment, ecology, animal rights
- Belong to education, arts, music or cultural activities
- Rejecting neighbors: Muslims
- Unpaid work religious or church organization
- Belong to political parties
- Rejecting neighbors: People who have AIDS
- Unpaid work human rights
- Important in a job: a responsible job
- Belong to professional associations
- A woman has to have children to be fulfilled
- Raised religiously
- Important in a job: a respected job
- Political system as it was before good for the country
- Important child qualities: hard work
- Important in a job: a useful job for society
- Environmental action: contributed to environmental organization
- Moments of prayer, meditation...
- Poverty compared to 10 years ago decreased
- Rejecting neighbors: Emotionally unstable people

- Rejecting neighbors: Homosexuals
- Abortion if not wanting more children
- Belong to social welfare service for elderly
- Rejecting neighbors: People with a criminal record
- Get comfort and strength from religion
- Unpaid work youth work

Global Hindus distinguish themselves also by scoring 25% or less than the global average on the following indicators:

- Ever felt upset because somebody criticized you
- Ever felt very lonely or remote from other people
- Ever felt depressed or very unhappy
- Ever felt on top of the world
- Ever felt restless
- Ever felt bored
- Sharing with parents: no sharing attitudes
- Sharing with parents: sexual attitudes
- Ever felt that things were going your way
- Ever felt proud because someone complimented you
- Ever felt pleased about having accomplished something
- Justifiable: adultery
- Belong to labor unions
- Churches give answers: the problems of family life
- Environmental action: recycle
- Justifiable: sex under the legal age of consent
- Ever felt very excited or interested
- Environmental action: chosen products that are better for environment
- Justifiable: homosexuality
- Justifiable: divorce
- Hard work does not bring success
- Churches give answers: moral problems
- Churches give answers: the social problems
- Justifiable: avoiding a fare on public transport
- Never pray to God outside of religious services (I)
- Active/Inactive membership of any other organization
- Never attend religious services
- No confidence: Armed Forces
- Justifiable: cheating on taxes
- Sharing with parents: political views
- Frequency watches TV

Global Muslims are 25% or more above the global average for the following indicators:

- Unpaid work peace movement
- Belong to peace movement

- Unpaid work local political action groups
- Rejecting neighbors: People with large families
- Unpaid work organization concerned with health
- Unpaid work political parties or groups
- Belong to local political actions
- Rejecting neighbors: Jews
- Unpaid work human rights
- Unpaid work environment, conservation, animal rights
- Unpaid work women's group
- Belong to women's group
- Important child qualities: religious faith
- Believe in: hell
- Rejecting neighbors: People of a different race
- Important in a job: a useful job for society
- Rejecting neighbors: Immigrants/foreign workers
- Rejecting neighbors: Left wing extremists
- Important in a job: good chances for promotion
- Belong to political parties
- Unpaid work religious or church organization
- Rejecting neighbors: Right wing extremists
- Unpaid work labor unions
- Unpaid work education, arts, music or cultural activities
- Belong to human rights
- Believe in: devil
- Belong to organization concerned with health
- Important in a job: meeting people
- Important in a job: a respected job
- Important in a job: not too much pressure
- Believe in: heaven
- Unpaid work youth work
- Churches give answers: the social problems
- Rejecting neighbors: People who have AIDS
- Justifiable: threatening workers who refuse to join a strike
- Rejecting neighbors: Homosexuals
- Belong to conservation, the environment, ecology, animal rights
- Belong to youth work
- Important in a job: a responsible job
- Get comfort and strength from religion
- Justifiable: political assassination
- Sharing with parents: attitudes towards religion
- Believe in: life after death
- A woman has to have children to be fulfilled
- Churches give answers: moral problems
- Churches give answers: the problems of family life
- Rejecting neighbors: Emotionally unstable people
- Active/Inactive membership of political party

- Unpaid work social welfare service for elderly, handicapped or deprived people
- God important in your life
- Moments of prayer, meditation
- Important child qualities: obedience
- Important in a job: good hours
- Important in a job: generous holidays
- Belong to social welfare service for elderly
- Justifiable: keeping money that you have found
- Rejecting neighbors: Political Extremists
- Important in a job: good job security
- Important in a job: an opportunity to use initiative
- Unpaid work sports or recreation

Global Muslims are 25% or more below the global average for the following indicators:

- Sharing with parents: no sharing attitudes
- Ever felt upset because somebody criticized you
- Justifiable: homosexuality
- Active/Inactive membership of charitable/humanitarian organization
- Belong to labor unions
- Ever felt restless
- Justifiable: euthanasia
- Active/Inactive membership of any other organization
- Ever felt very lonely or remote from other people
- Justifiable: prostitution
- Ever felt bored
- Justifiable: suicide
- Sharing with parents: sexual attitudes
- Ever felt depressed or very unhappy
- Active/Inactive membership of sport or recreation
- Religion not important in life
- Abortion when child physically handicapped
- Justifiable: abortion
- Active/Inactive membership of church or religious organization
- Never pray to God outside of religious services (I)
- Not important for successful marriage: Religious beliefs
- Unpaid work other groups
- Ever felt proud because someone complimented you
- Active/Inactive membership of art, music, educational
- Politicians who don't believe in God are fit for public office
- Ever felt on top of the world
- Active/Inactive membership of environmental organization
- Justifiable: divorce
- Not important for successful marriage: Same social background
- Ever felt that things were going your way

Global Orthodox are 25% or more above the global average for the following indicators:

- Unpaid work labor unions
- Important child qualities: hard work
- Rejecting neighbors: Emotionally unstable people
- Abortion if not wanting more children
- Rejecting neighbors: People who have AIDS
- Abortion when woman not married
- Rejecting neighbors: Homosexuals
- Ever felt on top of the world
- A woman has to have children to be fulfilled
- Active/Inactive membership of labor unions
- Ever felt very lonely or remote from other people
- Rejecting neighbors: People with large families
- Ever felt proud because someone complimented you
- Rejecting neighbors: Muslims
- Rejecting neighbors: Jews

Global Orthodox are 25% or more below the global average for the following indicators:

- Belong to human rights
- Unpaid work women's group
- Active/Inactive membership of any other organization
- Belong to reiigious organization
- Belong to social welfare service for elderly
- Belong to sports or recreation
- Active/Inactive membership of sport or recreation
- Belong to other groups
- Unpaid work social welfare service for elderly, handicapped or deprived people
- Unpaid work youth work
- Unpaid work religious or church organization
- Unpaid work human rights
- Belong to women's group
- Belong to local political actions
- Belong to peace movement
- Environmental action: attend meeting, signed petition
- Environmental action: contributed to environmental organization
- Active/Inactive membership of art, music, educational
- Active/Inactive membership of charitable/humanitarian organization
- Active/Inactive membership of environmental organization
- Active/Inactive membership of church or religious organization
- Belong to conservation, the environment, ecology, animal rights
- Belong to youth work
- Belong to organization concerned with health
- Unpaid work sports or recreation
- Active/Inactive membership of professional organization

- Unpaid work other groups
- Unpaid work professional associations
- Unpaid work education, arts, music or cultural activities
- Unpaid work organization concerned with health
- Unpaid work local political action groups
- Justifiable: homosexuality
- Environmental action: recycle
- Belong to education, arts, music or cultural activities
- Belong to professional associations
- Environmental action: chosen products that are better for environment
- Satisfaction with financial situation of household
- Unpaid work political parties or groups

Global Protestants are 25% or more above the global average for the following indicators:

- Belong to religious organization
- Belong to other groups
- Belong to labor unions
- Active/Inactive membership of sport or recreation
- Active/Inactive membership of church or religious organization
- Belong to sports or recreation
- Unpaid work other groups
- Active/Inactive membership of any other organization
- Active/Inactive membership of charitable/humanitarian organization
- Belong to youth work
- Belong to social welfare service for elderly
- Belong to professional associations
- Unpaid work youth work
- Belong to women's group
- Active/Inactive membership of art, music, educational
- Active/Inactive membership of professional organization
- Environmental action: recycle
- Belong to organization concerned with health
- Unpaid work sports or recreation
- Belong to human rights
- Environmental action: contributed to environmental organization
- Unpaid work organization concerned with health
- Environmental action: chosen products that are better for environment
- Unpaid work religious or church organization
- Belong to education, arts, music or cultural activities
- Belong to political parties
- Belong to local political actions

Global Protestants are 25% or more below the global average for the following indicators:
- Rejecting neighbors: Jews
- Rejecting neighbors: People who have AIDS
- Rejecting neighbors: People with large families
- Important child qualities: hard work
- Rejecting neighbors: Homosexuals
- A woman has to have children to be fulfilled
- Rejecting neighbors: People of a different race
- Believe in: hell
- Unpaid work political parties or groups

The factor analytical interpretation of the differences from the global means is now the following:

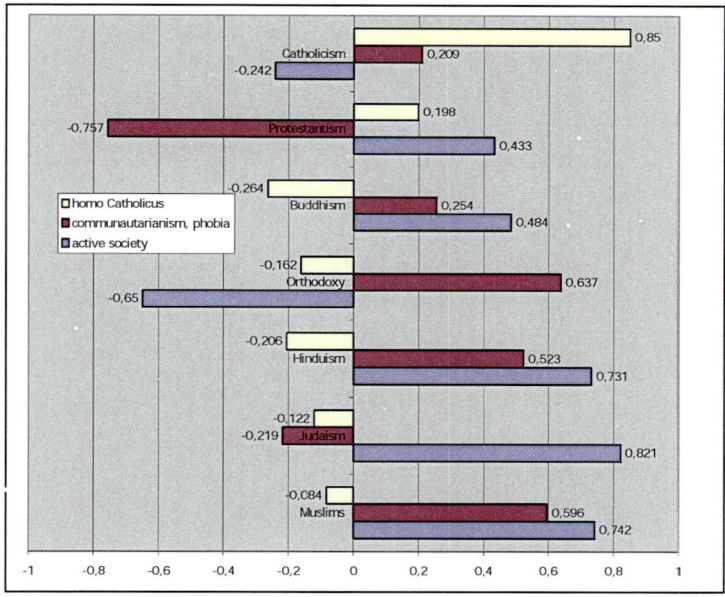

Graph 23. The factor analytical results of value system differences.

Note: based on a factor analysis of the percentage differences of ALL *World Values Survey* variables, all waves, from the global mean, working with the subsamples of the following religious groups: Muslims; Judaism; Hinduism; Orthodoxy; Buddhism; Protestantism; Catholicism; Practicing Orthodoxy; Practicing Islam; Practicing Catholicism; Practicing Protestantism. "Practicing" was understood to comprise all those religious denomination members, whose regular religious service attendance rate was once greater or equal to once a month or more frequent. Only those WVS variables, which rendered themselves for a multivariate analysis due to their scales, were included in the final analysis. As a further rule, we included only those variables with more than 50 global observations even for the smallest religious groups in question. The list of variables, the global means, and the percentage differences from the global means are all documented in the appendix to this work. Our results are based on SPSS XIV calculations, Innsbruck University, 2008. We used standard orthogonal factor rotation, and the *Eigenvalue* criterion *Eigenvalues* greater or equal to 1. The free data download in SPSS format is available from the WVS Website (data downloads).

In the light of our quantitative analysis of the World Values Survey data, the following consequences for research on global political culture can be drawn. All denominations are being described—not by what they aim to be, but what the sociological WVS data show their members currently believing:

- Buddhism has a higher degree of commitment towards the active society, and a small, but also existent element of phobia and communautarianism
- Catholicism is characterized by a relatively high degree of the "fiesta" factor, by a somewhat higher degree of phobias and by a somewhat lower degree of the active society
- Hinduism is characterized by a high degree of commitment towards an active society, but unfortunately did not overcome as yet the phobias and the communautarianism, so characteristic also of the countries of the Orthodox political culture. The fiesta factor is not present in this political culture
- Real existing Islam in the world currently characterized, like Hinduism, by a combination of high commitments towards the active society, but unfortunately also many of the phobias and the communautarianism, present also in global Hinduism.
- Judaism is characterized by a very high degree of commitment towards the active society, and by the notable absence of phobia + communautarianism and also by the absence of the "fiesta" factor. The data of the WVS suggest that Judaism is indeed the religion of the active society, of global tolerance and liberal values, often also regarding marriage and family matters
- Orthodox political cultures in many ways combine the politically most unstable mix of all global political/religious cultures: a very high degree of phobias and communautarianism, and a very low degree of commitment towards an active society.
- Protestantism is characterized by a strong rejection of phobias and communautarianism, by a higher commitment to the active society and somewhat also by the "fiesta" factor

We will now analyze the performances of the numerically biggest global practicing religious communities, i.e. practicing Catholics, practicing Muslims, practicing Orthodox and practicing Protestants.

In all four denominations, the practicing component is more active in organizations of the "active society" than the total, i.e. practicing believers are more involved in organizations of the active society than the passive members of each denomination. But there is an alarming phenomenon of Orthodox phobia and communautarianism: while all other denominations show a phobia and communautarianism reducing aspect of regular religious service attendance, in accordance with the fact that all religions of the "book" demand from their members tolerance and respect of humankind, it is the religiously active segment of the Orthodox denomination, which is more xenophobic and more longing towards communautarianism forms of order than the Orthodox average, and, hence, the secular Orthodox population. Needless to say that not only the Catholic regular practitioners, but also the practicing segment of the other Christian denominations share with the Catholics a good part of the "fiesta" factor, while practically there are no differences between practicing Muslims and secular Muslims in this respect.

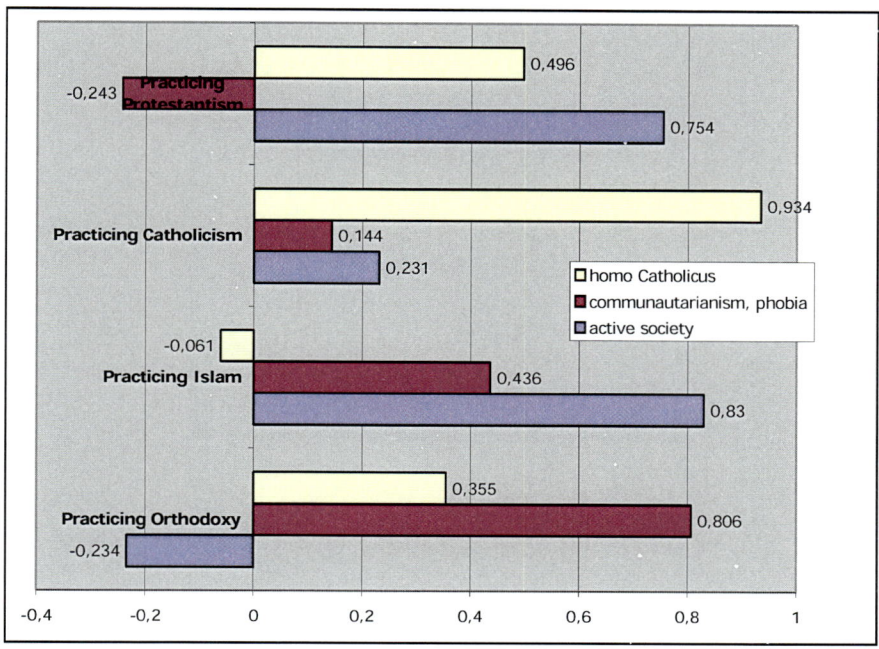

Graph 24. The factor analytical results of value system differences among practicing Protestants, Catholics, Muslims, and Orthodox Christians

Note: based on a factor analysis of the percentage differences of ALL *World Values Survey* variables, all waves, from the global mean, working with the subsamples of the following religious groups: Muslims; Judaism; Hinduism; Orthodoxy; Buddhism; Protestantism; Catholicism; Practicing Orthodoxy; Practicing Islam; Practicing Catholicism; Practicing Protestantism. "Practicing" was understood to comprise all those religious denomination members, whose regular religious service attendance rate was once greater or equal to once a month or more frequent. Only those WVS variables, which rendered themselves for a multivariate analysis due to their scales, were included in the final analysis. As a further rule, we included only those variables with more than 50 global observations even for the smallest religious groups in question. The list of variables, the global means, and the percentage differences from the global means are all documented in the appendix to this work. Our results are based on SPSS XIV calculations, Innsbruck University, 2008. We used standard orthogonal factor rotation, and the *Eigenvalue* criterion *Eigenvalues* greater or equal to 1. The free data download in SPSS format is available from the WVS Website (data downloads).

The results of this analysis are fairly radical – Islam cannot be portrayed as the most intolerant political culture of the world, and it is the revival of xenophobic and often anti-Semitic attitudes in Orthodox Europe and in the Buddhist and the Hindu world, which should cause the greatest alarm among policy planners and policy makers. Islam and Judaism are religions, which strictly affect everyday life, and it is not prayer-day alone, but everyday life, which decides over your "assets" in "heaven" "above". Christianity, especially Catholic Christianity, runs the danger of merely sticking towards a tradition, and not really translating itself into activities from "Monday" to "Friday". In addition, it is shown that – especially in our multicultural Europe – the active society has a great chance of becoming the glue, which brings all these different traditions and believes together in a positive and future-oriented competition.

A Digression on the Images of the "Other": A Nineteenth-Century Art and a twenty-first Century Internet Image Exploration

Having analyzed the structures of the opinions of the adherents of the major world religions in comparison to the global sample, we have come to the conclusion that in reality

- active society,
- phobias and the
- *"fiesta"* of the *"homo Catholicus"*

are the determining underlying currents, explaining 4/5 of the variance of the percentage differences from the global means along more than 290 variables of the World Values Survey. Our results are partially optimistic about the possibilities to overcome phobias in the Muslim world, and especially the active society component of the real existing belief structures of the Muslim *Umma* permit us to say that in globally secularizing societies, Islam is rather an asset and not a burden on development.

In the following, we will contrast these images with the images of three of the most famous nineteenth-century European artists, whose works featured "the Orient" in a very "orientalist" way (Jean Léone Gérôme; Jean Auguste Dominique Ingres; Eugène Delacroix). At the height of French colonialism and the brutal conquest of Algeria, and the still existing rigid moral conduct structures of post-revolutionary France in the nineteenth century, these artists depicted the "Orient" as the lustful, lascivious and brute "other" to be conquered by the banner of French-inspired Enlightenment. The globally available images of Islam and Muslims on the Internet, as evidenced by the search engine "Google", today, are a different story.

As it is well-known, Google is the most used search engine on the Web with a 53.6% market share, ahead of Yahoo! (19.9%) and Live Search (12.9%) (http://en.wikipedia.org/wiki/Google). Google's search engines analyze the structure of the Web to calculate a quality ranking for each Web page (see also: "The Anatomy of a Large-Scale Hypertextual Web Search Engine" by Sergey Brin and Lawrence Page, Computer Science Department, Stanford University, Stanford, CA 94305, available at http://infolab.stanford.edu/~backrub/google.html).

Citation analysis is an important resource that has largely gone unused before in Web search engines. Google thus aims to provide a measure of the "citation importance" of a page that should correspond well with people's subjective ideas of the importance of a page. Because of this, *"Pagerank"*, designed by Google, was planned to be a way to prioritize the results of Web keyword searches.

Given the structure of the search results, we can safely assume that the reprinted 15 images of "Islam" and "Muslims" unfortunately correspond to the most widely circulating global imaginary about Islam and Muslims around the globe. While sexual repressive Europe imagined the world of the Orient as the sexually permissive and brute "other", which has to be civilized, the twenty-first century presents Islam and Muslims as "the headscarf" and the "veil", which has to be "liberated", and Muslim "political and religious violence", which is "threatening" and has to be "repressed".

What a contrast between the "lustful ladies" in the "Turkish bath" in 1862, imagined by Jean Auguste Dominique Ingres, and the "veiled Internet ladies" of August 28, 2008!

What a difference between the lustful slave-owners, deliberating the unveiled "advantages" of the nude non-Muslim slave, painted by Jean Léone Gérôme in 1866, and the hordes of "slaughtering" and "angry people", said to represent "Islam" or "Muslims" by August 28, 2008!

What a contrast between the Internet images of the "Djihad warriors" of 2008 and the bearded pre-Islamic oriental (painted by Eugène Delacroix in 1827), who slaughters the naked lady upon order by the ancient king Sardanapalus, who watches all this as his worldly possessions are destroyed and who ordered his own concubines to be murdered by his Oriental mercenaries before he sets himself on fire, once he learns that he is faced with military defeat!

WESTERN ORIENTALIST IMAGES OF THE ORIENTAL WORLD IN THE NINETEENTH CENTURY

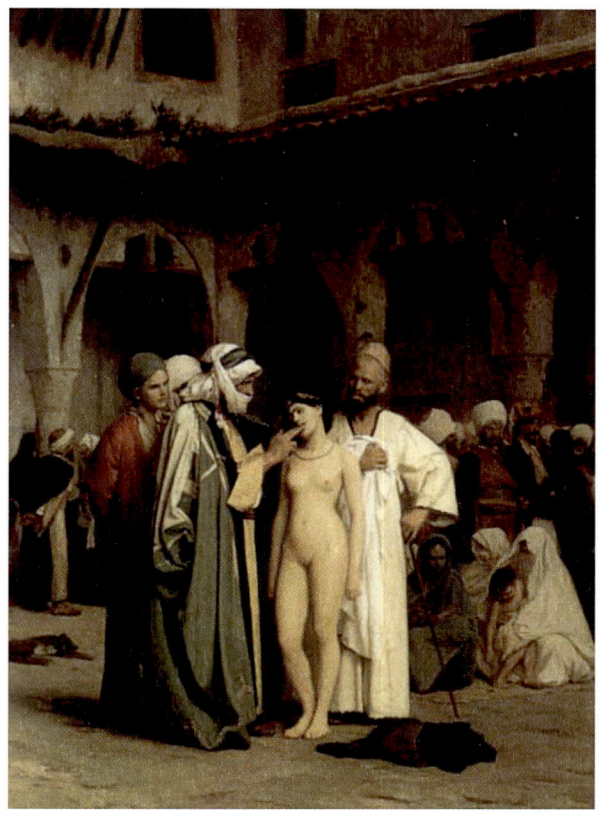

The Slave Market
Signed lower right Jean Léone Gérôme 1866
Oil on canvas/huile sur toile
Size 33.25 x 25 in (84.3 x 63 cm)
Location: as of 2007 at Francine Clark Art Institute, Williamstown

Jean Auguste Dominique Ingres
The Turkish Bath, 1862, oil on canvas, diam. 108 cm, Louvre.
(Photo credit: http://en.wikipedia.org/wiki/Jean_Auguste_Dominique_Ingres)

Detail of the painting *Death of Sardanapalus (La Mort de Sardanapale)*, oil on canvas dated 1827 by Eugène Delacroix, 392 x 496 cm or 12' 1" x 16' 3". Musee du Louvre, Paris. (Photo credit: http://www.artchive.com/artchive/d/delacroix/delacroix_sardanapalus_cut.jpg)

Sardanapalus was the last king of Assyria. Sardanapalus watches as his worldly possessions are destroyed. Sardanapalus ordered his possessions destroyed and concubines murdered before he sets himself on fire, once he learns that he is faced with military defeat. *Death of Sardanapalus* is based on a play, *Sardanapalus*, written by Lord Byron.

THE TOP GLOBAL INTERNET IMAGES OF "ISLAM" IN THE TWENTY-FIRST CENTURY AS EVIDENCED BY THE GOOGLE IMAGE SEARCH ENGINE

As of August 28, 2008

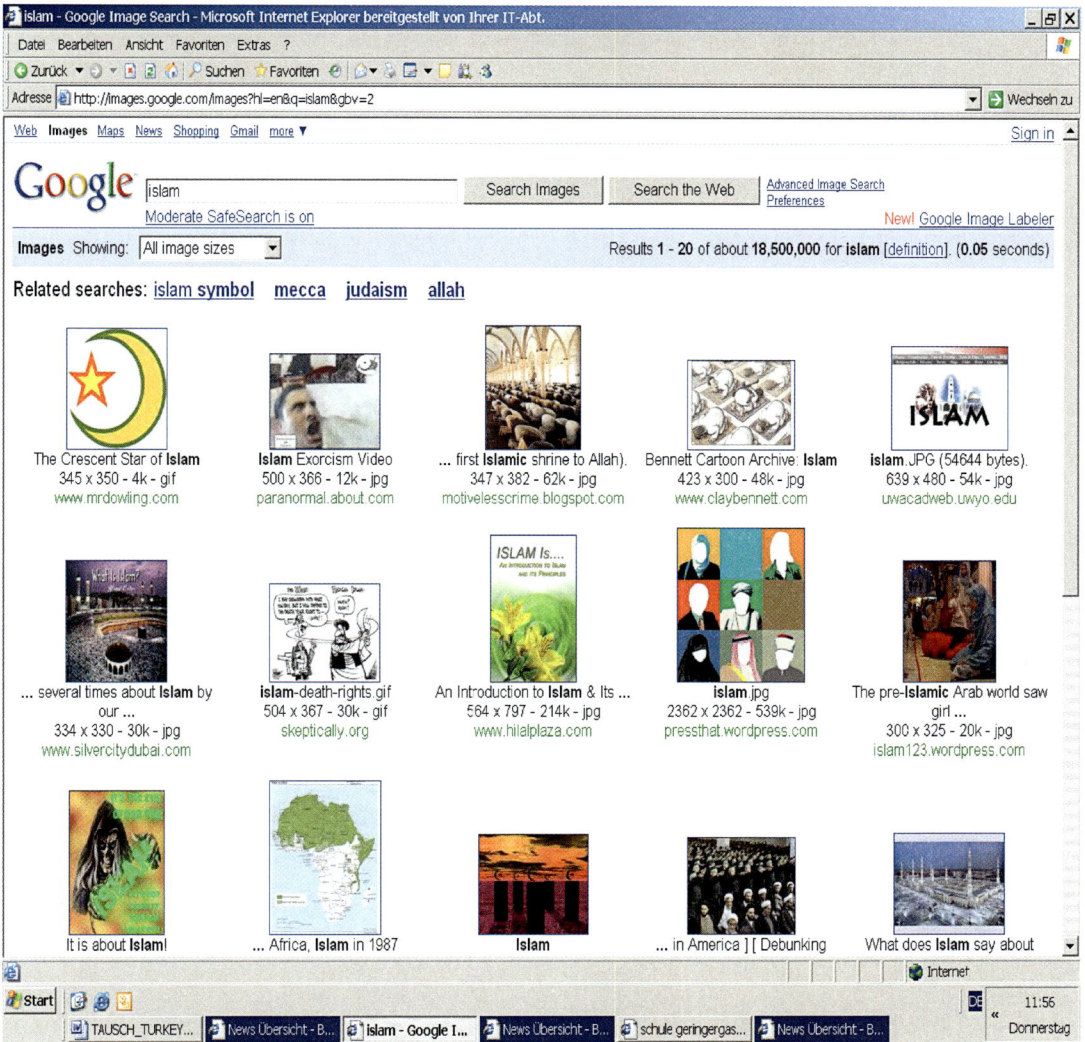

THE STRUCTURE OF GLOBAL PREJUDICES

The research design for the following analysis on the individual level of the tens of thousands of pooled global citizens from all World Values Survey waves and of the tens of thousands of pooled global Muslim respondents from all World Values Survey waves is completely different from the earlier investigations.

The Top Global Internet Images of "Muslims" in the Twenty-first Century as Evidenced by the Google Image Search Engine

As of August 28, 2008

This time, we look into the determinants of the global phobias on a global scale (pooled results of all WVS surveys, all times, all countries) and on the level of the Muslim respondents in the WVS (all times, all countries), with *listwise* deletion of missing values.

The variables for our analysis are:

- Anti-egalitarian position on income equality scale
- Believe in: God
- Child qualities: tolerance and respect for other people
- Competition harmful (Competition good or harmful)
- For state ownership of business
- Highest educational level attained
- Income level
- Never attend religious services (How often do you attend religious services?)
- No family savings during past year (Family savings during past year)
- Rejecting neighbors: Homosexuals
- Rejecting neighbors: Immigrants/foreign workers
- Rejecting neighbors: Jews
- Rejecting neighbors: People of a different race
- right wing (self positioning in political scale)

What interrelations exist between these variables on the level of global society, and on the level of the Muslim global sample? Short of a confirmatory factor analytical design, which might be the subject of future research, we opted for a standard orthogonal factor analytical research design, which looks into the way, in, which the following indicators of tolerance and phobias

- Child qualities: tolerance and respect for other people
- Rejecting neighbors: Homosexuals
- Rejecting neighbors: Immigrants/foreign workers
- Rejecting neighbors: Jews
- Rejecting neighbors: People of a different race

are being determined by the "classical" political science variables:

Educational level
Income levels and savings
Left-right scale
Position on competition policy
Position on state ownership
Religious dimension

Contradicting hypotheses about these phenomena abound around the globe. Are religious people more tolerant or less tolerant than secular people? Is the rejection of homosexuals the same stereotype or a different stereotype, than, say, phobia of immigrants, racism or Anti-Semitism? Is the global right wing less tolerant than the global left-wing?

Our 6 extracted factors with *Eigenvalues* above or equal to one in our standard-type SPSS XIV/XV factor analysis, based on more than 200.000 representative respondents around the globe in more than 80 countries since the 1980s shows that among the 6 extracted factors, which together explain almost 60% of total variance of all the variables used in this analysis, the most important factor is indeed the "phobia of the other", or "phobia of multiculturalism" be it the foreign worker, the Jew, the person of a different race, while homophobia is a different factor, which must not be confounded with the typical "xenophobia/racism" dimension.

It should be also emphasized that the "political" or "social" background-variables show relatively weak loadings with this dimension. As squared factor loadings correspond to explained percentages of variance, it can be said that secularism, for example (never attending religious services) is far less strongly and negatively connected with the phobia factor than expected by many. The phobia factor explains some 15% of total variance.

The next important factor, upper strata, reflects the life perspectives and the dimensions of thinking of the well-to-do on this earth. But interestingly enough, the connections of the richer people around the globe with the hard-core values of economic liberalism such as competition policy, income redistribution, and private ownership are far weaker than most would expect. Interestingly enough, also the political affiliation of the upper strata with the political right is far weaker than expected, and in fact explains far less than 10% of the variance of the political left-right scale.

The next factor is secularism. But while secular people are in their majority politically at home on the left and not on the right-wing, and tend to be somewhat richer and more educated than their religious counterparts, and are also in favor of state interventions rather than a pure market economy, the great hope of followers of secularism around the globe that with secularism comes tolerance is rather decidedly to be rejected. Nowadays, there is also a marked positive relationship between secularism and Anti-Semitism, i.e. we are confronted in the 21st Century by a phenomenon of "pagan Anti-Semitism".

Our results about the contemporary etatist mentality present also some surprising and interesting aspects. It is not so much the political left, but the political right nowadays, which feels attracted to this kind of perspective. Competition is seen as harmful, one is in favor of state-owned businesses, and one accumulated some family savings over the life cycle, and one believes somewhat in God but one rejects tolerance as a value in education. The conservative etatist mentality also accepts homosexual neighbors, while the profile *vis-à-vis* the other "multicultural groups" is unclear.

The next factor, anti-egalitarianism, is an interesting and also frightening combination of anti-egalitarianism, savings poverty, a decided yes to state ownership of the means of production, homophobia and – interestingly enough – the theoretical support for the thesis that tolerance and respect for other people are important qualities of a child. The adherents of this model tend to identify themselves rather with the political right, and not with the political left; they in some way represent the "socialism of the desperate".

The last factor, which achieved an Eigenvalue greater or equal to 1, is homophobia. Homophobes rather tend to disregard tolerance in education; they will be – *ceteris paribus* – rather in favor of state ownership of the means of production and they will be interestingly enough rather left-wing and not right-wing. Homophobia is a phenomenon of the educated and the rather well-to-do, but interestingly, homophobes will be also rather anti-Semites, but not xenophobes.

"Who Are We"?: A Factor Analysis of Global Value Differences

Table 18. world wide prejudices – a factor analytical model, based on global citizenry (pooled analysis of the total World Values Survey respondents' data base)

Global society

Matrix of components (a)						
	Component					
	Phobia	Upper strata	Secularism	Etatist mentality	Anti-egalitarianists	Homophobia
Believe in: God	0.238	-0.057	-0.68	0.268	0.013	0.111
Child qualities: tolerance and respect for other people	-0.084	0.053	0.035	-0.159	0.477	-0.313
Competition harmful (Competition good or harmful)	0	-0.461	0.245	0.58	0.096	0.127
No family savings during past year (Family savings during past year)	0.088	-0.461	0.013	-0.387	0.179	-0.136
Highest educational level attained	-0.245	0.595	0.236	0.116	0.008	0.166
Never attend religious services (How often do you attend religious services)	-0.314	-0.065	0.656	-0.174	0.025	-0.142
Anti-egalitarian position on „Income equality" scale	0.031	0.367	-0.084	-0.093	0.672	-0.067
Income level	-0.184	0.657	0.164	0.26	0.006	0.218
Rejecting neighbors: Homosexuals	0.218	-0.035	-0.073	-0.435	0.214	0.749
Rejecting neighbors: Immigrants/foreign workers	0.782	0.136	0.241	0.028	-0.027	-0.112
Rejecting neighbors: Jews	0.717	0.08	0.252	-0.091	-0.053	0.152
Rejecting neighbors: People of a different race	0.769	0.149	0.201	0.083	-0.048	-0.194
For state ownership of business	0.025	-0.417	0.308	0.414	0.427	0.254
right wing (self positioning in political scale)	0.183	0.181	-0.301	0.242	0.275	-0.244
Extraction method: principal components						
a	6 component(s) extracted					

Statistical properties of the model:

Explained total variance						
Component	Initial Eigenvalues			Sum of squared factor loadings for extraction		
	Total	% of total variance	Cumulated %	Total	% of total variance	Cumulated %
1	2.063	14.733	14.733	2.063	14.733	14.733
2	1.61	11.498	26.232	1.61	11.498	26.232
3	1.396	9.975	36.206	1.396	9.975	36.206
4	1.139	8.137	44.343	1.139	8.137	44.343
5	1.03	7.36	51.703	1.03	7.36	51.703
6	1.004	7.171	58.875	1.004	7.171	58.875

Communalities	
	Extraction (percentage of variance explained by the model)
Highest educational level attained	0.51
No family savings during past year (Family savings during past year)	0.421
Income level	0.608
Believe in: God	0.607
Never attend religious services (How often do you attend religious services)	0.585
Child qualities: tolerance and respect for other people	0.362
Rejecting neighbors: People of a different race	0.701
Rejecting neighbors: Immigrants/foreign workers	0.702
Rejecting neighbors: Homosexuals	0.851
Rejecting neighbors: Jews	0.618
right wing (self positioning in political scale)	0.35
Anti-egalitarian position on „Income equality" scale	0.607
For state ownership of business	0.687
Competition harmful (Competition good or harmful)	0.634
Extraction method: principal components	

SPSS XIV and XV calculations, University Computing Center, Innsbruck University, based on the data of this work and our own calculations from World Values Survey, 3rd and 4th wave, http://www.worldvaluessurvey.org/.

The all important question now is of course, whether the *"Umma"* – the community of Muslim believers – as reflected in the World Values Survey – shares these value structures, or whether there are other forces at work, which sharply distinguish the *Umma* from the non-believers. It should be emphasized at the outset that the present study deals with the real existing people around the globe and not with an imagined and idealized *Umma*.

Are religious Muslims more tolerant or less tolerant than secular Muslims? Is the rejection of homosexuals the same stereotype or a different stereotype, than, say, phobia of immigrants, racism or Anti-Semitism also in the world of the *Umma?* Is the Muslim right wing less tolerant or more tolerant than the Muslim left-wing? To make a long story short, we have come to the surprising conclusion here that the contemporary ideological landscape, as analyzed by our global factor analysis with almost 30.000 Muslim representative respondents, is far nearer to the political causal mechanisms, so well-known to European sociology from the 1930s to the days of the first appearance of the "guest workers" in Europe during the 1960s. In theoretical terms, our analysis would suggest far more classical answers to the contemporary crisis of the Muslim world than many would suggest – i.e., to concentrate on the "bread and butter issues" of a decent worker's and trade union movement, to try to integrate migrants and nationals in the Muslim countries themselves, et cetera.

Our again 6 extracted factors with *Eigenvalues* above or equal to one in our standard-type SPSS XIV/XV factor analysis, based on around 30.000 representative Muslim respondents around the globe in more than 60 countries since the 1980s shows that among the 6 extracted factors, which together explain again almost 60% of total variance of all the variables used in this analysis, the most important factor is indeed – just as in the case of global society - the "phobia of the other", or "phobia of multiculturalism" or "Muslim racism" against foreign workers, and persons of a different race. Muslim racists, in contrast to non-Muslim racists (see above) tend to be decidedly tolerant of homosexuals, but they tend to be somewhat anti-Semitic, be of upper class origin, and they will be decidedly politically right-wing and they will hold anti-egalitarian positions on income inequality. So in a way, their mindset will rather better reflect the classical picture of racism and xenophobia, which sociology had from the days of the 1930s through to the days of the "guest worker economy" in the 1960s. Muslim xenophobes will also be – *ceteris paribus* – more often to be seen at prayer services than their non-xenophobic Muslim counterparts. It should be emphasized that the "social" background-variables show medium loadings with this dimension. As squared factor loadings correspond to explained percentages of variance, it can be said that Muslim racists are not secularists. The racism factor explains again some 15% of total variance. The existence of such a strong, xenophobic phenomenon in the Muslim world and also among the Muslims in the developed, Western democracies raises the question about the political strategies of the right and left in Western democracies, including Turkey, to balance such tendencies.

The next important factor, Muslim poverty, reflects the life perspectives and the dimensions of thinking of the Muslim poor. Interestingly enough, the connections of the Muslim poor around the globe with the hard-core values of left wing ideology are still in force, such as their rejection of competition policy, their favoring income redistribution, their rejection of private ownership. But these identities tend to be weaker than most would expect, Interestingly enough, also the political affiliation of the lower strata with the political left are far weaker than expected, and in fact explain far less than 10% of the variance of the political left-right-scale. The Muslim poor share the common phobias – rejecting immigrants, Jews, people of a different race, but not homosexuals.

The next factor is Muslim secularism. But while secular Muslims also – like their global counterparts - are in their majority more left than right-wing, and tend to be somewhat richer and more educated than their religious counterparts, they will be very much in favor of state interventions and will also think that competition is harmful. Their mindset corresponds neatly to the mindset of "Arab socialism", "Kemalism", "Third Worldism", and there is only a weak and lamentably enough positive relationship between secularism and phobias.

The next three factors are in total difference to the global sample. Muslim Anti-Semitism rather reminds us of the typical *petite bourgeoisie* Anti-Semitism sociology is so familiar with in the Europe of the 1930s – anti-Semites will be strongly in favor of competition, they will reject state ownership, but in contrast to the Europe of the 1930s they will be somewhat sympathizing with the Left, and they will be rather secular. They will share several other phobias, most notably against homosexuals.

Finally, there will be two strings of tolerance at work among the global *Umma* – a kind of decided secular tolerance movement, rejecting Anti-Semitism, and interestingly enough combining anti-egalitarian positions with a relatively low socio-economic status. Together with their religious counterpart, they will be strongly of the opinion that tolerance is an important factor in education.

The religiously tolerant current received a somewhat higher education and enjoys a higher income, is politically rather on the left and is also in favor of state ownership, but does not transpose its theoretical commitment towards tolerance and respect in education into the daily practice of not rejecting Jews and/or homosexuals, and is at best indifferent *vis-à-vis* immigrants and people of a different race.

Needless to say - the political conclusions from our analysis this time are only partially optimistic. To be sure, factors 1 – 3 of our analysis are pretty similar in their structure for both global society and the *Umma*.

Racism, poverty and *petite bourgeoisie* thinking prolong and deepen such phenomena as Muslim Anti-Semitism, and the religiously tolerant currents "exclude" Jews from their discourse. Only the current of "secular tolerance" inspires some hope here, but in many ways, it will be not strong enough to influence several Muslim societies from the fatal projections of their real existing problems onto scapegoats. The task of building up true workers movements and workers parties, social democracies in the classical sense of the European word of the 1930s through to the mid 1970s would be very high on the agenda. From the viewpoint of liberal Western democracy, including secular Turkey, the quantitative and qualitative leap of the religious current of tolerance into a religious democratic mass movement with a social and economic agenda comparable to parties like the CDU/CSU in the 1950s, 1960s and early 1970s would be and in the case of the Turkish AKP was a highly welcome. Last but not least, the secularist but upper-class current, which is the fruit of "Arab socialism", "secular Kemalism" *et cetera* at least would have the potential to become a true socio-liberal movement. Compared to the tendencies of Muslim racism and Muslim poverty/global racism and global upper class identities, it is clear how important it would be to act politically to save the Muslim world from the siren calls of religious fanatism and secular anti-imperialist anti-Zionism, which brought the region to nowhere during the last 60 years, and to save the globe from the siren calls of etatism and anti-egalitarianism as the unifying characteristics of the populist movements around the globe in the early 21st Century.

Table 19. Worldwide prejudices – a factor analytical model, based on the global *Umma* (pooled analysis of the total World Values Survey Muslim respondents data base)

MUSLIMS Matrix of components (a)

	Component					
	Muslim racism	Muslim poverty	Muslim secularism	Muslim Anti-Semitism	Muslim secular tolerance	Muslim religiously motivated tolerance
	Component					
Believe in: God	0.192	0.084	-0.382	-0.284	-0.402	0.469
Child qualities: tolerance and respect for other people	0.024	-0.038	-0.052	0.164	0.581	0.678
Competition harmful (Competition good or harmful)	-0.145	0.459	0.478	-0.408	-0.045	0.061
No family savings during past year (Family savings during past year)	-0.298	0.429	-0.3	0.024	0.304	0.069
Highest educational level attained	0.066	-0.475	0.403	0.131	-0.073	0.182
Never attend religious services (How often do you attend religious services)	-0.235	-0.019	0.543	0.246	0.376	-0.172
Anti-egalitarian position on „Income equality" scale	0.448	-0.331	-0.08	-0.126	0.318	0.143
Income level	0.232	-0.514	0.39	-0.041	-0.291	0.216
Rejecting neighbors: Homosexuals	-0.593	0.06	-0.025	0.35	-0.263	0.231
Rejecting neighbors: Immigrants/foreign workers	0.698	0.326	0.116	0.234	-0.012	0.007
Rejecting neighbors: Jews	0.258	0.401	0.144	0.608	-0.244	0.164
Rejecting neighbors: People of a different race	0.742	0.337	0.067	0.097	0.02	-0.096
For state ownership of business	0.042	0.353	0.412	-0.536	0.054	0.204
right wing (self positioning in political scale)	0.399	-0.216	-0.248	-0.122	0.16	-0.229
Extraction method: principal components						
a	6 component(s) extracted					

Statistical properties of the model:

Explained total variance						
Component	Initial Eigenvalues			Sum of squared factor loadings for extraction		
	Total	% of total variance	Cumulated %	Total	% of total variance	Cumulated %
1	2.077	14.838	14.838	2.077	14.838	14.838
2	1.559	11.134	25.971	1.559	11.134	25.971
3	1.352	9.661	35.632	1.352	9.661	35.632
4	1.227	8.763	44.395	1.227	8.763	44.395
5	1.085	7.748	52.143	1.085	7.748	52.143
6	1.002	7.16	59.304	1.002	7.16	59.304

Communalities	
	Extraction (percentage of variance explained by the model)
Child qualities: tolerance and respect for other people	0.83
Rejecting neighbors: People of a different race	0.687
Rejecting neighbors: Immigrants/foreign workers	0.661
Rejecting neighbors: Homosexuals	0.6
Rejecting neighbors: Jews	0.704
right wing (self positioning in political scale)	0.36
Anti-egalitarian position on „Income equality" scale	0.454
Believe in: God	0.652
Competition harmful (Competition good or harmful)	0.632
For state ownership of business	0.627
Highest educational level attained	0.448
Income level	0.604
No family savings during past year (Family savings during past year)	0.461
Never attend religious services (How often do you attend religious services)	0.582
Extraction method: principal components	

SPSS XIV and XV calculations, University Computing Center, Innsbruck University, based on the data of this work and our own calculations from World Values Survey, 3rd and 4th wave, http://www.worldvaluessurvey.org/.

Chapter 10

BY WAY OF CONCLUSION: HOW MUCH SECULARIZATION IS NECESSARY, AND HOW MUCH SECULARIZATION IS RECOMMENDABLE?

A standard dictionary definition has it that:

"Scylla [...] was one of the two monsters in Greek mythology (the other being Charybdis) that lived on either side of a narrow channel of water. The two sides of the strait were within an arrow's range of each other—so close that sailors attempting to avoid Charybdis would pass too close to Scylla and vice versa. The phrase between Scylla and Charybdis has come to mean being in a state where one is between two dangers and moving away from one will cause you to be in danger from the other."[33]

One of the surprising conclusions of this work is that the sophisticated analysis of the World Values Survey shows that the dimension of the active society is absolutely necessary for advanced and also for the transformation and the developing democracies. The dimension of the active society and the religious or post-religious humanistic convictions, which are necessary to fuel such a system of an active society, become all the more important as societies transform themselves from the "traditional" to the "modern" spectrum in the sense of Inglehart's theory.

Religious conservatives in many countries, in Latin America, in the Middle East and North Africa, in India, in Eastern Europe and the former USSR, fearing a dwindling role of religion around the globe, observe the dwindling global role of religion, but they get it all wrong in their analysis. They will blame female emancipation as the arch-enemy, responsible for what they perceive as the destruction of religious values, the family and what have you. Enlightened liberals of all sorts, inside and outside the European Union, will by contrast push relentlessly for what they term "anti-discrimination policy", and they will underline the role of gender policy in the evolving democratic systems. Note at this point, perhaps, that EURLEX[34], the data archive for the existing *Acquis Communautaire,* i.e., the European Union law, which has to be implemented by all acceding countries, lists "discrimination" 1292 times, "gender" 109 times, "sexual orientation" 18 times, "homosexual" 12 times,

---

[33] http://en.wikipedia.org/wiki/Scylla.
[34] http://eur-lex.europa.eu/RECH_mot.do.

"lesbian" two times, while the term "Muslim" appears only 18 times, "Christianity" only six times, and "religion" in general only 39 times! The European Union, seen in such a way, is "top-less", and all the former talk of the EU as a "Christian Club" to the contrary, it is a "Club" of the (ultra)liberal market economy plus – well plus some anti-discrimination policy. A critic at this point might also remark that the word "wage" appears throughout the "Acquis" only 66 times, while the term "market" appears 14221 times!

For the empirical political scientist, sharing humanistic and liberal values, neither the vision of the religious conservatives nor the vision of the ultraliberal anti-discriminationists is correct.

The most recent figures, published by the UNDP, about the share of female parliamentarians in the legislative lower assemblies around the globe convey indeed a vivid testimony about the fact, where the traditional thought patterns and gender roles are weakest and where they are strongest. 1:0 for the anti-discriminationists, and indeed there can be only zero tolerance towards gender discrimination, and all liberal and progressive forces around the globe should support what the UNDP calls "gender empowerment".

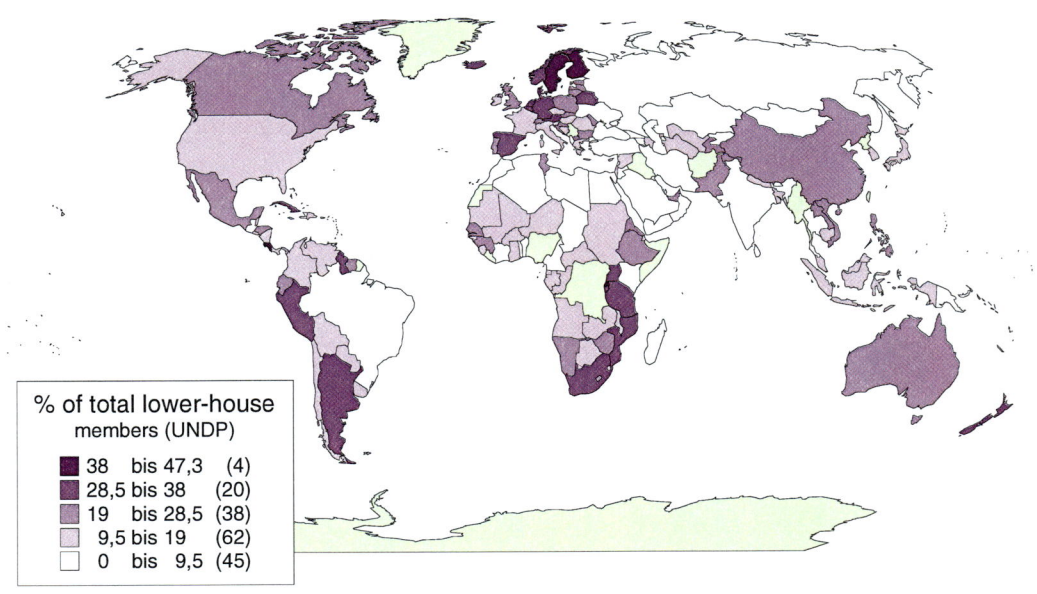

Map 12. Female parliamentarians as % of all lower-house members.

Note: UNDP data from http://hdr.undp.org/en/statistics/. The UNDP also collects data on "gender empowerment", which highly correlates with our indicator, but these data are available for far fewer countries than the female parliamentary share.

Explanatory note: "bis" is shorthand for "ranging from … to"; countries with missing values are marked in green color.

Current West European thinking seems to imply that all forms of household composition and formation should be treated equally by policy, including social policy, i.e. that what is perceived to be as an existing discrimination of homosexual couples, single parents *et cetera* in all laws should be ended, and that homosexual couples should be given the right to adopt children, et cetera.

Nowadays, the word "family" appears only 461 times in the "Acquis", and most of these references are to such combined terms as "family members", "family allowances", "family benefits" ... The fact is that in most European countries, and in many other countries around the globe, a growing number of people regard the institution of marriage as outdated. A still larger number of people is not willing anymore even to consider a religious ceremony in the context of marriage; and this kind of thinking made heavy inroads in Catholic Latin America, in South Africa and interestingly enough also in Muslim Kyrgyzstan and in Muslim Iran, as well as in Muslim Bangladesh and in Orthodox Russia.

The countries still regarding "marriage" not as being outdated are quickly named here – above all the United States of America, but also Japan, Protestant Iceland, Catholic Croatia and Poland, the Catholic Dominican Republic and religiously plural Tanzania, and Muslim Morocco, Egypt, Turkey, Pakistan and Indonesia.

One now could argue that all this is a matter of individual choice, and that no societal consequences are connected with such patterns. And here, the match between the religious conservatives around the globe and the "progressives" in such divergent countries as France or Iran could be tilted in favor of the religious conservatives, insofar as our empirical analyses clearly show that there are *certain societal limits to such a state of affairs.*

One very clear consequence of the erosion of the model of marriage (and mind you, the WVS question was NOT about religious marriage, but marriage IN GENERAL) is sexual permissiveness, which in the UNDP-type of index developed here is understood to be the combination of three syndromes:

- The rejection of the model of marriage as such
- Adultery is permissible
- Casual sex is acceptable

France and Slovenia lead the field here, with a large chunk of the European continent – the UK, the BENELUX countries, Germany, Spain, Greece, Sweden and Estonia as well as Belarus following behind in a group. The third group of medium permissiveness is constituted by Portugal, Ireland, Italy, the Central European countries, the Ukraine, Russia, the rest of the Baltic States, and Finland, while Croatia, Romania, and Poland are the least sexually permissive European societies.

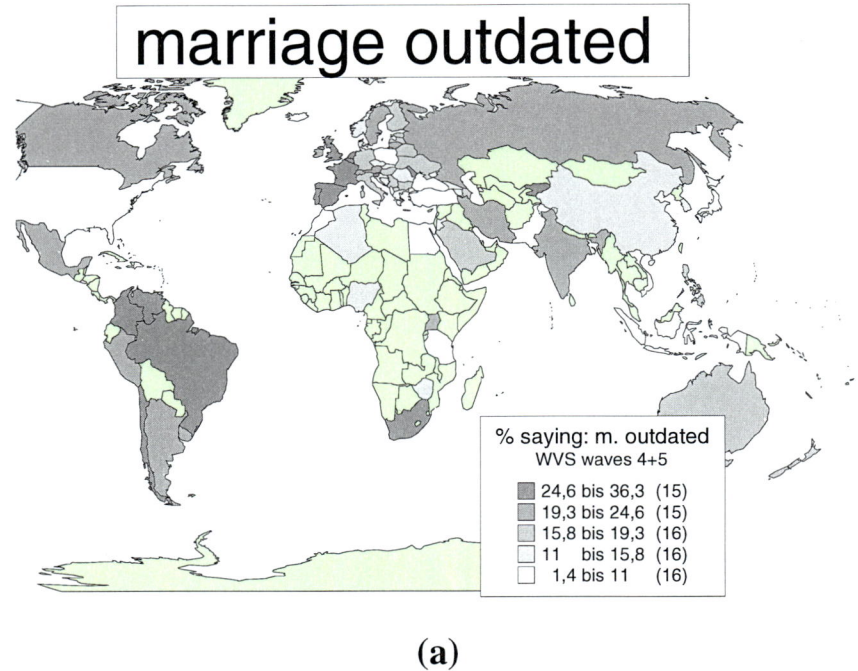

(a)

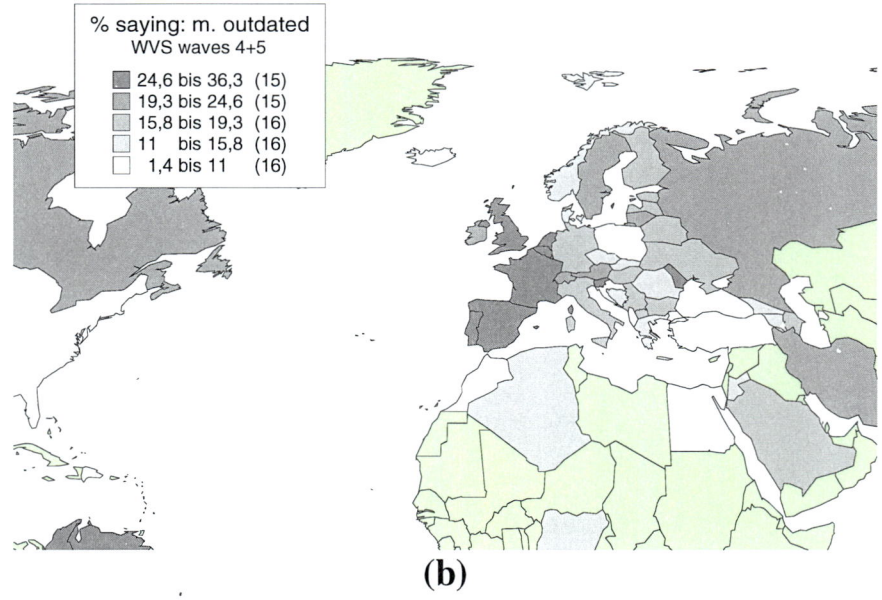

(b)

Map 13 a-b. Marriage outdated (continued).

Note: World Values Survey country results (wave 3+4).
Explanatory note: "bis" is shorthand for "ranging from ... to"; countries with missing values are marked in green color.

One very clear consequence of the erosion of the model of marriage (and mind you, the WVS question was NOT about religious marriage, but marriage IN GENERAL) is sexual permissiveness, which in the UNDP-type of index developed here is understood to be the combination of three syndromes:

- The rejection of the model of marriage as such
- Adultery is permissible
- Casual sex is acceptable

France and Slovenia lead the field here, with a large chunk of the European continent – the UK, the BENELUX countries, Germany, Spain, Greece, Sweden and Estonia as well as Belarus following behind in a group. The third group of medium permissiveness is constituted by Portugal, Ireland, Italy, the Central European countries, the Ukraine, Russia, the rest of the Baltic States, and Finland, while Croatia, Romania, and Poland are the least sexually permissive European societies.

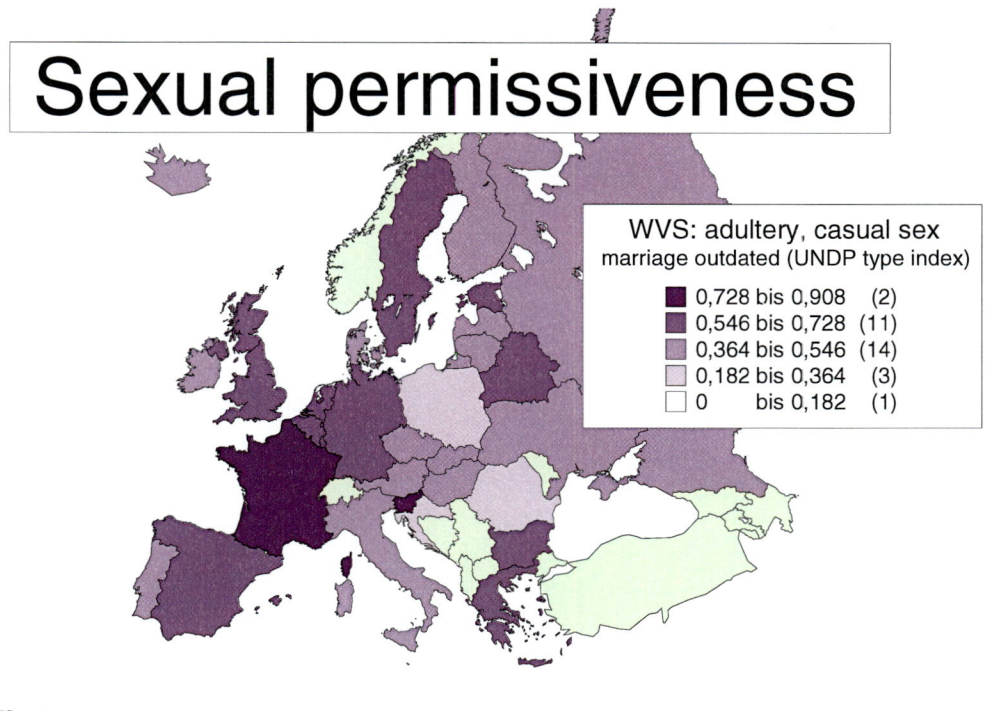

Map 14. Sexual permissiveness index.

Note: non-parametric standard UNDP-type index of the World Values Survey country results (wave 3+4) the three specified sexual permissiveness variables
Explanatory note: "bis" is shorthand for "ranging from ... to"; countries with missing values are marked in green color

The raw data, which were used in the index construction, are quoted in Table 20:

Table 20. Sexual permissiveness – the raw data

	Adultery justifiable (mean response on a 10 point scale)	Casual sex justifiable (mean response on a 10 point scale)	Marriage outdated institution (% of total adult resident population saying this)
Iceland [1999]	1.47	4.97	8.3
Sweden [1999]	2.38	4.8	20.4
Greece [1999]	2.95	4.62	15.7
Slovenia [1999]	3.47	4.08	27.4
Spain [1999]	2.48	3.92	17.5
France [1999]	3.52	3.91	36.3
Belarus [2000]	3.3	3.89	17
Netherlands [1999]	2.65	3.76	25
Finland [2000]	2.36	3.75	18
Denmark [1999]	2.1	3.69	15
Luxembourg [1999]	2.48	3.5	32.8
Great Britain [1999]	2.31	3.44	25.9
Slovakia [1999]	3.19	3.24	11.5
Germany West [1999]	2.83	3.19	18.6
Estonia [1999]	3.33	3.09	15.8
Italy [1999]	2.75	3.07	17
Austria [1999]	2.44	3.05	20.1
Czech Republic [1999]	2.81	2.91	11.4
Russian Federation [1999]	2.65	2.84	21.7
Bulgaria [1999]	3.37	2.77	17.9
Ukraine [1999]	2.49	2.77	18
Portugal [1999]	2.47	2.76	25.6
Hungary [1999]	2.1	2.74	17.1
Belgium [1999]	2.55	2.69	30.6
Ireland [1999]	1.82	2.66	22.3
Croatia [1999]	2.48	2.6	8.3
Lithuania [1999]	2.34	2.41	20.5
Latvia [1999]	3.04	2.36	16.4
Poland [1999]	1.94	2.35	9.3
Romania [1999]	1.98	2	12.5
Malta [1999]	1.11	1.13	6.7

Note: World Values Survey country results (wave 3+4) the three specified sexual permissiveness variables.

The provocative question in this context then is: which trade-off exists between the erosion of the institution of civil heterosexual marriage and societal decay? For this reason, we calculated again a UNDP type of index, this time called the clean hands index, composed of the acceptance of bribery, cheating on taxes, and acceptance of government benefits fraud.

"Clean hands" index
- Mean acceptance level: bribery
- Mean acceptance level: cheating on taxes

- Mean acceptance level: government benefits fraud

The most lamentable results, shown in white color, are to be observed in ultra-permissive societies like France, Belarus, Belgium, et cetera, while the countries most immune against the combination of bribery, cheating on taxes and government benefits fraud are the family-value–oriented countries like Morocco, Egypt, and Turkey. The match is now 1:1, definitely:

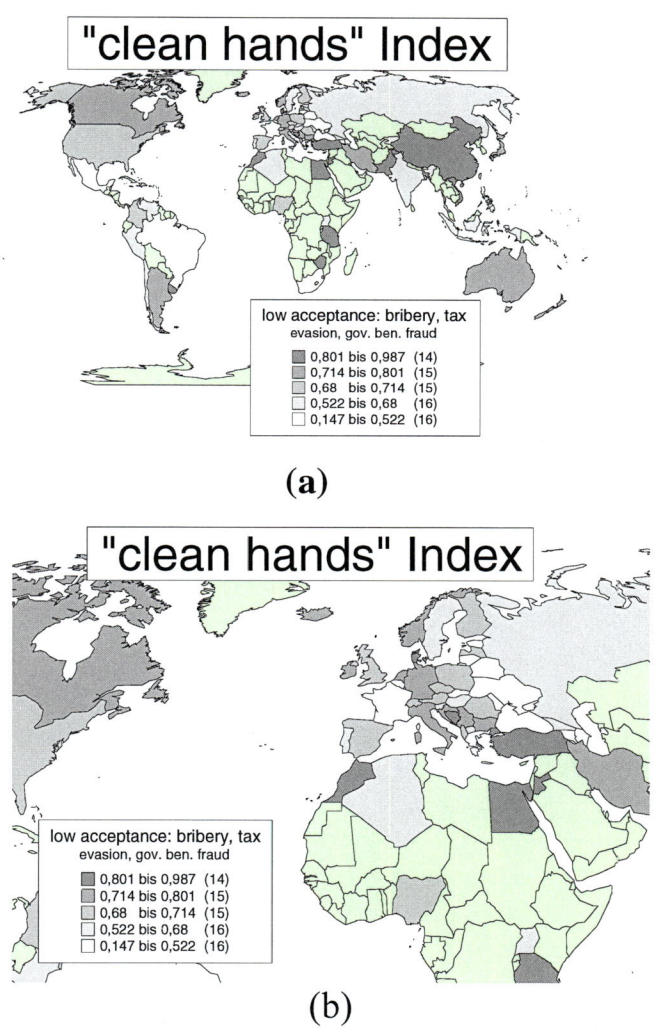

Map 15 a-b. "Clean hands" index (continued).

Note: non-parametric standard UNDP-type index of the World Values Survey country results (wave 3+4) for the voluntary work variables: social welfare service for elderly, handicapped or deprived people; religious or church organization; education, arts, music or cultural activities; labor unions; political parties or groups; local political action groups; human rights; environment, conservation, animal rights; professional associations; youth work; sports or recreation; women's group; peace movement; organization concerned with health; other groups.

Explanatory note: "bis" is shorthand for "ranging from … to"; countries with missing values are marked in green color.

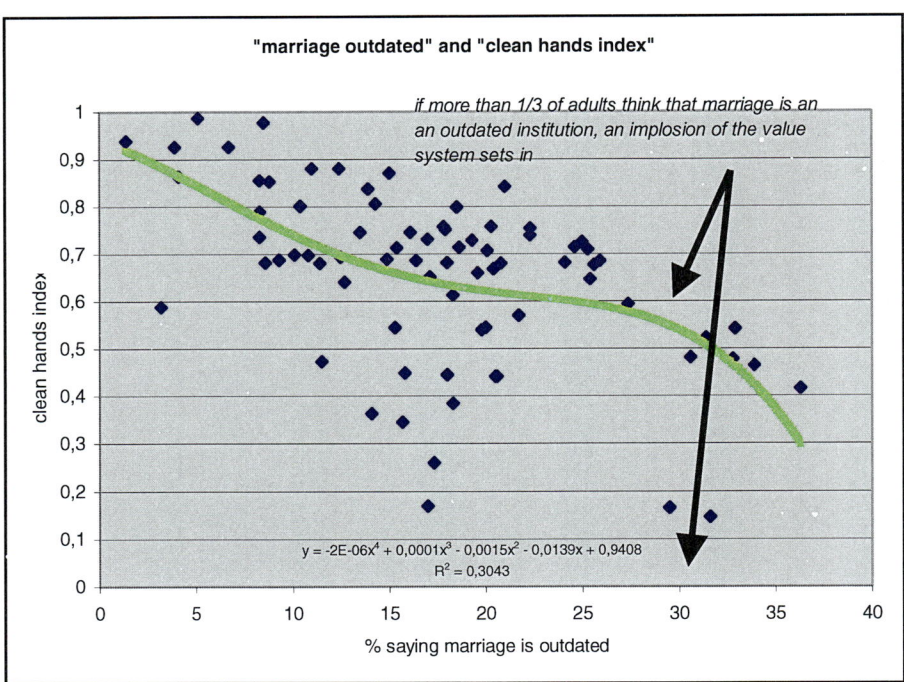

Graph 25. The erosion of the institution of marriage and the erosion of the value system.

SPSS XIV and XV calculations, University Computing Center, Innsbruck University, based on the data of this work and our own calculations from World Values Survey, 3rd and 4th wave, http://www.worldvaluessurvey.org/.

Being an empirical political scientist, we now can also estimate the "trigger levels" of sexual permissiveness, beyond which a society will increasingly face the danger of a social implosion, constituted by bribery, tax evasion and government benefits fraud. Our estimate, well usable for policy planners and religious and civil society leaders around the globe is that a society must under any circumstances avoid a situation where more than 1/3 of the adult population assumes that marriage is outdated.

Our next empirical test deals with the hotly contested question – how much secularization is necessary, or for that matter, even possible? Or do we really need a stronger religious consciousness throughout the globe? Does frequent religious service attendance make people more tolerant, less accepting corruption, more optimistic or less optimistic about the market economy, does it drive them politically to the right or to the left, and what are the effects on such policy areas as economic inequality?

Are empty Churches, Mosques, Synagogues and Temples really in the interest of enlightened humanity? Our empirical analysis tests the effects of falling religious service attendance rates on societal attitudes and behavior, using a partial correlation analyses between religious service non-attendance rates with 77 key World Values Survey indicators for the four separate global religious groups: Catholics, Muslims, Orthodox and Protestants. A sophisticated research design, looking at the correlations of religious service non-attendance versus attendance rates (high numerical values: no attendance, low numerical values: daily attendance) in the global Catholic, Muslim *et cetera* sample with the 77 variables, has to exclude the obvious intervening effects of poverty and education in the game. Religious sociology around the globe fairly reasonably assumes that religious service attendance rates among the poor are higher than among the rich, and they also assume that the same holds for the trade-off with education. Thus we did not run bi-variate correlations, but partial SPSS XIV and XV correlations, keeping constant the WVS variables: Highest educational level attained and Income level.

Our investigation now looks into the partial effects of religious service non-attendance among the separate global samples of global Catholics, Muslims, Orthodox and Protestants:

Anti-egalitarian position on the income equality scale

1. Basic kinds of attitudes concerning society
2. Competition harmful (Competition good or harmful)
3. For state ownership of business
4. Government responsibility
5. Hard work brings success
6. Job taking of the unemployed
7. Justifiable: abortion
8. Justifiable: adultery
9. Justifiable: avoiding a fare on public transport
10. Justifiable: buy stolen goods
11. Justifiable: cheating on taxes
12. Justifiable: claiming government benefits
13. Justifiable: divorce
14. Justifiable: drinking alcohol
15. Justifiable: driving under influence of alcohol
16. Justifiable: euthanasia
17. Justifiable: experiments with human embryos
18. Justifiable: failing to report damage you've done accidentally to a parked vehicle
19. Justifiable: fighting with the police
20. Justifiable: having casual sex
21. Justifiable: homosexuality
22. Justifiable: joyriding
23. Justifiable: keeping money that you have found
24. Justifiable: killing in self-defense
25. Justifiable: lying
26. Justifiable: manipulation of food
27. Justifiable: paying cash
28. Justifiable: political assassination
29. Justifiable: prostitution
30. Justifiable: sex under the legal age of consent
31. Justifiable: smoking in public places
32. Justifiable: someone accepting a bribe
33. Justifiable: speeding over the limit
34. Justifiable: suicide
35. Justifiable: taking soft drugs

36 Justifiable: threatening workers who refuse to join a strike
37 Justifiable: throwing away litter
38 Lack of confidence: Armed Forces
39 Lack of confidence: Churches
40 Lack of confidence: Education System
41 Lack of confidence: Health Care System
42 Lack of confidence: Justice System
43 Lack of confidence: Labor Unions
44 Lack of confidence: Major Companies
45 Lack of confidence: NATO
46 Lack of confidence: Parliament
47 Lack of confidence: Social Security System
48 Lack of confidence: Television
49 Lack of confidence: The Civil Services
50 Lack of confidence: The Environmental Protection Movement
51 Lack of confidence: The European Union
52 Lack of confidence: The Government
53 Lack of confidence: The Police
54 Lack of confidence: The Political Parties
55 Lack of confidence: The Press
56 Lack of confidence: The United Nations
57 Lack of confidence: The Women's Movement
58 Rejecting neighbors: Drug addicts
59 Rejecting neighbors: Emotionally unstable people
60 Rejecting neighbors: Evangelists
61 Rejecting neighbors: Gypsies
62 Rejecting neighbors: Heavy drinkers
63 Rejecting neighbors: Homosexuals
64 Rejecting neighbors: Immigrants/foreign workers
65 Rejecting neighbors: Jews
66 Rejecting neighbors: Militant minority
67 Rejecting neighbors: Muslims
68 Rejecting neighbors: People not from country of origin
69 Rejecting neighbors: People of a different race
70 Rejecting neighbors: People of a different religion
71 Rejecting neighbors: People of the same religion
72 Rejecting neighbors: People who have AIDS
73 Rejecting neighbors: People with a criminal record
74 Rejecting neighbors: Zoroastrians
75 Self positioning in political left-right scale on the right
76 Wealth accumulation

A high non-attendance of religious services is interpreted here as a simple, crude indicator of secularization. The results of this exercise are now given in Table 21. It tells us that for example, the fear about competition among Muslims will increase stronger with secularization than among the other religious global groups in question.

Table 21. Is everybody better off with empty churches, mosques, synagogues and temples? The effects of falling religious service attendance rates on societal attitudes and behavior, partial correlation analyses with the constants: highest educational level attained and Income level; the effects of religious service non-attendance on global Catholics, Muslims, Orthodox and Protestants

IRRESPECTIVE OF EDUCATION AND INCOME LEVELS (PARTIAL CORRELATION ANALYSIS, ALL RESPONDENTS WORLD VALUES SURVEY; ALL WAVES)	CATHOLICISM	ISLAM	ORTHODOXY	PROTESTANTISM
Basic kinds of attitudes concerning society	-0.028	0.002	0.011	0.041
Competition harmful (Competition good or harmful)	0.018	0.112	0.003	0.013
Government responsibility	0.023	0.006	0.013	-0.137
Hard work brings success	0.064	0.186	0.093	0.131
Anti-egalitarian position on „Income equality" scale	-0.046	-0.051	0.019	-0.05
Job taking of the unemployed	0.012	0.105	0.079	0.014
Justifiable: abortion	0.313	0.139	0.149	0.367
Justifiable: adultery	0.236	-0.054	0.085	0.115
Justifiable: avoiding a fare on public transport	0.064	0.055	0.049	0.05
Justifiable: buy stolen goods	0.084	0.064	0.028	0.049
Justifiable: cheating on taxes	0.079	0.061	0.059	0.151
Justifiable: claiming government benefits	0.066	0.027	-0.011	-0.005
Justifiable: divorce	0.279	0.111	0.118	0.347
Justifiable: drinking alcohol	0.12	0.066	.	0.072
Justifiable: driving under influence of alcohol	0.078	-0.091	0.011	0.006
Justifiable: euthanasia	0.265	0.11	0.145	0.303
Justifiable: experiments with human embryos	0.101	0.074	0.129	0.102
Justifiable: failing to report damage you've done accidentally to a parked vehicle	0.078	-0.12	0.018	0.026
Justifiable: fighting with the police	0.132	-0.041	0.018	0.031
Justifiable: having casual sex	0.251	0.038	0.038	0.255
Justifiable: homosexuality	0.175	0.053	0.015	0.294
Justifiable: joyriding	0.039	-0.186	-0.032	0.018
Justifiable: keeping money that you have found	0.178	-0.316	-0.002	0.049
Justifiable: killing in self-defense	0.136	0.062	0.206	0.086
Justifiable: lying	0.18	-0.115	0.044	0.101
Justifiable: manipulation of food	0.079	0.138	0.108	0.1
Justifiable: paying cash	0.131	-0.009	0.002	0.184
Justifiable: political assassination	0.05	-0.108	0.025	-0.004

Table 21. (Continued)

IRRESPECTIVE OF EDUCATION AND INCOME LEVELS (PARTIAL CORRELATION ANALYSIS, ALL RESPONDENTS WORLD VALUES SURVEY; ALL WAVES)	CATHOLICISM	ISLAM	ORTHODOXY	PROTESTANTISM
Justifiable: prostitution	0.199	0.036	0.069	0.23
Justifiable: sex under the legal age of consent	0.21	-0.058	0.002	0.048
Justifiable: smoking in public places	0.152	0.046	0.036	0.168
Justifiable: someone accepting a bribe	0.056	0.068	0.003	0.004
Justifiable: speeding over the limit	0.089	0.029	0.043	0.13
Justifiable: suicide	0.169	0.063	0.08	0.196
Justifiable: taking soft drugs	0.119	-0.108	-0.006	0.125
Justifiable: threatening workers who refuse to join a strike	0.05	-0.218	-0.019	0.019
Justifiable: throwing away litter	0.031	-0.08	-0.011	0.084
Lack of confidence: Armed Forces	0.14	0.081	0.033	0.095
Lack of confidence: Churches	0.465	0.241	0.345	0.524
Lack of confidence: Education System	0.118	0.111	0.049	0.074
Lack of confidence: Health Care System	0.039	0.047	0.038	0.02
Lack of confidence: Justice System	0.083	0.161	0.054	0.022
Lack of confidence: Labor Unions	0.055	0.075	0.027	0.017
Lack of confidence: Major Companies	0.099	0.078	0.028	0.132
Lack of confidence: NATO	0.084	0.062	0.024	0.028
Lack of confidence: Parliament	0.089	0.097	0.033	0.074
Lack of confidence: Social Security System	0.071	0.113	0.005	0.093
Lack of confidence: Television	0.066	0.071	0.037	0.129
Lack of confidence: The Civil Services	0.101	0.097	0.034	0.146
Lack of confidence: The Environmental Protection Movement	0.06	0.047	-0.024	0.112
Lack of confidence: The European Union	0.053	0	0.019	0.053
Lack of confidence: The Government	0.099	0.079	0.041	0.131
Lack of confidence: The Police	0.097	0.014	0.055	-0.056
Lack of confidence: The Political Parties	0.064	0.108	0.053	0.108
Lack of confidence: The Press	0.05	0.091	0.052	0.139
Lack of confidence: The United Nations	0.078	0.064	0.007	0.071
Lack of confidence: The Women's Movement	0.092	0.023	0.039	0.16

IRRESPECTIVE OF EDUCATION AND INCOME LEVELS (PARTIAL CORRELATION ANALYSIS, ALL RESPONDENTS WORLD VALUES SURVEY; ALL WAVES)	CATHOLICISM	ISLAM	ORTHODOXY	PROTESTANTISM
For state ownership of business	-0.013	0.007	0.038	-0.053
Rejecting neighbors: Drug addicts	-0.054	0.052	0.025	-0.016
Rejecting neighbors: Emotionally unstable people	-0.023	0.064	0.023	-0.087
Rejecting neighbors: Evangelists	-0.064	.	.	0.189
Rejecting neighbors: Gypsies	-0.038	-0.121	-0.032	-0.045
Rejecting neighbors: Heavy drinkers	-0.056	0.033	-0.017	-0.105
Rejecting neighbors: Homosexuals	-0.089	0.039	0.025	-0.242
Rejecting neighbors: Immigrants/foreign workers	-0.015	-0.025	-0.019	-0.058
Rejecting neighbors: Jews	-0.041	0.053	-0.074	-0.094
Rejecting neighbors: Militant minority	-0.013	0.081	.	.
Rejecting neighbors: Muslims	-0.026	0.113	-0.061	-0.019
Rejecting neighbors: People not from country of origin	0.436	-0.043	.	.
Rejecting neighbors: People of a different race	-0.036	-0.046	-0.056	-0.081
Rejecting neighbors: People of a different religion	-0.004	0.033	-0.08	-0.086
Rejecting neighbors: People of the same religion	-0.082	0.053	.	.
Rejecting neighbors: People who have AIDS	-0.077	0.042	0.024	-0.164
Rejecting neighbors: People with a criminal record	-0.121	-0.004	-0.085	-0.174
Rejecting neighbors: Zoroastrians	0.024	-0.033	.	.
Self positioning in political left-right scale on the right	-0.152	-0.141	-0.112	-0.078
Wealth accumulation	-0.075	-0.01	0.006	-0.058

SPSS XIV and XV calculations, University Computing Center, Innsbruck University, based on the data of this work and our own calculations from World Values Survey, 3rd and 4th wave, http://www.worldvaluessurvey.org/.

The results for the Muslims are given in Table 22 in descending order. The most notable increases in the process of secularization among the global Muslims are to be observed for:

- Lack of confidence: Churches
- Hard work brings success
- Lack of confidence: Justice System
- Justifiable: abortion
- Justifiable: manipulation of food

Table 22. The effects of secularism on Islam

IRRESPECTIVE OF EDUCATION AND INCOME LEVELS (PARTIAL CORRELATION ANALYSIS, ALL RESPONDENTS WORLD VALUES SURVEY; ALL WAVES)	THE EFFECTS OF RELIGIOUS SECULARISM (=NON-ATTENDANCE OF RELIGIOUS SERVICES) ON ISLAM
Lack of confidence: Churches	0.241
Hard work brings success	0.186
Lack of confidence: Justice System	0.161
Justifiable: abortion	0.139
Justifiable: manipulation of food	0.138
Lack of confidence: Social Security System	0.113
Rejecting neighbors: Muslims	0.113
Competition harmful (Competition good or harmful)	0.112
Justifiable: divorce	0.111
Lack of confidence: Education System	0.111
Justifiable: euthanasia	0.11
Lack of confidence: The Political Parties	0.108
Job taking of the unemployed	0.105
Lack of confidence: The Civil Services	0.097
Lack of confidence: Parliament	0.097
Lack of confidence: The Press	0.091
Lack of confidence: Armed Forces	0.081
Lack of confidence: The Government	0.079
Lack of confidence: Major Companies	0.078
Lack of confidence: Labor Unions	0.075
Justifiable: experiments with human embryos	0.074
Lack of confidence: Television	0.071
Justifiable: someone accepting a bribe	0.068
Justifiable: buy stolen goods	0.064
Lack of confidence: The United Nations	0.064
Rejecting neighbors: Emotionally unstable people	0.064
Justifiable: suicide	0.063
Lack of confidence: NATO	0.062
Justifiable: cheating on taxes	0.061
Justifiable: avoiding a fare on public transport	0.055
Justifiable: homosexuality	0.053
Rejecting neighbors: Jews	0.053
Rejecting neighbors: Drug addicts	0.052
Lack of confidence: The Environmental Protection Movement	0.047
Lack of confidence: Health Care System	0.047
Justifiable: smoking in public places	0.046
Rejecting neighbors: People who have AIDS	0.042
Rejecting neighbors: Homosexuals	0.039
Justifiable: having casual sex	0.038
Justifiable: prostitution	0.036
Rejecting neighbors: People of a different religion	0.033

IRRESPECTIVE OF EDUCATION AND INCOME LEVELS (PARTIAL CORRELATION ANALYSIS, ALL RESPONDENTS WORLD VALUES SURVEY; ALL WAVES)	THE EFECTS OF RELIGIOUS SECULARISM (=NON-ATTENDANCE OF RELIGIOUS SERVICES) ON ISLAM
Rejecting neighbors: People of a different religion	0.033
Rejecting neighbors: Heavy drinkers	0.033
Justifiable: speeding over the limit	0.029
Justifiable: claiming government benefits	0.027
Lack of confidence: The Women's Movement	0.023
Lack of confidence: The Police	0.014
For state ownership of business	0.007
Government responsibility	0.006
Basic kinds of attitudes concerning society	0.002
Lack of confidence: The European Union	0
Rejecting neighbors: People with a criminal record	-0.004
Justifiable: paying cash	-0.009
Wealth accumulation	-0.01
Rejecting neighbors: Immigrants/foreign workers	-0.025
Rejecting neighbors: People of a different race	-0.046
Anti-egalitarian position on „Income equality" scale	-0.051
Justifiable: adultery	-0.054
Justifiable: sex under the legal age of consent	-0.058
Justifiable: throwing away litter	-0.08
Justifiable: driving under influence of alcohol	-0.091
Justifiable: taking soft drugs	-0.108
Justifiable: political assassination	-0.108
Justifiable: lying	-0.115
Rejecting neighbors: Gypsies	-0.121
Self positioning in political left-right scale on the right	-0.141
Justifiable: joyriding	-0.186
Justifiable: keeping money that you have found	-0.316

SPSS XIV and XV calculations, University Computing Center, Innsbruck University, based on the data of this work and our own calculations from World Values Survey, 3rd and 4th wave, http://www.worldvaluessurvey.org/.

The most notable decreases along the process of secularization are to be observed for the following variables:

- Justifiable: keeping money that you have found
- Justifiable: joyriding
- Self positioning in political left-right scale on the right
- Rejecting neighbors: Gypsies
- Justifiable: lying

It has to be noted that the observed effects in all religious groups around the world are rather small.

In general, it can be safely assumed that secularization does NOT have the general and beneficial effects, which secularists around the globe assume to have. Although the tendency to justify political assassinations decreases among secular Muslims and secular Protestants, and increases among secular Catholics and secular Orthodox, the effects explain a rather small percentage of total variance (squared partial correlations). The direct comparison between the "secularization paths" of the 4 large global denominations however yields quite interesting results: Muslims are the religious denomination, whose "yes" to the "American dream" ("hard work brings success") is strongly secularization-driven:

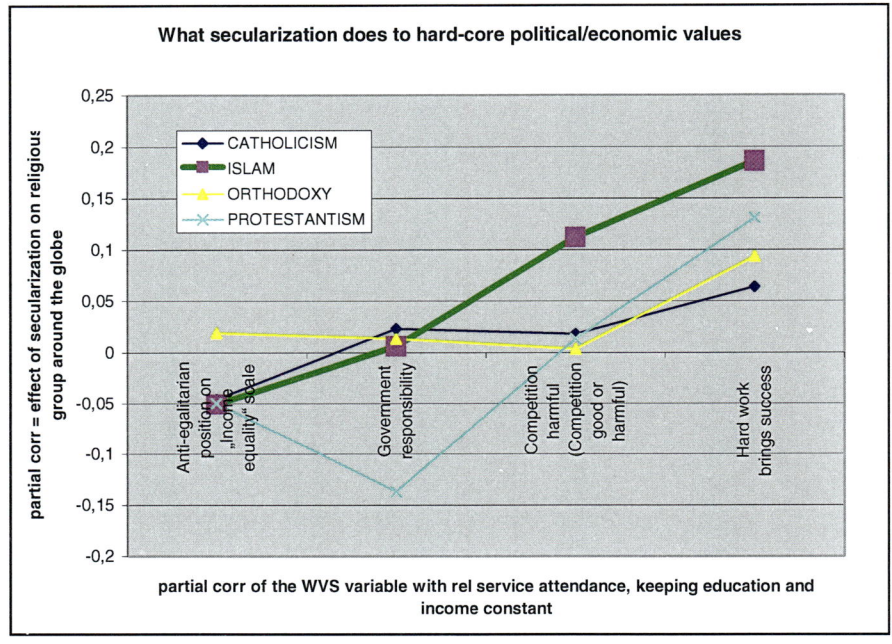

Graph 26. The effects of secularism on hard-core political and economic values.

SPSS XIV and XV calculations, University Computing Center, Innsbruck University, based on the data of this work and our own calculations from World Values Survey, 3rd and 4th wave, http://www.worldvaluessurvey.org/.

It is not religious service attendance, but religious service non-attendance, i.e., secularization, that is numerically positively correlated with an increasing rejection of Jewish neighbors. i.e., *ceteris paribus* – several phobias, including Muslim-self-hatred – notably increase with growing secularization.

Increasing secularization also leads – *ceteris paribus* – towards an increase in the lack of trust in the major state institutions.

Interestingly enough, Muslim secularization, *in tandem* with other global religions, also leads to decay in societal values:

Thus in order to further strengthen the alliance of Enlightenment, there is no need for Muslims to give up their spirituality. This is the positive and optimistic message of this work.

By Way of Conclusion 257

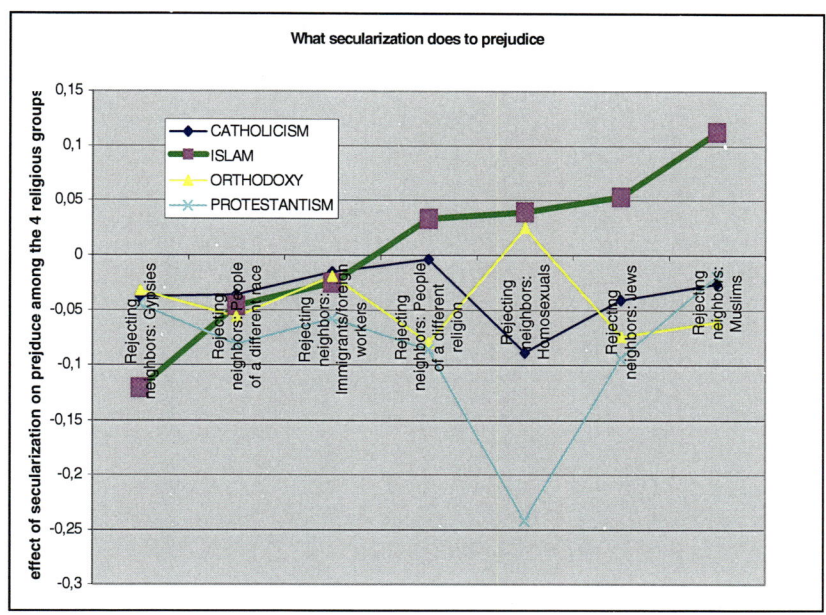

Graph 27. The effects of secularism on prejudice.

SPSS XIV and XV calculations, University Computing Center, Innsbruck University, based on the data of this work and our own calculations from World Values Survey, 3rd and 4th wave, http://www.worldvaluessurvey.org/.

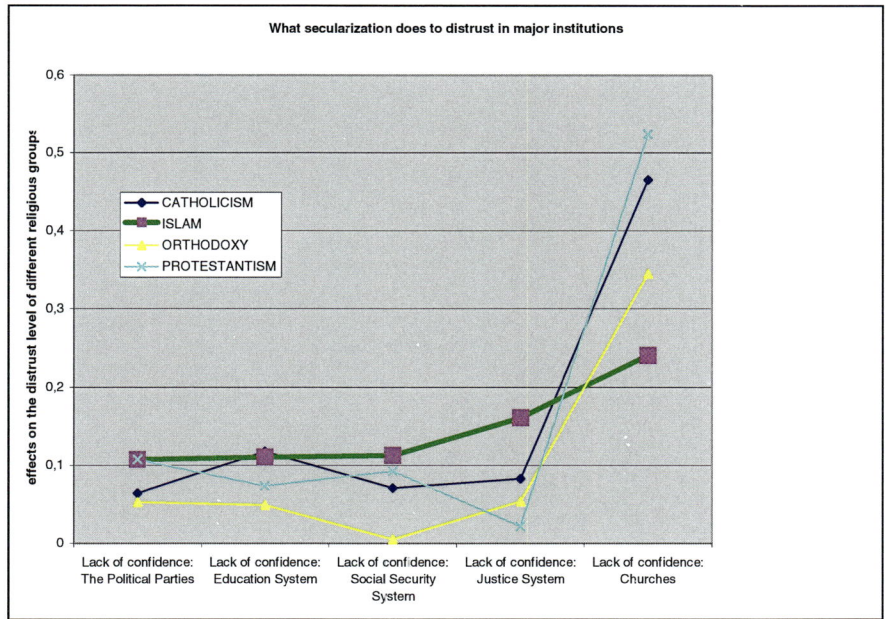

Graph 28. the effects of secularism on distrust in major institutions.

SPSS XIV and XV calculations, University Computing Center, Innsbruck University, based on the data of this work and our own calculations from World Values Survey, 3rd and 4th wave, http://www.worldvaluessurvey.org/.

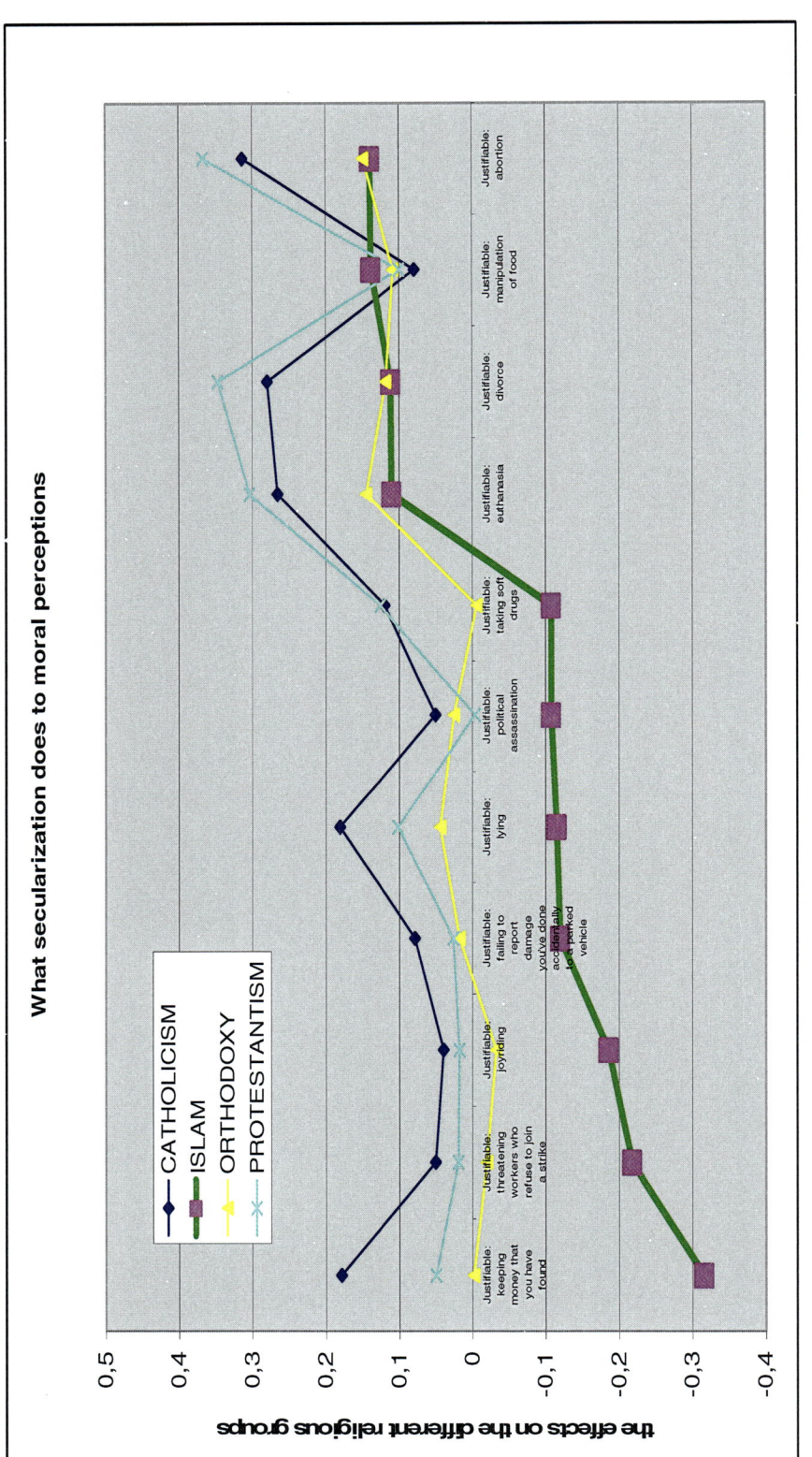

Graph 29. the effects of secularism on moral perceptions.

SPSS XIV and XV calculations, University Computing Center, Innsbruck University, based on the data of this work and our own calculations from World Values Survey, 3rd and 4th wave, http://www.worldvaluessurvey.org/

Appendix I

ANALYSIS OF WVS DATA: METHODOLOGICAL NOTES ON SAMPLE SIZE, ERROR PROBABILITY, SAMPLE COMPOSITION, ET CETERA

THE METHODOLOGY*

http://www.worldvaluessurvey.org/

University of Michigan

Our own analysis (online data analysis)

Number of respondents	At 10 % confidence interval - error range (the real value could be plus or minus the given values in %)
5	36.7
10	25.9
15	21.2
20	18.3
25	16.4
30	15
35	13.9
40	13
45	12.2
50	11.6
55	11.1
60	10.6
65	10.2
70	9.8
75	9.5
80	9.2

---

* Note for all the tables: Results with n < 50 are to be interpreted with extreme care. True results might be +- 11.6% off the mark. See also: Appendix Table above for +- error range at the 10% confidence interval.

Number of respondents	At 10 % confidence interval - error range (the real value could be plus or minus the given values in %)
85	8.9
90	8.6
95	8.4
100	8.2
110	7.8
120	7.5
130	7.2
140	6.9
150	6.7
160	6.5
170	6.3
180	6.1
190	5.9
200	5.8
210	5.7
220	5.5
230	5.4
240	5.3
250	5.2
260	5.1
270	5
280	4.9
300	4.7
320	4.6
340	4.4
360	4.3
380	4.2
400	4.1
420	4
440	3.9
460	3.8
480	3.7
500	3.7
550	3.5
600	3.3
650	3.2
700	3.1
750	3
800	2.9
850	2.8
900	2.7
950	2.7
1000	2.6

The World Sample: Persons belonging to a religious confession

BASE=267875	Male	Female	Total	Religious group in %
Total	46.9	53.1	204303	100
Roman Catholic	45.9	54.1	87053	42.6097512
Protestant	46.9	53.1	37522	18.36585855
Muslim	51.5	48.5	30039	14.70316148
Orthodox	42.4	57.6	20397	9.98370068
Hindu	54.4	45.6	5977	2.925556649
Buddhist	47.7	52.3	4076	1.995075941
Other	44.4	55.6	3705	1.813482915
Free church/Non denominational church	46	54	2182	1.068021517
Sunni	52.5	47.5	1956	0.957401507
Jew	46.4	53.6	1741	0.852165656
Evangelical	43.7	56.3	1672	0.81839229
Armenian Apostolic Church	44.4	55.6	1654	0.809581847
The Church of Sweden	51.1	48.9	853	0.417517119
Shia	44.4	55.6	829	0.405769861
Independent African Church (e.g., ZCC, Shembe, et cetera)	43.2	56.8	652	0.319133836
Pentecostal	41.5	58.5	572	0.27997631
Other: Taiwan (Taoism, protestant fundamentalism, ancient cults)	49.9	50.1	343	0.167887892
Catholic: doesn't follow rules	50	50	332	0.162503732
Ancestral worshipping	46.7	53.3	304	0.148798598
Zionist	42.1	57.9	290	0.141946031
Anglican	47.6	52.4	278	0.136072402
Christian	50.8	49.2	225	0.110130541
Al-Hadis	44.7	55.3	221	0.108172665
Jehovah witnesses	44.5	55.5	168	0.082230804
Other: Brazil: Espirit, Candomblé, Umbanda, Esoterism, Occultism	40	60	165	0.080762397
Taoist	56.5	43.5	115	0.056288943
Iglesia ni Cristo (INC)	54.4	45.6	81	0.039646995
Tac	54.5	45.5	73	0.035731242
Sikh	53.3	46.7	68	0.033283897
Shenism (Chinese Religion)	42.9	57.1	65	0.03181549
C and S Celestial	40.6	59.4	63	0.030836552
Seven Day Adventist	52.9	47.1	61	0.029857613
Jain	64.1	35.9	56	0.027410268
Gregorian	54.1	45.9	44	0.021536639
Baptist	58.9	41.1	42	0.020557701

The World Sample (Continued)'

BASE=267875	Male	Female	Total	Religious group in %
Independent Church	35.7	64.3	42	0.020557701
Aglipayan	54.7	45.3	36	0.017620887
Born again	45.5	54.5	32	0.01566301
Greek Catholic	54.1	45.9	30	0.014684072
Israelita Nuevo Pacto Universal (FREPAP)	41.7	58.3	24	0.011747258
Presbyterian	54.5	45.5	22	0.01076832
Confucianism	66.7	33.3	21	0.010278851
Other: Philippines (less 0.5%)	55	45	20	0.009789381
Druse	64.7	35.3	17	0.008320974
Church of Christ	77.9	22.1	16	0.007831505
Mormon	59.3	40.7	16	0.007831505
Jesus is Lord (JIL)	27.2	72.8	12	0.005873629
United	10.5	89.5	11	0.00538416
Lutheran	11.5	88.5	10	0.004894691
Qadiani	25	75	9	0.004405222
Zoroastrian	44.4	55.6	9	0.004405222
Cao dai	25	75	8	0.003915753
Hussite	87.5	12.5	8	0.003915753
Mennonite	39.2	60.8	8	0.003915753
Filipinista	65.5	34.5	6	0.002936814
Other: Christian com	66.7	33.3	6	0.002936814
United Church of Christ in the Philippines (UCCP)	16.9	83.1	6	0.002936814
Methodists	40.4	59.6	5	0.002447345
New Testament Christ/Biblist	40.9	59.1	5	0.002447345
Assembly of God	100	0	4	0.001957876
Essid	100	0	4	0.001957876
Mita	50	50	4	0.001957876
Alliance	100	0	3	0.001468407
Native	0	100	3	0.001468407
Paganism	35	65	3	0.001468407
Spiritista	31.3	68.7	3	0.001468407
The Worldwide Church of God	50	50	3	0.001468407
Christian Reform	0	100	2	0.000978938
El Shaddai	0	100	2	0.000978938
Faith in god	100	0	2	0.000978938
Ka-a Elica	100	0	2	0.000978938

BASE=267875	Male	Female	Total	Religious group in %
Other: Oriental'	50	50	2	0.000978938
Theosofists	100	0	2	0.000978938
Unitarian	0	100	2	0.000978938
Brgy. Sang Birhen	100	0	1	0.000489469
Christian Fellowship	0	100	1	0.000489469
Hoa hao	100	0	1	0.000489469
Jesus Miracle Crusade	0	100	1	0.000489469
Self Lealisation Fellowship	0	100	1	0.000489469
Sisewiss	0	100	1	0.000489469
Spiritualists	0	100	1	0.000489469
Wicca	0	100	1	0.000489469

Source: Our own compilations, based on the official Website of the *World Values Survey (WVS)* Project, http://www.worldvaluessurvey.org./. Our calculations are based on the WVS data (Download survey data files) and the SPSS XIV statistics program, Innsbruck University. All waves of the WVS surveys are integrated into the data file. To weight for country population size, we used the WVS routine: weights 1000. The sample comprised 204303 representative interview partners with available data on religious confession, gender and age of the respondent. The following WVS surveys were part of our investigation: Albania [1998], Albania [2002], Algeria [2002], Argentina [1984], Argentina [1991], Argentina [1995], Argentina [1999], Armenia [1997], Australia [1981], Australia [1995], Austria [1990], Austria [1999], Azerbaijan [1997], Bangladesh [1996], Bangladesh [2002], Belarus [1990], Belarus [1996], Belarus [2000], Belgium [1981], Belgium [1990], Belgium [1999], Bosnia and Herzegovina [1998], Bosnia and Herzegovina [2001], Brazil [1991], Brazil [1997], Bulgaria [1990], Bulgaria [1997], Bulgaria [1999], Canada [1982], Canada [1990], Canada [2000], Chile [1990], Chile [1996], Chile [2000], China [1990], China [1995], China [2001], Colombia [1997], Colombia [1998], Croatia [1996], Croatia [1999], Czech Republic [1990], Czech Republic [1991], Czech Republic [1998], Czech Republic [1999], Denmark [1981], Denmark [1990], Denmark [1999], Dominican Republic [1996], Egypt [2000], El Salvador [1999], Estonia [1990], Estonia [1996], Estonia [1999], Finland [1990], Finland [1996], Finland [2000], France [1981], France [1990], France [1999], Georgia [1996], Germany East [1990], Germany East [1997], Germany East [1999], Germany West [1981], Germany West [1990], Germany West [1997], Germany West [1999], Great Britain [1981], Great Britain [1990], Great Britain [1998], Great Britain [1999], Greece [1999], Hungary [1982], Hungary [1991], Hungary [1998], Hungary [1999], Iceland [1984], Iceland [1990], Iceland [1999], India [1990], India [1995], India [2001], Indonesia [2001], Iran (Islamic Republic of) [2000], Iraq [2004], Ireland [1981], Ireland [1990], Ireland [1999], Israel [2001], Italy [1981], Italy [1990], Italy [1999], Japan [1981], Japan [1990], Japan [1995], Japan [2000], Jordan [2001], Kyrgyzstan [2003], Latvia [1990], Latvia [1996], Latvia [1999], Lithuania [1990], Lithuania [1997], Lithuania [1999], Luxembourg [1999], Macedonia, Republic of [1998], Macedonia, Republic of [2001], Malta [1983], Malta [1991], Malta [1999], Mexico [1990], Mexico [1996], Mexico [2000], Montenegro [1996], Montenegro [2001], Morocco [2001], Morocco [2001], Netherlands [1981], Netherlands [1990], Netherlands [1999], New Zealand [1998], Nigeria [1990], Nigeria [1995], Nigeria [2000], Northern Ireland [1981], Northern Ireland [1990], Northern Ireland [1999], Norway [1982], Norway [1990], Norway [1996], Pakistan [1997], Pakistan [2001], Peru [1996], Peru [2001], Philippines [1996], Philippines [2001], Poland [1989], Poland [1990], Poland [1997], Poland [1999], Portugal [1990], Portugal [1999], Puerto Rico [1995], Puerto Rico [2001], Republic of Korea [1982], Republic of Korea [1990], Republic of Korea [1996], Republic of Korea [2001],

Republic of Moldova [1996], Republic of Moldova [2002], Romania [1993], Romania [1998], Romania [1999], Russian Federation [1990], Russian Federation [1995], Russian Federation [1999], Saudi Arabia [2003], Serbia [1996], Serbia [2001], Singapore [2002], Slovakia [1990], Slovakia [1991], Slovakia [1998], Slovakia [1999], Slovenia [1992], Slovenia [1995], Slovenia [1999], South Africa [1990], South Africa [1996], South Africa [2001], Spain [1981], Spain [1990], Spain [1990], Spain [1995], Spain [1999], Spain [2000], Sweden [1982], Sweden [1990], Sweden [1996], Sweden [1999], Switzerland [1989], Switzerland [1996], Taiwan [1994], Tanzania, United Republic Of [2001], Turkey [1990], Turkey [1996], Turkey [2001], Turkey [2001], Uganda [2001], Ukraine [1996], Ukraine [1999], United States [1982], United States [1990], United States [1995], United States [1999], Uruguay [1996], Venezuela [1996], Venezuela [2000], Viet Nam [2001], Zimbabwe [2001].

The WVS sample Euro-Islam (EU-27 + EEA + EFTA) includes Austria [1999], Belgium [1999] Bulgaria [1999], Czech Republic [1999], Denmark [1999], Estonia [1999], Finland [2000], France [1999] East Germany [1999], West Germany [1999], Great Britain [1999], Greece [1999], Hungary [1999], Iceland [1999] Ireland [1999], Italy [1999], Latvia [1999], Lithuania [1999], Luxembourg [1999], Malta [1999], Netherlands [1999], Northern Ireland [1999], Norway [1996], Poland [1999], Portugal [1999], Romania [1999], Slovakia [1999], Slovenia [1999], Spain [2000], Sweden [1999], and Switzerland [1996]. There were 36569 interview partners with basic data such as age or gender. The results have an error margin of +- 0.00 at a significance level of 10%. There were 240 Muslims in the sample, which implies an error margin of +-2.0%. The WVS sample of the EU-27 + EEA + EFTA has a certain bias against the Muslim communities in Western countries such as France, Spain and Italy. The number of Muslim interview partners of the WVS project in the EU-27, EEA + EFTA were: Austria [4], Belgium [34], Bulgaria [109], Czech Republic [0], Denmark [5], Estonia [5], Finland [0], France [1], East Germany [1], West Germany [26], Great Britain [10], Greece [0], Hungary [0], Iceland [0], Ireland [0], Italy [0], Latvia [1], Lithuania [0], Luxembourg [8], Malta [0], Netherlands [10], Northern Ireland [0], Norway [4], Poland [0], Portugal [0], Romania [0], Slovakia [0], Slovenia [11], Spain [1], Sweden [4], Switzerland [6]. Thus our results about Euro-Islam have to be interpreted with caution.

THE "WVS UMMA" AND THE INCOME CATEGORY

Selected samples: Albania [1998], Albania [2002], Algeria [2002], Argentina [1984], Argentina [1991], Argentina [1995], Argentina [1999], Armenia [1997], Australia [1981], Australia [1995], Austria [1990], Austria [1999], Azerbaijan [1997], Bangladesh [1996], Bangladesh [2002], Belarus [1990], Belarus [1996], Belarus [2000], Belgium [1981], Belgium [1990], Belgium [1999], Bosnia and Herzegovina [1998], Bosnia and Herzegovina [2001], Brazil [1991], Brazil [1997], Bulgaria [1990], Bulgaria [1997], Bulgaria [1999], Canada [1982], Canada [1990], Canada [2000], Chile [1990], Chile [1996], Chile [2000], China [1990], China [1995], China [2001], Colombia [1997], Colombia [1998], Croatia [1996], Croatia [1999], Czech Republic [1990], Czech Republic [1991], Czech Republic [1998], Czech Republic [1999], Denmark [1981], Denmark [1990], Denmark [1999], Dominican Republic [1996], Egypt [2000], El Salvador [1999], Estonia [1990], Estonia [1996], Estonia [1999], Finland [1990], Finland [1996], Finland [2000], France [1981], France [1990], France [1999], Georgia [1996], Germany East [1990], Germany East [1997], Germany East [1999], Germany West [1981], Germany West [1990], Germany West [1997], Germany West [1999], Great Britain [1981], Great Britain [1990], Great Britain [1998], Great Britain [1999], Greece [1999], Hungary [1982], Hungary [1991], Hungary [1998], Hungary

[1999], Iceland [1984], Iceland [1990], Iceland [1999], India [1990], India [1995], India [2001], Indonesia [2001], Iran (Islamic Republic of) [2000], Iraq [2004], Ireland [1981], Ireland [1990], Ireland [1999], Israel [2001], Italy [1981], Italy [1990], Italy [1999], Japan [1981], Japan [1990], Japan [1995], Japan [2000], Jordan [2001], Kyrgyzstan [2003], Latvia [1990], Latvia [1996], Latvia [1999], Lithuania [1990], Lithuania [1997], Lithuania [1999], Luxembourg [1999], Macedonia, Republic of [1998], Macedonia, Republic of [2001], Malta [1983], Malta [1991], Malta [1999], Mexico [1990], Mexico [1996], Mexico [2000], Montenegro [1996], Montenegro [2001], Morocco [2001], Morocco [2001], Netherlands [1981], Netherlands [1990], Netherlands [1999], New Zealand [1998], Nigeria [1990], Nigeria [1995], Nigeria [2000], Northern Ireland [1981], Northern Ireland [1990], Northern Ireland [1999], Norway [1982], Norway [1990], Norway [1996], Pakistan [1997], Pakistan [2001], Peru [1996], Peru [2001], Philippines [1996], Philippines [2001], Poland [1989], Poland [1990], Poland [1997], Poland [1999], Portugal [1990], Portugal [1999], Puerto Rico [1995], Puerto Rico [2001], Republic of Korea [1982], Republic of Korea [1990], Republic of Korea [1996], Republic of Korea [2001], Republic of Moldova [1996], Republic of Moldova [2002], Romania [1993], Romania [1998], Romania [1999], Russian Federation [1990], Russian Federation [1995], Russian Federation [1999], Saudi Arabia [2003], Serbia [1996], Serbia [2001], Singapore [2002], Slovakia [1990], Slovakia [1991], Slovakia [1998], Slovakia [1999], Slovenia [1992], Slovenia [1995], Slovenia [1999], South Africa [1990], South Africa [1996], South Africa [2001], Spain [1981], Spain [1990], Spain [1990], Spain [1995], Spain [1999], Spain [2000], Sweden [1982], Sweden [1990], Sweden [1996], Sweden [1999], Switzerland [1989], Switzerland [1996], Taiwan [1994], Tanzania, United Republic Of [2001], Turkey [1990], Turkey [1996], Turkey [2001], Turkey [2001], Uganda [2001], Ukraine [1996], Ukraine [1999], United States [1982], United States [1990], United States [1995], United States [1999], Uruguay [1996], Venezuela [1996], Venezuela [2000], Viet Nam [2001], Zimbabwe [2001]

No data on religion were asked in the following surveys:

- Algeria [2002]
- Belarus [1990]
- China [1995]
- Great Britain [1998]
- Morocco [2001]
- Poland [1989]
- Poland [1999]

There is no person classified in "Muslim" category in the following surveys (the Pakistan surveys categorized respondents by the following religious categories: Al-Hadis, Qadiani, Shia, and Sunni).

	WVS interview partners with data on gender and religion of the respondent	Muslims in the sample
Argentina [1984]	875	0
Argentina [1995]	920	0
Argentina [1999]	1112	0
Armenia [1997]	1695	0
Austria [1990]	1215	0
Brazil [1997]	1009	0
Chile [1990]	1223	0
Chile [1996]	874	0
Chile [2000]	789	0
Colombia [1997]	2733	0
Colombia [1998]	2782	0
Croatia [1999]	890	0
Czech Republic [1990]	829	0
Czech Republic [1991]	392	0
Czech Republic [1998]	481	0
Czech Republic [1999]	630	0
Denmark [1981]	1116	0
Dominican Republic [1996]	310	0
El Salvador [1999]	1054	0
Finland [1990]	517	0
Finland [2000]	906	0
Germany East [1990]	510	0
Germany East [1997]	244	0
Germany West [1981]	1183	0
Germany West [1990]	1870	0
Greece [1999]	1089	0
Hungary [1991]	581	0
Hungary [1998]	502	0
Hungary [1999]	563	0
Iceland [1984]	915	0
Iceland [1990]	686	0
Iceland [1999]	922	0
Ireland [1990]	959	0
Ireland [1999]	921	0
Italy [1981]	1261	0
Italy [1990]	1709	0
Italy [1999]	1635	0
Japan [1981]	726	0
Japan [1990]	321	0
Japan [1995]	354	0

	WVS interview partners with data on gender and religion of the respondent	Muslims in the sample
Japan [2000]	562	0
Lithuania [1990]	624	0
Lithuania [1999]	822	0
Malta [1983]	466	0
Malta [1991]	383	0
Malta [1999]	987	0
Mexico [1990]	1292	0
Mexico [2000]	1231	0
Netherlands [1981]	754	0
Northern Ireland [1981]	298	0
Northern Ireland [1990]	271	0
Northern Ireland [1999]	845	0
Pakistan [1997]	718	**0**
Pakistan [2001]	1417	**0**
Peru [1996]	1121	0
Peru [2001]	1408	0
Philippines [1996]	1199	0
Philippines [2001]	1076	0
Poland [1990]	944	0
Poland [1997]	1106	0
Portugal [1990]	858	0
Portugal [1999]	883	0
Puerto Rico [1995]	934	0
Puerto Rico [2001]	627	0
Republic of Korea [1990]	881	0
Republic of Moldova [2002]	931	0
Romania [1999]	1107	0
Russian Federation [1990]	670	0
Slovakia [1990]	806	0
Slovakia [1991]	364	0
Slovakia [1998]	950	0
Slovakia [1999]	1022	0
Spain [1981]	2097	0
Sweden [1990]	840	0
Switzerland [1989]	1278	0
Taiwan [1994]	617	0
Uruguay [1996]	510	0
Venezuela [1996]	1081	0
Venezuela [2000]	871	0
Viet Nam [2001]	535	0

The WVS data imply the following Table. It has to be noted that the Iraq survey mentions—somewhat misleadingly—the following religious denominations: Christian, Muslim, Orthodox, Roman Catholic, Shia, and Sunni. Our analysis thus works with almost 30.000 interview partners in 63 countries around the globe:

1. Albania
2. Argentina
3. Australia
4. Austria
5. Azerbaijan
6. Bangladesh
7. Belarus
8. Belgium
9. Bosnia and Herzegovina
10. Brazil
11. Bulgaria
12. Canada
13. China
14. Croatia
15. Denmark
16. Denmark
17. Egypt
18. Estonia
19. Finland
20. France
21. Georgia
22. Germany East
23. Germany West
24. Great Britain
25. Hungary
26. India
27. Indonesia
28. Iran (Islamic Republic of)
29. Iraq
30. Ireland
31. Israel
32. Jordan
33. Kyrgyzstan
34. Latvia
35. Lithuania
36. Luxembourg
37. Macedonia, Republic of
38. Mexico
39. Montenegro
40. Morocco
41. Netherlands

42 New Zealand
43 Nigeria
44 Norway
45 Republic of Korea
46 Republic of Moldova
47 Romania
48 Russian Federation
49 Saudi Arabia
50 Serbia
51 Singapore
52 Slovenia
53 South Africa
54 Spain
55 Sweden
56 Switzerland
57 Tanzania, United Republic Of
58 Turkey
59 Uganda
60 Ukraine
61 Ukraine
62 United States
63 Zimbabwe

The WVS data imply the following Table:

The Muslim respondents in the World Values Survey

	WVS interview partners with data on gender and religion of the respondent	Muslims in the sample	Implied Muslim share per total population	Overall reliability of results for conclusions about the social situations of Muslims in the country (% error margin at 10% significance level)
Albania [1998]	980	701	71.53	3.1
Albania [2002]	867	580	66.9	3.4
Argentina [1991]	844	2	0.24	57.98
Australia [1981]	1081	25	2.31	16.4
Australia [1995]	1646	14	0.85	21.92
Austria [1999]	1312	4	0.3	41
Azerbaijan [1997]	1869	1821	97.43	1.92
Bangladesh [1996]	1519	1306	85.98	2.27
Bangladesh [2002]	1498	1378	91.99	2.21
Belarus [1996]	1310	2	0.15	57.98
Belarus [2000]	518	2	0.39	57.98
Belgium [1981]	866	6	0.69	33.48
Belgium [1990]	1882	6	0.32	33.48

The Muslim respondents in the World Values Survey (Continued)

	WVS interview partners with data on gender and religion of the respondent	Muslims in the sample	Implied Muslim share per total population	Overall reliability of results for conclusions about the social situations of Muslims in the country (% error margin at 10% significance level)
Belgium [1999]	1199	34	2.84	14.06
Bosnia and Herzegovina [1998]	841	326	38.76	4.54
Bosnia and Herzegovina [2001]	892	485	54.37	3.72
Brazil [1991]	1399	2	0.14	57.98
Bulgaria [1990]	331	66	19.94	10.09
Bulgaria [1997]	709	126	17.77	7.31
Bulgaria [1999]	696	109	15.66	7.85
Canada [1982]	1116	1	0.09	82
Canada [1990]	1268	6	0.47	33.48
Canada [2000]	1302	23	1.77	17.1
China [1990]	32	13	40.63	22.74
China [2001]	60	4	6.67	41
Croatia [1996]	1023	14	1.37	21.92
Denmark [1990]	943	4	0.42	41
Denmark [1999]	910	5	0.55	36.67
Egypt [2000]	2999	2830	94.36	1.54
Estonia [1990]	128	1	0.78	82
Estonia [1996]	273	3	1.1	47.34
Estonia [1999]	249	1	0.4	82
Finland [1996]	866	2	0.23	57.98
France [1981]	885	5	0.56	36.67
France [1990]	614	10	1.63	25.93
France [1999]	925	1	0.11	82
Georgia [1996]	1875	5	0.27	36.67
Germany East [1999]	334	1	0.3	82
Germany West [1997]	766	7	0.91	30.99
Germany West [1999]	887	26	2.93	16.08
Great Britain [1981]	1056	4	0.38	41
Great Britain [1990]	853	6	0.7	33.48
Great Britain [1999]	823	10	1.22	25.93
Hungary [1982]	1354	6	0.44	33.48
India [1990]	2471	138	5.58	6.98
India [1995]	1955	245	12.53	5.24
India [2001]	1842	217	11.78	5.57
Indonesia [2001]	999	929	92.99	2.69

Appendix I

	WVS interview partners with data on gender and religion of the respondent	Muslims in the sample	Implied Muslim share per total population	Overall reliability of results for conclusions about the social situations of Muslims in the country (% error margin at 10% significance level)
India [2001]	1842	217	11.78	5.57
Indonesia [2001]	999	929	92.99	2.69
Iran (Islamic Republic of) [2000]	2498	2457	98.36	1.65
Iraq [2004]	2311	1418	61.36	2.18
Ireland [1981]	1198	1	0.08	82
Israel [2001]	1198	114	9.52	7.68
Jordan [2001]	1223	1164	95.18	2.4
Kyrgyzstan [2003]	884	774	87.56	2.95
Latvia [1990]	324	1	0.31	82
Latvia [1996]	680	4	0.59	41
Latvia [1999]	597	1	0.17	82
Lithuania [1997]	845	1	0.12	82
Luxembourg [1999]	852	8	0.94	28.99
Macedonia, Republic of [1998]	707	239	33.8	5.3
Macedonia, Republic of [2001]	903	266	29.46	5.03
Mexico [1996]	1787	3	0.17	47.34
Montenegro [1996]	223	51	22.87	11.48
Montenegro [2001]	1013	221	21.82	5.52
Morocco [2001]	1013	1012	99.9	2.58
Netherlands [1990]	513	5	0.97	36.67
Netherlands [1999]	448	10	2.23	25.93
New Zealand [1998]	969	4	0.41	41
Nigeria [1990]	946	248	26.22	5.21
Nigeria [1995]	1960	544	27.76	3.52
Nigeria [2000]	2004	640	31.94	3.24
Norway [1982]	1006	2	0.2	57.98
Norway [1990]	1115	3	0.27	47.34
Norway [1996]	1018	7	0.69	30.99
Republic of Korea [1982]	502	2	0.4	57.98
Republic of Korea [1996]	747	1	0.13	82
Republic of Korea [2001]	756	2	0.26	57.98
Republic of Moldova [1996]	824	1	0.12	82
Romania [1993]	1038	2	0.19	57.98
Romania [1998]	1194	2	0.17	57.98
Russian Federation [1995]	1090	104	9.54	8.04

The Muslim respondents in the World Values Survey (Continued)

	WVS interview partners with data on gender and religion of the respondent	Muslims in the sample	Implied Muslim share per total population	Overall reliability of results for conclusions about the social situations of Muslims in the country (% error margin at 10% significance level)
Russian Federation [1999]	1255	74	5.9	9.53
Saudi Arabia [2003]	1496	1457	97.39	2.15
Serbia [1996]	1001	73	7.29	9.6
Serbia [2001]	1106	52	4.7	11.37
Singapore [2002]	1212	236	19.47	5.34
Slovenia [1992]	758	16	2.11	20.5
Slovenia [1995]	760	10	1.32	25.93
Slovenia [1999]	701	11	1.57	24.72
South Africa [1990]	2494	113	4.53	7.71
South Africa [1996]	2521	47	1.86	11.96
South Africa [2001]	2492	84	3.37	8.95
Spain [1990]	2278	1	0.04	82
Spain [1990]	1258	1	0.08	82
Spain [1995]	1033	2	0.19	57.98
Spain [1999]	981	3	0.31	47.34
Spain [2000]	1004	1	0.1	82
Sweden [1982]	888	1	0.11	82
Sweden [1996]	925	4	0.43	41
Sweden [1999]	770	4	0.52	41
Switzerland [1996]	1090	6	0.55	33.48
Tanzania, United Republic Of [2001]	1135	466	41.06	3.8
Turkey [1990]	51	34	66.67	14.06
Turkey [1996]	1590	1560	98.11	2.08
Turkey [2001]	3329	3310	99.43	1.43
Turkey [2001]	1178	1176	99.83	2.39
Uganda [2001]	993	169	17.02	6.31
Ukraine [1996]	1757	6	0.34	33.48
Ukraine [1999]	635	3	0.47	47.34
United States [1982]	2183	4	0.18	41
United States [1990]	1335	2	0.15	57.98
United States [1995]	1195	7	0.59	30.99
United States [1999]	891	3	0.34	47.34
Zimbabwe [2001]	857	5	0.58	36.67
Total	128605	29765	23.14	0.48

The variable key to the World Values Survey, ordered alphabetically

Variable label in the WVS	Variable label should read (because of highest and lowest numerical values)
[Country] needs foreign military cooperation to combat terrorism	[Country] needs no foreign military cooperation to combat terrorism
[Country] should have close relations with France	No multivariate analysis [Country] should have close relations with France
[Country] should have close relations with United States	No multivariate analysis [Country] should have close relations with United States
[Country]s environmental problems can be solved without any international agreements to handle them	disagree: a[Country]s environmental problems can be solved without any international agreements to handle them
10th commandment applies for myself	10th commandment does not apply for myself
10th commandment applies to most people	10th commandment does not apply to most people
1st commandment applies for myself	1st commandment does not apply for myself
1st commandment applies to most people	1st commandment does not apply to most people
2nd commandment applies for myself	2nd commandment does not apply for myself
2nd commandment applies to most people	2nd commandment does not apply to most people
3rd commandment applies for myself	3rd commandment does not apply for myself
3rd commandment applies to most people	3rd commandment does not apply to most people
4th commandment applies for myself	4th commandment does not apply for myself
4th commandment applies to most people	4th commandment does not apply to most people
5th commandment applies for myself	5th commandment does not apply for myself
5th commandment applies to most people	5th commandment does not apply to most people
6th commandment applies for myself	6th commandment does not apply for myself
6th commandment applies to most people	6th commandment does not apply to most people
7th commandment applies for myself	7th commandment does not apply for myself
7th commandment applies to most people	7th commandment does not apply to most people
8th commandment applies for myself	8th commandment does not apply for myself
8th commandment applies to most people	8th commandment does not apply to most people
9th commandment applies for myself	9th commandment does not apply for myself
9th commandment applies to most people	9th commandment does not apply to most people
A man has to have children to be fulfilled	A man has to have children to be fulfilled
A truly Islamic country should not have a parliament with the right to pass laws	A truly Islamic country should not have a parliament with the right to pass laws
A woman has to have children to be fulfilled	A woman has to have children to be fulfilled
Abortion if not wanting more children	Abortion if not wanting more children
Abortion when child physically handicapped	Abortion when child physically handicapped
Abortion when the mothers health is at risk	Abortion when the mothers health is at risk
Abortion when woman not married	Abortion when woman not married
Active/Inactive membership of any other organization	Active/Inactive membership of any other organization

The variable key to the World Values Survey, ordered alphabetically (Continued)

Variable label in the WVS	Variable label should read (because of highest and lowest numerical values)
Active/Inactive membership of art, music, educational	Active/Inactive membership of art, music, educational
Active/Inactive membership of charitable/humanitarian organization	Active/Inactive membership of charitable/humanitarian organization
Active/Inactive membership of church or religious organization	Active/Inactive membership of church or religious organization
Active/Inactive membership of environmental organization	Active/Inactive membership of environmental organization
Active/Inactive membership of labor unions	Active/Inactive membership of labor unions
Active/Inactive membership of political party	Active/Inactive membership of political party
Active/Inactive membership of professional organization	Active/Inactive membership of professional organization
Active/Inactive membership of sport or recreation	Active/Inactive membership of sport or recreation
Age	Age
Age recoded	Age recoded
Age recoded (3 intervals)	Age recoded (3 intervals)
Aggression from neighboring country	No aggression from neighboring country
Aims of country: first choice	No multivariate analysis Aims of country: first choice
Aims of country: second choice	No multivariate analysis Aims of country: second choice
Aims of respondent: first choice	No multivariate analysis Aims of respondent: first choice
Aims of respondent: first choice (GB 5 cat)	No multivariate analysis Aims of respondent: first choice (GB 5 cat)
Aims of respondent: second choice	No multivariate analysis Aims of respondent: second choice
Aims of respondent: second choice (GB 5 cat)	No multivariate analysis Aims of respondent: second choice (GB 5 cat)
All talk about the environment make people anxious	Disagree with opinion: all talk about the environment make people anxious
Allow more freedom for individuals	Disagreement with: Allow more freedom for individuals
Amount of help for less developed countries	No multivariate analysis Amount of help for less developed countries
Approval: Anti-apartheid movement	No approval: Anti-apartheid movement
Approval: Anti-nuclear energy movement	No approval: Anti-nuclear energy movement
Approval: Disarmament movement	No approval: Disarmament movement
Approval: Ecology movement or nature protection	No approval: Ecology movement or nature protection
Approval: Human rights movement	No approval: Human rights movement
Approval: Women's movement	No approval: Women's movement
Are you close to this party	No multivariate analysis Are you close to this party
Are you supervising someone	Are you supervising someone
Are you the chief wage earner in your house	Are you the chief wage earner in your house
Attendance religious services 12 years old	Never attended religious services 12 years old
Autonomy Index	Autonomy Index

Appendix I

Variable label in the WVS	Variable label should read (because of highest and lowest numerical values)
Basic kinds of attitudes concerning society	No multivariate analysis Basic kinds of attitudes concerning society
Been divorced	Been divorced
Being a housewife just as fulfilling	Disagreement with: Being a housewife just as fulfilling
Being a housewife just as fulfilling (5 cat)	No multivariate analysis Being a housewife just as fulfilling (5 cat)
Believe in: angels	Believe in: angels
Believe in: devil	Believe in: devil
Believe in: God	Believe in: God
Believe in: heaven	Believe in: heaven
Believe in: hell	Believe in: hell
Believe in: life after death	Believe in: life after death
Believe in: people have a soul	Believe in: people have a soul
Believe in: re-incarnation	Believe in: re-incarnation
Believe in: resurrection of the dead	Believe in: resurrection of the dead
Believe in: sin	Believe in: sin
Believe in: supernatural forces	Do not believe in: supernatural forces
Believe in: telepathy	Believe in: telepathy
Belong to animal rights	Belong to animal rights
Belong to conservation, the environment, ecology	Belong to conservation, the environment, ecology
Belong to conservation, the environment, ecology, animal rights	Belong to conservation, the environment, ecology, animal rights
Belong to education, arts, music or cultural activities	Belong to education, arts, music or cultural activities
Belong to human rights	Belong to human rights
Belong to labor unions	Belong to labor unions
Belong to local political actions	Belong to local political actions
Belong to none	No multivariate analysis Belong to none
Belong to organization concerned with health	Belong to organization concerned with health
Belong to other groups	Belong to other groups
Belong to peace movement	Belong to peace movement
Belong to political parties	Belong to political parties
Belong to professional associations	Belong to professional associations
Belong to religious denomination	Belong to religious denomination
Belong to religious organization	Belong to religious organization
Belong to social welfare service for elderly	Belong to social welfare service for elderly
Belong to sports or recreation	Belong to sports or recreation
Belong to women's group	Belong to women's group
Belong to youth work	Belong to youth work

The variable key to the World Values Survey, ordered alphabetically (Continued)

Variable label in the WVS	Variable label should read (because of highest and lowest numerical values)
Belong: consumer groups	Belong: consumer groups
Better if more people with strong religious beliefs in public office	Worse if more people with strong religious beliefs in public office
Born in this country: birth country	Born in this country: birth country
By requiring man treat all wives equally, Islam true intent is prohibit taking more than one wife	By requiring man treat all wives equally, Islam true intent is prohibit taking more than one wife
Chance to escape from poverty	No multivariate analysis Chance to escape from poverty
Chief wage earner employed now	Chief wage earner employed now
Chief wage earner profession/job	Chief wage earner profession/job
Child needs a home with father and mother	Child needs a home with father and mother
Child qualities: tolerance and respect for other people	Child qualities: tolerance and respect for other people
Church(es) influence on national politics	Church(es) no influence on national politics
Churches give answers: moral problems	Churches give answers: moral problems
Churches give answers: people's spiritual needs	Churches give answers: people's spiritual needs
Churches give answers: the problems of family life	Churches give answers: the problems of family life
Churches give answers: the social problems	Churches give answers: the social problems
Churches speak out on: abortion	Churches speak out on: abortion
Churches speak out on: disarmament	Churches speak out on: disarmament
Churches speak out on: ecology and environmental issues	Churches speak out on: ecology and environmental issues
Churches speak out on: euthanasia	Churches speak out on: euthanasia
Churches speak out on: extramarital affairs	Churches speak out on: extramarital affairs
Churches speak out on: government policy	Churches speak out on: government policy
Churches speak out on: homosexuality	Churches speak out on: homosexuality
Churches speak out on: racial discrimination	Churches speak out on: racial discrimination
Churches speak out on: third world problems	Churches speak out on: third world problems
Churches speak out on: unemployment	Churches speak out on: unemployment
Citizen of [country]	Citizen of [country]
Citizenship	Citizenship
Civil marriage is very important because it helps maintain the family	Civil marriage is very important because it helps maintain the family
Close to any particular party	Not close to any particular party
Combating unemployment, we have to accept environmental problems	disagree with: combating unemployment, we have to accept environmental problems
Compatriots do: accepting a bribe	Compatriots do not: accepting a bribe
Compatriots do: accepting a bribe (5 cat)	No multivariate analysis Compatriots do: accepting a bribe (5 cat)
Compatriots do: avoiding a fare on public transport	Compatriots do not: avoiding a fare on public transport

Appendix I

Variable label in the WVS	Variable label should read (because of highest and lowest numerical values)
Compatriots do: avoiding a fare on public transport (5 cat)	No multivariate analysis Compatriots do not: avoiding a fare on public transport (5 cat)
Compatriots do: cheating on taxes	Compatriots do not: cheating on taxes
Compatriots do: cheating on taxes (5 cat)	No multivariate analysis Compatriots do not: cheating on taxes (5 cat)
Compatriots do: claiming state benefits	Compatriots do not: claiming state benefits
Compatriots do: claiming state benefits (5 cat)	No multivariate analysis Compatriots do not: claiming state benefits (5 cat)
Compatriots do: driving under the influence of alcohol	Compatriots do not: driving under the influence of alcohol
Compatriots do: driving under the influence of alcohol (5 cat)	No multivariate analysis Compatriots do not: driving under the influence of alcohol (5 cat)
Compatriots do: having casual sex	Compatriots do not: having casual sex
Compatriots do: having casual sex (5 cat)	No multivariate analysis Compatriots do not: having casual sex (5 cat)
Compatriots do: lying in own interest	Compatriots do not: lying in own interest
Compatriots do: lying in own interest (5 cat)	No multivariate analysis Compatriots do not: lying in own interest (5 cat)
Compatriots do: paying in cash	Compatriots do not: paying in cash
Compatriots do: paying in cash (5 cat)	No multivariate analysis Compatriots do not: paying in cash (5 cat)
Compatriots do: speeding over the limit in build up areas	Compatriots do not: speeding over the limit in build up areas
Compatriots do: speeding over the limit in build up areas (5 cat)	No multivariate analysis Compatriots do not: speeding over the limit in build up areas (5 cat)
Compatriots do: taking soft drugs	Compatriots do not: taking soft drugs
Compatriots do: taking soft drugs (5 cat)	No multivariate analysis Compatriots do not: taking soft drugs (5 cat)
Compatriots do: throwing away litter	Compatriots do not: throwing away litter
Compatriots do: throwing away litter (5 cat)	No multivariate analysis Compatriots do not: throwing away litter (5 cat)
Competition good or harmful	Competition harmful
Concerned with elderly people	not concerned with elderly people
Concerned with Europeans	not concerned with Europeans
Concerned with fellow countrymen	not concerned with fellow countrymen
Concerned with human kind	not concerned with human kind
Concerned with immediate family	not concerned with immediate family
Concerned with immigrants	not concerned with immigrants
Concerned with people in the neighborhood	not concerned with people in the neighborhood
Concerned with people in the region	not concerned with people in the region
Concerned with sick and disabled people	not concerned with sick and disabled people
Concerned with unemployed people	not concerned with unemployed people
Confidence respondent during the interview	Confidence respondent during the interview
Confidence: Armed Forces	No confidence: Armed Forces
Confidence: Churches	No confidence: Churches

The variable key to the World Values Survey, ordered alphabetically (Continued)

Variable label in the WVS	Variable label should read (because of highest and lowest numerical values)
Confidence: East African Cooperation (EAC)	No confidence: East African Cooperation (EAC)
Confidence: Education System	No confidence: Education System
Confidence: Health Care System	No confidence: Health Care System
Confidence: Justice System	No confidence: Justice System
Confidence: Labor Unions	No confidence: Labor Unions
Confidence: Local/Regional Government	No confidence: Local/Regional Government
Confidence: Major Companies	No confidence: Major Companies
Confidence: NATO	No confidence: NATO
Confidence: Other television	no confidence: Other television
Confidence: Parliament	No confidence: Parliament
Confidence: SADC/SADEC	No confidence: SADC/SADEC
Confidence: Social Security System	No confidence: Social Security System
Confidence: Television	No confidence: Television
Confidence: The "Movimiento en pro de Vieques"(Puerto Rico)	No confidence: The "Movimiento en pro de Vieques"(Puerto Rico)
Confidence: The Americans	no confidence: The Americans
Confidence: The Andean pact	No confidence: The Andean pact
Confidence: The APEC	No confidence: The APEC
Confidence: The Arab League	No confidence: The Arab League
Confidence: The Association of South East Asian Nations -ASEAN	No confidence: The Association of South East Asian Nations -ASEAN
Confidence: The Civil Services	No confidence: The Civil Services
Confidence: The Civil Society Groups	no confidence: The Civil Society Groups
Confidence: The ECO	No confidence: The ECO
Confidence: The Environmental Protection Movement	No confidence: The Environmental Protection Movement
Confidence: The European Union	No confidence: The European Union
Confidence: The Free Commerce Treaty (Tratado de libre comercio)	No confidence: The Free Commerce Treaty (Tratado de libre comercio)
Confidence: The Government	No confidence: The Government
Confidence: The Mercosur	No confidence: The Mercosur
Confidence: The NAFTA	No confidence: The NAFTA
Confidence: The Organization for African Unity-OAU	No confidence: The Organization for African Unity-OAU
Confidence: The Police	No confidence: The Police
Confidence: The Political Parties	No confidence: The Political Parties
Confidence: The Presidency	no confidence: The Presidency
Confidence: The Press	No confidence: The Press

Appendix I

Variable label in the WVS	Variable label should read (because of highest and lowest numerical values)
Confidence: The SAARC	No confidence: The SAARC
Confidence: The United American States Organization (Organización de Estados Unidos Americanos - OEA)	No confidence: The United American States Organization (Organización de Estados Unidos Americanos - OEA)
Confidence: The United Nations	No confidence: The United Nations
Confidence: The Women's Movement	No confidence: The Women's Movement
Consult horoscope	Never consult horoscope
Country - wave	Country - wave
Country - wave	Country - wave
Country - wave - study - set - year	Country - wave - study - set - year
Country - year	Country - year
Country - year	Country - year
Country cannot solve crime problems by itself	Country can solve crime problems by itself
Country cannot solve employment problems by itself	Country can solve employment problems by itself
Country cannot solve environmental problems by itself	Country can solve environmental problems by itself
Country is run by big interest vs. for all people's benefit	Country is run for all people's benefit
Country/region	Country/region
Country/regions [with split ups]	Country/regions [with split ups]
Country2 - wave - study - set – year	Country2 - wave - study - set - year
Cultural invasion by the west	No cultural invasion by the west
Current society: Egalitarian vs. competitive society	Current society: competitive society
Current society: Extensive welfare vs. low taxes	Current society: low taxes
Current society: Regulated vs. responsible society	Current society: responsible society
Date interview	Date interview
Death has meaning if you believe in God	No multivariate analysis Death has meaning if you believe in God
Death is a natural resting point	No multivariate analysis Death is a natural resting point
Death is inevitable	No multivariate analysis Death is inevitable
Degree of pride in your work	No pride in your work
Democracies are indecisive and have too much squabbling	Disagreement with: Democracies are indecisive and have too much squabbling
Democracies aren't good at maintaining order	Disagreement with: Democracies aren't good at maintaining order
Democracy is a Western form of government that is not compatible with Islam	Democracy is a Western form of government that is not compatible with Islam
Democracy may have problems but is better	Disagreement with: Democracy may have problems but is better
Dislike being with people with different ideas	like being with people with different ideas
Divorce: none of these	No multivariate analysis Divorce: none of these
Divorce: when can not have children	Divorce: when can not have children
Divorce: when can not stand relatives	Divorce: when can not stand relatives

The variable key to the World Values Survey, ordered alphabetically (Continued)

Variable label in the WVS	Variable label should read (because of highest and lowest numerical values)
Divorce: when financially broke	Divorce: when financially broke
Divorce: when partner has ceased to love	Divorce: when partner has ceased to love
Divorce: when partner ill for a long time	Divorce: when partner ill for a long time
Divorce: when partner is a heavy drinker	Divorce: when partner is a heavy drinker
Divorce: when partner is unfaithful	Divorce: when partner is unfaithful
Divorce: when partner is violent	Divorce: when partner is violent
Divorce: when personalities do not watch	Divorce: when personalities do not watch
Divorce: when sexual relationship is not satisfactory	Divorce: when sexual relationship is not satisfactory
Do you drink more or less than others	No multivariate analysis Do you drink more or less than others
Do you ever feel very lonely	never lonely
Do you ever regret having done something	Never regret having done something
Do you have a lucky charm	Do you have a lucky charm
Do you live with your parents	Do you live with your parents
Do you or your spouse belong to a labor union	Do you or your spouse belong to a labor union
Do you own your home or rent it	Do you own your home or rent it
Do you think most people try to take advantage of you	No multivariate analysis Do you think most people try to take advantage of you
Economic aid to poorer countries	Economic aid to poorer countries should be reduced
Education (country specific)	Education (country specific)
Education level (recoded)	Education level (recoded)
Effect of market economic reforms	No multivariate analysis Effect of market economic reforms
Employed	Employed
Employment status	Employment status
Enjoy sexual freedom	No multivariate analysis Enjoy sexual freedom
Environmental action: attend meeting, signed petition	Environmental action: attend meeting, signed petition
Environmental action: chosen products that are better for environment	Environmental action: chosen products that are better for environment
Environmental action: contributed to environmental organization	Environmental action: contributed to environmental organization
Environmental action: recycle	Environmental action: recycle
Environmental action: reduce water consumption	Environmental action: reduce water consumption
Equilibrated weight-1000	Equilibrated weight-1000
Equilibrated weight-1000 [with split ups]	Equilibrated weight-1000 [with split ups]
Equilibrated weight-1500	Equilibrated weight-1500
Equilibrated weight-1500 [with split ups]	Equilibrated weight-1500 [with split ups]
Ethnic group	Ethnic group

Appendix I

Variable label in the WVS	Variable label should read (because of highest and lowest numerical values)
Ever felt bored	Ever felt bored
Ever felt depressed or very unhappy	Ever felt depressed or very unhappy
Ever felt on top of the world	Ever felt on top of the world
Ever felt pleased about having accomplished something	Ever felt pleased about having accomplished something
Ever felt proud because someone complimented you	Ever felt proud because someone complimented you
Ever felt restless	Ever felt restless
Ever felt that things were going your way	Ever felt that things were going your way
Ever felt upset because somebody criticized you	Ever felt upset because somebody criticized you
Ever felt very excited or interested	Ever felt very excited or interested
Ever felt very lonely or remote from other people	Ever felt very lonely or remote from other people
Expected satisfaction with your life in 5 years	Expected satisfaction with your life in 5 years
Experience altered outlook on life	Experience altered outlook on life
Exploitation of local resources	No exploitation of local resources
Exposure to the culture of the US and other Western countries harmful effect on our country	Exposure to the culture of the US and other Western countries harmful effect on our country
Extent of political corruption	wide extent of political corruption in the country
Fairness: One secretary is paid more	Fairness: One secretary is paid more
Family important in life	Family not important in life
Family savings during past year	No family savings during past year
Fathers are well suited for looking after children	Disagreement with: Fathers are well suited for looking after children
Fathers are well suited for looking after children (5 cat)	No multivariate analysis Fathers are well suited for looking after children (5 cat)
Feeling of happiness	Feeling of unhappiness
Feeling of happiness thinking of the environment (GB)	Feeling of unhappiness thinking of the environment (GB)
Feeling that life is meaningless	Never feeling that life is meaningless
Felt close to a powerful life force	Felt close to a powerful life force
Felt in touch with someone dead	Felt in touch with someone dead
Felt in touch with someone far away	Felt in touch with someone far away
File version (yyyymmdd)	File version (yyyymmdd)
Financial situation of household in 12months	Financial situation of household got worse in 12months
Firm party leader vs. Cooperating party leader	Cooperating party leader good
Firms and freedom	State should control firms
First choice, if looking for a job	No multivariate analysis First choice, if looking for a job
Following instructions at work	No multivariate analysis Following instructions at work
Former religious denomination	No multivariate analysis Former religious denomination
Free and fair elections will reduce terrorism	Free and fair elections will reduce terrorism
Free market economy right for country future	Wrong: Free market economy right for country future

The variable key to the World Values Survey, ordered alphabetically (Continued)

Variable label in the WVS	Variable label should read (because of highest and lowest numerical values)
Freedom decision taking in job	Freedom decision taking in job
Freedom or equality	No multivariate analysis Freedom or equality
Frequency watches TV	Frequency watches TV
Friends important in life	Friends not important in life
Future changes: A simple and more natural lifestyle	Bad future changes: A simple and more natural lifestyle
Future changes: Greater respect for authority	Bad future changes: Greater respect for authority
Future changes: Less emphasis on money and material possessions	Bad future changes: Less emphasis on money and material possessions
Future changes: Less importance placed on work	Bad future changes: Less importance placed on work
Future changes: More emphasis on family life	Bad future changes: More emphasis on family life
Future changes: More emphasis on individual	Bad future changes: More emphasis on individual
Future changes: More emphasis on technology	Bad future changes: More emphasis on technology
Future changes: More power to local authorities	Bad future changes: More power to local authorities
Geographical groups belonging to first	Geographical groups belonging to first
Geographical groups belonging to first (country specific)	Geographical groups belonging to first (country specific)
Geographical groups belonging to least of all	Geographical groups belonging to least of all
Geographical groups belonging to least of all (country specific)	Geographical groups belonging to least of all (country specific)
Geographical groups belonging to second	Geographical groups belonging to second
Geographical groups belonging to second (country specific)	Geographical groups belonging to second (country specific)
Get comfort and strength from religion	Get comfort and strength from religion
Give authorities information to help justice	Disagree to give authorities information to help justice
Good human relationships	No multivariate analysis Good human relationships
Government order vs. freedom	No multivariate analysis Government order vs. freedom
Government protects freedom	Government does not protect freedom
Government protects religion	Government does not protect religion
Government responsibility	Government responsibility vs. private responsibility
Government should reduce environmental pollution	Government should not reduce environmental pollution
Had formal education	Had formal education
Hard work brings success	Hard work does not bring success
Have you been married before	Have you been married before
Have you had any children	Have you had any children
Highest educational level attained	Highest educational level attained
House or apartment	House or apartment
How business and industry should be managed	No multivariate analysis How business and industry should be managed

Appendix I

Variable label in the WVS	Variable label should read (because of highest and lowest numerical values)
How business and industry should be managed (Poland)	No multivariate analysis How business and industry should be managed (Poland)
How frequently do you perform in the mosque	How frequently do you perform in the mosque
How frequently do you perform the five prescribed prayers of the Islam	How frequently do you perform the five prescribed prayers of the Islam
How important is God in your life	God important in your life
How important: building a prosperous society	How important: building a prosperous society
How important: building a successful professional future	How important: building a successful professional future
How important: daily prayer	How important: daily prayer
How important: forming a happy secure family	How important: forming a happy secure family
How long unemployed	How long unemployed
How many are still living at home	How many are still living at home
How many children do you have	How many children do you have
How many people work in your department-organization	How many people work in your department-organization
How much do you trust your family	Mistrust your family
How much freedom of choice and control	Much freedom of choice and control
How much is the government doing against poverty	No multivariate analysis How much is the government doing against poverty
How often discusses political matters with friends	Never discusses political matters with friends
How often do you attend religious services	Never attend religious services
How often do you drink alcohol	do not drink alcohol
How often follows politics in the news	Never follow politics in the news
How proud of nationality	How proud of nationality
How serious is alcoholism	How serious is alcoholism
How serious is illegal drug-taking	How serious is illegal drug-taking
How strict were your parents	No strict parents
Human and nature	No multivariate analysis Human and nature
Humanity has a bright or bleak future	No multivariate analysis Humanity has a bright or bleak future
Humiliating to receive money without having to work for it	Disagreement with: Humiliating to receive money without having to work for it
Humiliating to receive money without having to work for it (4 cat)	No multivariate analysis Humiliating to receive money without having to work for it (4 cat)
Husband and wife should both contribute to income	Disagreement with: Husband and wife should both contribute to income
Husband and wife should both contribute to income (5 cat)	No multivariate analysis Husband and wife should both contribute to income (5 cat)
I could do nothing about an unjust law	Disagreement with: I could do nothing about an unjust law
Ideal number of children	Ideal number of children
If country pursues policies harmful to Muslims, Islam permits killing civilians in that country	If country pursues policies harmful to Muslims, Islam permits killing civilians in that country
If don't know, which party appeals to you most	No multivariate analysis If don't know, which party appeals to you most

The variable key to the World Values Survey, ordered alphabetically (Continued)

Variable label in the WVS	Variable label should read (because of highest and lowest numerical values)
If only one child allowed: boy or girl	No multivariate analysis If only one child allowed: boy or girl
If Palestinian state established and peace with Israel, Islam would not oppose existence of Israel	If Palestinian state established and peace with Israel, Islam would not oppose existence of Israel
If you feel sad and want to talk to someone, to whom do you usually turn to	If you feel sad and want to talk to someone, to whom do you usually turn to
Immigrant policy	favoring a restrictive immigrant policy
Immigrants and their customs and traditions	No multivariate analysis Immigrants and their customs and traditions
Importance of eliminating big income inequalities	No importance of eliminating big income inequalities
Importance of eliminating big income inequalities (4 cat)	No multivariate analysis No importance of eliminating big income inequalities (4 cat)
Importance of equalizing chances for education	No importance of equalizing chances for education
Importance of equalizing chances for education (4 cat)	No multivariate analysis No importance of equalizing chances for education (4 cat)
Importance of guaranteeing basic needs for all	No importance of guaranteeing basic needs for all
Importance of guaranteeing basic needs for all (4 cat)	No multivariate analysis No importance of guaranteeing basic needs for all (4 cat)
Importance of recognizing people on their merits	No importance of recognizing people on their merits
Importance of recognizing people on their merits (4 cat)	No multivariate analysis No importance of recognizing people on their merits (4 cat)
Importance of religion in the future	No multivariate analysis Importance of religion in the future
Important child qualities: determination perseverance	Important child qualities: determination perseverance
Important child qualities: feeling of responsibility	Important child qualities: feeling of responsibility
Important child qualities: good manners	Important child qualities: good manners
Important child qualities: hard work	Important child qualities: hard work
Important child qualities: honesty	Important child qualities: honesty
Important child qualities: imagination	Important child qualities: imagination
Important child qualities: independence	Important child qualities: independence
Important child qualities: leadership	Important child qualities: leadership
Important child qualities: loyalty	Important child qualities: loyalty
Important child qualities: obedience	Important child qualities: obedience
Important child qualities: patience	Important child qualities: patience
Important child qualities: politeness and neatness	Important child qualities: politeness and neatness
Important child qualities: religious faith	Important child qualities: religious faith
Important child qualities: self-control	Important child qualities: self-control
Important child qualities: thrift saving money and things	Important child qualities: thrift saving money and things
Important child qualities: unselfishness	Important child qualities: unselfishness
Important for successful marriage: Adequate income	Not important for successful marriage: Adequate income

Appendix I

Variable label in the WVS	Variable label should read (because of highest and lowest numerical values)
Important for successful marriage: Agreement on politics	Not important for successful marriage: Agreement on politics
Important for successful marriage: Apart from in-laws	Not important for successful marriage: Apart from in-laws
Important for successful marriage: Children	Not important for successful marriage: Children
Important for successful marriage: Faithfulness	Not important for successful marriage: Faithfulness
Important for successful marriage: Good housing	Not important for successful marriage: Good housing
Important for successful marriage: Happy sexual relationship	Not important for successful marriage: Happy sexual relationship
Important for successful marriage: Religious beliefs	Not important for successful marriage: Religious beliefs
Important for successful marriage: Respect and appreciation	Not important for successful marriage: Respect and appreciation
Important for successful marriage: Same ethnic background	Not important for successful marriage: Same ethnic background
Important for successful marriage: Same social background	Not important for successful marriage: Same social background
Important for successful marriage: Sharing household chores	Not important for successful marriage: Sharing household chores
Important for successful marriage: Spending time together	Not important for successful marriage: Spending time together
Important for successful marriage: Tastes and interests in common	Not important for successful marriage: Tastes and interests in common
Important in a job: a job that is interesting	Important in a job: a job that is interesting
Important in a job: a job that meets one's abilities	Important in a job: a job that meets one's abilities
Important in a job: a respected job	Important in a job: a respected job
Important in a job: a responsible job	Important in a job: a responsible job
Important in a job: a useful job for society	Important in a job: a useful job for society
Important in a job: an opportunity to use initiative	Important in a job: an opportunity to use initiative
Important in a job: generous holidays	Important in a job: generous holidays
Important in a job: good chances for promotion	Important in a job: good chances for promotion
Important in a job: good hours	Important in a job: good hours
Important in a job: good job security	Important in a job: good job security
Important in a job: good pay	Important in a job: good pay
Important in a job: good physical working conditions	Important in a job: good physical working conditions
Important in a job: meeting people	Important in a job: meeting people
Important in a job: none of these	No multivariate analysis Important in a job: none of these
Important in a job: not too much pressure	Important in a job: not too much pressure
Important in a job: pleasant people to work with	Important in a job: pleasant people to work with
Important in a job: that you can achieve something	Important in a job: that you can achieve something
Important in a job: to have time off at the weekends	Important in a job: to have time off at the weekends
Important in successful marriage: Discussing problems	Not important in successful marriage: Discussing problems
Important in successful marriage: Talking	Important in successful marriage: Talking

The variable key to the World Values Survey, ordered alphabetically (Continued)

Variable label in the WVS	Variable label should read (because of highest and lowest numerical values)
Important in successful marriage: Understanding and tolerance	Important in successful marriage: Understanding and tolerance
Important: Religious service birth	Important: Religious service birth
Important: Religious service death	Important: Religious service death
Important: Religious service marriage	Important: Religious service marriage
Importation of goods	No multivariate analysis Importation of goods
In democracy, the economic system runs badly	Disagreement with: In democracy, the economic system runs badly
Income (country specific)	Income (country specific)
Income equality	anti-egalitarian position on income equality
Income level	High income level
Increase in taxes if used to prevent environmental pollution	No increase in taxes if used to prevent environmental pollution
Interest in politics	No interest in politics
Interest in politics (ii)	No multivariate analysis Interest in politics (ii)
Interviewer number	Interviewer number
Is the chief wage earner employed now	Is the chief wage earner employed now
Is there good and evil in everyone	Basically good in everyone
Islam requires that political rights of non Muslims should be inferior to those of Muslims	Islam requires that political rights of non Muslims should be inferior to those of Muslims
Islam requires woman to dress modestly but does not require cover face with veil	Islam requires woman to dress modestly but does not require cover face with veil
Islam requires country with majority of Muslims be governed by men of Islamic learning	Islam requires country with majority of Muslims be governed by men of Islamic learning
It is necessary to fight terrorism by military means	Disagreement with: It is necessary to fight terrorism by military means
Job best way for women to be independent	Disagreement with: Job best way for women to be independent
Job best way for women to be independent (5 cat)	No multivariate analysis Job best way for women to be independent (5 cat)
Job profession/industry (2 digit isco88)	Job profession/industry (2 digit isco88)
Job profession/industry (3 digit isco88)	Job profession/industry (3 digit isco88)
Job profession/industry (4 digit isco88)	Job profession/industry (4 digit isco88)
Job satisfaction	High job satisfaction
Job taking of the unemployed	Against Labor market reforms: Unemployed have a right to refuse offered jobs
Jobs scarce: Employers should give priority to (nation) people than immigrants	No multivariate analysis Jobs scarce: Employers should give priority to (nation) people than immigrants
Jobs scarce: Jobs to local people	No multivariate analysis Jobs scarce: Jobs to local people
Jobs scarce: Men should have more right to a job than women	No multivariate analysis Jobs scarce: Men should have more right to a job than women
Jobs scarce: older people should be forced to retire	No multivariate analysis Jobs scarce: older people should be forced to retire

Variable label in the WVS	Variable label should read (because of highest and lowest numerical values)
Justifiable: abortion	Justifiable: abortion
Justifiable: adultery	Justifiable: adultery
Justifiable: avoiding a fare on public transport	Justifiable: avoiding a fare on public transport
Justifiable: buy stolen goods	Justifiable: buy stolen goods
Justifiable: cheating on taxes	Justifiable: cheating on taxes
Justifiable: claiming government benefits	Justifiable: claiming government benefits
Justifiable: divorce	Justifiable: divorce
Justifiable: drinking alcohol	Justifiable: drinking alcohol
Justifiable: driving under influence of alcohol	Justifiable: driving under influence of alcohol
Justifiable: euthanasia	Justifiable: euthanasia
Justifiable: experiments with human embryos	Justifiable: experiments with human embryos
Justifiable: failing to report damage you've done accidentally to a parked vehicle	Justifiable: failing to report damage you've done accidentally to a parked vehicle
Justifiable: fighting with the police	Justifiable: fighting with the police
Justifiable: having casual sex	Justifiable: having casual sex
Justifiable: homosexuality	Justifiable: homosexuality
Justifiable: joyriding	Justifiable: joyriding
Justifiable: keeping money that you have found	Justifiable: keeping money that you have found
Justifiable: killing in self-defense	Justifiable: killing in self-defense
Justifiable: lying	Justifiable: lying
Justifiable: manipulation of food	Justifiable: manipulation of food
Justifiable: paying cash	Justifiable: paying cash
Justifiable: political assassination	Justifiable: political assassination
Justifiable: prostitution	Justifiable: prostitution
Justifiable: sex under the legal age of consent	Justifiable: sex under the legal age of consent
Justifiable: smoking in public places	Justifiable: smoking in public places
Justifiable: someone accepting a bribe	Justifiable: someone accepting a bribe
Justifiable: speeding over the limit	Justifiable: speeding over the limit
Justifiable: suicide	Justifiable: suicide
Justifiable: taking soft drugs	Justifiable: taking soft drugs
Justifiable: threatening workers who refuse to join a strike	Justifiable: threatening workers who refuse to join a strike
Justifiable: throwing away litter	Justifiable: throwing away litter
Language at home	Language at home
Language in, which interview was conducted	Language in, which interview was conducted
Laws: people's wishes	Ejecting laws based on secular people's wishes
Least liked allow: demonstrate	No multivariate analysis Least liked allow: demonstrate
Least liked allow: hold office	No multivariate analysis Least liked allow: hold office

The variable key to the World Values Survey, ordered alphabetically (Continued)

Variable label in the WVS	Variable label should read (because of highest and lowest numerical values)
Least liked allow: teach	No multivariate analysis Least liked allow: teach
Least liked group in society	No multivariate analysis Least liked group in society
Legally married to partner	Legally married to partner
Leisure time important in life	Leisure not time important in life
Life has no meaning	No multivariate analysis Life has no meaning
Life is meaningful because God exits	No multivariate analysis Life is meaningful because God exits
Living day to day because of uncertain future	No multivariate analysis Living day to day because of uncertain future
Long-term relationship is necessary to be happy	Disagreement with: Long-term relationship is necessary to be happy
Look forward to work after weekend	No multivariate analysis Look forward to work after weekend
Lucky charm protects	Lucky charm protects
Major changes in life	Major changes in life: one should act boldly
Make effort to live up to what my friends expect	Disagreement with: Make effort to live up to what my friends expect
Marital status	Marital status
Marriage is an out-dated institution	No multivariate analysis Marriage is an out-dated institution
Men are less able to handle emotions	Disagreement with: Men are less able to handle emotions
Men are less able to handle emotions (5 cat)	No multivariate analysis Men are less able to handle emotions (5 cat)
Men make better political leaders than women do	Disagreement with: Men make better political leaders than women do
Moments of prayer, meditation...	Moments of prayer, meditation...
Monarchy is a form of government that is compatible with Islam	Monarchy is a form of government that is compatible with Islam
More than one wife	strongly disagree: More than one wife
Most important: first choice	No multivariate analysis Most important: first choice
Most important: second choice	No multivariate analysis Most important: second choice
Most people can be trusted	You cannot be too careful (most people cannot be trusted)
National goals: Fighting rising prices	Not important as a national goal: Fighting rising prices
National goals: free speech	Not important as a national goal: free speech
National goals: Giving people more say	Not important as a national goal: Giving people more say
National goals: Maintaining order in the nation	Not important as a national goal: Maintaining order in the nation
Nationalism is incompatible with Islam because Islam requires 'Umma'	Nationalism is incompatible with Islam because Islam requires 'Umma'
Neighbors: Black people	Rejecting neighbors: Black people
Neighbors: British	Rejecting neighbors: British
Neighbors: Chinese or Philippino Chinese	Rejecting neighbors: Chinese or Philippino Chinese

Appendix I

Variable label in the WVS	Variable label should read (because of highest and lowest numerical values)
Neighbors: Christians	Rejecting neighbors: Christians
Neighbors: Colored people	Rejecting neighbors: Colored people
Neighbors: Drug addicts	Rejecting neighbors: Drug addicts
Neighbors: Emotionally unstable people	Rejecting neighbors: Emotionally unstable people
Neighbors: Evangelists	Rejecting neighbors: Evangelists
Neighbors: French	Rejecting neighbors: French
Neighbors: Gypsies	Rejecting neighbors: Gypsies
Neighbors: Haitians	Rejecting neighbors: Haitians
Neighbors: Heavy drinkers	Rejecting neighbors: Heavy drinkers
Neighbors: Hindus	Rejecting neighbors: Hindus
Neighbors: Homosexuals	Rejecting neighbors: Homosexuals
Neighbors: Immigrants/foreign workers	Rejecting neighbors: Immigrants/foreign workers
Neighbors: Indians	Rejecting neighbors: Indians
Neighbors: Indians or Lebanese	Rejecting neighbors: Indians or Lebanese
Neighbors: Iranian	Rejecting neighbors: Iranian
Neighbors: Jews	Rejecting neighbors: Jews
Neighbors: Jews, Arabs, Asians, gypsies, etc	Rejecting neighbors: Jews, Arabs, Asians, gypsies, etc
Neighbors: Jordanian	Rejecting neighbors: Jordanian
Neighbors: Kildani	Rejecting neighbors: Kildani
Neighbors: Kurds, Esids	Rejecting neighbors: Kurds, Esids
Neighbors: Kuwaiti	Rejecting neighbors: Kuwaiti
Neighbors: Left wing extremists	Rejecting neighbors: Left wing extremists
Neighbors: Members of ETA (terrorists)	Rejecting neighbors: Members of ETA (terrorists)
Neighbors: Members of minority religious sects or cults	Rejecting neighbors: Members of minority religious sects or cults
Neighbors: Members of new religious movements	Rejecting neighbors: Members of new religious movements
Neighbors: Militant minority	Rejecting neighbors: Militant minority
Neighbors: Muslims	Rejecting neighbors: Muslims
Neighbors: North-American persons	Rejecting neighbors: North-American persons
Neighbors: People not from country of origin	Rejecting neighbors: People not from country of origin
Neighbors: People of a different race	Rejecting neighbors: People of a different race
Neighbors: People of a different religion	Rejecting neighbors: People of a different religion
Neighbors: People of the same religion	Rejecting neighbors: People of the same religion
Neighbors: People who have AIDS	Rejecting neighbors: People who have AIDS
Neighbors: People with a criminal record	Rejecting neighbors: People with a criminal record
Neighbors: People with large families	Rejecting neighbors: People with large families

The variable key to the World Values Survey, ordered alphabetically (Continued)

Variable label in the WVS	Variable label should read (because of highest and lowest numerical values)
Neighbors: Political Extremists	Rejecting neighbors: Political Extremists
Neighbors: Protestants	Rejecting neighbors: Protestants
Neighbors: Right wing extremists	Rejecting neighbors: Right wing extremists
Neighbors: Shia	Rejecting neighbors: Shia
Neighbors: Spiritists	Rejecting neighbors: Spiritists
Neighbors: Students	Rejecting neighbors: Students
Neighbors: Sunnis	Rejecting neighbors: Sunnis
Neighbors: Trafficants	Rejecting neighbors: Trafficants
Neighbors: Turkish	Rejecting neighbors: Turkish
Neighbors: Unmarried mothers	Rejecting neighbors: Unmarried mothers
Neighbors: White people	Rejecting neighbors: White people
Neighbors: Witchdoctors and related labels	Rejecting neighbors: Witchdoctors and related labels
Neighbors: Zoroastrians	Rejecting neighbors: Zoroastrians
New and old ideas	New ideas better than old ones
Number of employees	Number of employees
Number of employees (recoded)	Number of employees (recoded)
Number of others working in the organization	Number of others working in the organization
Number of others working in the organization (recoded)	Number of others working in the organization (recoded)
Number of people in household	Number of people in household
Number of people in household aged 11-15	Number of people in household aged 11-15
Number of people in household aged 13-17	Number of people in household aged 13-17
Number of people in household aged 1-4	Number of people in household aged 1-4
Number of people in household aged 16-17	Number of people in household aged 16-17
Number of people in household aged 5-10	Number of people in household aged 5-10
Number of people in household aged 5-12	Number of people in household aged 5-12
Number of people in household of 18+	Number of people in household of 18+
Number of people in household under age of 1	Number of people in household under age of 1
Number of people in household under age of 5	Number of people in household under age of 5
Number of supervised people	Number of supervised people
Number of supervised people (recoded)	Number of supervised people (recoded)
Nurse refusing legal abortion on religious grounds	No multivariate analysis Nurse refusing legal abortion on religious grounds
Often exploited in your job	Never exploited in your job
Older peoples trust in young people	Older peoples trust in young people
On the whole respondent looked	On the whole respondent looked

Variable label in the WVS	Variable label should read (because of highest and lowest numerical values)
One needs children	One needs children
One of main goals in life has been to make my parents proud	Disagreement with: One of main goals in life has been to make my parents proud
Only laws of the Shari´a	Rejecting laws of the Shari´a
Opinion about 11th September airliners crash action by religious fundamentalists	No multivariate analysis Opinion about 11th September airliners crash action by religious fundamentalists
Opinion about scientific advances	No multivariate analysis Opinion about scientific advances
Opinion about the problem of Palestine and Israel	No multivariate analysis Opinion about the problem of Palestine and Israel
Opinion European union	Opinion European union
Opinion on terrorism	No multivariate analysis Opinion on terrorism
Original respondent number	Original respondent number
Our government should be made much more open to the public	Disagreement with: Our government should be made much more open to the public
Paid free days: don't know	Paid free days: don't know
Paid free days: find additional work to avoid boredom	Paid free days: find additional work to avoid boredom
Paid free days: find extra work for money	Paid free days: find extra work for money
Paid free days: none of these	Paid free days: none of these
Paid free days: run own business in spare time	Paid free days: run own business in spare time
Paid free days: spend the time relaxing	Paid free days: spend the time relaxing
Paid free days: spend time on hobbies	Paid free days: spend time on hobbies
Paid free days: spend time with family and friends	Paid free days: spend time with family and friends
Paid free days: use spare time for voluntary work	Paid free days: use spare time for voluntary work
Paid free days: use spare time to study	Paid free days: use spare time to study
Parents responsibilities to their children	Parents responsibilities to their children
Party that would never vote	No multivariate analysis Party that would never vote
People should not have to work if they don't want to	Disagreement with: People should not have to work if they don't want to
People should not have to work if they don't want to (4 cat)	No multivariate analysis People should not have to work if they don't want to (4 cat)
People who don't work turn lazy	Disagreement with: People who don't work turn lazy
People who don't work turn lazy (4 cat)	No multivariate analysis People who don't work turn lazy (4 cat)
People's will to help each other today	No multivariate analysis People's will to help each other today
Personal characteristics: Changes, worry or welcome possibility	Personal characteristics: Changes welcome possibility
Personal characteristics: I am good at getting what I want	Personal characteristics: I am good at getting what I want
Personal characteristics: I am rarely unsure about how I should behave	Personal characteristics: I am rarely unsure about how I should behave
Personal characteristics: I enjoy convincing others of my opinion	Personal characteristics: I enjoy convincing others of my opinion
Personal characteristics: I like to assume responsibility	Personal characteristics: I like to assume responsibility
Personal characteristics: I often give others advice	Personal characteristics: I often give others advice

The variable key to the World Values Survey, ordered alphabetically (Continued)

Variable label in the WVS	Variable label should read (because of highest and lowest numerical values)
Personal characteristics: I own many things others envy me for	Personal characteristics: I own many things others envy me for
Personal characteristics: I serve as a model for others	Personal characteristics: I serve as a model for others
Personal characteristics: I usually count on being successful in everything I do	Personal characteristics: I usually count on being successful in everything I do
Personal characteristics: None of the above	No multivariate analysis Personal characteristics: None of the above
Personal God vs. Spirit or Life Force	No multivariate analysis Personal God vs. Spirit or Life Force
Persuading friends, relatives or fellow workers	Never persuading friends, relatives or fellow workers
Political action: attending lawful demonstrations	Would never do (political action): attending lawful demonstrations
Political action: damaging things, breaking windows, street violence	Would never do (political action): damaging things, breaking windows, street violence
Political action: joining in boycotts	Would never do (political action): joining in boycotts
Political action: joining unofficial strikes	Would never do (political action): joining unofficial strikes
Political action: occupying buildings or factories	Would never do (political action): occupying buildings or factories
Political action: personal violence	Would never do (political action): personal violence
Political action: signing a petition	Would never do (political action): signing a petition
Political parties serve the social and political needs of people	Disagree: Political parties serve the social and political needs of people
Political reform is moving too rapidly	Disagreement with: Political reform is moving too rapidly
Political system: Having a democratic political system	Bad political system: Having a democratic political system
Political system: Having a strong leader	Bad political system: Having a strong leader
Political system: Having experts make decisions	Bad political system: Having experts make decisions
Political system: Having the army rule	Bad political system: Having the army rule
Politicians who don't believe in God are unfit for public office[35]	Politicians who don't believe in God are fit for public office
Politics important in life	Politics not important in life
Post-Materialist index 12-item	Post-Materialist index 12-item
Post-Materialist index 4-item	Post-Materialist index 4-item

---

[35] It is not only important, but very important to state here that this variable, due to the distribution of the highest and the lowest numerical values in the World Values Survey, has to be interpreted in the multivariate analysis as "Politicians who don´t believe in God are fit for public office". However, the analysis of fundamentalist thought patterns above also took properly care of the distribution of the highest and the lowest numerical values, and correctly measures the percentages of those who think that "Politicians who don´t believe in God are unfit for public office". The WVS wording of the F102 WVS question is: "How much do you agree or disagree with each of the following statement: Politicians who do not believe in God are unfit for public office.
    1 Agree strongly
    2 Agree
    3 Neither agree or disagree
    4 Disagree
    5 Strongly disagree"

Appendix I

Variable label in the WVS	Variable label should read (because of highest and lowest numerical values)
Poverty compared to 10 years ago	Poverty compared to 10 years ago decreased
Pray to God outside of religious services (I)	Never pray to God outside of religious services (I)
Pray to God outside of religious services (ii)	No multivariate analysis Pray to God outside of religious services (ii)
Prepared to help elderly people	Not prepared to help elderly people
Prepared to help immediate family	Not prepared to help immediate family
Prepared to help immigrants	Not prepared to help immigrants
Prepared to help people in the neighborhood	Not prepared to help people in the neighborhood
Prepared to help sick and disabled people	Not prepared to help sick and disabled people
Pre-school child suffers with working mother	Disagreement with: Pre-school child suffers with working mother
Pre-school child suffers with working mother (5 cat)	No multivariate analysis Pre-school child suffers with working mother (5 cat)
Private vs. state ownership of business	state ownership vs. private ownership of business
Problem if women have more income than husband	Disagreement with: Problem if women have more income than husband
Profession/industry (2 digit isco88)	Profession/industry (2 digit isco88)
Profession/industry (3 digit isco88)	Profession/industry (3 digit isco88)
Profession/industry (4 digit isco88)	Profession/industry (4 digit isco88)
Profession/job	Profession/job
Prohibiting or allowing books that attack religion	No multivariate analysis Prohibiting or allowing books that attack religion
Protecting environment and fighting pollution is less urgent than suggested	Protecting environment and fighting pollution is more urgent than suggested
Protecting environment vs. Economic growth	No multivariate analysis Protecting environment vs. Economic growth
Raised religiously	Raised religiously
Rapid implementation of market reforms have negative impact on national stability	Disagree: rapid implementation of market reforms have negative impact on national stability
Rate political system as it was before	Political system as it was before good for the country
Rate political system for governing country	Political system good for governing country
Rate political system in ten years	Political system in ten years good for the country
Reason to help: Do something in return for immigrants	No reason to help: Do something in return for immigrants
Reason to help: Do something in return for immigrants (2 cat)	No multivariate analysis No reason to help: Do something in return for immigrants (2 cat)
Reason to help: Do something in return for old people	No reason to help: Do something in return for old people
Reason to help: Do something in return for old people (2 cat)	No multivariate analysis No reason to help: Do something in return for old people (2 cat)
Reason to help: In the interest of society	No reason to help: In the interest of society
Reason to help: In the interest of society	No reason to help: In the interest of society
Reason to help: In the interest of society (2 cat)	No multivariate analysis No reason to help: In the interest of society (2 cat)
Reason to help: In the interest of society (2 cat)	No multivariate analysis No reason to help: In the interest of society (2 cat)

The variable key to the World Values Survey, ordered alphabetically (Continued)

Variable label in the WVS	Variable label should read (because of highest and lowest numerical values)
Reason to help: Moral duty to help elderly people	No reason to help: Moral duty to help elderly people
Reason to help: Moral duty to help elderly people (2 cat)	No multivariate analysis No reason to help: Moral duty to help elderly people (2 cat)
Reason to help: Moral duty to help immigrants	No reason to help: Moral duty to help immigrants
Reason to help: Moral duty to help immigrants (2 cat)	No multivariate analysis No reason to help: Moral duty to help immigrants (2 cat)
Reason to help: Own interest	No reason to help: Own interest
Reason to help: Own interest	No reason to help: Own interest
Reason to help: Own interest (2 cat)	No multivariate analysis No reason to help: Own interest (2 cat)
Reason to help: Own interest (2 cat)	No multivariate analysis No reason to help: Own interest (2 cat)
Reason to help: Sympathize with immigrants	No reason to help: Sympathize with immigrants
Reason to help: Sympathize with immigrants (2 cat)	No multivariate analysis No reason to help: Sympathize with immigrants (2 cat)
Reason to help: Sympathize with old people	No reason to help: Sympathize with old people
Reason to help: Sympathize with old people (2 cat)	No multivariate analysis No reason to help: Sympathize with old people (2 cat)
Reasons voluntary work: Bring about social or political change	Reasons voluntary work: Bring about social or political change
Reasons voluntary work: Compassion for those in need	Reasons voluntary work: Compassion for those in need
Reasons voluntary work: Did not want to, but could not refuse	Reasons voluntary work: Did not want to, but could not refuse
Reasons voluntary work: For social reasons	Reasons voluntary work: For social reasons
Reasons voluntary work: Gain new skills and useful experience	Reasons voluntary work: Gain new skills and useful experience
Reasons voluntary work: Help disadvantaged people	Reasons voluntary work: Help disadvantaged people
Reasons voluntary work: Identifying with people who suffer	Reasons voluntary work: Identifying with people who suffer
Reasons voluntary work: Make a contribution to my local community	Reasons voluntary work: Make a contribution to my local community
Reasons voluntary work: Opportunity to repay something	Reasons voluntary work: Opportunity to repay something
Reasons voluntary work: Personal satisfaction	Reasons voluntary work: Personal satisfaction
Reasons voluntary work: Religious belief	Reasons voluntary work: Religious belief
Reasons voluntary work: Sense of duty, moral, obligation	Reasons voluntary work: Sense of duty, moral, obligation
Reasons voluntary work: Solidarity with the poor and disadvantaged	Reasons voluntary work: Solidarity with the poor and disadvantaged
Reasons voluntary work: Time on my hands	Reasons voluntary work: Time on my hands
Region where the interview was conducted	Region where the interview was conducted
Regularly read a daily newspaper	Regularly read a daily newspaper
Relationship between you and your father	No close relationship between you and your father
Relationship between you and your mother	No close relationship between you and your mother
Relationship between your parents	No close relationship between your parents

Appendix I

Variable label in the WVS	Variable label should read (because of highest and lowest numerical values)
Relationship working mother	Disagreement with: Relationship working mother
Relationship working mother (5 cat)	No multivariate analysis Relationship working mother (5 cat)
Religion important in life	Religion not important in life
Religion is a cause of terrorism	Religion is a cause of terrorism
Religions limit democratic processes	Religions limit democratic processes
Religious denomination	No multivariate analysis Religious denomination
Religious leaders should not influence government	Religious leaders should influence government
Religious leaders should not influence how people vote	Religious leaders should influence how people vote
Religious person	Religious person
Respect and love for parents	no respect and love for parents
Respect for individual human rights nowadays	No respect for individual human rights nowadays
Respondent interested during the interview	Respondent interested during the interview
Responsibility housing	State responsibility for housing
Responsibility pension	State responsibility for pensions
Satisfaction job security	Satisfaction job security
Satisfaction with financial situation of household	Satisfaction with financial situation of household
Satisfaction with home life	High satisfaction with home life
Satisfaction with the people in national office	Dissatisfaction with the people in national office
Satisfaction with the way democracy develops	Dissatisfaction with the way democracy develops
Satisfaction with your life	Satisfaction with your life
Satisfaction with your life 5 years ago	Satisfaction with your life five years ago
Scale of incomes	Scale of incomes
Second choice if looking for a job	No multivariate analysis Second choice if looking for a job
Seen events that happened far away	Seen events that happened far away
Self positioning in political scale	Right wing versus left wing (Self positioning in political scale)
Service to others important in life	Service to others not important in life
Set	Set
Sex	Sex
Sex cannot entirely be left to individual choice	No multivariate analysis Sex cannot entirely be left to individual choice
Sharing with parents: attitudes towards religion	Sharing with parents: attitudes towards religion
Sharing with parents: don't know or missing	Sharing with parents: don't know or missing
Sharing with parents: moral standards´	Sharing with parents: moral standards´
Sharing with parents: no sharing attitudes	Sharing with parents: no sharing attitudes
Sharing with parents: political views	Sharing with parents: political views
Sharing with parents: sexual attitudes	Sharing with parents: sexual attitudes

The variable key to the World Values Survey, ordered alphabetically (Continued)

Variable label in the WVS	Variable label should read (because of highest and lowest numerical values)
Sharing with parents: social attitudes	Sharing with parents: social attitudes
Sharing with partner: attitudes towards religion	Sharing with partner: attitudes towards religion
Sharing with partner: don't know or missing	Sharing with partner: don't know or missing
Sharing with partner: moral standards	Sharing with partner: moral standards
Sharing with partner: no sharing attitudes	Sharing with partner: no sharing attitudes
Sharing with partner: political views	Sharing with partner: political views
Sharing with partner: sexual attitudes	Sharing with partner: sexual attitudes
Sharing with partner: social attitudes	Sharing with partner: social attitudes
Size of town	Size of town
Size of town (country specific)	Size of town (country specific)
Social class (subjective)	Low Social class (subjective)
Society aimed: egalitarian vs. competitive	Society aimed: competitive
Society aimed: extensive welfare vs. low taxes	Society aimed: low taxes
Society aimed: regulated vs. responsible society	Society aimed: responsible society
Socio-economic status of respondent	Low Socio-economic status of respondent
Some US Policies toward other countries are good and some are bad	Some US Policies toward other countries are good and some are bad
Sorrow has meaning if you believe in God	No multivariate analysis Sorrow has meaning if you Believe in God
Spend leisure time with: don't know	No multivariate analysis What children should learn 1
Spend leisure time: all equally	No multivariate analysis No multivariate analysis What children should learn 1
Spend leisure time: alone	Spend leisure time: alone
Spend leisure time: in a lively place	Spend leisure time: in a lively place
Spend leisure time: with family	Spend leisure time: with family
Spend leisure time: with friends	Spend leisure time: with friends
Spend time with colleagues from work	Not spend time with colleagues from work
Spend time with colleagues from work (filtered)	No multivariate analysis Spend time with colleagues from work (filtered)
Spend time with friends	Not spend time with friends
Spend time with parents or other relatives	Not spend time with parents or other relatives
Spend time with people at sport, culture, communal organization	Not spend time with people at sport, culture, communal organization
Spend time with people at sport, culture, communal organization (filtered)	No multivariate analysis Spend time with people at sport, culture, communal organization (filtered)
Spend time with people at your church, mosque or synagogue	Not spend time with people at your church, mosque or synagogue
Spend time with people at your church, mosque or synagogue (filtered)	No multivariate analysis Spend time with people at your church, mosque or synagogue (filtered)
Stable relationship	Stable relationship

Appendix I

Variable label in the WVS	Variable label should read (because of highest and lowest numerical values)
Stable relationship before	Stable relationship before
State of health (subjective)	State of health very bad (subjective)
Statement: good and evil	No multivariate analysis Statement: good and evil
Statement: religion and truth	No multivariate analysis Statement: religion and truth
Stealing food punished less: poor thief	Stealing food punished less: poor thief
Stealing food punished less: poor thief (4 cat)	Stealing food punished less: poor thief (4 cat)
Stealing food punished less: shop part of a supermarket chain	Stealing food punished less: shop part of a supermarket chain
Stealing food punished less: shop part of a supermarket chain (4 cat)	Stealing food punished less: shop part of a supermarket chain (4 cat)
Stealing food punished less: young thief	Stealing food punished less: young thief
Stealing food punished less: young thief (4 cat)	Stealing food punished less: young thief (4 cat)
Stick to own affairs	Disagree to stick to own affairs
Stick to religion vs. Explore different traditions	explore different religious traditions
Study	Study
SURVIVAL/SELF-EXPRESSION VALUES	SURVIVAL/SELF-EXPRESSION VALUES
Taking horoscope into account in daily life	Not taking horoscope into account in daily life
The content of [Country] education contributes to religious extremism	The content of [Country] education contributes to religious extremism
The culture of US and other Western countries has many positive attributes	The culture of US and other Western countries has many positive attributes
The economic system needs fundamental changes	Disagreement with: The economic system needs fundamental changes
The main aim of imprisonment	No multivariate analysis The main aim of imprisonment
Thinking about death	Never thinking about death
Thinking about meaning and purpose of life	Never thinking about meaning and purpose life
Time at the end of interview	Time at the end of interview
Time for prayer and meditation in all schools	Rejecting time for prayer and meditation in all schools
To develop talents you need to have a job	Disagreement with: to develop talents you need to have a job
To develop talents you need to have a job (4 cat)	No multivariate analysis To develop talents you need to have a job (4 cat)
Total length of interview	Total length of interview
Tradition vs. high economic growth	No multivariate analysis Tradition vs. high economic growth
TRADITIONAL/SECULAR RATIONAL VALUES	TRADITIONAL/SECULAR RATIONAL VALUES
Traits in a woman: Woman being independent	Not important Traits in a woman: Woman being independent
Traits in a woman: Woman being sociable	Not important Traits in a woman: Woman being sociable
Traits in a woman: Woman educated	Not important Traits in a woman: Woman educated
Traits in a woman: Woman good mother	Not important Traits in a woman: Woman good mother
Traits in a woman: Woman good wife	Not important Traits in a woman: Woman good wife

The variable key to the World Values Survey, ordered alphabetically (Continued)

Variable label in the WVS	Variable label should read (because of highest and lowest numerical values)
Traits in a woman: Woman having work outside home	Not important Traits in a woman: Woman having work outside home
Traits in a woman: Woman maintaining her family	Not important Traits in a woman: Woman maintaining her family
Traits in a woman: Woman religious	Not important Traits in a woman: Woman religious
Traits in a woman: Woman wearing veil	Not important Traits in a woman: Woman wearing veil
Trust: Americans	Trust: Americans
Trust: Arabs	Trust: Arabs
Trust: Argentines	Trust: Argentines
Trust: Asian South Africans	Trust: Asian South Africans
Trust: Black South Africans	Trust: Black South Africans
Trust: Blacks	Trust: Blacks
Trust: Central Americans	Trust: Central Americans
Trust: Chinese	Trust: Chinese
Trust: Chinese Hui Nationality	Trust: Chinese Hui Nationality
Trust: Chinese residents in Japan	Trust: Chinese residents in Japan
Trust: Chinese Zhuan Nationality	Trust: Chinese Zhuan Nationality
Trust: Colored South Africans	Trust: Colored South Africans
Trust: Czechs	Trust: Czechs
Trust: East Germans	Trust: East Germans
Trust: English	Trust: English
Trust: Europeans	Trust: Europeans
Trust: French Canadians	Trust: French Canadians
Trust: Germans	Trust: Germans
Trust: Ghanaians	Trust: Ghanaians
Trust: Greeks	Trust: Greeks
Trust: Gypsies	Trust: Gypsies
Trust: Hausas	Trust: Hausas
Trust: Hungarians	Trust: Hungarians
Trust: Igbos	Trust: Igbos
Trust: Immigrants	Trust: Immigrants
Trust: Indian Hindus	Trust: Indian Hindus
Trust: Indian Non-Hindus	Trust: Indian Non-Hindus
Trust: Indians	Trust: Indians
Trust: Iranians	Trust: Iranians
Trust: Italians	Trust: Italians

Variable label in the WVS	Variable label should read (because of highest and lowest numerical values)
Trust: Japanese	Trust: Japanese
Trust: Jews	Trust: Jews
Trust: Korean residents in Japan	Trust: Korean residents in Japan
Trust: Koreans	Trust: Koreans
Trust: Latin Americans	Trust: Latin Americans
Trust: Mapuche Indians	Trust: Mapuche Indians
Trust: Mestizo	Trust: Mestizo
Trust: Mexicans	Trust: Mexicans
Trust: Moroccans	Trust: Moroccans
Trust: Nepalis	Trust: Nepalis
Trust: Other people in country	Trust: Other people in country
Trust: Pakistanis	Trust: Pakistanis
Trust: Pascuences	Trust: Pascuences
Trust: Peruvians	Trust: Peruvians
Trust: Poles	Trust: Poles
Trust: Portuguese	Trust: Portuguese
Trust: Russians	Trust: Russians
Trust: Slovaks	Trust: Slovaks
Trust: Soviet Union people	Trust: Soviet Union people
Trust: West Germans	Trust: West Germans
Trust: White South Africans	Trust: White South Africans
Trust: Xhosas	Trust: Xhosas
Trust: Yorubas	Trust: Yorubas
Trust: Your friends	Trust: Your friends
Trust: Your neighborhood	Trust: Your neighborhood
Trust: Zulus	Trust: Zulus
Try to get the best out of life	No multivariate analysis Try to get the best out of life
TV most important entertainment	TV not most important entertainment
Type of habitat	Type of habitat
Unfair to give work to handicapped people when able bodied people can't find jobs	No multivariate analysis Unfair to give work to handicapped people when able bodied people can't find jobs
Unified respondent number	Unified respondent number
University is more important for a boy than for a girl	Disagreement with: University is more important for a boy than for a girl
Unpaid work animal rights	Unpaid work animal rights
Unpaid work consumer groups	Unpaid work consumer groups
Unpaid work education, arts, music or cultural activities	Unpaid work education, arts, music or cultural activities

The variable key to the World Values Survey, ordered alphabetically (Continued)

Variable label in the WVS	Variable label should read (because of highest and lowest numerical values)
Unpaid work environment, conservation, animal rights	Unpaid work environment, conservation, animal rights
Unpaid work environment, conservation, ecology	Unpaid work environment, conservation, ecology
Unpaid work human rights	Unpaid work human rights
Unpaid work labor unions	Unpaid work labor unions
Unpaid work local political action groups	Unpaid work local political action groups
Unpaid work none	Unpaid work none
Unpaid work organization concerned with health	Unpaid work organization concerned with health
Unpaid work other groups	Unpaid work other groups
Unpaid work peace movement	Unpaid work peace movement
Unpaid work political parties or groups	Unpaid work political parties or groups
Unpaid work professional associations	Unpaid work professional associations
Unpaid work religious or church organization	Unpaid work religious or church organization
Unpaid work social welfare service for elderly, handicapped or deprived people	Unpaid work social welfare service for elderly, handicapped or deprived people
Unpaid work sports or recreation	Unpaid work sports or recreation
Unpaid work women's group	Unpaid work women's group
Unpaid work youth work	Unpaid work youth work
Using violence for political goals not justified	Using violence for political goals justified
Violation of Islam for male and female university students to attend classes together	Violation of Islam for male and female university students to attend classes together
Wave	Wave
Way of spending leisure time	No multivariate analysis No multivariate analysis What children should learn 1
Wealth accumulation	Wealth accumulation does not harm others
Weight	Weight
Weight [with split ups]	Weight [with split ups]
Western democracy is the best political system for country	No multivariate analysis Western democracy is the best political system for country
What age did you complete your education	What age did you complete your education
What age did you complete your education (recoded in intervals)	What age did you complete your education (recoded in intervals)
What children should learn 1	No multivariate analysis What children should learn 1
What children should learn 2	No multivariate analysis What children should learn 1
What thing are you proud of in your country -1st	What thing are you proud of in your country -1st
What thing are you proud of in your country -2nd	What thing are you proud of in your country -2nd
When came to country	When came to country
When you are home, do you feel aggressive	When you are home, do you feel never aggressive
When you are home, do you feel anxious	When you are home, do you feel never anxious

Appendix I

Variable label in the WVS	Variable label should read (because of highest and lowest numerical values)
When you are home, do you feel happy	When you are home, do you feel never happy
When you are home, do you feel relaxed	When you are home, do you feel unrelaxed
When you are home, do you feel secure	When you are home, do you feel never secure
When you were growing up, did your father or mother have more influence in the affairs of the house	When you were growing up, did your father or mother have more influence in the affairs of the house
Where r lived after married	Where r lived after married
Which former religious denomination	No multivariate analysis, which former religious denomination
Which is more important as a basis for marriage: parents' approval or love	Which is more important as a basis for marriage: parents' approval or love
Which of the following best describes you	Which of the following best describes you
Which party would you vote for: first choice	No multivariate analysis, which party would you vote for: first choice
Which party would you vote for: second choice	No multivariate analysis, which party would you vote for: second choice
While US policies toward other countries are often bad, most ordinary Americans are good people	While US policies toward other countries are often bad, most ordinary Americans are good people
Who should decide: aid to developing countries	No multivariate analysis Who should decide: aid to developing countries
Who should decide: human rights	No multivariate analysis Who should decide: human rights
Who should decide: international peacekeeping	No multivariate analysis Who should decide: international peacekeeping
Who should decide: protection of the environment	No multivariate analysis Who should decide: protection of the environment
Who should decide: refugees	No multivariate analysis Who should decide: refugees
Why are people in need	No multivariate analysis Why are people in need
Why are there people living in need: first	No multivariate analysis Why are there people living in need: first
Why are there people living in need: second	No multivariate analysis Why are there people living in need: second
Why people work	No multivariate analysis Why people work
Why people work: don't know	Why people work: don't know
Why people work: I do the best I can regardless of pay	Why people work: I do the best I can regardless of pay
Why people work: I never had a paid job	Why people work: I never had a paid job
Why people work: I wouldn't work if work interfered my life	Why people work: I wouldn't work if work interfered my life
Why people work: I wouldn't work if I didn't have to	Why people work: I wouldn't work if I didn't have to
Why people work: work is like a business transaction	Why people work: work is like a business transaction
Why people work: work most important in my life	Why people work: work most important in my life
Wife must obey	strongly disagree: Wife must obey
Will there be war in your country in the next 5 years	There will be war in your country in the next 5 years+C44
Willingness to fight for country	No multivariate analysis Willingness to fight for country
Woman as a single parent	No multivariate analysis Woman as a single parent
Woman should not work outside unless forced to do so	No multivariate analysis Woman should not work outside unless forced to do so

The variable key to the World Values Survey, ordered alphabetically (Continued)

Variable label in the WVS	Variable label should read (because of highest and lowest numerical values)
Women want a home and children	Disagreement with: Women want a home and children
Women want a home and children (5 cat)	No multivariate analysis Women want a home and children (5 cat)
Work compared with Leisure	Work more important than leisure
Work important in life	Work not important in life
Work is a duty towards society	Disagreement with: Work is a duty towards society
Work is a duty towards society (4 cat)	No multivariate analysis Work is a duty towards society (4 cat)
Work should come first even if it means less spare time	Disagreement with: Work should come first even if it means less spare time
Work should come first even if it means less spare time (4 cat)	No multivariate analysis Work should come first even if it means less spare time (4 cat)
Work: accomplish personal goals	Disagreement with: Work: accomplish personal goals
Work: stay up late to finish	Disagreement with: Work: stay up late to finish
Work: until satisfied with results	disagreement with: Work: until satisfied with results
Worth risking life for: another's life	Worth risking life for: another's life
Worth risking life for: don't know	No multivariate analysis Worth risking life for: don't know
Worth risking life for: freedom	Worth risking life for: freedom
Worth risking life for: justice	Worth risking life for: justice
Worth risking life for: my country	Worth risking life for: my country
Worth risking life for: other	No multivariate analysis Worth risking life for: other
Worth risking life for: peace	Worth risking life for: peace
Worth risking life for: religion	Worth risking life for: religion
Would buy things at a 20% higher price if it helped to protect environment	Would not buy things at a 20% higher price if it helped to protect environment
Would give part of my income for the environment	No part of my income for the environment
Would persist to immigrate abroad if R's economic situation was better	No multivariate analysis Would persist to immigrate abroad if R's economic situation was better
Year of birth	Year of birth
Year survey	Year survey
Year/month of end-fieldwork	Year/month of end-fieldwork
Year/month of start-fieldwork	Year/month of start-fieldwork
Young peoples trust in older people	Young peoples trust in older people

Appendix II

WHAT THE GALLUP BOOKLET UNFORTUNATELY DOES NOT TELL YOU: WHAT MUSLIMS REALLY THINK – THE DATA FROM THE WORLD VALUES SURVEY, WITH A FULL DOCUMENTATION AND THE ORIGINAL SPSS XIV/XV TABLES, AND THE MOST IMPORTANT SURVEY RESULTS FOR THE MUSLIM GLOBAL SAMPLE FROM THE WORLD VALUES SURVEY[36]

FREQUENCIES ACCORDING TO THE SPSS XIV (WEIGHTS: 1000)

Translation of the SPSS XIV Innsbruck University German language terms into English

Fehlend – missing
Total – total
Gültig – valid
Gültige Prozente – valid percentages
Häufigkeit – Frequency
Kumulierte Prozente – cumulated percentages
Prozent – percent

---

[36] WVS, SPSS, wave 1 + 2 + 3 + 4.

GLOBAL MUSLIM TRUST IN CENTRAL SOCIETAL INSTITUTIONS

Satisfaction with the way democracy develops

		Häufigkeit	Prozent	Gültige Prozente	Kumulierte Prozente
Gültig	Very satisfied	1069	5.7	10.3	10.3
	Rather satisfied	4222	22.5	40.6	50.8
	Not very satisfied	3519	18.7	33.8	84.6
	Not at all satisfied	1599	8.5	15.4	100.0
	Gesamt	10410	55.4	100.0	
Fehlend	Not asked	7403	39.4		
	No answer	183	1.0		
	Don't know	798	4.2		
	Gesamt	8383	44.6		
Gesamt		18793	100.0		

Satisfaction with the way democracy develops

		Häufigkeit	Prozent	Gültige Prozente	Kumulierte Prozente
Gültig	Very satisfied	1069	5.7	10.3	10.3
	Rather satisfied	4222	22.5	40.6	50.8
	Not very satisfied	3519	18.7	33.8	84.6
	Not at all satisfied	1599	8.5	15.4	100.0
	Gesamt	10410	55.4	100.0	
Fehlend	Not asked	7403	39.4		
	No answer	183	1.0		
	Don´t know	798	4.2		
	Gesamt	8383	44.6		
Gesamt		18793	100.0		

Appendix II

Confidence: churches

		Häufigkeit	Prozent	Gültige Prozente	Kumulierte Prozente
Gültig	A great deal	9266	49.3	51.5	51.5
	Quite a lot	5019	26.7	27.9	79.4
	Not very much	2365	12.6	13.1	92.5
	None at all	1343	7.1	7.5	100.0
	Gesamt	17993	95.7	100.0	
Fehlend	Missing; Unknown	4	.0		
	Not asked	255	1.4		
	No answer	88	.5		
	Don't know	453	2.4		
	Gesamt	801	4.3		
Gesamt		18793	100.0		

Confidence: armed forces

		Häufigkeit	Prozent	Gültige Prozente	Kumulierte Prozente
Gültig	A great deal	5485	29.2	34.4	34.4
	Quite a lot	5533	29.4	34.7	69.2
	Not very much	3419	18.2	21.5	90.6
	None at all	1490	7.9	9.4	100.0
	Gesamt	15927	84.7	100.0	
Fehlend	Missing; unknown	1	.0		
	Not asked	2196	11.7		
	No answer	49	.3		
	Don't know	620	3.3		
	Gesamt	2866	15.3		
Gesamt		18793	100.0		

Confidence: education system

		Häufigkeit	Prozent	Gültige Prozente	Kumulierte Prozente
Gültig	A great deal	624	3.3	35.3	35.3
	Quite a lot	592	3.1	33.5	68.8
	Not very much	330	1.8	18.6	87.4
	None at all	222	1.2	12.6	100.0
	Gesamt	1768	9.4	100.0	
Fehlend	Not asked	16993	90.4		
	No answer	12	.1		
	Don't know	21	.1		
	Gesamt	17025	90.6		
Gesamt		18793	100.0		

Confidence: the press

		Häufigkeit	Prozent	Gültige Prozente	Kumulierte Prozente
Gültig	A great deal	2379	12.7	14.1	14.1
	Quite a lot	5860	31.2	34.8	49.0
	Not very much	5960	31.7	35.4	84.4
	None at all	2628	14.0	15.6	100.0
	Gesamt	16827	89.5	100.0	
Fehlend	Missing; unknown	3	.0		
	Not asked	861	4.6		
	No answer	85	.5		
	Don't know	1017	5.4		
	Gesamt	1966	10.5		
Gesamt		18793	100.0		

Confidence: labour unions

		Häufigkeit	Prozent	Gültige Prozente	Kumulierte Prozente
Gültig	A great deal	1804	9.6	12.9	12.9
	Quite a lot	4576	24.3	32.6	45.5
	Not very much	4949	26.3	35.3	80.8
	None at all	2693	14.3	19.2	100.0
	Gesamt	14022	74.6	100.0	
Fehlend	Missing; unknown	8	.0		
	Not asked	1831	9.7		
	No answer	178	.9		
	Don't know	2753	14.7		
	Gesamt	4771	25.4		
Gesamt		18793	100.0		

Confidence: the police

		Häufigkeit	Prozent	Gültige Prozente	Kumulierte Prozente
Gültig	A great deal	4101	21.8	25.2	25.2
	Quite a lot	5620	29.9	34.5	59.7
	Not very much	4000	21.3	24.6	84.2
	None at all	2567	13.7	15.8	100.0
	Gesamt	16289	86.7	100.0	
Fehlend	Missing; unknown	1	.0		
	Not asked	1836	9.8		
	No answer	92	.5		
	Don't know	575	3.1		
	Gesamt	2505	13.3		
Gesamt		18793	100.0		

Confidence: Parliament

		Häufigkeit	Prozent	Gültige Prozente	Kumulierte Prozente
Gültig	A great deal	2989	15.9	19.1	19.1
	Quite a lot	5417	28.8	34.6	53.7
	Not very much	4151	22.1	26.5	80.2
	None at all	3098	16.5	19.8	100.0
	Gesamt	15655	83.3	100.0	
Fehlend	Missing; unknown	2	.0		
	Not asked	1834	9.8		
	No answer	120	.6		
	Don´t know	1182	6.3		
	Gesamt	3139	16.7		
Gesamt		18793	100.0		

Confidence: the civil services

		Häufigkeit	Prozent	Gültige Prozente	Kumulierte Prozente
Gültig	A great deal	3050	16.2	18.9	18.9
	Quite a lot	6180	32.9	38.2	57.1
	Not very much	4543	24.2	28.1	85.2
	None at all	2396	12.8	14.8	100.0
	Gesamt	16170	86.0	100.0	
Fehlend	Missing; unknown	1	.0		
	Not asked	863	4.6		
	No answer	144	.8		
	Don´t know	1615	8.6		
	Gesamt	2623	14.0		
Gesamt		18793	100.0		

Confidence: social security system

		Häufigkeit	Prozent	Gültige Prozente	Kumulierte Prozente
Gültig	A great deal	416	2.2	24.8	24.8
	Quite a lot	665	3.5	39.6	64.4
	Not very much	350	1.9	20.9	85.3
	None at all	247	1.3	14.7	100.0
	Gesamt	1679	8.9	100.0	
Fehlend	Not asked	17012	90.5		
	No answer	36	.2		
	Don´t know	67	.4		
	Gesamt	17115	91.1		
Gesamt		18793	100.0		

Confidence: television

		Häufigkeit	Prozent	Gültige Prozente	Kumulierte Prozente
Gültig	A great deal	2470	13.1	15.3	15.3
	Quite a lot	6324	33.7	39.1	54.3
	Not very much	5365	28.5	33.1	87.5
	None at all	2030	10.8	12.5	100.0
	Gesamt	16189	86.1	100.0	
Fehlend	Missing; unknown	1	.0		
	Not asked	1808	9.6		
	No answer	67	.4		
	Don't know	729	3.9		
	Gesamt	2605	13.9		
Gesamt		18793	100.0		

Confidence: the government

		Häufigkeit	Prozent	Gültige Prozente	Kumulierte Prozente
Gültig	A great deal	3478	18.5	23.1	23.1
	Quite a lot	5349	28.5	35.5	58.5
	Not very much	3790	20.2	25.1	83.7
	None at all	2459	13.1	16.3	100.0
	Gesamt	15077	80.2	100.0	
Fehlend	Missing; unknown	4	.0		
	Not asked	2745	14.6		
	No answer	111	.6		
	Don't know	857	4.6		
	Gesamt	3717	19.8		
Gesamt		18793	100.0		

Confidence: the political parties

		Häufigkeit	Prozent	Gültige Prozente	Kumulierte Prozente
Gültig	A great deal	1537	8.2	11.1	11.1
	Quite a lot	3952	21.0	28.4	39.5
	Not very much	5032	26.8	36.2	75.7
	None at all	3381	18.0	24.3	100.0
	Gesamt	13902	74.0	100.0	
Fehlend	Missing; unknown	2	.0		
	Not asked	3247	17.3		
	No answer	138	.7		
	Don't know	1504	8.0		
	Gesamt	4891	26.0		
Gesamt		18793	100.0		

Confidence: major companies

		Häufigkeit	Prozent	Gültige Prozente	Kumulierte Prozente
Gültig	A great deal	2201	11.7	15.4	15.4
	Quite a lot	5084	27.1	35.6	51.0
	Not very much	4396	23.4	30.7	81.7
	None at all	2617	13.9	18.3	100.0
	Gesamt	14297	76.1	100.0	
Fehlend	Missing; unknown	2	.0		
	Not asked	2000	10.6		
	No answer	123	.7		
	Don´t know	2370	12.6		
	Gesamt	4496	23.9		
Gesamt		18793	100.0		

Confidence: the environmental protection movement

		Häufigkeit	Prozent	Gültige Prozente	Kumulierte Prozente
Gültig	A great deal	2713	14.4	20.3	20.3
	Quite a lot	5250	27.9	39.2	59.5
	Not very much	3520	18.7	26.3	85.8
	None at all	1908	10.2	14.2	100.0
	Gesamt	13391	71.3	100.0	
Fehlend	Missing; unknown	11	.1		
	Not asked	2722	14.5		
	No answer	135	.7		
	Don´t know	2535	13.5		
	Gesamt	5403	28.7		
Gesamt		18793	100.0		

Confidence: the women´s movement

		Häufigkeit	Prozent	Gültige Prozente	Kumulierte Prozente
Gültig	A great deal	2529	13.5	18.8	18.8
	Quite a lot	4888	26.0	36.4	55.3
	Not very much	3509	18.7	26.1	81.4
	None at all	2495	13.3	18.6	100.0
	Gesamt	13421	71.4	100.0	
Fehlend	Missing; unknown	8	.0		
	Not asked	2722	14.5		
	No answer	116	.6		
	Don´t know	2527	13.4		
	Gesamt	5372	28.6		
Gesamt		18793	100.0		

Confidence: health care system

		Häufigkeit	Prozent	Gültige Prozente	Kumulierte Prozente
Gültig	A great deal	243	1.3	20.6	20.6
	Quite a lot	443	2.4	37.5	58.1
	Not very much	239	1.3	20.2	78.3
	None at all	257	1.4	21.7	100.0
	Gesamt	1181	6.3	100.0	
Fehlend	Not asked	17576	93.5		
	No answer	7	.0		
	Don't know	29	.2		
	Gesamt	17612	93.7		
Gesamt		18793	100.0		

Confidence: justice system

		Häufigkeit	Prozent	Gültige Prozente	Kumulierte Prozente
Gültig	A great deal	1473	7.8	22.9	22.9
	Quite a lot	2487	13.2	38.6	61.5
	Not very much	1735	9.2	26.9	88.4
	None at all	744	4.0	11.6	100.0
	Gesamt	6438	34.3	100.0	
Fehlend	Missing; unknown	3	.0		
	Not asked	12048	64.1		
	No answer	33	.2		
	Don't know	271	1.4		
	Gesamt	12355	65.7		
Gesamt		18793	100.0		

Confidence: the European Union

		Häufigkeit	Prozent	Gültige Prozente	Kumulierte Prozente
Gültig	A great deal	1485	7.9	23.2	23.2
	Quite a lot	2213	11.8	34.6	57.8
	Not very much	1519	8.1	23.8	81.6
	None at all	1171	6.2	18.3	99.9
	9	8	.0	.1	100.0
	Gesamt	6396	34.0	100.0	
Fehlend	Missing; unknown	10	.1		
	Not asked	11361	60.5		
	No answer	25	.1		
	Don't know	1001	5.3		
	Gesamt	12398	66.0		
Gesamt		18793	100.0		

Confidence: NATO

		Häufigkeit	Prozent	Gültige Prozente	Kumulierte Prozente
Gültig	A great deal	1120	6.0	24.9	24.9
	Quite a lot	1475	7.9	32.8	57.8
	Not very much	986	5.2	21.9	79.7
	None at all	911	4.8	20.3	100.0
	Gesamt	4493	23.9	100.0	
Fehlend	Not asked	13628	72.5		
	No answer	21	.1		
	Don´t know	650	3.5		
	Gesamt	14300	76.1		
Gesamt		18793	100.0		

Confidence: the United Nations

		Häufigkeit	Prozent	Gültige Prozente	Kumulierte Prozente
Gültig	A great deal	3247	17.3	21.9	21.9
	Quite a lot	4530	24.1	30.5	52.4
	Not very much	3217	17.1	21.7	74.0
	None at all	3855	20.5	26.0	100.0
	Gesamt	14848	79.0	100.0	
Fehlend	Missing; Unknown	9	.0		
	Not asked	895	4.8		
	No answer	138	.7		
	Don´t know	2904	15.5		
	Gesamt	3945	21.0		
Gesamt		18793	100.0		

WHAT GLOBAL MUSLIMS THINK IS PERMISSIBLE AND WHAT IS NOT PERMISSIBLE

Justifiable: claiming government benefits

		Häufigkeit	Prozent	Gültige Prozente	Kumulierte Prozente
Gültig	Never justifiable	10366	55.2	66.4	66.4
	2	1215	6.5	7.8	74.2
	3	808	4.3	5.2	79.4
	4	578	3.1	3.7	83.1
	5	805	4.3	5.2	88.3
	6	489	2.6	3.1	91.4
	7	320	1.7	2.1	93.5
	8	271	1.4	1.7	95.2
	9	204	1.1	1.3	96.5
	Always justifiable	543	2.9	3.5	100.0
	Gesamt	15601	83.0	100.0	
Fehlend	Missing; Unknown	2	.0		
	Not asked	2499	13.3		
	No answer	34	.2		
	Don't know	657	3.5		
	Gesamt	3192	17.0		
Gesamt		18793	100.0		

Justifiable: avoiding a fare on public transport

		Häufigkeit	Prozent	Gültige Prozente	Kumulierte Prozente
Gültig	Never justifiable	10507	55.9	71.1	71.1
	2	1294	6.9	8.8	79.9
	3	886	4.7	6.0	85.8
	4	451	2.4	3.1	88.9
	5	620	3.3	4.2	93.1
	6	236	1.3	1.6	94.7
	7	157	.8	1.1	95.8
	8	144	.8	1.0	96.7
	9	90	.5	.6	97.3
	Always justifiable	393	2.1	2.7	100.0
	Gesamt	14778	78.6	100.0	
Fehlend	Not asked	3728	19.8		
	No answer	22	.1		
	Don't know	265	1.4		
	Gesamt	4015	21.4		
Gesamt		18793	100.0		

Justifiable: cheating on taxes

		Häufigkeit	Prozent	Gültige Prozente	Kumulierte Prozente
Gültig	Never justifiable	11263	59.9	75.6	75.6
	2	1118	5.9	7.5	83.1
	3	694	3.7	4.7	87.8
	4	406	2.2	2.7	90.5
	5	479	2.5	3.2	93.7
	6	211	1.1	1.4	95.1
	7	165	.9	1.1	96.2
	8	146	.8	1.0	97.2
	9	96	.5	.6	97.9
	Always justifiable	318	1.7	2.1	100.0
	Gesamt	14896	79.3	100.0	
Fehlend	Not asked	3471	18.5		
	No answer	20	.1		
	Don't know	406	2.2		
	Gesamt	3897	20.7		
Gesamt		18793	100.0		

Justifiable: someone accepting a bribe

		Häufigkeit	Prozent	Gültige Prozente	Kumulierte Prozente
Gültig	Never justifiable	13792	73.4	82.4	82.4
	2	1007	5.4	6.0	88.5
	3	606	3.2	3.6	92.1
	4	334	1.8	2.0	94.1
	5	354	1.9	2.1	96.2
	6	181	1.0	1.1	97.3
	7	113	.6	.7	98.0
	8	109	.6	.7	98.6
	9	60	.3	.4	99.0
	Always justifiable	173	.9	1.0	100.0
	Gesamt	16729	89.0	100.0	
Fehlend	Not asked	1792	9.5		
	No answer	21	.1		
	Don't know	252	1.3		
	Gesamt	2064	11.0		
Gesamt		18793	100.0		

Justifiable: homosexuality

		Häufigkeit	Prozent	Gültige Prozente	Kumulierte Prozente
Gültig	Never justifiable	12268	65.3	87.4	87.4
	2	550	2.9	3.9	91.4
	3	313	1.7	2.2	93.6
	4	213	1.1	1.5	95.1
	5	320	1.7	2.3	97.4
	6	102	.5	.7	98.1
	7	77	.4	.6	98.7
	8	58	.3	.4	99.1
	9	30	.2	.2	99.3
	Always justifiable	98	.5	.7	100.0
	Gesamt	14029	74.6	100.0	
Fehlend	Missing; unknown	2	.0		
	Not asked	4257	22.7		
	No answer	33	.2		
	Don't know	472	2.5		
	Gesamt	4764	25.4		
Gesamt		18793	100.0		

Justifiable: prostitution

		Häufigkeit	Prozent	Gültige Prozente	Kumulierte Prozente
Gültig	Never justifiable	11238	59.8	85.2	85.2
	2	659	3.5	5.0	90.2
	3	385	2.0	2.9	93.1
	4	262	1.4	2.0	95.1
	5	308	1.6	2.3	97.4
	6	121	.6	.9	98.4
	7	62	.3	.5	98.8
	8	41	.2	.3	99.1
	9	38	.2	.3	99.4
	Always justifiable	77	.4	.6	100.0
	Gesamt	13190	70.2	100.0	
Fehlend	Missing; unknown	1	.0		
	Not asked	5381	28.6		
	No answer	16	.1		
	Don't know	205	1.1		
	Gesamt	5603	29.8		
Gesamt		18793	100.0		

Justifiable: abortion

		Häufigkeit	Prozent	Gültige Prozente	Kumulierte Prozente
Gültig	Never justifiable	9773	52.0	62.1	62.1
	2	922	4.9	5.9	68.0
	3	902	4.8	5.7	73.7
	4	724	3.9	4.6	78.3
	5	1396	7.4	8.9	87.2
	6	647	3.4	4.1	91.3
	7	430	2.3	2.7	94.1
	8	416	2.2	2.6	96.7
	9	184	1.0	1.2	97.9
	Always justifiable	332	1.8	2.1	100.0
	Gesamt	15727	83.7	100.0	
Fehlend	Missing; unknown	1	.0		
	Not asked	2652	14.1		
	No answer	20	.1		
	Don´t know	394	2.1		
	Gesamt	3066	16.3		
Gesamt		18793	100.0		

Justifiable: divorce

		Häufigkeit	Prozent	Gültige Prozente	Kumulierte Prozente
Gültig	Never justifiable	6856	36.5	41.2	41.2
	2	885	4.7	5.3	46.5
	3	1142	6.1	6.9	53.4
	4	1091	5.8	6.6	59.9
	5	2999	16.0	18.0	77.9
	6	1117	5.9	6.7	84.7
	7	816	4.3	4.9	89.6
	8	637	3.4	3.8	93.4
	9	326	1.7	2.0	95.3
	Always justifiable	776	4.1	4.7	100.0
	Gesamt	16644	88.6	100.0	
Fehlend	Missing; unknown	1	.0		
	Not asked	1792	9.5		
	No answer	33	.2		
	Don´t know	324	1.7		
	Gesamt	2149	11.4		
Gesamt		18793	100.0		

Justifiable: euthanasia

		Häufigkeit	Prozent	Gültige Prozente	Kumulierte Prozente
Gültig	Never justifiable	11151	59.3	72.4	72.4
	2	965	5.1	6.3	78.6
	3	626	3.3	4.1	82.7
	4	322	1.7	2.1	84.8
	5	827	4.4	5.4	90.1
	6	307	1.6	2.0	92.1
	7	234	1.2	1.5	93.7
	8	269	1.4	1.7	95.4
	9	173	.9	1.1	96.5
	Always justifiable	536	2.9	3.5	100.0
	Gesamt	15411	82.0	100.0	
Fehlend	Missing; unknown	2	.0		
	Not asked	2503	13.3		
	No answer	40	.2		
	Don´t know	837	4.5		
	Gesamt	3382	18.0		
Gesamt		18793	100.0		

Justifiable: suicide

		Häufigkeit	Prozent	Gültige Prozente	Kumulierte Prozente
Gültig	Never justifiable	13878	73.8	87.1	87.1
	2	773	4.1	4.9	92.0
	3	386	2.1	2.4	94.4
	4	228	1.2	1.4	95.8
	5	296	1.6	1.9	97.7
	6	91	.5	.6	98.3
	7	85	.5	.5	98.8
	8	58	.3	.4	99.2
	9	26	.1	.2	99.3
	Always justifiable	107	.6	.7	100.0
	Gesamt	15928	84.8	100.0	
Fehlend	Missing; unknown	1	.0		
	Not asked	2496	13.3		
	No answer	38	.2		
	Don´t know	330	1.8		
	Gesamt	2866	15.2		
Gesamt		18793	100.0		

Justifiable: drinking alcohol

		Häufigkeit	Prozent	Gültige Prozente	Kumulierte Prozente
Gültig	Never justifiable	5784	30.8	87.7	87.7
	2	252	1.3	3.8	91.6
	3	129	.7	2.0	93.5
	4	67	.4	1.0	94.5
	5	151	.8	2.3	96.8
	6	44	.2	.7	97.5
	7	34	.2	.5	98.0
	8	28	.1	.4	98.4
	9	23	.1	.3	98.8
	Always justifiable	80	.4	1.2	100.0
	Gesamt	6593	35.1	100.0	
Fehlend	Not asked	12158	64.7		
	No answer	11	.1		
	Don´t know	31	.2		
	Gesamt	12201	64.9		
Gesamt		18793	100.0		

Justifiable: joyriding

		Häufigkeit	Prozent	Gültige Prozente	Kumulierte Prozente
Gültig	Never justifiable	1360	7.2	82.6	82.6
	2	102	.5	6.2	88.8
	3	73	.4	4.4	93.2
	4	38	.2	2.3	95.5
	5	38	.2	2.3	97.8
	6	10	.1	.6	98.4
	7	5	.0	.3	98.7
	8	4	.0	.2	98.9
	9	6	.0	.4	99.3
	Always justifiable	12	.1	.7	100.0
	Gesamt	1646	8.8	100.0	
Fehlend	Not asked	17121	91.1		
	No answer	7	.0		
	Don´t know	20	.1		
	Gesamt	17147	91.2		
Gesamt		18793	100.0		

Justifiable: taking soft drugs

		Häufigkeit	Prozent	Gültige Prozente	Kumulierte Prozente
Gültig	Never justifiable	1513	8.1	85.7	85.7
	2	89	.5	5.1	90.8
	3	44	.2	2.5	93.3
	4	49	.3	2.7	96.0
	5	22	.1	1.2	97.2
	6	12	.1	.7	97.9
	7	8	.0	.5	98.4
	8	7	.0	.4	98.8
	9	3	.0	.1	98.9
	Always justifiable	19	.1	1.1	100.0
	Gesamt	1766	9.4	100.0	
Fehlend	Not asked	16993	90.4		
	No answer	7	.0		
	Don't know	28	.1		
	Gesamt	17027	90.6		
Gesamt		18793	100.0		

Justifiable: lying

		Häufigkeit	Prozent	Gültige Prozente	Kumulierte Prozente
Gültig	Never justifiable	1220	6.5	68.8	68.8
	2	133	.7	7.5	76.3
	3	119	.6	6.7	83.0
	4	69	.4	3.9	86.9
	5	87	.5	4.9	91.7
	6	48	.3	2.7	94.5
	7	25	.1	1.4	95.9
	8	23	.1	1.3	97.1
	9	13	.1	.7	97.9
	Always justifiable	38	.2	2.1	100.0
	Gesamt	1773	9.4	100.0	
Fehlend	Not asked	16993	90.4		
	No answer	8	.0		
	Don't know	18	.1		
	Gesamt	17020	90.6		
Gesamt		18793	100.0		

Justifiable: adultery

		Häufigkeit	Prozent	Gültige Prozente	Kumulierte Prozente
Gültig	Never justifiable	485	2.6	60.4	60.4
	2	53	.3	6.6	67.0
	3	57	.3	7.1	74.1
	4	54	.3	6.8	80.8
	5	49	.3	6.1	86.9
	6	28	.1	3.5	90.4
	7	14	.1	1.7	92.1
	8	20	.1	2.4	94.5
	9	16	.1	2.0	96.5
	Always justifiable	28	.1	3.5	100.0
	Gesamt	804	4.3	100.0	
Fehlend	Not asked	17968	95.6		
	No answer	6	.0		
	Don't know	15	.1		
	Gesamt	17989	95.7		
Gesamt		18793	100.0		

Justifiable: throwing away litter

		Häufigkeit	Prozent	Gültige Prozente	Kumulierte Prozente
Gültig	Never justifiable	1295	6.9	79.4	79.4
	2	111	.6	6.8	86.1
	3	93	.5	5.7	91.8
	4	56	.3	3.4	95.3
	5	39	.2	2.4	97.7
	6	14	.1	.9	98.5
	7	4	.0	.2	98.8
	8	7	.0	.4	99.2
	9	3	.0	.2	99.4
	Always justifiable	10	.1	.6	100.0
	Gesamt	1632	8.7	100.0	
Fehlend	Not asked	17140	91.2		
	No answer	4	.0		
	Don't know	18	.1		
	Gesamt	17162	91.3		
Gesamt		18793	100.0		

Justifiable: driving under influence of alcohol

		Häufigkeit	Prozent	Gültige Prozente	Kumulierte Prozente
Gültig	Never justifiable	1508	8.0	85.5	85.5
	2	102	.5	5.8	91.4
	3	54	.3	3.1	94.4
	4	49	.3	2.8	97.2
	5	17	.1	1.0	98.2
	6	3	.0	.2	98.3
	7	6	.0	.3	98.7
	8	6	.0	.3	99.0
	9	3	.0	.2	99.2
	Always justifiable	15	.1	.8	100.0
	Gesamt	1763	9.4	100.0	
Fehlend	Not asked	17012	90.5		
	No answer	4	.0		
	Don't know	14	.1		
	Gesamt	17030	90.6		
Gesamt		18793	100.0		

Justifiable: paying cash

		Häufigkeit	Prozent	Gültige Prozente	Kumulierte Prozente
Gültig	Never justifiable	968	5.1	82.1	82.1
	2	63	.3	5.4	87.5
	3	42	.2	3.6	91.1
	4	22	.1	1.9	93.0
	5	31	.2	2.6	95.6
	6	16	.1	1.4	97.0
	7	9	.0	.7	97.8
	8	8	.0	.7	98.5
	9	5	.0	.4	98.9
	Always justifiable	13	.1	1.1	100.0
	Gesamt	1178	6.3	100.0	
Fehlend	Not asked	17576	93.5		
	No answer	5	.0		
	Don't know	34	.2		
	Gesamt	17615	93.7		
Gesamt		18793	100.0		

Justifiable: having casual sex

		Häufigkeit	Prozent	Gültige Prozente	Kumulierte Prozente
Gültig	Never justifiable	896	4.8	75.3	75.3
	2	65	.3	5.4	80.7
	3	65	.3	5.5	86.2
	4	27	.1	2.2	88.4
	5	69	.4	5.8	94.2
	6	24	.1	2.0	96.2
	7	7	.0	.5	96.8
	8	14	.1	1.2	98.0
	9	4	.0	.3	98.3
	Always justifiable	21	.1	1.7	100.0
	Gesamt	1191	6.3	100.0	
Fehlend	Not asked	17576	93.5		
	No answer	8	.0		
	Don´t know	18	.1		
	Gesamt	17603	93.7		
Gesamt		18793	100.0		

Justifiable: smoking in public places

		Häufigkeit	Prozent	Gültige Prozente	Kumulierte Prozente
Gültig	Never justifiable	819	4.4	68.9	68.9
	2	76	.4	6.4	75.3
	3	74	.4	6.2	81.5
	4	47	.2	3.9	85.4
	5	90	.5	7.6	93.0
	6	32	.2	2.7	95.8
	7	19	.1	1.6	97.3
	8	13	.1	1.1	98.4
	9	5	.0	.4	98.8
	Always justifiable	15	.1	1.2	100.0
	Gesamt	1188	6.3	100.0	
Fehlend	Not asked	17576	93.5		
	No answer	7	.0		
	Don´t know	22	.1		
	Gesamt	17605	93.7		
Gesamt		18793	100.0		

Justifiable: speeding over the limit

		Häufigkeit	Prozent	Gültige Prozente	Kumulierte Prozente
Gültig	Never justifiable	1016	5.4	85.2	85.2
	2	74	.4	6.2	91.4
	3	49	.3	4.1	95.6
	4	13	.1	1.1	96.7
	5	20	.1	1.7	98.3
	6	4	.0	.3	98.7
	7	6	.0	.5	99.1
	8	6	.0	.5	99.7
	9	2	.0	.1	99.8
	Always justifiable	2	.0	.2	100.0
	Gesamt	1192	6.3	100.0	
Fehlend	Not asked	17576	93.5		
	No answer	5	.0		
	Don't know	20	.1		
	Gesamt	17601	93.7		
Gesamt		18793	100.0		

Justifiable: sex under the legal age of consent

		Häufigkeit	Prozent	Gültige Prozente	Kumulierte Prozente
Gültig	Never justifiable	360	1.9	55.9	55.9
	2	47	.3	7.3	63.2
	3	44	.2	6.8	70.0
	4	39	.2	6.1	76.1
	5	44	.2	6.8	82.9
	6	22	.1	3.4	86.3
	7	23	.1	3.6	89.9
	8	15	.1	2.3	92.2
	9	19	.1	2.9	95.2
	Always justifiable	31	.2	4.8	100.0
	Gesamt	645	3.4	100.0	
Fehlend	Not asked	18122	96.4		
	No answer	2	.0		
	Don't know	25	.1		
	Gesamt	18149	96.6		
Gesamt		18793	100.0		

Justifiable: political assassination

		Häufigkeit	Prozent	Gültige Prozente	Kumulierte Prozente
Gültig	Never justifiable	393	2.1	63.9	63.9
	2	55	.3	8.9	72.9
	3	33	.2	5.3	78.2
	4	40	.2	6.5	84.7
	5	32	.2	5.3	90.0
	6	18	.1	2.9	92.9
	7	10	.1	1.7	94.6
	8	12	.1	2.0	96.5
	9	6	.0	1.1	97.6
	Always justifiable	15	.1	2.4	100.0
	Gesamt	615	3.3	100.0	
Fehlend	Not asked	18144	96.5		
	No answer	4	.0		
	Don´t know	31	.2		
	Gesamt	18178	96.7		
Gesamt		18793	100.0		

Justifiable: experiments with human embryos

		Häufigkeit	Prozent	Gültige Prozente	Kumulierte Prozente
Gültig	Never justifiable	74	.4	85.6	85.6
	2	1	.0	1.1	86.7
	3	2	.0	2.0	88.7
	4	1	.0	1.2	89.9
	5	3	.0	3.3	93.2
	6	1	.0	1.6	94.8
	7	1	.0	1.0	95.7
	9	1	.0	1.2	96.9
	Always justifiable	3	.0	3.1	100.0
	Gesamt	86	.5	100.0	
Fehlend	Not asked	18704	99.5		
	No answer	1	.0		
	Don´t know	2	.0		
	Gesamt	18707	99.5		
Gesamt		18793	100.0		

Justifiable: manipulation of food

		Häufigkeit	Prozent	Gültige Prozente	Kumulierte Prozente
Gültig	Never justifiable	61	.3	71.2	71.2
	2	3	.0	3.7	75.0
	3	4	.0	4.4	79.4
	4	3	.0	3.1	82.5
	5	7	.0	8.8	91.3
	6	1	.0	1.8	93.1
	7	1	.0	1.4	94.5
	8	2	.0	1.8	96.3
	9	2	.0	2.6	98.9
	Always justifiable	1	.0	1.1	100.0
	Gesamt	85	.5	100.0	
Fehlend	Not asked	18704	99.5		
	No answer	2	.0		
	Don't know	3	.0		
	Gesamt	18708	99.5		
Gesamt		18793	100.0		

Justifiable: buying stolen goods

		Häufigkeit	Prozent	Gültige Prozente	Kumulierte Prozente
Gültig	Never justifiable	3413	18.2	74.5	74.5
	2	383	2.0	8.4	82.8
	3	280	1.5	6.1	88.9
	4	177	.9	3.9	92.8
	5	156	.8	3.4	96.2
	6	76	.4	1.7	97.9
	7	23	.1	.5	98.4
	8	22	.1	.5	98.9
	9	10	.1	.2	99.1
	Always justifiable	43	.2	.9	100.0
	Gesamt	4583	24.4	100.0	
Fehlend	Missing; unknown	1	.0		
	Not asked	14083	74.9		
	No answer	8	.0		
	Don't know	118	.6		
	Gesamt	14210	75.6		
Gesamt		18793	100.0		

Justifiable: keeping money that you have found

		Häufigkeit	Prozent	Gültige Prozente	Kumulierte Prozente
Gültig	Never justifiable	180	1.0	40.4	40.4
	2	33	.2	7.3	47.7
	3	27	.1	6.0	53.6
	4	20	.1	4.5	58.1
	5	52	.3	11.7	69.8
	6	35	.2	8.0	77.8
	7	24	.1	5.5	83.2
	8	22	.1	5.0	88.2
	9	21	.1	4.7	92.9
	Always justifiable	32	.2	7.1	100.0
	Gesamt	446	2.4	100.0	
Fehlend	Not asked	18340	97.6		
	No answer	2	.0		
	Don't know	6	.0		
	Gesamt	18348	97.6		
Gesamt		18793	100.0		

Justifiable: fighting with the police

		Häufigkeit	Prozent	Gültige Prozente	Kumulierte Prozente
Gültig	Never justifiable	283	1.5	50.1	50.1
	2	38	.2	6.8	56.9
	3	52	.3	9.3	66.1
	4	49	.3	8.6	74.7
	5	71	.4	12.6	87.3
	6	21	.1	3.6	91.0
	7	10	.1	1.7	92.7
	8	11	.1	1.9	94.5
	9	10	.1	1.8	96.4
	Always justifiable	21	.1	3.6	100.0
	Gesamt	565	3.0	100.0	
Fehlend	Not asked	18210	96.9		
	No answer	2	.0		
	Don't know	16	.1		
	Gesamt	18228	97.0		
Gesamt		18793	100.0		

Justifiable: failing to report damage you've caused with a parked vehicle

		Häufigkeit	Prozent	Gültige Prozente	Kumulierte Prozente
Gültig	Never justifiable	238	1.3	53.5	53.5
	2	49	.3	11.1	64.6
	3	48	.3	10.9	75.5
	4	37	.2	8.3	83.8
	5	32	.2	7.2	90.9
	6	14	.1	3.0	94.0
	7	6	.0	1.2	95.2
	8	3	.0	.7	95.9
	9	1	.0	.3	96.2
	Always justifiable	17	.1	3.8	100.0
	Gesamt	445	2.4	100.0	
Fehlend	Not asked	18338	97.6		
	No answer	2	.0		
	Don't know	9	.0		
	Gesamt	18348	97.6		
Gesamt		18793	100.0		

Justifiable: threatening workers who refuse to join a strike

		Häufigkeit	Prozent	Gültige Prozente	Kumulierte Prozente
Gültig	Never justifiable	316	1.7	56.5	56.5
	2	48	.3	8.5	65.0
	3	38	.2	6.8	71.8
	4	38	.2	6.7	78.5
	5	54	.3	9.6	88.2
	6	26	.1	4.6	92.8
	7	14	.1	2.5	95.3
	8	9	.0	1.6	96.9
	9	4	.0	.8	97.7
	Always justifiable	13	.1	2.3	100.0
	Gesamt	559	3.0	100.0	
Fehlend	Not asked	18210	96.9		
	No answer	2	.0		
	Don't know	22	.1		
	Gesamt	18234	97.0		
Gesamt		18793	100.0		

Justifiable: killing in self-defence

		Häufigkeit	Prozent	Gültige Prozente	Kumulierte Prozente
Gültig	Never justifiable	179	1.0	31.7	31.7
	2	36	.2	6.4	38.1
	3	49	.3	8.7	46.8
	4	51	.3	9.0	55.8
	5	45	.2	8.0	63.8
	6	35	.2	6.2	70.0
	7	24	.1	4.3	74.3
	8	33	.2	5.7	80.0
	9	25	.1	4.5	84.5
	Always justifiable	87	.5	15.5	100.0
	Gesamt	565	3.0	100.0	
Fehlend	Not asked	18210	96.9		
	No answer	1	.0		
	Don´t know	17	.1		
	Gesamt	18228	97.0		
Gesamt		18793	100.0		

28.3% PERCENT RACISTS : WHOM GLOBAL MUSLIMS ACCEPT AND WHOM THEY REJECT AS NEIGHBORS

Neighbours: people with a criminal record

		Häufigkeit	Prozent	Gültige Prozente	Kumulierte Prozente
Gültig	Not mentioned	6338	33.7	34.1	34.1
	Mentioned	12227	65.1	65.9	100.0
	Gesamt	18565	98.8	100.0	
Fehlend	Not asked	223	1.2		
	No answer	1	.0		
	Don´t know	4	.0		
	Gesamt	228	1.2		
Gesamt		18793	100.0		

Neighbours: people of a different race

		Häufigkeit	Prozent	Gültige Prozente	Kumulierte Prozente
Gültig	Not mentioned	12871	68.5	71.7	71.7
	Mentioned	5080	27.0	28.3	100.0
	Gesamt	17950	95.5	100.0	
Fehlend	Not asked	838	4.5		
	No answer	1	.0		
	Don´t know	4	.0		
	Gesamt	843	4.5		
Gesamt		18793	100.0		

Neighbours: heavy drinkers

		Häufigkeit	Prozent	Gültige Prozente	Kumulierte Prozente
Gültig	Not mentioned	5709	30.4	33.6	33.6
	Mentioned	11276	60.0	66.4	100.0
	Gesamt	16985	90.4	100.0	
Fehlend	Not asked	1803	9.6		
	No answer	1	.0		
	Don´t know	4	.0		
	Gesamt	1808	9.6		
Gesamt		18793	100.0		

Neighbours: emotionally unstable people

		Häufigkeit	Prozent	Gültige Prozente	Kumulierte Prozente
Gültig	Not mentioned	8288	44.1	46.2	46.2
	Mentioned	9668	51.4	53.8	100.0
	Gesamt	17955	95.5	100.0	
Fehlend	Not asked	833	4.4		
	No answer	1	.0		
	Don´t know	4	.0		
	Gesamt	838	4.5		
Gesamt		18793	100.0		

Neighbours: Muslims

		Häufigkeit	Prozent	Gültige Prozente	Kumulierte Prozente
Gültig	Not mentioned	3555	18.9	83.8	83,8
	Mentioned	687	3.7	16.2	100,0
	Gesamt	4243	22.6	100.0	
Fehlend	Not asked	14545	77.4		
	No answer	2	.0		
	Don't know	4	.0		
	Gesamt	14551	77.4		
Gesamt		18793	100.0		

Neighbours: immigrants/foreign workers

		Häufigkeit	Prozent	Gültige Prozente	Kumulierte Prozente
Gültig	Not mentioned	12573	66.9	70.0	70.0
	Mentioned	5377	28.6	30.0	100.0
	Gesamt	17950	95.5	100.0	
Fehlend	Not asked	837	4.5		
	No answer	2	.0		
	Don't know	4	.0		
	Gesamt	843	4.5		
Gesamt		18793	100.0		

Neighbours: people who have AIDS

		Häufigkeit	Prozent	Gültige Prozente	Kumulierte Prozente
Gültig	Not mentioned	6777	36.1	37.8	37.8
	Mentioned	11134	59.2	62.2	100.0
	Gesamt	17911	95.3	100.0	
Fehlend	Not asked	878	4.7		
	Don't know	4	.0		
	Gesamt	883	4.7		
Gesamt		18793	100.0		

Neighbours: drug addicts

		Häufigkeit	Prozent	Gültige Prozente	Kumulierte Prozente
Gültig	Not mentioned	4997	26.6	27.9	27.9
	Mentioned	12913	68.7	72.1	100.0
	Gesamt	17910	95.3	100.0	
Fehlend	Not asked	878	4.7		
	No answer	1	.0		
	Don't know	4	.0		
	Gesamt	884	4.7		
Gesamt		18793	100.0		

Neighbours: homosexuals

		Häufigkeit	Prozent	Gültige Prozente	Kumulierte Prozente
Gültig	Not mentioned	5679	30.2	33.5	33.5
	Mentioned	11261	59.9	66.5	100.0
	Gesamt	16940	90.1	100.0	
Fehlend	Not asked	1849	9.8		
	Don't know	4	.0		
	Gesamt	1853	9.9		
Gesamt		18793	100.0		

Neighbours: Jews

		Häufigkeit	Prozent	Gültige Prozente	Kumulierte Prozente
Gültig	Not mentioned	4163	22.2	65.7	65.7
	Mentioned	2173	11.6	34.3	100.0
	Gesamt	6336	33.7	100.0	
Fehlend	Not asked	12451	66.3		
	No answer	2	.0		
	Don't know	4	.0		
	Gesamt	12457	66.3		
Gesamt		18793	100.0		

Neighbours: people of a different religion

		Häufigkeit	Prozent	Gültige Prozente	Kumulierte Prozente
Gültig	Not mentioned	6611	35.2	66.9	66.9
	Mentioned	3272	17.4	33.1	100.0
	Gesamt	9883	52.6	100.0	
Fehlend	Not asked	8911	47.4		
Gesamt		18793	100.0		

Neighbours: People of the same religion

		Häufigkeit	Prozent	Gültige Prozente	Kumulierte Prozente
Gültig	Not mentioned	51	,3	47,5	47,5
	Mentioned	57	,3	52,5	100,0
	Gesamt	108	,6	100,0	
Fehlend	Not asked	18685	99,4		
Gesamt		18793	100,0		

Neighbours: militant minority

		Häufigkeit	Prozent	Gültige Prozente	Kumulierte Prozente
Gültig	Not mentioned	474	2.5	51.2	51.2
	Mentioned	451	2.4	48.8	100.0
	Gesamt	925	4.9	100.0	
Fehlend	Not asked	17868	95.1		
Gesamt		18793	100.0		

Neighbours: Zoroastrians

		Häufigkeit	Prozent	Gültige Prozente	Kumulierte Prozente
Gültig	Not mentioned	829	4.4	85.4	85.4
	Mentioned	142	.8	14.6	100.0
	Gesamt	970	5.2	100.0	
Fehlend	Not asked	17823	94.8		
Gesamt		18793	100.0		

Neighbours: people not from country of origin

		Häufigkeit	Prozent	Gültige Prozente	Kumulierte Prozente
Gültig	Not mentioned	807	4.3	84.8	84.8
	Mentioned	145	.8	15.2	100.0
	Gesamt	952	5.1	100.0	
Fehlend	Not asked	17841	94.9		
Gesamt		18793	100.0		

Neighbours: Gypsies

		Häufigkeit	Prozent	Gültige Prozente	Kumulierte Prozente
Gültig	Not mentioned	787	4.2	45.3	45.3
	Mentioned	948	5.0	54.7	100.0
	Gesamt	1735	9.2	100.0	
Fehlend	Not asked	17054	90.7		
	Don't know	4	.0		
	Gesamt	17058	90.8		
Gesamt		18793	100.0		

GLOBAL MUSLIM ATTITUDES ON MARRIAGE, GENDER ROLES AND THE FAMILY

Marriage is an out-dated institution

		Häufigkeit	Prozent	Gültige Prozente	Kumulierte Prozente
Gültig	Disagree	14711	78.3	84.5	84.5
	Agree	2691	14.3	15.5	100.0
	Gesamt	17402	92.6	100.0	
Fehlend	Missing; unknown	5	.0		
	Not asked	705	3.8		
	No answer	92	.5		
	Don't know	589	3.1		
	Gesamt	1391	7.4		
Gesamt		18793	100.0		

Woman as a single parent

		Häufigkeit	Prozent	Gültige Prozente	Kumulierte Prozente
Gültig	Disapprove	11719	62.4	70.4	70.4
	Approve	2110	11.2	12.7	83.1
	Depends	2460	13.1	14.8	97.9
	3	350	1.9	2.1	100.0
	Gesamt	16639	88.5	100.0	
Fehlend	Missing; unknown	16	.1		
	Not asked	1562	8.3		
	No answer	110	.6		
	Don't know	467	2.5		
	Gesamt	2155	11.5		
Gesamt		18793	100.0		

Enjoy sexual freedom

		Häufigkeit	Prozent	Gültige Prozente	Kumulierte Prozente
Gültig	Agree	756	4.0	18.6	18.6
	Disagree	1672	8.9	41.2	59.8
	Neither	1634	8.7	40.2	100.0
	Gesamt	4062	21.6	100.0	
Fehlend	Missing; unknown	227	1.2		
	Not asked	14121	75.1		
	No answer	11	.1		
	Don't know	372	2.0		
	Gesamt	14731	78.4		
Gesamt		18793	100.0		

If only one child allowed: boy or girl

		Häufigkeit	Prozent	Gültige Prozente	Kumulierte Prozente
Gültig	Boy	1772	9.4	37.2	37.2
	Girl	1546	8.2	32.5	69.7
	No difference	1442	7.7	30.3	100.0
	Gesamt	4761	25.3	100.0	
Fehlend	Missing; unknown	9	.0		
	Not asked	13920	74.1		
	No answer	4	.0		
	Don't know	99	.5		
	Gesamt	14032	74.7		
Gesamt		18793	100.0		

Long-term relationship is necessary to be happy

		Häufigkeit	Prozent	Gültige Prozente	Kumulierte Prozente
Gültig	Agree strongly	450	2.4	38.5	38.5
	Agree	474	2.5	40.5	79.0
	Neither agree or disagree	112	.6	9.6	88.6
	Disagree	89	.5	7.6	96.2
	Strongly disagree	45	.2	3.8	100.0
	Gesamt	1171	6.2	100.0	
Fehlend	Not asked	17576	93.5		
	No answer	16	.1		
	Don't know	31	.2		
	Gesamt	17623	93.8		
Gesamt		18793	100.0		

Important for succesful marriage: Faithfulness

		Häufigkeit	Prozent	Gültige Prozente	Kumulierte Prozente
Gültig	Very	1560	8.3	93.7	93.7
	Rather	93	.5	5.6	99.3
	Not very	12	.1	.7	100.0
	Gesamt	1665	8.9	100.0	
Fehlend	Not asked	17121	91.1		
	No answer	2	.0		
	Don't know	6	.0		
	Gesamt	17128	91.1		
Gesamt		18793	100.0		

Important for succesful marriage: adequate income

		Häufigkeit	Prozent	Gültige Prozente	Kumulierte Prozente
Gültig	Very	1203	6.4	72.3	72.3
	Rather	366	1.9	22.0	94.3
	Not very	95	.5	5.7	100.0
	Gesamt	1665	8.9	100.0	
Fehlend	Not asked	17121	91.1		
	No answer	4	.0		
	Don't know	3	.0		
	Gesamt	17129	91.1		
Gesamt		18793	100.0		

Important for successful marriage: same social background

		Häufigkeit	Prozent	Gültige Prozente	Kumulierte Prozente
Gültig	Very	886	4.7	54.4	54.4
	Rather	401	2.1	24.6	79.0
	Not very	342	1.8	21.0	100.0
	Gesamt	1628	8.7	100.0	
Fehlend	Not asked	17121	91.1		
	No answer	7	.0		
	Don't know	38	.2		
	Gesamt	17165	91.3		
Gesamt		18793	100.0		

Important for succesful marriage: respect and appreciation

		Häufigkeit	Prozent	Gültige Prozente	Kumulierte Prozente
Gültig	Very	1497	8.0	89.7	89.7
	Rather	149	.8	8.9	98.7
	Not very	22	.1	1.3	100.0
	Gesamt	1669	8.9	100.0	
Fehlend	Not asked	17121	91.1		
	No answer	1	.0		
	Don't know	3	.0		
	Gesamt	17125	91.1		
Gesamt		18793	100.0		

Important for succesful marriage: religious beliefs

		Häufigkeit	Prozent	Gültige Prozente	Kumulierte Prozente
Gültig	Very	1141	6.1	68.8	68.8
	Rather	296	1.6	17.9	86.7
	Not very	221	1.2	13.3	100.0
	Gesamt	1658	8.8	100.0	
Fehlend	Not asked	17121	91.1		
	No answer	5	.0		
	Don't know	9	.0		
	Gesamt	17135	91.2		
Gesamt		18793	100.0		

Important for succesful marriage: good housing

		Häufigkeit	Prozent	Gültige Prozente	Kumulierte Prozente
Gültig	Very	945	5.0	56.8	56.8
	Rather	536	2.9	32.2	89.0
	Not very	183	1.0	11.0	100.0
	Gesamt	1663	8.9	100.0	
Fehlend	Not asked	17121	91.1		
	No answer	5	.0		
	Don't know	4	.0		
	Gesamt	17130	91.1		
Gesamt		18793	100.0		

Important for succesful marriage: agreement on politics

		Häufigkeit	Prozent	Gültige Prozente	Kumulierte Prozente
Gültig	Very	584	3.1	35.9	35.9
	Rather	422	2.2	25.9	61.9
	Not very	620	3.3	38.1	100.0
	Gesamt	1626	8.7	100.0	
Fehlend	Not asked	17121	91.1		
	No answer	18	.1		
	Don't know	28	.2		
	Gesamt	17167	91.3		
Gesamt		18793	100.0		

Important in succesful marriage: understanding and tolerance

		Häufigkeit	Prozent	Gültige Prozente	Kumulierte Prozente
Gültig	Very	1442	7.7	86.7	86.7
	Rather	197	1.1	11.9	98.6
	Not very	23	.1	1.4	100.0
	Gesamt	1662	8.8	100.0	
Fehlend	Not asked	17121	91.1		
	No answer	4	.0		
	Don't know	6	.0		
	Gesamt	17131	91.2		
Gesamt		18793	100.0		

Important for succesful marriage: apart from in-laws

		Häufigkeit	Prozent	Gültige Prozente	Kumulierte Prozente
Gültig	Very	826	4.4	49.9	49.9
	Rather	406	2.2	24.5	74.5
	Not very	422	2.2	25.5	100.0
	Gesamt	1654	8.8	100.0	
Fehlend	Not asked	17121	91.1		
	No answer	5	.0		
	Don't know	14	.1		
	Gesamt	17139	91.2		
Gesamt		18793	100.0		

Important for succesful marriage: happy sexual relationship

		Häufigkeit	Prozent	Gültige Prozente	Kumulierte Prozente
Gültig	Very	1278	6.8	78.2	78.2
	Rather	308	1.6	18.8	97.0
	Not very	49	.3	3.0	100.0
	Gesamt	1635	8.7	100.0	
Fehlend	Not asked	17121	91.1		
	No answer	21	.1		
	Don't know	17	.1		
	Gesamt	17158	91.3		
Gesamt		18793	100.0		

Important for succesful marriage: sharing household chores

		Häufigkeit	Prozent	Gültige Prozente	Kumulierte Prozente
Gültig	Very	868	4.6	52.4	52.4
	Rather	494	2.6	29.8	82.2
	Not very	295	1.6	17.8	100.0
	Gesamt	1657	8.8	100.0	
Fehlend	Not asked	17121	91.1		
	No answer	7	.0		
	Don't know	9	.0		
	Gesamt	17136	91.2		
Gesamt		18793	100.0		

Important for succesful marriage: children

		Häufigkeit	Prozent	Gültige Prozente	Kumulierte Prozente
Gültig	Very	1338	7.1	80.5	80.5
	Rather	269	1.4	16.2	96.7
	Not very	55	.3	3.3	100.0
	Gesamt	1662	8.8	100.0	
Fehlend	Not asked	17121	91.1		
	No answer	4	.0		
	Don´t know	7	.0		
	Gesamt	17132	91.2		
Gesamt		18793	100.0		

Important in succesful marriage: discussing problems

		Häufigkeit	Prozent	Gültige Prozente	Kumulierte Prozente
Gültig	Very	982	5.2	81.5	81.5
	Rather	199	1.1	16.6	98.0
	Not very	24	.1	2.0	100.0
	Gesamt	1205	6.4	100.0	
Fehlend	Not asked	17576	93.5		
	No answer	4	.0		
	Don´t know	8	.0		
	Gesamt	17588	93.6		
Gesamt		18793	100.0		

Important for succesful marriage: spending time together

		Häufigkeit	Prozent	Gültige Prozente	Kumulierte Prozente
Gültig	Very	860	4.6	71.6	71.6
	Rather	285	1.5	23.8	95.4
	Not very	55	.3	4.6	100.0
	Gesamt	1200	6.4	100.0	
Fehlend	Not asked	17576	93.5		
	No answer	3	.0		
	Don´t know	14	.1		
	Gesamt	17593	93.6		
Gesamt		18793	100.0		

Important in succesful marriage: talking

		Häufigkeit	Prozent	Gültige Prozente	Kumulierte Prozente
Gültig	Very	784	4.2	65.9	65.9
	Rather	281	1.5	23.6	89.5
	Not very	124	.7	10.5	100.0
	Gesamt	1189	6.3	100.0	
Fehlend	Not asked	17576	93.5		
	No answer	11	.1		
	Don't know	17	.1		
	Gesamt	17604	93.7		
Gesamt		18793	100.0		

Important for succesful marriage: same ethnic background

		Häufigkeit	Prozent	Gültige Prozente	Kumulierte Prozente
Gültig	Very	71	.4	40.4	40.4
	Rather	41	.2	23.5	63.9
	Not very	63	.3	36.1	100.0
	Gesamt	175	.9	100.0	
Fehlend	Not asked	18603	99.0		
	No answer	7	.0		
	Don't know	8	.0		
	Gesamt	18619	99.1		
Gesamt		18793	100.0		

Important for succesful marriage: tastes and interests in common

		Häufigkeit	Prozent	Gültige Prozente	Kumulierte Prozente
Gültig	Very	280	1.5	61.8	61.8
	Rather	110	.6	24.3	86.1
	Not very	63	.3	13.9	100.0
	Gesamt	453	2.4	100.0	
Fehlend	Not asked	18338	97.6		
	No answer	3	.0		
	Gesamt	18341	97.6		
Gesamt		18793	100.0		

GLOBAL MUSLIM ATTITUDES ON GLOBAL POLITICS

Willingness to fight for country

		Häufigkeit	Prozent	Gültige Prozente	Kumulierte Prozente
Gültig	No	1667	8.9	16.6	16.6
	Yes	8383	44.6	83.4	100.0
	Gesamt	10050	53.5	100.0	
Fehlend	Missing; unknown	5	.0		
	Not asked	7187	38.2		
	No answer	26	.1		
	Don't know	1526	8.1		
	Gesamt	8743	46.5		
Gesamt		18793	100.0		

Will there be war in your country in the next five years?

		Häufigkeit	Prozent	Gültige Prozente	Kumulierte Prozente
Gültig	Not at all likely	3	.0	22.6	22.6
	2	2	.0	12.8	35.4
	3	4	.0	26.8	62.1
	4	1	.0	6.5	68.6
	5	1	.0	5.4	74.1
	6	0	.0	3.1	77.2
	7	1	.0	8.3	85.5
	8	1	.0	3.9	89.4
	9	1	.0	8.0	97.4
	Very likely	0	.0	2.6	100.0
	Gesamt	15	.1	100.0	
Fehlend	Not asked	18774	99.9		
	Don't know	4	.0		
	Gesamt	18778	99.9		
Gesamt		18793	100.0		

Future changes: less emphasis on money and material possessions

		Häufigkeit	Prozent	Gültige Prozente	Kumulierte Prozente
Gültig	Good thing	9034	48.1	51.6	51.6
	Don't mind	3268	17.4	18.7	70.3
	Bad thing	5200	27.7	29.7	100.0
	Gesamt	17502	93.1	100.0	
Fehlend	Missing; unknown	5	.0		
	Not asked	614	3.3		
	No answer	134	.7		
	Don't know	539	2.9		
	Gesamt	1292	6.9		
Gesamt		18793	100.0		

Future changes: less importance placed on work

		Häufigkeit	Prozent	Gültige Prozente	Kumulierte Prozente
Gültig	Good thing	3247	17.3	18.4	18.4
	Don't mind	2939	15.6	16.7	35.1
	Bad thing	11460	61.0	64.9	100.0
	Gesamt	17646	93.9	100.0	
Fehlend	Missing; unknown	4	.0		
	Not asked	614	3.3		
	No answer	133	.7		
	Don't know	397	2.1		
	Gesamt	1147	6.1		
Gesamt		18793	100.0		

Future changes: more emphasis on technology

		Häufigkeit	Prozent	Gültige Prozente	Kumulierte Prozente
Gültig	Good thing	14238	75.8	81.0	81.0
	Don't mind	2572	13.7	14.6	95.6
	Bad thing	769	4.1	4.4	100.0
	Gesamt	17578	93.5	100.0	
Fehlend	Missing; unknown	4	.0		
	Not asked	612	3.3		
	No answer	142	.8		
	Don't know	457	2.4		
	Gesamt	1215	6.5		
Gesamt		18793	100.0		

Future changes: more emphasis on individual

		Häufigkeit	Prozent	Gültige Prozente	Kumulierte Prozente
Gültig	Good thing	1526	8.1	90.3	90.3
	Don't mind	105	.6	6.2	96.5
	Bad thing	58	.3	3.5	100.0
	Gesamt	1689	9.0	100.0	
Fehlend	Missing; unknown	1	.0		
	Not asked	17006	90.5		
	No answer	39	.2		
	Don't know	59	.3		
	Gesamt	17104	91.0		
Gesamt		18793	100.0		

Future changes: greater respect for authority

		Häufigkeit	Prozent	Gültige Prozente	Kumulierte Prozente
Gültig	Good thing	11680	62.1	66.6	66.6
	Don't mind	4377	23.3	25.0	91.6
	Bad thing	1479	7.9	8.4	100.0
	Gesamt	17536	93.3	100.0	
Fehlend	Missing; Unknown	7	.0		
	Not asked	614	3.3		
	No answer	170	.9		
	Don't know	467	2.5		
	Gesamt	1258	6.7		
Gesamt		18793	100.0		

Future changes: more emphasis on family life

		Häufigkeit	Prozent	Gültige Prozente	Kumulierte Prozente
Gültig	Good thing	16360	87.1	91.7	91.7
	Don't mind	1105	5.9	6.2	97.8
	Bad thing	385	2.0	2.2	100.0
	Gesamt	17849	95.0	100.0	
Fehlend	Missing; Unknown	3	.0		
	Not asked	612	3.3		
	No answer	97	.5		
	Don't know	232	1.2		
	Gesamt	944	5.0		
Gesamt		18793	100.0		

Future changes: a simple and more natural lifestyle

		Häufigkeit	Prozent	Gültige Prozente	Kumulierte Prozente
Gültig	Good thing	1247	6.6	73.5	73.5
	Don't mind	255	1.4	15.1	88.6
	Bad thing	193	1.0	11.4	100.0
	Gesamt	1696	9.0	100.0	
Fehlend	Missing; Unknown	1	.0		
	Not asked	16995	90.4		
	No answer	37	.2		
	Don't know	65	.3		
	Gesamt	17098	91.0		
Gesamt		18793	100.0		

Future changes: more power to local authorities

		Häufigkeit	Prozent	Gültige Prozente	Kumulierte Prozente
Gültig	Good thing	652	3.5	58.0	58.0
	Don't mind	236	1.3	21.0	79.0
	Bad thing	236	1.3	21.0	100.0
	Gesamt	1124	6.0	100.0	
Fehlend	Not asked	17576	93.5		
	No answer	16	.1		
	Don't know	77	.4		
	Gesamt	17669	94.0		
Gesamt		18793	100.0		

Opinion about scientific advances

		Häufigkeit	Prozent	Gültige Prozente	Kumulierte Prozente
Gültig	Will help	10791	57.4	67.8	67.8
	Will harm	1408	7.5	8.8	76.6
	Some of each	3720	19.8	23.4	100.0
	Gesamt	15919	84.7	100.0	
Fehlend	Missing; unknown	39	.2		
	Not asked	1866	9.9		
	No answer	82	.4		
	Don't know	886	4.7		
	Gesamt	2874	15.3		
Gesamt		18793	100.0		

GLOBAL MUSLIM ATTITUDES ON POLITICS AND DEMOCRACY

Interest in politics (i)

		Häufigkeit	Prozent	Gültige Prozente	Kumulierte Prozente
Gültig	Very interested	2215	11.8	12.7	12.7
	Somewhat interested	5790	30.8	33.1	45.8
	Not very interested	5236	27.9	30.0	75.8
	Not at all interested	4236	22.5	24.2	100.0
	Gesamt	17478	93.0	100.0	
Fehlend	Missing; Unknown	1	.0		
	Not asked	1021	5.4		
	No answer	32	.2		
	Don´t know	262	1.4		
	Gesamt	1316	7.0		
Gesamt		18793	100.0		

Interest in politics (ii)

		Häufigkeit	Prozent	Gültige Prozente	Kumulierte Prozente
Gültig	Active interest	3	.0	14.6	14.6
	Interest but inactive	5	.0	26.5	41.1
	Not greater than other	4	.0	21.0	62.1
	Not at all interested	7	.0	37.9	100.0
	Gesamt	18	.1	100.0	
Fehlend	Not asked	18774	99.9		
	No answer	1	.0		
	Gesamt	18775	99.9		
Gesamt		18793	100.0		

Political action: signing a petition

		Häufigkeit	Prozent	Gültige Prozente	Kumulierte Prozente
Gültig	Have done	2227	11.8	15.1	15.1
	Might do	5048	26.9	34.3	49.5
	Would never do	7430	39.5	50.5	100.0
	Gesamt	14706	78.2	100.0	
Fehlend	Missing; Unknown	6	.0		
	Not asked	2573	13.7		
	No answer	64	.3		
	Don´t know	1444	7.7		
	Gesamt	4088	21.8		
Gesamt		18793	100.0		

Political action: joining in boycotts

		Häufigkeit	Prozent	Gültige Prozente	Kumulierte Prozente
Gültig	Have done	1264	6.7	8.6	8.6
	Might do	3851	20.5	26.2	34.7
	Would never do	9608	51.1	65.3	100.0
	Gesamt	14723	78.3	100.0	
Fehlend	Missing; unknown	6	.0		
	Not asked	2573	13.7		
	No answer	72	.4		
	Don't know	1419	7.5		
	Gesamt	4071	21.7		
Gesamt		18793	100.0		

Political action: attending lawful demonstrations

		Häufigkeit	Prozent	Gültige Prozente	Kumulierte Prozente
Gültig	Have done	1753	9.3	11.7	11.7
	Might do	5053	26.9	33.7	45.3
	Would never do	8205	43.7	54.7	100.0
	Gesamt	15011	79.9	100.0	
Fehlend	Missing; Unknown	4	.0		
	Not asked	2573	13.7		
	No answer	71	.4		
	Don't know	1133	6.0		
	Gesamt	3782	20.1		
Gesamt		18793	100.0		

Political action: joining unofficial strikes

		Häufigkeit	Prozent	Gültige Prozente	Kumulierte Prozente
Gültig	Have done	521	2.8	3.5	3.5
	Might do	1865	9.9	12.7	16.2
	Would never do	12306	65.5	83.8	100.0
	Gesamt	14692	78.2	100.0	
Fehlend	Missing; Unknown	8	.0		
	Not asked	2730	14.5		
	No answer	87	.5		
	Don't know	1277	6.8		
	Gesamt	4101	21.8		
Gesamt		18793	100.0		

Political action: occupying buildings or factories

		Häufigkeit	Prozent	Gültige Prozente	Kumulierte Prozente
Gültig	Have done	185	1.0	1.3	1.3
	Might do	1064	5.7	7.2	8.5
	Would never do	13474	71.7	91.5	100.0
	Gesamt	14723	78.3	100.0	
Fehlend	Missing; unknown	8	.0		
	Not asked	2732	14.5		
	No answer	110	.6		
	Don't know	1222	6.5		
	Gesamt	4070	21.7		
Gesamt		18793	100.0		

Political action: damaging things, breaking windows, street violence

		Häufigkeit	Prozent	Gültige Prozente	Kumulierte Prozente
Gültig	Might do	0	.0	2.2	2.2
	Would never do	18	.1	97.8	100.0
	Gesamt	18	.1	100.0	
Fehlend	Not asked	18774	99.9		
	No answer	1	.0		
	Gesamt	18775	99.9		
Gesamt		18793	100.0		

Political action: personal violence

		Häufigkeit	Prozent	Gültige Prozente	Kumulierte Prozente
Gültig	Have done	0	.0	2.3	2.3
	Might do	1	.0	3.5	5.8
	Would never do	16	.1	94.2	100.0
	Gesamt	17	.1	100.0	
Fehlend	Not asked	18774	99.9		
	No answer	1	.0		
	Don't know	1	.0		
	Gesamt	18776	99.9		
Gesamt		18793	100.0		

Freedom or equality

		Häufigkeit	Prozent	Gültige Prozente	Kumulierte Prozente
Gültig	Freedom above equality	744	4.0	44.5	44.5
	Equality above freedom	859	4.6	51.4	95.9
	Neither	69	.4	4.1	100.0
	Gesamt	1671	8.9	100.0	
Fehlend	Not asked	16994	90.4		
	No answer	43	.2		
	Don't know	86	.5		
	Gesamt	17122	91.1		
Gesamt		18793	100.0		

Self positioning in political scale

		Häufigkeit	Prozent	Gültige Prozente	Kumulierte Prozente
Gültig	Left	854	4.5	7.2	7.2
	2	416	2.2	3.5	10.7
	3	774	4.1	6.5	17.1
	4	858	4.6	7.2	24.3
	5	3169	16.9	26.6	50.9
	6	1373	7.3	11.5	62.4
	7	982	5.2	8.2	70.7
	8	1126	6.0	9.4	80.1
	9	628	3.3	5.3	85.4
	Right	1743	9.3	14.6	100.0
	Gesamt	11922	63.4	100.0	
Fehlend	Missing; unknown	67	.4		
	Not asked	2703	14.4		
	No answer	382	2.0		
	Don't know	3719	19.8		
	Gesamt	6871	36.6		
Gesamt		18793	100.0		

Basic kinds of attitudes concerning society

		Häufigkeit	Prozent	Gültige Prozente	Kumulierte Prozente
Gültig	Society must be radically changed	2158	11.5	15.0	15.0
	Society must be gradually improved by reforms	8927	47.5	62.1	77.1
	Society must be valiantly defended	3294	17.5	22.9	100.0
	Gesamt	14379	76.5	100.0	
Fehlend	Missing; unknown	15	.1		
	Not asked	3012	16.0		
	No answer	120	.6		
	Don't know	1267	6.7		
	Gesamt	4415	23.5		
Gesamt		18793	100.0		

Income equality

		Häufigkeit	Prozent	Gültige Prozente	Kumulierte Prozente
Gültig	Incomes should be made more equal	2554	13.6	14.3	14.3
	2	968	5.2	5.4	19.8
	3	999	5.3	5.6	25.4
	4	961	5.1	5.4	30.8
	5	1967	10.5	11.0	41.8
	6	1496	8.0	8.4	50.2
	7	1693	9.0	9.5	59.7
	8	2040	10.9	11.5	71.2
	9	1368	7.3	7.7	78.9
	We need larger income differences as incentives	3758	20.0	21.1	100.0
	Gesamt	17804	94.7	100.0	
Fehlend	Missing; unknown	22	.1		
	Not asked	85	.4		
	No answer	143	.8		
	Don't know	740	3.9		
	Gesamt	990	5.3		
Gesamt		18793	100.0		

Private vs. state ownership of business

		Häufigkeit	Prozent	Gültige Prozente	Kumulierte Prozente
Gültig	Private ownership of business should be increased	3124	16.6	18.4	18.4
	2	1133	6.0	6.7	25.0
	3	1538	8.2	9.0	34.1
	4	1279	6.8	7.5	41.6
	5	2690	14.3	15.8	57.4
	6	1289	6.9	7.6	65.0
	7	1064	5.7	6.3	71.3
	8	1249	6.6	7.3	78.6
	9	1067	5.7	6.3	84.9
	Government ownership of business should be increased	2573	13.7	15.1	100.0
	Gesamt	17006	90.5	100.0	
Fehlend	Missing; unknown	13	.1		
	Not asked	614	3.3		
	No answer	146	.8		
	Don´t know	1014	5.4		
	Gesamt	1787	9.5		
Gesamt		18793	100.0		

Government responsibility

		Häufigkeit	Prozent	Gültige Prozente	Kumulierte Prozente
Gültig	People should take more responsibility	2093	11.1	11.6	11.6
	2	747	4.0	4.1	15.8
	3	1179	6.3	6.6	22.3
	4	1086	5.8	6.0	28.4
	5	1351	7.2	7.5	35.9
	6	2325	12.4	12.9	48.8
	7	1235	6.6	6.9	55.7
	8	1602	8.5	8.9	64.6
	9	1684	9.0	9.4	73.9
	The government should take more responsibility	4695	25.0	26.1	100.0
	Gesamt	17995	95.8	100.0	
Fehlend	Missing; unknown	18	.1		
	Not asked	46	.2		
	No answer	135	.7		
	Don´t know	598	3.2		
	Gesamt	798	4.2		
Gesamt		18793	100.0		

Job taking of the unemployed

		Häufigkeit	Prozent	Gültige Prozente	Kumulierte Prozente
Gültig	Unemployed should take any job	165	.9	25.3	25.3
	2	62	.3	9.5	34.9
	3	58	.3	9.0	43.8
	4	62	.3	9.5	53.3
	5	79	.4	12.2	65.5
	6	39	.2	5.9	71.4
	7	40	.2	6.1	77.5
	8	49	.3	7.5	85.1
	9	24	.1	3.7	88.8
	Unemployed have a right to refuse a job	73	.4	11.2	100.0
	Gesamt	652	3.5	100.0	
Fehlend	Not asked	17987	95.7		
	No answer	8	.0		
	Don't know	146	.8		
	Gesamt	18142	96.5		
Gesamt		18793	100.0		

GLOBAL MUSLIM ATTITUDES ON THE MARKET ECONOMY

Competition good or harmful

		Häufigkeit	Prozent	Gültige Prozente	Kumulierte Prozente
Gültig	Competition is good	4083	21,7	39,3	39,3
	2	1186	6,3	11,4	50,7
	3	1270	6,8	12,2	63,0
	4	999	5,3	9,6	72,6
	5	1126	6,0	10,8	83,4
	6	444	2,4	4,3	87,7
	7	291	1,5	2,8	90,5
	8	330	1,8	3,2	93,7
	9	153	,8	1,5	95,2
	Competition is harmful	503	2,7	4,8	100,0
	Gesamt	10386	55,3	100,0	
Fehlend	Missing; unknown	18	,1		
	Not asked	7801	41,5		
	No answer	43	,2		

Competition good or harmful (Continued)

		Häufigkeit	Prozent	Gültige Prozente	Kumulierte Prozente
	Don't know	545	2,9		
	Gesamt	8407	44,7		
Gesamt		18793	100,0		

Hard work brings success

		Häufigkeit	Prozent	Gültige Prozente	Kumulierte Prozente
Gültig	In the long run, hard work usually brings a better life	1828	9,7	34,8	34,8
	2	683	3,6	13,0	47,8
	3	507	2,7	9,7	57,5
	4	467	2,5	8,9	66,4
	5	484	2,6	9,2	75,6
	6	222	1,2	4,2	79,8
	7	233	1,2	4,4	84,2
	8	232	1,2	4,4	88,6
	9	146	,8	2,8	91,4
	Hard work doesn't generally bring success - it's more a matter of other factors	450	2,4	8,6	100,0
	Gesamt	5252	27,9	100,0	
Fehlend	Missing; unknown	14	,1		
	Not asked	13311	70,8		
	No answer	18	,1		
	Don't know	199	1,1		
	Gesamt	13541	72,1		
Gesamt		18793	100,0		

Wealth accumulation

		Häufigkeit	Prozent	Gültige Prozente	Kumulierte Prozente
Gültig	People can only get rich at the expense of others	534	2,8	10,5	10,5
	2	232	1,2	4,6	15,1
	3	258	1,4	5,1	20,2
	4	348	1,8	6,9	27,1
	5	634	3,4	12,5	39,6
	6	371	2,0	7,3	46,9
	7	495	2,6	9,8	56,7
	8	584	3,1	11,5	68,2
	9	435	2,3	8,6	76,8
	Wealth can grow so there's enough for everyone	1178	6,3	23,2	100,0
	Gesamt	5069	27,0	100,0	
Fehlend	Missing; unknown	57	,3		
	Not asked	13311	70,8		
	No answer	19	,1		
	Don't know	338	1,8		
	Gesamt	13724	73,0		
Gesamt		18793	100,0		

Firms and freedom

		Häufigkeit	Prozent	Gültige Prozente	Kumulierte Prozente
Gültig	State should give more freedom to firms	112	,6	10,2	10,2
	2	66	,4	6,0	16,2
	3	55	,3	5,0	21,2
	4	65	,3	5,9	27,2
	5	110	,6	10,0	37,2
	6	57	,3	5,2	42,4
	7	60	,3	5,5	47,9
	8	117	,6	10,6	58,5
	9	120	,6	10,9	69,3
	State should control firms more effectively	337	1,8	30,7	100,0
	Gesamt	1101	5,9	100,0	
Fehlend	Not asked	17576	93,5		
	No answer	25	,1		
	Don't know	92	,5		
	Gesamt	17693	94,1		
Gesamt		18793	100,0		

Responsibility pension

		Häufigkeit	Prozent	Gültige Prozente	Kumulierte Prozente
Gültig	Individual responsibility for pension	121	,6	12,0	12,0
	2	43	,2	4,2	16,2
	3	33	,2	3,3	19,5
	4	36	,2	3,6	23,1
	5	71	,4	7,0	30,1
	6	43	,2	4,2	34,3
	7	52	,3	5,1	39,4
	8	71	,4	7,0	46,4
	9	117	,6	11,5	57,9
	State responsibility for pension	427	2,3	42,1	100,0
	Gesamt	1015	5,4	100,0	
Fehlend	Not asked	17736	94,4		
	No answer	8	,0		
	Don´t know	34	,2		
	Gesamt	17778	94,6		
Gesamt		18793	100,0		

Responsibility housing

		Häufigkeit	Prozent	Gültige Prozente	Kumulierte Prozente
Gültig	Individual responsibility for housing	450	2,4	40,9	40,9
	2	117	,6	10,6	51,5
	3	85	,5	7,7	59,3
	4	46	,2	4,2	63,5
	5	99	,5	9,0	72,5
	6	61	,3	5,5	78,0
	7	39	,2	3,6	81,5
	8	53	,3	4,8	86,3
	9	35	,2	3,1	89,4
	State responsibility for housing	116	,6	10,6	100,0
	Gesamt	1101	5,9	100,0	
Fehlend	Not asked	17662	94,0		
	No answer	8	,0		
	Don´t know	22	,1		
	Gesamt	17693	94,1		
Gesamt		18793	100,0		

GLOBAL MUSLIM EXPECTATIONS FOR THE FUTURE

Major changes in life

		Häufigkeit	Prozent	Gültige Prozente	Kumulierte Prozente
Gültig	One should be cautious about major changes in life	1249	6,6	24,1	24,1
	2	421	2,2	8,1	32,3
	3	417	2,2	8,1	40,4
	4	418	2,2	8,1	48,4
	5	561	3,0	10,8	59,3
	6	354	1,9	6,8	66,1
	7	340	1,8	6,6	72,7
	8	403	2,1	7,8	80,5
	9	333	1,8	6,4	86,9
	One should act boldly to achieve	677	3,6	13,1	100,0
	Gesamt	5173	27,5	100,0	
Fehlend	Missing; unknown	21	,1		
	Not asked	13266	70,6		
	No answer	30	,2		
	Don´t know	302	1,6		
	Gesamt	13620	72,5		
Gesamt		18793	100,0		

New and old ideas

		Häufigkeit	Prozent	Gültige Prozente	Kumulierte Prozente
Gültig	Ideas that stood test of time are generally best	1258	6,7	16,4	16,4
	2	434	2,3	5,7	22,1
	3	393	2,1	5,1	27,3
	4	439	2,3	5,7	33,0
	5	928	4,9	12,1	45,1
	6	559	3,0	7,3	52,4
	7	635	3,4	8,3	60,8
	8	765	4,1	10,0	70,8
	9	563	3,0	7,4	78,1
	New ideas are generally better than old ones	1675	8,9	21,9	100,0
	Gesamt	7649	40,7	100,0	

New and old ideas (Continued)

		Häufigkeit	Prozent	Gültige Prozente	Kumulierte Prozente
Fehlend	Missing; unknown	23	,1		
	Not asked	10606	56,4		
	No answer	14	,1		
	Don't know	502	2,7		
	Gesamt	11144	59,3		
Gesamt		18793	100,0		

GLOBAL MUSLIM ATTITUDES ON THE POLITICAL PROCESS

Rate political system for governing country

		Häufigkeit	Prozent	Gültige Prozente	Kumulierte Prozente
Gültig	Bad	1798	9,6	14,6	14,6
	2	822	4,4	6,7	21,3
	3	1149	6,1	9,3	30,7
	4	1221	6,5	9,9	40,6
	5	2494	13,3	20,3	60,9
	6	1657	8,8	13,5	74,4
	7	1130	6,0	9,2	83,6
	8	913	4,9	7,4	91,0
	9	414	2,2	3,4	94,4
	Very good	689	3,7	5,6	100,0
	Gesamt	12287	65,4	100,0	
Fehlend	Missing; unknown	7	,0		
	Not asked	5758	30,6		
	No answer	90	,5		
	Don't know	652	3,5		
	Gesamt	6507	34,6		
Gesamt		18793	100,0		

Rate political system as it was before

		Häufigkeit	Prozent	Gültige Prozente	Kumulierte Prozente
Gültig	Bad	1135	6,0	10,8	10,8
	2	564	3,0	5,4	16,2
	3	867	4,6	8,3	24,5
	4	852	4,5	8,1	32,6
	5	1554	8,3	14,8	47,4
	6	985	5,2	9,4	56,8
	7	1074	5,7	10,2	67,1
	8	1388	7,4	13,2	80,3
	9	659	3,5	6,3	86,6
	Very good	1406	7,5	13,4	100,0
	Gesamt	10484	55,8	100,0	
Fehlend	Missing; unknown	14	,1		
	Not asked	7720	41,1		
	No answer	34	,2		
	Don´t know	541	2,9		
	Gesamt	8309	44,2		
Gesamt		18793	100,0		

Rate political system in ten years

		Häufigkeit	Prozent	Gültige Prozente	Kumulierte Prozente
Gültig	Bad	361	1,9	9,0	9,0
	2	104	,6	2,6	11,5
	3	146	,8	3,6	15,2
	4	113	,6	2,8	18,0
	5	406	2,2	10,1	28,1
	6	375	2,0	9,3	37,4
	7	503	2,7	12,5	49,9
	8	772	4,1	19,2	69,0
	9	538	2,9	13,4	82,4
	Very good	709	3,8	17,6	100,0
	Gesamt	4026	21,4	100,0	
Fehlend	Missing; unknown	138	,7		
	Not asked	13480	71,7		
	No answer	46	,2		
	Don´t know	1103	5,9		
	Gesamt	14767	78,6		
Gesamt		18793	100,0		

Political system: having a strong leader

		Häufigkeit	Prozent	Gültige Prozente	Kumulierte Prozente
Gültig	Very good	2047	10,9	13,9	13,9
	Fairly good	2984	15,9	20,3	34,2
	Bad	4653	24,8	31,6	65,8
	Very bad	5031	26,8	34,2	100,0
	Gesamt	14715	78,3	100,0	
Fehlend	Missing; unknown	3	,0		
	Not asked	1708	9,1		
	No answer	112	,6		
	Don't know	2255	12,0		
	Gesamt	4079	21,7		
Gesamt		18793	100,0		

Political system: having experts make decisions

		Häufigkeit	Prozent	Gültige Prozente	Kumulierte Prozente
Gültig	Very good	3412	18,2	24,1	24,1
	Fairly good	6038	32,1	42,7	66,9
	Fairly bad	2906	15,5	20,6	87,4
	Very bad	1775	9,4	12,6	100,0
	Gesamt	14130	75,2	100,0	
Fehlend	Missing; unknown	4	,0		
	Not asked	1708	9,1		
	No answer	122	,7		
	Don't know	2828	15,1		
	Gesamt	4663	24,8		
Gesamt		18793	100,0		

Political system: having the army rule

		Häufigkeit	Prozent	Gültige Prozente	Kumulierte Prozente
Gültig	Very good	1830	9,7	12,9	12,9
	Fairly good	2922	15,5	20,6	33,5
	Fairly bad	3686	19,6	26,0	59,6
	Very bad	5730	30,5	40,4	100,0
	Gesamt	14169	75,4	100,0	
Fehlend	Missing; unknown	4	,0		
	Not asked	2652	14,1		
	No answer	112	,6		
	Don't know	1857	9,9		
	Gesamt	4625	24,6		
Gesamt		18793	100,0		

Political system: having a democratic political system

		Häufigkeit	Prozent	Gültige Prozente	Kumulierte Prozente
Gültig	Very good	8609	45,8	57,2	57,2
	Fairly good	5491	29,2	36,5	93,6
	Fairly bad	669	3,6	4,4	98,0
	Very bad	294	1,6	2,0	100,0
	Gesamt	15063	80,2	100,0	
Fehlend	Missing; unknown	3	,0		
	Not asked	1708	9,1		
	No answer	121	,6		
	Don't know	1898	10,1		
	Gesamt	3730	19,8		
Gesamt		18793	100,0		

Firm party leader vs. cooperative party leader

		Häufigkeit	Prozent	Gültige Prozente	Kumulierte Prozente
Gültig	Firm party leader	1140	6,1	26,6	26,6
	Cooperative party leader	3139	16,7	73,4	100,0
	Gesamt	4279	22,8	100,0	
Fehlend	Missing; unknown	16	,1		
	Not asked	13861	73,8		
	No answer	11	,1		
	Don't know	627	3,3		
	Gesamt	14514	77,2		
Gesamt		18793	100,0		

Political system: having the army rule

		Häufigkeit	Prozent	Gültige Prozente	Kumulierte Prozente
Gültig	Very good	1830	9,7	12,9	12,9
	Fairly good	2922	15,5	20,6	33,5
	Fairly bad	3686	19,6	26,0	59,6
	Very bad	5730	30,5	40,4	100,0
	Gesamt	14169	75,4	100,0	
Fehlend	Missing; Unknown	4	,0		
	Not asked	2652	14,1		
	No answer	112	,6		
	Don't know	1857	9,9		
	Gesamt	4625	24,6		
Gesamt		18793	100,0		

In democracy, the economic system runs badly

		Häufigkeit	Prozent	Gültige Prozente	Kumulierte Prozente
Gültig	Agree strongly	1096	5,8	7,4	7,4
	Agree	2878	15,3	19,6	27,0
	Disagree	8001	42,6	54,4	81,4
	Strongly disagree	2740	14,6	18,6	100,0
	Gesamt	14714	78,3	100,0	
Fehlend	Missing; unknown	6	,0		
	Not asked	895	4,8		
	No answer	129	,7		
	Don't know	3049	16,2		
	Gesamt	4079	21,7		
Gesamt		18793	100,0		

Democracies are indecisive and have too much squabbling

		Häufigkeit	Prozent	Gültige Prozente	Kumulierte Prozente
Gültig	Agree strongly	1587	8,4	10,7	10,7
	Agree	4653	24,8	31,4	42,1
	Disagree	6445	34,3	43,5	85,7
	Strongly disagree	2121	11,3	14,3	100,0
	Gesamt	14806	78,8	100,0	
Fehlend	Missing; unknown	5	,0		
	Not asked	895	4,8		
	No answer	137	,7		
	Don't know	2950	15,7		
	Gesamt	3987	21,2		
Gesamt		18793	100,0		

Democracies aren't good at maintaining order

		Häufigkeit	Prozent	Gültige Prozente	Kumulierte Prozente
Gültig	Agree strongly	1231	6,5	8,3	8,3
	Agree	3294	17,5	22,2	30,6
	Disagree	7432	39,5	50,2	80,8
	Strongly disagree	2848	15,2	19,2	100,0
	Gesamt	14804	78,8	100,0	
Fehlend	Missing; unknown	5	,0		
	Not asked	895	4,8		
	No answer	145	,8		
	Don't know	2944	15,7		
	Gesamt	3989	21,2		
Gesamt		18793	100,0		

Democracy may have problems but is better

		Häufigkeit	Prozent	Gültige Prozente	Kumulierte Prozente
Gültig	Agree strongly	7136	38,0	46,4	46,4
	Agree	6408	34,1	41,7	88,1
	Disagree	1311	7,0	8,5	96,7
	Strongly disagree	510	2,7	3,3	100,0
	Gesamt	15365	81,8	100,0	
Fehlend	Missing; unknown	5	,0		
	Not asked	895	4,8		
	No answer	128	,7		
	Don´t know	2400	12,8		
	Gesamt	3429	18,2		
Gesamt		18793	100,0		

Respect for individual human rights nowadays

		Häufigkeit	Prozent	Gültige Prozente	Kumulierte Prozente
Gültig	There is a lot of respect for individual human rights	1803	9,6	13,5	13,5
	There is some respect	5226	27,8	39,2	52,7
	There is not much respect	3995	21,3	29,9	82,6
	There is no respect at all	2323	12,4	17,4	100,0
	Gesamt	13347	71,0	100,0	
Fehlend	Not asked	4850	25,8		
	No answer	30	,2		
	Don´t know	567	3,0		
	Gesamt	5447	29,0		
Gesamt		18793	100,0		

Satisfaction with the people in national office

		Häufigkeit	Prozent	Gültige Prozente	Kumulierte Prozente
Gültig	Very satisfied	1514	8,1	10,5	10,5
	Fairly satisfied	5540	29,5	38,5	49,1
	Fairly dissatisfied	5054	26,9	35,2	84,3
	Very dissatisfied	2263	12,0	15,7	100,0
	Gesamt	14371	76,5	100,0	
Fehlend	Missing; unknown	6	,0		
	Not asked	3531	18,8		
	No answer	80	,4		
	Don't know	805	4,3		
	Gesamt	4423	23,5		
Gesamt		18793	100,0		

Free market economy right for country future

		Häufigkeit	Prozent	Gültige Prozente	Kumulierte Prozente
Gültig	Right	406	2,2	75,0	75,0
	Wrong	136	,7	25,0	100,0
	Gesamt	541	2,9	100,0	
Fehlend	Not asked	17863	95,0		
	No answer	389	2,1		
	Gesamt	18252	97,1		
Gesamt		18793	100,0		

Country is run by big interest vs. for all people's benefit

		Häufigkeit	Prozent	Gültige Prozente	Kumulierte Prozente
Gültig	Run by a few big interests	9972	53,1	68,3	68,3
	Run for all the people	4631	24,6	31,7	100,0
	Gesamt	14602	77,7	100,0	
Fehlend	Missing; unknown	7	,0		
	Not asked	1606	8,5		
	No answer	163	,9		
	Don't know	2415	12,9		
	Gesamt	4191	22,3		
Gesamt		18793	100,0		

GLOBAL MUSLIM ATTITUDES ON GLOBAL POVERTY

Economic aid to poorer countries

		Häufigkeit	Prozent	Gültige Prozente	Kumulierte Prozente
Gültig	A lot more than we do now	1252	6,7	21,2	21,2
	Somewhat more than we do now	2154	11,5	36,5	57,8
	About the right amount/same	1	,0	,0	57,8
	Somewhat less than we do now	1275	6,8	21,6	79,4
	A lot less than we do now	1212	6,4	20,6	100,0
	Gesamt	5894	31,4	100,0	
Fehlend	Not asked	11293	60,1		
	No answer	32	,2		
	Don't know	1575	8,4		
	Gesamt	12900	68,6		
Gesamt		18793	100,0		

Poverty compared to 10 years ago

		Häufigkeit	Prozent	Gültige Prozente	Kumulierte Prozente
Gültig	Larger share	3207	17,1	68,7	68,7
	Same share	796	4,2	17,0	85,7
	Smaller share	666	3,5	14,3	100,0
	Gesamt	4669	24,8	100,0	
Fehlend	Missing; Unknown	0	,0		
	Not asked	13913	74,0		
	No answer	11	,1		
	Don't know	199	1,1		
	Gesamt	14124	75,2		
Gesamt		18793	100,0		

Why are people in need?

		Häufigkeit	Prozent	Gültige Prozente	Kumulierte Prozente
Gültig	Poor because of laziness and lack of will power	1059	5,6	24,1	24,1
	Poor because of an unfair society	3279	17,4	74,8	98,9
	Other answer	49	,3	1,1	100,0
	Gesamt	4386	23,3	100,0	
Fehlend	Missing; unknown	11	,1		
	Not asked	13913	74,0		
	No answer	40	,2		
	Don't know	444	2,4		
	Gesamt	14408	76,7		
Gesamt		18793	100,0		

Chance to escape from poverty

		Häufigkeit	Prozent	Gültige Prozente	Kumulierte Prozente
Gültig	They have a chance	1821	9,7	41,0	41,0
	There is very little chance	2625	14,0	59,0	100,0
	Gesamt	4447	23,7	100,0	
Fehlend	Missing; unknown	11	,1		
	Not asked	13914	74,0		
	No answer	34	,2		
	Don't know	389	2,1		
	Gesamt	14347	76,3		
Gesamt		18793	100,0		

GLOBAL MUSLIM RELIGIOUS BELIEFS

Believe in God

		Häufigkeit	Prozent	Gültige Prozente	Kumulierte Prozente
Gültig	No	287	1,5	1,6	1,6
	Yes	18151	96,6	98,4	100,0
	Gesamt	18438	98,1	100,0	
Fehlend	Missing; unknown	11	,1		
	Not asked	149	,8		
	No answer	15	,1		
	Don´t know	181	1,0		
	Gesamt	356	1,9		
Gesamt		18793	100,0		

Believe in life after death

		Häufigkeit	Prozent	Gültige Prozente	Kumulierte Prozente
Gültig	No	3172	16,9	18,2	18,2
	Yes	14223	75,7	81,8	100,0
	Gesamt	17395	92,6	100,0	
Fehlend	Missing; unknown	17	,1		
	Not asked	116	,6		
	No answer	39	,2		
	Don´t know	1227	6,5		
	Gesamt	1398	7,4		
Gesamt		18793	100,0		

Believe in: people have a soul

		Häufigkeit	Prozent	Gültige Prozente	Kumulierte Prozente
Gültig	No	1330	7,1	8,0	8,0
	Yes	15217	81,0	92,0	100,0
	Gesamt	16547	88,0	100,0	
Fehlend	Missing; Unknown	12	,1		
	Not asked	1333	7,1		
	No answer	30	,2		
	Don´t know	873	4,6		
	Gesamt	2246	12,0		
Gesamt		18793	100,0		

Believe in hell

		Häufigkeit	Prozent	Gültige Prozente	Kumulierte Prozente
Gültig	No	2292	12,2	13,2	13,2
	Yes	15126	80,5	86,8	100,0
	Gesamt	17418	92,7	100,0	
Fehlend	Missing; unknown	21	,1		
	Not asked	116	,6		
	No answer	39	,2		
	Don't know	1200	6,4		
	Gesamt	1375	7,3		
Gesamt		18793	100,0		

Believe in heaven

		Häufigkeit	Prozent	Gültige Prozente	Kumulierte Prozente
Gültig	No	1834	9,8	10,5	10,5
	Yes	15687	83,5	89,5	100,0
	Gesamt	17521	93,2	100,0	
Fehlend	Missing; unknown	19	,1		
	Not asked	116	,6		
	No answer	32	,2		
	Don't know	1106	5,9		
	Gesamt	1273	6,8		
Gesamt		18793	100,0		

Believe in sin

		Häufigkeit	Prozent	Gültige Prozente	Kumulierte Prozente
Gültig	No	1017	5,4	16,5	16,5
	Yes	5130	27,3	83,5	100,0
	Gesamt	6147	32,7	100,0	
Fehlend	Missing; unknown	20	,1		
	Not asked	12063	64,2		
	No answer	16	,1		
	Don't know	547	2,9		
	Gesamt	12646	67,3		
Gesamt		18793	100,0		

Believe in telepathy

		Häufigkeit	Prozent	Gültige Prozente	Kumulierte Prozente
Gültig	No	990	5,3	87,9	87,9
	Yes	136	,7	12,1	100,0
	Gesamt	1126	6,0	100,0	
Fehlend	Not asked	17576	93,5		
	No answer	18	,1		
	Don't know	73	,4		
	Gesamt	17667	94,0		
Gesamt		18793	100,0		

Believe in reincarnation

		Häufigkeit	Prozent	Gültige Prozente	Kumulierte Prozente
Gültig	No	1078	5,7	68,8	68,8
	Yes	488	2,6	31,2	100,0
	Gesamt	1566	8,3	100,0	
Fehlend	Not asked	17017	90,5		
	No answer	51	,3		
	Don't know	160	,8		
	Gesamt	17227	91,7		
Gesamt		18793	100,0		

Believe in angels

		Häufigkeit	Prozent	Gültige Prozente	Kumulierte Prozente
Gültig	No	16	,1	62,2	62,2
	Yes	10	,1	37,8	100,0
	Gesamt	26	,1	100,0	
Fehlend	Not asked	18763	99,8		
	Don't know	5	,0		
	Gesamt	18768	99,9		
Gesamt		18793	100,0		

Believe in devil

		Häufigkeit	Prozent	Gültige Prozente	Kumulierte Prozente
Gültig	No	1546	8,2	32,3	32,3
	Yes	3237	17,2	67,7	100,0
	Gesamt	4783	25,4	100,0	
Fehlend	Missing; unknown	21	,1		
	Not asked	13280	70,7		
	No answer	15	,1		
	Don't know	696	3,7		
	Gesamt	14011	74,6		
Gesamt		18793	100,0		

Believe in resurrection of the dead

		Häufigkeit	Prozent	Gültige Prozente	Kumulierte Prozente
Gültig	No	116	,6	23,6	23,6
	Yes	374	2,0	76,4	100,0
	Gesamt	490	2,6	100,0	
Fehlend	Not asked	18243	97,1		
	No answer	26	,1		
	Don't know	35	,2		
	Gesamt	18303	97,4		
Gesamt		18793	100,0		

Stick to religion vs. explore different traditions

		Häufigkeit	Prozent	Gültige Prozente	Kumulierte Prozente
Gültig	To stick to a particular faith	14	,1	49,1	49,1
	2	0	,0	,6	49,8
	3	1	,0	4,2	54,0
	4	1	,0	4,9	58,9
	5	2	,0	7,3	66,2
	6	1	,0	4,4	70,6
	7	3	,0	9,1	79,7
	8	2	,0	7,3	87,0
	9	1	,0	3,4	90,4
	To explore teachings of different religious traditions	3	,0	9,6	100,0
	Gesamt	28	,1	100,0	

Stick to religion vs. explore different traditions (Continued)

		Häufigkeit	Prozent	Gültige Prozente	Kumulierte Prozente
Fehlend	Not asked	18765	99,9		
	No answer	0	,0		
	Don´t know	0	,0		
	Gesamt	18766	99,9		
Gesamt		18793	100,0		

Personal God vs. spirit or life force

		Häufigkeit	Prozent	Gültige Prozente	Kumulierte Prozente
Gültig	Personal God	387	2,1	59,5	59,5
	Spirit or life force	180	1,0	27,7	87,2
	Don´t know what to think	64	,3	9,9	97,1
	No spirit God or life force	19	,1	2,9	100,0
	Gesamt	650	3,5	100,0	
Fehlend	Not asked	18096	96,3		
	No answer	13	,1		
	Don´t know	35	,2		
	Gesamt	18143	96,5		
Gesamt		18793	100,0		

How important is God in your life?

		Häufigkeit	Prozent	Gültige Prozente	Kumulierte Prozente
Gültig	Not at all important	291	1,5	1,6	1,6
	2	148	,8	,8	2,4
	3	204	1,1	1,1	3,5
	4	197	1,0	1,1	4,5
	5	459	2,4	2,5	7,0
	6	350	1,9	1,9	8,9
	7	604	3,2	3,2	12,1
	8	966	5,1	5,2	17,3
	9	1229	6,5	6,6	23,9
	Very important	14156	75,3	76,1	100,0
	Gesamt	18604	99,0	100,0	
Fehlend	Missing; unknown	14	,1		
	Not asked	9	,0		
	No answer	17	,1		
	Don´t know	149	,8		
	Gesamt	189	1,0		
Gesamt		18793	100,0		

Get comfort and strength from religion

		Häufigkeit	Prozent	Gültige Prozente	Kumulierte Prozente
Gültig	No	1256	6,7	7,2	7,2
	Yes	16157	86,0	92,8	100,0
	Gesamt	17413	92,7	100,0	
Fehlend	Missing; unknown	14	,1		
	Not asked	396	2,1		
	No answer	108	,6		
	Don't know	863	4,6		
	Gesamt	1380	7,3		
Gesamt		18793	100,0		

Moments of prayer, meditation

		Häufigkeit	Prozent	Gültige Prozente	Kumulierte Prozente
Gültig	No	767	4,1	13,0	13,0
	Yes	5112	27,2	87,0	100,0
	Gesamt	5879	31,3	100,0	
Fehlend	Not asked	12705	67,6		
	No answer	14	,1		
	Don't know	195	1,0		
	Gesamt	12915	68,7		
Gesamt		18793	100,0		

Pray to God outside of religious services (i)

		Häufigkeit	Prozent	Gültige Prozente	Kumulierte Prozente
Gültig	Every day	4503	24,0	57,1	57,1
	More than once a week	1036	5,5	13,1	70,2
	Once a week	542	2,9	6,9	77,1
	At least once a month	428	2,3	5,4	82,5
	Several times a year	469	2,5	5,9	88,5
	Less often	412	2,2	5,2	93,7
	Never	496	2,6	6,3	100,0
	Gesamt	7887	42,0	100,0	
Fehlend	Not asked	10723	57,1		
	No answer	58	,3		
	Don't know	125	,7		
	Gesamt	10906	58,0		
Gesamt		18793	100,0		

Pray to God outside of religious services (ii)

		Häufigkeit	Prozent	Gültige Prozente	Kumulierte Prozente
Gültig	Often	280	1,5	63,6	63,6
	Sometimes	80	,4	18,3	81,9
	Hardly ever	24	,1	5,3	87,2
	Only in times of crisis	30	,2	6,8	94,0
	Never	26	,1	6,0	100,0
	Gesamt	440	2,3	100,0	
Fehlend	Not asked	18347	97,6		
	No answer	1	,0		
	Don´t know	5	,0		
	Gesamt	18353	97,7		
Gesamt		18793	100,0		

Politicians who don't believe in God are unfit for public office

		Häufigkeit	Prozent	Gültige Prozente	Kumulierte Prozente
Gültig	Agree strongly	4542	24,2	43,4	43,4
	Agree	2462	13,1	23,5	66,9
	Neither agree or disagree	1086	5,8	10,4	77,3
	Disagree	1605	8,5	15,3	92,6
	Strongly disagree	775	4,1	7,4	100,0
	Gesamt	10471	55,7	100,0	
Fehlend	Not asked	7724	41,1		
	No answer	28	,1		
	Don´t know	571	3,0		
	Gesamt	8323	44,3		
Gesamt		18793	100,0		

Religious leaders should not influence how people vote

		Häufigkeit	Prozent	Gültige Prozente	Kumulierte Prozente
Gültig	Agree strongly	3212	17,1	31,2	31,2
	Agree	4136	22,0	40,2	71,4
	Neither agree or disagree	1158	6,2	11,2	82,6
	Disagree	1254	6,7	12,2	94,8
	Strongly disagree	535	2,8	5,2	100,0
	Gesamt	10294	54,8	100,0	
Fehlend	Not asked	7724	41,1		
	No answer	28	,2		
	Don´t know	746	4,0		
	Gesamt	8499	45,2		
Gesamt		18793	100,0		

Better if more people with strong religious beliefs in public office

		Häufigkeit	Prozent	Gültige Prozente	Kumulierte Prozente
Gültig	Agree strongly	2145	11,4	25,2	25,2
	Agree	2488	13,2	29,3	54,5
	Neither agree or disagree	1575	8,4	18,5	73,1
	Disagree	1695	9,0	19,9	93,0
	Strongly disagree	594	3,2	7,0	100,0
	Gesamt	8498	45,2	100,0	
Fehlend	Not asked	9649	51,3		
	No answer	42	,2		
	Don´t know	604	3,2		
	Gesamt	10295	54,8		
Gesamt		18793	100,0		

Religious leaders should not influence government

		Häufigkeit	Prozent	Gültige Prozente	Kumulierte Prozente
Gültig	Agree strongly	2046	10,9	30,9	30,9
	Agree	2763	14,7	41,8	72,7
	Neither agree or disagree	836	4,4	12,6	85,4
	Disagree	735	3,9	11,1	96,5
	Strongly disagree	230	1,2	3,5	100,0
	Gesamt	6610	35,2	100,0	
Fehlend	Not asked	11519	61,3		
	No answer	18	,1		
	Don´t know	646	3,4		
	Gesamt	12183	64,8		
Gesamt		18793	100,0		

Nurse refusing legal abortion on religious grounds

		Häufigkeit	Prozent	Gültige Prozente	Kumulierte Prozente
Gültig	Agree strongly	15	,1	34,4	34,4
	Agree	18	,1	39,6	74,0
	Neither agree or disagree	4	,0	8,6	82,6
	Disagree	5	,0	11,9	94,5
	Strongly disagree	2	,0	5,5	100,0
	Gesamt	44	,2	100,0	
Fehlend	Not asked	18746	99,7		
	Don´t know	3	,0		
	Gesamt	18749	99,8		
Gesamt		18793	100,0		

Time for prayer and meditation in all schools

		Häufigkeit	Prozent	Gültige Prozente	Kumulierte Prozente
Gültig	Agree strongly	268	1,4	25,8	25,8
	Agree	392	2,1	37,8	63,6
	Neither agree or disagree	153	,8	14,8	78,3
	Disagree	160	,9	15,4	93,7
	Strongly disagree	65	,3	6,3	100,0
	Gesamt	1038	5,5	100,0	
Fehlend	Not asked	17679	94,1		
	No answer	15	,1		
	Don´t know	62	,3		
	Gesamt	17756	94,5		
Gesamt		18793	100,0		

Government protects freedom

		Häufigkeit	Prozent	Gültige Prozente	Kumulierte Prozente
Gültig	Agree strongly	1736	9,2	36,7	36,7
	Agree	2037	10,8	43,1	79,8
	Neither agree or disagree	365	1,9	7,7	87,5
	Disagree	449	2,4	9,5	97,0
	Strongly disagree	141	,7	3,0	100,0
	Gesamt	4728	25,2	100,0	
Fehlend	Not asked	13739	73,1		
	Don´t know	327	1,7		
	Gesamt	14066	74,8		
Gesamt		18793	100,0		

Government protects religion

		Häufigkeit	Prozent	Gültige Prozente	Kumulierte Prozente
Gültig	Agree strongly	2237	11,9	47,1	47,1
	Agree	1900	10,1	40,0	87,0
	Neither agree or disagree	237	1,3	5,0	92,0
	Disagree	277	1,5	5,8	97,9
	Strongly disagree	102	,5	2,1	100,0
	Gesamt	4752	25,3	100,0	
Fehlend	Not asked	13739	73,1		
	Don´t know	302	1,6		
	Gesamt	14041	74,7		
Gesamt		18793	100,0		

Laws: people's wishes

		Häufigkeit	Prozent	Gültige Prozente	Kumulierte Prozente
Gültig	Agree strongly	2367	12,6	44,0	44,0
	Agree	1711	9,1	31,8	75,8
	Neither agree or disagree	654	3,5	12,2	87,9
	Disagree	353	1,9	6,6	94,5
	Strongly disagree	298	1,6	5,5	100,0
	Gesamt	5383	28,6	100,0	
Fehlend	Not asked	13158	70,0		
	No answer	10	,1		
	Don't know	243	1,3		
	Gesamt	13410	71,4		
Gesamt		18793	100,0		

Only laws of the Shari´a

		Häufigkeit	Prozent	Gültige Prozente	Kumulierte Prozente
Gültig	Agree strongly	2194	11,7	41,8	41,8
	Agree	1380	7,3	26,3	68,1
	Neither agree or disagree	823	4,4	15,7	83,7
	Disagree	524	2,8	10,0	93,7
	Strongly disagree	331	1,8	6,3	100,0
	Gesamt	5252	27,9	100,0	
Fehlend	Not asked	13158	70,0		
	No answer	25	,1		
	Don't know	358	1,9		
	Gesamt	13541	72,1		
Gesamt		18793	100,0		

Prohibiting or allowing books that attack religion

		Häufigkeit	Prozent	Gültige Prozente	Kumulierte Prozente
Gültig	Definitely should be banned	578	3,1	56,9	56,9
	Probably should be banned	209	1,1	20,5	77,4
	Probably should be allowed	147	,8	14,5	91,9
	Definitely should be allowed	61	,3	6,0	97,9
	Can't choose	21	,1	2,1	100,0
	Gesamt	1017	5,4	100,0	
Fehlend	Not asked	17756	94,5		
	Don't know	21	,1		
	Gesamt	17777	94,6		
Gesamt		18793	100,0		

Church(es) influence on national politics

		Häufigkeit	Prozent	Gültige Prozente	Kumulierte Prozente
Gültig	Yes, absolutely	264	1,4	27,4	27,4
	Yes, think so	323	1,7	33,6	61,0
	No, I don't think they have	250	1,3	25,9	86,9
	No, absolutely not	126	,7	13,1	100,0
	Gesamt	963	5,1	100,0	
Fehlend	Not asked	17749	94,4		
	No answer	8	,0		
	Don't know	73	,4		
	Gesamt	17830	94,9		
Gesamt		18793	100,0		

GLOBAL MUSLIM SOCIAL DATA

Family savings during past year

		Häufigkeit	Prozent	Gültige Prozente	Kumulierte Prozente
Gültig	Save money	3183	16,9	20,5	20,5
	Just get by	8393	44,7	54,0	74,5
	Spent some savings and borrowed money	2118	11,3	13,6	88,2
	Spent savings and borrowed money	1838	9,8	11,8	100,0
	Gesamt	15532	82,6	100,0	
Fehlend	Missing; Unknown	214	1,1		
	Not asked	1952	10,4		
	No answer	469	2,5		
	Don't know	628	3,3		
	Gesamt	3262	17,4		
Gesamt		18793	100,0		

Social class (subjective)

		Häufigkeit	Prozent	Gültige Prozente	Kumulierte Prozente
Gültig	Upper class	375	2,0	2,3	2,3
	Upper middle class	3311	17,6	20,4	22,7
	Lower middle class	6371	33,9	39,2	61,8
	Working class	3895	20,7	23,9	85,8
	Lower class	2312	12,3	14,2	100,0
	Gesamt	16264	86,5	100,0	
Fehlend	Missing; Unknown	12	,1		
	Not asked	1858	9,9		
	No answer	87	,5		
	Don't know	573	3,0		
	Gesamt	2529	13,5		
Gesamt		18793	100,0		

Scale of incomes

		Häufigkeit	Prozent	Gültige Prozente	Kumulierte Prozente
Gültig	Lower step	1452	7,7	8,6	8,6
	second step	2354	12,5	13,9	22,5
	Third step	2863	15,2	16,9	39,4
	Fourth step	3004	16,0	17,8	57,2
	Fifth step	2626	14,0	15,5	72,7
	Sixth step	1792	9,5	10,6	83,3
	Seventh step	1329	7,1	7,9	91,2
	Eigth step	810	4,3	4,8	95,9
	Nineth step	448	2,4	2,6	98,6
	Tenth step	237	1,3	1,4	100,0
	11	0	,0	,0	100,0
	Gesamt	16916	90,0	100,0	
Fehlend	Missing; Unknown	19	,1		
	Not asked	28	,2		
	No answer	563	3,0		
	Don't know	1266	6,7		
	Gesamt	1877	10,0		
Gesamt		18793	100,0		

Income level

		Häufigkeit	Prozent	Gültige Prozente	Kumulierte Prozente
Gültig	Low	6109	32,5	37,2	37,2
	Medium	6456	34,4	39,3	76,5
	High	3870	20,6	23,5	100,0
	Gesamt	16435	87,5	100,0	
Fehlend	Not asked	2358	12,5		
Gesamt		18793	100,0		

Appendix III

IBN KHALDOUN REVISITED: A FACTOR ANALYTICAL MODEL OF CENTRAL WORLD VALUES SURVEY INDICATORS

		Initial	Extraction
mean left-right position	VAR00001	1	0.238
not satisfied with democracy	VAR00002	1	0.405
openly racist	VAR00003	1	0.501
openly anti-Semitic	VAR00004	1	0.256
belief in hell	VAR00005	1	0.681
only God-believing politicians	VAR00006	1	0.491
mean acceptability homosexuality	VAR00007	1	0.783
mean acceptance competition	VAR00008	1	0.228
secularization rate (never attending rel.	VAR00009	1	0.245
always respect parents	VAR00010	1	0.734
education for tolerance and respect important	VAR00011	1	0.43
never praying	VAR00012	1	0.309
thrift important in education	VAR00013	1	0.141
mean workaholic scale	VAR00014	1	0.11
jobs scarce men have rights	VAR00015	1	0.626
belong voluntary welfare elderly	VAR00016	1	0.41
unpaid social welfare work	VAR00017	1	0.323
just can't be too careful	VAR00018	1	0.385
mean satisfaction income	VAR00019	1	0.138
mean acceptance government benefits fraud	VAR00020	1	0.301
cheating taxes	VAR00021	1	0.516
taking bribes	VAR00022	1	0.409
unpaid work religious organizations	VAR00023	1	0.313
for less materialism	VAR00024	1	0.161
emphasis on authority good	VAR00025	1	0.213
income differences good	VAR00026	1	0.127
government sector	VAR00027	1	0.226
Confidence in the EU	VAR00028	1	0.157
rejecting foreign workers	VAR00029	1	0.497
rejecting homosexual neighbor	VAR00030	1	0.523
never occupy building/factory	VAR00031	1	0.122
Islamophobia	VAR00032	1	0.259

	Total	% of variance	cumulated %
1	7.653	23.915	23.915
2	3.603	11.26	35.175

		traditional versus secular attitudes	cheating versus active society
mean left-right position	VAR00001	0.335	-0.355
not satisfied with democracy	VAR00002	0.294	0.564
openly racist	VAR00003	0.651	-0.278
openly anti-Semitic	VAR00004	0.498	0.092
belief in hell	VAR00005	0.805	-0.179
only God-believing politicians	VAR00006	0.633	-0.301
mean acceptability homosexuality	VAR00007	-0.877	-0.114
mean acceptance competition	VAR00008	-0.385	0.282
secularization rate (never attending rel. Services)	VAR00009	-0.472	-0.147
always respect parents	VAR00010	0.849	0.115
education for tolerance and respect important	VAR00011	-0.557	-0.346
never praying	VAR00012	-0.53	0.17
thrift important in education	VAR00013	0.26	0.27
mean workaholic scale	VAR00014	0.327	-0.058
jobs scarce men have rights	VAR00015	0.787	-0.08
belong voluntary welfare elderly	VAR00016	-0.091	-0.634
unpaid social welfare work	VAR00017	0.194	-0.534
just can't be too careful	VAR00018	0.446	0.431
mean satisfaction income	VAR00019	-0.311	-0.203
mean acceptance government benefits fraud	VAR00020	0.111	0.537
cheating taxes	VAR00021	-0.281	0.661
taking bribes	VAR00022	-0.02	0.639
unpaid work religious organizations	VAR00023	0.365	-0.424
for less materialism	VAR00024	-0.399	-0.034
emphasis on authority good	VAR00025	0.416	-0.199
income differences good	VAR00026	0.329	-0.135
government sector	VAR00027	0.452	0.148
Confidence in the EU	VAR00028	0.375	0.129
rejecting foreign workers	VAR00029	0.685	-0.168
rejecting homosexual neighbor	VAR00030	0.635	0.347
never occupy building/factory	VAR00031	0.342	0.068
Islamophobia	VAR00032	0.382	0.336

Screeplot

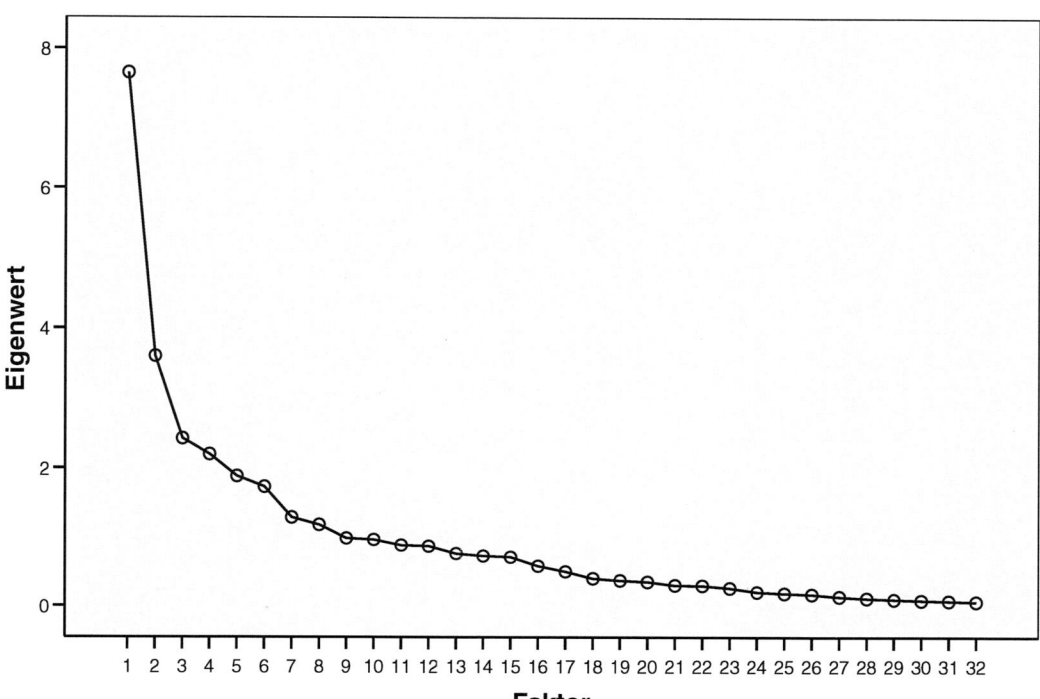

Factor scores

	traditional	intransparent, inactive	predicted value	bad performance low transparency and low activity even at high levels of development)	good performance
Viet Nam [2001]	0.451	-2.216	0.325	-2.541	2.541
United States [1999]	-0.666	-1.554	0.364	-1.918	1.918
China [2001]	0.458	-1.501	0.321	-1.822	1.822
Tanzania, United Republic Of [2001]	1.286	-2.247	-0.512	-1.735	1.735
Canada [2000]	-1.179	-1.157	-0.033	-1.124	1.124
Iran (Islamic Republic of) [2000]	0.542	-0.729	0.267	-0.996	0.996
Australia [1995]	-0.937	-0.765	0.187	-0.952	0.952
Egypt [2000]	1.559	-1.804	-0.936	-0.868	0.868
Bangladesh [2002]	2.184	-2.993	-2.183	-0.810	0.810
Ireland [1999]	-0.610	-0.415	0.392	-0.807	0.807
Dominican Republic [1996]	0.231	-0.373	0.430	-0.803	0.803
Colombia [1998]	0.133	-0.329	0.462	-0.791	0.791

Factor Scores (Continued)

	traditional	intransparent, inactive	predicted value	bad performance low transparency and low activity even at high levels of development)	good performance
Iceland [1999]	-1.643	-1.349	-0.616	-0.732	0.732
New Zealand [1998]	-1.123	-0.577	0.023	-0.600	0.600
Uruguay [1996]	-0.842	-0.307	0.257	-0.564	0.564
Japan [2000]	-0.563	-0.139	0.412	-0.551	0.551
Israel [2001]	-0.491	-0.091	0.440	-0.530	0.530
Argentina [1999]	-0.443	-0.055	0.455	-0.510	0.510
Iraq [2004]	0.960	-0.599	-0.103	-0.496	0.496
Italy [1999]	-0.558	-0.077	0.414	-0.491	0.491
Morocco [2001]	1.186	-0.852	-0.376	-0.477	0.477
Jordan [2001]	1.258	-0.942	-0.473	-0.470	0.470
Malta [1999]	0.740	-0.345	0.113	-0.459	0.459
Singapore [2002]	0.398	-0.093	0.355	-0.447	0.447
Uganda [2001]	0.856	-0.425	0.005	-0.430	0.430
Venezuela [2000]	0.576	-0.182	0.244	-0.425	0.425
Nigeria [2000]	0.970	-0.530	-0.114	-0.416	0.416
Norway [1996]	-1.405	-0.677	-0.290	-0.386	0.386
Finland [2000]	-1.355	-0.613	-0.229	-0.384	0.384
Saudi Arabia [2003]	0.945	-0.429	-0.087	-0.343	0.343
Zimbabwe [2001]	1.212	-0.665	-0.410	-0.255	0.255
Austria [1999]	-0.971	-0.078	0.160	-0.238	0.238
Switzerland [1996]	-1.316	-0.414	-0.183	-0.232	0.232
India [2001]	0.798	-0.163	0.061	-0.224	0.224
Great Britain [1999]	-1.206	-0.265	-0.061	-0.204	0.204
Chile [2000]	-0.423	0.399	0.461	-0.062	0.062
Peru [2001]	0.498	0.256	0.296	-0.040	0.040
Serbia [2001]	-0.218	0.516	0.497	0.019	-0.019
Bosnia and Herzegovina [2001]	0.316	0.421	0.395	0.025	-0.025
Mexico [2000]	0.387	0.403	0.361	0.042	-0.042
Sweden [1999]	-2.120	-1.371	-1.439	0.068	-0.068
El Salvador [1999]	0.868	0.063	-0.007	0.070	-0.070
Poland [1999]	0.259	0.491	0.420	0.071	-0.071
Czech Republic [1999]	-0.993	0.224	0.141	0.082	-0.082
Croatia [1999]	-0.075	0.583	0.497	0.086	-0.086
Bulgaria [1999]	0.141	0.552	0.460	0.093	-0.093
Portugal [1999]	-0.573	0.503	0.408	0.095	-0.095
Spain [2000]	-1.011	0.228	0.126	0.102	-0.102
Indonesia [2001]	1.320	-0.455	-0.561	0.106	-0.106
South Africa [2001]	0.743	0.218	0.110	0.108	-0.108
Latvia [1999]	-0.398	0.592	0.467	0.124	-0.124

	traditional	intransparent, inactive	predicted value	bad performance low transparency and low activity even at high levels of development)	good performance
Germany West [1999]	-1.380	-0.112	-0.260	0.148	-0.148
Pakistan [2001]	1.223	-0.164	-0.425	0.261	-0.261
Slovenia [1999]	-0.661	0.628	0.366	0.261	-0.261
Algeria [2002]	1.452	-0.491	-0.761	0.270	-0.270
Luxembourg [1999]	-1.233	0.223	-0.090	0.312	-0.312
Hungary [1999]	-0.152	0.826	0.500	0.327	-0.327
Kyrgyzstan [2003]	0.564	0.694	0.252	0.442	-0.442
Denmark [1999]	-2.153	-1.026	-1.504	0.478	-0.478
Slovakia [1999]	-0.065	1.004	0.497	0.507	-0.507
Republic of Korea [2001]	1.066	0.299	-0.224	0.523	-0.523
Albania [2002]	0.982	0.433	-0.128	0.560	-0.560
Macedonia, Republic of [2001]	0.549	0.828	0.263	0.565	-0.565
Belgium [1999]	-1.232	0.493	-0.089	0.582	-0.582
Romania [1999]	0.740	0.734	0.114	0.621	-0.621
Netherlands [1999]	-2.379	-1.336	-1.981	0.645	-0.645
Greece [1999]	-0.757	1.027	0.312	0.714	-0.714
Estonia [1999]	-0.626	1.187	0.384	0.803	-0.803
Georgia [1996]	0.905	0.831	-0.044	0.875	-0.875
Philippines [2001]	1.061	0.745	-0.218	0.964	-0.964
Azerbaijan [1997]	0.610	1.192	0.219	0.973	-0.973
Brazil [1997]	0.073	1.594	0.477	1.117	-1.117
Russian Federation [1999]	-0.257	1.743	0.493	1.250	-1.250
Ukraine [1999]	0.084	1.757	0.474	1.283	-1.283
Turkey [2001]	1.464	0.523	-0.780	1.303	-1.303
Lithuania [1999]	0.098	1.816	0.471	1.345	-1.345
France [1999]	-1.603	0.799	-0.558	1.357	-1.357
Belarus [2000]	-0.218	1.973	0.497	1.476	-1.476
Armenia [1997]	0.780	1.664	0.078	1.586	-1.586
Republic of Moldova [2002]	0.909	2.443	-0.048	2.492	-2.492

GLOBAL VALUES ON A COUNTRY-TO-COUNTRY BASIS

The following appendix Table summarizes the WVS country values for the following 30 central World Values Survey variables:

1. mean left-right position
2. not satisfied with democracy
3. openly racist
4. openly anti-Semitic
5. belief in hell
6. only God-believing politicians
7. mean acceptability homosexuality
8. mean acceptance competition
9. secularization rate (never attending rel. Services)
10. always respect parents
11. education for tolerance and respect important
12. never praying
13. thrift important in education
14. mean workaholic scale
15. jobs scarce men have rights
16. belong voluntary welfare elderly
17. unpaid social welfare work
18. just can't be too careful
19. mean satisfaction income
20. mean acceptance government benefits fraud
21. unpaid work religious organizations
22. for less materialism
23. emphasis on authority good
24. income differences good
25. government sector
26. Confidence in the EU
27. rejecting foreign workers
28. rejecting homosexual neighbor
29. never occupy building/factory
30. Islamophobia

The world value system according to the WVS – mean average positions or percentages (percentages per total adult resident population) (Part 1)

	mean left-right position	not satisfied with democracy	openly racist	openly anti-Semitic	belief in hell	only God-believing politicians	mean acceptability homosexuality	mean acceptance competition	secularization rate (never attending rel. services)	always respect parents
Albania [2002]	5.34	27.2	30.4	17	41	17.5	1.48	2.97	23.3	86.8
Algeria [2002]	6.22	20.8	28		98.8	55.9	1.26		27.2	92.9
Argentina [1999]	5.99	17.8	4.5	6.4	43.7	14.5	4.33	4.17	28.1	88
Armenia [1997]	5.39	30.3	19.2		36.4		2.03	4.07	13.5	92.8
Australia [1995]	5.34		4.8		41.1		4.6	3.2	44.1	74
Austria [1999]	5.42	2.9	6.7	8.3	18.3	4.8	5.36	3.19	17	65
Azerbaijan [1997]	5.54	4.6	12.2		59		1.41	3.51	16.8	91.5
Bangladesh [2002]	7.56	3.3	71.7	20.4	95.4	31.9	1.05	2.87	3.7	89.9
Belarus [2000]	5.68	27.8	16.5	14.8	35.1	7.5	2.91	3.67	27.8	70.9
Belgium [1999]	5.25	15.7	16.5	13	16.1	3.4	5.4	4.8	46.5	65.2
Bosnia and Herzegovina [2001]	5.09	19.1	13.2	28	60.3	5.5	1.98	3.05	13.8	91.2
Brazil [1997]	5.9		2.8		49.1		3.16	3.43	7.6	92.7
Bulgaria [1999]	5.85	22.7	28.1	18.1	30	9.5	2.6	3.5	27.4	81.9
Canada [2000]	5.55	6	3.4	3.8	50.3	6.8	5.44	3.52	29.1	77.6
Chile [2000]	5.23	11.5	9	8.8	65.4	14.8	3.98	4.76	22.4	87.3
China [2001]		0.9	14.6				1.14	2.72	89.6	94.5
Colombia [1998]	6.63		2		40.4		2.55		7	91
Croatia [1999]	5.27	24.6	19.5	18.2	57.1	9.2	2.41	2.91	10.4	71.5
Czech Republic [1999]	5.96	13	9.8	4.4	13.1	2.5	5.47	3.25	57.5	73.8
Denmark [1999]	5.51	3	7.4	2.5	9.5	1.3	6.59	4.02	42.7	35.9
Dominican Republic [1996]	6.63		18.5		67.7		3.26	3.33	13.7	85.7
Egypt [2000]		0.1	65.8	16.5	100	70.1	1.01		25.1	95.2
El Salvador [1999]	6.3				76.4		2.03	3.75	12.1	93.6
Estonia [1999]	5.93	12.3	15.2	11.2	16.2	3.8	2.98	4.39	37.7	71.9
Finland [2000]	5.77	4.3	12.4	8.6	31.3	3.7	4.94	4.28	26.2	63.2
France [1999]	4.86	11.4	8.9	5.9	19.6	4	5.27	4.73	60.4	74.7
Georgia [1996]	5.93	22.5	9.5		59.3		1.56	3.18	13.7	91.3
Germany West [1999]	5.43	4.8	4.3	4.5	22.5	3.8	5.83	3.81	22.4	49.4

The world value system according to the WVS (Part 1 - Continued)

	mean left-right position	not satisfied with democracy	openly racist	openly anti-Semitic	belief in hell	only God-believing politicians	mean acceptability homosexuality	mean acceptance competition	secularization rate (never attending rel. services)	always respect parents
Great Britain [1999]	5.08	11.3	8.6	6.2	35.3	3.4	4.89	4.01	55.8	65.1
Greece [1999]	5.13	9	14.4	18.7	40.9	17.9	4.95	4.34	4.7	69.1
Hungary [1999]	5.1	11.9			20.2	5.9	1.45	3.75	42.7	82.7
Iceland [1999]	5.78	4.5	3.1	4.1	17.5	2.6	7.19	2.7	32.3	60.7
India [2001]	5.66	7.9	41.8		68.5	18.5	3.08	3.21	3.1	88.8
Indonesia [2001]	6.62	12.1	34.7		99.9	60.4	1.13		0.8	90.2
Iran (Islamic Republic of) [2000]	4.82	9.7	24.2		98.2		1.25		4.1	89.1
Iraq [2004]				83.4	99.3	70.7			44.9	
Ireland [1999]	5.64	6.6	12.4	11.2	53.5	4.2	4.27	3.84	9.4	71.9
Israel [2001]	5.09						4.89			
Italy [1999]	5.36	11.4	15.6	12.9	49	4.6	4.83	4.16	13.9	79.4
Japan [2000]	5.7	6.3			30.1	2.3	4.36	4.17	8.6	71.6
Jordan [2001]	5.91	7.9	20		99.3	69.5	1.05		41.9	93.9
Kyrgyzstan [2003]	6.2	16.8	18.4	20.4	69.8	10.6	1.77	3.59	31.2	93.9
Latvia [1999]	5.83	10.3	4.8	5.2	28.4	5.8	1.9	3.43	34.6	77.1
Lithuania [1999]	5.41	22	9.8	23	68.2	7.9	1.88	3.99	16	82.7
Luxembourg [1999]	5.37	2.2	6.3	8.3	21.6	5.5	5.9	4.45	32.7	58.8
Macedonia, Republic of [2001]	5.21	38	19	20	46.5	19	1.93	2.85	7	91
Malta [1999]	5.8	3.8	18.6	20.8	80.6	10.9	2.58	3.2	4.2	91.1
Mexico [2000]	6.65	20.7	15.2		74.6	16.7	3.58	3.92	6.1	90.2
Morocco [2001]	5.72	16.1	13.7			76.3		2.23	35.3	98.2
Netherlands [1999]	5.09	2	5	1.6	13.8	0.6	7.82	4.68	48.3	31.9
New Zealand [1998]	5.79		3		34.8		4.74	3.49	44.4	63.6
Nigeria [2000]	5.51	9.2	30.4		93.6	57.4	1.5		0.6	94.3
Norway [1996]	5.57		8.2		19.7		5.71	3.54	41.8	52
Pakistan [2001]	5.94	40.5	6.5		100	82.4	1.05			94.4
Peru [2001]	5.69	10.5	11.2		65.2		2.62	3.4	4.9	90.7
Philippines [2001]	6.45	9.9	21.3		92.5	26.9	3.88	4.03	0.9	93.8
Poland [1999]	5.35	13.2	17.2	25.1	65.6	7.1	2.9	3.99	5.3	86.5

	mean left-right position	not satisfied with democracy	openly racist	openly anti-Semitic	belief in hell	only God-believing politicians	mean acceptability homosexuality	mean acceptance competition	secularization rate (never attending rel. services)	always respect parents
Portugal [1999]	5.27	3.2	7.6	10.8	37.8	2.8	3.19	4.45	15.3	82.6
Republic of Korea [2001]	5.35	8.4	34.7	40.9		2.9	2.77	4.1	16	92.2
Republic of Moldova [2002]	5.58	32	11	25	64.7	12.9	2.32	3.98	6.8	90.4
Romania [1999]	5.83	26.9	24.2	23.2	71.4	25.2	1.91	2.74	7.5	83.6
Russian Federation [1999]	4.92	50	8.1	11.4	35.7	7.1	2.2	4.09	50.1	84.2
Saudi Arabia [2003]			37.7		99.5		1.38		15.4	92.2
Serbia [2001]	5.52	14.2	6.1		18	9.6	1.96	3.39	13.8	87
Singapore [2002]			4.7		79.1		2.57	3.29	12.5	93.3
Slovakia [1999]	5.14	23.7	17	9.9	46.1	9	4.91	3.59	23.1	73.6
Slovenia [1999]	4.99	10.6	12	16.8	20.3	2.5	4.62	3.24	30.1	78.2
South Africa [2001]	5.68	9.9	23.6	24.4	60.5	24.5	3.16	3.59	10.3	90.8
Spain [2000]	4.69	5	11.5	34.2	40.1	1.9	6.17	4.29	33.1	87.4
Sweden [1999]	5.34	5.7	2.5	2.1	9.5	1.7	7.65	3.46	45.6	43.9
Switzerland [1996]	5.31		8.7		20.5		6.45	3.18	33.1	66.3
Tanzania, United Republic Of [2001]	6.75	7.1	16.7		95.6	54.7	1.15	3.05	2.3	90.7
Turkey [2001]	5.91	50.6	33.9	61.9	92.7	29.7	1.55	3.85	32.3	83.5
Uganda [2001]	5.55	5	18.2	22.2	76.5	26	1.25	2.56	1	89.9
Ukraine [1999]	5.48	35.8	10.5	10.4	38.1	13.4	2.35	4.05	30.4	85.7
United States [1999]	5.8	6.9	8	9.1	74.6	17.8	4.75	3.4	14.8	77.2
Uruguay [1996]	5.67		6.8	10.4	25.2		3.95	4.73	54.4	77.9
Venezuela [2000]	6.32	11.5	15.5			36.3	2.44	3.84	14.2	94
Viet Nam [2001]	9.05	0.1	32.2		17.1	5.2	1.65	3.79	49.4	99.3
Zimbabwe [2001]	3.66	25.4	19.8	19.3	79.4	15.7	1.1	2.47	11.3	96.2

The world value system according to the WVS (Part 2)

	Education for tolerance and respect important	never praying	thrift important in education	mean workaholic scale	jobs scarce men have rights	belong voluntary welfare elderly	unpaid social welfare work	just can't be too careful	mean satisfaction income	mean acceptance government benefits fraud
Albania [2002]	80	10.8	54.9	4.3	46.7	13.6	10.8	75.6	4.76	1.92
Algeria [2002]	54		17.9	4.57	67.5	10.9	18.9	88.8	5.92	3.02
Argentina [1999]	70.4	15.7	14.9	4.24	25.7	4.7	2.7	84.6	5.51	2.59
Armenia [1997]	48.4		38.2	3.42	59.9			75.3	3.63	3.24
Australia [1995]	80.7		18.9	3.07	25.5			60.1	6.38	1.73
Austria [1999]	71.4	20.2	47.6		26.7	6.6	2.3	66.1		2.17
Azerbaijan [1997]	59.1		59.3	3.21	63.6			79.5	4.56	2.42
Bangladesh [2002]	70.9	0.1	57.3	4.43	68.2	17.2	19.4	76.5	5.57	1.35
Belarus [2000]	72.2	30	46.2		24.8	1.3	2.5	58.1		3.48
Belgium [1999]	83	39.8	43.3		25.1	12.3	5.9	69.3		2.39
Bosnia and Herzegovina [2001]	71.7	15.3	37.2	3.86	26.5	1.5	1.1	84.2	4.87	1.67
Brazil [1997]	59.4		38.6	3.91	35.6			97.2	5.48	3.2
Bulgaria [1999]	59.3	47.2	39.1		38.9	1.3	1.5	73.1		1.86
Canada [2000]	80.6	18.9	27.1	3.3	14.6	13.2	9.6	61.2	6.92	1.87
Chile [2000]	76	9.3	34.4	3.65	25.2	6.7	5.9	77.2	5.66	3.33
China [2001]	72.6		57.2	4.17	45.1	2.9	56	45.5	5.65	2.13
Colombia [1998]	69.4		20.3	4.26	29.2			88.8	8	2.13
Croatia [1999]		19			29	2.1	1.1	81.6		1.58
Czech Republic [1999]	63	62.2	31.7		18.4	6.5	3.4	76.1		1.87
Denmark [1999]	87.3	51.8	9.6		6.2	6.5	4	33.5		1.38
Dominican Republic [1996]	67.9		11.3	3.94	15.1			73.6	5.74	2.19
Egypt [2000]	64.6		8	3.64	89.6			62.1	5.26	1.82
El Salvador [1999]	58.8		29.8	4.37	27.2			85.4	6.28	2.69
Estonia [1999]	71.3	56.7	44.6		13.5	3.3	2.6	77.2		3.19
Finland [2000]	82.7	20.7	22.6		9.9	10.4	7.2	42		2.3
France [1999]	85.2	55	37.7		21.8	5.6	4.1	77.8		3.39
Georgia [1996]	54.1		31.9	3.48	64.5			81.3	3.07	2.91

	Education for tolerance and respect important	never praying	thrift important in education	mean workaholic scale	jobs scarce men have rights	belong voluntary welfare elderly	unpaid social welfare work	just can't be too careful	mean satisfaction income	mean acceptance government benefits fraud
Germany West [1999]	73.6	29.2	35.2		27.2	4.2	2	67.1		1.84
Great Britain [1999]	83.5	48.3	33		22.9	6.7	13.4	70.3		1.99
Greece [1999]	52.5	14.6	29.9		19.9	6.5	7.6	76.3		4.04
Hungary [1999]	65.6	36.6	41.5		24.7	1.9	2.5	78.2		1.7
Iceland [1999]	84.3	18.8	20.5		3.5	17.4	8.7	58.9		1.75
India [2001]	63.2	4.3	61.9	3.7	57.2	7.1	6.3	59	4.96	2.34
Indonesia [2001]	62.6		52	3.52	52.2			48.4	6.46	3.88
Iran (Islamic Republic of) [2000]	59	2.7	29.6	4.01	72.8			34.7	5.75	2.7
Iraq [2004]	77.8	5.3	28.2		77.6			52.4	5.43	
Ireland [1999]	75	8.9	22.6		15.4	5.8	3.8	64.2		1.89
Israel [2001]	81.9		19.8	2.55		6.4	5.1	76.5		
Italy [1999]	75	12.9	34.7		27			67.4		1.88
Japan [2000]	71.2	16.3	48.1	2.98	31.8	9.4	5.4	56.9	6.17	2.09
Jordan [2001]	67.3		19.4	1.62	80.4			72.3	5.09	1.7
Kyrgyzstan [2003]	65.5	14.2	43	3.95	49.1	8.1	3.7	83.3	5.68	2.77
Latvia [1999]	69.5	34.8	45.1		19.8	1.5	1.8	82.9		2.12
Lithuania [1999]	57.6	33.8	42.3		24.4	0.7	0.6	75.1		2.55
Luxembourg [1999]	78.1	33.8	48.5		26.2	14.2	6.9	74		2.86
Macedonia, Republic of [2001]	75.3	16.3	39.5	4.08	42.7	7.2	4.8	86.5	4.44	3
Malta [1999]	61	2.9	53.5		47.4	2.4	4.9	79.3		1.37
Mexico [2000]	70.6	5.7	39.3	4	33.7	7.2	5.3	78.7	6.54	3.75
Morocco [2001]	74.3	13	35.6	3.92	87.2	1.3		76.1	5.08	1.68
Netherlands [1999]	91.1	49.3	21.6		12.4	21.2	9.3	40.2		1.52
New Zealand [1998]	77.9		25.1	2.98	13.1			50.9	6.46	1.87
Nigeria [2000]	59.1		10.3	4.13	60.3			74.4	6.28	1.97
Norway [1996]	65.9		13.2	3.16	14.4			34.7	6.74	1.64
Pakistan [2001]	53		55.4		67.4			69.2	3.52	1.53
Peru [2001]	72.6	3.2	23.5	4.13	15.1	4.1	3.3	89.3	5.11	3.49

The world value system according to the WVS (Part 2 - Continued)

	Education for tolerance and respect important	never praying	thrift important in education	mean workaholic scale	jobs scarce men have rights	belong voluntary welfare elderly	unpaid social welfare work	just can't be too careful	mean satisfaction income	mean acceptance government benefits fraud
Philippines [2001]	60.1	0.1	45.3	4.24	69	8	10	91.6	5.83	3.57
Poland [1999]	80.1	4.4	38.3		34.9	3	2.2	81.1		2.36
Portugal [1999]	65.4	17.1	35.7		29.5	2	0.8	90		2.03
Republic of Korea [2001]	64.7	3.3	67.5	3.49	38.7	9.4	9.1	72.7	5.79	
Republic of Moldova [2002]	77.9	5.2	42.1	3.6	45	3.7	7.4	85.3	4.07	3.85
Romania [1999]	58.3	6.5	30.7		37.9	1.7	1	89.9		1.82
Russian Federation [1999]	67.1	55.6	51.3		36.4	1.5	0.5	76.3		2.3
Saudi Arabia [2003]	56.4		31.5	4.42	69.7	3.3	1.3	47	7.23	2.65
Serbia [2001]	64.5	26.5	30.8	3.64	31.3	7.1	11.6	81.2	3.86	2.12
Singapore [2002]	69.8	12.2	43.8	3.22	30	6.6	6.1	83.1	6.6	2.66
Slovakia [1999]	57	21.5	38.6		24.1	5.4	4.9	84.3		2.91
Slovenia [1999]	70.1		35.4	3.96	17.8	8.5	6.7	78.3	4.65	2.82
South Africa [2001]	74.1	4.3	37.1	2.78	31.8	2.7	2	88.2	6.27	2.89
Spain [2000]	77	30.5	31.4		16.6	20.8	9.1	66		2.11
Sweden [1999]	92.5		30.5	2.98	2.3			33.7	7.47	2.08
Switzerland [1996]	79.3		35	4.45	27.4	26.9	24.6	59	3.48	2.07
Tanzania, United Republic Of [2001]	83.6	0.8	53.5		27.2	0.2	0.3	91.9		1.62
Turkey [2001]	57.5	3.7	30.1	4.25	61.8	12.2	11.4	93.2	4.83	1.24
Uganda [2001]	56.8	0.6	10.7	3.1	40.7	1.9	0.6	92.4	6.53	1.98
Ukraine [1999]	65.5	38.7	50.4	3.28	30.8	16.8	14	72.8	6.7	2.83
United States [1999]	79.5	6.4	22.8	4.05	9.9			64.2	6.19	2.18
Uruguay [1996]	69.7		26.6		27.9	6.6		77.9	5.95	1.75
Venezuela [2000]	79.6	2.2	39	4	31.4	26.5	28.7	84.1	3.2	2.98
Viet Nam [2001]	67.9	48.4	48.1	4.67	48.5	8.5	6.6	58.9		2.13
Zimbabwe [2001]	78.2	6.4	20.5		40.3			88.1		1.67

The world value system according to the WVS (Part 3)

	unpaid work religious organizations	for less materialism	emphasis on authority good	income differences good	government sector	Confidence in the EU	Rejecting foreign workers	rejecting homosexual neighbor	never occupy building/factory	Islamophobia
Albania [2002]	14.6	36.7	34.2	5.96	3.85	41.3	16.5	82.6	97.9	30.4
Algeria [2002]	13.5	39.9	62.6	8.09	5.06	5	23.5	80.7	94.6	
Argentina [1999]	9.2	64.2	72.1	4.92	5.68		5.9	22.1	89.1	6.2
Armenia [1997]		58.7	62.7	6.4	6.17	13.2	21.6	83.3	86.4	
Australia [1995]		68.7	72.9	5.58	3.8		4.6	24.7	80.6	
Austria [1999]	7	50	39	4.63	3.41	6.1	12.2	25.4	89.7	15.4
Azerbaijan [1997]		64	60.6	5.9	5.57	4.4	19.9	90.7	96.7	
Bangladesh [2002]	40.5	36.4	91.5	7.56	5.31		67.1	4.9	92.6	
Belarus [2000]	4.1	47.5	72.4	5.27	5.24	6.5	17.1	63.3	95.3	26.6
Belgium [1999]	5.5	67	63.1	5.49		7.3	18.2	17.4	68.5	22
Bosnia and Herzegovina [2001]	4.5	53.9	26.3	6.1	4.63	14	24.8	64.2	87.5	12.8
Brazil [1997]		64.5	83	5.71	5.21		3.6	26.3	81.1	
Bulgaria [1999]	1.8	57.7	68.8	6.12		11	24.6	53.9	82.8	21.2
Canada [2000]	18.4	65.4	66.4	5.44	3.88		4.2	16.9	78.9	6.5
Chile [2000]	16.5	64.5	56	4	5.92		10.7	32.8	86.1	7.4
China [2001]	4.3	46.9	63.7	6.26	6.79	4.3	16	73.2		
Colombia [1998]		59.4	88.5	6.2	6.56			14.9	87.5	
Croatia [1999]	5.3	77.2	55.7	4.08	4.64	6.6	21.7	52.8	80.8	26.5
Czech Republic [1999]	2.8	48.7	52.3	5.48	4.71	7.6	19.4	19.7	88.8	15.2
Denmark [1999]	3.3	70	38.2			2.1	10.6	8	85.1	16.3
Dominican Republic [1996]		51.7	55.9	7.7	6.34		17.5	48.7	67.8	
Egypt [2000]		55.6	86.2	8.23	6.68		42.3	0.4	95.1	
El Salvador [1999]		42.5	85.8	6.83	6.11			78.3	94.4	
Estonia [1999]	2.8	54.1	43.9	6.88	5.74	3.5	20.9	46.2	94.9	22.2
Finland [2000]	7.8	66.1	39.4	4.56	4.22	1.7	13	21.3	84.9	19.3
France [1999]	3.1	70.9	68.7	4.83	4.03	6.5	12	15.6	55.7	16
Georgia [1996]		70.3	75.3	7.6	5.67	12.5	10.9	77	97.2	
Germany West [1999]	6.4	53.7	42.6		3.82	5.1	7.4	13.2	85.6	10.2
Great Britain [1999]	6.3	65.7	70.7	5.61	4.72	4.7	15.5	24.3	81.7	13.6
Greece [1999]	6.1	78.1	17.1			2.9	13.7	26.8	46	20.9
Hungary [1999]	5.4	45.1	68.7			9			95.1	
Iceland [1999]	4.6	61.5	46.9	5.66	3.67	3.4	3	7.9	87.1	11.6
India [2001]	14.3	42.7	43.4	4.18	6.04		38.2	28.8	82.9	
Indonesia [2001]		27	37.4	7.18	5.86		40.2	54.6	86.4	
Iran (Islamic Republic of) [2000]		55.8	71.4	5.66	5.66		9.6	0.9		
Iraq [2004]				5.42	6.93					
Ireland [1999]	7.6	69.5	77.4	6.07	4.23	12.3	12.1	27.4	81	13.6
Israel [2001]		74.8	58.7	3.77					92.3	
Italy [1999]	6.7	70.6	51.3	6.02	4.11	15.7	16.5	28.7	74.4	17.2
Japan [2000]	3.2	39	4.2	5.72	4.49				92.2	
Jordan [2001]		59.1	90.4	7.43	5.79		39.9	98.4	99.5	
Kyrgyzstan 2003]	1.3	60.7	50.7	5.44	5.75	15.5	19.8	66	93.5	14.6
Latvia [1999]	3.8	31.8	48.9			4.3	9.8	45.5	95.7	14.5

The world value system according to the WVS (Part 3 – Continued))

	unpaid work religious organizations	for less materialism	emphasis on authority	income differences	government sector	Confidence in the EU	Rejecting foreign workers	rejecting homosexual neighbor	never occupy building/facto ry	Islamophobia
Lithuania [1999]	4.2	45.6	44	4.81	4.94	1.2	23.6	67.5	86.5	33.1
Luxembourg [1999]	6.1	70.7	52.8	6.75		12.6	8.4	18.6	80	14.2
Macedonia, Republic of [2001]	8.5	51.5	48.5	5.33	3.77	16.1	18.6	53.5	83.3	26.2
Malta [1999]	12.7	81.4	92.2			19.3	15.3	39.6	85.5	27.8
Mexico [2000]	19.6	58.3	75.9	5.02	5.57		14.3	44.6	90.8	17
Morocco [2001]		65.3	90.4	7.44	5.15	9.6	19.1	93	95.8	
Netherlands [1999]	11.4	60	66.6	6.16	4.38	2.5	5	6.2	71.7	11.9
New Zealand [1998]		56.3	52.7	5.34	4.35		5.4	22.3	79.3	
Nigeria [2000]		62.8	82.8	6.25			28	73.6	58.2	
Norway [1996]		60.9	31.5	5.27	4.45	3.4	9.8	14.3	87.9	19.3
Pakistan [2001]		70	62.4	3.83	5.01		29.1		99.3	
Peru [2001]	20.3	49.2	80.4	7.52	6.45		10.9	49.2	86	13.5
Philippines [2001]	29.6	49.1	69.7	6.46	6.42		15.3	23.6	93	26.4
Poland [1999]	3.7	60.1	54.5	6.09	5.78	9.3	23.5	55.2	81.4	23.8
Portugal [1999]	2.6	57.2	77.7		4.72	7.4	2.5	25.2	76.8	7.9
Republic of Korea [2001]	26.9	52.8	19.4	6.55	4.83			46.8	82.4	57.3
Republic of Moldova [2002]	15.7	46	48.1	6.69	6.53	17.1	18.8	77.4	86.7	44.4
Romania [1999]	3.6	65.5	84.5	3.69	4.38	8.5	21.1	65.2	94	31.4
Russian Federation [1999]	0.5	45.4	56.2	7.15	6.11	3	11.1	57.9	90.9	13.7
Saudi Arabia [2003]		55.7	73	6.72	5.51		33.1			
Serbia [2001]	1.2	51.1	55	5.78	4.62	3.6	7.8	49.1	81.5	13.6
Singapore [2002]	12	37.9	52.3	6.88	4.75		25.9	45.7		
Slovakia [1999]	13.1	61.3	68.1			9.6	22.9	44	84.5	24.5
Slovenia [1999]	4.5	62.8	43.3	4.05		7.4	16	44.3	74.5	22.6
South Africa [2001]	37.4	35.3	72.7	5.4	5.51		30.6	46.2	74.7	23.9
Spain [2000]	4.4	72.3	61.4	5.07	5.53	8	10.8	14.8	84.8	15.4
Sweden [1999]	23.4	67.3	22.2			3.1	2.8	6.1	78.4	9
Switzerland [1996]		68.3	30.6	4.82	3.28	6.3	10	18.5	85.8	18.5
Tanzania, United Republic Of [2001]	61.9	60.4	82.2	4.97	5.14		17.5	74.1	93.9	12.6
Turkey [2001]	0.7	72.4	65.1	3.55	5.17	12	45.4	90	95.2	
Uganda [2001]	38.7	24.7	73.3	7.22	3.7		13	76.1	45.1	14.2
Ukraine [1999]	2.3	44.3	63.8	7.35	5.6	8.6	14.9	65.7	93.9	24
United States [1999]	38	65.2	70.3	5.72	3.52		10.1	23.3	70.9	10.7
Uruguay [1996]		74.9	58.1	5.09	5.46		7.1	31.9	75.9	
Venezuela [2000]		48.4	91.2	5.58	5.64		17.9	57.4	90	
Viet Nam [2001]	9.6	57.9	80.1	6.33	5.39		32.9	38.6	76.7	27
Zimbabwe [2001]	54	27.9	89.7	6.94	4.3		20.5	66.5	95.7	17.7

Appendix IV

THE ACTIVE SOCIETY INDEX

The "active society index" is a non-parametric standard UNDP-type index of the World Values Survey country results (wave 3+4) for the voluntary work variables:

1. social welfare service for elderly, handicapped or deprived people
2. religious or church organization
3. education, arts, music or cultural activities
4. labor unions
5. political parties or groups
6. local political action groups
7. human rights
8. environment, conservation, animal rights
9. professional associations
10. youth work
11. sports or recreation
12. women's group
13. peace movement
14. organization concerned with health

World Values Survey University of Michigan – volunteer work per total population, countries of the world system (Part 1)

BASE n=110193	Social welfare service for elderly, handicapped or deprived people	religious or church organization	education, arts, music or cultural activities	labor unions	political parties or groups	local political action groups	human rights
Tanzania, United Republic Of [2001]	24.6	61.9	25.5	20.7	21.3	23.3	19.6
Bangladesh [2002]	19.4	40.5	28.5	13.9	22.9	24.3	10.7
Viet Nam [2001]	28.7	9.6	15.8	9.8	23.8	25.8	1.3
China [2001]	56	4.3	16.4	7.2	9.9	14.1	4.6
United States [1999]	14	38	19.8	3.2	7	7.2	2.9
Uganda [2001]	11.4	38.7	16.3	4	6.1	6.1	3
Algeria [2002]	18.9	13.5	11.9		5.8	7	5.5
Philippines [2001]	10	29.6	4	3.3	4	6.5	5.3
Albania [2002]	10.8	14.6	9.8	4.4	11.4	7.7	2.4
South Africa [2001]	6.7	37.4	7.1	4.9	6.2	4.9	1.3
Sweden [1999]	9.1	23.4	11.3	10.3	4.4	5.5	4.5
Canada [2000]	9.6	18.4	11.2	3.4	2.7	5.1	2.5
India [2001]	6.3	14.3	11.6	6.6	8.2	5.3	2.2
Zimbabwe [2001]	6.6	54	4.1	1.1	4.7	1.9	0.5
Republic of Korea [2001]	9.1	26.9	8.5	2.4	2.2	6.9	1.3
Greece [1999]	7.6	6.1	13.8	4.5	5.2	6.7	5.7
Netherlands [1999]	9.3	11.4	15.9	2.1	2.7	3.9	4.2
Great Britain [1999]	13.4	6.3	2.8	2.3	1.4	1.7	4.3
Slovakia [1999]	6.1	13.1	5.5	5.8	4.8	6.7	0.1
Republic of Moldova [2002]	7.4	15.7	9	7.9	5	3	2.2
TOTAL world	7	12.7	7.2	3.7	4.1	4.2	2.1
Chile [2000]	5.9	16.5	7	2.4	1.8	3.7	1.6
Mexico [2000]	5.3	19.6	5.3	2.3	3.5	4.2	1.4

BASE n=110193	Social welfare service for elderly, handicapped or deprived people	religious or church organization	education, arts, music or cultural activities	labor unions	political parties or groups	local political action groups	human rights
Peru [2001]	3.3	20.3	9.5	2.7	3.3	4.2	1.6
Macedonia, Republic of [2001]	4.8	8.5	7.1	1.7	8.1	3.3	2
Belgium [1999]	5.9	5.5	9.2	2.2	2.6	2.4	4
Finland [2000]	7.2	7.8	4.8	4.1	2.7	1.6	3.1
Luxembourg [1999]	6.9	6.1	8.3	2.9	2.7	2.9	5.1
Singapore [2002]	11.6	12	6.4	1.1	0.3	2	0.6
Denmark [1999]	4	3.3	5.4	3.8	2.6	3	1.2
Ireland [1999]	3.8	7.6	4.3	1.5	1.7	3.7	1.7
Slovenia [1999]	4.9	4.5	6.7	3.3	1.3	5.8	0.4
Iceland [1999]	8.7	4.6	5.9	3.1	3.4	0.7	1.3
Malta [1999]	4.9	12.7	3.7	2	4.3	3.7	1.5
Czech Republic [1999]	3.4	2.8	5.8	2.9	2.1	2	0.4
Austria [1999]	2.3	7	6.7	2	3.2	1.1	0.8
Italy [1999]	5.1	6.7	6	2.2	2.3	1.8	1.9
France [1999]	4.1	3.1	4.8	1.4	0.7	1.5	0.8
Croatia [1999]	1.1	5.3	2.7	3.7	1.6	1	0.4
Argentina [1999]	2.7	9.2	3.8	0.7	3.1	2.7	0.3
Bosnia and Herzegovina [2001]	1.1	4.5	2.7	1.9	3.1	1.2	0.3
Germany West [1999]	2	6.4	2.7	0.3	0.9	0.4	0.2
Kyrgyzstan [2003]	3.7	1.3	2.8	3.4	1	2.3	1.1
Latvia [1999]	1.8	3.8	4.4	2.3	0.9	1.7	0.3
Estonia [1999]	2.6	2.8	5.5	0.5	1.4	1.8	0.2
Japan [2000]	5.4	3.2	3.9	0.6	1.2	0.4	0.3
Hungary [1999]	2.5	5.4	3	1.3	1.1	1.3	0.2
Belarus [2000]	2.5	4.1	2	5.3	0.8	0.9	0.7

World Values Survey University of Michigan (Part 1 - Continued)

BASE n=110193	Social welfare service for elderly, handicapped or deprived people	religious or church organization	education, arts, music or cultural activities	labor unions	political parties or groups	local political action groups	human rights
Spain [2000]	2	4.4	2.8	1.5	1.3	1.5	1.5
Bulgaria [1999]	1.5	1.8	2.4	3.1	2.8	0.8	0.2
Romania [1999]	1	3.6	1.7	5.8	1.8	0.6	0.4
Poland [1999]	2.2	3.7	1.8	2.2	0.5	1.3	0.1
Portugal [1999]	0.8	2.6	2.3	0.3	0.5	0.6	0.6
Ukraine [1999]	0.6	2.3	1.8	3.9	1.3	1	0.2
Lithuania [1999]	0.6	4.2	1.5	1.2	1.2	0.6	0.1
Serbia [2001]	1.3	1.2	0.8	1.9	1.2	0.3	0.2
Russian Federation [1999]	0.5	0.5	0.4	3.6	0.3	0.6	
Turkey [2001]	0.3	0.7	1.2	0.9	2.9	0.2	0.2

World Values Survey University of Michigan (Part 2)

BASE n=110193	Environment, conservation, animal rights	professional associations	youth work	sports or recreation	women's group	peace movement	organization concerned with health	other groups	Average volunteer engagement
Tanzania, United Republic Of [2001]	21.1	20.3	19.6	30.5	23.1	4.3	21.1		24.06
Bangladesh [2002]	19.4		13.7	25	13.4	26.9	21.8	2.1	20.18
Viet Nam [2001]	7.9	10.4	13.9	18.1	26.9	6.8	15.1		15.28
China [2001]	27.7	3.6	9.8	12.7	15	16	24	1.6	14.86
United States [1999]	8.5	10.8	21.8	18.7	8.2	2	11.1	15	12.55
Uganda [2001]	8	4.7	17.6	20.4	12.4	6	9.5		11.73
Algeria [2002]	6	8.9	9.9	14.7	5.6				9.79
Philippines [2001]	8.8	2.4	6.4	12.2	9	10.5	9.3		8.66
Albania [2002]	7	7.2	8.8	8.2	9.3	3.4	8.3		8.09
South Africa [2001]	1.5	1.9	6.8	15.3	7.7	3.7	5		7.89
Sweden [1999]	3.8	4.3	5.1	17.6	2.1	0.4	2.7	10.3	7.65
Canada [2000]	4.4	6.1	8.1	12.9	4.5	1	8.4	8.1	7.09
India [2001]	5.3	5.6	5.1	8.9	5.5	4	7.1	5.4	6.76
Zimbabwe [2001]	1.2	2.2	3.8	3.8	6.5	1.1	2.7		6.73
Republic of Korea [2001]	4.5	4.1	3.4	11.8	3.9	1.8			6.68
Greece [1999]	9.5	5.5	4.6	8.9	3	5.3	5.4	4.5	6.42
Netherlands [1999]	2.3	3.4	4.6	17.4	2.3	0.6	7	6.4	6.23
Great Britain [1999]	7.8	7.8	15.3	4	1.3	4.3	10		5.91
Slovakia [1999]	2	3	5.6	13.4	4.7	0.1	3.7	6.1	5.38
Republic of Moldova [2002]	4.2	3.8	3.7	4.1	2.6	2	3.8		5.31
TOTAL world	3.7	3.1	4.9	8.9	3.8	2.2	4.5	3.8	5.06
Chile [2000]	2	2.3	4.1	12	4.5	2.2	2.9		4.92

World Values Survey University of Michigan (Part 2 – Continued))

BASE n=110193	Environment, conservation, animal rights	professional associations	youth work	sports or recreation	women's group	peace movement	organization concerned with health	other groups	Average volunteer engagement
Mexico [2000]	3	1.5	3.7	7.1	3.3	3	5.2		4.89
Peru [2001]	2.2	3.2	4.8	8.2	4.9	0.4	3.8	0.1	4.83
Macedonia, Republic of [2001]	3.1	2.8	3.4	8.7	3.9	2.8	4.8		4.64
Belgium [1999]	3.5	2.7	4.6	7.9	2.9	1	4.6	7	4.40
Finland [2000]	2	2	4.5	12	2	0.9	4.2	5.6	4.30
Luxembourg [1999]	4.3	1.4	5.7	8.7	2.3	1.4	2.9	1.9	4.23
Singapore [2002]	1.2	0.8	7.7	6.1	0.5	0.7	4.2		3.94
Denmark [1999]	2.2	3.8	5.1	14.2	0.8	0.4	1	6.5	3.82
Ireland [1999]	0.9	3	4.5	13	2.7	0.7	2.8	4	3.73
Slovenia [1999]	2.9	2.7	3.5	8.4	1.3	0.6	2.1	5.9	3.62
Iceland [1999]	1.3	3	3.4	11.4	2.3	0.1	1.9	1.7	3.52
Malta [1999]	1.8	1.7	3.2	5.6	1.5	0.5	1.6	1.9	3.37
Czech Republic [1999]	3.2	2.4	5.7	10.5	1.1	0.2	3.1	4.4	3.33
Austria [1999]	2.1	1.5	2.1	8.7	2.4	0.1	2.5	4	3.10
Italy [1999]	1.8	3.2	2.9	6.2	0.4	0.9	2.9	1.6	3.06
France [1999]	0.9	1.3	1.5	8.7	0.1	0.3	1.5	6.1	2.45
Croatia [1999]	1.5	2.2	1.5	6.7	2.2	0.6	1.6	3.1	2.35
Argentina [1999]	1.4	1	2.1	2.6	0.7	0.3	2.1	2	2.31
Bosnia and Herzegovina [2001]	1.5	1.1	1.5	7.2	1.8	0.2	1.8		2.14
Germany West [1999]	1	0.6	1.8	7.2	1.6	0.1	1.4	2.3	1.93
Kyrgyzstan [2003]	1.2	1.2	1.8	2.3	2.1	0.9	1.7		1.91
Latvia [1999]	0.5	0.5	0.7	6.2	0.3	0.1	0.5	4.7	1.91

BASE n=110193	Environment, conservation, animal rights	professional associations	youth work	sports or recreation	women's group	peace movement	organization concerned with health	other groups	Average volunteer engagement
Estonia [1999]	1.1	1.5	1.9	3.4	1.4	0.4	0.7	2.9	1.87
Japan [2000]	1.2	1.3	1	3.3	1.2	0.7	1.5		1.80
Hungary [1999]	1.8	1.9	1.1	2.6	0.2	0.4	1.2	1.8	1.72
Belarus [2000]	2.2	0.6	0.9	1.2	0.5	0.6	1.7	1.2	1.68
Spain [2000]	1.2	0.6	0.7	2.8	0.7	0.4	1.5		1.64
Bulgaria [1999]	1.2	1.6	1.4	3.7	0.8	0.4	0.6	1.5	1.59
Romania [1999]	0.6	1	0.5	1.2	0.3		0.6	1.5	1.47
Poland [1999]	0.5	1.3	0.7	2.2	0.5		0.7	2.1	1.41
Portugal [1999]	0.4	0.6	0.9	4.3	0.1	0.1	1	2.5	1.17
Ukraine [1999]	0.3	0.6	0.9	0.8	0.3		0.6	1	1.11
Lithuania [1999]	0.4	0.2	1.1	2.2	0.2	0.1	0.5	2.1	1.08
Serbia [2001]	0.3	0.8	0.3	3.4	0.4		0.4		0.96
Russian Federation [1999]	0.4	0.3	0.3	1.3	0.3		0.3	0.7	0.73
Turkey [2001]	0.2	0.7	0.5	0.6	0.2	0.1	0.3	1.2	0.68

Relative Index numbers UNDP-Method (non-parametric index)

Country code (1)	social welfare service for elderly, handicapped or deprived people	religious or church organization	education, arts, music or cultural activities	labor unions	political parties or groups	local political action groups	human rights	environment, conservation, animal rights
Tanzania, United Republic Of [2001]	0.436	1.000	0.893	1.000	0.894	0.902	1.000	0.760
Bangladesh [2002]	0.343	0.651	1.000	0.667	0.962	0.941	0.544	0.698
Viet Nam [2001]	0.510	0.148	0.548	0.466	1.000	1.000	0.062	0.280
China [2001]	1.000	0.062	0.569	0.338	0.409	0.543	0.231	1.000
United States [1999]	0.246	0.611	0.690	0.142	0.285	0.273	0.144	0.302
Uganda [2001]	0.199	0.622	0.566	0.181	0.247	0.230	0.149	0.284
Algeria [2002]	0.334	0.212	0.409		0.234	0.266	0.277	0.211
Albania [2002]	0.189	0.230	0.335	0.201	0.472	0.293	0.118	0.247
Philippines [2001]	0.174	0.474	0.128	0.147	0.157	0.246	0.267	0.313
Sweden [1999]	0.158	0.373	0.388	0.490	0.174	0.207	0.226	0.131
India [2001]	0.108	0.225	0.399	0.309	0.336	0.199	0.108	0.185
Greece [1999]	0.131	0.091	0.477	0.206	0.209	0.254	0.287	0.338
South Africa [2001]	0.115	0.601	0.238	0.225	0.251	0.184	0.062	0.047
Canada [2000]	0.167	0.292	0.384	0.152	0.102	0.191	0.123	0.153
Great Britain [1999]	0.235	0.094	0.085	0.098	0.047	0.059	0.215	0.276
Netherlands [1999]	0.162	0.178	0.552	0.088	0.102	0.145	0.210	0.076
Republic of Korea [2001]	0.158	0.430	0.288	0.103	0.081	0.262	0.062	0.156
Slovakia [1999]	0.104	0.205	0.181	0.270	0.191	0.254	0.000	0.065
Republic of Moldova [2002]	0.127	0.248	0.306	0.373	0.200	0.109	0.108	0.145
Zimbabwe [2001]	0.113	0.871	0.132	0.039	0.187	0.066	0.021	0.036
Peru [2001]	0.054	0.322	0.324	0.118	0.128	0.156	0.077	0.073
Macedonia, Republic of [2001]	0.081	0.130	0.238	0.069	0.332	0.121	0.097	0.105
Chile [2000]	0.101	0.261	0.235	0.103	0.064	0.137	0.077	0.065
Luxembourg [1999]	0.118	0.091	0.281	0.127	0.102	0.105	0.256	0.149
Mexico [2000]	0.090	0.311	0.174	0.098	0.136	0.156	0.067	0.102
Belgium [1999]	0.101	0.081	0.313	0.093	0.098	0.086	0.200	0.120
Finland [2000]	0.124	0.119	0.157	0.186	0.102	0.055	0.154	0.065

Country code (1)	social welfare service for elderly, handicapped or deprived people	religious or church organization	education, arts, music or cultural activities	labor unions	political parties or groups	local political action groups	human rights	environment, conservation, animal rights
Denmark [1999]	0.066	0.046	0.178	0.172	0.098	0.109	0.056	0.073
Ireland [1999]	0.063	0.116	0.139	0.059	0.060	0.137	0.082	0.025
Iceland [1999]	0.151	0.067	0.196	0.137	0.132	0.020	0.062	0.040
Slovenia [1999]	0.083	0.065	0.224	0.147	0.043	0.219	0.015	0.098
Singapore [2002]	0.203	0.187	0.214	0.039	0.000	0.070	0.026	0.036
Czech Republic [1999]	0.056	0.037	0.192	0.127	0.077	0.070	0.015	0.109
Malta [1999]	0.083	0.199	0.117	0.083	0.170	0.137	0.072	0.058
Italy [1999]	0.086	0.101	0.199	0.093	0.085	0.063	0.092	0.058
Austria [1999]	0.036	0.106	0.224	0.083	0.123	0.035	0.036	0.069
Croatia [1999]	0.014	0.078	0.082	0.167	0.055	0.031	0.015	0.047
Bosnia and Herzegovina [2001]	0.014	0.065	0.082	0.078	0.119	0.039	0.010	0.047
Argentina [1999]	0.043	0.142	0.121	0.020	0.119	0.098	0.010	0.044
France [1999]	0.068	0.042	0.157	0.054	0.017	0.051	0.036	0.025
Kyrgyzstan [2003]	0.061	0.013	0.085	0.152	0.030	0.082	0.051	0.036
Estonia [1999]	0.041	0.037	0.181	0.010	0.047	0.063	0.005	0.033
Belarus [2000]	0.039	0.059	0.057	0.245	0.021	0.027	0.031	0.073
Bulgaria [1999]	0.022	0.021	0.071	0.137	0.106	0.023	0.005	0.036
Germany West [1999]	0.031	0.096	0.082	0.000	0.026	0.008	0.005	0.029
Latvia [1999]	0.027	0.054	0.142	0.098	0.026	0.059	0.010	0.011
Japan [2000]	0.092	0.044	0.125	0.015	0.038	0.008	0.010	0.036
Hungary [1999]	0.039	0.080	0.093	0.049	0.034	0.043	0.005	0.058
Spain [2000]	0.031	0.064	0.085	0.059	0.043	0.051	0.072	0.036
Romania [1999]	0.013	0.050	0.046	0.270	0.064	0.016	0.015	0.015
Poland [1999]	0.034	0.052	0.050	0.093	0.009	0.043	0.000	0.011
Ukraine [1999]	0.005	0.029	0.050	0.176	0.043	0.031	0.005	0.004
Portugal [1999]	0.009	0.034	0.068	0.000	0.009	0.016	0.026	0.007
Serbia [2001]	0.018	0.011	0.014	0.078	0.038	0.004	0.005	0.004
Lithuania [1999]	0.005	0.060	0.039	0.044	0.038	0.016	0.000	0.007
Russian Federation [1999]	0.004	0.000	0.000	0.162	0.000	0.016	-0.005	0.007
Turkey [2001]	0.000	0.003	0.028	0.029	0.111	0.000	0.005	0.000

Relative Index numbers UNDP-Method (non-parametric index) (Continued)

Country code (1)	professional associations	youth work	spots or recreation	women's group	peace movement	organization concerned with health	UNDP active society ("Etzioni")-Index
Tanzania, United Republic Of [2001]	1.000	0.898	1.000	0.858	0.157	0.878	0.834
Bangladesh [2002]		0.623	0.816	0.496	1.000	0.907	0.742
Viet Nam [2001]	0.507	0.633	0.585	1.000	0.250	0.624	0.544
China [2001]	0.169	0.442	0.405	0.556	0.593	1.000	0.523
United States [1999]	0.527	1.000	0.605	0.302	0.071	0.456	0.404
Uganda [2001]	0.224	0.805	0.662	0.459	0.220	0.388	0.374
Algeria [2002]	0.433	0.447	0.472	0.205			0.318
Albania [2002]	0.348	0.395	0.254	0.343	0.123	0.338	0.278
Philippines [2001]	0.109	0.284	0.388	0.332	0.388	0.380	0.271
Sweden [1999]	0.204	0.223	0.569	0.075	0.011	0.101	0.238
India [2001]	0.269	0.223	0.278	0.201	0.146	0.287	0.234
Greece [1999]	0.264	0.200	0.278	0.108	0.194	0.215	0.232
South Africa [2001]	0.085	0.302	0.492	0.284	0.134	0.198	0.230
Canada [2000]	0.294	0.363	0.411	0.164	0.034	0.342	0.227
Great Britain [1999]	0.378	0.698	0.114	0.045	0.157	0.409	0.208
Netherlands [1999]	0.159	0.200	0.562	0.082	0.019	0.283	0.201
Republic of Korea [2001]	0.194	0.144	0.375	0.142	0.063		0.189
Slovakia [1999]	0.139	0.247	0.428	0.172	0.000	0.143	0.171
Republic of Moldova [2002]	0.179	0.158	0.117	0.093	0.071	0.148	0.170
Zimbabwe [2001]	0.100	0.163	0.107	0.239	0.037	0.101	0.158
Peru [2001]	0.149	0.209	0.254	0.179	0.011	0.148	0.157
Macedonia, Republic of [2001]	0.129	0.144	0.271	0.142	0.101	0.190	0.154
Chile [2000]	0.104	0.177	0.381	0.164	0.078	0.110	0.147
Luxembourg [1999]	0.060	0.251	0.271	0.082	0.049	0.110	0.147
Mexico [2000]	0.065	0.158	0.217	0.119	0.108	0.207	0.143
Belgium [1999]	0.124	0.200	0.244	0.104	0.034	0.181	0.141
Finland [2000]	0.090	0.195	0.381	0.071	0.030	0.165	0.135
Denmark [1999]	0.179	0.223	0.455	0.026	0.011	0.030	0.123

Country code (1)	professional associations	youth work	sports or recreation	women's group	peace movement	organization concerned with health	UNDP active society ("Etzioni")-Index
Ireland [1999]	0.139	0.195	0.415	0.097	0.022	0.105	0.118
Iceland [1999]	0.139	0.144	0.361	0.082	0.000	0.068	0.114
Slovenia [1999]	0.124	0.149	0.261	0.045	0.019	0.076	0.112
Singapore [2002]	0.030	0.344	0.184	0.015	0.022	0.165	0.110
Czech Republic [1999]	0.109	0.251	0.331	0.037	0.004	0.118	0.110
Malta [1999]	0.075	0.135	0.167	0.052	0.015	0.055	0.101
Italy [1999]	0.149	0.121	0.187	0.011	0.030	0.110	0.099
Austria [1999]	0.065	0.084	0.271	0.086	0.000	0.093	0.094
Croatia [1999]	0.100	0.056	0.204	0.078	0.019	0.055	0.072
Bosnia and Herzegovina [2001]	0.045	0.056	0.221	0.063	0.004	0.063	0.065
Argentina [1999]	0.040	0.084	0.067	0.022	0.007	0.076	0.064
France [1999]	0.055	0.056	0.271	0.000	0.007	0.051	0.064
Kyrgyzstan [2003]	0.050	0.070	0.057	0.075	0.030	0.059	0.061
Estonia [1999]	0.065	0.074	0.094	0.049	0.011	0.017	0.052
Belarus [2000]	0.020	0.028	0.020	0.015	0.019	0.059	0.051
Bulgaria [1999]	0.070	0.051	0.104	0.026	0.011	0.013	0.050
Germany West [1999]	0.020	0.070	0.221	0.056	0.000	0.046	0.049
Latvia [1999]	0.015	0.019	0.187	0.007	0.000	0.008	0.047
Japan [2000]	0.055	0.033	0.090	0.041	0.022	0.051	0.047
Hungary [1999]	0.085	0.037	0.067	0.004	0.011	0.038	0.046
Spain [2000]	0.020	0.019	0.074	0.022	0.011	0.051	0.045
Romania [1999]	0.040	0.009	0.020	0.007		0.013	0.044
Poland [1999]	0.055	0.019	0.054	0.015		0.017	0.035
Ukraine [1999]	0.020	0.028	0.007	0.007		0.013	0.032
Portugal [1999]	0.020	0.028	0.124	0.000	0.000	0.030	0.026
Serbia [2001]	0.030	0.000	0.094	0.011		0.004	0.024
Lithuania [1999]	0.000	0.037	0.054	0.004	0.000	0.008	0.022
Russian Federation [1999]	0.005	0.000	0.023	0.007		0.000	0.017
Turkey [2001]	0.025	0.009	0.000	0.004	0.000	0.000	0.015

Appendix V

ISLAM AND ENLIGHTENMENT: THE POSSIBLE WAY AHEAD— A QUANTITATIVE VIEW; THE CROSS-NATIONAL DETERMINANTS OF ECONOMIC GROWTH, THE ACTIVE SOCIETY, GLOBAL TOLERANCE, TRADITIONAL VALUES, THE INTRANSPARENT SOCIETY AND *ASABIYYA*

Global tolerance index						
Summary of the model						
Model	R	R-Square	Corrected R-Square	Standard error of the estimate		
1,000	.862(a)	0.742	0.685	0.093		
a	Independent variables: (Constant), VAR00012, VAR00006, VAR00001, VAR00008, VAR00009, VAR00002, VAR00003, VAR00004, VAR00005, VAR00007, VAR00010, VAR00011					
ANOVA(b)						
Model		Sum of squares	df	Mean of squares	F	Significance
1,000	Regression	1,347	12,000	0.112	12.970	.000(a)
	Residuals	0,467	54,000	0.009		
	Total	1,815	66,000			
a	Independent variables: (Constant), VAR00012, VAR00006, VAR00001, VAR00008, VAR00009, VAR00002, VAR00003, VAR00004, VAR00005, VAR00007, VAR00010, VAR00011					
b	Dependent variable: VAR00013					

Coefficients(a)

Model Global tolerance index		Non-standardized coefficients		Standardized coefficients	T	Significance
		B	Standard error	Beta		
1,000	(Constant)	3.187	0.950		3.356	0.001
Dummy for being landlocked	VAR00001	-0.031	0.036	-0.072	-0.850	0.399
Dummy for transition economy	VAR00002	0.002	0.040	0.006	0.053	0.958
Urbanization ratio, 1990	VAR00003	0.000	0.001	0.019	0.146	0.884
(I-S)/GNP	VAR00004	0.001	0.002	0.088	0.805	0.424
State interventionism (absence of ec. freedom)	VAR00005	0.035	0.032	0.155	1.119	0.268
MNC PEN 1995	VAR00006	0.000	0.001	0.017	0.200	0.842
Low comparative international price level (ERD)	VAR00007	0.004	0.021	0.030	0.173	0.864
EU membership (EU-15)	VAR00008	0.039	0.036	0.099	1.086	0.282
Muslims as % of total population	VAR00009	-0.001	0.000	-0.284	-3.365	0.001
ln(GDP PPP pc)	VAR00010	-0.739	0.238	-4.551	-3.100	0.003
ln (GDP PPP pc)^2	VAR00011	0.049	0.014	5.212	3.382	0.001
World Bank pension reform	VAR00012	0.091	0.034	0.213	2.687	0.010

Active society index

Summary of the model

Model	R	R-Square	Corrected R-Square	Standard error of the estimate		
1,000	.858(a)	0.736	0.655	0.101		
a	Independent variables: (Constant), VAR00012, VAR00002, VAR00009, VAR00006, VAR00001, VAR00008, VAR00003, VAR00004, VAR00005, VAR00007, VAR00010, VAR00011					

ANOVA(b)

Model		Sum of squares	df	Mean of squares	F	Significance
1,000	Regression	1,114	12,000	0.093	9.062	.000(a)
	residuals	0,400	39,000	0.010		
	Total	1,514	51,000			
a	Independent variables: (Constant), VAR00012, VAR00002, VAR00009, VAR00006, VAR00001, VAR00008, VAR00003, VAR00004, VAR00005, VAR00007, VAR00010, VAR00011					
b	dependent variable: VAR00014					

Coefficients(a)

Model Active society index		Non-standardized coefficients		Standardized coefficients	T	Significance

Active society index						
Summary of the model						
		B	Standard error	Beta		
1,000	(Constant)	6.560	1.195		5.488	0.000
Dummy for being landlocked	VAR00001	-0.077	0.043	-0.177	-1.793	0.081
Dummy for transition economy	VAR00002	-0.075	0.048	-0.200	-1.578	0.123
Urbanization ratio, 1990	VAR00003	-0.003	0.001	-0.342	-1.950	0.058
(I-S)/GNP	VAR00004	0.000	0.002	-0.021	-0.166	0.869
State Interventionism (absence of ec. freedom)	VAR00005	0.037	0.043	0.147	0.848	0.401
MNC PEN 1995	VAR00006	0.001	0.001	0.106	1.044	0.303
Low comparative international price level (ERD)	VAR00007	0.007	0.026	0.054	0.260	0.796
EU membership (EU-15)	VAR00008	-0.070	0.044	-0.185	-1.584	0.121
Muslims as % of total population	VAR00009	0.000	0.001	0.050	0.537	0.594
Ln (GDP PPP pc)	VAR00010	-1.453	0.304	-8.337	-4.778	0.000
ln (GDP PPP pc)^2	VAR00011	0.083	0.019	8.234	4.411	0.000
World Bank pension reform	VAR00012	0.048	0.042	0.116	1.160	0.253
a	Dependent variable: VAR00014					

Traditional values						
Summary of the model						
Model	R	R-Square	corrected R-Square	Standard error of the estimate		
1,000	.912(a)	0.833	0.799	0.461		
a	Independent variables: (Constant), VAR00012, VAR00002, VAR00006, VAR00009, VAR00008, VAR00001, VAR00003, VAR00004, VAR00005, VAR00007, VAR00010, VAR00011					
ANOVA(b)						
Model		Sum of squares	df	Mean of squares	F	Significance
1,000	Regression	63,422	12,000	5.285	24.863	.000(a)
	Residuals	12,754	60,000	0.213		
	Total	76,176	72,000			
a	Independent variables: (Constant), VAR00012, VAR00002, VAR00006, VAR00009, VAR00008, VAR00001, VAR00003, VAR00004, VAR00005, VAR00007, VAR00010, VAR00011					
b	Dependent variable: VAR00015					
Coefficients(a)						

Traditional values						
Summary of the model						
Model	R	R-Square	corrected R-Square	Standard error of the estimate		
Model Active society index		Non-standardized coefficients		Standardized coefficients	T	Significance
		B	Standard error	Beta		
1,000	(Constant)	-10.901	4.577		-2.382	0.020
Dummy for being landlocked	VAR00001	0.090	0.174	0.034	0.515	0.608
Dummy for transition economy	VAR00002	-0.194	0.180	-0.082	-1.078	0.285
Urbanization ratio, 1990	VAR00003	-0.005	0.005	-0.099	-1.027	0.308
(I-S)/GNP	VAR00004	-0.013	0.008	-0.121	-1.486	0.143
State interventionism (absence of ec. freedom)	VAR00005	-0.249	0.151	-0.172	-1.655	0.103
MNC PEN 1995	VAR00006	-0.002	0.005	-0.030	-0.467	0.642
Low comparative international price level (ERD)	VAR00007	-0.056	0.098	-0.072	-0.568	0.572
EU membership (EU-15)	VAR00008	-0.562	0.170	-0.222	-3.303	0.002
Muslims as % of total population	VAR00009	0.007	0.002	0.225	3.497	0.001
ln(GDP PPP pc)	VAR00010	3.674	1.145	3.552	3.208	0.002
ln (GDP PPP pc)^2	VAR00011	-0.256	0.069	-4.304	-3.708	0.000
World Bank pension reform	VAR00012	-0.416	0.151	-0.165	-2.750	0.008
a	Dependent variable: VAR00015					

Intransparent, inactive society						
Summary of the model						
Model	R	R-Square	corrected R-Square	standard error of the estimate		
1,000	.797(a)	0.635	0.562	0.672		
a	Independent variables: (Constant), VAR00012, VAR00002, VAR00006, VAR00009, VAR00008, VAR00001, VAR00003, VAR00004, VAR00005, VAR00007, VAR00010, VAR00011					
ANOVA(b)						
Model		Sum of squares	df	Mean of squares	F	Significance
1,000	Regression	47,122	12,000	3.927	8.698	.000(a)
	residuals	27,086	60,000	0.451		
	Total	74,208	72,000			
a	Independent variables: (Constant), VAR00012, VAR00002, VAR00006, VAR00009, VAR00008, VAR00001, VAR00003, VAR00004, VAR00005, VAR00007, VAR00010, VAR00011					
b	dependent variable: VAR00016					

Appendix V

Intransparent, inactive society						
Summary of the model						
Coefficients(a)						
Model Intransparent, inactive society		Non-standardized coefficients		Standardized coefficients	T	Significance
		B	Standard error	Beta		
1,000	(Constant)	-29.609	6.670		-4.439	0.000
Dummy for being landlocked	VAR00001	0.669	0.254	0.254	2.637	0.011
Dummy for transition economy	VAR00002	0.919	0.262	0.393	3.503	0.001
Urbanization ratio, 1990	VAR00003	0.013	0.007	0.277	1.937	0.058
(I-S)/GNP	VAR00004	0.009	0.012	0.089	0.746	0.459
State interventionism (absence of ec. freedom)	VAR00005	-0.049	0.220	-0.034	-0.222	0.825
MNC PEN 1995	VAR00006	0.002	0.008	0.020	0.207	0.836
Low comparative international price level (ERD)	VAR00007	-0.218	0.143	-0.284	-1.522	0.133
EU-membership (EU-15)	VAR00008	0.474	0.248	0.190	1.911	0.061
Muslims as % of total population	VAR00009	-0.007	0.003	-0.226	-2.382	0.020
ln(GDP PPP pc)	VAR00010	7.263	1.669	7.114	4.351	0.000
ln (GDP PPP pc)^2	VAR00011	-0.443	0.101	-7.542	-4.401	0.000
World Bank pension reform	VAR00012	-0.624	0.221	-0.250	-2.829	0.006
a	Dependent variable: VAR00016					

Performance Inglehart/Etzioni scale						
Summary of the model						
Model	R	R-Square	corrected R-Square	standard error of the estimate		
1,000	.708(a)	0.501	0.401	0.663		
a	Independent variables: (Constant), VAR00012, VAR00002, VAR00006, VAR00009, VAR00008, VAR00001, VAR00003, VAR00004, VAR00005, VAR00007, VAR00010, VAR00011					
ANOVA(b)						
Model		Sum of squares	df	Mean of squares	F	Significance
1,000	Regression	26,522	12,000	2.210	5.025	.000(a)
	residuals	26,390	60,000	0,440		
	Total	52,912	72,000			
a	Independent variables: (Constant), VAR00012, VAR00002, VAR00006, VAR00009, VAR00008, VAR00001, VAR00003, VAR00004, VAR00005, VAR00007, VAR00010, VAR00011					
b	Dependent variable: VAR00017					
Coefficients(a)						
Model Performance Inglehart/Etzioni scale		Non-standardized coefficients		Standardized coefficients	T	Significance
		B	Standard error	Beta		
1,000	(Constant)	16.528	6.584		2.510	0.015
Dummy for being landlocked	VAR00001	-0.551	0.250	-0.248	-2.202	0.032
Dummy for transition economy	VAR00002	-0.791	0.259	-0.400	-3.052	0.003
Urbanization ratio, 1990	VAR00003	-0.016	0.007	-0.397	-2.380	0.021
(I-S)/GNP	VAR00004	0.001	0.012	0.016	0.117	0.907
State interventionism (absence of ec. freedom)	VAR00005	0.139	0.217	0.115	0.642	0.523
MNC PEN 1995	VAR00006	0.008	0.008	0.111	1.000	0.321
Low comparative international price level (ERD)	VAR00007	0.083	0.141	0.128	0.584	0.561
EU membership (EU-15)	VAR00008	-0.881	0.245	-0.418	-3.595	0.001
Muslims as % of total population	VAR00009	-0.001	0.003	-0.060	-0.546	0.587
ln(GDP PPP pc)	VAR00010	-4.166	1.648	-4.832	-2.528	0.014
ln (GDP PPP pc)^2	VAR00011	0.266	0.099	5.366	2.679	0.010
World Bank pension reform	VAR00012	0.304	0.218	0.144	1.399	0.167

Appendix VI

MAPPING THE WORLD CIVILIZATIONS: IS ISLAM COMPATIBLE WITH ENLIGHTENMENT? A FACTOR ANALYTICAL MODEL

Global scales with country weights

The original data
(Part 1)

	N Muslim sample	Minimum	Maximum	Global Islam mean	Global Protestantism – mean	Global Catholicism - mean
[Country]'s environmental problems can be solved without any international agreements to handle them	3814	1	4	2,270	2,620	2,400
A woman has to have children to be fulfilled	18138	0	1	0,830	0,440	0,580
Abortion if not wanting more children	1719	0	1	0,380	0,450	0,280
Abortion when woman not married	1699	0	1	0,380	0,420	0,270
Active/Inactive membership of any other organization	4861	0	2	0,110	0,330	0,180
Active/Inactive membership of art, music, educational	4890	0	2	0,190	0,400	0,260
Active/Inactive membership of charitable/humanitarian organization	4886	0	2	0,110	0,340	0,210
Active/Inactive membership of church or religious organization	4889	0	2	0,340	0,870	0,690
Active/Inactive membership of environmental organization	4884	0	2	0,100	0,170	0,140
Active/Inactive membership of labor unions	4890	0	2	0,210	0,330	0,190
Active/Inactive membership of political party	4891	0	2	0,270	0,210	0,170
Active/Inactive membership of professional organization	4888	0	2	0,160	0,290	0,200
Active/Inactive membership of sport or recreation	4870	0	2	0,230	0,640	0,390
Amount of help for less developed countries	3170	1	3	2,550	2,460	2,560

The original data (Part 1 - Continued)

	N Muslim sample	Minimum	Maximum	Global Islam mean	Global Protestantism – mean	Global Catholicism - mean
Being a housewife just as fulfilling	16569	1	4	2,210	2,230	2,160
Believe in: devil	4783	0	1	0,680	0,340	0,490
Believe in: God	18438	0	1	0,980	0,840	0,950
Believe in: heaven	17521	0	1	0,900	0,590	0,710
Believe in: hell	17418	0	1	0,870	0,340	0,510
Believe in: life after death	17395	0	1	0,820	0,610	0,700
Believe in: people have a soul	16547	0	1	0,920	0,780	0,850
Believe in: re-incarnation	1566	0	1	0,310	0,270	0,290
Believe in: sin	6147	0	1	0,830	0,620	0,790
Belong to conservation, the environment, ecology, animal rights	5529	0	1	0,070	0,060	0,040
Belong to education, arts, music or cultural activities	5663	0	1	0,120	0,130	0,090
Belong to human rights	5663	0	1	0,050	0,040	0,020
Belong to labor unions	5663	0	1	0,090	0,310	0,100
Belong to local political actions	5644	0	1	0,090	0,050	0,040
Belong to organization concerned with health	5644	0	1	0,080	0,070	0,040
Belong to other groups	5642	0	1	0,050	0,110	0,050
Belong to peace movement	5644	0	1	0,060	0,020	0,010
Belong to political parties	5661	0	1	0,120	0,090	0,050
Belong to professional associations	5663	0	1	0,080	0,110	0,050
Belong to religious organization	5663	0	1	0,200	0,340	0,180
Belong to social welfare service for elderly	5663	0	1	0,090	0,110	0,060
Belong to sports or recreation	5644	0	1	0,120	0,250	0,130
Belong to women's group	5644	0	1	0,080	0,060	0,040
Belong to youth work	5663	0	1	0,070	0,080	0,050
Better if more people with strong religious beliefs in public office	8498	1	5	2,540	3,080	3,010
Chance to escape from poverty	4447	1	2	1,590	1,480	1,630
Child needs a home with father and mother	17826	0	1	0,960	0,810	0,900
Child qualities: tolerance and respect for other people	18790	0	1	0,650	0,700	0,650
Churches give answers: moral problems	11193	0	1	0,760	0,490	0,610
Churches give answers: people's spiritual needs	11114	0	1	0,810	0,680	0,770
Churches give answers: the problems of family life	11205	0	1	0,690	0,460	0,580
Churches give answers: the social problems	10758	0	1	0,610	0,370	0,470
Competition harmful (Competition good or harmful)	10386	1	10	3,240	3,370	3,660

Appendix VI

	N Muslim sample	Minimum	Maximum	Global Islam mean	Global Protestantism – mean	Global Catholicism - mean
Confidence: Armed Forces	15927	1	4	2,060	2,310	2,410
Confidence: Churches	17993	1	4	1,770	2,180	1,990
Confidence: Education System	1768	1	4	2,080	2,160	2,150
Confidence: Justice System	6438	1	4	2,270	2,270	2,530
Confidence: Labor Unions	14022	1	4	2,610	2,630	2,790
Confidence: Major Companies	14297	1	4	2,520	2,520	2,570
Confidence: NATO	4493	1	4	2,380	2,550	2,660
Confidence: Parliament	15655	1	4	2,470	2,530	2,710
Confidence: Social Security System	1679	1	4	2,260	2,390	2,470
Confidence: Television	16189	1	4	2,430	2,480	2,510
Confidence: The Civil Services	16170	1	4	2,390	2,490	2,660
Confidence: The Environmental Protection Movement	13391	1	4	2,350	2,370	2,270
Confidence: The Government	15077	1	4	2,350	2,590	2,660
Confidence: The Police	16289	1	4	2,310	2,100	2,450
Confidence: The Political Parties	13902	1	4	2,740	2,870	3,000
Confidence: The Press	16827	1	4	2,530	2,690	2,600
Confidence: The United Nations	14848	1	4	2,520	2,320	2,390
Confidence: The Women's Movement	13421	1	4	2,440	2,500	2,510
Country is run by big interest vs. for all people's benefit	14602	1	2	1,320	1,370	1,310
Democracies are indecisive and have too much squabbling	14806	1	4	2,610	2,560	2,450
Democracies aren't good at maintaining order	14804	1	4	2,800	2,870	2,710
Democracy may have problems but is better	15365	1	4	1,690	1,690	1,710
Do you think most people try to take advantage of you	10762	1	2	1,440	1,490	1,420
Economic aid to poorer countries	5894	1	5	2,840	2,680	2,720
Education level (recoded)	18444	1	3	1,720	1,850	1,800
Enjoy sexual freedom	4062	1	3	2,220	1,970	1,960
Environmental action: attend meeting, signed petition	4560	0	1	0,130	0,180	0,190
Environmental action: chosen products that are better for environment	3543	0	1	0,420	0,660	0,480
Environmental action: contributed to environmental organization	4529	0	1	0,140	0,200	0,180
Environmental action: recycle	3563	0	1	0,370	0,710	0,450
Environmental action: reduce water consumption	3808	0	1	0,580	0,510	0,510
Extent of political corruption	4047	1	4	2,910	2,460	2,940
Fairness: One secretary is paid more	17093	0	2	0,840	0,850	0,840
Family important in life	18616	1	4	1,060	1,130	1,130

The original data (Part 1 - Continued)

	N Muslim sample	Minimum	Maximum	Global Islam mean	Global Protestantism - mean	Global Catholicism - mean
No family savings during past year (Family savings during past year)	15532	1	4	2,170	1,950	2,210
Feeling of happiness	18565	1	4	2,040	1,790	1,950
Firm party leader vs. Cooperating party leader	4279	1	2	1,730	1,760	1,740
First choice, if looking for a job	9109	1	4	1,880	2,460	2,190
Following instructions at work	17134	1	3	1,810	1,750	1,860
Freedom or equality	1671	1	3	1,600	1,450	1,560
Frequency watches TV	10523	1	4	2,580	2,550	2,560
Friends important in life	18478	1	4	1,650	1,590	1,770
Future changes: A simple and more natural lifestyle	1696	1	3	1,380	1,250	1,170
Future changes: Greater respect for authority	17536	1	3	1,420	1,710	1,440
Future changes: Less emphasis on money and material possessions	17502	1	3	1,780	1,600	1,580
Future changes: Less importance placed on work	17646	1	3	2,470	2,330	2,310
Future changes: More emphasis on family life	17849	1	3	1,110	1,100	1,090
Future changes: More emphasis on individual	1689	1	3	1,130	1,160	1,180
Future changes: More emphasis on technology	17578	1	3	1,230	1,580	1,410
Get comfort and strength from religion	17413	0	1	0,930	0,620	0,790
Good human relationships	12924	1	5	1,380	1,290	1,410
Government order vs. freedom	4755	1	2	1,200	1,390	1,450
Government responsibility	17995	1	10	6,430	5,060	5,640
Government should reduce environmental pollution	5629	1	4	1,920	2,400	2,030
Had formal education	16775	0	1	0,890	0,980	0,980
Hard work brings success	5252	1	10	3,740	4,280	4,620
Highest educational level attained	18444	1	8	3,980	4,460	4,310
How business and industry should be managed	15290	1	4	2,040	1,740	1,920
How important is God in your life	18604	1	10	9,190	6,350	7,850
How many children do you have	18202	0	15	2,310	1,980	2,030
How much freedom of choice and control	17791	1	10	6,040	7,100	6,880
How much is the government doing against poverty	4533	1	3	2,730	2,560	2,660
How often discusses political matters with friends	18397	1	3	2,200	2,080	2,190

Appendix VI

	N Muslim sample	Minimum	Maximum	Global Islam mean	Global Protestantism - mean	Global Catholicism - mean
Never attend religious services (How often do you attend religious services)	18438	1	8	3,890	5,010	3,740
How often follows politics in the news	5517	1	5	2,380	2,140	2,230
How proud of nationality	18000	1	4	1,440	1,610	1,540
Humanity has a bright or bleak future	3851	1	5	1,280	1,480	1,540
Humiliating to receive money without having to work for it	5504	1	5	2,050	2,770	2,490
Husband and wife should both contribute to income	17134	1	4	1,820	1,940	1,780
Ideal number of children	16593	0	10	2,990	2,750	2,800
If only one child allowed: boy or girl	4761	1	3	1,930	2,330	2,100
Immigrant policy	15529	1	4	2,450	2,510	2,520
Important child qualities: determination perseverance	18181	0	1	0,320	0,320	0,290
Important child qualities: feeling of responsibility	18790	0	1	0,590	0,680	0,680
Important child qualities: good manners	14497	0	1	0,860	0,740	0,730
Important child qualities: hard work	18181	0	1	0,610	0,320	0,480
Important child qualities: imagination	18181	0	1	0,190	0,210	0,160
Important child qualities: independence	18790	0	1	0,440	0,510	0,390
Important child qualities: obedience	18790	0	1	0,460	0,320	0,380
Important child qualities: religious faith	18786	0	1	0,600	0,260	0,380
Important child qualities: thrift saving money and things	18790	0	1	0,370	0,280	0,340
Important child qualities: unselfishness	18181	0	1	0,260	0,270	0,260
Important for successful marriage: Adequate income	1665	1	3	1,330	1,880	1,700
Important for successful marriage: Agreement on politics	1626	1	3	2,020	2,590	2,500
Important for successful marriage: Apart from in-laws	1654	1	3	1,760	1,830	1,800
Important for successful marriage: Children	1662	1	3	1,230	1,570	1,400
Important for successful marriage: Faithfulness	1665	1	3	1,070	1,130	1,150
Important for successful marriage: Good housing	1663	1	3	1,540	1,780	1,710
Important for successful marriage: Happy sexual relationship	1635	1	3	1,250	1,390	1,410
Important for successful marriage: Religious beliefs	1658	1	3	1,440	2,220	2,000

The original data (Part 1 - Continued)

	N Muslim sample	Minimum	Maximum	Global Islam mean	Global Protestantism - mean	Global Catholicism - mean
Important for successful marriage: Respect and appreciation	1669	1	3	**1,120**	1,140	1,160
Important for successful marriage: Same social background	1628	1	3	**1,670**	2,280	2,150
Important for successful marriage: Sharing household chores	1657	1	3	**1,650**	1,780	1,820
Important in a job: a job that is interesting	17946	0	1	**0,640**	0,670	0,580
Important in a job: a job that meets one's abilities	18072	0	1	**0,770**	0,560	0,600
Important in a job: a respected job	18070	0	1	**0,730**	0,370	0,450
Important in a job: a responsible job	18069	0	1	**0,640**	0,460	0,450
Important in a job: a useful job for society	1794	0	1	**0,780**	0,370	0,440
Important in a job: an opportunity to use initiative	17753	0	1	**0,600**	0,500	0,460
Important in a job: generous holidays	18070	0	1	**0,400**	0,250	0,290
Important in a job: good chances for promotion	1794	0	1	**0,640**	0,320	0,400
Important in a job: good hours	17944	0	1	**0,660**	0,480	0,490
Important in a job: good job security	18075	0	1	**0,850**	0,660	0,670
Important in a job: good pay	18076	0	1	**0,920**	0,710	0,790
Important in a job: meeting people	1667	0	1	**0,720**	0,470	0,450
Important in a job: none of these	1553	0	1	**0,860**	0,610	0,670
Important in a job: not too much pressure	18070	0	1	**0,600**	0,330	0,380
Important in a job: pleasant people to work with	1800	0	1	**0,820**	0,760	0,670
Important in a job: that you can achieve something	17945	0	1	**0,710**	0,660	0,550
Important in successful marriage: Understanding and tolerance	1662	1	3	**1,150**	1,190	1,230
Important: Religious service birth	1714	0	1	**0,610**	0,740	0,890
Important: Religious service death	1753	0	1	**0,940**	0,880	0,920
Important: Religious service marriage	1735	0	1	**0,860**	0,770	0,900
Importation of goods	4563	1	2	**1,630**	1,630	1,710
In democracy, the economic system runs badly	14714	1	4	**2,840**	2,880	2,700

Appendix VI

	N Muslim sample	Minimum	Maximum	Global Islam mean	Global Protestantism - mean	Global Catholicism - mean
Anti-egalitarian position on Income equality" scale	17804	1	10	6,080	5,820	5,850
Income level	16435	1	3	1,860	1,930	1,960
Increase in taxes if used to prevent environmental pollution	10007	1	4	2,250	2,370	2,410
Interest in politics	17478	1	4	2,660	2,450	2,730
Is the chief wage earner employed now	9480	0	1	0,830	0,800	0,780
Jobs scarce: Employers should give priority to (nation) people than immigrants	17428	1	3	1,300	1,440	1,320
Jobs scarce: Men should have more right to a job than women	18221	1	3	1,500	1,870	1,810
Jobs scarce: older people should be forced to retire	5175	0	9	1,640	1,760	1,750
Justifiable: abortion	15727	1	10	2,510	4,420	3,330
Justifiable: avoiding a fare on public transport	14778	1	10	1,970	2,090	2,470
Justifiable: buy stolen goods	4583	1	10	1,710	1,530	1,740
Justifiable: cheating on taxes	14896	1	10	1,830	2,360	2,440
Justifiable: claiming government benefits	15601	1	10	2,320	1,840	2,470
Justifiable: divorce	16644	1	10	3,580	5,360	4,670
Justifiable: driving under influence of alcohol	1763	1	10	1,380	1,390	1,550
Justifiable: euthanasia	15411	1	10	2,140	4,540	3,620
Justifiable: homosexuality	14029	1	10	1,400	3,980	3,290
Justifiable: joyriding	1646	1	10	1,470	1,310	1,390
Justifiable: lying	1773	1	10	2,080	2,320	2,700
Justifiable: prostitution	13190	1	10	1,430	2,810	2,610
Justifiable: someone accepting a bribe	16729	1	10	1,540	1,560	1,810
Justifiable: suicide	15928	1	10	1,370	2,570	2,190
Justifiable: taking soft drugs	1766	1	10	1,430	1,650	1,560
Justifiable: throwing away litter	1632	1	10	1,540	1,920	1,760
Least liked allow: demonstrate	3716	0	1	0,110	0,160	0,090
Least liked allow: hold office	3836	0	1	0,080	0,080	0,060
Least liked allow: teach	3729	0	1	0,100	0,060	0,070
Leisure time important in life	18321	1	4	2,080	1,770	1,890
Major changes in life	5173	1	10	4,890	5,910	5,130
Make effort to live up to what my friends expect	14440	1	4	2,180	2,600	2,450
Marriage is an out-dated institution	17402	0	1	0,150	0,140	0,150
Men make better political leaders than women do	15806	1	4	2,080	2,720	2,580
Moments of prayer, meditation...	5879	0	1	0,870	0,630	0,790
Most people can be trusted	17803	1	2	1,730	1,570	1,750

The original data (Part 1 - Continued)

	N Muslim sample	Minimum	Maximum	Global Islam mean	Global Protestantism - mean	Global Catholicism - mean
Rejecting neighbors: Drug addicts	17910	0	1	0,720	0,680	0,650
Rejecting neighbors: Emotionally unstable people	17955	0	1	0,540	0,310	0,340
Rejecting neighbors: Heavy drinkers	16985	0	1	0,660	0,530	0,560
Rejecting neighbors: Homosexuals	16940	0	1	0,660	0,320	0,430
Rejecting neighbors: Immigrants/foreign workers	17950	0	1	0,300	0,130	0,140
Rejecting neighbors: Jews	6336	0	1	0,340	0,090	0,150
Rejecting neighbors: Left wing extremists	1653	0	1	0,580	0,270	0,320
Rejecting neighbors: Muslims	4243	0	1	0,160	0,190	0,190
Rejecting neighbors: People of a different race	17950	0	1	0,280	0,110	0,130
Rejecting neighbors: People of a different religion	9883	0	1	0,330	0,250	0,190
Rejecting neighbors: People who have AIDS	17911	0	1	0,620	0,250	0,370
Rejecting neighbors: People with a criminal record	18565	0	1	0,660	0,420	0,540
Rejecting neighbors: People with large families	1667	0	1	0,290	0,070	0,100
Rejecting neighbors: Political Extremists	4941	0	2	0,650	0,450	0,430
Rejecting neighbors: Right wing extremists	1651	0	1	0,560	0,280	0,310
New and old ideas	7649	1	10	5,940	5,270	5,340
One of main goals in life has been to make my parents proud	16276	1	4	1,480	2,090	1,800
Opinion about scientific advances	15919	1	3	1,560	1,830	1,830
Parents responsibilities to their children	17615	1	3	1,250	1,400	1,310
People should not have to work if they don't want to	5398	1	5	3,090	3,510	3,320
People who don't work turn lazy	5507	1	5	1,910	2,590	2,230
Political action: attending lawful demonstrations	15011	1	3	2,430	2,210	2,310
Political action: joining in boycotts	14723	1	3	2,570	2,340	2,570
Political action: joining unofficial strikes	14692	1	3	2,800	2,660	2,730
Political action: occupying buildings or factories	14723	1	3	2,900	2,850	2,830
Political action: signing a petition	14706	1	3	2,350	1,670	1,970
Political system: Having a democratic political system	15063	1	4	1,510	1,570	1,660

	N Muslim sample	Minimum	Maximum	Global Islam mean	Global Protestantism - mean	Global Catholicism - mean
Political system: Having a strong leader	14715	1	4	2,860	3,130	2,870
Political system: Having experts make decisions	14130	1	4	2,220	2,550	2,340
Political system: Having the army rule	14169	1	4	2,940	3,590	3,370
Politicians who don't believe in God are unfit for public office	10471	1	5	2,200	3,390	3,320
Politics important in life	18093	1	4	2,650	2,640	2,830
Poverty compared to 10 years ago	4669	1	3	1,460	1,510	1,400
Pray to God outside of religious services (I)	7887	1	7	2,310	3,490	2,860
For state ownership of business	17006	1	10	5,240	4,220	4,860
Problem if women have more income than husband	4429	1	4	2,340	2,630	2,470
Protecting environment vs. Economic growth	14785	1	3	1,560	1,550	1,540
Raised religiously	5405	0	1	0,760	0,630	0,870
Rate political system as it was before	10484	1	10	5,780	5,380	4,950
Rate political system for governing country	12287	1	10	4,880	5,180	4,850
Rate political system in ten years	4026	1	10	6,800	5,900	6,310
Religion important in life	18477	1	4	1,380	2,250	1,900
Religious leaders should not influence government	6610	1	5	2,140	2,340	2,210
Religious leaders should not influence how people vote	10294	1	5	2,200	2,150	2,090
Religious person	17563	1	3	1,160	1,330	1,170
Respect and love for parents	17789	1	2	1,090	1,330	1,170
Respect for individual human rights nowadays	13347	1	4	2,510	2,130	2,390
Respondent interested during the interview	16938	1	3	1,530	1,470	1,560
Satisfaction with financial situation of household	17325	1	10	5,320	6,460	5,950
Satisfaction with the people in national office	14371	1	4	2,560	2,590	2,760
Satisfaction with the way democracy develops	10410	1	4	2,540	2,400	2,520
Satisfaction with your life	18643	1	10	5,890	7,450	7,020
Scale of incomes	16916	1	11	4,310	5,100	4,680
right wing (self positioning in political scale)	11922	1	10	5,910	5,690	5,720
Service to others important in life	10167	1	4	1,710	1,600	1,600
Social class (subjective)	16264	1	5	3,270	3,290	3,390
Socio-economic status of respondent	1497	1	4	2,910	2,550	2,680

The original data (Part 1 - Continued)

	N Muslim sample	Minimum	Maximum	Global Islam mean	Global Protestantism - mean	Global Catholicism - mean
Spend time with colleagues from work	10942	1	4	2,340	2,480	2,710
Spend time with friends	12429	1	4	1,610	1,530	1,760
Spend time with parents or other relatives	11238	1	4	1,440	1,600	1,520
Spend time with people at sport, culture, communal organization	10457	1	4	3,200	2,720	3,020
Spend time with people at your church, mosque or synagogue	10198	1	4	2,460	2,700	2,680
State of health (subjective)	17262	1	5	2,120	2,040	2,310
Thinking about meaning and purpose of life	16391	1	4	1,670	1,880	1,870
To develop talents you need to have a job	5436	1	5	1,810	2,340	2,160
Tradition vs. high economic growth	4439	1	5	1,650	1,480	1,520
TV most important entertainment	9540	1	4	2,230	2,650	2,440
University is more important for a boy than for a girl	16236	1	4	2,780	3,200	3,010
Unpaid work education, arts, music or cultural activities	5662	0	1	0,100	0,050	0,050
Unpaid work environment, conservation, animal rights	5529	0	1	0,060	0,030	0,020
Unpaid work human rights	5662	0	1	0,040	0,020	0,010
Unpaid work labor unions	5662	0	1	0,050	0,030	0,030
Unpaid work local political action groups	5643	0	1	0,080	0,030	0,030
Unpaid work none	1366	0	1	0,920	0,630	0,740
Unpaid work organization concerned with health	5641	0	1	0,070	0,040	0,030
Unpaid work other groups	2385	0	1	0,020	0,050	0,030
Unpaid work peace movement	5643	0	1	0,060	0,010	0,010
Unpaid work political parties or groups	5662	0	1	0,090	0,030	0,020
Unpaid work professional associations	4743	0	1	0,030	0,030	0,020
Unpaid work religious or church organization	5662	0	1	0,170	0,130	0,110
Unpaid work social welfare service for elderly, handicapped or deprived people	5662	0	1	0,080	0,070	0,050
Unpaid work sports or recreation	5643	0	1	0,100	0,110	0,070
Unpaid work women's group	5643	0	1	0,060	0,030	0,020
Unpaid work youth work	5662	0	1	0,060	0,060	0,040
Using violence for political goals not justified	4437	1	4	1,610	1,570	1,860
What age did you complete your education (recoded in intervals)	12905	1	10	6,370	6,710	5,860
Willingness to fight for country	10050	0	1	0,830	0,770	0,690

The original data (Part 1 - Continued)

	N Muslim sample	Minimum	Maximum	Global Islam mean	Global Protestantism - mean	Global Catholicism - mean
Woman as a single parent	16639	0	3	**0,490**	0,870	0,890
Work compared with Leisure	15428	1	5	**3,870**	3,520	3,720
Work important in life	18430	1	4	**1,320**	1,540	1,430
Work is a duty towards society	5470	1	5	**1,960**	2,300	2,190
Work should come first even if it means less spare time	5463	1	5	**1,920**	2,750	2,550
Work: accomplish personal goals	4698	1	4	**1,860**	1,800	1,870
Work: stay up late to finish	4607	1	4	**2,040**	2,400	2,200
Work: until satisfied with results	4558	1	4	**1,670**	1,610	1,700
Would buy things at a 20% higher price if it helped to protect environment	4360	1	4	**2,470**	2,640	2,520
Would give part of my income for the environment	5544	1	4	**2,090**	2,200	2,230

The original data (Part 2)

	Global Judaism - mean	Global Orthodoxy - mean	Global Hinduism - mean	Global Buddhism - mean	Global Catholicism - (practicing) - mean	Global citizens - mean
[Country]'s environmental problems can be solved without any international agreements to handle them	2,670	2,390	2,030	2,330	2,370	2,460
A woman has to have children to be fulfilled	0,600	0,800	0,860	0,710	0,580	0,610
Abortion if not wanting more children	0,570	0,600	0,570	0,490	0,150	0,440
Abortion when woman not married	0,530	0,540	0,670	0,550	0,160	0,400
Active/Inactive membership of any other organization	0,310	0,080	0,140	0,230	0,200	0,200
Active/Inactive membership of art, music, educational	0,280	0,150	0,310	0,170	0,300	0,270
Active/Inactive membership of charitable/humanitarian organization	0,400	0,120	0,210	0,200	0,280	0,210
Active/Inactive membership of church or religious organization	0,550	0,300	0,420	0,390	1,000	0,520
Active/Inactive membership of environmental organization	0,120	0,080	0,150	0,100	0,160	0,140
Active/Inactive membership of labor unions	0,180	0,350	0,210	0,160	0,170	0,270

The original data (Part 2 Continued)

	Global Judaism - mean	Global Orthodoxy - mean	Global Hinduism - mean	Global Buddhism - mean	Global Catholicism - (practicing) - mean	Global citizens - mean
Active/Inactive membership of political party	0,220	0,180	0,230	0,120	0,190	0,200
Active/Inactive membership of professional organization	0,230	0,130	0,200	0,160	0,210	0,200
Active/Inactive membership of sport or recreation	0,320	0,190	0,320	0,380	0,390	0,380
Amount of help for less developed countries	2,640	2,650	2,510	2,350	2,520	2,550
Being a housewife just as fulfilling	2,150	2,220	2,380	1,960	2,130	2,190
Believe in: devil	0,320	0,430	0,360	0,400	0,620	0,410
Believe in: God	0,890	0,900	0,950	0,690	1,000	0,830
Believe in: heaven	0,530	0,480	0,600	0,530	0,880	0,600
Believe in: hell	0,390	0,430	0,550	0,480	0,650	0,460
Believe in: life after death	0,530	0,470	0,570	0,600	0,830	0,600
Believe in: people have a soul	0,750	0,690	0,790	0,780	0,930	0,770
Believe in: re-incarnation	0,280	0,340	0,960	0,590	0,300	0,280
Believe in: sin	0,630	0,770	0,720	0,460	0,910	0,670
Belong to conservation, the environment, ecology, animal rights	0,110	0,030	0,080	0,050	0,040	0,050
Belong to education, arts, music or cultural activities	0,220	0,070	0,160	0,120	0,090	0,100
Belong to human rights	0,060	0,010	0,030	0,020	0,020	0,030
Belong to labor unions	0,130	0,160	0,090	0,070	0,100	0,170
Belong to local political actions	0,090	0,020	0,070	0,070	0,050	0,040
Belong to organization concerned with health	0,090	0,030	0,090	0,080	0,050	0,050
Belong to other groups	0,090	0,030	0,070	0,060	0,050	0,060
Belong to peace movement	0,040	0,010	0,060	0,030	0,020	0,020
Belong to political parties	0,130	0,060	0,110	0,050	0,050	0,070
Belong to professional associations	0,160	0,050	0,100	0,070	0,060	0,070
Belong to religious organization	0,340	0,070	0,210	0,220	0,250	0,170
Belong to social welfare service for elderly	0,140	0,030	0,090	0,090	0,070	0,070
Belong to sports or recreation	0,240	0,070	0,130	0,150	0,130	0,150
Belong to women's group	0,100	0,020	0,070	0,060	0,050	0,040
Belong to youth work	0,120	0,030	0,060	0,060	0,060	0,050
Better if more people with strong religious beliefs in public office	3,190	2,770	3,210	3,360	2,720	3,050
Chance to escape from poverty	1,580	1,740	1,460	1,170	1,580	1,600

Appendix VI

	Global Judaism - mean	Global Orthodoxy - mean	Global Hinduism - mean	Global Buddhism - mean	Global Catholicism - (practicing) - mean	Global citizens - mean
Child needs a home with father and mother	0,860	0,960	0,930	0,930	0,910	0,890
Child qualities: tolerance and respect for other people	0,780	0,640	0,590	0,540	0,650	0,670
Churches give answers: moral problems	0,620	0,630	0,360	0,450	0,720	0,560
Churches give answers: people's spiritual needs	0,780	0,790	0,540	0,570	0,860	0,700
Churches give answers: the problems of family life	0,600	0,520	0,280	0,340	0,700	0,510
Churches give answers: the social problems	0,500	0,340	0,270	0,210	0,570	0,410
Competition harmful (Competition good or harmful)	3,410	3,400	2,870	3,960	3,660	3,530
Confidence: Armed Forces	2,410	2,140	1,670	2,170	2,290	2,330
Confidence: Churches	2,320	2,080	1,760	2,720	1,630	2,220
Confidence: Education System	2,340	2,180	1,960	2,190	2,070	2,190
Confidence: Justice System	2,450	2,580	2,150	2,130	2,470	2,480
Confidence: Labor Unions	2,790	2,880	2,530	2,530	2,740	2,750
Confidence: Major Companies	2,490	2,740	2,370	2,660	2,480	2,600
Confidence: NATO	2,450	3,110	2,770	2,740	2,600	2,730
Confidence: Parliament	2,550	2,880	2,280	2,600	2,630	2,670
Confidence: Social Security System	2,550	2,730	2,230	1,910	2,420	2,480
Confidence: Television	2,510	2,640	2,390	2,330	2,470	2,510
Confidence: The Civil Services	2,640	2,760	2,230	2,390	2,570	2,600
Confidence: The Environmental Protection Movement	2,360	2,540	2,350	2,150	2,210	2,330
Confidence: The Government	2,640	2,720	2,430	2,450	2,570	2,600
Confidence: The Police	2,430	2,640	2,660	2,210	2,350	2,430
Confidence: The Political Parties	2,830	3,080	2,560	2,730	2,950	2,920
Confidence: The Press	2,590	2,760	2,200	2,300	2,580	2,620
Confidence: The United Nations	2,350	2,670	2,350	2,290	2,330	2,480
Confidence: The Women's Movement	2,390	2,650	2,410	2,260	2,430	2,510
Country is run by big interest vs. for all people's benefit	1,340	1,230	1,400	1,430	1,340	1,310
Democracies are indecisive and have too much squabbling	2,610	2,430	2,370	2,560	2,460	2,490

The original data (Part 2 - Continued)

	Global Judaism - mean	Global Orthodoxy - mean	Global Hinduism - mean	Global Buddhism - mean	Global Catholicism - (practicing) - mean	Global citizens - mean
Democracies aren't good at maintaining order	2,800	2,610	2,660	2,800	2,710	2,740
Democracy may have problems but is better	1,660	1,840	1,600	1,910	1,720	1,740
Do you think most people try to take advantage of you	1,490	1,320	1,410	1,490	1,430	1,430
Economic aid to poorer countries	2,830	3,010	2,790	2,580	2,690	2,760
Education level (recoded)	2,110	1,920	1,870	1,980	1,800	1,840
Enjoy sexual freedom	2,150	2,060	2,010	2,210	2,010	2,010
Environmental action: attend meeting, signed petition	0,150	0,080	0,180	0,180	0,210	0,150
Environmental action: chosen products that are better for environment	0,500	0,360	0,300	0,720	0,490	0,500
Environmental action: contributed to environmental organization	0,170	0,080	0,200	0,160	0,220	0,150
Environmental action: recycle	0,460	0,340	0,270	0,800	0,480	0,490
Environmental action: reduce water consumption	0,380	0,400	0,400	0,700	0,560	0,500
Extent of political corruption	2,740	3,010	2,940	2,640	2,920	2,870
Fairness: One secretary is paid more	0,850	0,870	0,750	0,800	0,840	0,850
Family important in life	1,140	1,150	1,140	1,120	1,100	1,150
No family savings during past year (Family savings during past year)	2,050	2,320	2,080	2,030	2,210	2,180
Feeling of happiness	1,940	2,360	2,000	1,900	1,890	1,990
Firm party leader vs. Cooperating party leader	1,650	1,710	1,620	1,690	1,720	1,740
First choice, if looking for a job	2,510	1,840	1,920	2,360	2,210	2,160
Following instructions at work	1,940	1,960	1,880	2,050	1,810	1,880
Freedom or equality	1,390	1,530	1,600	1,680	1,560	1,530
Frequency watches TV	2,320	2,840	1,890	2,720	2,570	2,590
Friends important in life	1,630	1,790	1,900	1,720	1,760	1,740
Future changes: A simple and more natural lifestyle	1,240	1,240	1,260	1,330	1,160	1,220
Future changes: Greater respect for authority	1,550	1,540	1,640	2,190	1,350	1,570
Future changes: Less emphasis on money and material possessions	1,410	1,810	1,920	1,770	1,570	1,650

Appendix VI

	Global Judaism - mean	Global Orthodoxy - mean	Global Hinduism - mean	Global Buddhism - mean	Global Catholicism - (practicing) - mean	Global citizens - mean
Future changes: Less importance placed on work	2,170	2,480	2,570	2,420	2,370	2,350
Future changes: More emphasis on family life	1,090	1,100	1,350	1,150	1,070	1,120
Future changes: More emphasis on individual	1,140	1,120	1,400	1,330	1,170	1,190
Future changes: More emphasis on technology	1,330	1,290	1,390	1,320	1,410	1,400
Get comfort and strength from religion	0,660	0,750	0,840	0,700	0,950	0,670
Good human relationships	1,380	1,410	1,570	1,220	1,410	1,370
Government order vs. freedom	1,530	1,410	1,240	1,160	1,420	1,410
Government responsibility	6,850	6,670	5,770	6,130	5,560	5,800
Government should reduce environmental pollution	1,960	1,940	2,290	2,270	2,060	2,120
Had formal education	0,930	0,990	0,750	0,960	0,970	0,940
Hard work brings success	4,490	4,420	2,790	3,900	4,490	4,440
Highest educational level attained	5,500	4,620	4,470	4,970	4,280	4,390
How business and industry should be managed	1,890	2,340	2,140	1,890	1,850	1,990
How important is God in your life	7,270	7,000	8,150	5,880	8,880	6,930
How many children do you have	1,750	1,630	2,500	1,970	2,260	1,920
How much freedom of choice and control	6,720	5,940	6,360	6,380	6,940	6,660
How much is the government doing against poverty	2,800	2,840	2,500	2,570	2,590	2,690
How often discusses political matters with friends	1,860	2,070	2,190	2,240	2,210	2,130
Never attend religious services (How often do you attend religious services)	4,580	4,550	3,320	4,890	2,000	4,720
How often follows politics in the news	1,520	2,060	2,780	2,130	2,260	2,230
How proud of nationality	1,530	1,820	1,360	1,810	1,450	1,640
Humanity has a bright or bleak future	1,400	1,450	1,240	1,330	1,480	1,480
Humiliating to receive money without having to work for it	2,440	2,290	1,980	2,420	2,450	2,480
Husband and wife should both contribute to income	1,870	1,650	1,890	2,070	1,800	1,810
Ideal number of children	2,920	2,650	2,240	2,570	2,960	2,710
If only one child allowed: boy or girl	1,970	1,950	2,010	2,170	2,140	2,060

The original data (Part 2 - Continued)

	Global Judaism - mean	Global Orthodoxy - mean	Global Hinduism - mean	Global Buddhism - mean	Global Catholicism - (practicing) - mean	Global citizens - mean
Immigrant policy	2,230	2,440	2,840	2,520	2,540	2,480
Important child qualities: determination perseverance	0,320	0,420	0,360	0,410	0,250	0,340
Important child qualities: feeling of responsibility	0,640	0,700	0,580	0,780	0,650	0,680
Important child qualities: good manners	0,690	0,690	0,870	0,770	0,740	0,740
Important child qualities: hard work	0,320	0,720	0,690	0,450	0,470	0,500
Important child qualities: imagination	0,250	0,160	0,210	0,150	0,140	0,190
Important child qualities: independence	0,610	0,430	0,420	0,610	0,330	0,450
Important child qualities: obedience	0,200	0,300	0,570	0,190	0,410	0,350
Important child qualities: religious faith	0,300	0,280	0,380	0,120	0,530	0,310
Important child qualities: thrift saving money and things	0,230	0,420	0,410	0,470	0,340	0,350
Important child qualities: unselfishness	0,430	0,250	0,300	0,280	0,270	0,270
Important for successful marriage: Adequate income	1,710	1,560	1,480	1,610	1,680	1,740
Important for successful marriage: Agreement on politics	2,530	2,550	2,470	2,430	2,450	2,530
Important for successful marriage: Apart from in-laws	1,730	1,770	2,220	2,550	1,820	1,810
Important for successful marriage: Children	1,470	1,280	1,240	1,550	1,360	1,450
Important for successful marriage: Faithfulness	1,250	1,220	1,080	1,190	1,090	1,190
Important for successful marriage: Good housing	1,690	1,560	1,720	1,990	1,680	1,730
Important for successful marriage: Happy sexual relationship	1,330	1,460	1,270	1,730	1,420	1,410
Important for successful marriage: Religious beliefs	2,030	2,070	1,780	2,090	1,760	2,190
Important for successful marriage: Respect and appreciation	1,110	1,190	1,200	1,310	1,150	1,170
Important for successful marriage: Same social background	2,070	2,230	1,710	1,990	2,070	2,240

Appendix VI

	Global Judaism - mean	Global Orthodoxy - mean	Global Hinduism - mean	Global Buddhism - mean	Global Catholicism - (practicing) - mean	Global citizens - mean
Important for successful marriage: Sharing household chores	1,820	1,720	1,490	2,130	1,810	1,800
Important in a job: a job that is interesting	0,690	0,620	0,620	0,490	0,580	0,610
Important in a job: a job that meets one's abilities	0,630	0,600	0,700	0,690	0,600	0,620
Important in a job: a respected job	0,420	0,540	0,650	0,430	0,480	0,470
Important in a job: a responsible job	0,490	0,360	0,660	0,560	0,460	0,460
Important in a job: a useful job for society	0,430	0,480	0,570	0,370	0,450	0,420
Important in a job: an opportunity to use initiative	0,540	0,390	0,540	0,450	0,450	0,480
Important in a job: generous holidays	0,310	0,340	0,360	0,450	0,280	0,310
Important in a job: good chances for promotion	0,460	0,430	0,700	0,150	0,410	0,370
Important in a job: good hours	0,510	0,500	0,550	0,550	0,500	0,510
Important in a job: good job security	0,700	0,690	0,830	0,680	0,680	0,680
Important in a job: good pay	0,780	0,880	0,900	0,690	0,790	0,800
Important in a job: meeting people	0,490	0,440	0,460	0,350	0,440	0,460
Important in a job: none of these	0,630	0,900	0,040	0,100	0,670	0,690
Important in a job: not too much pressure	0,360	0,350	0,440	0,520	0,380	0,390
Important in a job: pleasant people to work with	0,700	0,660	0,700	0,480	0,670	0,690
Important in a job: that you can achieve something	0,630	0,560	0,630	0,520	0,560	0,580
Important in successful marriage: Understanding and tolerance	1,160	1,260	1,200	1,320	1,210	1,230
Important: Religious service birth	0,750	0,870	0,740	0,490	0,960	0,720
Important: Religious service death	0,840	0,920	0,750	0,920	0,980	0,810
Important: Religious service marriage	0,810	0,870	0,800	0,620	0,980	0,740
Importation of goods	1,520	1,560	1,770	1,520	1,730	1,640
In democracy, the economic system runs badly	2,850	2,610	2,540	2,810	2,690	2,750
Anti-egalitarian position on Income equality" scale	4,470	5,900	5,010	6,090	5,960	5,970
Income level	2,010	1,920	2,050	1,940	1,950	1,950

The original data (Part 2 - Continued)

	Global Judaism - mean	Global Orthodoxy - mean	Global Hinduism - mean	Global Buddhism - mean	Global Catholicism - (practicing) - mean	Global citizens - mean
Increase in taxes if used to prevent environmental pollution	2,310	2,310	2,330	2,190	2,390	2,350
Interest in politics	2,240	2,680	2,720	2,410	2,730	2,620
Is the chief wage earner employed now	0,770	0,740	0,940	0,860	0,770	0,810
Jobs scarce: Employers should give priority to (nation) people than immigrants	1,650	1,390	1,210	1,380	1,310	1,370
Jobs scarce: Men should have more right to a job than women	1,860	1,790	1,590	1,890	1,790	1,780
Jobs scarce: older people should be forced to retire	1,860	1,590	2,050	2,390	1,750	1,760
Justifiable: abortion	5,190	4,400	3,050	3,550	2,530	3,900
Justifiable: avoiding a fare on public transport	2,500	3,010	1,660	1,960	2,310	2,430
Justifiable: buy stolen goods	1,630	1,810	1,510	1,520	1,620	1,740
Justifiable: cheating on taxes	2,440	2,720	1,730	1,640	2,320	2,400
Justifiable: claiming government benefits	2,290	2,560	1,990	2,110	2,330	2,350
Justifiable: divorce	6,400	5,010	3,080	4,240	3,940	4,910
Justifiable: driving under influence of alcohol	1,480	1,500	1,350	1,670	1,460	1,540
Justifiable: euthanasia	4,500	4,040	3,130	4,590	2,900	4,000
Justifiable: homosexuality	4,740	2,200	1,970	2,460	2,910	3,200
Justifiable: joyriding	1,380	1,410	1,410	1,510	1,350	1,400
Justifiable: lying	3,460	2,940	2,510	2,410	2,410	2,730
Justifiable: prostitution	3,340	2,130	1,990	2,080	2,190	2,560
Justifiable: someone accepting a bribe	1,460	1,780	1,530	1,660	1,720	1,740
Justifiable: suicide	2,640	2,030	1,940	2,430	1,890	2,330
Justifiable: taking soft drugs	2,390	1,530	1,290	1,470	1,410	1,670
Justifiable: throwing away litter	1,710	1,700	1,460	1,650	1,730	1,820
Least liked allow: demonstrate	0,110	0,070	0,150	0,120	0,090	0,110
Least liked allow: hold office	0,060	0,030	0,130	0,170	0,060	0,060
Least liked allow: teach	0,080	0,050	0,130	0,150	0,080	0,070
Leisure time important in life	1,910	2,020	2,390	1,980	1,890	1,930
Major changes in life	5,390	5,110	5,110	4,370	5,040	5,360
Make effort to live up to what my friends expect	2,330	2,400	2,290	2,340	2,410	2,410

Appendix VI

	Global Judaism - mean	Global Orthodoxy - mean	Global Hinduism - mean	Global Buddhism - mean	Global Catholicism - (practicing) - mean	Global citizens - mean
Marriage is an out-dated institution	0,130	0,160	0,190	0,160	0,110	0,170
Men make better political leaders than women do	2,560	2,310	2,390	2,400	2,550	2,440
Moments of prayer, meditation...	0,730	0,730	0,870	0,620	0,920	0,660
Most people can be trusted	1,700	1,780	1,630	1,650	1,740	1,700
Rejecting neighbors: Drug addicts	0,710	0,770	0,690	0,590	0,680	0,690
Rejecting neighbors: Emotionally unstable people	0,400	0,570	0,520	0,490	0,340	0,400
Rejecting neighbors: Heavy drinkers	0,590	0,700	0,650	0,550	0,580	0,590
Rejecting neighbors: Homosexuals	0,360	0,630	0,610	0,510	0,460	0,470
Rejecting neighbors: Immigrants/foreign workers	0,110	0,190	0,360	0,240	0,140	0,170
Rejecting neighbors: Jews	0,110	0,200	0,490	0,300	0,170	0,160
Rejecting neighbors: Left wing extremists	0,380	0,390	0,710	0,450	0,320	0,330
Rejecting neighbors: Muslims	0,170	0,250	0,320	0,280	0,200	0,200
Rejecting neighbors: People of a different race	0,100	0,180	0,360	0,200	0,140	0,150
Rejecting neighbors: People of a different religion	0,100	0,270	0,380	0,320	0,200	0,260
Rejecting neighbors: People who have AIDS	0,350	0,570	0,640	0,440	0,410	0,420
Rejecting neighbors: People with a criminal record	0,550	0,660	0,690	0,440	0,590	0,540
Rejecting neighbors: People with large families	0,130	0,140	0,340	0,390	0,100	0,110
Rejecting neighbors: Political Extremists	0,400	0,480	0,580	0,520	0,390	0,510
Rejecting neighbors: Right wing extremists	0,500	0,380	0,630	0,530	0,290	0,330
New and old ideas	4,950	5,050	4,520	4,380	5,370	5,290
One of main goals in life has been to make my parents proud	1,940	1,940	1,590	2,070	1,690	1,840
Opinion about scientific advances	1,740	1,700	1,800	2,080	1,830	1,780
Parents responsibilities to their children	1,390	1,340	1,270	1,480	1,260	1,360
People should not have to work if they don't want to	3,210	3,110	2,950	3,250	3,290	3,250
People who don't work turn lazy	2,030	2,260	1,870	2,030	2,190	2,280
Political action: attending lawful demonstrations	2,160	2,220	2,290	2,480	2,360	2,270

The original data (Part 2 - Continued)

	Global Judaism - mean	Global Orthodoxy - mean	Global Hinduism - mean	Global Buddhism - mean	Global Catholicism - (practicing) - mean	Global citizens - mean
Political action: joining in boycotts	2,460	2,590	2,320	2,440	2,610	2,490
Political action: joining unofficial strikes	2,600	2,690	2,690	2,760	2,770	2,700
Political action: occupying buildings or factories	2,870	2,830	2,870	2,840	2,850	2,830
Political action: signing a petition	1,800	2,230	2,090	1,840	2,010	1,950
Political system: Having a democratic political system	1,510	1,710	1,560	1,720	1,650	1,650
Political system: Having a strong leader	3,000	2,660	2,400	2,700	2,860	2,870
Political system: Having experts make decisions	2,510	2,250	2,140	2,380	2,370	2,350
Political system: Having the army rule	3,480	3,310	3,110	3,300	3,310	3,340
Politicians who don't believe in God are unfit for public office	3,180	3,070	2,890	3,270	3,070	3,120
Politics important in life	2,520	2,880	2,750	2,240	2,790	2,740
Poverty compared to 10 years ago	1,250	1,180	1,860	2,470	1,450	1,430
Pray to God outside of religious services (I)	3,240	3,600	2,450	4,060	1,780	3,510
For state ownership of business	4,450	5,250	5,340	4,870	4,900	4,930
Problem if women have more income than husband	2,570	2,610	2,400	2,470	2,470	2,510
Protecting environment vs. Economic growth	1,700	1,580	1,720	1,560	1,510	1,570
Raised religiously	0,560	0,570	0,910	0,570	0,950	0,650
Rate political system as it was before	5,480	5,120	7,190	5,620	4,990	5,200
Rate political system for governing country	4,910	3,890	4,890	5,490	5,040	4,690
Rate political system in ten years	6,810	6,270	5,520	5,750	6,370	6,180
Religion important in life	1,960	2,080	1,710	2,370	1,500	2,170
Religious leaders should not influence government	2,080	2,130	2,180	2,200	2,330	2,190
Religious leaders should not influence how people vote	1,940	1,970	2,350	2,160	2,170	2,090
Religious person	1,370	1,220	1,210	1,510	1,080	1,370
Respect and love for parents	1,270	1,140	1,130	1,140	1,130	1,210
Respect for individual human rights nowadays	2,440	2,830	2,050	2,180	2,280	2,470
Respondent interested during the interview	1,580	1,710	1,560	1,830	1,550	1,580

Appendix VI

	Global Judaism - mean	Global Orthodoxy - mean	Global Hinduism - mean	Global Buddhism - mean	Global Catholicism - (practicing) - mean	Global citizens - mean
Satisfaction with financial situation of household	5,860	4,080	5,910	6,090	6,210	5,660
Satisfaction with the people in national office	2,760	3,020	2,490	2,610	2,680	2,750
Satisfaction with the way democracy develops	2,570	2,980	2,300	2,310	2,460	2,620
Satisfaction with your life	6,940	5,180	6,310	6,650	7,260	6,640
Scale of incomes	4,260	4,510	4,010	4,770	4,670	4,720
right wing (self positioning in political scale)	4,900	5,260	5,930	6,260	6,030	5,580
Service to others important in life	1,680	2,100	1,730	2,200	1,530	1,760
Social class (subjective)	2,780	3,450	3,170	3,170	3,400	3,350
Socio-economic status of respondent	1,990	2,930	2,270	2,600	2,700	2,620
Spend time with colleagues from work	2,590	2,410	2,170	2,510	2,720	2,520
Spend time with friends	1,570	1,720	1,960	1,990	1,770	1,710
Spend time with parents or other relatives	1,590	1,600	1,550	1,640	1,550	1,520
Spend time with people at sport, culture, communal organization	2,740	3,360	3,190	3,140	2,970	3,090
Spend time with people at your church, mosque or synagogue	2,620	3,030	2,310	3,080	2,090	2,820
State of health (subjective)	2,130	2,590	2,280	2,430	2,280	2,260
Thinking about meaning and purpose of life	1,780	1,780	2,020	1,860	1,850	1,840
To develop talents you need to have a job	1,760	2,020	1,990	2,000	2,170	2,110
Tradition vs. high economic growth	1,460	1,490	1,800	1,530	1,500	1,540
TV most important entertainment	2,500	2,550	2,240	2,150	2,420	2,400
University is more important for a boy than for a girl	2,990	2,900	2,720	2,800	3,000	2,960
Unpaid work education, arts, music or cultural activities	0,110	0,040	0,130	0,070	0,050	0,060
Unpaid work environment, conservation, animal rights	0,070	0,030	0,060	0,030	0,020	0,030
Unpaid work human rights	0,040	0,010	0,030	0,010	0,020	0,020
Unpaid work labor unions	0,040	0,050	0,060	0,020	0,030	0,030
Unpaid work local political action groups	0,060	0,020	0,060	0,050	0,030	0,030
Unpaid work none	0,660	0,770	0,610	0,700	0,710	0,710
Unpaid work organization concerned with health	0,060	0,020	0,090	0,040	0,040	0,030
Unpaid work other groups	0,070	0,020	0,050	0,050	0,030	0,030

The original data (Part 2 - Continued)

	Global Judaism - mean	Global Orthodoxy - mean	Global Hinduism - mean	Global Buddhism - mean	Global Catholicism - (practicing) - mean	Global citizens - mean
Unpaid work peace movement	0,030	0,010	0,050	0,020	0,010	0,010
Unpaid work political parties or groups	0,070	0,030	0,080	0,030	0,030	0,040
Unpaid work professional associations	0,100	0,020	0,050	0,030	0,020	0,030
Unpaid work religious or church organization	0,220	0,050	0,160	0,090	0,150	0,100
Unpaid work social welfare service for elderly, handicapped or deprived people	0,110	0,030	0,070	0,100	0,060	0,060
Unpaid work sports or recreation	0,130	0,050	0,090	0,070	0,070	0,080
Unpaid work women's group	0,070	0,010	0,060	0,050	0,030	0,030
Unpaid work youth work	0,110	0,020	0,050	0,040	0,040	0,040
Using violence for political goals not justified	1,640	1,830	1,580	1,830	1,890	1,770
What age did you complete your education (recoded in intervals)	7,250	6,860	5,990	6,570	5,810	6,410
Willingness to fight for country	0,830	0,820	0,890	0,690	0,710	0,740
Woman as a single parent	0,910	0,930	1,180	0,740	0,810	0,860
Work compared with Leisure	2,820	3,650	4,070	3,370	3,850	3,660
Work important in life	1,600	1,520	1,210	1,540	1,410	1,460
Work is a duty towards society	2,220	2,390	1,870	2,090	2,110	2,250
Work should come first even if it means less spare time	2,240	2,400	2,140	2,680	2,490	2,510
Work: accomplish personal goals	1,840	1,750	2,040	2,090	1,890	1,850
Work: stay up late to finish	2,330	2,200	2,080	2,330	2,140	2,220
Work: until satisfied with results	1,850	1,710	1,840	1,870	1,690	1,690
Would buy things at a 20% higher price if it helped to protect environment	2,500	2,550	2,580	2,360	2,530	2,520
Would give part of my income for the environment	2,120	2,150	2,020	2,080	2,230	2,190

Percentage differences to the global average (Part 1)

	Muslims	Judaism	Hinduism	Orthodoxy	Buddhism	Protestantism
A woman has to have children to be fulfilled	36,1	-1,6	41,0	31,1	16,4	-27,9
Abortion if not wanting more children	-13,6	29,5	29,5	36,4	11,4	2,3
Abortion when child physically handicapped	-35,6	9,6	-8,2	2,7	1,4	9,6
Abortion when the Mother's health is at risk	-17,2	6,9	2,3	-6,9	6,9	9,2
Abortion when woman not married	-5,0	32,5	67,5	35,0	37,5	5,0
Active/Inactive membership of any other organization	-45,0	55,0	-30,0	-60,0	15,0	65,0
Active/Inactive membership of art, music, educational	-29,6	3,7	14,8	-44,4	-37,0	48,1
Active/Inactive membership of charitable/humanitarian organization	-47,6	90,5	0,0	-42,9	-4,8	61,9
Active/Inactive membership of church or religious organization	-34,6	5,8	-19,2	-42,3	-25,0	67,3
Active/Inactive membership of environmental organization	-28,6	-14,3	7,1	-42,9	-28,6	21,4
Active/Inactive membership of labor unions	-22,2	-33,3	-22,2	29,6	-40,7	22,2
Active/Inactive membership of political party	35,0	10,0	15,0	-10,0	-40,0	5,0
Active/Inactive membership of professional organization	-20,0	15,0	0,0	-35,0	-20,0	45,0
Active/Inactive membership of sport or recreation	-39,5	-15,8	-15,8	-50,0	0,0	68,4
Against Labor market reforms: unemployed have a right to refuse offered jobs	-6,6	3,3	-16,5	14,4	-1,6	-7,8
Anti-egalitarian position on income equality	1,8	-25,1	-16,1	-1,2	2,0	-2,5
Bad future changes: A simple and more natural lifestyle	13,1	1,6	3,3	1,6	9,0	2,5
Bad future changes: Greater respect for authority	-9,6	-1,3	4,5	-1,9	39,5	8,9

Percentage differences to the global average (Part 1 - Continued)

	Muslims	Judaism	Hinduism	Orthodoxy	Buddhism	Protestantism
Bad future changes: Less emphasis on money and material possessions	7,9	-14,5	16,4	9,7	7,3	-3,0
Bad future changes: Less importance placed on work	5,1	-7,7	9,4	5,5	3,0	-0,9
Bad future changes: More emphasis on family life	-0,9	-2,7	20,5	-1,8	2,7	-1,8
Bad future changes: More emphasis on individual	-5,0	-4,2	17,6	-5,9	11,8	-2,5
Bad future changes: More emphasis on technology	-12,1	-5,0	-0,7	-7,9	-5,7	12,9
Bad political system: Having a democratic political system	-8,5	-8,5	-5,5	3,6	4,2	-4,8
Bad political system: Having a strong leader	-0,3	4,5	-16,4	-7,3	-5,9	9,1
Bad political system: Having experts make decisions	-5,5	6,8	-8,9	-4,3	1,3	8,5
Bad political system: Having the army rule	-12,0	4,2	-6,9	-0,9	-1,2	7,5
Believe in: devil	65,9	-22,0	-12,2	4,9	-2,4	-17,1
Believe in: God	18,1	7,2	14,5	8,4	-16,9	1,2
Believe in: heaven	50,0	-11,7	0,0	-20,0	-11,7	-1,7
Believe in: hell	89,1	-15,2	19,6	-6,5	4,3	-26,1
Believe in: life after death	36,7	-11,7	-5,0	-21,7	0,0	1,7
Believe in: people have a soul	19,5	-2,6	2,6	-10,4	1,3	1,3
Believe in: re-incarnation	10,7	0,0	242,9	21,4	110,7	-3,6
Believe in: sin	23,9	-6,0	7,5	14,9	-31,3	-7,5
Belong to conservation, the environment, ecology, animal rights	40,0	120,0	60,0	-40,0	0,0	20,0
Belong to education, arts, music or cultural activities	20,0	120,0	60,0	-30,0	20,0	30,0
Belong to human rights	66,7	100,0	0,0	-66,7	-33,3	33,3
Belong to labor unions	-47,1	-23,5	-47,1	-5,9	-58,8	82,4
Belong to local political actions	125,0	125,0	75,0	-50,0	75,0	25,0
Belong to organization concerned with health	60,0	80,0	80,0	-40,0	60,0	40,0
Belong to other groups	-16,7	50,0	16,7	-50,0	0,0	83,3
Belong to peace movement	200,0	100,0	200,0	-50,0	50,0	0,0
Belong to political parties	71,4	85,7	57,1	-14,3	-28,6	28,6

Appendix VI

	Muslims	Judaism	Hinduism	Orthodoxy	Buddhism	Protestantism
Belong to professional associations	14,3	128,6	42,9	-28,6	0,0	57,1
Belong to religious organization	17,6	100,0	23,5	-58,8	29,4	100,0
Belong to social welfare service for elderly	28,6	100,0	28,6	-57,1	28,6	57,1
Belong to sports or recreation	-20,0	60,0	-13,3	-53,3	0,0	66,7
Belong to women's group	100,0	150,0	75,0	-50,0	50,0	50,0
Belong to youth work	40,0	140,0	20,0	-40,0	20,0	60,0
Child needs a home with father and mother	7,9	-3,4	4,5	7,9	4,5	-9,0
Child qualities: tolerance and Respect for other people	-3,0	16,4	-11,9	-4,5	-19,4	4,5
Churches give answers: moral problems	35,7	10,7	-35,7	12,5	-19,6	-12,5
Churches give answers: people's spiritual needs	15,7	11,4	-22,9	12,9	-18,6	-2,9
Churches give answers: the problems of family life	35,3	17,6	-45,1	2,0	-33,3	-9,8
Churches give answers: the social problems	48,8	22,0	-34,1	-17,1	-48,8	-9,8
Competition harmful	-8,2	-3,4	-18,7	-3,7	12,2	-4,5
Cooperating party leader good	-0,6	-5,2	-6,9	-1,7	-2,9	1,1
Country is run for all people's benefit	0,8	2,3	6,9	-6,1	9,2	4,6
Disagree: a[Country]'s environmental problems can be solved without any international agreements to handle them	-7,7	8,5	-17,5	-2,8	-5,3	6,5
Disagreement with: Being a housewife just as fulfilling	0,9	-1,8	8,7	1,4	-10,5	1,8
Disagreement with: Democracies are indecisive and have too much squabbling	4,8	4,8	-4,8	-2,4	2,8	2,8
Disagreement with: Democracies aren't good at maintaining order	2,2	2,2	-2,9	-4,7	2,2	4,7
Disagreement with: Democracy may have problems but is better	-2,9	-4,6	-8,0	5,7	9,8	-2,9
Disagreement with: Humiliating to receive money without having to work for it	-17,3	-1,6	-20,2	-7,7	-2,4	11,7

Percentage differences to the global average (Part 1 - Continued)

	Muslims	Judaism	Hinduism	Orthodoxy	Buddhism	Protestantism
Disagreement with: Husband and wife should both contribute to income	0,6	3,3	4,4	-8,8	14,4	7,2
Disagreement with: In democracy, the economic system runs badly	3,3	3,6	-7,6	-5,1	2,2	4,7
Disagreement with: Job best way for women to be independent	2,8	-1,9	6,1	-6,6	22,6	1,4
Disagreement with: Make effort to live up to what my friends expect	-9,5	-3,3	-5,0	-0,4	-2,9	7,9
Disagreement with: Men make better political leaders than women do	-14,8	4,9	-2,0	-5,3	-1,6	11,5
Disagreement with: One of main goals in life has been to make my parents proud	-19,6	5,4	-13,6	5,4	12,5	13,6
Disagreement with: People should not have to work if they don't want to	-4,9	-1,2	-9,2	-4,3	0,0	8,0
Disagreement with: Pre-school child suffers with working mother	-4,1	5,9	-24,7	-0,9	-8,2	11,4
Disagreement with: Problem if women have more income than husband	-6,8	2,4	-4,4	4,0	-1,6	4,8
Disagreement with: Relationship working mother	6,4	-6,4	10,3	-8,4	-0,5	-4,4
Disagreement with: to develop talents you need to have a job	-14,2	-16,6	-5,7	-4,3	-5,2	10,9
Disagreement with: University is more important for a boy than for a girl	-6,1	1,0	-8,1	-2,0	-5,4	8,1
Disagreement with: Women want a home and children	-22,9	11,5	-24,3	-11,5	-12,8	11,9
Disagreement with: Work is a duty towards society	-12,9	-1,3	-16,9	6,2	-7,1	2,2
Disagreement with: Work should come first even if it means less spare time	-23,5	-10,8	-14,7	-4,4	6,8	9,6

Appendix VI

	Muslims	Judaism	Hinduism	Orthodoxy	Buddhism	Protestantism
Disagreement with: Work: accomplish personal goals	0,5	-0,5	10,3	-5,4	13,0	-2,7
Disagreement with: Work: stay up late to finish	-8,1	5,0	-6,3	-0,9	5,0	8,1
disagreement with: Work: until satisfied with results	-1,2	9,5	8,9	1,2	10,7	-4,7
Disagreement with: People who don't work turn lazy	-16,2	-11,0	-18,0	-0,9	-11,0	13,6
Dissatisfaction with the people in national office	-6,9	0,4	-9,5	9,8	-5,1	-5,8
Dissatisfaction with the way democracy develops	-3,1	-1,9	-12,2	13,7	-11,8	-8,4
Economic aid to poorer countries should be reduced	2,9	2,5	1,1	9,1	-6,5	-2,9
Environmental action: attend meeting, signed petition	-13,3	0,0	20,0	-46,7	20,0	20,0
Environmental action: chosen products that are better for environment	-16,0	0,0	-40,0	-28,0	44,0	32,0
Environmental action: contributed to environmental organization	-6,7	13,3	33,3	-46,7	6,7	33,3
Environmental action: recycle	-24,5	-6,1	-44,9	-30,6	63,3	44,9
Environmental action: reduce water consumption	16,0	-24,0	-20,0	-20,0	40,0	2,0
Ever felt bored	-41,4	-4,0	-68,7	24,2	-75,8	-9,1
Ever felt depressed or very unhappy	-40,0	-10,0	-72,0	24,0	-75,0	-10,0
Ever felt on top of the world	-28,7	-14,9	-71,3	31,7	-73,3	-7,9
Ever felt pleased about having accomplished something	-22,7	2,1	-49,5	9,3	-46,4	-2,1
Ever felt proud because someone complimented you	-32,0	-11,3	-58,8	25,8	-67,0	-7,2
Ever felt restless	-46,5	-7,1	-69,7	18,2	-73,7	-8,1
Ever felt that things were going your way	-25,3	-8,1	-60,6	18,2	-71,7	-5,1
Ever felt upset because somebody criticized you	-62,2	-4,1	-76,5	22,4	-78,6	-9,2
Ever felt very excited or interested	-17,2	-1,0	-44,4	24,2	-62,6	-7,1
Ever felt very lonely or remote from other people	-44,4	-4,0	-75,8	27,3	-79,8	-11,1

Percentage differences to the global average (Part 1 - Continued)

	Muslims	Judaism	Hinduism	Orthodoxy	Buddhism	Protestantism
Ever felt very excited or interested	-17,2	-1,0	-44,4	24,2	-62,6	-7,1
Ever felt very lonely or remote from other people	-44,4	-4,0	-75,8	27,3	-79,8	-11,1
Fairness: One secretary is paid more	-1,2	0,0	-11,8	2,4	-5,9	0,0
Family not important in life	-7,8	-0,9	-0,9	0,0	-2,6	-1,7
favoring a restrictive immigrant policy	-1,2	-10,1	14,5	-1,6	1,6	1,2
Feeling of unhappiness	2,5	-2,5	0,5	18,6	-4,5	-10,1
Frequency watches TV	-0,4	-10,4	-27,0	9,7	5,0	-1,5
Friends not important in life	-5,2	-6,3	9,2	2,9	-1,1	-8,6
Get comfort and strength from religion	38,8	-1,5	25,4	11,9	4,5	-7,5
God important in your life	32,6	4,9	17,6	1,0	-15,2	-8,4
Government responsibility vs. private responsibility	10,9	18,1	-0,5	15,0	5,7	-12,8
Government should not reduce environmental pollution	-9,4	-7,5	8,0	-8,5	7,1	13,2
Hard work does not bring success	-15,8	1,1	-37,2	-0,5	-12,2	-3,6
High income level	-4,6	3,1	5,1	-1,5	-0,5	-1,0
High satisfaction with home life	-6,1	-6,3	-5,9	-12,6	-8,2	4,5
Ideal number of children	10,3	7,7	-17,3	-2,2	-5,2	1,5
Important child qualities: determination perseverance	-5,9	-5,9	5,9	23,5	20,6	-5,9
Important child qualities: feeling of responsibility	-13,2	-5,9	-14,7	2,9	14,7	0,0
Important child qualities: good manners	16,2	-6,8	17,6	-6,8	4,1	0,0
Important child qualities: hard work	22,0	-36,0	38,0	44,0	-10,0	-36,0
Important child qualities: imagination	0,0	31,6	10,5	-15,8	-21,1	10,5
Important child qualities: independence	-2,2	35,6	-6,7	-4,4	35,6	13,3
Important child qualities: obedience	31,4	-42,9	62,9	-14,3	-45,7	-8,6
Important child qualities: religious faith	93,5	-3,2	22,6	-9,7	-61,3	-16,1
Important child qualities: thrift saving money and things	5,7	-34,3	17,1	20,0	34,3	-20,0
Important child qualities: unselfishness	-3,7	59,3	11,1	-7,4	3,7	0,0

	Muslims	Judaism	Hinduism	Orthodoxy	Buddhism	Protestantism
Important in a job: a job that is interesting	4,9	13,1	1,6	1,6	-19,7	9,8
Important in a job: a job that meets one's abilities	24,2	1,6	12,9	-3,2	11,3	-9,7
Important in a job: a respected job	55,3	-10,6	38,3	14,9	-8,5	-21,3
Important in a job: a responsible job	39,1	6,5	43,5	-21,7	21,7	0,0
Important in a job: a useful job for society	85,7	2,4	35,7	14,3	-11,9	-11,9
Important in a job: an opportunity to use initiative	25,0	12,5	12,5	-18,8	-6,3	4,2
Important in a job: generous holidays	29,0	0,0	16,1	9,7	45,2	-19,4
Important in a job: good chances for promotion	73,0	24,3	89,2	16,2	-59,5	-13,5
Important in a job: good hours	29,4	0,0	7,8	-2,0	7,8	-5,9
Important in a job: good job security	25,0	2,9	22,1	1,5	0,0	-2,9
Important in a job: good pay	15,0	-2,5	12,5	10,0	-13,8	-11,3
Important in a job: meeting people	56,5	6,5	0,0	-4,3	-23,9	2,2
Important in a job: not too much pressure	53,8	-7,7	12,8	-10,3	33,3	-15,4
Important in a job: pleasant people to work with	18,8	1,4	1,4	-4,3	-30,4	10,1
Important in a job: that you can achieve something	22,4	8,6	8,6	-3,4	-10,3	13,8
Important in successful marriage: Understanding and tolerance	-6,5	-5,7	-2,4	2,4	7,3	-3,3
Important: Religious service birth	-15,3	4,2	2,8	20,8	-31,9	2,8
Important: Religious service death	16,0	3,7	-7,4	13,6	13,6	8,6
Important: Religious service marriage	16,2	9,5	8,1	17,6	-16,2	4,1
Justifiable: abortion	-35,6	33,1	-21,8	12,8	-9,0	13,3
Justifiable: adultery	0,8	31,8	-47,5	5,1	-4,3	-14,5
Justifiable: avoiding a fare on public transport	-18,9	2,9	-31,7	23,9	-19,3	-14,0
Justifiable: buy stolen goods	-1,7	-6,3	-13,2	4,0	-12,6	-12,1
Justifiable: cheating on taxes	-23,8	1,7	-27,9	13,3	-31,7	-1,7
Justifiable: claiming government benefits	-1,3	-2,6	-15,3	8,9	-10,2	-21,7
Justifiable: divorce	-27,1	30,3	-37,3	2,0	-13,6	9,2
Justifiable: driving under influence of alcohol	-10,4	-3,9	-12,3	-2,6	8,4	-9,7

Percentage differences to the global average (Part 1 - Continued)

	Muslims	Judaism	Hinduism	Orthodoxy	Buddhism	Protestantism
Justifiable: euthanasia	-46,5	12,5	-21,8	1,0	14,8	13,5
Justifiable: failing to report damage you've done accidentally to a parked vehicle	20,2	2,4	-15,9	-1,4	-9,1	-14,4
Justifiable: fighting with the police	14,2	0,8	-7,9	-7,5	30,7	-17,7
Justifiable: homosexuality	-56,3	48,1	-38,4	-31,3	-23,1	24,4
Justifiable: joyriding	5,0	-1,4	0,7	0,7	7,9	-6,4
Justifiable: keeping money that you have found	28,5	37,1	-19,5	12,3	-28,1	-17,9
Justifiable. killing in self-defense	-15,9	20,5	-14,8	-6,1	-11,8	-4,3
Justifiable: lying	-23,8	26,7	-8,1	7,7	-11,7	-15,0
Justifiable: political assassination	37,1	23,4	-0,6	6,0	19,8	-11,4
Justifiable: prostitution	-44,1	30,5	-22,3	-16,8	-18,8	9,8
Justifiable: sex under the legal age of consent	18,0	10,7	-44,7	16,8	-14,3	-17,2
Justifiable: someone accepting a bribe	-11,5	-16,1	-12,1	2,3	-4,6	-10,3
Justifiable: suicide	-41,2	13,3	-16,7	-12,9	4,3	10,3
Justifiable: taking soft drugs	-14,4	43,1	-22,8	-8,4	-12,0	-1,2
Justifiable: threatening workers who refuse to join a strike	42,0	-2,8	-8,3	-0,6	-9,9	-6,1
Justifiable: throwing away litter	-15,4	-6,0	-19,8	-6,6	-9,3	5,5
Leisure not time important in life	7,8	-1,0	23,8	4,7	2,6	-8,3
Low Social class (subjective)	-2,4	-17,0	-5,4	3,0	-5,4	-1,8
Low Socio-economic status of respondent	11,1	-24,0	-13,4	11,8	-0,8	-2,7
Major changes in life: one should act boldly	-8,8	0,6	-4,7	-4,7	-18,5	10,3
Moments of prayer, meditation...	31,8	10,6	31,8	10,6	-6,1	-4,5
Much freedom of choice and control	-9,3	0,9	-4,5	-10,8	-4,2	6,6
Rejecting neighbors: Drug addicts	4,3	2,9	0,0	11,6	-14,5	-1,4
Rejecting neighbors: Emotionally unstable people	35,0	0,0	30,0	42,5	22,5	-22,5
Rejecting neighbors: Heavy drinkers	11,9	0,0	10,2	18,6	-6,8	-10,2
Rejecting neighbors: Homosexuals	40,4	-23,4	29,8	34,0	8,5	-31,9

Appendix VI

	Muslims	Judaism	Hinduism	Orthodoxy	Buddhism	Protestantism
Rejecting neighbors: Immigrants/foreign workers	76,5	-35,3	111,8	11,8	41,2	-23,5
Rejecting neighbors: Jews	112,5	-31,3	206,3	25,0	87,5	-43,8
Rejecting neighbors: Left wing extremists	75,8	15,2	115,2	18,2	36,4	-18,2
Rejecting neighbors: Muslims	-20,0	-15,0	60,0	25,0	40,0	-5,0
Rejecting neighbors: People of a different race	86,7	-33,3	140,0	20,0	33,3	-26,7
Rejecting neighbors: People who have AIDS	47,6	-16,7	52,4	35,7	4,8	-40,5
Rejecting neighbors: People with a criminal record	22,2	1,9	27,8	22,2	-18,5	-22,2
Rejecting neighbors: People with large families	163,6	18,2	209,1	27,3	254,5	-36,4
Rejecting neighbors: Political Extremists	27,5	-21,6	13,7	-5,9	2,0	-11,8
Rejecting neighbors: Right wing extremists	69,7	51,5	90,9	15,2	60,6	-15,2
Never attend religious services	-17,6	-3,0	-29,7	-3,6	3,6	6,1
Never discusses political matters with friends	3,3	-12,7	2,8	-2,8	5,2	-2,3
Never follow politics in the news	6,7	-31,8	24,7	-7,6	-4,5	-4,0
Never persuading friends, relatives or fellow workers	-5,7	-2,8	2,0	-11,8	-2,0	0,8
Never pray to God outside of religious services (I)	-34,2	-7,7	-30,2	2,6	15,7	-0,6
Never thinking about death	-22,5	-3,3	10,2	-4,1	-9,0	-1,6
Never thinking about meaning and purpose life	-9,2	-3,3	9,8	-3,3	1,1	2,2
New ideas better than old ones	12,3	-6,4	-14,6	-4,5	-17,2	-0,4
No confidence: Armed Forces	-11,6	3,4	-28,3	-8,2	-6,9	-0,9
No confidence: Churches	-20,3	4,5	-20,7	-6,3	22,5	-1,8
No confidence: Education System	-5,0	6,8	-10,5	-0,5	0,0	-1,4
No confidence: Justice System	-8,5	-1,2	-13,3	4,0	-14,1	-8,5
No confidence: Labor Unions	-5,1	1,5	-8,0	4,7	-8,0	-4,4
No confidence: Major Companies	-3,1	-4,2	-8,8	5,4	2,3	-3,1

Percentage differences to the global average (Part 1 - Continued)

	Muslims	Judaism	Hinduism	Orthodoxy	Buddhism	Protestantism
No confidence: NATO	-12,8	-10,3	1,5	13,9	0,4	-6,6
No confidence: Parliament	-7,5	-4,5	-14,6	7,9	-2,6	-5,2
No confidence: Social Security System	-8,9	2,8	-10,1	10,1	-23,0	-3,6
No confidence: Television	-3,2	0,0	-4,8	5,2	-7,2	-1,2
No confidence: The Civil Services	-8,1	1,5	-14,2	6,2	-8,1	-4,2
No confidence: The Environmental Protection Movement	0,9	1,3	0,9	9,0	-7,7	1,7
No confidence: The Government	-9,6	1,5	-6,5	4,6	-5,8	-0,4
No confidence: The Police	-4,9	0,0	9,5	8,6	-9,1	-13,6
No confidence: The Political Parties	-6,2	-3,1	-12,3	5,5	-6,5	-1,7
No confidence: The Press	-3,4	-1,1	-16,0	5,3	-12,2	2,7
No confidence: The United Nations	1,6	-5,2	-5,2	7,7	-7,7	-6,5
No confidence: The Women's Movement	-2,8	-4,8	-4,0	5,6	-10,0	-0,4
No increase in taxes if used to prevent environmental pollution	-4,3	-1,7	-0,9	-1,7	-6,8	0,9
No interest in politics	1,5	-14,5	3,8	2,3	-8,0	-6,5
no part of my income for the environment	-4,6	-3,2	-7,8	-1,8	-5,0	0,5
no respect and love for parents	-9,9	5,0	-6,6	-5,8	-5,8	9,9
No respect for individual human rights nowadays	1,6	-1,2	-17,0	14,6	-11,7	-13,8
Not important for successful marriage: Adequate income	-23,6	-1,7	-14,9	-10,3	-7,5	8,0
Not important for successful marriage: Agreement on politics	-20,2	0,0	-2,4	0,8	-4,0	2,4
Not important for successful marriage: Apart from in-laws	-2,8	-4,4	22,7	-2,2	40,9	1,1
Not important for successful marriage: Children	-15,2	1,4	-14,5	-11,7	6,9	8,3
Not important for successful marriage: Faithfulness	-10,1	5,0	-9,2	2,5	0,0	-5,0
Not important for successful marriage: Good housing	-11,0	-2,3	-0,6	-9,8	15,0	2,9

Appendix VI

	Muslims	Judaism	Hinduism	Orthodoxy	Buddhism	Protestantism
Not important for successful marriage: Happy sexual relationship	-11,3	-5,7	-9,9	3,5	22,7	-1,4
Not important for successful marriage: Religious beliefs	-34,2	-7,3	-18,7	-5,5	-4,6	1,4
Not important for successful marriage: Respect and appreciation	-4,3	-5,1	2,6	1,7	12,0	-2,6
Not important for successful marriage: Same social background	-25,4	-7,6	-23,7	-0,4	-11,2	1,8
Not important for successful marriage: Sharing household chores	-8,3	1,1	-17,2	-4,4	18,3	-1,1
Not important for successful marriage: Tastes and interests in common	-12,1	-8,1	-7,5	-5,2	12,1	2,9
Not spend time with colleagues from work	-7,1	2,8	-13,9	-4,4	-0,4	-1,6
Not spend time with friends	-5,8	-8,2	14,6	0,6	16,4	-10,5
Not spend time with parents or other relatives	-5,3	4,6	2,0	5,3	7,9	5,3
Not spend time with people at sport, culture, communal organization	3,6	-11,3	3,2	8,7	1,6	-12,0
Not spend time with people at your church, mosque or synagogue	-12,8	-7,1	-18,1	7,4	9,2	-4,3
Parents responsibilities to their children	-8,1	2,2	-6,6	-1,5	8,8	2,9
Political system as it was before good for the country	11,2	5,4	38,3	-1,5	8,1	3,5
Political system good for governing country	4,1	4,7	4,3	-17,1	17,1	10,4
Political system in ten years good for the country	10,0	10,2	-10,7	1,5	-7,0	-4,5
Politicians who don't believe in God are fit for public office	-29,5	1,9	-7,4	-1,6	4,8	8,7
Politics not important in life	-3,3	-8,0	0,4	5,1	-18,2	-3,6
Poverty compared to 10 years ago decreased	2,1	-12,6	30,1	-17,5	72,7	5,6
Raised religiously	16,9	-13,8	40,0	-12,3	-12,3	-3,1
Religion not important in life	-36,4	-9,7	-21,2	-4,1	9,2	3,7
Religious leaders should influence government	-2,3	-5,0	-0,5	-2,7	0,5	6,8

Percentage differences to the global average (Part 1 - Continued)

	Muslims	Judaism	Hinduism	Orthodoxy	Buddhism	Protestantism
Religious leaders should influence how people vote	5,3	-7,2	12,4	-5,7	3,3	2,9
No religious person	-15,3	0,0	-11,7	-10,9	10,2	-2,9
Right wing versus left wind (right wing (self positioning in political scale))	5,9	-12,2	6,3	-5,7	12,2	2,0
Satisfaction with financial situation of household	-6,0	3,5	4,4	-27,9	7,6	14,1
Satisfaction with your life	-11,3	4,5	-5,0	-22,0	0,2	12,2
Scale of incomes	-8,7	-9,7	-15,0	-4,4	1,1	8,1
Service to others not important in life	-2,8	-4,5	-1,7	19,3	25,0	-9,1
Sharing with parents: attitudes towards religion	36,9	10,8	23,1	16,9	-15,4	4,6
Sharing with parents: moral standards'	23,9	5,6	14,1	7,0	-12,7	2,8
Sharing with parents: no sharing attitudes	-77,8	-55,6	-66,7	0,0	-44,4	-22,2
Sharing with parents: political views	-11,6	4,7	-27,9	-9,3	-41,9	9,3
Sharing with parents: sexual attitudes	-40,7	11,1	-66,7	11,1	-33,3	11,1
Sharing with parents: social attitudes	17,5	6,3	22,2	4,8	-27,0	3,2
State of health very bad (subjective)	-6,2	-5,8	0,9	14,6	7,5	-9,7
state ownership vs. private ownership of business	6,3	-9,7	8,3	6,5	-1,2	-14,4
TV not most important entertainment	-7,1	4,2	-6,7	6,2	-10,4	10,4
Unpaid work education, arts, music or cultural activities	66,7	83,3	116,7	-33,3	16,7	-16,7
Unpaid work environment, conservation, animal rights	100,0	133,3	100,0	0,0	0,0	0,0
Unpaid work human rights	100,0	100,0	50,0	-50,0	-50,0	0,0
Unpaid work labor unions	66,7	33,3	100,0	66,7	-33,3	0,0
Unpaid work local political action groups	166,7	100,0	100,0	-33,3	66,7	0,0
Unpaid work organization concerned with health	133,3	100,0	200,0	-33,3	33,3	33,3
Unpaid work other groups	-33,3	133,3	66,7	-33,3	66,7	66,7

	Muslims	Judaism	Hinduism	Orthodoxy	Buddhism	Protestantism
Unpaid work peace movement	500,0	200,0	400,0	0,0	100,0	0,0
Unpaid work political parties or groups	125,0	75,0	100,0	-25,0	-25,0	-25,0
Unpaid work professional associations	0,0	233,3	66,7	-33,3	0,0	0,0
Unpaid work religious or church organization	70,0	120,0	60,0	-50,0	-10,0	30,0
Unpaid work social welfare service for elderly, handicapped or deprived people	33,3	83,3	16,7	-50,0	66,7	16,7
Unpaid work sports or recreation	25,0	62,5	12,5	-37,5	-12,5	37,5
Unpaid work women's group	100,0	133,3	100,0	-66,7	66,7	0,0
Unpaid work youth work	50,0	175,0	25,0	-50,0	0,0	50,0
Using violence for political goals justified	-9,0	-7,3	-10,7	3,4	3,4	-11,3
Wealth accumulation does not harm others	-0,3	0,8	-10,8	-4,7	5,3	0,9
wide extent of political corruption in the country	1,4	-4,5	2,4	4,9	-8,0	-14,3
Work more important than leisure	5,7	-23,0	11,2	-0,3	-7,9	-3,8
Work not important in life	-9,6	9,6	-17,1	4,1	5,5	5,5
Worse if more people with strong religious beliefs in public office	-16,7	4,6	5,2	-9,2	10,2	1,0
would never do (political action): attending lawful demonstrations	7,0	-4,8	0,9	-2,2	9,3	-2,6
would never do (political action): joining in boycotts	3,2	-1,2	-6,8	4,0	-2,0	-6,0
would never do (political action): joining unofficial strikes	3,7	-3,7	-0,4	-0,4	2,2	-1,5
would never do (political action): occupying buildings or factories	2,5	1,4	1,4	0,0	0,4	0,7
would never do (political action): signing a petition	20,5	-7,7	7,2	14,4	-5,6	-14,4
Would not buy things at a 20% higher price if it helped to protect environment	-2,0	-0,8	2,4	1,2	-6,3	4,8
You cannot be too careful (most people cannot be trusted)	1,8	0,0	-4,1	4,7	-2,9	-7,6

Percentage differences to the global average (Part 2)

	Catholicism	Practicing Orthodoxy	Practicing Islam	Practicing Catholicism	Practicing Protestantism
A woman has to have children to be fulfilled	-4,9	34,4	41,0	-4,9	-16,4
Abortion if not wanting more children	-36,4	-4,5	-36,4	-61,4	-43,2
Abortion when child physically handicapped	-13,7	-21,9	-45,2	-31,5	-11,0
Abortion when the Mother's health is at risk	-8,0	-14,9	-19,5	-17,2	3,4
Abortion when woman not married	-32,5	-2,5	-27,5	-57,5	-40,0
Active/Inactive membership of any other organization	-10,0	-45,0	-20,0	5,0	80,0
Active/Inactive membership of art, music, educational	-3,7	-29,6	-11,1	11,1	81,5
Active/Inactive membership of charitable/humanitarian organization	-4,9	34,4	41,0	-4,9	-16,4
Active/Inactive membership of church or religious organization	-36,4	-4,5	-36,4	-61,4	-43,2
Active/Inactive membership of environmental organization	-13,7	-21,9	-45,2	-31,5	-11,0
Active/Inactive membership of labor unions	-8,0	-14,9	-19,5	-17,2	3,4
Active/Inactive membership of political party	-32,5	-2,5	-27,5	-57,5	-40,0
Active/Inactive membership of professional organization	-10,0	-45,0	-20,0	5,0	80,0
Active/Inactive membership of sport or recreation	-3,7	-29,6	-11,1	11,1	81,5
Active/Inactive membership of charitable/humanitarian organization	0,0	-14,3	-33,3	33,3	119,0
Active/Inactive membership of church or religious organization	32,7	25,0	5,8	82,7	178,8
Active/Inactive membership of environmental organization	0,0	-28,6	7,1	21,4	57,1
Active/Inactive membership of labor unions	-29,6	22,2	-29,6	-29,6	0,0
Active/Inactive membership of political party	-15,0	20,0	60,0	0,0	65,0
Active/Inactive membership of professional organization	0,0	-35,0	0,0	10,0	70,0
Active/Inactive membership of sport or recreation	2,6	-50,0	-23,7	2,6	52,6
Against Labor market reforms: unemployed have a right to refuse offered jobs	-6,2	3,1	-12,3	-7,0	-8,4
Anti-egalitarian position on income equality	-2,0	-6,4	5,4	-0,5	1,2
Bad future changes: A simple and more natural lifestyle	-4,1	-3,3	9,8	-5,7	0,0
Bad future changes: Greater respect for authority	-8,3	-3,8	-12,1	-13,4	-6,4
Bad future changes: Less emphasis on money and material possessions	-4,2	9,1	9,7	-5,5	-2,4
Bad future changes: Less importance placed on work	-1,7	5,5	6,4	0,4	0,9

	Catholicism	Practicing Orthodoxy	Practicing Islam	Practicing Catholicism	Practicing Protestantism
Bad future changes: More emphasis on family life	-2,7	-0,9	-0,9	-4,5	-3,6
Bad future changes: More emphasis on individual	-0,8	-5,0	-5,0	-0,8	0,0
Bad future changes: More emphasis on technology	0,7	-4,3	-12,1	0,7	7,1
Bad political system: Having a democratic political system	0,6	3,0	-9,7	0,6	-4,8
Bad political system: Having a strong leader	0,0	-10,8	1,0	-0,7	5,6
Bad political system: Having experts make decisions	-0,4	-2,6	-5,5	0,4	6,8
Bad political system: Having the army rule	0,9	-3,6	-12,9	-1,2	3,6
Believe in: devil	19,5	53,7	104,9	51,2	56,1
Believe in: God	14,5	18,1	20,5	19,3	19,3
Believe in: heaven	18,3	21,7	61,7	43,3	46,7
Believe in: hell	10,9	41,3	102,2	41,3	43,5
Believe in: life after death	16,7	16,7	45,0	36,7	40,0
Believe in: people have a soul	10,4	11,7	26,0	20,8	22,1
Believe in: re-incarnation	3,6	35,7	10,7	7,1	10,7
Believe in: sin	17,9	35,8	31,3	34,3	28,4
Belong to conservation, the environment, ecology, animal rights	-20,0	-20,0	80,0	-20,0	40,0
Belong to education, arts, music or cultural activities	-10,0	-20,0	70,0	0,0	90,0
Belong to human rights	-33,3	-33,3	133,3	0,0	66,7
Belong to labor unions	-41,2	-35,3	-41,2	-47,1	-17,6
Belong to local political actions	0,0	-25,0	225,0	25,0	75,0
Belong to organization concerned with health	-20,0	-40,0	140,0	0,0	80,0
Belong to other groups	-16,7	-50,0	0,0	-16,7	66,7
Belong to peace movement	-50,0	-50,0	350,0	0,0	50,0
Belong to political parties	-28,6	0,0	128,6	-28,6	57,1
Disagreement with: Democracies are indecisive and have too much squabbling	-1,6	-3,2	4,8	-1,6	3,2
Disagreement with: Democracies aren't good at maintaining order	-1,1	-5,5	2,6	-1,1	2,6
Disagreement with: Democracy may have problems but is better	-1,7	5,7	-3,4	-1,7	2,3
Disagreement with: Humiliating to receive money without having to work for it	0,4	-10,5	-19,4	-1,6	5,2
Disagreement with: Husband and wife should both contribute to income	-1,7	-9,4	2,8	-1,1	4,4
Disagreement with: In democracy, the economic system runs badly	-1,8	-7,3	3,6	-2,2	2,5
Disagreement with: Job best way for women to be independent	0,0	-7,5	8,5	2,8	8,5
Disagreement with: Make effort to live up to what my friends expect	1,7	-0,8	-8,7	-0,4	0,4

Percentage differences to the global average (Part 2 - Continued)

	Catholicism	Practicing Orthodoxy	Practicing Islam	Practicing Catholicism	Practicing Protestantism
Disagreement with: Men make better political leaders than women do	5,7	-4,5	-16,4	4,9	1,2
Disagreement with: One of main goals in life has been to make my parents proud	-2,2	2,2	-20,7	-7,6	-4,3
Disagreement with: People should not have to work if they don't want to	2,2	-2,8	-0,3	1,8	8,0
Disagreement with: Pre-school child suffers with working mother	-5,5	0,5	-5,0	-8,2	2,7
Disagreement with: Problem if women have more income than husband	-1,6	2,0	-10,8	-2,4	-2,4
Disagreement with: Relationship working mother	3,9	-8,4	10,8	5,9	2,0
Disagreement with: to develop talents you need to have a job	2,4	-7,1	-13,3	2,8	4,3
Disagreement with: University is more important for a boy than for a girl	1,7	-2,7	-9,5	1,0	3,7
Disagreement with: Women want a home and children	-3,2	-16,5	-28,9	-5,0	2,8
Disagreement with: Work is a duty towards society	-2,7	-0,9	-20,0	-6,2	-6,2
Disagreement with: Work should come first even if it means less spare time	1,6	-7,6	-26,3	-1,2	-2,8
Disagreement with: Work: accomplish personal goals	1,1	-8,1	2,2	1,6	-1,1
Disagreement with: Work: stay up late to finish	-0,9	-4,1	-7,7	-4,5	5,9
Disagreement with: Work: until satisfied with results	0,6	-2,4	-3,6	-0,6	-3,6
Disagreement with: People who don't work turn lazy	-2,2	-3,9	-19,3	-4,4	1,3
Dissatisfaction with the people in national office	0,4	7,6	-10,5	-1,8	-7,3
Dissatisfaction with the way democracy develops	-3,8	11,1	-5,7	-5,3	-9,2
Economic aid to poorer countries should be reduced	-1,4	8,0	0,0	-3,3	-0,7
Environmental action: attend meeting, signed petition	26,7	-40,0	6,7	40,0	20,0
Environmental action: chosen products that are better for environment	-4,0	-24,0	-10,0	-4,0	20,0
Environmental action: contributed to environmental organization	20,0	-26,7	20,0	40,0	40,0
Environmental action: recycle	-8,2	-24,5	-14,3	-6,1	28,6
Environmental action: reduce water consumption	2,0	-16,0	8,0	10,0	10,0
Ever felt bored	1,0	3,0	-59,6	0,0	-11,1
Ever felt depressed or very unhappy	-1,0	-1,0	-53,0	-2,0	-13,0
Ever felt on top of the world	-2,0	7,9	-38,6	-2,0	-8,9
Ever felt pleased about having accomplished something	1,0	1,0	-25,8	1,0	-1,0

Appendix VI

	Catholicism	Practicing Orthodoxy	Practicing Islam	Practicing Catholicism	Practicing Protestantism
Ever felt very excited or interested	0,0	10,1	-23,2	0,0	-6,1
Ever felt very lonely or remote from other people	1,0	-1,0	-59,6	0,0	-15,2
Fairness: One secretary is paid more	-1,2	-1,2	-2,4	-1,2	-2,4
Family not important in life	-1,7	-0,9	-8,7	-4,3	-5,2
favoring a restrictive immigrant policy	1,6	-1,6	-0,4	1,6	-0,8
Feeling of unhappiness	-2,0	16,6	0,5	-4,5	-11,1
Frequency watches TV	-1,2	10,0	-6,2	-1,5	-3,9
Friends not important in life	1,7	4,6	-5,2	1,1	-7,5
Get comfort and strength from religion	17,9	38,8	46,3	40,3	41,8
God important in your life	13,3	22,5	38,7	27,1	27,0
Government responsibility vs. private responsibility	-2,8	15,3	10,3	-4,0	-5,0
Government should not reduce environmental pollution	-4,2	-9,0	-12,3	-2,8	8,5
Hard work does not bring success	4,1	-9,7	-26,8	0,7	-12,4
High income level	0,5	-5,6	-6,2	-0,5	-2,1
High satisfaction with home life	1,9	-5,4	0,1	5,1	6,0
Ideal number of children	3,3	4,1	14,0	9,2	11,8
Important child qualities: determination perseverance	-14,7	2,9	-8,8	-23,5	-17,6
Important child qualities: feeling of responsibility	0,0	-4,4	-17,6	-2,9	-11,8
Important child qualities: good manners	-1,4	0,0	20,3	0,0	1,4
Important child qualities: hard work	-4,0	42,0	20,0	-6,0	-8,0
Important child qualities: imagination	-15,8	-15,8	5,3	-26,3	-15,8
Important child qualities: independence	-13,3	-17,8	-2,2	-24,4	-8,9
Important child qualities: obedience	8,6	-5,7	37,1	17,1	22,9
Important child qualities: religious faith	22,6	54,8	129,0	67,7	80,6
Ever felt very excited or interested	0,0	10,1	-23,2	0,0	-6,1
Ever felt very lonely or remote from other people	1,0	-1,0	-59,6	0,0	-15,2
Fairness: One secretary is paid more	-1,2	-1,2	-2,4	-1,2	-2,4
Family not important in life	-1,7	-0,9	-8,7	-4,3	-5,2
favoring a restrictive immigrant policy	1,6	-1,6	-0,4	1,6	-0,8
Feeling of unhappiness	-2,0	16,6	0,5	-4,5	-11,1
Frequency watches TV	-1,2	10,0	-6,2	-1,5	-3,9
Friends not important in life	1,7	4,6	-5,2	1,1	-7,5
Get comfort and strength from religion	17,9	38,8	46,3	40,3	41,8
God important in your life	13,3	22,5	38,7	27,1	27,0
Government responsibility vs. private responsibility	-2,8	15,3	10,3	-4,0	-5,0
Government should not reduce environmental pollution	-4,2	-9,0	-12,3	-2,8	8,5
Hard work does not bring success	4,1	-9,7	-26,8	0,7	-12,4
High income level	0,5	-5,6	-6,2	-0,5	-2,1

Percentage differences to the global average (Part 2 - Continued)

	Catholicism	Practicing Orthodoxy	Practicing Islam	Practicing Catholicism	Practicing Protestantism
High satisfaction with home life	1,9	-5,4	0,1	5,1	6,0
Ideal number of children	3,3	4,1	14,0	9,2	11,8
Important child qualities: determination perseverance	-14,7	2,9	-8,8	-23,5	-17,6
Important child qualities: feeling of responsibility	0,0	-4,4	-17,6	-2,9	-11,8
Important child qualities: good manners	-1,4	0,0	20,3	0,0	1,4
Important child qualities: hard work	-4,0	42,0	20,0	-6,0	-8,0
Important child qualities: imagination	-15,8	-15,8	5,3	-26,3	-15,8
Important child qualities: independence	-13,3	-17,8	-2,2	-24,4	-8,9
Important child qualities: obedience	8,6	-5,7	37,1	17,1	22,9
Important child qualities: religious faith	22,6	54,8	129,0	67,7	80,6
Important child qualities: thrift saving money and things	-2,9	20,0	5,7	-2,9	-20,0
Important child qualities: unselfishness	-3,7	-14,8	-7,4	-3,7	-3,7
Important in a job: a job that is interesting	-4,9	-1,6	6,6	-6,6	6,6
Important in a job: a job that meets one's abilities	-3,2	-3,2	27,4	-3,2	-1,6
Important in a job: a respected job	-4,3	21,3	59,6	2,1	-4,3
Important in a job: a responsible job	-2,2	-15,2	50,0	0,0	15,2
Important in a job: a useful job for society	4,8	31,0	97,6	9,5	4,8
Important in a job: an opportunity to use initiative	-4,2	-16,7	31,3	-4,2	6,3
Important in a job: generous holidays	-6,5	9,7	25,8	-9,7	-3,2
Important in a job: good chances for promotion	8,1	27,0	89,2	10,8	-5,4
Important in a job: good hours	-3,9	0,0	25,5	-3,9	-2,0
Important in a job: good job security	-1,5	7,4	26,5	-1,5	1,5
Important in a job: good pay	-1,3	10,0	13,8	-2,5	-10,0
Important in a job: meeting people	-2,2	2,2	56,5	-4,3	4,3
Important in a job: not too much pressure	-2,6	-5,1	51,3	0,0	-2,6
Important in a job: pleasant people to work with	-2,9	-1,4	24,6	-2,9	2,9
Important in a job: that you can achieve something	-5,2	-1,7	25,9	-5,2	15,5
Important in successful marriage: Understanding and tolerance	0,0	-0,8	-9,8	-1,6	-4,9
Important: Religious service birth	23,6	26,4	-6,9	31,9	19,4
Important: Religious service death	13,6	17,3	16,0	19,8	18,5
Important: Religious service marriage	21,6	27,0	24,3	31,1	27,0
Justifiable: abortion	-14,6	-7,9	-47,7	-32,8	-23,3
Justifiable: adultery	-7,8	-11,8	4,3	-23,1	-26,3

Appendix VI

	Catholicism	Practicing Orthodoxy	Practicing Islam	Practicing Catholicism	Practicing Protestantism
Justifiable: avoiding a fare on public transport	1,6	13,6	-23,9	-3,3	-18,5
Justifiable: buy stolen goods	0,0	-2,9	-8,6	-6,9	-18,4
Justifiable: cheating on taxes	1,7	2,5	-30,4	-4,2	-20,0
Justifiable: claiming government benefits	5,1	5,5	-5,5	0,0	-22,1
Justifiable: divorce	-4,9	-11,0	-34,6	-18,5	-17,9
Justifiable: driving under influence of alcohol	0,6	-7,8	-7,1	-5,2	-11,7
Justifiable: euthanasia	-9,5	-17,0	-54,8	-25,5	-17,8
Justifiable: failing to report damage you've done accidentally to a parked vehicle	0,5	-9,1	27,4	-5,8	-13,9
Justifiable: fighting with the police	-6,3	-16,1	13,8	-15,4	-20,9
Justifiable: homosexuality	2,8	-36,9	-58,8	-8,1	-15,6
Justifiable: joyriding	-0,7	0,0	22,9	-3,6	-7,9
Justifiable: keeping money that you have found	2,6	7,6	47,4	-8,9	-20,9
Justifiable: killing in self-defense	-1,8	-23,8	-14,6	-7,8	-8,1
Justifiable: lying	-1,1	-2,9	-16,1	-12,1	-24,9
Justifiable: political assassination	-6,0	-1,8	49,7	-9,6	-9,6
Justifiable: prostitution	2,0	-27,7	-46,5	-11,7	-18,0
Justifiable: sex under the legal age of consent	-4,5	2,5	22,5	-19,7	-23,8
Justifiable: someone accepting a bribe	4,0	-2,3	-19,0	-0,6	-10,9
Justifiable: suicide	-6,0	-25,3	-45,5	-17,6	-14,2
Justifiable: taking soft drugs	-6,6	-16,8	-7,8	-15,0	-16,2
Justifiable: threatening workers who refuse to join a strike	-5,0	-2,2	61,3	-8,3	-10,5
Justifiable: throwing away litter	-3,3	-8,2	-8,2	-5,5	-4,9
Leisure not time important in life	-2,1	5,2	8,8	-2,1	-4,7
Low Social class (subjective)	1,2	3,6	-0,9	1,5	0,9
Low Socio-economic status of respondent	2,3	13,4	12,2	3,4	-4,6
Major changes in life: one should act boldly	-4,3	-7,8	-6,0	-6,5	-1,7
Moments of prayer, meditation...	19,7	37,9	45,5	39,4	39,4
Much freedom of choice and control	3,3	-11,4	-8,3	4,2	5,7
Rejecting neighbors: Drug addicts	-5,8	10,1	2,9	-2,9	-1,4
Rejecting neighbors: Emotionally unstable people	-15,0	37,5	27,5	-15,0	-7,5
Rejecting neighbors: Heavy drinkers	-5,1	22,0	11,9	-3,4	0,0
Rejecting neighbors: Homosexuals	-8,5	31,9	40,4	-4,3	-2,1
Rejecting neighbors: Immigrants/foreign workers	-17,6	23,5	82,4	-17,6	-5,9
Rejecting neighbors: Jews	-6,3	56,3	112,5	0,0	-18,8
Rejecting neighbors: Left wing extremists	-3,0	15,2	69,7	-3,0	3,0
Rejecting neighbors: Muslims	-5,0	50,0	-35,0	-5,0	-5,0
Rejecting neighbors: People of a different race	-13,3	46,7	100,0	-6,7	-6,7

Percentage differences to the global average (Part 2 - Continued)

	Catholicism	Practicing Orthodoxy	Practicing Islam	Practicing Catholicism	Practicing Protestantism
Rejecting neighbors: People who have AIDS	-11,9	35,7	45,2	-7,1	-21,4
Rejecting neighbors: People with a criminal record	0,0	31,5	24,1	7,4	-1,9
Rejecting neighbors: People with large families	-9,1	45,5	145,5	-9,1	0,0
Rejecting neighbors: Political Extremists	-15,7	-7,8	41,2	-19,6	-21,6
Rejecting neighbors: Right wing extremists	-6,1	9,1	51,5	-9,1	-6,1
Never attend religious services	-20,8	-49,8	-65,7	-55,9	-55,5
Never discusses political matters with friends	2,8	0,0	0,9	3,8	-0,9
Never follow politics in the news	0,0	-3,6	5,8	0,0	0,9
Never persuading friends, relatives or fellow workers	3,7	-10,2	-11,0	5,3	2,8
Never pray to God outside of religious services (I)	-18,5	-36,5	-53,6	-45,3	-51,0
Never thinking about death	-2,0	-10,7	-32,8	-5,3	-13,1
Never thinking about meaning and purpose life	1,6	-6,5	-11,4	-0,5	-12,5
New ideas better than old ones	0,9	-3,6	21,2	1,1	-2,8
No confidence: Armed Forces	3,4	-10,7	-15,9	-1,3	-5,6
No confidence: Churches	-10,4	-26,1	-31,5	-25,2	-27,9
No confidence: Education System	-1,8	-6,4	-8,2	-5,5	-3,7
No confidence: Justice System	2,0	0,4	-14,9	-0,4	-8,1
No confidence: Labor Unions	1,5	2,2	-8,0	0,0	-3,6
No confidence: Major Companies	-1,2	3,1	-6,5	-4,2	-7,7
No confidence: NATO	-2,6	12,1	-15,8	-4,4	-7,3
No confidence: Parliament	1,5	4,9	-10,5	-0,4	-6,7
No confidence: Social Security System	-0,4	7,7	-12,9	-2,8	-8,5
No confidence: Television	0,0	2,0	-6,4	-1,2	-4,4
No confidence: The Civil Services	2,3	3,1	-12,3	-0,4	-9,2
No confidence: The Environmental Protection Movement	-2,6	9,4	-2,6	-4,7	-2,1
No confidence: The Government	2,3	1,5	-12,7	0,0	-3,8
No confidence: The Police	0,8	4,1	-6,6	-2,1	-10,3
No confidence: The Political Parties	2,7	1,7	-9,6	1,4	-3,1
No confidence: The Press	-0,8	2,3	-7,6	-1,9	-2,3
No confidence: The United Nations	-3,6	8,1	-0,8	-5,2	-9,3
No confidence: The Women's Movement	0,0	3,6	-4,4	-2,8	-5,6
No increase in taxes if used to prevent environmental pollution	2,6	-1,7	-6,4	1,3	0,4
No interest in politics	4,2	3,8	-1,9	4,6	-6,9
no part of my income for the environment	1,8	-3,7	-5,9	0,9	-0,5
no respect and love for parents	-3,3	-9,1	-10,7	-6,6	-2,5

	Catholicism	Practicing Orthodoxy	Practicing Islam	Practicing Catholicism	Practicing Protestantism
No respect for individual human rights nowadays	-3,2	13,8	0,0	-6,1	-9,3
Not important for successful marriage: Adequate income	-2,3	-11,5	-25,3	-2,9	4,0
Not important for successful marriage: Agreement on politics	-1,2	-2,4	-19,8	-3,6	-1,6
Not important for successful marriage: Apart from in-laws	-0,6	-1,1	-1,7	1,1	3,3
Not important for successful marriage: Children	-3,4	-14,5	-20,0	-6,2	0,0
Not important for successful marriage: Faithfulness	1,1	-7,2	-8,9	0,6	0,6
Not important for successful marriage: Good housing	-3,5	-11,6	-20,8	-4,0	-2,9
Not important for successful marriage: Happy sexual relationship	7,5	-4,0	-16,7	7,5	-7,9
Not important for successful marriage: Religious beliefs	2,9	3,5	-9,9	4,1	-10,5
Not important for successful marriage: Respect and appreciation	0,0	5,3	-6,6	0,7	5,3
Not important for successful marriage: Same social background	-2,3	6,1	-1,9	-4,9	-13,6
Not important for successful marriage: Sharing household chores	-5,0	-14,2	-33,0	-22,7	-39,7
Not important for successful marriage: Tastes and interests in common	-3,7	-5,1	-8,8	-7,4	-4,4
Not spend time with colleagues from work	-4,8	-2,9	14,8	-4,2	0,6
Not spend time with friends	3,4	-15,4	4,3	6,4	9,6
Not spend time with parents or other relatives	2,1	3,7	8,7	2,1	-2,6
Not spend time with people at sport, culture, communal organization	6,4	-17,6	-34,6	-1,9	-16,3
Not spend time with people at your church, mosque or synagogue	1,1	-7,2	-8,9	0,6	0,6
Parents responsibilities to their children	-3,5	-11,6	-20,8	-4,0	-2,9
Political system as it was before good for the country	7,5	-4,0	-16,7	7,5	-7,9
Political system good for governing country	2,9	3,5	-9,9	4,1	-10,5
Political system in ten years good for the country	0,0	5,3	-6,6	0,7	5,3
Politicians who don't believe in God are fit for public office	-2,3	6,1	-1,9	-4,9	-13,6
Politics not important in life	3,3	5,8	-6,6	1,5	-8,0
Poverty compared to 10 years ago decreased	-2,1	-16,1	11,2	0,0	7,0
Raised religiously	33,8	26,2	41,5	44,6	30,8
Religion not important in life	-12,4	-26,3	-45,6	-29,0	-33,6
Religious leaders should influence government	0,9	3,7	0,0	6,4	20,1
Religious leaders should influence how people vote	0,0	-0,5	5,7	4,3	11,0
No religious person	-14,6	-22,6	-21,2	-21,2	-20,4

Percentage differences to the global average (Part 2 - Continued)

	Catholicism	Practicing Orthodoxy	Practicing Islam	Practicing Catholicism	Practicing Protestantism
Right wing versus left wind (right wing (self positioning in political scale))	2,5	-0,7	11,8	7,0	5,6
Satisfaction with financial situation of household	5,1	-25,6	-4,4	8,5	11,7
Satisfaction with your life	5,7	-20,3	-11,0	8,6	8,3
Scale of incomes	-0,8	-11,4	-9,1	-3,0	2,8
Service to others not important in life	-9,1	17,6	-5,1	-13,1	-12,5
Sharing with parents: attitudes towards religion	13,8	29,2	44,6	27,7	23,1
Sharing with parents: moral standards	4,2	19,7	29,6	9,9	14,1
Sharing with parents: no sharing attitudes	-22,2	-44,4	-88,9	-55,6	-44,4
Sharing with parents: political views	2,3	-7,0	-16,3	11,6	16,3
Sharing with parents: sexual attitudes	3,7	37,0	-51,9	18,5	33,3
Sharing with parents: social attitudes	3,2	19,0	28,6	7,9	12,7
State of health very bad (subjective)	2,2	15,0	-5,8	1,3	-9,3
state ownership vs. private ownership of business	-1,4	7,3	5,9	0,0	-11,4
TV not most important entertainment	1,7	5,8	-7,1	1,3	4,6
Unpaid work education, arts, music or cultural activities	-16,7	-16,7	150,0	-16,7	50,0
Unpaid work environment, conservation, animal rights	-33,3	0,0	200,0	-33,3	33,3
Unpaid work human rights	-50,0	-50,0	250,0	0,0	0,0
Unpaid work labor unions	0,0	66,7	166,7	-33,3	-33,3
Unpaid work local political action groups	0,0	0,0	300,0	0,0	33,3
Unpaid work organization concerned with health	0,0	0,0	233,3	33,3	100,0
Unpaid work other groups	0,0	-33,3	-33,3	0,0	133,3
Unpaid work peace movement	0,0	0,0	800,0	0,0	100,0
Unpaid work political parties or groups	-50,0	0,0	250,0	-25,0	25,0
Unpaid work professional associations	-33,3	-33,3	33,3	-33,3	66,7
Unpaid work religious or church organization	10,0	30,0	200,0	60,0	260,0
Unpaid work social welfare service for elderly, handicapped or deprived people	-16,7	-33,3	100,0	0,0	100,0
Unpaid work sports or recreation	-12,5	-37,5	87,5	-12,5	25,0
Unpaid work women's group	-33,3	-33,3	166,7	0,0	133,3
Unpaid work youth work	0,0	-25,0	100,0	0,0	125,0
Using violence for political goals justified	5,1	2,8	-10,7	6,8	-5,6
Wealth accumulation does not harm others	1,2	-5,9	-1,4	3,6	2,0
wide extent of political corruption in the country	2,4	3,1	1,4	2,1	-7,3

	Catholicism	Practicing Orthodoxy	Practicing Islam	Practicing Catholicism	Practicing Protestantism
Work more important than leisure	1,6	2,7	8,2	4,9	3,8
Work not important in life	-2,1	2,1	-14,4	-3,4	2,1
Worse if more people with strong religious beliefs in public office	-1,3	-24,3	-22,6	-10,8	-25,2
would never do (political action): attending lawful demonstrations	1,8	-0,4	6,2	4,0	1,3
would never do (political action): joining in boycotts	3,2	4,8	1,6	4,4	-2,0
would never do (political action): joining unofficial strikes	1,1	0,0	2,6	2,6	1,9
would never do (political action): occupying buildings or factories	0,0	0,4	1,8	0,7	0,0
would never do (political action): signing a petition	1,0	14,4	19,0	3,1	-6,7
Would not buy things at a 20% higher price if it helped to protect environment	0,0	2,0	-4,8	-0,8	3,2
You cannot be too careful (most people cannot be trusted)	2,9	4,7	1,8	2,4	-4,1

GLOBAL ISLAM: +25% OR MORE DEVIATION FROM GLOBAL CITIZENRY

Unpaid work peace movement
Belong to peace movement
Unpaid work local political action groups
Rejecting neighbors: People with large families
Unpaid work organization concerned with health
Belong to local political actions
Unpaid work political parties or groups
Rejecting neighbors: Jews
Belong to women's group
Unpaid work environment, conservation, animal rights
Unpaid work human rights
Unpaid work women's group
Important child qualities: religious faith
Believe in: hell
Rejecting neighbors: People of a different race
Important in a job: a useful job for society
Rejecting neighbors: Immigrants/foreign workers
Rejecting neighbors: Left wing extremists
Important in a job: good chances for promotion
Belong to political parties
Unpaid work religious or church organization
Rejecting neighbors: Right wing extremists

Belong to human rights
Unpaid work education, arts, music or cultural activities
Unpaid work labor unions
Believe in: devil
Belong to organization concerned with health
Important in a job: meeting people
Important in a job: a respected job
Important in a job: not too much pressure
Believe in: heaven
Unpaid work youth work
Churches give answers: the social problems
Rejecting neighbors: People who have AIDS
Justifiable: threatening workers who refuse to join a strike
Rejecting neighbors: Homosexuals
Belong to conservation, the environment, ecology, animal rights
Belong to youth work
Important in a job: a responsible job
Get comfort and strength from religion
Justifiable: political assassination
Sharing with parents: attitudes towards religion
Believe in: life after death
A woman has to have children to be fulfilled
Churches give answers: moral problems
Churches give answers: the problems of family life
Active/Inactive membership of political party
Rejecting neighbors: Emotionally unstable people
Unpaid work social welfare service for elderly, handicapped or deprived people
God important in your life
Moments of prayer, meditation...
Important child qualities: obedience
Important in a job: good hours
Important in a job: generous holidays
Belong to social welfare service for elderly
Justifiable: keeping money that you have found
Rejecting neighbors: Political Extremists
Important in a job: an opportunity to use initiative
Important in a job: good job security
Unpaid work sports or recreation

GLOBAL ISLAM: -25% OR MORE DEVIATION FROM WORLD CITIZENRY

Sharing with parents: no sharing attitudes
Ever felt upset because somebody criticized you
Justifiable: homosexuality
Active/Inactive membership of charitable/humanitarian organization
Belong to labor unions
Ever felt restless
Justifiable: euthanasia
Active/Inactive membership of any other organization
Ever felt very lonely or remote from other people
Justifiable: prostitution
Ever felt bored
Justifiable: suicide
Sharing with parents: sexual attitudes
Ever felt depressed or very unhappy
Active/Inactive membership of sport or recreation
Religion not important in life
Abortion when child physically handicapped
Justifiable: abortion
Active/Inactive membership of church or religious organization
Never pray to God outside of religious services (I)
Not important for successful marriage: Religious beliefs
Unpaid work other groups
Ever felt proud because someone complimented you
Active/Inactive membership of art, music, educational
Politicians who don't believe in God are fit for public office
Ever felt on top of the world
Active/Inactive membership of environmental organization
Justifiable: divorce
Not important for successful marriage: Same social background
Ever felt that things were going your way

GLOBAL ORTHODOXY: +25% OR MORE DEVIATION FROM GLOBAL CITIZENRY

Unpaid work labor unions
Important child qualities: hard work
Rejecting neighbors: Emotionally unstable people
Abortion if not wanting more children
Rejecting neighbors: People who have AIDS
Abortion when woman not married
Rejecting neighbors: Homosexuals

Ever felt on top of the world
A woman has to have children to be fulfilled
Active/Inactive membership of labor unions
Ever felt very lonely or remote from other people
Rejecting neighbors: People with large families
Ever felt proud because someone complimented you
Rejecting neighbors: Muslims
Rejecting neighbors: Jews

GLOBAL ORTHODOXY: -25% OR MORE DEVIATION FROM WORLD CITIZENRY

Belong to human rights
Unpaid work women's group
Active/Inactive membership of any other organization
Belong to religious organization
Belong to social welfare service for elderly
Belong to sports or recreation
Active/Inactive membership of sport or recreation
Belong to other groups
Unpaid work social welfare service for elderly, handicapped or deprived people
Unpaid work youth work
Unpaid work human rights
Unpaid work religious or church organization
Belong to local political actions
Belong to women's group
Belong to peace movement
Environmental action: attend meeting, signed petition
Environmental action: contributed to environmental organization
Active/Inactive membership of art, music, educational
Active/Inactive membership of charitable/humanitarian organization
Active/Inactive membership of environmental organization
Active/Inactive membership of church or religious organization
Belong to youth work
Belong to conservation, the environment, ecology, animal rights
Belong to organization concerned with health
Unpaid work sports or recreation
Active/Inactive membership of professional organization
Unpaid work other groups
Unpaid work professional associations
Unpaid work local political action groups
Unpaid work education, arts, music or cultural activities
Unpaid work organization concerned with health
Justifiable: homosexuality

Environmental action: recycle
Belong to education, arts, music or cultural activities
Belong to professional associations
Environmental action: chosen products that are better for environment
Satisfaction with financial situation of household
Unpaid work political parties or groups

GLOBAL PRACTICING ORTHODOXY: +25% OR MORE DEVIATION FROM GLOBAL CITIZENRY

Unpaid work labor unions
Rejecting neighbors: Jews
Important child qualities: religious faith
Believe in: devil
Rejecting neighbors: Muslims
Rejecting neighbors: People of a different race
Rejecting neighbors: People with large families
Important child qualities: hard work
Believe in: hell
Churches give answers: moral problems
Get comfort and strength from religion
Moments of prayer, meditation...
Rejecting neighbors: Emotionally unstable people
Sharing with parents: sexual attitudes
Believe in: sin
Rejecting neighbors: People who have AIDS
Believe in: re-incarnation
Churches give answers: the problems of family life
A woman has to have children to be fulfilled
Rejecting neighbors: Homosexuals
Rejecting neighbors: People with a criminal record
Important in a job: a useful job for society
Unpaid work religious or church organization
Sharing with parents: attitudes towards religion
Churches give answers: people's spiritual needs
Important in a job: good chances for promotion
Important: Religious service marriage
Important: Religious service birth
Raised religiously
Active/Inactive membership of church or religious organization

GLOBAL PRACTICING ORTHODOXY: -25% OR MORE DEVIATION FROM WORLD CITIZENRY

Belong to sports or recreation
Unpaid work human rights
Belong to peace movement
Belong to other groups
Active/Inactive membership of sport or recreation
Never attend religious services
Active/Inactive membership of any other organization
Sharing with parents: no sharing attitudes
Belong to social welfare service for elderly
Belong to organization concerned with health
Environmental action: attend meeting, signed petition
Unpaid work sports or recreation
Justifiable: homosexuality
Never pray to God outside of religious services (I)
Belong to labor unions
Active/Inactive membership of professional organization
Unpaid work professional associations
Unpaid work women's group
Belong to human rights
Unpaid work social welfare service for elderly, handicapped or deprived people
Unpaid work other groups
Active/Inactive membership of art, music, educational
Belong to professional associations
Active/Inactive membership of environmental organization
Justifiable: prostitution
Environmental action: contributed to environmental organization
Religion not important in life
No confidence: Churches
Satisfaction with financial situation of household
Justifiable: suicide
Belong to local political actions
Unpaid work youth work
Belong to women's group

GLOBAL PRACTICING ISLAM: + 25% OR MORE DEVIATION FROM GLOBAL CITIZENRY

Unpaid work peace movement
Belong to peace movement
Unpaid work local political action groups
Unpaid work human rights

Unpaid work political parties or groups
Unpaid work organization concerned with health
Belong to local political actions
Unpaid work environment, conservation, animal rights
Unpaid work religious or church organization
Unpaid work women's group
Unpaid work labor unions
Unpaid work education, arts, music or cultural activities
Rejecting neighbors: People with large families
Belong to organization concerned with health
Belong to human rights
Important child qualities: religious faith
Belong to political parties
Belong to women's group
Rejecting neighbors: Jews
Believe in: devil
Believe in: hell
Unpaid work social welfare service for elderly, handicapped or deprived people
Unpaid work youth work
Rejecting neighbors: People of a different race
Important in a job: a useful job for society
Belong to religious organization
Important in a job: good chances for promotion
Unpaid work sports or recreation
Rejecting neighbors: Immigrants/foreign workers
Belong to conservation, the environment, ecology, animal rights
Belong to youth work
Belong to social welfare service for elderly
Belong to education, arts, music or cultural activities
Rejecting neighbors: Left wing extremists
Churches give answers: the social problems
Believe in: heaven
Justifiable: threatening workers who refuse to join a strike
Active/Inactive membership of political party
Important in a job: a respected job
Important in a job: meeting people
Rejecting neighbors: Right wing extremists
Important in a job: not too much pressure
Important in a job: a responsible job
Justifiable: political assassination
Justifiable: keeping money that you have found
Get comfort and strength from religion
Moments of prayer, meditation...
Rejecting neighbors: People who have AIDS
Churches give answers: the problems of family life
Believe in: life after death

Sharing with parents: attitudes towards religion
Belong to professional associations
Churches give answers: moral problems
Raised religiously
Rejecting neighbors: Political Extremists
A woman has to have children to be fulfilled
Rejecting neighbors: Homosexuals
God important in your life
Important child qualities: obedience
Unpaid work professional associations
Important in a job: an opportunity to use initiative
Believe in: sin
Sharing with parents: moral standards´
Sharing with parents: social attitudes
Rejecting neighbors: Emotionally unstable people
Justifiable: failing to report damage you've done accidentally to a parked vehicle
Important in a job: a job that meets one's abilities
Important in a job: good job security
Believe in: people have a soul
Important in a job: that you can achieve something
Important in a job: generous holidays
Important in a job: good hours

GLOBAL PRACTICING ISLAM: -25% OR MORE DEVIATION FROM WORLD CITIZENRY

Sharing with parents: no sharing attitudes
Ever felt upset because somebody criticized you
Never attend religious services
Ever felt restless
Ever felt very lonely or remote from other people
Ever felt bored
Justifiable: homosexuality
Justifiable: euthanasia
Never pray to God outside of religious services (I)
Ever felt depressed or very unhappy
Sharing with parents: sexual attitudes
Justifiable: abortion
Justifiable: prostitution
Religion not important in life
Justifiable: suicide
Abortion when child physically handicapped
Ever felt proud because someone complimented you
Belong to labor unions
Not important for successful marriage: Religious beliefs

Ever felt on top of the world
Abortion if not wanting more children
Rejecting neighbors: Muslims
Politicians who don't believe in God are fit for public office
Justifiable: divorce
Unpaid work other groups
Active/Inactive membership of charitable/humanitarian organization
Not spend time with people at your church, mosque or synagogue
Never thinking about death
Ever felt that things were going your way
No confidence: Churches
Justifiable: cheating on taxes
Active/Inactive membership of labor unions
Disagreement with: Women want a home and children
Abortion when woman not married
Hard work does not bring success
Disagreement with: Work should come first even if it means less spare time
Not important for successful marriage: Same social background
Ever felt pleased about having accomplished something
Not important for successful marriage: Adequate income

FACTOR ANALYTICAL MODEL OF GLOBAL CIVILIZATIONS

		Communalities	
		Initial	Extraction
Muslims	VAR00001	1,0	0,9
Judaism	VAR00002	1,0	0,7
Hinduism	VAR00003	1	0,85
Orthodoxy	VAR00004	1	0,854
Buddhism	VAR00005	1	0,368
Protestantism	VAR00006	1	0,8
Catholicism	VAR00007	1	0,824
Practicing Orthodoxy	VAR00008	1	0,83
Practicing Islam	VAR00009	1	0,883
Practicing Catholicism	VAR00010	1	0,945
Practicing Protestantism	VAR00011	1	0,873

EXPLAINED TOTAL VARIANCE

Component	Initial *Eigenvalues*			Sums of squared factor loadings for extraction		
	Total	% of variance	cumulated %	Total	% of variance	cumulated %
1	4,026	36,604	36,604	4,026	36,604	36,604
2	2,684	24,396	60,999	2,684	24,396	60,999
3	2,169	19,717	80,716	2,169	19,717	80,716
4	,836	7,598	88,314			
5	,480	4,363	92,677			
6	,278	2,530	95,207			
7	,244	2,215	97,422			
8	,157	1,423	98,846			
9	,062	,566	99,412			
10	,048	,432	99,844			
11	,017	,156	100,000			

Extraction method: principal components.

	Factor 1 Active society	Factor 2 communautarianism, phobia	homo Catholicus
A woman has to have children to be fulfilled	-0,372	1,799	-0,482
Abortion if not wanting more children	-0,585	-0,030	-3,278
Abortion when child physically handicapped	-0,493	-0,883	-1,368
Abortion when the mothers health is at risk	-0,164	-0,625	-0,703
Abortion when woman not married	-0,240	0,264	-3,182
Active/Inactive membership of any other organization	1,156	-2,975	0,407
Active/Inactive membership of art, music, educational	0,666	-2,033	0,955
Active/Inactive membership of charitable/humanitarian organization	1,307	-2,252	1,832
Active/Inactive membership of church or religious organization	1,046	-1,297	5,117
Active/Inactive membership of environmental organization	0,367	-1,424	1,078
Active/Inactive membership of labor unions	-0,970	-0,209	-1,266
Active/Inactive membership of political party	0,431	0,112	0,185
Active/Inactive membership of professional organization	0,650	-1,870	0,834
Active/Inactive membership of sport or recreation	0,536	-2,659	0,709
Against Labor market reforms: Unemployed have a right to refuse offered jobs	-0,575	0,187	-0,403

Appendix VI

	Factor 1 Active society	Factor 2 communautarianism, phobia	homo Catholicus
Anti-egalitarian position on income equality	-0,400	-0,039	-0,021
Bad future changes: A simple and more natural lifestyle	-0,118	0,048	-0,307
Bad future changes: Greater respect for authority	-0,128	-0,184	-0,735
Bad future changes: Less emphasis on money and material possessions	-0,323	0,472	-0,265
Bad future changes: Less importance placed on work	-0,273	0,290	0,008
Bad future changes: More emphasis on family life	-0,210	0,096	-0,223
Bad future changes: More emphasis on individual	-0,161	0,003	-0,089
Bad future changes: More emphasis on technology	-0,221	-0,408	0,242
Bad political system: Having a democratic political system	-0,465	0,161	0,074
Bad political system: Having a strong leader	-0,161	-0,449	0,104
Bad political system: Having experts make decisions	-0,172	-0,274	0,137
Bad political system: Having the army rule	-0,292	-0,264	0,118
Believe in: devil	0,150	1,856	2,649
Believe in: God	-0,151	0,636	1,290
Believe in: heaven	0,346	0,672	2,287
Believe in: hell	0,449	1,839	1,809
Believe in: life after death	0,276	0,427	1,992
Believe in: people have a soul	0,056	0,331	1,177
Believe in: re-incarnation	0,901	2,297	-0,303
Believe in: sin	-0,328	1,162	1,993
Belong to conservation, the environment, ecology, animal rights	1,694	-0,964	-1,193
Belong to education, arts, music or cultural activities	1,885	-1,027	-0,106
Belong to human rights	2,081	-1,824	-0,736
Belong to labor unions	-0,504	-2,782	-2,139
Belong to local political actions	3,134	-0,028	0,389
Belong to organization concerned with health	2,461	-1,009	-0,799
Belong to other groups	1,351	-2,949	-0,490
Belong to peace movement	4,029	0,692	-2,695
Belong to political parties	1,533	-0,378	-1,379
Belong to professional associations	1,888	-1,932	-0,980
Belong to religious organization	3,251	-2,338	3,407
Belong to social welfare service for elderly	2,353	-2,142	0,320
Belong to sports or recreation	1,046	-2,815	-0,564
Belong to women's group	3,398	-1,085	1,203
Belong to youth work	2,439	-1,647	1,236

	Factor 1 Active society	Factor 2 communautarianism, phobia	homo Catholicus
Child needs a home with father and mother	-0,343	0,496	0,102
Child qualities: tolerance and respect for other people	-0,241	-0,341	-0,079
Churches give answers: moral problems	-0,231	1,069	1,588
Churches give answers: people's spiritual needs	-0,317	0,671	1,323
Churches give answers: the problems of family life	-0,111	0,789	2,119
Churches give answers: the social problems	0,203	0,491	2,213
Competition harmful	-0,408	-0,009	0,241
Cooperating party leader good	-0,324	-0,086	0,028
Country is run for all people's benefit	-0,067	-0,098	0,100
Disagree: a[Country]s environmental problems can be solved without any international agreements to handle them	-0,304	-0,322	-0,073
Disagreement with: Being a housewife just as fulfilling	-0,272	0,035	-0,045
Disagreement with: Democracies are indecisive and have too much squabbling	-0,154	-0,088	-0,038
Disagreement with: Democracies aren't good at maintaining order	-0,147	-0,177	-0,007
Disagreement with: Democracy may have problems but is better	-0,368	0,199	-0,030
Disagreement with: Humiliating to receive money without having to work for it	-0,309	-0,603	0,134
Disagreement with: Husband and wife should both contribute to income	-0,003	-0,272	-0,086
Disagreement with: In democracy, the economic system runs badly	-0,142	-0,232	-0,067
Disagreement with: Job best way for women to be independent	0,000	-0,053	0,043
Disagreement with: Make effort to live up to what my friends expect	-0,336	-0,167	0,181
Disagreement with: Men make better political leaders than women do	-0,250	-0,334	0,448
Disagreement with: One of main goals in life has been to make my parents proud	-0,384	-0,254	-0,175
Disagreement with: People should not have to work if they don't want to	-0,210	-0,224	0,282
Disagreement with: Pre-school child suffers with working mother	-0,306	-0,365	-0,185
Disagreement with: Problem if women have more income than husband	-0,356	-0,049	-0,026
Disagreement with: Relationship working mother	-0,133	0,026	0,278
Disagreement with: to develop talents you need to have a job	-0,357	-0,361	0,319
Disagreement with: University is more important for a boy than for a girl	-0,284	-0,236	0,233

	Factor 1 Active society	Factor 2 communautarianism, phobia	homo Catholicus
Disagreement with: Women want a home and children	-0,298	-0,895	-0,088
Disagreement with: Work is a duty towards society	-0,541	-0,148	-0,164
Disagreement with: Work should come first even if it means less spare time	-0,434	-0,437	0,117
Disagreement with: Work: accomplish personal goals	-0,126	-0,003	0,000
Disagreement with: Work: stay up late to finish	-0,217	-0,259	-0,047
Disagreement with: Work: until satisfied with results	-0,208	0,131	-0,072
Disagreement with: People who don't work turn lazy	-0,456	-0,460	0,030
Dissatisfaction with the people in national office	-0,552	0,258	0,034
Dissatisfaction with the way democracy develops	-0,626	0,361	-0,181
Economic aid to poorer countries should be reduced	-0,383	0,285	-0,040
Environmental action: attend meeting, signed petition	0,534	-1,048	1,938
Environmental action: chosen products that are better for environment	0,238	-1,327	-0,088
Environmental action: contributed to environmental organization	0,830	-1,087	1,982
Environmental action: recycle	0,367	-1,605	-0,223
Environmental action: reduce water consumption	0,061	-0,260	0,286
Ever felt bored	-1,481	-0,292	0,418
Ever felt depressed or very unhappy	-1,494	-0,334	0,259
Ever felt on top of the world	-1,478	-0,051	0,285
Ever felt pleased about having accomplished something	-0,880	-0,302	0,382
Ever felt proud because someone complimented you	-1,357	-0,138	0,375
Ever felt restless	-1,447	-0,511	0,442
Ever felt that things were going your way	-1,194	-0,365	0,214
Ever felt upset because somebody criticized you	-1,591	-0,557	0,420
Ever felt very excited or interested	-1,107	0,095	0,341
Ever felt very lonely or remote from other people	-1,579	-0,332	0,373
Fairness: One secretary is paid more	-0,370	-0,033	0,002
Family not important in life	-0,376	-0,028	-0,129
favoring a restrictive immigrant policy	-0,249	0,075	0,130
Feeling of unhappiness	-0,595	0,661	-0,148
Frequency watches TV	-0,555	0,237	0,047
Friends not important in life	-0,430	0,311	0,092
Get comfort and strength from religion	0,100	1,435	2,053

	Factor 1 Active society	Factor 2 communautarianism, phobia	homo Catholicus
God important in your life	0,025	0,882	1,473
Government responsibility vs. private responsibility	-0,337	0,665	-0,218
Government should not reduce environmental pollution	-0,099	-0,447	-0,112
Hard work does not bring success	-0,651	-0,324	0,199
High income level	-0,260	-0,064	0,001
High satisfaction with home life	-0,201	-0,305	0,368
Ideal number of children	-0,150	0,057	0,549
Important child qualities: determination perseverance	-0,553	0,364	-1,311
Important child qualities: feeling of responsibility	-0,473	-0,077	-0,130
Important child qualities: good manners	-0,031	0,165	-0,019
Important child qualities: hard work	-0,921	2,034	-0,272
Important child qualities: imagination	0,029	-0,771	-1,249
Important child qualities: independence	0,130	-0,629	-1,310
Important child qualities: obedience	-0,006	0,403	0,963
Important child qualities: religious faith	0,599	1,806	3,478
Important child qualities: thrift saving money and things	-0,629	1,170	-0,360
Important child qualities: unselfishness	0,159	-0,403	-0,396
Important in a job: a job that is interesting	-0,149	-0,220	-0,164
Important in a job: a job that meets one's abilities	-0,013	0,323	-0,305
Important in a job: a respected job	-0,117	1,376	-0,142
Important in a job: a responsible job	0,611	0,026	-0,207
Important in a job: a useful job for society	0,200	1,626	0,503
Important in a job: an opportunity to use initiative	0,270	-0,361	-0,256
Important in a job: generous holidays	-0,069	0,911	-0,719
Important in a job: good chances for promotion	0,182	1,606	0,611
Important in a job: good hours	-0,037	0,317	-0,287
Important in a job: good job security	-0,036	0,452	-0,059
Important in a job: good pay	-0,409	0,593	-0,098
Important in a job: meeting people	0,114	0,258	-0,039
Important in a job: not too much pressure	0,241	0,589	-0,333
Important in a job: pleasant people to work with	-0,115	-0,161	0,043
Important in a job: that you can achieve something	0,124	-0,165	-0,119
Important in successful marriage: Understanding and tolerance	-0,394	0,082	-0,046
Important: Religious service birth	-0,601	0,682	2,078

Appendix VI

	Factor 1 Active society	Factor 2 communautarianism, phobia	homo Catholicus
Important: Religious service death	-0,150	0,569	1,205
Important: Religious service marriage	-0,206	0,877	1,936
Justifiable: abortion	-0,627	-0,729	-1,374
Justifiable: adultery	-0,522	-0,192	-1,060
Justifiable: avoiding a fare on public transport	-1,003	0,439	0,045
Justifiable: buy stolen goods	-0,629	0,134	-0,222
Justifiable: cheating on taxes	-0,906	-0,088	0,073
Justifiable: claiming government benefits	-0,737	0,523	0,102
Justifiable: divorce	-0,555	-0,746	-0,610
Justifiable: driving under influence of alcohol	-0,447	-0,034	-0,206
Justifiable: euthanasia	-0,561	-0,914	-1,063
Justifiable: failing to report damage you've done accidentally to a parked vehicle	-0,321	0,171	-0,246
Justifiable: fighting with the police	-0,183	0,078	-0,975
Justifiable: homosexuality	-0,255	-1,933	-0,038
Justifiable: joyriding	-0,243	0,247	-0,176
Justifiable: keeping money that you have found	-0,371	0,596	-0,201
Justifiable: killing in self-defense	-0,323	-0,594	-0,372
Justifiable: lying	-0,628	0,043	-0,494
Justifiable: political assassination	0,067	0,494	-0,697
Justifiable: prostitution	-0,431	-1,223	-0,253
Justifiable: sex under the legal age of consent	-0,689	0,377	-0,740
Justifiable: someone accepting a bribe	-0,657	0,107	0,131
Justifiable: suicide	-0,390	-1,086	-0,733
Justifiable: taking soft drugs	-0,230	-0,656	-0,706
Justifiable: threatening workers who refuse to join a strike	-0,086	0,328	-0,427
Justifiable: throwing away litter	-0,408	-0,457	-0,139
Leisure not time important in life	-0,234	0,445	-0,173
Low Social class (subjective)	-0,452	0,151	0,213
Low Socio-economic status of respondent	-0,541	0,532	0,302
Major changes in life: one should act boldly	-0,293	-0,461	-0,172
Moments of prayer, meditation...	0,122	1,311	2,110
much freedom of choice and control	-0,176	-0,428	0,325
Rejecting neighbors: drug addicts	-0,398	0,280	-0,146
Rejecting neighbors: emotionally unstable people	-0,431	1,716	-1,029
Rejecting neighbors: heavy drinkers	-0,429	0,796	-0,150
Rejecting neighbors: homosexuals	-0,493	1,793	-0,482
Rejecting neighbors: immigrants/foreign workers	0,376	1,903	-1,420
Rejecting neighbors: Jews	0,778	3,761	-0,947

	Factor 1 Active society	Factor 2 communautarianism, phobia	homo Catholicus
Rejecting neighbors: left wing extremists	0,609	1,767	-0,612
Rejecting neighbors: Muslims	-0,530	1,347	-0,199
Rejecting neighbors: people of a different race	0,408	2,635	-0,900
Rejecting neighbors: people who have AIDS	-0,500	2,116	-0,845
Rejecting neighbors: people with a criminal record	-0,448	1,336	0,291
Rejecting neighbors: people with large families	2,119	4,163	-2,014
Rejecting neighbors: political extremists	-0,172	0,229	-1,246
Rejecting neighbors: right wing extremists	0,740	1,407	-1,038
Never attend religious services	-0,756	-1,365	-2,655
Never discusses political matters with friends	-0,285	0,145	0,236
Never follow politics in the news	-0,263	0,148	0,052
Never persuading friends, relatives or fellow workers	-0,196	-0,273	0,318
Never pray to God outside of religious services (I)	-0,849	-0,962	-2,262
Never thinking about death	-0,474	-0,307	-0,247
Never thinking about meaning and purpose life	-0,323	-0,110	-0,006
New ideas better than old ones	-0,284	-0,039	0,175
No confidence: armed forces	-0,429	-0,405	0,148
No confidence: churches	-0,441	-0,680	-1,317
No confidence: education system	-0,324	-0,162	-0,201
No confidence: justice system	-0,584	0,080	0,119
No confidence: labor unions	-0,456	0,110	0,124
No confidence: major companies	-0,457	0,143	-0,121
No confidence: NATO	-0,627	0,401	-0,140
No confidence: parliament	-0,562	0,191	0,106
No confidence: social security system	-0,621	0,148	0,055
No confidence: television	-0,423	0,085	0,039
No confidence: the civil services	-0,550	0,106	0,130
No confidence: the environmental protection movement	-0,392	0,212	-0,082
No confidence: the government	-0,454	0,027	0,159
No confidence: the police	-0,521	0,395	-0,061
No confidence: the political parties	-0,489	0,072	0,220
No confidence: the press	-0,462	-0,040	0,069
No confidence: the United Nations	-0,502	0,299	-0,196
No confidence: the women's movement	-0,463	0,111	0,023
No increase in taxes if used to prevent environmental pollution	-0,325	-0,053	0,220
No interest in politics	-0,465	0,302	0,319
No part of my income for the environment	-0,348	-0,103	0,167

	Factor 1 Active society	Factor 2 communautarianism, phobia	homo Catholicus
No religious person	-0,338	-0,646	-1,255
No respect and love for parents	-0,244	-0,472	-0,201
No respect for individual human rights nowadays	-0,656	0,507	-0,184
Not important for successful marriage: adequate income	-0,342	-0,653	0,000
Not important for successful marriage: agreement on politics	-0,426	-0,199	-0,048
Not important for successful marriage: apart from in-laws	-0,013	0,182	-0,108
Not important for successful marriage: children	-0,222	-0,637	-0,232
Not important for successful marriage: faithfulness	-0,435	-0,056	-0,316
Not important for successful marriage: good housing	-0,159	-0,358	-0,111
Not important for successful marriage: happy sexual relationship	-0,368	0,124	0,053
Not important for successful marriage: religious beliefs	-0,627	-0,807	-0,902
Not important for successful marriage: respect and appreciation	-0,313	0,104	-0,099
Not important for successful marriage: same social background	-0,609	-0,423	-0,214
Not important for successful marriage: sharing household chores	-0,263	-0,171	0,039
Not important for successful marriage: tastes and interests in common	-0,312	-0,349	-0,246
Not spend time with colleagues from work	-0,396	-0,089	0,478
Not spend time with friends	-0,367	0,385	0,108
Not spend time with parents or other relatives	-0,246	0,079	0,121
Not spend time with people at sport, culture, communal organization	-0,521	0,463	-0,258
Not spend time with people at your church, mosque or synagogue	-0,755	-0,202	-1,037
Parents responsibilities to their children	-0,284	-0,198	-0,318
Political system as it was before good for the country	0,077	0,133	-0,343
Political system good for governing country	0,156	-0,435	0,291
Political system in ten years good for the country	-0,281	0,187	0,197
Politicians who don't believe in God are fit for public office	-0,485	-0,529	0,079
Politics not important in life	-0,539	0,219	0,267
Poverty compared to 10 years ago decreased	0,365	-0,118	-0,349
Raised religiously	0,056	0,964	2,745
Religion not important in life	-0,688	-0,869	-1,406
Religious leaders should influence government	-0,143	-0,055	0,445

	Factor 1 Active society	Factor 2 communautarianism, phobia	homo Catholicus
Religious leaders should influence how people vote	-0,080	0,024	0,225
Right wing versus left wind (right wing (self positioning in political scale)	-0,109	0,102	0,325
Satisfaction with financial situation of household	0,194	-0,850	0,439
Satisfaction with your life	0,003	-0,763	0,509
Scale of incomes	-0,309	-0,420	-0,017
Service to others not important in life	-0,534	0,645	-0,713
Sharing with parents: attitudes towards religion	0,014	1,041	1,516
Sharing with parents: moral standards	-0,080	0,593	0,666
Sharing with parents: no sharing attitudes	-1,799	-1,388	-2,339
Sharing with parents: political views	-0,352	-0,637	0,769
Sharing with parents: sexual attitudes	-0,833	-0,124	1,451
Sharing with parents: social attitudes	-0,115	0,495	0,622
State of health very bad (subjective)	-0,572	0,617	0,124
State ownership vs. private ownership of business	-0,449	0,544	-0,093
TV not most important entertainment	-0,351	-0,060	0,308
Unpaid work education, arts, music or cultural activities	1,854	0,343	-1,278
Unpaid work environment, conservation, animal rights	1,993	0,664	-2,303
Unpaid work human rights	2,169	-0,798	-2,175
Unpaid work labor unions	-0,116	2,727	-0,881
Unpaid work local political action groups	2,815	1,418	-0,480
Unpaid work organization concerned with health	3,347	0,881	0,865
Unpaid work other groups	2,079	-2,164	0,442
Unpaid work peace movement	7,352	5,445	-1,549
Unpaid work political parties or groups	1,972	0,929	-2,624
Unpaid work professional associations	2,057	-1,496	-2,195
Unpaid work religious or church organization	3,233	-0,140	3,573
Unpaid work social welfare service for elderly, handicapped or deprived people	2,059	-1,168	-0,453
Unpaid work sports or recreation	1,167	-1,504	-0,663
Unpaid work women's group	3,374	-0,626	-1,186
Unpaid work youth work	2,564	-1,747	0,611
Using violence for political goals justified	-0,528	0,272	0,363
Wealth accumulation does not harm others	-0,213	-0,136	0,175
wide extent of political corruption in the country	-0,471	0,396	0,126
Work more important than leisure	-0,333	0,264	0,299

	Factor 1 Active society	Factor 2 communautarianism, phobia	homo Catholicus
Work not important in life	-0,336	-0,139	-0,048
Worse if more people with strong religious beliefs in public office	-0,309	-0,522	-0,593
Would never do (political action): attending lawful demonstrations	-0,194	0,156	0,182
Would never do (political action): joining in boycotts	-0,381	0,275	0,286
Would never do (political action): joining unofficial strikes	-0,251	0,104	0,161
Would never do (political action): occupying buildings or factories	-0,233	0,058	0,074
Would never do (political action): signing a petition	-0,433	0,835	0,125
Would not buy things at a 20% higher price if it helped to protect environment	-0,285	-0,023	0,117
You cannot be too careful (most people cannot be trusted)	-0,402	0,301	0,201

The World Value System According to the WVS – Mean Average Positions or Percentages
(Percentages per Total Adult Resident Population)
(Part 1)

	mean left-right position	not satisfied with democracy	openly racist	openly anti-Semitic	belief in hell	only God-believing politicians	mean acceptability homosexuality	mean acceptance competition	secularization rate (never attending rel. Services)
Albania [2002]	5,34	27,2	30,4	17	41	17,5	1,48	2,97	23,3
Algeria [2002]	6,22	20,8	28		98,8	55,9	1,26		27,2
Argentina [1999]	5,99	17,8	4,5	6,4	43,7	14,5	4,33	4,17	28,1
Armenia [1997]	5,39	30,3	19,2		36,4		2,03	4,07	13,5
Australia [1995]	5,34		4,8		41,1		4,6	3,2	44,1
Austria [1999]	5,42	2,9	6,7	8,3	18,3	4,8	5,36	3,19	17
Azerbaijan [1997]	5,54	4,6	12,2		59		1,41	3,51	16,8
Bangladesh [2002]	7,56	3,3	71,7	20,4	95,4	31,9	1,05	2,87	3,7
Belarus [2000]	5,68	27,8	16,5	14,8	35,1	7,5	2,91	3,67	27,8
Belgium [1999]	5,25	15,7	16,5	13	16,1	3,4	5,4	4,8	46,5
Bosnia and Herzegovina [2001]	5,09	19,1	13,2	28	60,3	5,5	1,98	3,05	13,8
Brazil [1997]	5,9		2,8		49,1		3,16	3,43	7,6
Bulgaria [1999]	5,85	22,7	28,1	18,1	30	9,5	2,6	3,5	27,4
Canada [2000]	5,55	6	3,4	3,8	50,3	6,8	5,44	3,52	29,1
Chile [2000]	5,23	11,5	9	8,8	65,4	14,8	3,98	4,76	22,4
China [2001]		0,9	14,6				1,14	2,72	89,6
Colombia [1998]	6,63		2		40,4		2,55		7
Croatia [1999]	5,27	24,6	19,5	18,2	57,1	9,2	2,41	2,91	10,4
Czech Republic [1999]	5,96	13	9,8	4,4	13,1	2,5	5,47	3,25	57,5
Denmark [1999]	5,51	3	7,4	2,5	9,5	1,3	6,59	4,02	42,7
Dominican Republic [1996]	6,63		18,5		67,7		3,26	3,33	13,7
Egypt [2000]		0,1	65,8	16,5	100	70,1	1,01		25,1
El Salvador [1999]	6,3				76,4		2,03	3,75	12,1
Estonia [1999]	5,93	12,3	15,2	11,2	16,2	3,8	2,98	4,39	37,7
Finland [2000]	5,77	4,3	12,4	8,6	31,3	3,7	4,94	4,28	26,2
France [1999]	4,86	11,4	8,9	5,9	19,6	4	5,27	4,73	60,4

	mean left-right position	not satisfied with democracy	openly racist	openly anti-Semitic	belief in hell	only God-believing politicians	mean acceptability homosexuality	mean acceptance competition	secularization rate (never attending rel. Services)
Georgia [1996]	5,93	22,5	9,5		59,3		1,56	3,18	13,7
Germany West [1999]	5,43	4,8	4,3	4,5	22,5	3,8	5,83	3,81	22,4
Great Britain [1999]	5,08	11,3	8,6	6,2	35,3	3,4	4,89	4,01	55,8
Greece [1999]	5,13	9	14,4	18,7	40,9	17,9	4,95	4,34	4,7
Hungary [1999]	5,1	11,9			20,2	5,9	1,45	3,75	42,7
Iceland [1999]	5,78	4,5	3,1	4,1	17,5	2,6	7,19	2,7	32,3
India [2001]	5,66	7,9	41,8		68,5	18,5	3,08	3,21	3,1
Indonesia [2001]	6,62	12,1	34,7		99,9	60,4	1,13		0,8
Iran (Islamic Republic of) [2000]	4,82	9,7	24,2		98,2		1,25		4,1
Iraq [2004]				83,4	99,3	70,7			44,9
Ireland [1999]	5,64	6,6	12,4	11,2	53,5	4,2	4,27	3,84	9,4
Israel [2001]	5,09						4,89		
Italy [1999]	5,36	11,4	15,6	12,9	49	4,6	4,83	4,16	13,9
Japan [2000]	5,7	6,3			30,1	2,3	4,36	4,17	8,6
Jordan [2001]	5,91	7,9	20		99,3	69,5	1,05		41,9
Kyrgyzstan [2003]	6,2	16,8	18,4	20,4	69,8	10,6	1,77	3,59	31,2
Latvia [1999]	5,83	10,3	4,8	5,2	28,4	5,8	1,9	3,43	34,6
Lithuania [1999]	5,41	22	9,8	23	68,2	7,9	1,88	3,99	16
Luxembourg [1999]	5,37	2,2	6,3	8,3	21,6	5,5	5,9	4,45	32,7
Macedonia, Republic of [2001]	5,21	38	19	20	46,5	19	1,93	2,85	7
Malta [1999]	5,8	3,8	18,6	20,8	80,6	10,9	2,58	3,2	4,2
Mexico [2000]	6,65	20,7	15,2		74,6	16,7	3,58	3,92	6,1
Morocco [2001]	5,72	16,1	13,7			76,3		2,23	35,3
Netherlands [1999]	5,09	2	5	1,6	13,8	0,6	7,82	4,68	48,3
New Zealand [1998]	5,79		3		34,8		4,74	3,49	44,4
Nigeria [2000]	5,51	9,2	30,4		93,6	57,4	1,5		0,6
Norway [1996]	5,57		8,2		19,7		5,71	3,54	41,8
Pakistan [2001]	5,94	40,5	6,5		100	82,4	1,05		
Peru [2001]	5,69	10,5	11,2		65,2		2,62	3,4	4,9
Philippines [2001]	6,45	9,9	21,3		92,5	26,9	3,88	4,03	0,9
Poland [1999]	5,35	13,2	17,2	25,1	65,6	7,1	2,9	3,99	5,3

The World Value System According to the WVS-(Part 1 - Continued)

	mean left-right position	not satisfied with democracy	openly racist	openly anti-Semitic	belief in hell	only God-believing politicians	mean acceptability homosexuality	mean acceptance competition	secularization rate (never attending rel. Services)
Portugal [1999]	5,27	3,2	7,6	10,8	37,8	2,8	3,19	4,45	15,3
Republic of Korea [2001]	5,35	8,4	34,7	40,9		2,9	2,77	4,1	16
Republic of Moldova [2002]	5,58	32	11	25	64,7	12,9	2,32	3,98	6,8
Romania [1999]	5,83	26,9	24,2	23,2	71,4	25,2	1,91	2,74	7,5
Russian Federation [1999]	4,92	50	8,1	11,4	35,7	7,1	2,2	4,09	50,1
Saudi Arabia [2003]			37,7		99,5		1,38		15,4
Serbia [2001]	5,52	14,2	6,1		18	9,6	1,96	3,39	13,8
Singapore [2002]			4,7		79,1		2,57	3,29	12,5
Slovakia [1999]	5,14	23,7	17	9,9	46,1	9	4,91	3,59	23,1
Slovenia [1999]	4,99	10,6	12	16,8	20,3	2,5	4,62	3,24	30,1
South Africa [2001]	5,68	9,9	23,6	24,4	60,5	24,5	3,16	3,59	10,3
Spain [2000]	4,69	5	11,5	34,2	40,1	1,9	6,17	4,29	33,1
Sweden [1999]	5,34	5,7	2,5	2,1	9,5	1,7	7,65	3,46	45,6
Switzerland [1996]	5,31		8,7		20,5		6,45	3,18	33,1
Tanzania, United Republic Of [2001]	6,75	7,1	16,7		95,6	54,7	1,15	3,05	2,3
Turkey [2001]	5,91	50,6	33,9	61,9	92,7	29,7	1,55	3,85	32,3
Uganda [2001]	5,55	5	18,2	22,2	76,5	26	1,25	2,56	1
Ukraine [1999]	5,48	35,8	10,5	10,4	38,1	13,4	2,35	4,05	30,4
United States [1999]	5,8	6,9	8	9,1	74,6	17,8	4,75	3,4	14,8
Uruguay [1996]	5,67		6,8	10,4	25,2		3,95	4,73	54,4
Venezuela [2000]	6,32	11,5	15,5			36,3	2,44	3,84	14,2
Viet Nam [2001]	9,05	0,1	32,2		17,1	5,2	1,65	3,79	49,4
Zimbabwe [2001]	3,66	25,4	19,8	19,3	79,4	15,7	1,1	2,47	11,3

The World Value System According to the WVS – (Part 2)

	always respect parents	education for tolerance and respect important	never praying	thrift important in education	mean workaholic scale	jobs scarce men have rights	belong voluntary welfare elderly	unpaid social welfare work	just can't be too careful	mean satisfaction income	mean acceptance government benefits fraud
Albania [2002]	86,8	80	10,8	54,9	4,3	46,7	13,6	10,8	75,6	4,76	1,92
Algeria [2002]	92,9	54		17,9	4,57	67,5	10,9	18,9	88,8	5,92	3,02
Argentina [1999]	88	70,4	15,7	14,9	4,24	25,7	4,7	2,7	84,6	5,51	2,59
Armenia [1997]	92,8	48,4		38,2	3,42	59,9			75,3	3,63	3,24
Australia [1995]	74	80,7		18,9	3,07	25,5			60,1	6,38	1,73
Austria [1999]	65	71,4	20,2	47,6		26,7	6,6	2,3	66,1		2,17
Azerbaijan [1997]	91,5	59,1		59,3	3,21	63,6			79,5	4,56	2,42
Bangladesh [2002]	89,9	70,9	0,1	57,3	4,43	68,2	17,2	19,4	76,5	5,57	1,35
Belarus [2000]	70,9	72,2	30	46,2		24,8	1,3	2,5	58,1		3,48
Belgium [1999]	65,2	83	39,8	43,3		25,1	12,3	5,9	69,3		2,39
Bosnia and Herzegovina [2001]	91,2	71,7	15,3	37,2	3,86	26,5	1,5	1,1	84,2	4,87	1,67
Brazil [1997]	92,7	59,4		38,6	3,91	35,6			97,2	5,48	3,2
Bulgaria [1999]	81,9	59,3	47,2	39,1		38,9	1,3	1,5	73,1		1,86
Canada [2000]	77,6	80,6	18,9	27,1	3,3	14,6	13,2	9,6	61,2	6,92	1,87
Chile [2000]	87,3	76	9,3	34,4	3,65	25,2	6,7	5,9	77,2	5,66	3,33
China [2001]	94,5	72,6		57,2	4,17	45,1	2,9	56	45,5	5,65	2,13
Colombia [1998]	91	69,4		20,3	4,26	29,2			88,8	8	2,13
Croatia [1999]	71,5		19			29	2,1	1,1	81,6		1,58
Czech Republic [1999]	73,8	63	62,2	31,7		18,4	6,5	3,4	76,1		1,87
Denmark [1999]	35,9	87,3	51,8	9,6		6,2	6,5	4	33,5		1,38
Dominican Republic [1996]	85,7	67,9		11,3	3,94	15,1			73,6	5,74	2,19
Egypt [2000]	95,2	64,6		8	3,64	89,6			62,1	5,26	1,82
El Salvador [1999]	93,6	58,8		29,8	4,37	27,2			85,4	6,28	2,69

The World Value System According to the WVS – (Part 2-Continued)

	always respect parents	education for tolerance and respect important	never praying	thrift important in education	mean workaholic scale	jobs scarce men have rights	belong voluntary welfare elderly	unpaid social welfare work	just can't be too careful	mean satisfaction income	mean acceptance government benefits fraud
Estonia [1999]	71,9	71,3	56,7	44,6		13,5	3,3	2,6	77,2		3,19
Finland [2000]	63,2	82,7	20,7	22,6		9,9	10,4	7,2	42		2,3
France [1999]	74,7	85,2	55	37,7		21,8	5,6	4,1	77,8		3,39
Georgia [1996]	91,3	54,1		31,9	3,48	64,5			81,3	3,07	2,91
Germany West [1999]	49,4	73,6	29,2	35,2		27,2	4,2	2	67,1		1,84
Great Britain [1999]	65,1	83,5	48,3	33		22,9	6,7	13,4	70,3		1,99
Greece [1999]	69,1	52,5	14,6	29,9		19,9	6,5	7,6	76,3		4,04
Hungary [1999]	82,7	65,6	36,6	41,5		24,7	1,9	2,5	78,2		1,7
Iceland [1999]	60,7	84,3	18,8	20,5		3,5	17,4	8,7	58,9		1,75
India [2001]	88,8	63,2	4,3	61,9	3,7	57,2	7,1	6,3	59	4,96	2,34
Indonesia [2001]	90,2	62,6		52	3,52	52,2			48,4	6,46	3,88
Iran (Islamic Republic of) [2000]	89,1	59	2,7	29,6	4,01	72,8			34,7	5,75	2,7
Iraq [2004]		77,8	5,3	28,2		77,6			52,4	5,43	
Ireland [1999]	71,9	75	8,9	22,6		15,4	5,8	3,8	64,2		1,89
Israel [2001]		81,9		19,8	2,55				76,5		
Italy [1999]	79,4	75	12,9	34,7		27	6,4	5,1	67,4		1,88
Japan [2000]	71,6	71,2	16,3	48,1	2,98	31,8	9,4	5,4	56,9	6,17	2,09
Jordan [2001]	93,9	67,3		19,4	1,62	80,4			72,3	5,09	1,7
Kyrgyzstan [2003]	93,9	65,5	14,2	43	3,95	49,1	8,1	3,7	83,3	5,68	2,77
Latvia [1999]	77,1	69,5	34,8	45,1		19,8	1,5	1,8	82,9		2,12
Lithuania [1999]	82,7	57,6	33,8	42,3		24,4	0,7	0,6	75,1		2,55
Luxembourg [1999]	58,8	78,1	33,8	48,5		26,2	14,2	6,9	74		2,86
Macedonia, Republic of [2001]	91	75,3	16,3	39,5	4,08	42,7	7,2	4,8	86,5	4,44	3

	always respect parents	education for tolerance and respect important	never praying	thrift important in education	mean workaholic scale	jobs scarce men have rights	belong voluntary welfare elderly	unpaid social welfare work	just can't be too careful	mean satisfaction income	mean acceptance government benefits fraud
Malta [1999]	91,1	61	2,9	53,5		47,4	2,4	4,9	79,3		1,37
Mexico [2000]	90,2	70,6	5,7	39,3	4	33,7	7,2	5,3	78,7	6,54	3,75
Morocco [2001]	98,2	74,3	13	35,6	3,92	87,2	1,3		76,1	5,08	1,68
Netherlands [1999]	31,9	91,1	49,3	21,6		12,4	21,2	9,3	40,2		1,52
New Zealand [1998]	63,6	77,9		25,1	2,98	13,1			50,9	6,46	1,87
Nigeria [2000]	94,3	59,1		10,3	4,13	60,3			74,4	6,28	1,97
Norway [1996]	52	65,9		13,2	3,16	14,4			34,7	6,74	1,64
Pakistan [2001]	94,4	53		55,4		67,4			69,2	3,52	1,53
Peru [2001]	90,7	72,6	3,2	23,5	4,13	15,1	4,1	3,3	89,3	5,11	3,49
Philippines [2001]	93,8	60,1	0,1	45,3	4,24	69	8	10	91,6	5,83	3,57
Poland [1999]	86,5	80,1	4,4	38,3		34,9	3	2,2	81,1		2,36
Portugal [1999]	82,6	65,4	17,1	35,7		29,5	2	0,8	90		2,03
Republic of Korea [2001]	92,2	64,7	3,3	67,5	3,49	38,7	9,4	9,1	72,7	5,79	
Republic of Moldova [2002]	90,4	77,9	5,2	42,1	3,6	45	3,7	7,4	85,3	4,07	3,85
Romania [1999]	83,6	58,3	6,5	30,7		37,9	1,7	1	89,9		1,82
Russian Federation [1999]	84,2	67,1	55,6	51,3		36,4	1,5	0,5	76,3		2,3
Saudi Arabia [2003]	92,2	56,4		31,5	4,42	69,7			47	7,23	2,65
Serbia [2001]	87	64,5	26,5	30,8	3,64	31,3	3,3	1,3	81,2	3,86	2,12
Singapore [2002]	93,3	69,8	12,2	43,8	3,22	30	7,1	11,6	83,1	6,6	2,66
Slovakia [1999]	73,6	57	21,5	38,6		24,1	6,6	6,1	84,3		2,91
Slovenia [1999]	78,2	70,1		35,4		17,8	5,4	4,9	78,3		2,82
South Africa [2001]	90,8	74,1	4,3	37,1	3,96	31,8	8,5	6,7	88,2	4,65	2,89
Spain [2000]	87,4	77	30,5	31,4	2,78	16,6	2,7	2	66	6,27	2,11
Sweden [1999]	43,9	92,5		30,5		2,3	20,8	9,1	33,7		2,08

The World Value System According to the WVS – (Part 2-Continued)

	always respect parents	education for tolerance and respect important	never praying	thrift important in education	mean workaholic scale	jobs scarce men have rights	belong voluntary welfare elderly	unpaid social welfare work	just can't be too careful	mean satisfaction income	mean acceptance government benefits fraud
Switzerland [1996]	66,3	79,3		35	2,98	27,4			59	7,47	2,07
Tanzania, United Republic Of [2001]	90,7	83,6	0,8	53,5	4,45	27,2	26,9	24,6	91,9	3,48	1,62
Turkey [2001]	83,5	57,5	3,7	30,1		61,8	0,2	0,3	93,2		1,24
Uganda [2001]	89,9	56,8	0,6	10,7	4,25	40,7	12,2	11,4	92,4	4,83	1,98
Ukraine [1999]	85,7	65,5	38,7	50,4		30,8	1,9	0,6	72,8		2,83
United States [1999]	77,2	79,5	6,4	22,8	3,1	9,9	16,8	14	64,2	6,53	2,18
Uruguay [1996]	77,9	69,7		26,6	3,28	27,9			77,9	6,7	1,75
Venezuela [2000]	94	79,6	2,2	39	4,05	31,4	6,6		84,1	6,19	2,98
Viet Nam [2001]	99,3	67,9	48,4	48,1	4	48,5	26,5	28,7	58,9	5,95	2,13
Zimbabwe [2001]	96,2	78,2	6,4	20,5	4,67	40,3	8,5	6,6	88,1	3,2	1,67

The World Value System According to the WVS – (Part 3)

	unpaid work religious organizations	for less materialism	emphasis on authority good	income differences good	government sector	Confidence in the EU	rejecting foreign workers	rejecting homosexual neighbor	never occupy building/factory	Islamophobia
Albania [2002]	14,6	36,7	34,2	5,96	3,85	41,3	16,5	82,6	97,9	30,4
Algeria [2002]	13,5	39,9	62,6	8,09	5,06	5	23,5	80,7	94,6	
Argentina [1999]	9,2	64,2	72,1	4,92	5,68		5,9	22,1	89,1	6,2
Armenia [1997]		58,7	62,7	6,4	6,17	13,2	21,6	83,3	86,4	
Australia [1995]		68,7	72,9	5,58	3,8		4,6	24,7	80,6	
Austria [1999]	7	50	39	4,63	3,41	6,1	12,2	25,4	89,7	15,4
Azerbaijan [1997]		64	60,6	5,9	5,57	4,4	19,9	90,7	96,7	
Bangladesh [2002]	40,5	36,4	91,5	7,56	5,31		67,1	4,9	92,6	
Belarus [2000]	4,1	47,5	72,4	5,27	5,24	6,5	17,1	63,3	95,3	26,6
Belgium [1999]	5,5	67	63,1	5,49		7,3	18,2	17,4	68,5	22
Bosnia and Herzegovina [2001]	4,5	53,9	26,3	6,1	4,63	14	24,8	64,2	87,5	12,8
Brazil [1997]		64,5	83	5,71	5,21		3,6	26,3	81,1	
Bulgaria [1999]	1,8	57,7	68,8	6,12		11	24,6	53,9	82,8	21,2
Canada [2000]	18,4	65,4	66,4	5,44	3,88		4,2	16,9	78,9	6,5
Chile [2000]	16,5	64,5	56	4	5,92		10,7	32,8	86,1	7,4
China [2001]	4,3	46,9	63,7	6,26	6,79	4,3	16	73,2		
Colombia [1998]		59,4	88,5	6,2	6,56			14,9	87,5	
Croatia [1999]	5,3	77,2	55,7	4,08	4,64	6,6	21,7	52,8	80,8	26,5
Czech Republic [1999]	2,8	48,7	52,3	5,48	4,71	7,6	19,4	19,7	88,8	15,2
Denmark [1999]	3,3	70	38,2			2,1	10,6	8	85,1	16,3
Dominican Republic [1996]		51,7	55,9	7,7	6,34		17,5	48,7	67,8	
Egypt [2000]		55,6	86,2	8,23	6,68		42,3	0,4	95,1	
El Salvador [1999]		42,5	85,8	6,83	6,11			78,3	94,4	
Estonia [1999]	2,8	54,1	43,9	6,88	5,74	3,5	20,9	46,2	94,9	22,2
Finland [2000]	7,8	66,1	39,4	4,56	4,22	1,7	13	21,3	84,9	19,3
France [1999]	3,1	70,9	68,7	4,83	4,03	6,5	12	15,6	55,7	16
Georgia [1996]		70,3	75,3	7,6	5,67	12,5	10,9	77	97,2	
Germany West [1999]	6,4	53,7	42,6		3,82	5,1	7,4	13,2	85,6	10,2
Great Britain [1999]	6,3	65,7	70,7	5,61	4,72	4,7	15,5	24,3	81,7	13,6

The World Value System According to the WVS – (Part 3 - Continued)

	unpaid work religious organizations	for less materialism	emphasis on authority good	income differences good	government sector	Confidence in the EU	rejecting foreign workers	rejecting homosexual neighbor	never occupy building/factory	Islamophobia
Greece [1999]	6,1	78,1	17,1			2,9	13,7	26,8	46	20,9
Hungary [1999]	5,4	45,1	68,7			9		7,9	95,1	
Iceland [1999]	4,6	61,5	46,9	5,66	3,67	3,4	3		87,1	11,6
India [2001]	14,3	42,7	43,4	4,18	6,04		38,2	28,8	82,9	
Indonesia [2001]		27	37,4	7,18	5,86		40,2	54,6	86,4	
Iran (Islamic Republic of) [2000]		55,8	71,4	5,66	5,66		9,6	0,9		
Iraq [2004]				5,42	6,93					
Ireland [1999]	7,6	69,5	77,4	6,07	4,23	12,3	12,1	27,4	81	13,6
Israel [2001]		74,8	58,7	3,77					92,3	
Italy [1999]	6,7	70,6	51,3	6,02	4,11	15,7	16,5	28,7	74,4	17,2
Japan [2000]	3,2	39	4,2	5,72	4,49				92,2	
Jordan [2001]		59,1	90,4	7,43	5,79		39,9	98,4	99,5	
Kyrgyzstan [2003]	1,3	60,7	50,7	5,44	5,75	15,5	19,8	66	93,5	14,6
Latvia [1999]	3,8	31,8	48,9			4,3	9,8	45,5	95,7	14,5
Lithuania [1999]	4,2	45,6	44	4,81	4,94	1,2	23,6	67,5	86,5	33,1
Luxembourg [1999]	6,1	70,7	52,8	6,75		12,6	8,4	18,6	80	14,2
Macedonia, Republic of [2001]	8,5	51,5	48,5	5,33	3,77	16,1	18,6	53,5	83,3	26,2
Malta [1999]	12,7	81,4	92,2			19,3	15,3	39,6	85,5	27,8
Mexico [2000]	19,6	58,3	75,9	5,02	5,57		14,3	44,6	90,8	17
Morocco [2001]		65,3	90,4	7,44	5,15	9,6	19,1	93	95,8	
Netherlands [1999]	11,4	60	66,6	6,16	4,38	2,5	5	6,2	71,7	11,9
New Zealand [1998]		56,3	52,7	5,34	4,35		5,4	22,3	79,3	
Nigeria [2000]		62,8	82,8	6,25			28	73,6	58,2	
Norway [1996]		60,9	31,5	5,27	4,45	3,4	9,8	14,3	87,9	19,3
Pakistan [2001]		70	62,4	3,83	5,01		29,1		99,3	
Peru [2001]	20,3	49,2	80,4	7,52	6,45		10,9	49,2	86	13,5
Philippines [2001]	29,6	49,1	69,7	6,46	6,42		15,3	23,6	93	26,4
Poland [1999]	3,7	60,1	54,5	6,09	5,78	9,3	23,5	55,2	81,4	23,8

	unpaid work religious organizations	for less materialism	emphasis on authority good	income differences good	government sector	Confidence in the EU	rejecting foreign workers	rejecting homosexual neighbor	never occupy building/factory	Islamophobia
Portugal [1999]	2,6	57,2	77,7		4,72	7,4	2,5	25,2	76,8	7,9
Republic of Korea [2001]	26,9	52,8	19,4	6,55	4,83		46,8	82,4		57,3
Republic of Moldova [2002]	15,7	46	48,1	6,69	6,53	17,1	18,8	77,4	86,7	44,4
Romania [1999]	3,6	65,5	84,5	3,69	4,38	8,5	21,1	65,2	94	31,4
Russian Federation [1999]	0,5	45,4	56,2	7,15	6,11	3	11,1	57,9	90,9	13,7
Saudi Arabia [2003]		55,7	73	6,72	5,51		33,1			
Serbia [2001]	1,2	51,1	55	5,78	4,62	3,6	7,8	49,1	81,5	13,6
Singapore [2002]	12	37,9	52,3	6,88	4,75		25,9	45,7		
Slovakia [1999]	13,1	61,3	68,1			9,6	22,9	44	84,5	24,5
Slovenia [1999]	4,5	62,8	43,3	4,05		7,4	16	44,3	74,5	22,6
South Africa [2001]	37,4	35,3	72,7	5,4	5,51		30,6	46,2	74,7	23,9
Spain [2000]	4,4	72,3	61,4	5,07	5,53	8	10,8	14,8	84,8	15,4
Sweden [1999]	23,4	67,3	22,2			3,1	2,8	6,1	78,4	9
Switzerland [1996]		68,3	30,6	4,82	3,28	6,3	10	18,5	85,8	18,5
Tanzania, United Republic Of [2001]	61,9	60,4	82,2	4,97	5,14		17,5	74,1	93,9	12,6
Turkey [2001]	0,7	72,4	65,1	3,55	5,17	12	45,4	90	95,2	
Uganda [2001]	38,7	24,7	73,3	7,22	3,7		13	76,1	45,1	14,2
Ukraine [1999]	2,3	44,3	63,8	7,35	5,6	8,6	14,9	65,7	93,9	24
United States [1999]	38	65,2	70,3	5,72	3,52		10,1	23,3	70,9	10,7
Uruguay [1996]		74,9	58,1	5,09	5,46		7,1	31,9	75,9	
Venezuela [2000]		48,4	91,2	5,58	5,64		17,9	57,4	90	
Viet Nam [2001]	9,6	57,9	80,1	6,33	5,39		32,9	38,6	76,7	27
Zimbabwe [2001]	54	27,9	89,7	6,94	4,3		20,5	66,5	95,7	17,7

Appendix VII

SECULARIZATION—HOW MUCH? SOME FURTHER MATERIALS ON THE SCYLLA AND CHARYBDIS ON THE PATH TO MODERNIZATION AND THE GOVERNANCE OF VALUE CHANGE

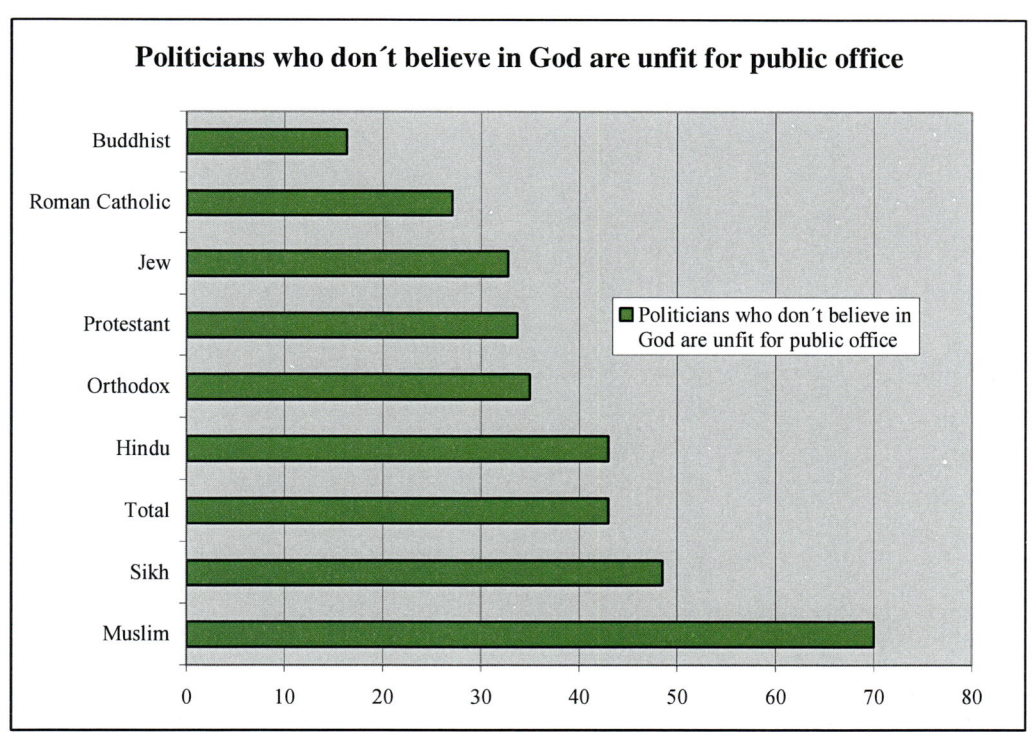

BASE=179850 global citizens, 67145 valid responses (100%).

Selected samples: Albania [1998], Albania [2002], Algeria [2002], Argentina [1995], Argentina [1999], Armenia [1997], Australia [1995], Austria [1999], Azerbaijan [1997], Bangladesh [1996], Bangladesh [2002], Belarus [1996], Belarus [2000], Belgium [1999], Bosnia and Herzegovina [1998], Bosnia and Herzegovina [2001], Brazil [1997], Bulgaria [1997], Bulgaria [1999], Canada [2000], Chile [1996], Chile [2000], China [1995], China [2001], Colombia [1997], Colombia [1998], Croatia [1996], Croatia [1999], Czech Republic [1998], Czech Republic [1999], Denmark [1999], Dominican Republic [1996], Egypt [2000], El Salvador [1999], Estonia [1996], Estonia [1999], Finland [1996], Finland [2000], France [1999], Georgia [1996], Germany East [1997],

Germany East [1999], Germany West [1997], Germany West [1999], Great Britain [1998], Great Britain [1999], Greece [1999], Hungary [1998], Hungary [1999], Iceland [1999], India [1995], India [2001], Indonesia [2001], Iran (Islamic Republic of) [2000], Iraq [2004], Ireland [1999], Israel [2001], Italy [1999], Japan [1995], Japan [2000], Jordan [2001], Kyrgyzstan [2003], Latvia [1996], Latvia [1999], Lithuania [1997], Lithuania [1999], Luxembourg [1999], Macedonia, Republic of [1998], Macedonia, Republic of [2001], Malta [1999], Mexico [1996], Mexico [2000], Montenegro [1996], Montenegro [2001], Morocco [2001], Morocco [2001], Netherlands [1999], New Zealand [1998], Nigeria [1995], Nigeria [2000], Northern Ireland [1999], Norway [1996], Pakistan [1997], Pakistan [2001], Peru [1996], Peru [2001], Philippines [1996], Philippines [2001], Poland [1997], Poland [1999], Portugal [1999], Puerto Rico [1995], Puerto Rico [2001], Republic of Korea [1996], Republic of Korea [2001], Republic of Moldova [1996], Republic of Moldova [2002], Romania [1998], Romania [1999], Russian Federation [1995], Russian Federation [1999], Saudi Arabia [2003], Serbia [1996], Serbia [2001], Singapore [2002], Slovakia [1998], Slovakia [1999], Slovenia [1995], Slovenia [1999], South Africa [1996], South Africa [2001], Spain [1995], Spain [1999], Spain [2000], Sweden [1996], Sweden [1999], Switzerland [1996], Taiwan [1994], Tanzania, United Republic Of [2001], Turkey [1996], Turkey [2001], Turkey [2001], Uganda [2001], Ukraine [1996], Ukraine [1999], United States [1995], United States [1999], Uruguay [1996], Venezuela [1996], Venezuela [2000], Viet Nam [2001], Zimbabwe [2001]

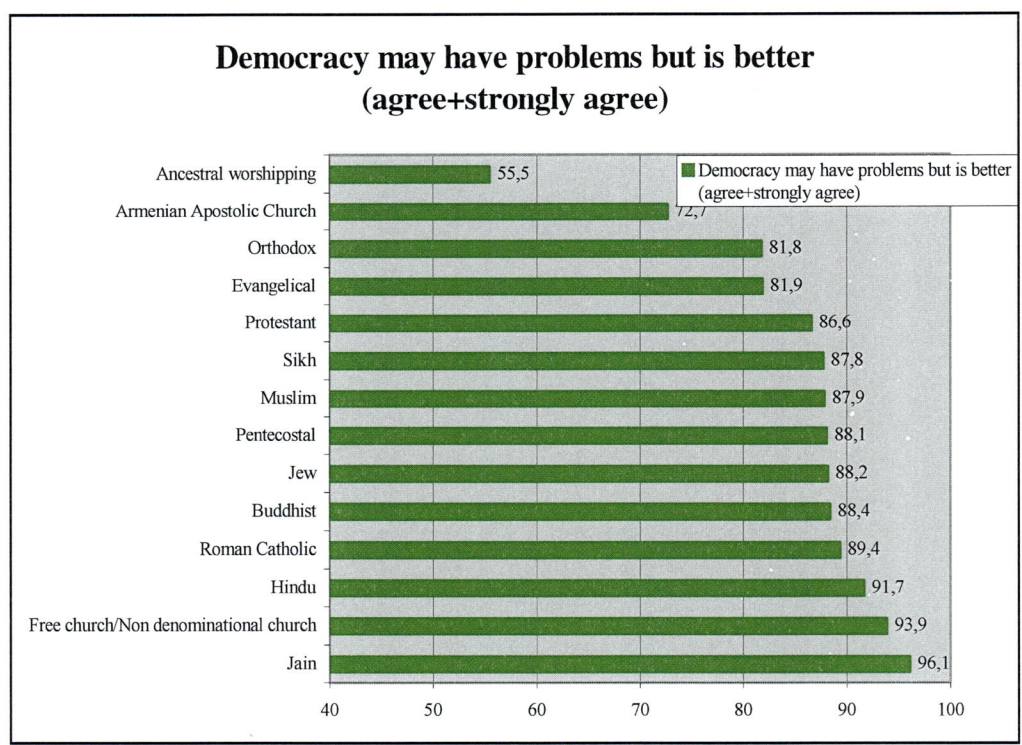

BASE=179850 global citizens; 114576 valid responses (100%).
Selected samples: Albania [1998], Albania [2002], Algeria [2002], Argentina [1995], Argentina [1999], Armenia [1997], Australia [1995], Austria [1999], Azerbaijan [1997], Bangladesh [1996], Bangladesh [2002], Belarus [1996], Belarus [2000], Belgium [1999], Bosnia and Herzegovina [1998], Bosnia and Herzegovina [2001], Brazil [1997], Bulgaria [1997], Bulgaria [1999], Canada [2000], Chile [1996], Chile [2000], China [1995], China [2001], Colombia [1997], Colombia [1998], Croatia [1996], Croatia [1999], Czech Republic [1998], Czech Republic [1999], Denmark

[1999], Dominican Republic [1996], Egypt [2000], El Salvador [1999], Estonia [1996], Estonia [1999], Finland [1996], Finland [2000], France [1999], Georgia [1996], Germany East [1997], Germany East [1999], Germany West [1997], Germany West [1999], Great Britain [1998], Great Britain [1999], Greece [1999], Hungary [1998], Hungary [1999], Iceland [1999], India [1995], India [2001], Indonesia [2001], Iran (Islamic Republic of) [2000], Iraq [2004], Ireland [1999], Israel [2001], Italy [1999], Japan [1995], Japan [2000], Jordan [2001], Kyrgyzstan [2003], Latvia [1996], Latvia [1999], Lithuania [1997], Lithuania [1999], Luxembourg [1999], Macedonia, Republic of [1998], Macedonia, Republic of [2001], Malta [1999], Mexico [1996], Mexico [2000], Montenegro [1996], Montenegro [2001], Morocco [2001], Morocco [2001], Netherlands [1999], New Zealand [1998], Nigeria [1995], Nigeria [2000], Northern Ireland [1999], Norway [1996], Pakistan [1997], Pakistan [2001], Peru [1996], Peru [2001], Philippines [1996], Philippines [2001], Poland [1997], Poland [1999], Portugal [1999], Puerto Rico [1995], Puerto Rico [2001], Republic of Korea [1996], Republic of Korea [2001], Republic of Moldova [1996], Republic of Moldova [2002], Romania [1998], Romania [1999], Russian Federation [1995], Russian Federation [1999], Saudi Arabia [2003], Serbia [1996], Serbia [2001], Singapore [2002], Slovakia [1998], Slovakia [1999], Slovenia [1995], Slovenia [1999], South Africa [1996], South Africa [2001], Spain [1995], Spain [1999], Spain [2000], Sweden [1996], Sweden [1999], Switzerland [1996], Taiwan [1994], Tanzania, United Republic Of [2001], Turkey [1996], Turkey [2001], Turkey [2001], Uganda [2001], Ukraine [1996], Ukraine [1999], United States [1995], United States [1999], Uruguay [1996], Venezuela [1996], Venezuela [2000], Viet Nam [2001], Zimbabwe [2001]

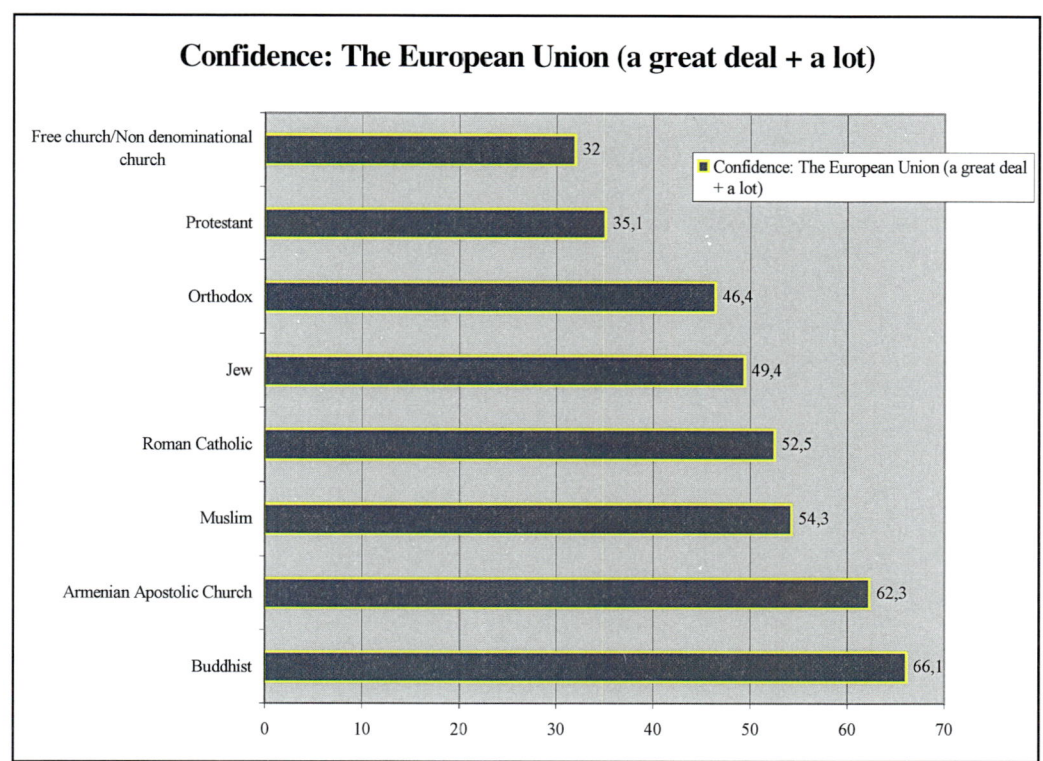

BASE=179850 global citizens; 57949 valid responses (100%).
Selected samples: Albania [1998], Albania [2002], Algeria [2002], Argentina [1995], Argentina [1999], Armenia [1997], Australia [1995], Austria [1999], Azerbaijan [1997], Bangladesh [1996], Bangladesh [2002], Belarus [1996], Belarus [2000], Belgium [1999], Bosnia and Herzegovina [1998], Bosnia and Herzegovina [2001], Brazil [1997], Bulgaria [1997], Bulgaria [1999], Canada

[2000], Chile [1996], Chile [2000], China [1995], China [2001], Colombia [1997], Colombia [1998], Croatia [1996], Croatia [1999], Czech Republic [1998], Czech Republic [1999], Denmark [1999], Dominican Republic [1996], Egypt [2000], El Salvador [1999], Estonia [1996], Estonia [1999], Finland [1996], Finland [2000], France [1999], Georgia [1996], Germany East [1997], Germany East [1999], Germany West [1997], Germany West [1999], Great Britain [1998], Great Britain [1999], Greece [1999], Hungary [1998], Hungary [1999], Iceland [1999], India [1995], India [2001], Indonesia [2001], Iran (Islamic Republic of) [2000], Iraq [2004], Ireland [1999], Israel [2001], Italy [1999], Japan [1995], Japan [2000], Jordan [2001], Kyrgyzstan [2003], Latvia [1996], Latvia [1999], Lithuania [1997], Lithuania [1999], Luxembourg [1999], Macedonia, Republic of [1998], Macedonia, Republic of [2001], Malta [1999], Mexico [1996], Mexico [2000], Montenegro [1996], Montenegro [2001], Morocco [2001], Morocco [2001], Netherlands [1999], New Zealand [1998], Nigeria [1995], Nigeria [2000], Northern Ireland [1999], Norway [1996], Pakistan [1997], Pakistan [2001], Peru [1996], Peru [2001], Philippines [1996], Philippines [2001], Poland [1997], Poland [1999], Portugal [1999], Puerto Rico [1995], Puerto Rico [2001], Republic of Korea [1996], Republic of Korea [2001], Republic of Moldova [1996], Republic of Moldova [2002], Romania [1998], Romania [1999], Russian Federation [1995], Russian Federation [1999], Saudi Arabia [2003], Serbia [1996], Serbia [2001], Singapore [2002], Slovakia [1998], Slovakia [1999], Slovenia [1995], Slovenia [1999], South Africa [1996], South Africa [2001], Spain [1995], Spain [1999], Spain [2000], Sweden [1996], Sweden [1999], Switzerland [1996], Taiwan [1994], Tanzania, United Republic Of [2001], Turkey [1996], Turkey [2001], Turkey [2001], Uganda [2001], Ukraine [1996], Ukraine [1999], United States [1995], United States [1999], Uruguay [1996], Venezuela [1996], Venezuela [2000], Viet Nam [2001], Zimbabwe [2001].

The graph rests on the combination of the values from:
Albania [1998]; Albania [2002]; Armenia [1997]; Austria [1999]; Azerbaijan [1997]; Belarus [1996]; Belarus [2000]; Belgium [1999]; Bosnia and Herzegovina [1998]; Bosnia and Herzegovina [2001]; Bulgaria [1997]; Bulgaria [1999]; China [2001]; Croatia [1996]; Croatia [1999]; Czech Republic [1998]; Czech Republic [1999]; Denmark [1999]; Estonia [1996]; Estonia [1999]; Finland [1996]; Finland [2000]; France [1999]; Georgia [1996]; Germany East [1997]; Germany East [1999]; Germany West [1997]; Germany West [1999]; Great Britain [1999]; Greece [1999]; Hungary [1998]; Hungary [1999]; Iceland [1999]; Ireland [1999]; Italy [1999]; Kyrgyzstan [2003]; Latvia [1996]; Latvia [1999]; Lithuania [1997]; Lithuania [1999]; Luxembourg [1999]; Macedonia, Republic of [1998]; Macedonia, Republic of [2001]; Malta [1999]; Montenegro [1996]; Montenegro [2001]; Netherlands [1999]; Northern Ireland [1999]; Norway [1996]; Poland [1997]; Poland [1999]; Portugal [1999]; Republic of Moldova [1996]; Republic of Moldova [2002]; Romania [1998]; Romania [1999]; Russian Federation [1995]; Russian Federation [1999]; Serbia [1996]; Serbia [2001]; Slovakia [1998]; Slovakia [1999]; Slovenia [1995]; Slovenia [1999]; Spain [1995]; Spain [1999]; Spain [2000]; Sweden [1996]; Sweden [1999]; Switzerland [1996]; Taiwan [1994]; Turkey [1996]; Turkey [2001]; Ukraine [1996]; Ukraine [1999];

On this item, there were no data collected for:
Algeria [2002]; Argentina [1995]; Argentina [1999]; Australia [1995]; Bangladesh [1996]; Bangladesh [2002]; Brazil [1997]; Canada [2000]; Chile [1996]; Chile [2000]; China [1995]; Colombia [1997]; Colombia [1998]; Dominican Republic [1996]; Egypt [2000]; El Salvador [1999]; Great Britain [1998]; India [1995]; India [2001]; Indonesia [2001]; Iran (Islamic Republic of) [2000]; Iraq [2004]; Israel [2001]; Japan [1995]; Japan [2000]; Jordan [2001]; Mexico [1996]; Mexico [2000]; Morocco [2001]; Morocco [2001]; New Zealand [1998]; Nigeria [1995]; Nigeria [2000]; Pakistan [1997]; Pakistan [2001]; Peru [1996]; Peru [2001];

Philippines [1996]; Philippines [2001]; Puerto Rico [1995]; Puerto Rico [2001]; Republic of Korea [1996]; Republic of Korea [2001]; Saudi Arabia [2003]; Singapore [2002]; South Africa [1996]; South Africa [2001]; Tanzania, United Republic Of [2001]; Turkey [2001]; Uganda [2001]; United States [1995]; United States [1999]; Uruguay [1996]; Venezuela [1996]; Venezuela [2000]; Viet Nam [2001]; Zimbabwe [2001].

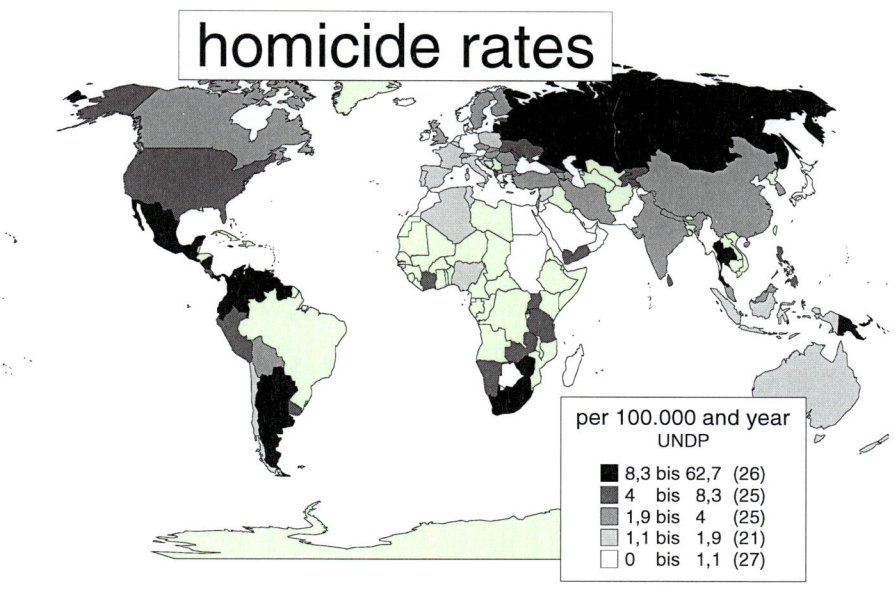

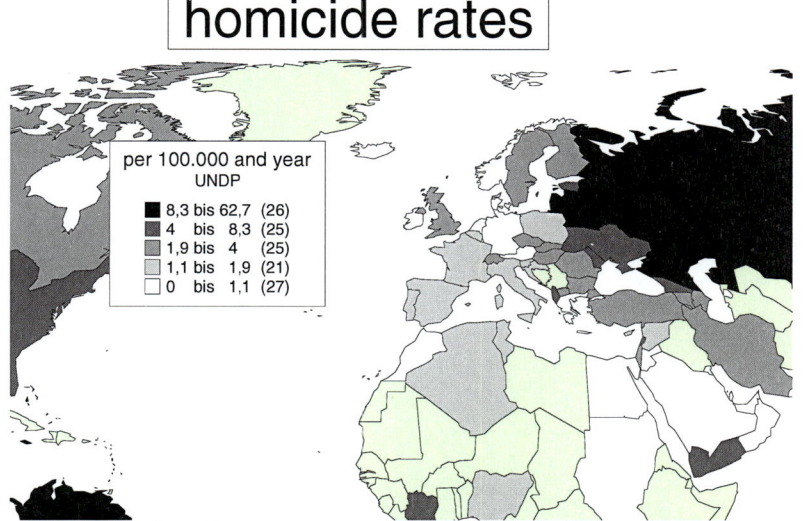

Source: Our own compilations from UNDP Statistics Office and Microsoft EXCEL 2000 Software. "Bis" is shorthand for: "ranging from ... to".

Maps: International comparison of homicide rates.

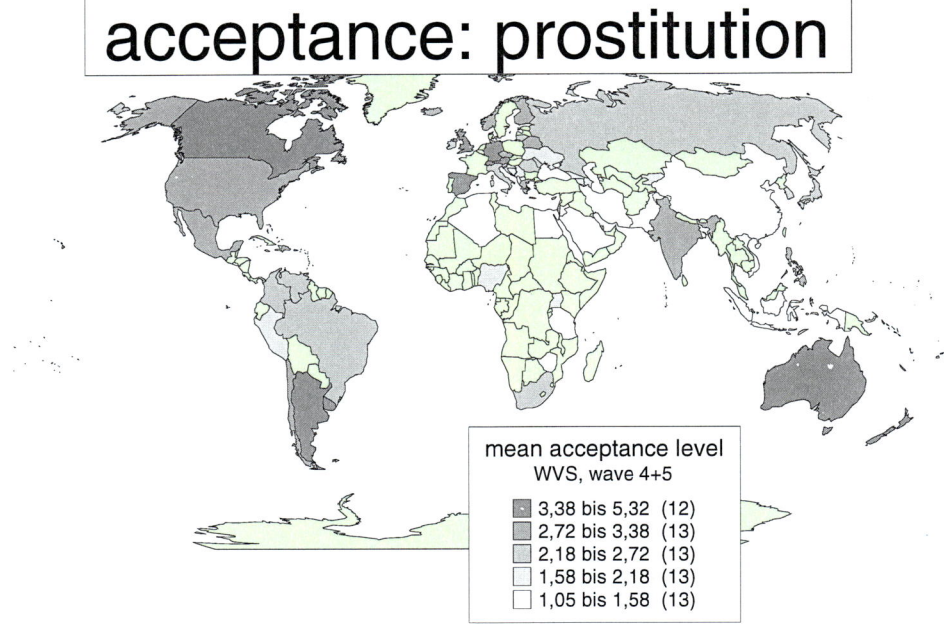

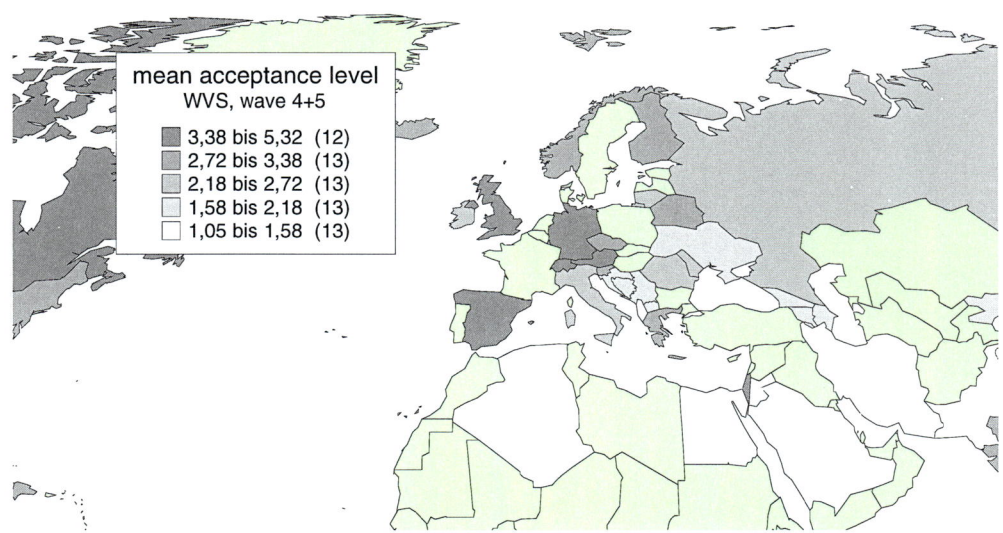

Maps. Acceptance of prostitution (continued).

Appendix VII

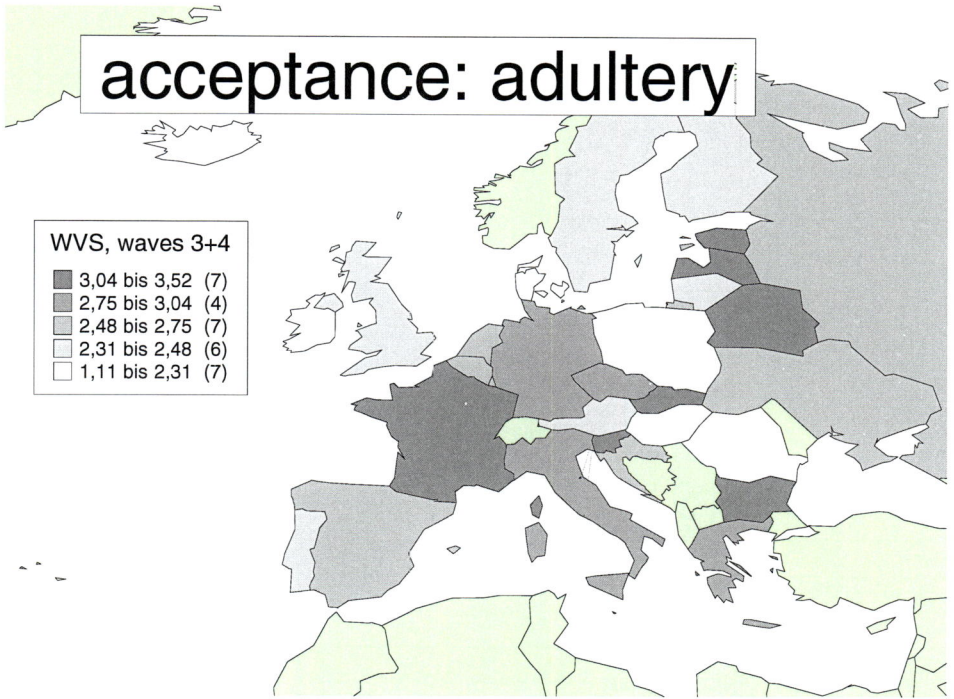

Map: Acceptance of adultery.

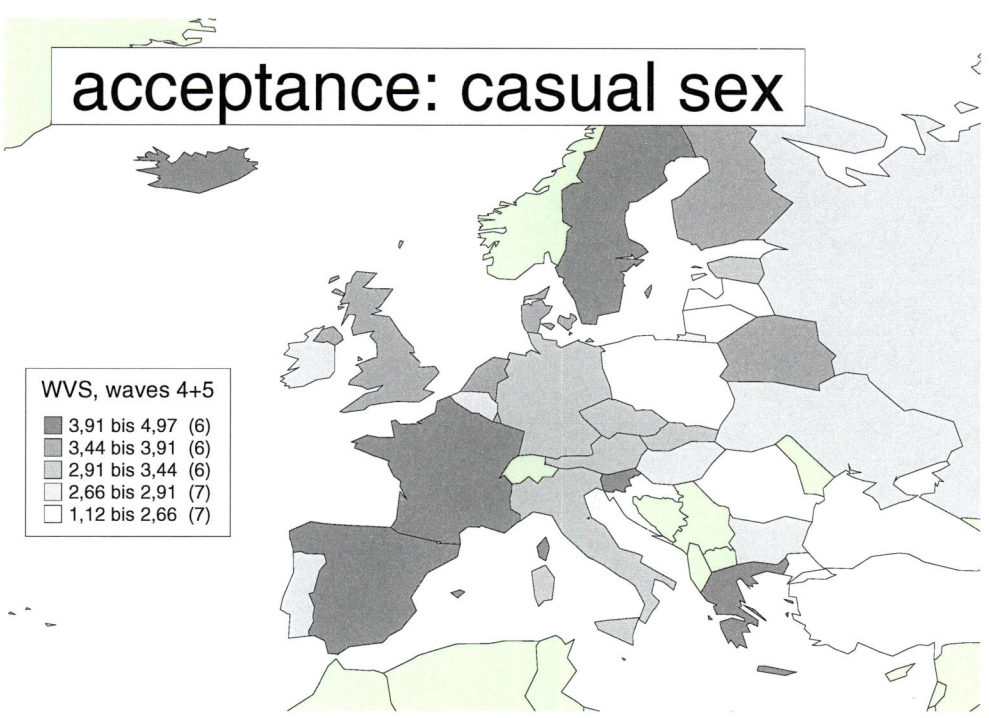

Map: Acceptance of casual sex.

Sexual permissiveness – the raw data

	Adultery justifiable (10-point scale, mean)	Casual sex justifiable (10-point scale, mean)	Marriage outdated institution (% of total adult resident population saying this)
Iceland [1999]	1,47	4,97	8,3
Sweden [1999]	2,38	4,8	20,4
Greece [1999]	2,95	4,62	15,7
Slovenia [1999]	3,47	4,08	27,4
Spain [1999]	2,48	3,92	17,5
France [1999]	3,52	3,91	36,3
Belarus [2000]	3,3	3,89	17
Netherlands [1999]	2,65	3,76	25
Finland [2000]	2,36	3,75	18
Denmark [1999]	2,1	3,69	15
Luxembourg [1999]	2,48	3,5	32,8
Great Britain [1999]	2,31	3,44	25,9
Slovakia [1999]	3,19	3,24	11,5
Germany West [1999]	2,83	3,19	18,6
Estonia [1999]	3,33	3,09	15,8
Italy [1999]	2,75	3,07	17
Austria [1999]	2,44	3,05	20,1
Czech Republic [1999]	2,81	2,91	11,4
Russian Federation [1999]	2,65	2,84	21,7
Bulgaria [1999]	3,37	2,77	17,9
Ukraine [1999]	2,49	2,77	18
Portugal [1999]	2,47	2,76	25,6
Hungary [1999]	2,1	2,74	17,1
Belgium [1999]	2,55	2,69	30,6
Ireland [1999]	1,82	2,66	22,3
Croatia [1999]	2,48	2,6	8,3
Lithuania [1999]	2,34	2,41	20,5
Latvia [1999]	3,04	2,36	16,4
Poland [1999]	1,94	2,35	9,3
Romania [1999]	1,98	2	12,5
Malta [1999]	1,11	1,13	6,7

Table: Sexual permissiveness – the index components

	Adultery justifiable	Casual sex justifiable	Marriage outdated institution	Sexual permissiveness index
France [1999]	1,000	0,724	1,000	0,908
Slovenia [1999]	0,979	0,768	0,699	0,816
Luxembourg [1999]	0,568	0,617	0,882	0,689
Greece [1999]	0,763	0,909	0,304	0,659
Belarus [2000]	0,909	0,719	0,348	0,658
Sweden [1999]	0,527	0,956	0,463	0,649
Netherlands [1999]	0,639	0,685	0,618	0,647
Belgium [1999]	0,598	0,406	0,807	0,604
Great Britain [1999]	0,498	0,602	0,649	0,583
Bulgaria [1999]	0,938	0,427	0,378	0,581
Estonia [1999]	0,921	0,510	0,307	0,580
Spain [1999]	0,568	0,727	0,365	0,553
Germany West [1999]	0,714	0,536	0,402	0,551
Portugal [1999]	0,564	0,424	0,639	0,542
Russian Federation [1999]	0,639	0,445	0,507	0,530
Finland [2000]	0,519	0,682	0,382	0,528
Slovakia [1999]	0,863	0,549	0,162	0,525
Italy [1999]	0,680	0,505	0,348	0,511
Austria [1999]	0,552	0,500	0,453	0,502
Latvia [1999]	0,801	0,320	0,328	0,483
Ukraine [1999]	0,573	0,427	0,382	0,460
Denmark [1999]	0,411	0,667	0,280	0,453
Czech Republic [1999]	0,705	0,464	0,159	0,443
Lithuania [1999]	0,510	0,333	0,466	0,437
Ireland [1999]	0,295	0,398	0,527	0,407
Iceland [1999]	0,149	1,000	0,054	0,401
Hungary [1999]	0,411	0,419	0,351	0,394
Croatia [1999]	0,568	0,383	0,054	0,335
Romania [1999]	0,361	0,227	0,196	0,261
Poland [1999]	0,344	0,318	0,088	0,250
Malta [1999]	0,000	0,000	0,000	0,000

The real destruction of family values in three (French speaking) European Union countries—France, Belgium, Luxembourg: marriage is an out-dated institution, total population.

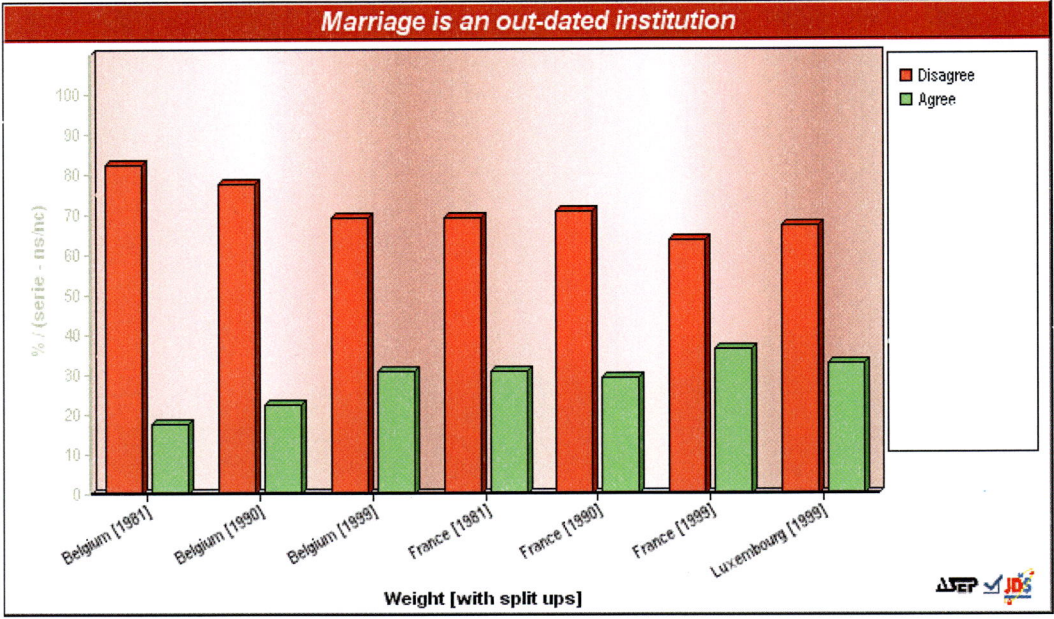

France, Belgium, Luxembourg: marriage is an out-dated institution, 15- to 29-year-old population

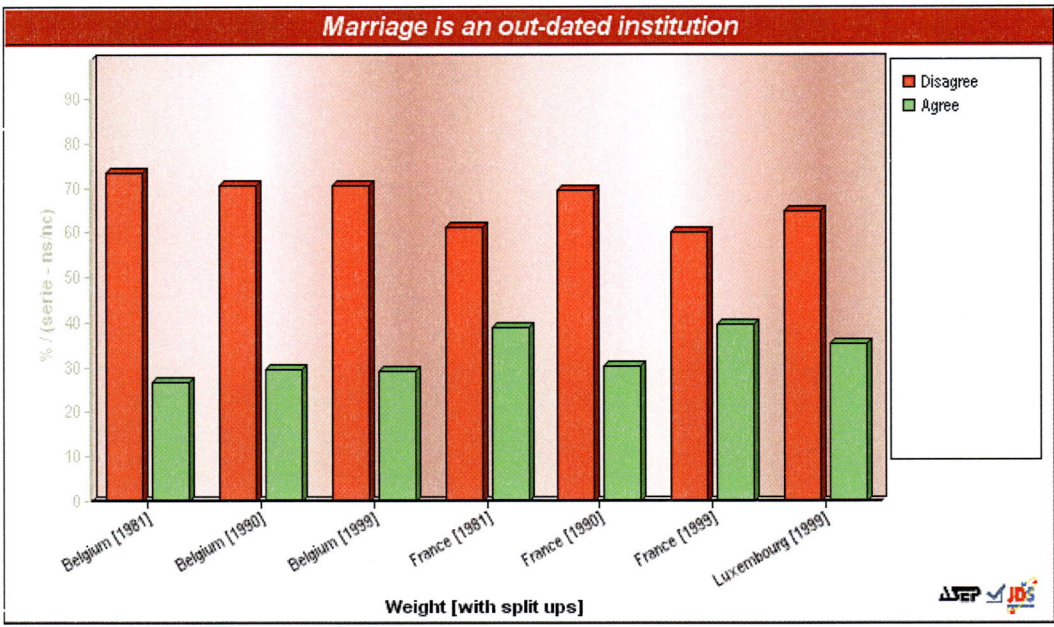

France, Belgium, Luxembourg: marriage is an out-dated institution, people never attending religious services, total population

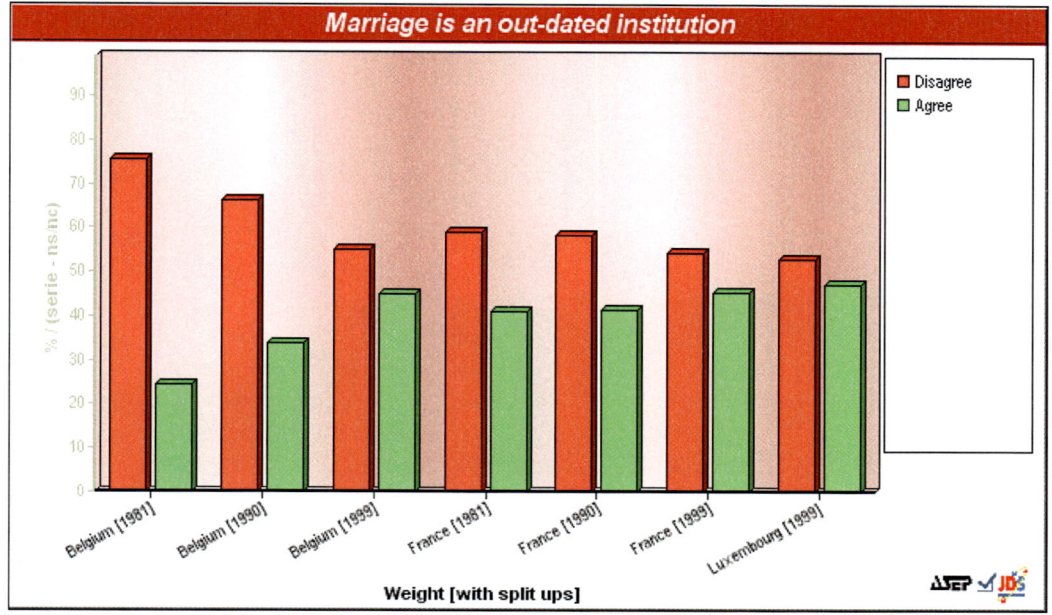

Cheating taxes around the globe and religious practice

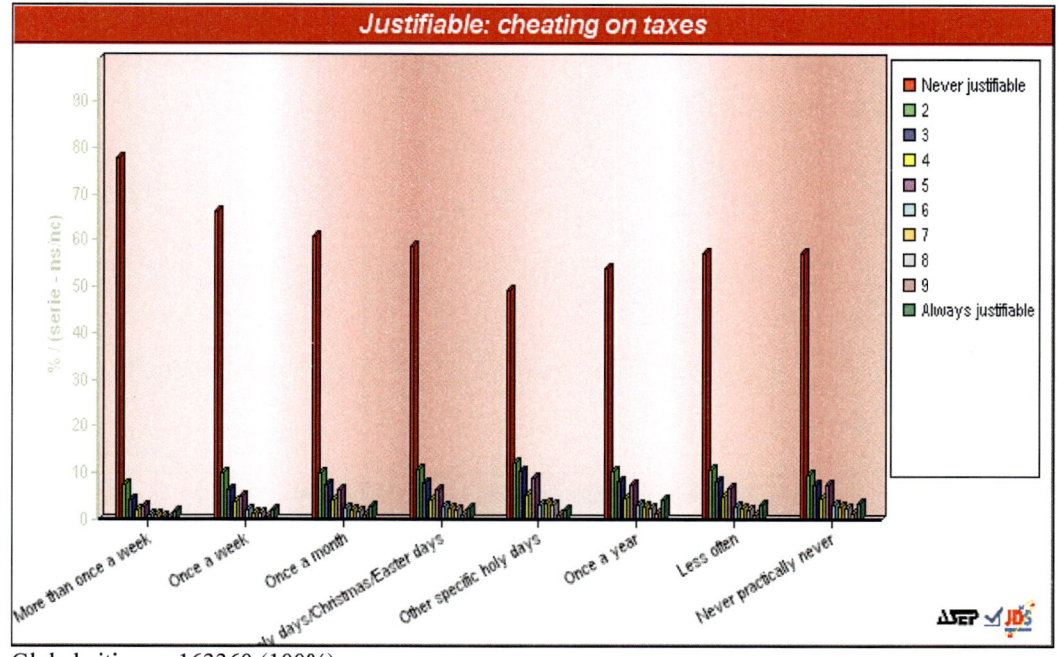

Global citizens: 163360 (100%).
Selected samples: Albania [1998], Albania [2002], Algeria [2002], Argentina [1995], Argentina [1999], Armenia [1997], Australia [1995], Austria [1999], Azerbaijan [1997], Bangladesh [1996], Bangladesh [2002], Belarus [1996], Belarus [2000], Belgium [1999], Bosnia and Herzegovina [1998], Bosnia and Herzegovina [2001], Brazil [1997], Bulgaria [1997], Bulgaria [1999], Canada

[2000], Chile [1996], Chile [2000], China [1995], China [2001], Colombia [1997], Colombia [1998], Croatia [1996], Croatia [1999], Czech Republic [1998], Czech Republic [1999], Denmark [1999], Dominican Republic [1996], Egypt [2000], El Salvador [1999], Estonia [1996], Estonia [1999], Finland [1996], Finland [2000], France [1999], Georgia [1996], Germany East [1997], Germany East [1999], Germany West [1997], Germany West [1999], Great Britain [1998], Great Britain [1999], Greece [1999], Hungary [1998], Hungary [1999], Iceland [1999], India [1995], India [2001], Indonesia [2001], Iran (Islamic Republic of) [2000], Iraq [2004], Ireland [1999], Israel [2001], Italy [1999], Japan [1995], Japan [2000], Jordan [2001], Kyrgyzstan [2003], Latvia [1996], Latvia [1999], Lithuania [1997], Lithuania [1999], Luxembourg [1999], Macedonia, Republic of [1998], Macedonia, Republic of [2001], Malta [1999], Mexico [1996], Mexico [2000], Montenegro [1996], Montenegro [2001], Morocco [2001], Morocco [2001], Netherlands [1999], New Zealand [1998], Nigeria [1995], Nigeria [2000], Northern Ireland [1999], Norway [1996], Pakistan [1997], Pakistan [2001], Peru [1996], Peru [2001], Philippines [1996], Philippines [2001], Poland [1997], Poland [1999], Portugal [1999], Puerto Rico [1995], Puerto Rico [2001], Republic of Korea [1996], Republic of Korea [2001], Republic of Moldova [1996], Republic of Moldova [2002], Romania [1998], Romania [1999], Russian Federation [1995], Russian Federation [1999], Saudi Arabia [2003], Serbia [1996], Serbia [2001], Singapore [2002], Slovakia [1998], Slovakia [1999], Slovenia [1995], Slovenia [1999], South Africa [1996], South Africa [2001], Spain [1995], Spain [1999], Spain [2000], Sweden [1996], Sweden [1999], Switzerland [1996], Taiwan [1994], Tanzania, United Republic Of [2001], Turkey [1996], Turkey [2001], Turkey [2001], Uganda [2001], Ukraine [1996], Ukraine [1999], United States [1995], United States [1999], Uruguay [1996], Venezuela [1996], Venezuela [2000], Viet Nam [2001], Zimbabwe [2001]

"CLEAN HANDS" INDEX

- Mean acceptance level: bribery
- Mean acceptance level: cheating on taxes
- Mean acceptance level: government benefits fraud

"Clean hands" index – the raw data

	Mean acceptance level: government benefits fraud		Mean acceptance level: cheating on taxes		Mean acceptance level: bribery
Turkey [2001]	1,24	Bangladesh [2002]	1,06	Bangladesh [2002]	1,03
Bangladesh [2002]	1,35	Turkey [2001]	1,18	Morocco [2001]	1,09
Malta [1999]	1,37	Pakistan [2001]	1,19	Malta [1999]	1,1
Denmark [1999]	1,38	Morocco [2001]	1,19	Turkey [2001]	1,12
Netherlands [1999]	1,52	Viet Nam [2001]	1,32	Jordan [2001]	1,13

	Mean acceptance level: government benefits fraud		Mean acceptance level: cheating on taxes		Mean acceptance level: bribery
Pakistan [2001]	1,53	Japan [2000]	1,46	Egypt [2000]	1,14
Croatia [1999]	1,58	Iran (Islamic Republic of) [2000]	1,47	Denmark [1999]	1,15
Tanzania, United Republic Of [2001]	1,62	Zimbabwe [2001]	1,52	Pakistan [2001]	1,15
Norway [1996]	1,64	Malta [1999]	1,54	Viet Nam [2001]	1,15
Bosnia and Herzegovina [2001]	1,67	Indonesia [2001]	1,54	Zimbabwe [2001]	1,21
Zimbabwe [2001]	1,67	Jordan [2001]	1,56	Argentina [1999]	1,26
Morocco [2001]	1,68	China [2001]	1,57	Iran (Islamic Republic of) [2000]	1,26
Hungary [1999]	1,7	Egypt [2000]	1,58	Iceland [1999]	1,27
Jordan [2001]	1,7	Tanzania, United Republic Of [2001]	1,73	Uruguay [1996]	1,27
Australia [1995]	1,73	Uruguay [1996]	1,73	Australia [1995]	1,28
Iceland [1999]	1,75	Bosnia and Herzegovina [2001]	1,76	Tanzania, United Republic Of [2001]	1,29
Uruguay [1996]	1,75	Venezuela [2000]	1,82	Serbia [2001]	1,29
Romania [1999]	1,82	Argentina [1999]	1,87	Norway [1996]	1,32
Egypt [2000]	1,82	Albania [2002]	1,88	China [2001]	1,34

"Clean hands" index – the raw data (Continued)

	Mean acceptance level: government benefits fraud		Mean acceptance level: cheating on taxes		Mean acceptance level: bribery
Germany West [1999]	1,84	Singapore [2002]	1,89	Bosnia and Herzegovina [2001]	1,37
Bulgaria [1999]	1,86	El Salvador [1999]	1,91	Finland [2000]	1,43
Czech Republic [1999]	1,87	Dominican Republic [1996]	1,95	Indonesia [2001]	1,45
Canada [2000]	1,87	Denmark [1999]	2	New Zealand [1998]	1,46
New Zealand [1998]	1,87	Bulgaria [1999]	2,01	Ireland [1999]	1,46
Italy [1999]	1,88	Algeria [2002]	2,01	Algeria [2002]	1,46
Ireland [1999]	1,89	Nigeria [2000]	2,03	El Salvador [1999]	1,47
Albania [2002]	1,92	Czech Republic [1999]	2,07	Macedonia, Republic of [2001]	1,47
Nigeria [2000]	1,97	Canada [2000]	2,08	Italy [1999]	1,5
Uganda [2001]	1,98	Serbia [2001]	2,09	Romania [1999]	1,52
Great Britain [1999]	1,99	Peru [2001]	2,11	Japan [2000]	1,53
Portugal [1999]	2,03	Hungary [1999]	2,12	Colombia [1998]	1,53
Switzerland [1996]	2,07	India [2001]	2,14	Poland [1999]	1,53
Sweden [1999]	2,08	Slovakia [1999]	2,15	Switzerland [1996]	1,54
Japan [2000]	2,09	Chile [2000]	2,15	United States [1999]	1,57
Latvia [1999]	2,12	Spain [2000]	2,16	Canada [2000]	1,6

	Mean acceptance level: government benefits fraud		Mean acceptance level: cheating on taxes		Mean acceptance level: bribery
Serbia [2001]	2,12	Austria [1999]	2,19	Austria [1999]	1,6
Colombia [1998]	2,13	Iceland [1999]	2,23	Singapore [2002]	1,6
China [2001]	2,13	Poland [1999]	2,23	Venezuela [2000]	1,62
Viet Nam [2001]	2,13	United States [1999]	2,28	Spain [2000]	1,63
Austria [1999]	2,17	Macedonia, Republic of [2001]	2,28	Croatia [1999]	1,64
United States [1999]	2,18	Colombia [1998]	2,29	Latvia [1999]	1,68
Dominican Republic [1996]	2,19	New Zealand [1998]	2,31	Bulgaria [1999]	1,69
Russian Federation [1999]	2,3	Mexico [2000]	2,31	Peru [2001]	1,72
Finland [2000]	2,3	Ireland [1999]	2,34	Germany West [1999]	1,73
India [2001]	2,34	Slovenia [1999]	2,34	Georgia [1996]	1,75
Poland [1999]	2,36	Germany West [1999]	2,35	Great Britain [1999]	1,77
Belgium [1999]	2,39	Latvia [1999]	2,36	Portugal [1999]	1,77
Azerbaijan [1997]	2,42	Italy [1999]	2,39	Slovenia [1999]	1,78
Lithuania [1999]	2,55	Sweden [1999]	2,41	Luxembourg [1999]	1,79
Argentina [1999]	2,59	Great Britain [1999]	2,42	Sweden [1999]	1,83
Singapore [2002]	2,66	Portugal [1999]	2,45	Russian Federation [1999]	1,84

"Clean hands" index – the raw data

	Mean acceptance level: government benefits fraud		Mean acceptance level: cheating on taxes		Mean acceptance level: bribery
El Salvador [1999]	2,69	Finland [2000]	2,46	India [2001]	1,88
Iran (Islamic Republic of) [2000]	2,7	Croatia [1999]	2,53	Dominican Republic [1996]	1,89
Kyrgyzstan [2003]	2,77	Switzerland [1996]	2,6	Nigeria [2000]	1,91
Slovenia [1999]	2,82	South Africa [2001]	2,7	Estonia [1999]	1,91
Ukraine [1999]	2,83	Norway [1996]	2,71	Kyrgyzstan [2003]	1,92
Luxembourg [1999]	2,86	Kyrgyzstan [2003]	2,73	Greece [1999]	1,93
South Africa [2001]	2,89	Georgia [1996]	2,74	Belgium [1999]	2
Slovakia [1999]	2,91	Netherlands [1999]	2,75	Ukraine [1999]	2,05
Georgia [1996]	2,91	Romania [1999]	2,79	Chile [2000]	2,05
Venezuela [2000]	2,98	France [1999]	3,06	Lithuania [1999]	2,08
Macedonia, Republic of [2001]	3	Russian Federation [1999]	3,09	France [1999]	2,08
Algeria [2002]	3,02	Philippines [2001]	3,14	Armenia [1997]	2,13
Estonia [1999]	3,19	Estonia [1999]	3,15	Uganda [2001]	2,14
Brazil [1997]	3,2	Greece [1999]	3,16	Mexico [2000]	2,17
Armenia [1997]	3,24	Luxembourg [1999]	3,38	Czech Republic [1999]	2,27
Chile [2000]	3,33	Uganda [2001]	3,42	Albania [2002]	2,38
France [1999]	3,39	Ukraine [1999]	3,45	South Africa [2001]	2,52

Appendix VII

	Mean acceptance level: government benefits fraud		Mean acceptance level: cheating on taxes		Mean acceptance level: bribery
Belarus [2000]	3,48	Brazil [1997]	3,59	Hungary [1999]	2,67
Peru [2001]	3,49	Azerbaijan [1997]	3,62	Azerbaijan [1997]	2,86
Philippines [2001]	3,57	Belgium [1999]	3,66	Republic of Moldova [2002]	2,93
Mexico [2000]	3,75	Armenia [1997]	3,68	Slovakia [1999]	2,94
Republic of Moldova [2002]	3,85	Lithuania [1999]	3,77	Belarus [2000]	3,09
Indonesia [2001]	3,88	Republic of Moldova [2002]	4,19	Philippines [2001]	3,21
Greece [1999]	4,04	Belarus [2000]	4,22	Brazil [1997]	4,02

"Clean Hands" index – the component indices

	Component index: Mean acceptance level: government benefits fraud		Component index: Mean acceptance level: cheating on taxes		Component index: Mean acceptance level: bribery	UNDP-type-Index *"manu politi"* society
Bangladesh [2002]	0,961	Bangladesh [2002]	1,000	Bangladesh [2002]	1,000	0,987
Turkey [2001]	1,000	Turkey [2001]	0,962	Turkey [2001]	0,970	0,977
Pakistan [2001]	0,896	Pakistan [2001]	0,959	Pakistan [2001]	0,960	0,938
Morocco [2001]	0,843	Morocco [2001]	0,959	Morocco [2001]	0,980	0,927
Malta [1999]	0,954	Malta [1999]	0,848	Malta [1999]	0,977	0,926

"Clean hands" index – the component indices (Continued)

	Component index: Mean acceptance level: government benefits fraud		Component index: Mean acceptance level: cheating on taxes		Component index: Mean acceptance level: bribery	UNDP-type-Index *"manu politi"* society
Jordan [2001]	0,836	Jordan [2001]	0,842	Jordan [2001]	0,967	0,881
Zimbabwe [2001]	0,846	Zimbabwe [2001]	0,854	Zimbabwe [2001]	0,940	0,880
Denmark [1999]	0,950	Denmark [1999]	0,703	Denmark [1999]	0,960	0,871
Egypt [2000]	0,793	Egypt [2000]	0,835	Egypt [2000]	0,963	0,864
Tanzania, United Republic Of [2001]	0,864	Tanzania, United Republic Of [2001]	0,788	Tanzania, United Republic Of [2001]	0,913	0,855
Viet Nam [2001]	0,682	Viet Nam [2001]	0,918	Viet Nam [2001]	0,960	0,853
Uruguay [1996]	0,818	Uruguay [1996]	0,788	Uruguay [1996]	0,920	0,842
Bosnia and Herzegovina [2001]	0,846	Bosnia and Herzegovina [2001]	0,778	Bosnia and Herzegovina [2001]	0,886	0,837
China [2001]	0,682	China [2001]	0,839	China [2001]	0,896	0,806
Japan [2000]	0,696	Japan [2000]	0,873	Japan [2000]	0,833	0,801
Australia [1995]	0,825	Australia [1995]	0,652	Australia [1995]	0,916	0,798
Iceland [1999]	0,818	Iceland [1999]	0,630	Iceland [1999]	0,920	0,789
Serbia [2001]	0,686	Serbia [2001]	0,674	Serbia [2001]	0,913	0,758
Iran (Islamic Republic of) [2000]	0,479	Iran (Islamic Republic of) [2000]	0,870	Iran (Islamic Republic of) [2000]	0,923	0,757
Canada [2000]	0,775	Canada [2000]	0,677	Canada [2000]	0,809	0,754
Bulgaria [1999]	0,779	Bulgaria [1999]	0,699	Bulgaria [1999]	0,779	0,752

Appendix VII

	Component index: Mean acceptance level: government benefits fraud		Component index: Mean acceptance level: cheating on taxes		Component index: Mean acceptance level: bribery	UNDP-type-Index *"manu politi"* society
Norway [1996]	0,857	Norway [1996]	0,478	Norway [1996]	0,903	0,746
New Zealand [1998]	0,775	New Zealand [1998]	0,604	New Zealand [1998]	0,856	0,745
Ireland [1999]	0,768	Ireland [1999]	0,595	Ireland [1999]	0,856	0,740
Croatia [1999]	0,879	Croatia [1999]	0,535	Croatia [1999]	0,796	0,736
Italy [1999]	0,771	Italy [1999]	0,579	Italy [1999]	0,843	0,731
Argentina [1999]	0,518	Argentina [1999]	0,744	Argentina [1999]	0,923	0,728
Netherlands [1999]	0,900	Netherlands [1999]	0,465	Netherlands [1999]	0,809	0,725
Germany West [1999]	0,786	Germany West [1999]	0,592	Germany West [1999]	0,766	0,714
Spain [2000]	0,689	Spain [2000]	0,652	Spain [2000]	0,799	0,714
Nigeria [2000]	0,739	Nigeria [2000]	0,693	Nigeria [2000]	0,706	0,713
Colombia [1998]	0,682	Colombia [1998]	0,611	Colombia [1998]	0,833	0,709
Austria [1999]	0,668	Austria [1999]	0,642	Austria [1999]	0,809	0,707
United States [1999]	0,664	United States [1999]	0,614	United States [1999]	0,819	0,699
Dominican Republic [1996]	0,661	Dominican Republic [1996]	0,718	Dominican Republic [1996]	0,712	0,697
Romania [1999]	0,793	Romania [1999]	0,453	Romania [1999]	0,836	0,694
El Salvador [1999]	0,482	El Salvador [1999]	0,731	El Salvador [1999]	0,853	0,689
Poland [1999]	0,600	Poland [1999]	0,630	Poland [1999]	0,833	0,688
Latvia [1999]	0,686	Latvia [1999]	0,589	Latvia [1999]	0,783	0,686

"Clean hands" index – the component indices (Continued)

	Component index: Mean acceptance level: government benefits fraud		Component index: Mean acceptance level: cheating on taxes		Component index: Mean acceptance level: bribery	UNDP-type-Index *"manu politi"* society
Great Britain [1999]	0,732	Great Britain [1999]	0,570	Great Britain [1999]	0,753	0,685
Albania [2002]	0,757	Albania [2002]	0,741	Albania [2002]	0,548	0,682
Switzerland [1996]	0,704	Switzerland [1996]	0,513	Switzerland [1996]	0,829	0,682
Finland [2000]	0,621	Finland [2000]	0,557	Finland [2000]	0,866	0,682
Czech Republic [1999]	0,775	Czech Republic [1999]	0,680	Czech Republic [1999]	0,585	0,680
Singapore [2002]	0,493	Singapore [2002]	0,737	Singapore [2002]	0,809	0,680
Portugal [1999]	0,718	Portugal [1999]	0,560	Portugal [1999]	0,753	0,677
Sweden [1999]	0,700	Sweden [1999]	0,573	Sweden [1999]	0,732	0,668
India [2001]	0,607	India [2001]	0,658	India [2001]	0,716	0,660
Hungary [1999]	0,836	Hungary [1999]	0,665	Hungary [1999]	0,452	0,651
Venezuela [2000]	0,379	Venezuela [2000]	0,759	Venezuela [2000]	0,803	0,647
Algeria [2002]	0,364	Algeria [2002]	0,699	Algeria [2002]	0,856	0,640
Macedonia, Republic of [2001]	0,371	Macedonia, Republic of [2001]	0,614	Macedonia, Republic of [2001]	0,853	0,613
Slovenia [1999]	0,436	Slovenia [1999]	0,595	Slovenia [1999]	0,749	0,593
Indonesia [2001]	0,057	Indonesia [2001]	0,848	Indonesia [2001]	0,860	0,588
Russian Federation [1999]	0,621	Russian Federation [1999]	0,358	Russian Federation [1999]	0,729	0,569
Peru [2001]	0,196	Peru [2001]	0,668	Peru [2001]	0,769	0,544

	Component index: Mean acceptance level: government benefits fraud		Component index: Mean acceptance level: cheating on taxes		Component index: Mean acceptance level: bribery	UNDP-type-Index *"manu politi"* society
Georgia [1996]	0,404	Georgia [1996]	0,468	Georgia [1996]	0,759	0,544
Kyrgyzstan [2003]	0,454	Kyrgyzstan [2003]	0,472	Kyrgyzstan [2003]	0,702	0,542
Uganda [2001]	0,736	Uganda [2001]	0,253	Uganda [2001]	0,629	0,539
Chile [2000]	0,254	Chile [2000]	0,655	Chile [2000]	0,659	0,522
Belgium [1999]	0,589	Belgium [1999]	0,177	Belgium [1999]	0,676	0,481
Luxembourg [1999]	0,421	Luxembourg [1999]	0,266	Luxembourg [1999]	0,746	0,478
Slovakia [1999]	0,404	Slovakia [1999]	0,655	Slovakia [1999]	0,361	0,473
South Africa [2001]	0,411	South Africa [2001]	0,481	South Africa [2001]	0,502	0,464
Estonia [1999]	0,304	Estonia [1999]	0,339	Estonia [1999]	0,706	0,449
Ukraine [1999]	0,432	Ukraine [1999]	0,244	Ukraine [1999]	0,659	0,445
Mexico [2000]	0,104	Mexico [2000]	0,604	Mexico [2000]	0,619	0,442
Lithuania [1999]	0,532	Lithuania [1999]	0,142	Lithuania [1999]	0,649	0,441
France [1999]	0,232	France [1999]	0,367	France [1999]	0,649	0,416
Azerbaijan [1997]	0,579	Azerbaijan [1997]	0,190	Azerbaijan [1997]	0,388	0,385
Armenia [1997]	0,286	Armenia [1997]	0,171	Armenia [1997]	0,632	0,363
Greece [1999]	0,000	Greece [1999]	0,335	Greece [1999]	0,699	0,345
Philippines [2001]	0,168	Philippines [2001]	0,342	Philippines [2001]	0,271	0,260
Belarus [2000]	0,200	Belarus [2000]	0,000	Belarus [2000]	0,311	0,170
Brazil [1997]	0,300	Brazil [1997]	0,199	Brazil [1997]	0,000	0,166

"Clean hands" index – the component indices (Continued)

	Component index: Mean acceptance level: government benefits fraud		Component index: Mean acceptance level: cheating on taxes		Component index: Mean acceptance level: bribery	UNDP-type-Index *"manu politi"* society
Republic of Moldova [2002]	0,068	Republic of Moldova [2002]	0,009	Republic of Moldova [2002]	0,365	0,147

THE DECAY OF ASABIYYA IN THE EU COUNTRIES : % PREPARED TO FIGHT FOR THE COUNTRY

	Prepared to fight for the country
Japan [2000]	25,1
Iraq [2004]	37,2
Spain [2000]	43
Germany West [1999]	47,7
Zimbabwe [2001]	53,6
Luxembourg [1999]	53,8
Austria [1999]	55
Uruguay [1996]	57
France [1999]	57,8
Chile [2000]	60,1
Italy [1999]	60,1
New Zealand [1998]	65
Argentina [1999]	65,3
Uganda [2001]	65,4
Canada [2000]	66,6
South Africa [2001]	68,2
El Salvador [1999]	69
Switzerland [1996]	69,3
Albania [2002]	71,7
Brazil [1997]	71,8
Lithuania [1999]	72,1
Serbia [2001]	72,1
Georgia [1996]	72,5
United States [1999]	72,7

	Prepared to fight for the country
Ukraine [1999]	73,6
Bosnia and Herzegovina [2001]	74,3
Mexico [2000]	74,3
Republic of Korea [2001]	74,6
Australia [1995]	74,8
Russian Federation [1999]	77
Dominican Republic [1996]	78,8
Macedonia, Republic of [2001]	79,7
Armenia [1997]	80,4
Israel [2001]	80,4
Peru [2001]	81,3
India [2001]	82,2
Venezuela [2000]	82,2
Romania [1999]	84,3
Belarus [2000]	84,4
Croatia [1999]	84,5
Slovenia [1999]	84,8
Republic of Moldova [2002]	84,9
Singapore [2002]	85,2
Kyrgyzstan [2003]	87
Philippines [2001]	87
Finland [2000]	87,5
Norway [1996]	88,6
Tanzania, United Republic Of [2001]	93,1
Morocco [2001]	95
Bangladesh [2002]	95,8
China [2001]	96,7
Azerbaijan [1997]	97,1
Viet Nam [2001]	97,8

Appendix VIII

MUSLIMS ARE NO SECURITY RISK IN A MULTICULTURAL EUROPE: A WORLD VALUES SURVEY COMPARISON OF EUROPEAN UNION, EEA AND EFTA COUNTRY OPINIONS ON MAJOR ISSUES AND SOCIAL REALITIES BY THE MAJOR RELIGIOUS GROUPS IN EUROPE

EDUCATIONAL ATTAINMENT

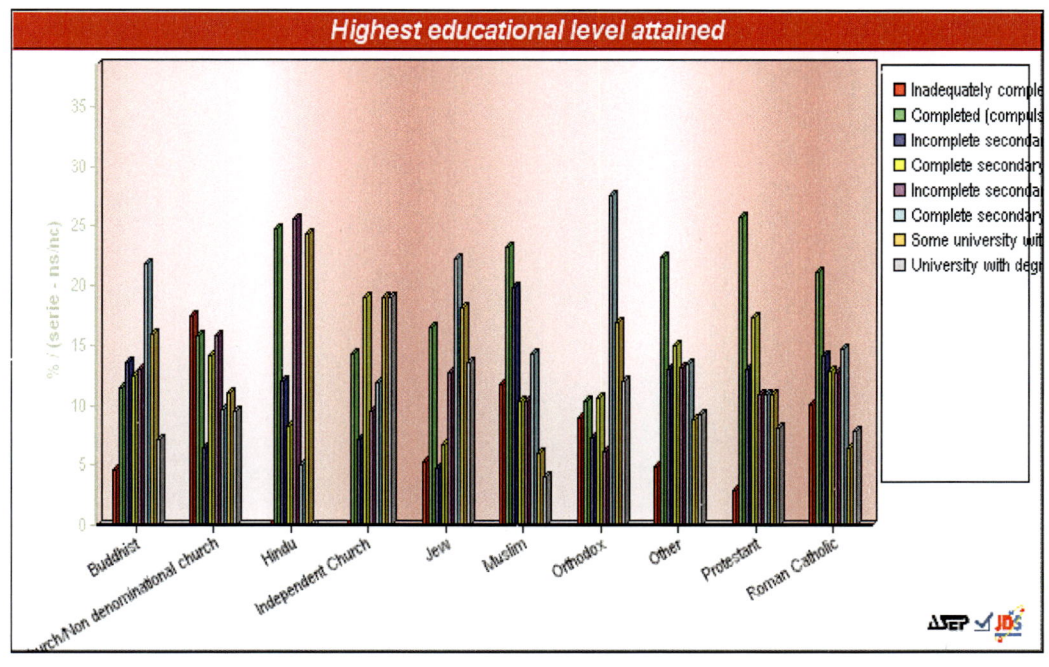

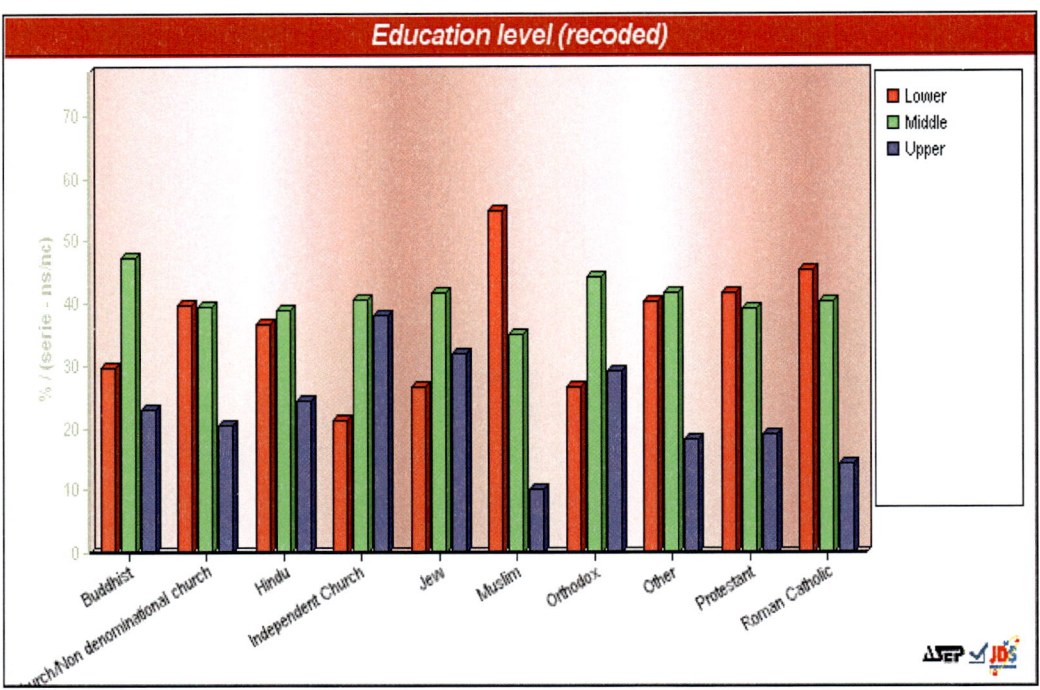

SOCIO-ECONOMIC STATUS

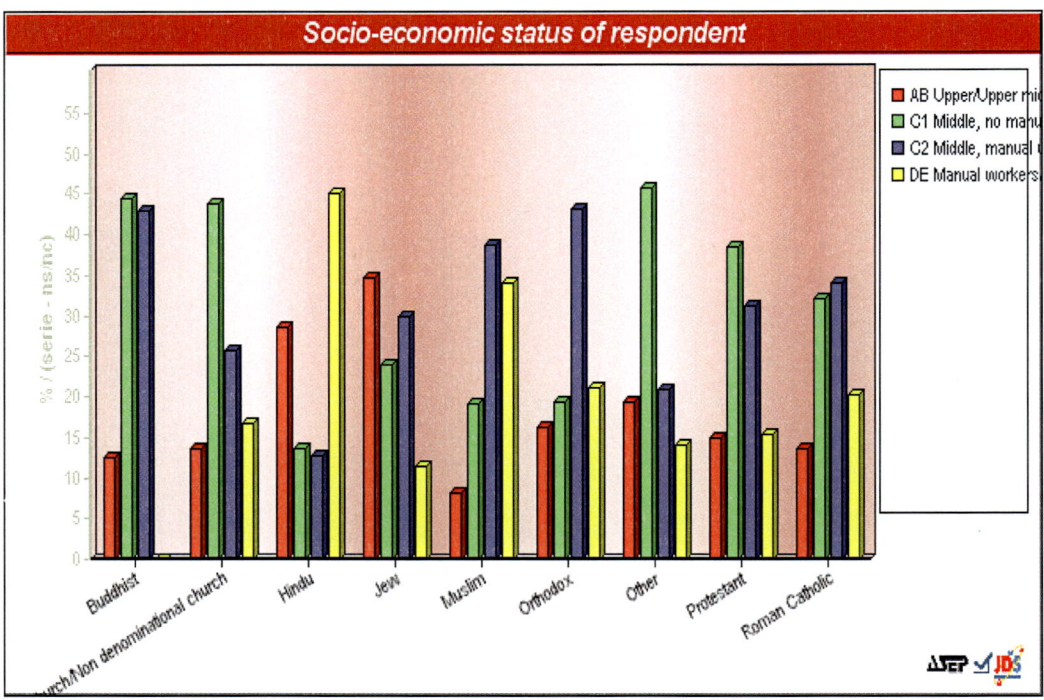

Appendix VIII 511

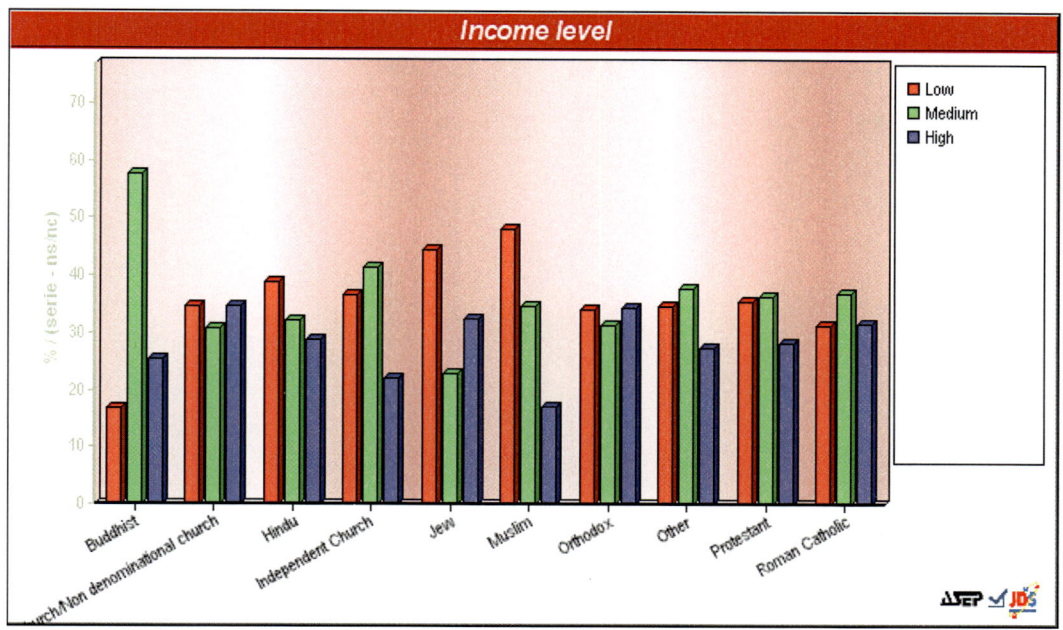

POLITICAL POSITIONS

Democracy

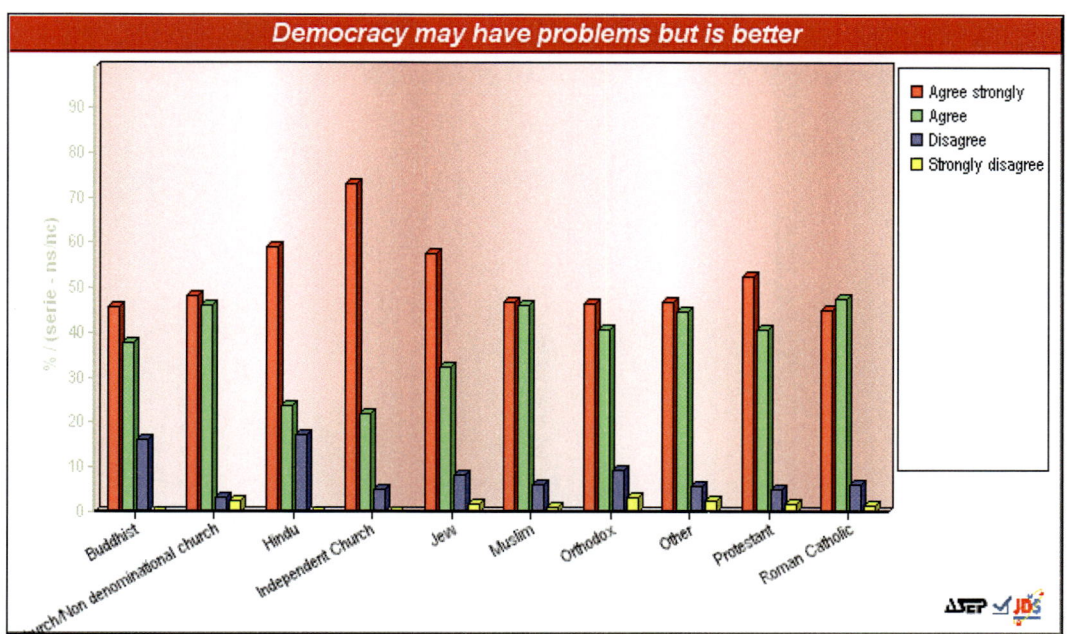

Left-Right Scale

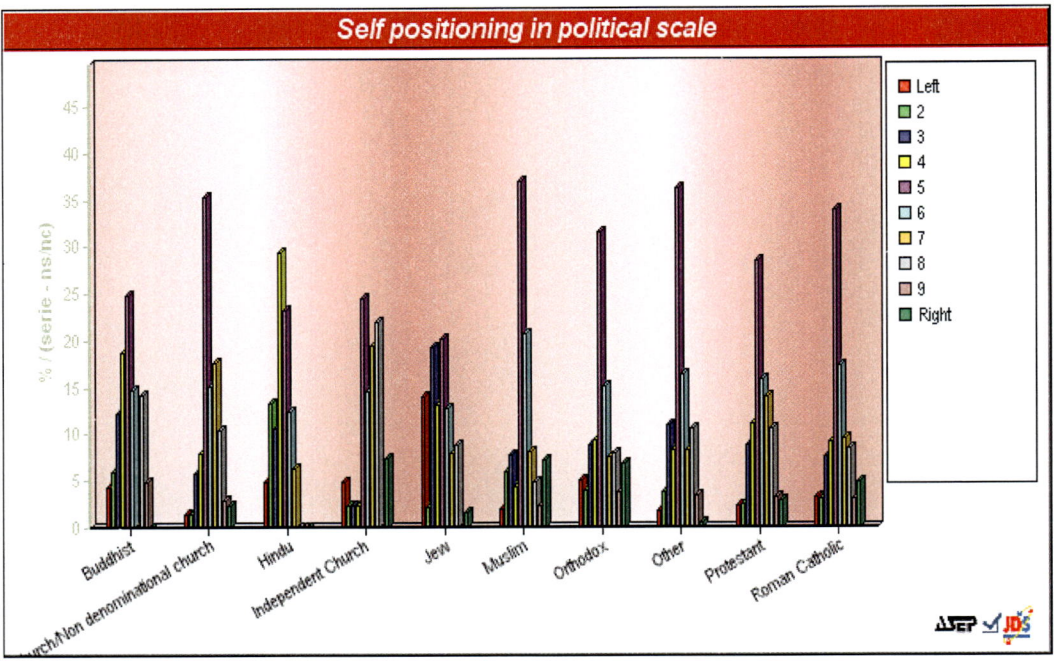

Proud of Nationality

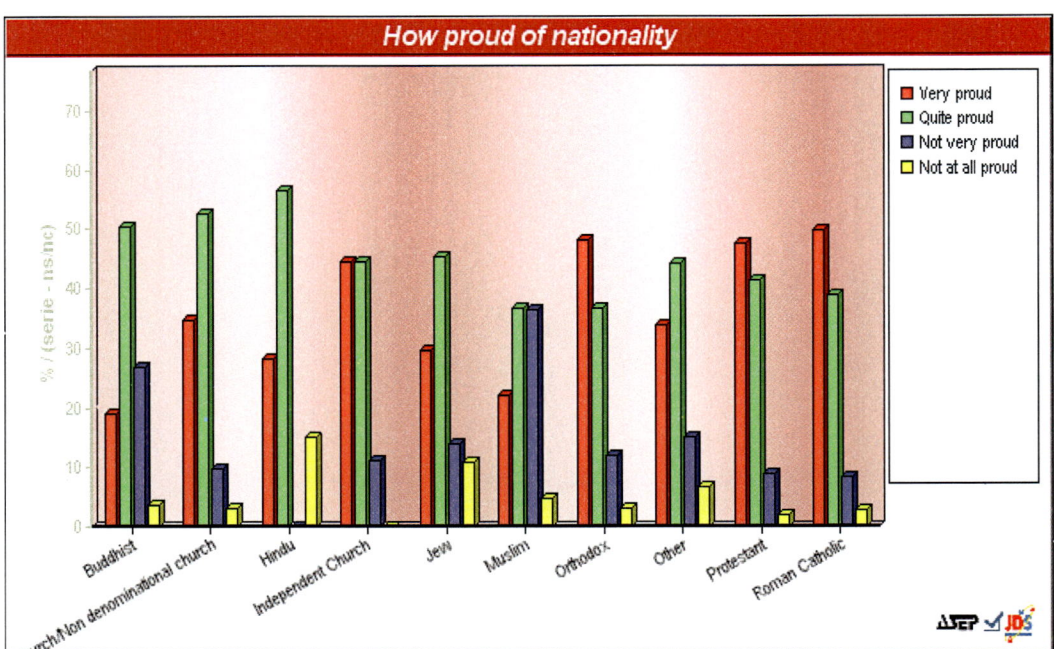

Politicians Who Don't Believe in God Are Unfit for Public Office

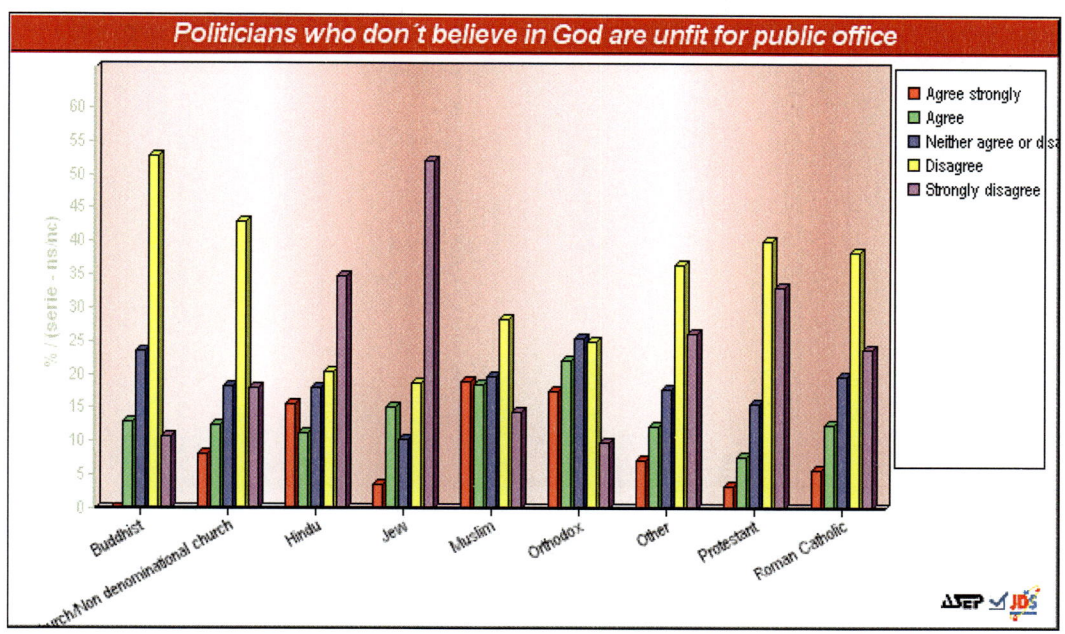

PREJUDICE

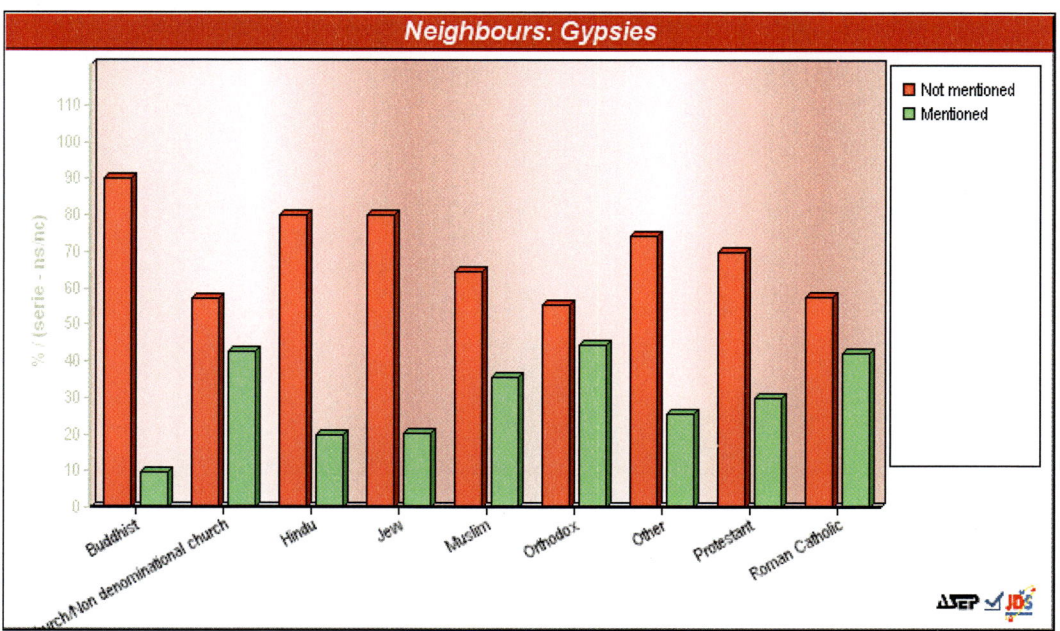

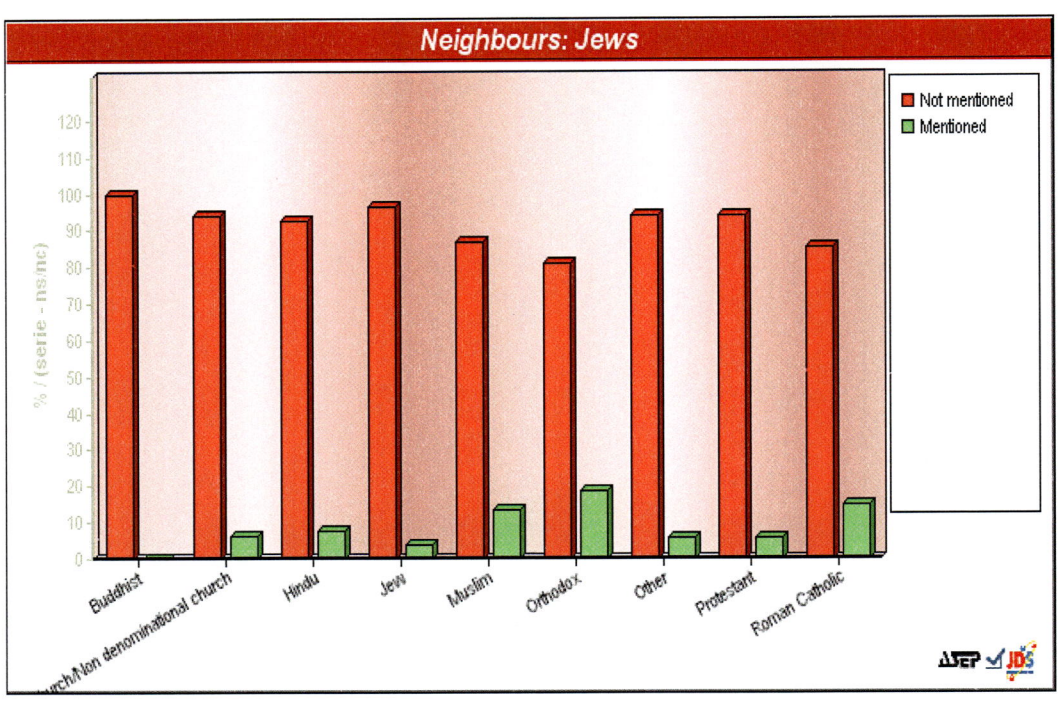

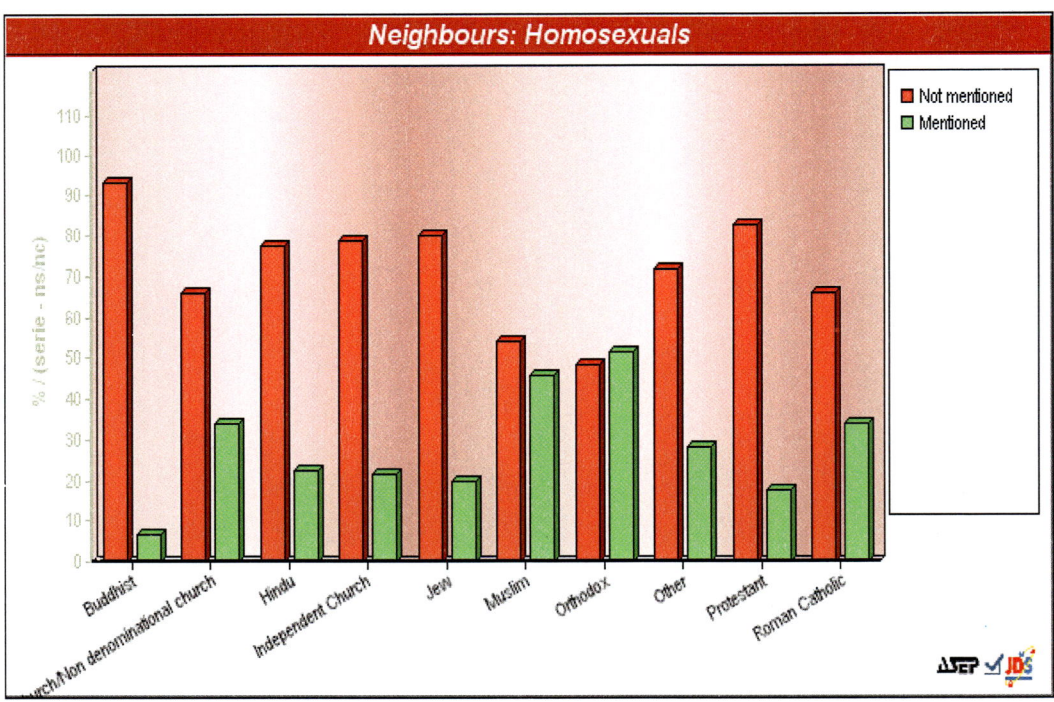

Appendix VIII

CONFIDENCE IN MAJOR SOCIAL INSTITUTIONS

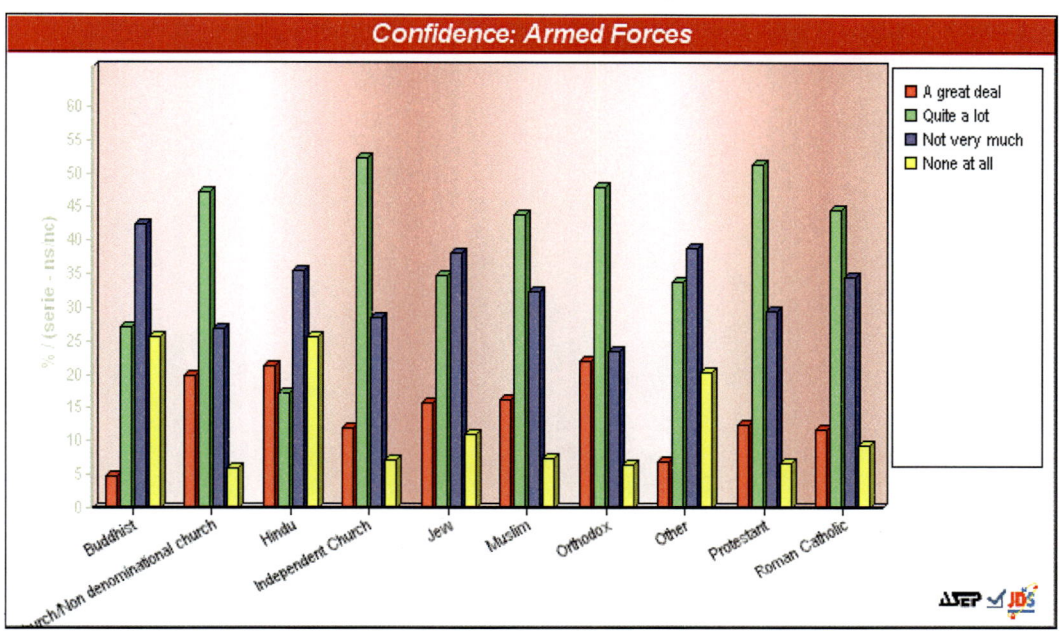

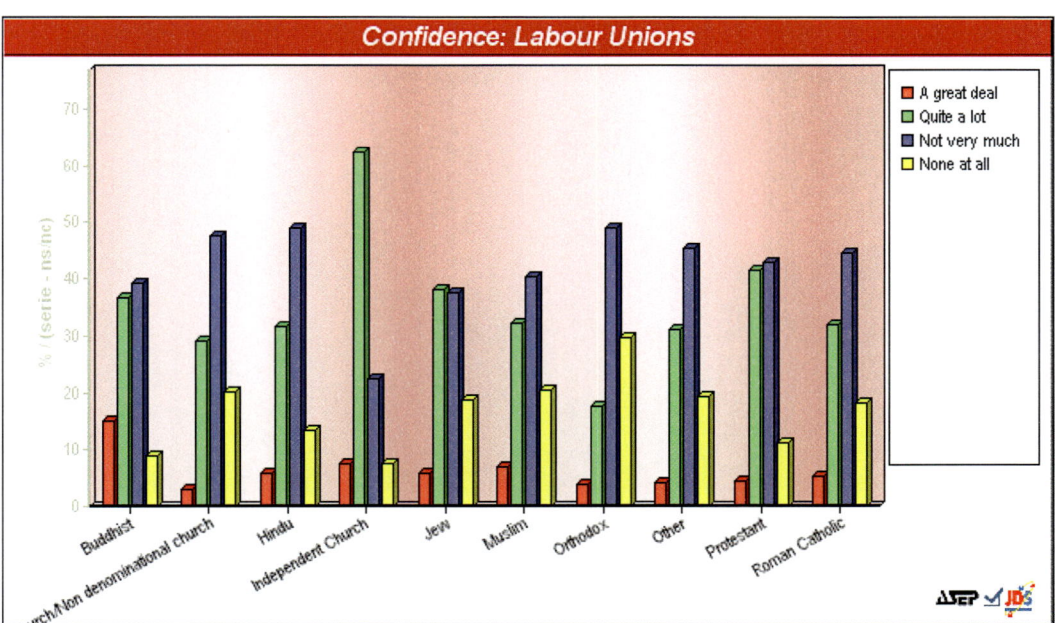

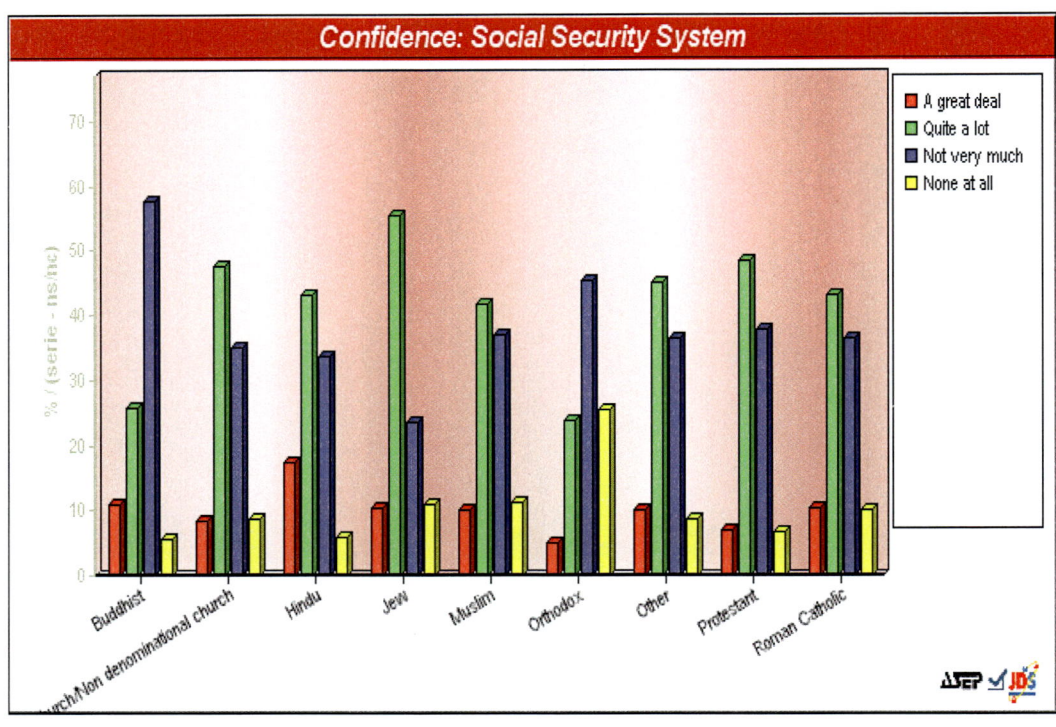

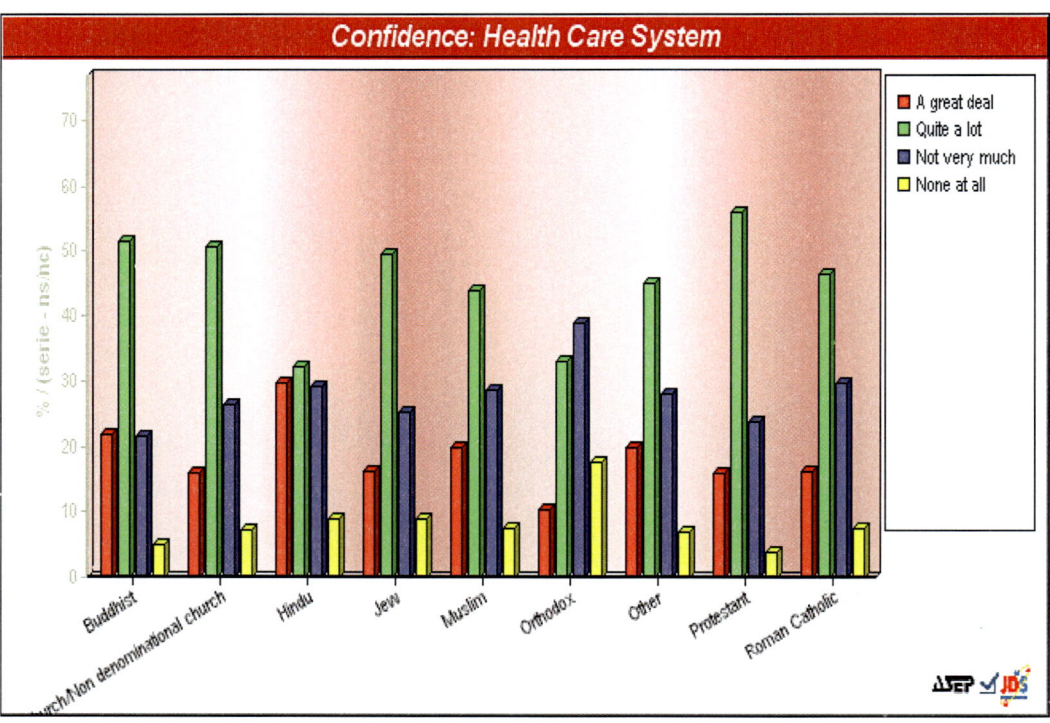

LAW AND ORDER

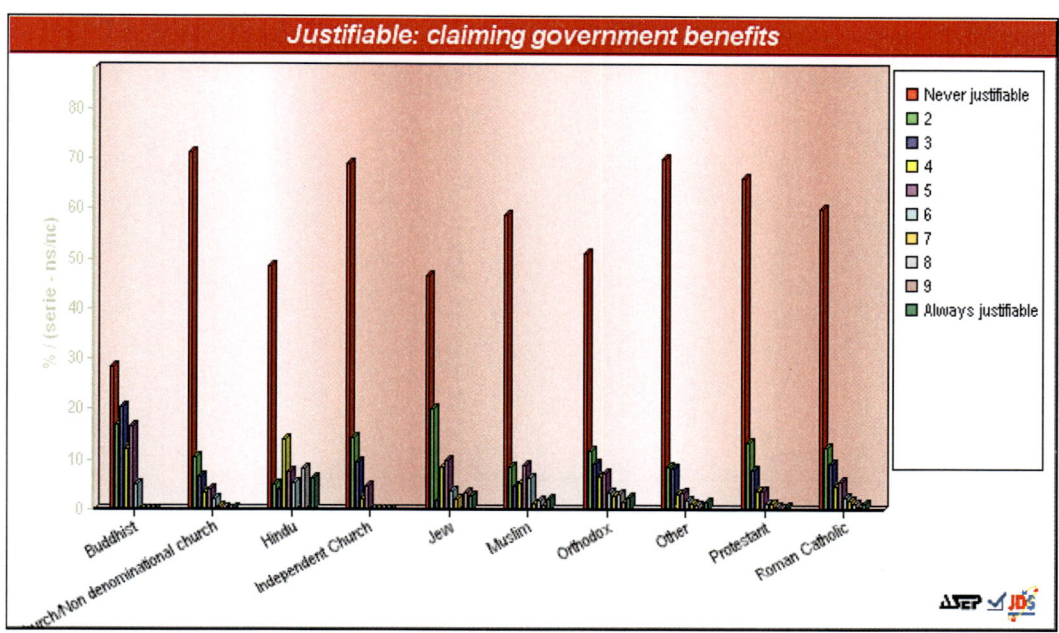

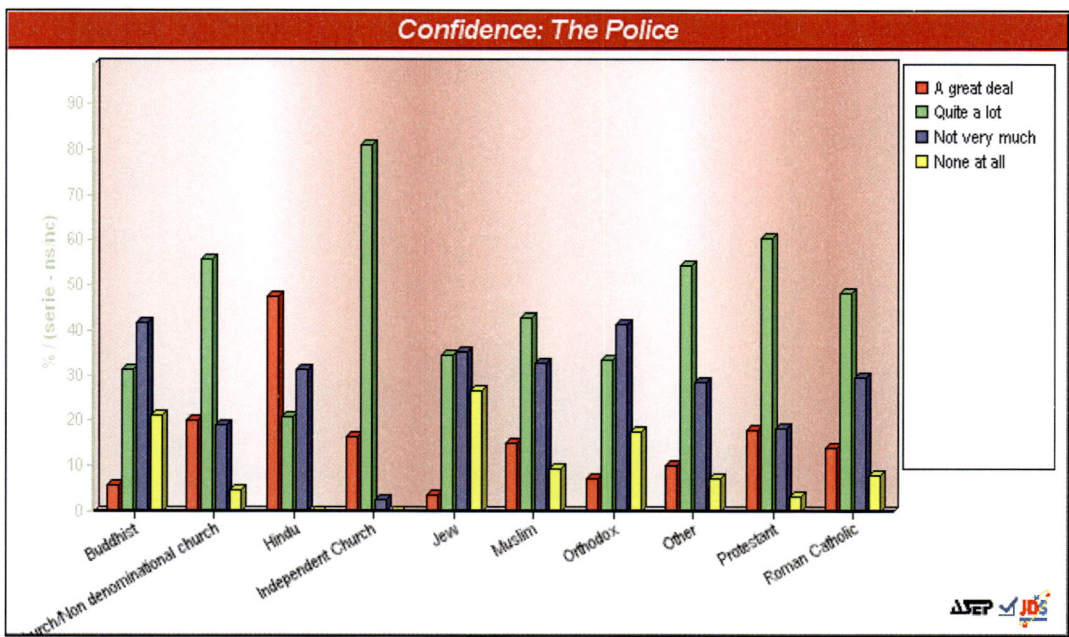

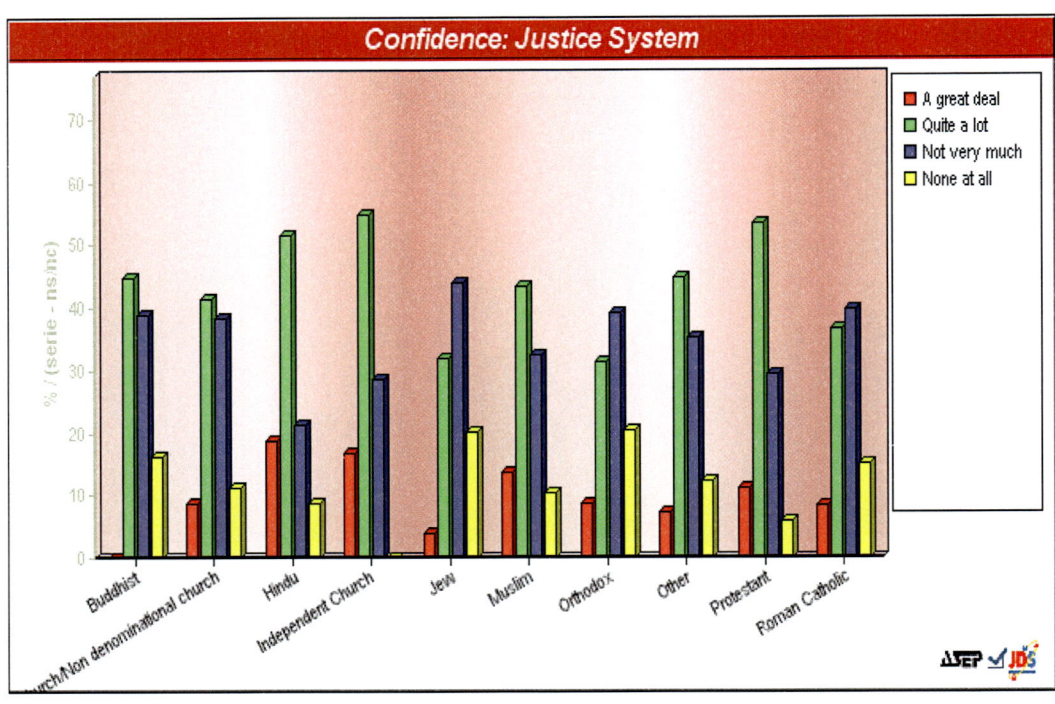
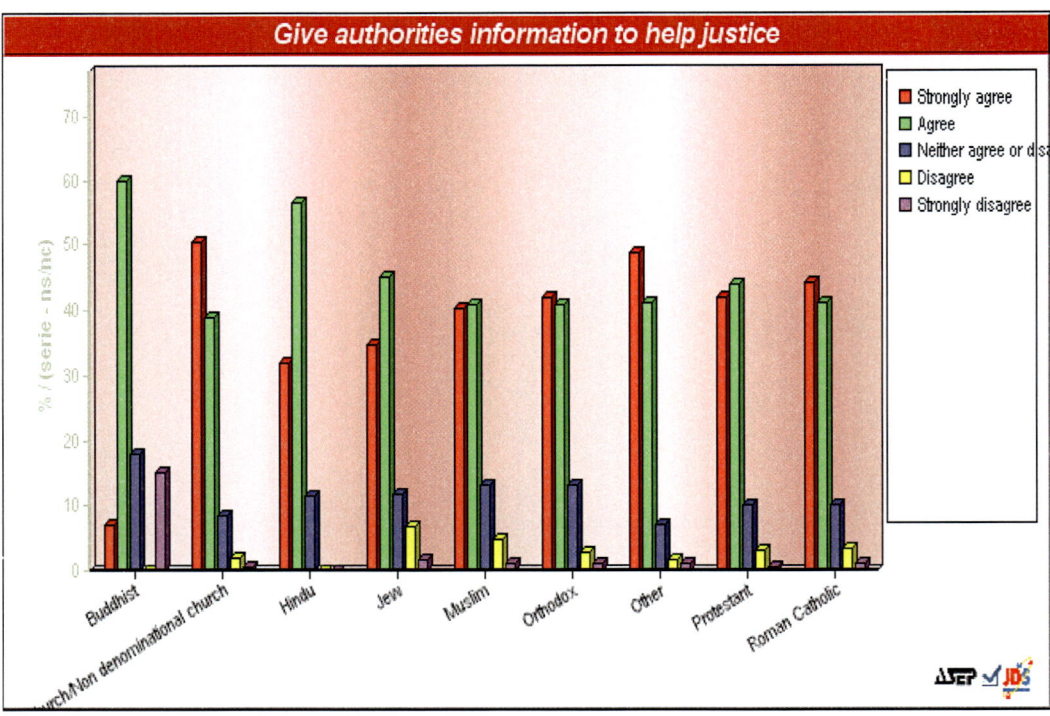

EUROPEAN INTEGRATION, ATLANTIC STRUCTURES, UNITED NATIONS

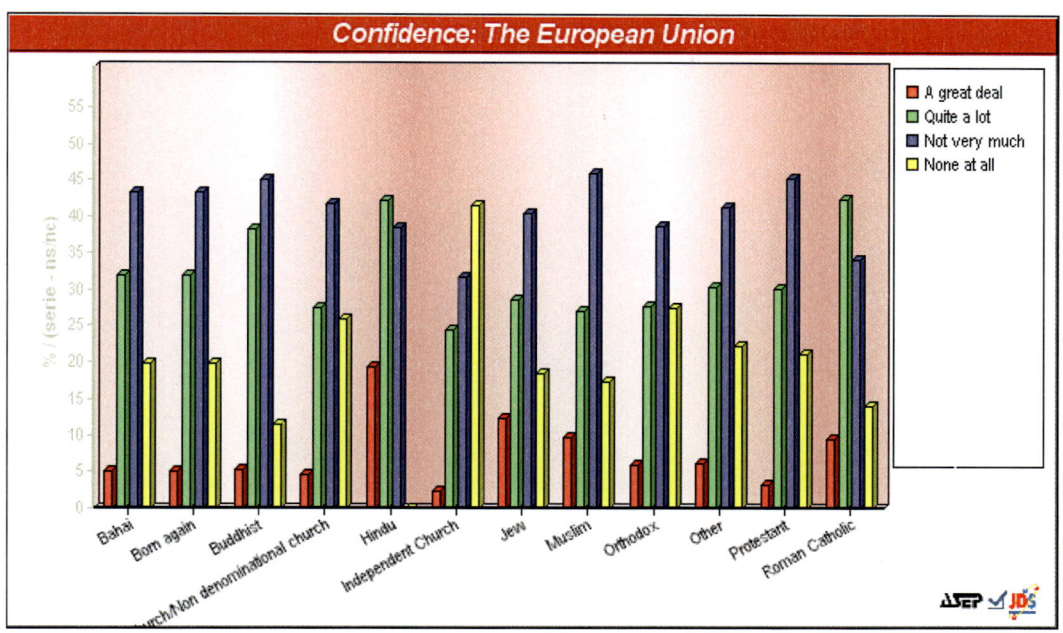

By Religious Practice

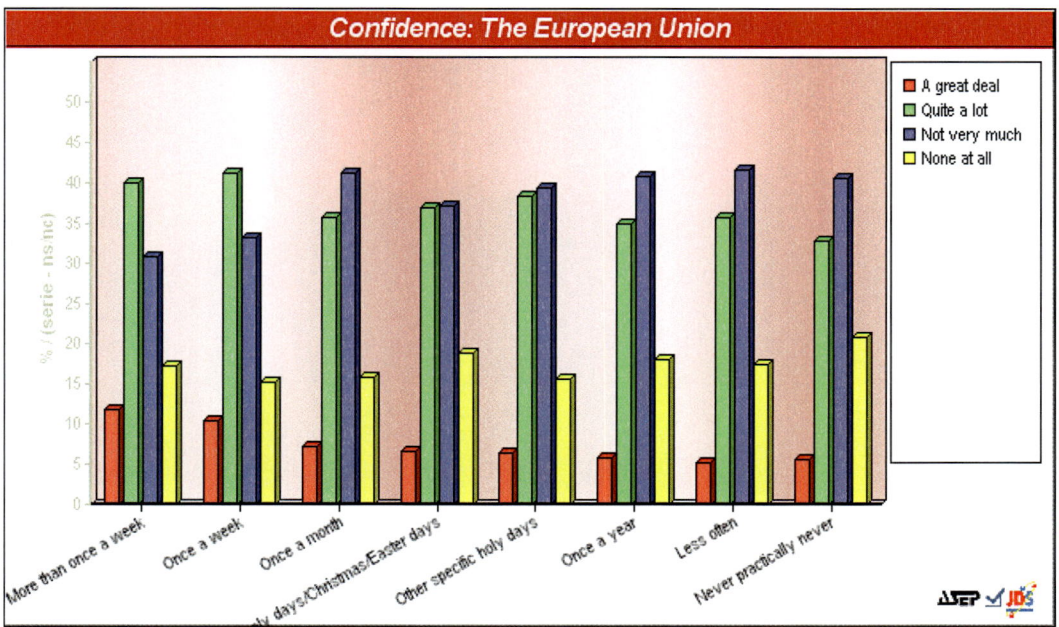

By Educational Level

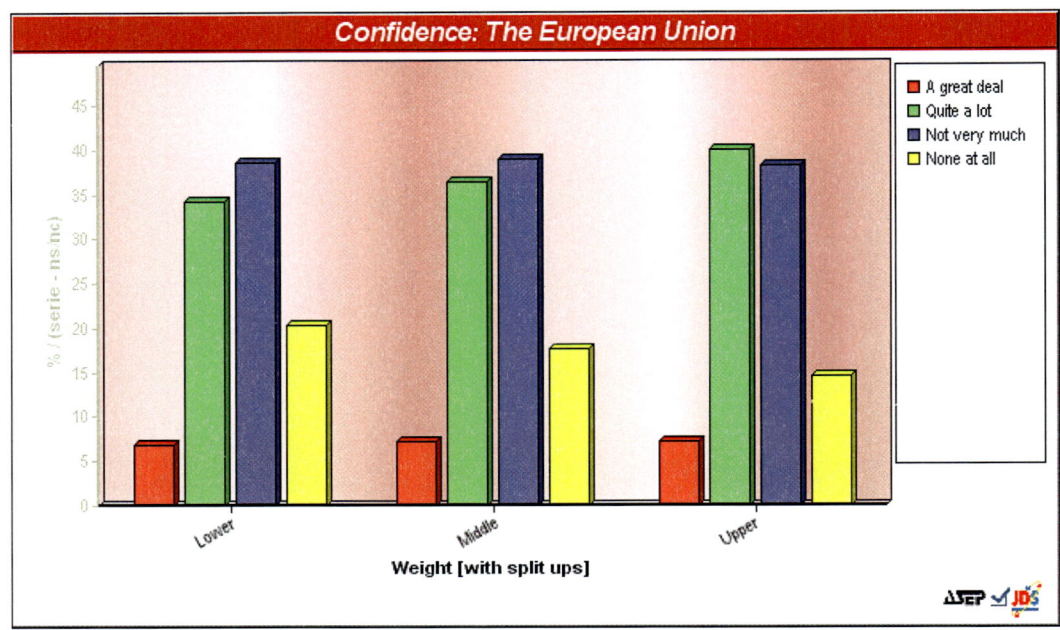

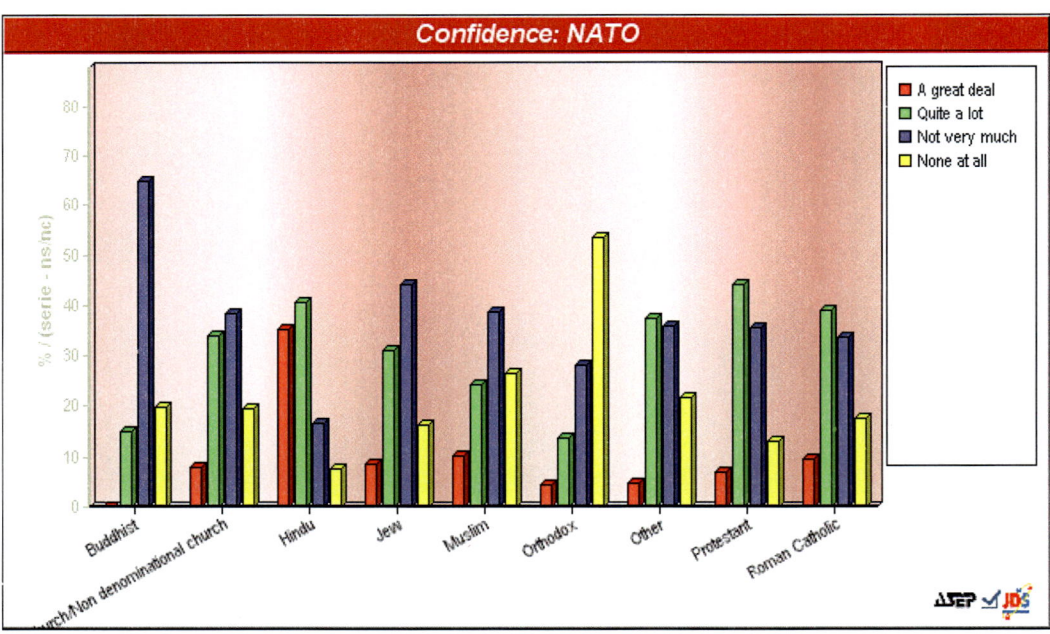

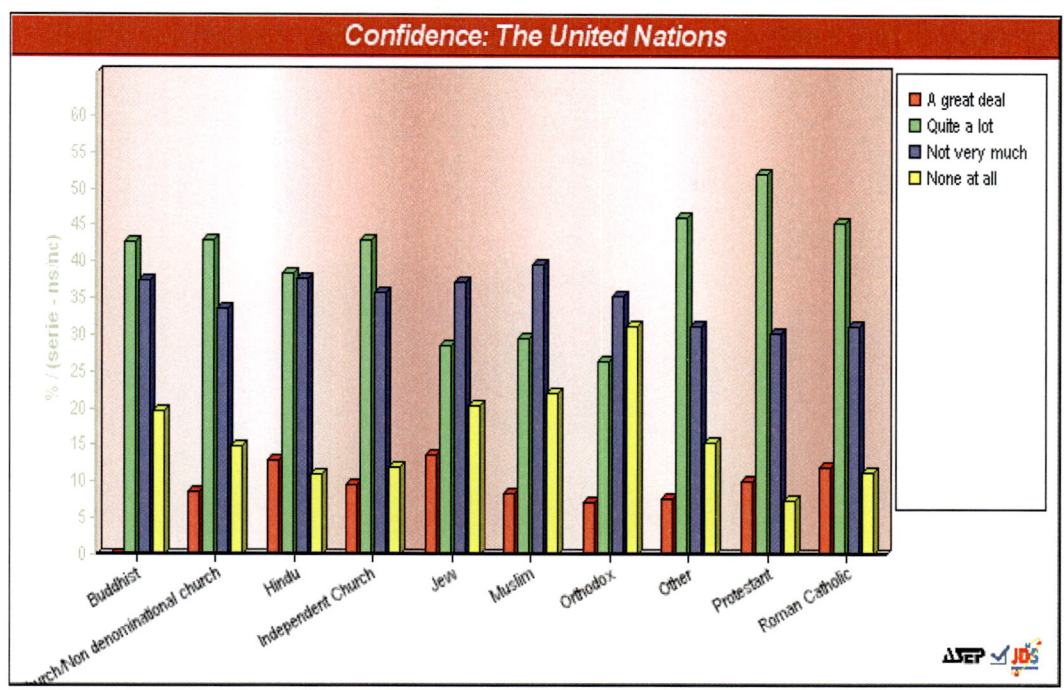

WILLINGNESS TO FIGHT FOR THE COUNTRY

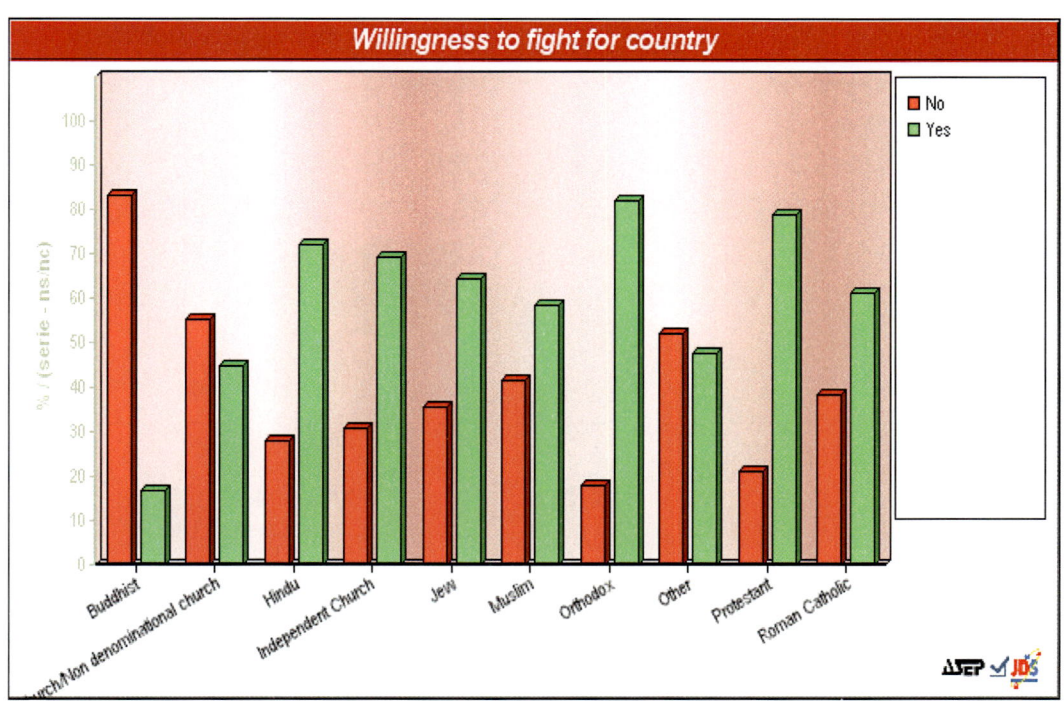

Willingness to Fight for the Country and Religious Practice

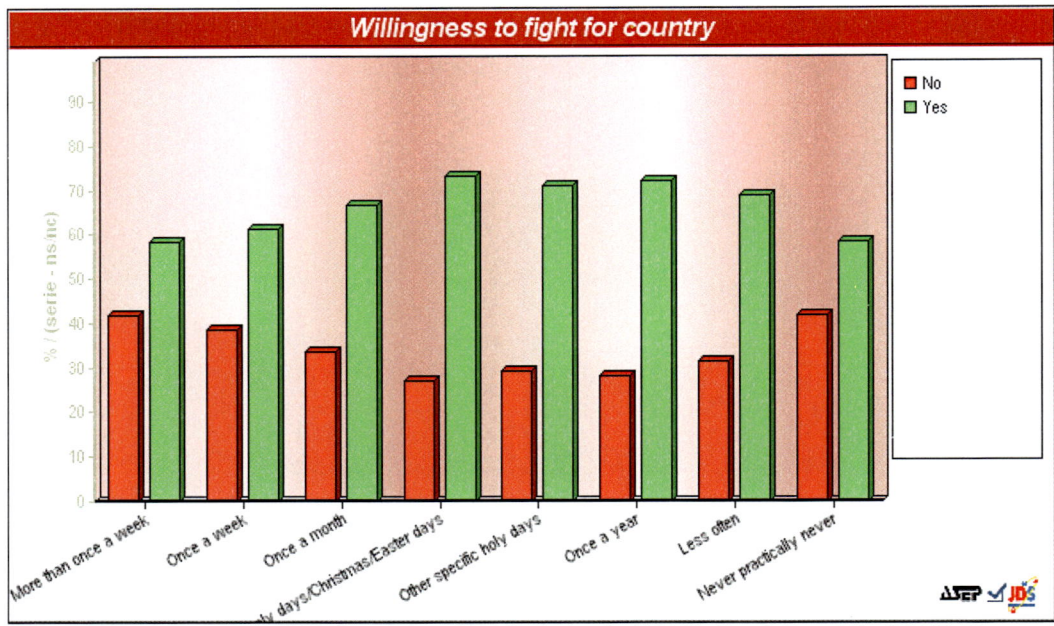

Selected samples: Austria [1999], Belgium [1999], Bulgaria [1999], Czech Republic [1999], Denmark [1999], Estonia [1999], Finland [2000], France [1999], Germany East [1999], Germany West [1999], Great Britain [1999], Greece [1999], Hungary [1999], Iceland [1999], Ireland [1999], Italy [1999], Latvia [1999], Lithuania [1999], Luxembourg [1999], Malta [1999], Netherlands [1999], Northern Ireland [1999], Norway [1996], Poland [1999], Portugal [1999], Romania [1999], Slovakia [1999], Slovenia [1999], Spain [2000], Sweden [1999], Switzerland [1996].

ON THE GLOBAL TGV LAÏCITÉ EXPRESS – WHAT HAPPENS WHEN PEOPLE DON'T ATTEND RELIGIOUS SERVICES, WITH EDUCATION AND INCOME CONSTANT (PARTIAL CORRELATIONS OF RELIGIOUS SERVICE NON-ATTENDANCE RATE WITH WVS INDICATORS)

Catholics

IRRESPECTIVE OF EDUCATION AND INCOME LEVELS (PARTIAL CORRELATION ANALYSIS, ALL RESPONDENTS WORLD VALUES SURVEY; ALL WAVES)	THE EFFECTS OF RELIGIOUS SECULARISM (=NON-ATTENDANCE OF RELIGIOUS SERVICES) ON CATHOLICISM
Lack of confidence: churches	0,465
Justifiable: abortion	0,313
Justifiable: divorce	0,279
Justifiable: euthanasia	0,265
Justifiable: having casual sex	0,251
Justifiable: adultery	0,236
Justifiable: sex under the legal age of consent	0,21

Appendix VIII

IRRESPECTIVE OF EDUCATION AND INCOME LEVELS (PARTIAL CORRELATION ANALYSIS, ALL RESPONDENTS WORLD VALUES SURVEY; ALL WAVES)	THE EFFECTS OF RELIGIOUS SECULARISM (=NON-ATTENDANCE OF RELIGIOUS SERVICES) ON CATHOLICISM
Justifiable: prostitution	0,199
Justifiable: lying	0.18
Justifiable: keeping money that you have found	0.178
Justifiable: homosexuality	0.175
Justifiable: suicide	0.169
Justifiable: smoking in public places	0.152
Lack of confidence: armed forces	0.14
Justifiable: paying cash	0.131
Justifiable: taking soft drugs	0.119
Lack of confidence: education system	0.118
Lack of confidence: the civil services	0.101
Justifiable: experiments with human embryos	0.101
Lack of confidence: the government	0.099
Lack of confidence: major companies	0.099
Lack of confidence: the police	0.097
Lack of confidence: the women's movement	0.092
Lack of confidence: Parliament	0.089
Justifiable: speeding over the limit	0.089
Justifiable: buy stolen goods	0.084
Lack of confidence: NATO	0.084
Lack of confidence: justice system	0.083
Justifiable: manipulation of food	0.079
Justifiable: cheating on taxes	0.079
Lack of confidence: the United Nations	0.078
Justifiable: driving under influence of alcohol	0.078
Lack of confidence: social security system	0.071
Lack of confidence: television	0.066
Justifiable: claiming government benefits	0.066
Hard work brings success	0.064
Lack of confidence: the political parties	0.064
Justifiable: avoiding a fare on public transport	0.064
Lack of confidence: the environmental protection movement	0.06
Justifiable: someone accepting a bribe	0.056
Lack of confidence: labor unions	0.055
Lack of confidence: the European Union	0.053
Lack of confidence: the press	0.05
Justifiable: political assassination	0.05
Lack of confidence: health care system	0.039
Justifiable: joyriding	0.039
Justifiable: throwing away litter	0.031
Government responsibility	0.023
Competition harmful (competition good or harmful)	0.018

IRRESPECTIVE OF EDUCATION AND INCOME LEVELS (PARTIAL CORRELATION ANALYSIS, ALL RESPONDENTS WORLD VALUES SURVEY; ALL WAVES)	THE EFFECTS OF RELIGIOUS SECULARISM (=NON-ATTENDANCE OF RELIGIOUS SERVICES) ON CATHOLICISM
Job taking of the unemployed	0.012
Rejecting neighbors: people of a different religion	-0.004
For state ownership of business	-0.013
Rejecting neighbors: immigrants/foreign workers	-0.015
Rejecting neighbors: emotionally unstable people	-0.023
Rejecting neighbors: Muslims	-0.026
Basic kinds of attitudes concerning society	-0.028
Rejecting neighbors: people of a different race	-0.036
Rejecting neighbors: Gypsies	-0.038
Rejecting neighbors: Jews	-0.041
Anti-egalitarian position on the income equality scale	-0.046
Rejecting neighbors: drug addicts	-0.054
Rejecting neighbors: heavy drinkers	-0.056
Wealth accumulation	-0.075
Rejecting neighbors: people who have AIDS	-0.077
Rejecting neighbors: homosexuals	-0.089
Rejecting neighbors: people with a criminal record	-0.121
Self positioning in political left-right scale on the right	-0.152

Orthodoxy

IRRESPECTIVE OF EDUCATION AND INCOME LEVELS (PARTIAL CORRELATION ANALYSIS, ALL RESPONDENTS WORLD VALUES SURVEY; ALL WAVES)	THE EFFECTS OF RELIGIOUS SECULARISM (=NON-ATTENDANCE OF RELIGIOUS SERVICES) ON ORTHODOXY
Lack of confidence: churches	0.345
Justifiable: abortion	0.149
Justifiable: euthanasia	0.145
Justifiable: experiments with human embryos	0.129
Justifiable: divorce	0.118
Justifiable: manipulation of food	0.108
Hard work brings success	0.093
Justifiable: adultery	0.085
Justifiable: suicide	0.08
Job taking of the unemployed	0.079
Justifiable: prostitution	0.069
Justifiable: cheating on taxes	0.059
Lack of confidence: the police	0.055

Appendix VIII

IRRESPECTIVE OF EDUCATION AND INCOME LEVELS (PARTIAL CORRELATION ANALYSIS, ALL RESPONDENTS WORLD VALUES SURVEY; ALL WAVES)	THE EFFECTS OF RELIGIOUS SECULARISM (=NON-ATTENDANCE OF RELIGIOUS SERVICES) ON ORTHODOXY
Lack of confidence: justice system	0.054
Lack of confidence: the political parties	0.053
Lack of confidence: the press	0.052
Lack of confidence: education system	0.049
Justifiable: avoiding a fare on public transport	0.049
Justifiable: lying	0.044
Justifiable: speeding over the limit	0.043
Lack of confidence: the government	0.041
Lack of confidence: the women's movement	0.039
Lack of confidence: health care system	0.038
Justifiable: having casual sex	0.038
For state ownership of business	0.038
Lack of confidence: television	0.037
Justifiable: smoking in public places	0.036
Lack of confidence: the civil services	0.034
Lack of confidence: Parliament	0.033
Lack of confidence: armed forces	0.033
Lack of confidence: major companies	0.028
Justifiable: buy stolen goods	0.028
Lack of confidence: labor unions	0.027
Rejecting neighbors: drug addicts	0.025
Rejecting neighbors: homosexuals	0.025
Justifiable: political assassination	0.025
Lack of confidence: NATO	0.024
Rejecting neighbors: people who have AIDS	0.024
Rejecting neighbors: emotionally unstable people	0.023
Lack of confidence: the European Union	0.019
Anti-egalitarian position on the income equality scale	0.019
Justifiable: homosexuality	0.015
Government responsibility	0.013
Basic kinds of attitudes concerning society	0.011
Justifiable: driving under influence of alcohol	0.011
Lack of confidence: the United Nations	0.007
Wealth accumulation	0.006
Lack of confidence: social security system	0.005
Competition harmful (competition good or harmful)	0.003
Justifiable: someone accepting a bribe	0.003
Justifiable: paying cash	0.002
Justifiable: sex under the legal age of consent	0.002

IRRESPECTIVE OF EDUCATION AND INCOME LEVELS (PARTIAL CORRELATION ANALYSIS, ALL RESPONDENTS WORLD VALUES SURVEY; ALL WAVES)	THE EFFECTS OF RELIGIOUS SECULARISM (=NON-ATTENDANCE OF RELIGIOUS SERVICES) ON ORTHODOXY
Justifiable: keeping money that you have found	-0.002
Justifiable: taking soft drugs	-0.006
Justifiable: claiming government benefits	-0.011
Justifiable: throwing away litter	-0.011
Rejecting neighbors: heavy drinkers	-0.017
Rejecting neighbors: immigrants/foreign workers	-0.019
Lack of confidence: the environmental protection movement	-0.024
Rejecting neighbors: Gypsies	-0.032
Justifiable: joyriding	-0.032
Rejecting neighbors: people of a different race	-0.056
Rejecting neighbors: Muslims	-0.061
Rejecting neighbors: Jews	-0.074
Rejecting neighbors: people of a different religion	-0.08
Rejecting neighbors: people with a criminal record	-0.085
Self positioning in political left-right scale on the right	-0.112

Protestantism

IRRESPECTIVE OF EDUCATION AND INCOME LEVELS (PARTIAL CORRELATION ANALYSIS, ALL RESPONDENTS WORLD VALUES SURVEY; ALL WAVES)	THE EFFECTS OF RELIGIOUS SECULARISM (=NON-ATTENDANCE OF RELIGIOUS SERVICES) ON PROTESTANTISM
Lack of confidence: churches	0.524
Justifiable: abortion	0.367
Justifiable: divorce	0.347
Justifiable: euthanasia	0.303
Justifiable: homosexuality	0.294
Justifiable: having casual sex	0.255
Justifiable: prostitution	0.23
Justifiable: suicide	0.196
Justifiable: paying cash	0.184
Justifiable: smoking in public places	0.168
Lack of confidence: the women's movement	0.16
Justifiable: cheating on taxes	0.151
Lack of confidence: the civil services	0.146
Lack of confidence: the press	0.139

IRRESPECTIVE OF EDUCATION AND INCOME LEVELS (PARTIAL CORRELATION ANALYSIS, ALL RESPONDENTS WORLD VALUES SURVEY; ALL WAVES)	THE EFFECTS OF RELIGIOUS SECULARISM (=NON-ATTENDANCE OF RELIGIOUS SERVICES) ON PROTESTANTISM
Lack of confidence: major companies	0.132
Hard work brings success	0.131
Lack of confidence: the government	0.131
Justifiable: speeding over the limit	0.13
Lack of confidence: television	0.129
Justifiable: taking soft drugs	0.125
Justifiable: adultery	0.115
Lack of confidence: the environmental protection movement	0.112
Lack of confidence: the political parties	0.108
Justifiable: experiments with human embryos	0.102
Justifiable: lying	0.101
Justifiable: manipulation of food	0.1
Lack of confidence: armed forces	0.095
Lack of confidence: social security system	0.093
Justifiable: throwing away litter	0.084
Lack of confidence: education system	0.074
Lack of confidence: Parliament	0.074
Lack of confidence: the United Nations	0.071
Lack of confidence: the European Union	0.053
Justifiable: avoiding a fare on public transport	0.05
Justifiable: buy stolen goods	0.049
Justifiable: keeping money that you have found	0.049
Justifiable: sex under the legal age of consent	0.048
Basic kinds of attitudes concerning society	0.041
Lack of confidence: NATO	0.028
Lack of confidence: justice system	0.022
Lack of confidence: health care system	0.02
Justifiable: joyriding	0.018
Lack of confidence: labor unions	0.017
Job taking of the unemployed	0.014
Competition harmful (competition good or harmful)	0.013
Justifiable: driving under influence of alcohol	0.006
Justifiable: someone accepting a bribe	0.004
Justifiable: political assassination	-0.004
Justifiable: claiming government benefits	-0.005
Rejecting neighbors: drug addicts	-0.016
Rejecting neighbors: Muslims	-0.019
Rejecting neighbors: Gypsies	-0.045

IRRESPECTIVE OF EDUCATION AND INCOME LEVELS (PARTIAL CORRELATION ANALYSIS, ALL RESPONDENTS WORLD VALUES SURVEY; ALL WAVES)	THE EFFECTS OF RELIGIOUS SECULARISM (=NON-ATTENDANCE OF RELIGIOUS SERVICES) ON PROTESTANTISM
Anti-egalitarian position on the income equality scale	-0.05
For state ownership of business	-0.053
Lack of confidence: the police	-0.056
Wealth accumulation	-0.058
Rejecting neighbors: immigrants/foreign workers	-0.058
Self positioning in political left-right scale on the right	-0.078
Rejecting neighbors: people of a different race	-0.081
Rejecting neighbors: people of a different religion	-0.086
Rejecting neighbors: emotionally unstable people	-0.087
Rejecting neighbors: Jews	-0.094
Rejecting neighbors: heavy drinkers	-0.105
Government responsibility	-0.137
Rejecting neighbors: people who have AIDS	-0.164
Rejecting neighbors: people with a criminal record	-0.174
Rejecting neighbors: homosexuals	-0.242

GENERAL SOURCES AND BIBLIOGRAPHY

Abdullah M. S. and Khoury A. Th. (1984), 'Mohammed für Christen. Eine Herausforderung' Freiburg, Basel, Wien: Herder.

Achen Ch. H. (1982), 'Interpreting and Using Regression' Beverly Hills: Sage University Papers.

Addison T. (2006), Focusing Fiscal Policy on Poverty Reduction, Redistribution and Growth. Wider Angle, 1.

Addison T. and A. Heshmati (2004), the New Global Determinants of FDI Flows to Developing Countries: The Impacts of ICT and Democratization, Research in Banking and Finance 4, 151-186.

Addo H. (1986), 'Imperialism: the permanent stage of capitalism' Tokyo: United Nations University.

Afheldt H. (1994), 'Wohlstand fuer niemand? Die Marktwirtschaft entlaesst ihre Kinder' Munich: Kunstmann.

Agénor P.R. (2003). Does Globalisation Hurt the Poor? (unpublished manuscript), World Bank: Washington DC. .

Aghion Ph. and Howitt P. (1992), "A Model of growth through Creative Destruction". Econometrica 60:2, pp. 323-51.

Aghion Ph. and Williamson J. G. (1998), 'Growth, Inequality and Globalization. Theory, History and Policy' Cambridge: at the University Press.

Agnew J. (2001), 'The New Global Economy: Time-Space Compression, Geopolitics, and Global Uneven Development' Journal of World-Systems Research, available at: http://jwsr.ucr.edu/index.phpVII, 2, Fall: 133-154.

Ahluwalia M. S. (1974), 'Income Inequality: Some Dimensions of the Problem' in 'Redistribution with Growth' (Chenery H.B. et al. (Eds.)), pp. 3 - 37, New York and Oxford: Oxford University Press.

Ahmed A. S. (2005), 'Ibn Khaldun and Anthropology: The Failure of Methodology in the Post 9/11 World.' Contemporary Sociology, Vol. 34, No. 6 (Nov. 2005), pp. 591-596.

Ahulwalia M. S. (1976), 'Inequality, Poverty and Development'. Journal of Development Economics 3, pps. 307-342.

Aiginger K. (2008), Performance Differences in Europe: Tentative Hypotheses on the Role of Institutions. WIFO Working Paper, REPEC/IDEAS, University of Connecticut.

Aiginger K. and Guger A. (2005), 'The European Socio-economic Model. Differences to the USA and Changes Over Time', London School of Economics – European Social Model Programme – Tandem Project to the British EU Presidency, 42 pages, available at: http://publikationen.wifo.ac.at/pls/wifosite/wifosite.wifo_search.frameset?p_filename=MONOGRAPHIEN/PRIVATE26369/S_2005_EUROPEAN_MODEL_25777$.PDF .

Aiginger K. and Guger A. (2005), ‚Das europäische Gesellschaftsmodell' Austrian Institute for Economic Research (WIFO) (Studie im Auftrag des Bundesministeriums für Wirtschaft und Arbeit, restricted).

Akerman J. (1936), 'Economic Progress and Economic Crises' London and Basingstoke: Macmillan.

Alber J. and P. Lenarz (2008), Wachsende soziale Ungleichheit in Europa. Die Lebensqualitaet unterer Einkommensschichten in der erweiterten Europaeischen Union, in: Informationsdienst Soziale Indikatoren; Mannheim: GESIS; January 2008: 1-5.

Albert M. (1991), Capitalisme contre Capitalisme, Paris: Editions du Seuil.

Albritton R. (2001), 'Phases of Capitalist Development: Booms, Crises, and Globalizations' Basingstoke and London: Palgrave.

Alderson A. and Nielsen F. (1999), ‚Income Inequality, Development and Dependence: A Reconsideration' American Sociological Review, 64, 4, August: 606 – 631.

Alderson A. S., Beckfield J. and Nielsen F. (2005), 'Income Inequality Trends in Core Societies' in 'The Future of World Society' (Herkenrath M. et al. (Eds.)) pp. 253 – 271; Sociological Institute, University of Zurich: Intelligent Book Production.

Almond G. (1991), 'Capitalism and Democracy' PS. Political Science and Politics, 24, 3, September: 467 - 474.

Amin S. (1976), 'Unequal Development: An Essay on the Social Formations of Peripheral Capitalism' New York: Monthly Review Press.

Amin S. (1989), 'Eurocentrism' Translated by Russell Moore. New York: Monthly Review Press.

Amin S. (1992), 'Empire of Chaos' New York: Monthly Review Press.

Amin S. (1994), 'Re-reading the postwar period: an intellectual itinerary' Translated by Michael Wolfers. New York: Monthly Review Press.

Amin S. (1997), 'Die Zukunft des Weltsystems. Herausforderungen der Globalisierung. Herausgegeben und aus dem Franzoesischen uebersetzt von Joachim Wilke' Hamburg: VSA.

Amnesty International (current issues), 'Jahresbericht' Frankfurt a.M.: Fischer TB.

An C. B. and Jeon S. H. (2006), "Demographic change and economic growth: An inverted-U shape relationship" Economics Letters, 92, (3): 447-454.

Andersen T.M. and T.T. Herbertsson (2003), Measuring Globalization. IZA Discussion Paper. 2003:817. Bonn: IZA.

Apps P. and R. Rees (2004), Fertility, taxation, and family policy, Scandinavian Journal of Economics, 106(4), 745-763.

Arcelus F., B. Sharma and G. Srinivasan (2005), Assessing the information content of the technology achievement index in the presence of the human development index, Economics Bulletin 15(4), 1-5.

Archibugi D. and A. Coco (2004), A New Indicator of Technological Capabilities for Developed and Developing Countries (ArCo), World Development 32(4), 629-654.

Armstrong K. (1992), 'Muhammad: a biography of the prophet' San Francisco, Calif.: Harper SanFrancisco.

Armstrong K. (1993), 'A history of God: the 4000-year quest of Judaism, Christianity, and Islam.' New York : A.A. Knopf: Distributed by Random House

Armstrong K. (2000), 'Islam: a short history'. New York: Modern Library

Armstrong K. (2006), 'Muhammad: a prophet for our time' New York: Atlas Books/HarperCollins

Arrighi G. (1995), 'The Long 20th Century. Money, Power, and the Origins of Our Times' London, New York: Verso.

Arrighi G. and Silver B. J. (1999), 'Chaos and Governance in the Modern World System' Minneapolis: University of Minnesota Press.

Arrighi G. et al. (1996), 'Modelling Zones of the World-Economy: A Polynomial Regression Analysis (1964-1994)' State University of New York at Binghamton: Fernand Braudel Center.

Arrighi G. et al. (1996), 'The Rise of East Asia in World Historical Perspective' State University of New York at Binghamton: Fernand Braudel Center.

Arrighi G., Hamashita T. and Selden M. (Eds.)(2003), 'Resurgence of East Asia: 500, 150 and 50 year perspectives' London; New York: Routledge, 2003.

Atkinson A. (2005), Atkinson Review: Final report: The measurement of government output and productivity for the national accounts, Palgrave Macmillan, Basingstoke.

Atkinson A.B., B. Cantillon, E. Marlier and B. Nolan (2002), Social Indicators: The EU and Social Inclusion, Oxford University Press, Oxford.

Atkinson A.B., E. Marlier and B. Nolan (2004), Indicators and targets for social inclusion in the European Union, Journal of Common Market Studies, 42(1), 47-75.

Australian Treasury (2001), 'Global poverty and inequality in the 20th Century: turning the corner? Australian Treasury, available at: http://www.treasury.gov.au/publications/EconomicPublications/EconomicRoundUp/2001CentenaryEdition/dowload/Round2.pdf.

Aydin H. et al. (2003), '"Euro-Islam". Das neue Islamverständnis der Muslime in der Migration". Stiftung Zentrum für Türkeistudien, Institut an der Universität Duisburg-Essen. Available at: http://www.renner-institut.at/download/texte/euroisla.pdf

Babones S. J. (2002), 'Population and Sample Selection Effects in Measuring International Income Inequality' Journal of World-Systems Research, available at: http://jwsr.ucr.edu/index.phpVIII, 1, Winter: 8 – 28.

Babones S. J. (2005), 'The Country-Level Income Structure of the World Economy' Journal of World-Systems Research, available at: http://jwsr.ucr.edu/index.phpXI, 1, July: 29 – 55.

Balakrishnan, P. (2003): "Globalisation, Growth and Justice", Economic and Political Weekly, June 26.

Balassa B. (1964),"The Purchasing Power Parity Doctrine: A Reappraisal", Journal of Political Economy, vol. 72, December, pp. 584-596.

Baldwin, R. E. and P. Martin (1999): "Two Waves of Globalization: Superficial Similarities, Fundamental Differences" NBER Working Paper 6904.

Balic S. (2001), ,Islam für Europa: neue Perspektiven einer alten Religion' Köln and Vienna: Böhlau

Bardakoglu A. (2006), 'Religion and Society. New Perspectives from Turkey.' Ankara: P.P.R.A.

Barr N. (1998), The Economics of the welfare state, 3rd edition, Stanford University Press, Stanford, CA.

Barro R. J. (1991), 'Economic Growth in a Cross Section of Countries.', Quarterly journal of economics, 106[2]: 407-43.

Barro R. J. (1994), 'Sources of economic growth.' Carnegie-Rochester conference series on public policy, 1994, vol. 40, pp. 1 .

Barro R. J. (1996), 'Democracy and Growth.' Journal of Economic Growth, 1996, vol. 1, no. 1, pp. 1 .

Barro R. J. (1996), 'Getting It Right. Markets and Choices in a Free Society' Cambridge, Mass.: MIT Press.

Barro R. J. (1999), 'Determinants of Democracy.' Journal of political economy, vol. 107, no. 6p2, pp. S158.

Barro R. J. (2000), 'Inequality and Growth in a Panel of Countries.' Journal of Economic Growth, 2000, vol. 5, no. 1, pp. 5 .

Barro R. J. (2001), 'Human Capital and Growth', American Economic Review, 2001, vol. 91, no. 2, pp. 12-17 .

Barro R. J. (2003), 'Economic Growth in a Cross Section of Countries' International Library of Critical Writings in Economics, 2003, vol. 159, no. 1, pp. 350-386 .

Barro R. J. (2004), 'Determinants of economic growth in a panel of countries' Annals of economics and finance, Beijing: Peking University Press Bd. 4 (2003), 2, pp. 231-275.

Barro R. J. (2004), 'Spirit of Capitalism Religion and Economic Development'. Harvard International Review, vol. 25, no. 4, pp. 64-67.

Barro R. J. and Grilli V. (1994), 'European Macroeconomics' Basingstoke and London: Macmillan.

Barro R. J. and McCleary R. M. (2003), 'Religion and Economic Growth across Countries Source' American Sociological Review, Volume 68, Number 5, 1 October 2003, pp. 760-781 .

Barro R. J. and McCleary R. M. (2003), 'Religion and Economic Growth' NBER Working Paper series, 2003, no. 9682, (entire).

Barro R. J. and McCleary R. M. (2004), 'Religion and economic growth' The Milken Institute review (Milken, Santa Monica, Cal.), 6 (2004), 2, S. 36-45.

Barro R. J. and Sala-i-Martin X. (1991), 'Convergence across States and Regions' Brookings Papers on Economic Activity, 1: 107 - 179.

Barro R. J. and Sala-i-Martin X. (1992), 'Convergence", Journal of Political Economy, vol. 100 (2), pp. 223-251.

Barro R. J. and Sala-i-Martin X. (1995/98), 'Wirtschaftswachstum (Economic Growth)' München: Oldenbourg (McGraw Hill, New York).

Barro R.J. and J-W. Lee (2000), International data on educational attainment: updates and implications, Centre for International Development at Harvard University, CID Working Paper 2000:42.

Bata, M. and A. J. Bergesen (2002a): "Global Inequality: An Introduction (to Special Issue on Global Economy – Part I)". Journal of World-System Research, 8 (1): 2-6.

Bata, M. and A. J. Bergesen (2002b): "Global Inequality: An Introduction (to Special Issue on Global Economy – Part II)", Journal of World-System Research, 8 (2): 146-48.

Baylis, J. and S. Smith (2001): "The Globalization of World Politics – An Introduction to International Relations", Oxford University Press.

Becker G. (1993), 'Europe Wastes Its Human Capital' The Wall Street Journal Europe, 18 - 19 June: 10.

Beer L. (1999), 'Income Inequality and Transnational Corporate Penetration' Journal of World Systems Research, 5, 1: 1 – 25.

Beer L. and Boswell T. (2002), 'The Resilience of Dependency Effects in Explaining Income Inequality in the Global Economy: A Cross-National Analysis, 1975 – 1995'. Journal of World-Systems Research, available at: http://jwsr.ucr.edu/index.phpVIII, 1, Winter 2002: 30 – 59.

Bello W. (1989), 'Confronting the Brave New World Economic Order: Toward a Southern Agenda for the 1990s' Alternatives, XIV, 2: 135 - 168.

Bello W. with Shea Cunningham and Bill Rau (1999), 'Dark Victory. The United States and Global Poverty' London: Pluto Press.

Beresford, B., Sloper, T. and Bradshaw, J. (2005), Physical Health, in Bradshaw, J. and Mayhew, E. (eds). The Well-being of Children in the UK (second edition). London: Save the Children, 65-107.

Berger P. L. (2001), ,Holy war, Inc.: inside the secret world of Osama bin Laden' New York: Free Press

Bergesen A. J. and Bata M. (2002), 'Global and National Inequality: Are They Connected?' Journal of World-Systems Research, available at: http://jwsr.ucr.edu/index.phpVIII, 1, Winter: 130 – 144.

Berry A. et al. (1981), 'The Level of World Inequality: How Much Canada One Say?' Document 38, Laboratoire d'Economie Politique, CNRS, 45, rue d'Ulm, F - 75230 Paris Cedex 05.

Berry W. D. and Feldman S. (1985), 'Multiple Regression in Practice' Beverly Hills: Sage University Papers.

Bevan, D. L. and A. K. Fosu (2003): "Globalization: An Overview". Journal of African Economies, 12 (1): 1-13.

Bhagwati J.N. (1989), 'Nation States in an International Framework: An Economist's Perspective' Alternatives, XIV, 2: 231 - 244.

Bhagwati, J. (2004): "Anti Globalization: Why?", Journal of Policy Modeling, Vol. 26, pp. 239-463.

Bhandari A. K. and A. Heshmati (2007), Measurement of Globalization and its Variations among Countries, Regions and over Time, in A. Heshmati and A. Tausch, Roadmap to

Bangalore? Globalization, the EU's Lisbon Process and the Structures of Global Inequality, Nova Science Publishers.

BM.I.SIAK (2006), 'Perspektiven und Herausforderungen in der Integration muslimischer MitbürgerInnen in Österreich' Federal Ministry of the Interior, Republic of Austria, available at: http://www.bmi.gv.at/downloadarea/asyl_fremdenwesen/Perspektiven_Herausforderungen.pdf

Boff L. (2005), 'Global civilization: challenges to society and to Christianity.' London; Oakville: Equinox Publishing.

Bolaky, B and C. Freund (2004): "Trade, Regulations, and Growth", World Bank Working Papers.

Bollen K. A. (1980), 'Issues in the Comparative Measurement of Political Democracy' American Sociological Review, 45: 370 - 390.

Bollen K. A. and Jackman R. W. (1985), 'Political Democracy and the Size Distribution of Income.' American Sociological Review, 46, pps. 651-659.

Bollen K. and Lennox, R. (1991) 'Conventional Wisdom on Measurement: A Structural Equation Perspective'. Psychological Bulletin, 110, 2, 305-14.

Bordo, M. D., Eichengreen, B., and Irwin, D. A., (1999): "Is Globalization Today Really Different than Globalization a Hundred Years Ago?" NBER Working Paper 7195, June

Bornschier V. (1976), 'Wachstum, Konzentration und Multinationalisierung von Industrieunternehmen' Frauenfeld and Stuttgart: Huber.

Bornschier V. (1988), 'Westliche Gesellschaft im Wandel' Frankfurt a.M./ New York: Campus.

Bornschier V. (1992), 'The Rise of the European Community. Grasping Towards Hegemony or Therapy against National Decline in the World Political Economy?'. Vienna: paper, presented at the First European Conference of Sociology, August 26 - 29.

Bornschier V. (1996), 'Western society in transition' New Brunswick, N.J.: Transaction Publishers.

Bornschier V. (1999), 'Hegemonic Transition, West European Unification and the Future Structure of the Core' in in 'The Future of Global Conflict' (Bornschier V. and Chase-Dunn Ch. K. (Eds.)), pp. 77 - 98, London, Thousand Oaks and New Delhi: Sage Publications.

Bornschier V. (2000), "State-building in Europe: the revitalization of Western European integration" Cambridge [England]; New York: Cambridge University Press

Bornschier V. (2002), 'Changing Income Inequality in the Second Half of the 20th Century: Preliminary Findings and Propositions for Explanations" Journal of World-Systems Research, available at: http://jwsr.ucr.edu/index.phpVIII, 1, Winter: 100 – 127.

Bornschier V. (2005), "Culture and politics in economic development" London; New York: Routledge

Bornschier V. (Ed.)(1994), 'Conflicts and new departures in world society' New Brunswick, N.J.: Transaction Publishers.

Bornschier V. and Ballmer-Cao, T. H. (1979), 'Income Inequality: A Cross-National Study of the Relationships between MNC-Penetration, Dimensions of the Power Structure and Income Distribution.' American Sociological Review, 44, pps. 438-506.

Bornschier V. and Chase-Dunn Ch. K (1985), 'Transnational Corporations and Underdevelopment' N.Y., N.Y.: Praeger.

Bornschier V. and Chase-Dunn Ch. K. (1999), 'Technological Change, Globalization and Hegemonic Rivalry' in 'The Future of Global Conflict' (Bornschier V. and Chase-Dunn Ch. K. (Eds.)), pp. 285-302, London, Thousand Oaks and New Delhi: Sage Publications. Bornschier V. and Heintz P., reworked and enlarged by Th. H. Ballmer - Cao and J. Scheidegger (1979), 'Compendium of Data for World Systems Analysis' Machine readable data file, Zurich: Department of Sociology, Zurich University.

Bornschier V. and Nollert M. (1994), 'Political Conflict and Labor Disputes at the Core: An Encompassing Review for the Post - War Era' in 'Conflicts and New Departures in World Society' (Bornschier V. and Lengyel P. (Eds.)), pp. 377 - 403, New Brunswick (U.S.A.) and London: Transaction Publishers, World Society Studies, Volume 3.

Bornschier V. and Suter Chr. (1992), 'Long Waves in the World System' in 'Waves, Formations and Values in the World System' (Bornschier V. and Lengyel P. (Eds.)), pp. 15 - 50, New Brunswick and London: Transaction Publishers.

Bornschier V. et al. (1980), 'Multinationale Konzerne, Wirtschaftspolitik und nationale Entwicklung im Weltsystem' Frankfurt a.M.: Campus.

Bornschier V., Chase-Dunn Ch. and Rubinson R. (1977), 'Cross-National Evidence of the Effects of Foreign Investment and Aid on Economic Growth and Inequality: A Survey of Findings and a Reanalysis.' American Journal of Sociology, 84, pps. 487-506.

Boswell T. (1989), 'Revolutions in the World System' Greenwich CT: Greenwood.

Boswell T. (1997), 'Review on George Modelski and William R. Thompson (1996)' Journal of World Systems Research, 3, 2, Spring 1977, electronic journal, available on the Internet at http://csf.colorado.edu/wsystems/jwsr.html.

Boswell T. (1999), 'Hegemony and Bifurcation Points in World History' in 'The Future of Global Conflict' (Bornschier V. and Chase-Dunn Ch. K. (Eds.)), pp. 263 - 284, London, Thousand Oaks and New Delhi: Sage Publications.

Boswell T. and Bergesen A. (1987), 'America's Changing Role in the World-System' New York: Frederic Praeger Publishers.

Boswell T. and Chase-Dunn Ch. K. (2000), 'The Spiral of Capitalism and Socialism. Toward Global Democracy' Boulder, Colorado: Lynne Rienner.

Boswell T. and Dixon W. J. (1990), 'Dependency and Rebellion: A Cross-National Analysis.' American Sociological Review, Vol. 55, No. 4 (Aug., 1990), pp. 540-559

Boswell T. and Dixon W. J. (1993), 'Marx's Theory of Rebellion: A Cross-National Analysis of Class Exploitation, Economic Development, and Violent Revolt.' American sociological review, 1993, vol. 58, no. 5, pp. 681 .

Boswell T. and Dixon W.J. (1990), 'Dependency and Rebellion: A Cross - National Analysis' American Sociological Review, 55, August: 540 - 559.

Boswell T. and Sweat M. (1991), 'Hegemony, Long Waves, and Major Wars: A Time Series Analysis of Systemic Dynamics, 1496 - 1967' International Studies Quarterly, 35, 2: 123-149.

Bowles, S. (2001): "A Future of Labour in the Global Economy", TIPS Working Paper, 4-2001.

Boyer R. and Y. Saillard [eds.] (1995), Théory de la Régulation. L'État des Savoirs: Paris: Editions La DécouverteandSyros.

Bradshaw J., Hoelscher, P. and Richardson, D. (2007), An Index of Child Well-being in the European Union, Social Indicators Research 80(1), 133-177.

Bradshaw Y. (1987), 'Urbanization and Underdevelopment: A Global Study of Modernization, Urban Bias, and Economic Dependency' American Sociological Review, 52: 224 - 239.

Bradshaw Y. and Huang J. (1991), 'Intensifying Global Dependency. Foreign Debt, Structural Adjustment, and Third - World Underdevelopment' Sociological Quarterly, 32, 3: 321 - 342.

Breedlove W. L. and Armer J. M. (1996), 'Economic Disarticulation and Social Development in Less-Developed Nations: A Cross-National Study of Intervening Structures.' Sociological focus, vol. 29, no. 4, pp. 359 ff.

Breedlove W. L. and Patrick N. D. (1988), 'International Stratification and Inequality 1960-1980'. International journal of contemporary sociology, 1988, vol. 25, no. 3/4, pp. 105.

Brenner R. (1998), 'Uneven Development and the Long Downturn: The Advanced Capitalist Economies from Boom to Stagnation, 1950-1998'. New Left Review, No. 229 (May-June), pp. 1-228.

Bronfenbrenner, U. (1979), The Ecology of Human Development. Experiments by Nature and Design. Cambridge, MA: Harvard University Press.

Bronfenbrenner, U. and Morris, P. (1998), The Ecology of Developmental Processes, in Damon, W. and Lerner, R. (eds). Handbook of Child Psychology (fifth edition, volume 1), Theoretical Models of Human Development, New York: Wiley.

Brooks, A.M. and Hanafin, S. (2005), Measuring Child Well-being. An Inventory of Key Indicators, Components and Indicator Selection Criteria to Support the Development of a National Set of Child Well-Being Indicators. Dublin: The National Children's Office. Available at http://www.nco.ie, last accessed at 05.11.2005.

Broswimmer F. J. (2003), 'Ecocide: A Short History of the Mass Extinction of Species'. London: Pluto Press.

Bsteh A. (1996), 'Peace for humanity: principles, problems, and perspectives of the future as seen by Muslims and Christians' New Delhi: Vikas Pub. House.

Bsteh A. and Anawati G. C. (1978), ,Der Gott des Christentums und des Islams' Mödling: Verl. St. Gabriel.

Bsteh A. and Dupré W. (2007), ,Christian faith in dialogue with Islam. Lectures, questions, interventions.' Mödling St. Gabriel Publ.

Bsteh A. and Khoury A. Th. (1994), 'Der Islam als Anfrage an christliche Theologie und Philosophie' Mödling : Verlag St. Gabriel.

Bullock B. and Firebaugh G. (1990), 'Guns and Butter? The Effect of Military, Economic and Social Development in the Third World'. Journal of Political and Military Sociology, 18:231-266.

Burns T. J. et al. (1994), 'Demography, Development, and Deforestation in a World-System Perspective'. International Journal of Comparative Sociology, 35(3-4):221-239.

Burns T. J., Kentor J. D. and Jorgenson, A. (2002), 'Trade Dependence, Pollution and Infant Mortality in Less Developed Countries: A Study of World-System Influences on National Outcomes' Department of Sociology, University of Utah, available at: http://www.irows.ucr.edu/andrew/papers/tradedep.doc.

Burns T. J., Kick E. L. and Davis B. L. (2003), 'Theorizing and Rethinking Linkages between the Natural Environment and the Modern World-System: Deforestation in the Late 20th Century' Journal of World-Systems Research, available at: http://jwsr.ucr.edu/index.phpVol. 9, Num. 2 (Summer 2003): 357 – 390.

Caminada K. and Goudswaard K. (2000), 'International trends in income inequality and social policy' ISSA Conference, Helsinki 'Social Security in the global village' available at: http://www.issa.int/pdf/helsinki2000/topic4/2goudswaard.PDF.

Canoy M. and F. Lerais (2007), Beyond GDP, Overview paper for the Beyond GDP conference. Bureau of European Policy Advisers (BEPA), European Commission. Available at: www.beyond-gdp.eu/download/bgdp-bp-bepa.pdf.

Cantanero, D., Pascual, M. and Sarabia, J.M. (2005) 'Effects of Income Inequality on Population Health: New Evidence from the European Community Household Panel. Applied Economics, 37, 87-91.

Caporaso J. A. (1978), 'Dependence, Dependency, and Power in the Global System: A Structural and Behavioral Analysis' International Organization, 32: 13 - 43.

Cardoso F. H. and Faletto E. (1971), 'Dependencia y desarrollo en América Latina' Mexico D.F.: editorial siglo I.

Carroll E. (2000), 'Globalization and social policy: social insurance quality, institutions, trade exposure and deregulation in 18 OECD nations, 1965-1995' ISSA Conference, Helsinki 'Social Security in the global village' available at: http://www.issa.int/engl/reunion/2000/helsinki/2prog.htm

Castells, M. (1996): "The Information Age: Economy, Society and Culture", Vol. 1; The Rise of the Networked Society, Blackwell Publishers Inc, USA.

Cervellati M. and Sunde U. (2005), "Human capital formation, life expectancy, and the process of development" American Economic Review, 95 (5): 1653-1672 DEC 2005

Chan St. (1989), 'Income Inequality among LDCs: A Comparative Analysis of Alternative Perspectives.' International Studies Quarterly, 33, pps. 45-65.

Chase-Dunn Ch. (1999), 'Globalization: A World-Systems Perspective' Journal of World-Systems Research, available at: http://jwsr.ucr.edu/index.phpV, 2: 165 – 185.

Chase-Dunn Ch. K. (1975), 'The Effects of International Economic Dependence on Development and Inequality: a Cross - national Study' American Sociological Review, 40: 720 - 738.

Chase-Dunn Ch. K. (1983), 'The Kernel of the Capitalist World Economy: Three Approaches' in 'Contending Approaches to World System Analysis' (Thompson W.R. (Ed.)), pp. 55 - 78, Beverly Hills: Sage.

Chase-Dunn Ch. K. (1984), 'The World - System Since 1950: What Has Really Changed?' in 'Labor in the Capitalist World - Economy' (Bergquist Ch. (Ed.)), pp. 75 - 104, Beverly Hills: Sage.

Chase-Dunn Ch. K. (1991), 'Global Formation: Structures of the World Economy' London, Oxford and New York: Basil Blackwell.

Chase-Dunn Ch. K. (1992), 'The Changing Role of Cities in World Systems' in 'Waves, Formations and Values in the World System' (Bornschier V. and Lengyel P. (Eds.)), pp. 51 - 87, New Brunswick and London: Transaction Publishers.

Chase-Dunn Ch. K. (1992), 'The National State as an Agent of Modernity' Problems of Communism, January - April: 29 - 37.

Chase-Dunn Ch. K. (1996), 'Conflict among Core States: World System Cycles and Trends' Department of Sociology, Johns Hopkins University, available from the Internet at http://csf.colorado.edu/wsystems/archive/papers/c-dandhall/warprop.htm.

Chase-Dunn Ch. K. (2000), 'World State Formation: Historical Processes and Emergent Necessity' Department of Sociology, Johns Hopkins University, available from the Internet at http://www.jhu.edu/.

Chase-Dunn Ch. K. (2005), 'Social Evolution and the Future of World Society' in 'The Future of World Society' (Herkenrath M. et al. (Eds.)) pp. 13 – 37; Sociological Institute, University of Zurich: Intelligent Book Production.

Chase-Dunn Ch. K. (Ed.), (1982), 'Socialist States in the World System' Beverly Hills and London: Sage.

Chase-Dunn Ch. K. and Boswell T. (2005), 'Global Democracy: a world systems perspective'. Forthcoming at Protosociology, available at: http://www.irows.ucr.edu/cd/courses/181/globdemo.htm

Chase-Dunn Ch. K. and Grimes P. (1995), 'World - Systems Analysis' Annual Review of Sociology, 21: 387 - 417.

Chase-Dunn Ch. K. and Hall Th. D. (1997), 'Rise and Demise. Comparing World - Systems' Boulder, Colorado: Westview Press.

Chase-Dunn Ch. K. and Podobnik B. (1995), 'The Next World War: World - System Cycles and Trends' Journal of World Systems Research 1, 6 (unpaginated electronic journal at World Wide Web site of the World System Network: http://csf.colorado.edu/wsystems/jwsr.html).

Chase-Dunn Ch., Kawano Y., and Brewer B. (2000), 'Trade Globalization since 1795: waves of integration in the world-system' American Sociological Review, 65: 77–95 (February).

Chenery H. and Syrquin M. (1975), 'Patterns of Development 1950-1970'. Oxford, London and New York: Oxford U. Press.

Clark R. (1992), 'Economic Dependency and Gender Differences in Labor - Force Sectoral Change in Non - Core Nations' Sociological Quarterly, 33, 1: 83 - 98.

Clark R. et al. (1991), 'Culture, Gender, and Labor - Force Participation. A Cross - National Study' Gender and Society, 5, 1: 47-66.

Clauss G. and Ebner H. (1978), 'Grundlagen der Statistik. Fuer Psychologen, Paedagogen und Soziologen' Berlin: Volk and Wissen.

Clesse A. (2008), The enlargement mess, Europe's World, 1, 2008, available freely online at: http://www.europesworld.org/EWSettings/Article/tabid/78/Default.aspx?Id=bc779ce3-5e4c-41fd-ba3a-8a48e0f4cff5

Collins, W. J. and Williamson J. G., (1999): "Capital Goods Prices, Global Capital Markets and Accumulation: 1870-1950" NBER Working Paper 7145.

Commonwealth of Australia, Office of the Status of Women (2000), 'Women and Poverty' available at: http://osw.dpmc.gov.au/content/publications/beijing/a_poverty.html.

Cook S. and H.J. Kwon (2007), Social Protection in East Asia in: Global Social Policy 7(2); London et altera: Sage, 2007: 223-229.

Coppel J. et al. (2001), 'Trends in Immigration and Economic Consequences' OECD Economics Department Working Papers, 284, available at: http://ideas.uqam.ca/ideas/data/Papers/oedoecdec284.html.

Corbetta R. and Dixon W. J. (2004), 'Multilateralism, Major Powers, and Militarized Disputes' Political Research Quarterly, vol. 57, no. 1, pp. 5-14.

Cornia G. A. (Ed.)(1993), 'Economies in Transition Studies, Regional Monitoring Report, 1' Firenze: UNICEF.

Cornia G. A. (Ed.)(1994), 'Economies in Transition Studies, Regional Monitoring Report, 2' Firenze: UNICEF.

Cornia G. A. (Ed.)(2004), 'Inequality, growth, and poverty in an era of liberalization and globalization' Oxford; New York: Oxford University Press.

Cornia G. A. and Kiiski S. (2002), 'Trends in Income Distribution in the Post WWII Period: Evidence and Interpretation' UNI WIDER available at http://www.wider.unu.edu/conference/conference-2001-1/cornia%20and%20kiiski.pdf.

Cornia G. A. and Paniccia R. (Eds.)(2000), 'Mortality crisis in transitional economies' Oxford; New York: Oxford University Press.

Cornia G. A., Addison T. and Kiiski S. (2003), 'Income Distribution Changes and their Impact in the Post-World War II Period' United Nations University, WIDER Institute Helsinki, Discussion Paper Wdp, 2003, no. 28, (entire).

Cornwall J. and Cornwall W. (2001), 'Capitalist Development in the Twentieth Century: An Evolutionary-Keynesian Analysis' Cambridge: Cambridge University Press, 2001.

Crafts N. (2000), 'Globalization and Growth in The Twentieth Century, IMF Working Paper, WP/00/44, International Monetary Fund, . Available at: http://www.imf.org/external/pubs/ft/wp/2000/wp0044.pdf

Crenshaw E. M. (1991), 'Foreign Investment as a Dependent Variable: Determinants of Foreign and Capital Penetration in Developing Nations, 1967 - 1978' Social Forces, 69, 4: 1169 - 1182.

Crenshaw E. M. (1992), 'Cross - National Determinants of Income Inequality: A Replication and Extension Using Ecological-Evolutionary Theory' Social Forces, 71: 339 - 363.

Crenshaw E. M. (1993), 'Polity, Economy and Technology: Alternative Explanations for Income Inequality.' Social forces, vol. 71, no. 3, pp. 807.

Crenshaw E. M. (1995), 'Democracy and Demographic Inheritance: The Influence of Modernity and Proto-Modernity on Political and Civil Rights, 1965 to 1980.' American sociological review, vol. 60, no. 5, pp. 702 ff.

Crenshaw E. M. and Ansari A. (1994), 'The Distribution of Income Across National Populations: Testing Multiple Paradigms.' Social Science Research, 23, 1, March, pps. 1-22.

Crenshaw E. M. and Jenkins J. C. (1996), 'Social Structure and Global Climate Change: Sociological Propositions Concerning the Greenhouse Effect.' Sociological focus, 1996, vol. 29, no. 4, pp. 341

Crenshaw E. M. and Oakey, D. R. (1998), ''Jump-Starting' Development: Hyperurbanization as a Long-Term Economic Investment.' Sociological focus, vol. 31, no. 4, pp. 321.

Crenshaw E. M.; Ameen A. Z.; and Christenson. M. (1997), 'Population Dynamics and Economic Development: Age-Specific Population Growth Rates and Economic Growth in Developing Countries, 1965 to 1990.' American sociological review, vol. 62, no. 6, pp. 974.

Crenshaw E. M.; Christenson M.; Oakey D. R. (2000), 'Demographic Transition in Ecological Focus.' American Sociological Review, vol. 65, no. 3, pp. 371.

Cutler et al. (1990), "An Aging Society: Opportunity or Challenge?" Brooking Papers on Economic Activity vol. 1 (1990).

Daguerre A. (2005), Hartz IV international. Hilfsbedürftige sollen arbeiten - und dankbar sein, Le Monde Diplomatique, August 2005, available at: http://www.monde-diplomatique.de/pm/2005/07/08/a0016.text.name,askBxa7Pw.n,0

Dasgupta P. (1995), 'An Inquiry into Well-Being and Destitution.' New York and Oxford: Oxford University Press.

Davis B. L., Kick E. L. and Burns T. J. (2004), 'Change Scores, Composites and Reliability Issues in Cross-National Development Research' International Journal of Comparative Sociology, vol. 45, no. 5, pp. 299-314.

Deininger K. and Squire L. (1996), 'A New Data Set Measuring Inequality", World Bank Economnic Review, vol. 10, pp. 565-591.

Delacroix J. and Ragin Ch. (1981), 'Structural Blockage: A Cross - National Study of Economic Dependency, State Efficacy, and Underdevelopment' American Journal of Sociology, 86, 6: 1311 - 1347.

Deutsch K. W. (1979), 'Tides Among Nations' New York: Free Press.

Deutsch K. W. (1982), 'Major Changes in Political Science' in 'International Handbook of Political Science' (Andrews W.G. (Ed.)), pp. 9 - 33, Westport, Con.: Greenwood Press.

Diez-Nicolás J. (2007), "Value Systems of Elites and Publics in the Mediterranean: Convergence and Divergence" in "Values and Perceptions of the Islamic and Middle Eastern Publics" (Moaddel M. (Ed.)), pp. 47 - 70, Houndmills, Basingstoke, Hampshire: Palgrave Macmillan.

Dittrich M. (2006), 'Muslims in Europe: addressing the challenges of radicalisation'. European Policy Centre in strategic partnership with the King Baudouin Foundation and the Comagnia di San Paolo, Brussels, available at http://www.theepc.be/TEWN/pdf/602431467_EPC%20Working%20Paper%2023%20Muslims%20in%20Europe.pdf

Dixon W. J. (1984), 'Trade Concentration, Economic Growth and the Provision of Basic Human Needs' Social Science Quarterly, 65: 761 - 774.

Dixon W. J. and Boswell T. (1996), 'Dependency, Disarticulation, and Denominator Effects: Another Look at Foreign Capital Penetration'. The american journal of sociology, 1996, vol. 102, no. 2, pp. 543.

Dixon W. J. and Boswell T. (1996), 'Differential Productivity, Negative Externalities, and Foreign Capital Dependency: Reply to Firebaugh.' The american journal of sociology, vol. 102, no. 2, pp. 576.

Dollar D. (2005), 'Globalization, Poverty, and Inequality since 1980.' World Bank Research Observer, vol. 20, no. 2, pp. 145-175.

Dollar D. and Kraay A. (2000), 'Growth Is Good for the Poor'. Development Research Group, The World Bank, available at: http://www.worldbank.org/research /growth /pdfiles/growthgoodforpoor.pdf; third (final) draft available at: http://www.worldbank.org/research/growth/pdfiles/GIGFTP3.pdf.

Dollar D. and Kraay A. (2001), 'Trade, Growth and Poverty' Finance and Development, 38, 3, available at: http://www.imf.org/external/pubs/ft/fandd/2001/09/dollar.htm.

Dollar, D and A. Kraay (2001): "Trade, Growth and Poverty", World Bank, Mimeo.

Dollar, D. and A. Kraay, (2002): "Institutions, Trade and Growth" Paper prepared for the Carnegie-Rochester Conference Series on Public Policy.

Dollar, D., and P. Collier (2001): Globalization, Growth and Poverty: Building an inclusive World Economy. Oxford: Oxford University Press.

Donno D. and Russett B. (2004), 'Islam, Authoritarianism, and Female Empowerment: What Are the Linkages?' World Politics, vol. 56, no. 4, pp. 582-607.

Dowrick, S. and Akmal M. (2001), 'Contradictory Trends in Global Income Inequality: A Tale of Two Biases", available from http://ecocomm.anu.edu.au/economics/staff/dowrick/dowrick.html .

Dreher A. (2005), Does Globalization Affect Growth? Empirical Evidence from a New Index. Department of Economics, University of Konstanz, Unpublished Manuscript.

Dunning J. H. (2001), 'Global Capitalism at Bay?' London and New York: Palgrave Macmillan.

Easterly W. (2001), 'The Lost Decades. Developing Countries' Stagnation In Spite of Policy Reform, 1980-98", Journal of Economic Growth, vol. 6, No.2, pp. 135-157.

Easterly W. (2002), 'Inequality does Cause Underdevelopment: New evidence'. Center for Global Development, Working Paper 1, January 2002, available at: http://www.cgdev.org/wp/cgd_wp001_rev.pdf.

Easterly W. G. (2000), 'The Middle Class Consensus and Economic Development'. (May 2000). World Bank Policy Research Working Paper No. 2346. Available at SSRN: http://ssrn.com/abstract=630718

Eckel C. (2003): "Labor Market Adjustments to Globalization: Unemployment versus Relative Wages". North American Journal of Economics and Finance, 14 (2): 173-88.

Ehrenfels O. R. L. W. Freiherr (1941), ,Mother-right in India, by Baron Omar Rolf Ehrenfels, PH.D." [London] H. Milford: Oxford university press

Ehrhardt-Martinez K.; Crenshaw E. M.; and Jenkins J. C. (2002), 'Deforestation and the Environmental Kuznets Curve: A Cross-National Investigation of Intervening Mechanisms'. Social Science Quarterly, Volume 83, Number 1, March, pp. 226-243 .

Elsenhans H. (1983), 'Rising mass incomes as a condition of capitalist growth: implications for the world economy' International Organization, 37, 1: 1 - 39.

Elsenhans H. (1992), 'Equality and development' Dhaka, Bangladesh: Centre for Social Studies: Distributor, Dana Publishers.

Elsenhans H. (1993), 'Europe-India: new perspectives in changing power structures in the international system.' [New Delhi]: Friedrich Ebert Stiftung.

Elsenhans H. (1996), 'State, class, and development'. New Delhi: Radiant Publishers.

Elsenhans H. (1999), 'A balanced European architecture: enlargement of the European Union to Central Europe and the Mediterranean = Une architecture européenne équilibré: l'ouverture de l'Union européenne vers l'Europe centrale et la Méditerranée' Paris: Publisud.

Elsenhans H. (Ed.)(1978), 'Migration und Wirtschaftsentwicklung' Frankfurt a.M.: Campus.

Elsenhans H. (Ed.)(1979), 'Agrarreform in der Dritten Welt' Frankfurt/Main; New York: Campus-Verlag.

Erdenir B. (2006), 'The Future of Europe: Islamophobia?' Secretariat General for EU Affairs (EUSG) of Turkey, available at: http://www.turkishpolicy.com/default. asp?show=fall_2005_erdenir (Turkish Policy Quarterly, 2006).

Esping-Andersen G. (1990), The Three Worlds of Welfare Capitalism. London: Polity Press.

Esping-Andersen G. (1996), Welfare States in Transition. London: Sage.

Esping-Andersen G. (1999/2000), Social Foundations of Postindustrial Economies, Oxford: Oxford University Press: 34 f.

Etzioni A. (1968), "The active society: a theory of societal and political processes." London, Collier-Macmillan; New York, Free Press

Etzioni A. (1996), "The new golden rule: community and morality in a democratic society" New York: Basic Books

European Commission (2000), Communication to the Council, the European Parliament, the Economic and Social Committee and the Committee of the Regions. Social Policy Agenda; Brussels 28.6.2000; COM(2000) 379 final.

European Commission (2003), Joint Report on Social Exclusion Summarising the Results of the Examination of the National Action Plans for Social Inclusion (2003-2005). Brussels.

European Commission (2003), Joint Report on Social Exclusion Summarising the Results of the Examination of the National Action Plans for Social Inclusion (2003-2005). Brussels.

European Commission (2005), A new start for the Lisbon Strategy, available at: http://europa.eu.int/growthandjobs/index_en.htm.

European Commission (2006), Joint report on Social Protection and Social Inclusion 2006, Directorate-General for Employment, Social Affairs and Equal Opportunities.

European Commission (2007), „Growing Regions, growing Europe. Fourth report on economic and social cohesion." Available at: http://ec.europa.eu/regional_ policy/sources /docoffic/official/repor_en.htm and http://ec.europa.eu/regional_policy/sources/docoffic/ official/reports/cohesion4/index_en.htm (including main regional data)

European Commission (2007), Joint report on Social Protection and Social Inclusion 2007, Directorate-General for Employment, Social Affairs and Equal Opportunities.

European Commission (2008), Proposal for a Joint Report on Social Protection and Social Inclusion 2008, COM (2008) 42 final, Directorate-General for Employment, Social Affairs and Equal Opportunities.

European Roundtable of Industrialists, ERT (2001), 'European Pensions. An Appeal for Reform'. Pension Schemes that Europe Can Really Afford' Brussels: ERT.

Evans P. B. and Timberlake M. (1980), 'Dependence, Inequality, and the Growth of the Tertiary: A Comparative Analysis of Less Developed Countries.' American Sociological Review, 45, August, pps. 531-552.

Fahey T. Et al. (2005), 'First European Quality of Life Survey: Income inequalities and deprivation' European Foundation for the Improvement of Living and Wokring Conditions, available at: http://www.eurofound.eu.int/pubdocs/2005/93/en/1/ef0593en. pdf

Fain H. D. et al. (1997), 'World-System Position, Tropical Climate, National Development, and Infant Mortality: A Cross-National Analysis of 86 Countries'. Human Ecology Review, 3:197-203.

Farell M.J. (1957), The measurement of productive efficiency, Journal of the Royal Statistical Society, Series A – General, 120, part 3, 253-281.

Ferrara, M., A. Hemerijck and M. Rhodes (2000), The future of social Europe: Recasting work and welfare in the new economy, Oeiras, Celta Editora.

Fiala R. (1992), 'The International System, Labor Force Structure, and the Growth and Distribution of National Income, 1950 - 1980' Sociological Perspectives, 35, 2: 249 - 282.

Field F., Member of Parliament, and Cacket B. (2007), Welfare isn't working. Child Poverty, Freely available at http://www.reform.co.uk/filestore /pdf/070611%20Welfare%20isn't% 20working%20-%20child%20poverty.pdf

Finance and Development (2002): "The Globalization of Finance", March 2002, Volume 39, Number 1.

Firebaugh G. (1992), 'Growth Effects of Foreign and Domestic Investment' American Journal of Sociology, 98: 105 - 130.

Firebaugh G. (1996), 'Does Foreign Capital Harm Poor Nations? New Estimates Based on Dixon and Boswells Measures of Capital Penetration' American Journal of Sociology, 2, 102: 563 - 575.

Firebaugh G. (1999), 'Empirics of World Income Inequality", American Journal of Sociology, vol.104, pp. 1597-1630.

Firebaugh G. (2000), 'The Trend in Between-Nation Income Inequality' Annual Review of Sociology, vol. 26, pp. 323-496.

Firebaugh G. (2002), 'The Myth of Growing Global Income Inequality' Paper, presented at Oxford University, available at http://www.nuff.ox.ac.uk/rc28/Papers/Firebaugh.PDF.

Firebaugh G. (2003), 'New geography of global income inequality' Cambridge, Mass.: Harvard University Press.

Firebaugh G. and Beck F. D. (1994), 'Does Economic Growth Benefit the Masses?' American Sociological Review, 59:631-653.

Firebaugh G. and Goesling B. (2004), 'Accounting for the Recent Decline in Global Income Inequality' American Journal of Sociology, vol. 110, no. 2, pp. 283-312.

Flechsig St. (1987), 'Raul Prebisch - ein bedeutender Oekonom Lateinamerikas und der Entwicklungslaender' Wirtschaftswissenschaft, 35, 5: 721 - 741.

Flechsig St. (1994), 'Raúl Prebisch (1901 - 1986) - ein bedeutendes theoretisches Vermaechtnis oder kein alter Hut' Utopie kreativ, 45/46, Juli/August: 136 - 155.

Flechsig St. (2000), 'The Heritage of Raúl Prebisch for a Humane World' in 'Globalization, Liberation Theology and the Social Sciences. An Analysis of the Contradictions of Modernity at the Turn of the Millennium' (Andreas Müller OFM et al.) Commack, New York: Nova Science.

Förster, M. and D'Ercole, M. (2005), Income Distribution and Poverty in OECD Countries in the Second Half of the 1990s. OECD Social, Employment and Migration Working Papers. Paris France, OECD.

Fox J. (2000), 'Religious Causes of Discrimination against Ethno-Religious Minorities'. International Studies Quarterly, Vol. 44, No. 3 (Sep., 2000), pp. 423-450.

Fox L. and Palmer E. (2000), 'New approaches to multi-pillar pension systems: What in the world is going on?' ISSA Conference, Helsinki 'Social Security in the global village' available at: http://www.issa.int/engl/reunion/2000/helsinki/2prog.htm

Frank A. G. (1992), 'Economic ironies in Europe: a world economic interpretation of East - West European politics' International Social Science Journal, 131, February: 41 - 56.

Frank A. G. (1994), 'World System History". University of Amsterdam, 23 April 1994, Prepared for presentation at the annual meeting of The New England Historical Association, Bentley College, Waltham, Mass., April 23, 1994, available at: http://www.hartford-hwp.com/archives/10/034.html.

Frank A. G. (1998), 'ReOrient: Global Economy in the Asian Age'. Ewing, USA: University of California Press.

Frank A. G. and Frank - Fuentes M. (1990), 'Widerstand im Weltsystem' Vienna: Promedia.

Frank A. G. and Gills B. (Eds.)(1993), 'The World System: Five Hundred or Five Thousand Years?' London and New York: Routledge, KeganandPaul.

Franzmeyer F./Brücker H. (1997), 'Europäische Union—Osterweiterung u. Arbeitskräfteemigration' - DIW Berlin, 1997 (DIW-Wochenbericht 5).

Frey R. S. and Field C. (2000), 'The determinants of Infant Mortality in the Less Developed Countries: A Cross-National Test of Five Theories' Social Indicators Research, 52, no. 3 (2000): 215-234.

Fukuyama F. (1991), 'Liberal Democracy as a Global Phenomenon' PS: Political Science and Politics (Washington D.C.), 24, 4: 659 - 664.

Futagami K. and T. Nakajima (2001), "Population Aging and Economic Growth". Journal of Macroeconomics 23, 31-44

Gabel S.G. and Kamerman S.B. (2006), Investing in Children: Public Commitment in Twenty-One Industrialized Countries, Social Service Review 80(2), 239-263.

Galbraith J. K. (2002), 'A perfect crime: global inequality' Daedalus, 2002, vol. 131, no. 1, pp. 11-25.

Galbraith J. K. and Berner M. (2001), 'Inequality and industrial change: a global view' Cambridge; New York: Cambridge University Press.

Galbraith J. K. and Kum H. (2005), 'Estimating the Inequality of Household Incomes: A Statistical Approach to the Creation of a Dense and Consistent Global Data Set.' The Review of Income and Wealth, Volume 51, Number 1, March, pp. 115-143.

Galbraith J. K. and Pitts J. W. (2002), 'Is Inequality Decreasing?' Foreign Affairs, 2002, vol. 81, no. 4, pp. 178-183.

Galbraith, J. K., D. R. Chowdhury and S. Shrivastava (2004): "Pay Inequality in the Indian Manufacturing, 1979-1998", UTIP Working Paper 2004:28.

Galtung J. (1969), 'Violence, Peace and Peace Research. Journal of Peace Research, 6 (3), 167-191.

Galtung J. (1971), 'A Structural Theory of Imperialism' Journal of Peace Research, 8, 2: 81 - 118.

Galtung J. (1994), 'Human Rights in Another Key'. Cambridge, United Kingdom: Polity Press.

Galtung J., Chase-Dunn, Ch. K. et al. (1985), 'Export Dependence and Economic Growth: a Reformulation and Respecification' Social Forces, Vol. 64, pp. 857 - 894.

Ghobarah H. et al. (2001), 'The Political Economy of Comparative Human Misery and Well-being' American Political Science Association Annual Meeting, San Francisco, available at: http://www.yale.edu/unsy/brussett/PoliticalEconomy(Dale_APSA)12.03.01.pdf.

Gholami R., Lee S. Y. T and Heshmati A. (2003), 'The Causal Relationship between Information and Communication Technology and Foreign Direct Investment' Helsinki: Wider Discussion Paper Wdp, 2003, no. 30, (entire)

Gierus J. (1998), 'Russia's Road to Modernity' Warsaw: Instytut Studiow Politycznych, Polskiej Akademii Nauk.

Giffin, K. (2003): "Economic Globalization and Institutions of Global Governance", Development and Change 34(5): 789-807.

Gissinger R. and Gleditsch N. P. (1999), 'Globalization and Conflict: Welfare, Distribution, and Political unrest' Journal of World-Systems Research, available at: http://jwsr.ucr.edu/index.php5, 2: 327–365.

Goesling B. (2001), 'Changing Income Inequalities within and between Nations: New Evidence' American Sociological Review, 66, 5, October: 745–761.

Goesling B. and Firebaugh G. (2004), 'The Trend in International Health Inequality' Population and Development Review, Volume 30, Number 1, March 2004, pp. 131-146.

Gogh I. (2001), Globalization and Regional Welfare Regimes. The East Asian Case, in: Global Social Policy; London et altera: Sage, 2001; 1(2): 163-189).

Goldfrank W. L. (1990), 'Fascism and the Great Transformation' in 'The Life and Work of Karl Polanyi' (Polanyi - Levitt K. (Ed.)), Montreal: Black Rose (quoted from the author's typescript).

Goldfrank W. L. (1999), 'Beyond Cycles of Hegemony: Economic, Social and Military Factors' in 'The Future of Global Conflict' (Bornschier V. and Chase-Dunn Ch. K. (Eds.)), pp. 66 - 76, London, Thousand Oaks and New Delhi: Sage Publications.

Goldfrank W. L. (1999), 'Ecology and the World-System' Westport, CT: Greenwood Press.

Goldstein J. S. (1985), 'Basic Human Needs: The Plateau Curve' World Development, 13, 5: 595 - 609.

Goldstein J. S. (1985), 'Kondratiev Waves as War Cycles' International Studies Quarterly, 29, 4: 411 - 444.

Goldstein J. S. (1988), 'Long Cycles. Prosperity and War in the Modern Age' New Haven and London: Yale University Press.

Goldstein J. S. (1996), 'International Relations' New York, N.Y.: Harper Collins, College Publishers, 2nd edition.

Goldstein J. S. (2001), 'War and Gender: How Gender Shapes the War System and Vice Versa' Cambridge: at the University Press, http://www.american.edu/academic.depts/sis/goldtext/wargendr.htm.

Goldstein J. S. (2005), 'The Predictive Power of Long Wave Theory, 1989-2004". Prepared for NATO conference on Kondratiev Waves and Warfare, Covilha, Portugal, Feb. 2005, available at: http://www.joshuagoldstein.com/jgkond.htm .

Gomory, R. E. and W. J. Baumol (2004): "Globalization: prospects, promise, and problems", Journal of Policy Modeling, Vol. 26, pp. 425-438.

Gough I. (2000), Global Capital: Human Needs and Social Policies. London: Palgrave.

Gough I. (2004), Human Well-Being and Social Structures. Relating the Universal and the Local, in: Global Social Policy, 4; London et altera: Sage, 2004:289-311; here: 301).

Gradstein M and Milanovic B. (2004), 'Does Liberte = Egalite? A Survey of the Empirical Links between Democracy and Inequality with Some Evidence on the Transition Economies' Journal of Economic Surveys, Volume 18, Number 4, September 2004, pp. 515-537 .

Gray C. and Weig D. (1999), 'Pension System Issues and Their Relation to Economic Growth' CAER II Discussion paper No. 41, Harvard Institute for International Development, available at: http://www.hiid.harvard.edu/projects/caer/papers/paper41/paper41.html.

Gray C. S. (2005), 'How Has War Changed Since the End of the Cold War?" Parameters. U.S. Army War College Quarterly, Spring 2005: 14-26, available at: http://carlisle-www.army.mil/usawc/Parameters/05spring/gray.htm .

Gregg, P., Washbrook, E., Propper, C. and Burgess, S. (2005), The Effects of a Mother's Return to Work Decision on Child Development in the UK, Economic Journal, 115, 48-80.

Grimes P. and Kentor J. (2003), 'Exporting the Greenhouse: Foreign Capital Penetration and CO_2 Emissions 1980–1996' Journal of World-Systems Research, available at: http://jwsr.ucr.edu/index.phpIX, 2, Summer: 261–275.

Grupp H. and M.E. Mogee (2004), Indicators of National Science and Technology Policy: How Robust are Composite Indicators?, Research Policy 33, 1373-1384.

Gurr T. R. (1994), 'Ethnic conflict in world politics' Boulder: Westview Press.

Gurr T. R. (1994), 'Peoples Against States: Ethnopolitical Conflict and the Changing World System' International Studies Quarterly, 38: 347 - 377.

Gwartney J. et al. (1998), 'The Size and Functions of Government and Economic Growth' Joint Economic Committee Study, United States Congress, http://www.house.gov/jec/growth/function/function.htm.

Hadden K. and London B. (1996), 'Educating Girls in the Third World: The Demographic, Basic Needs, and Economic Benefits'. International journal of comparative sociology, 1996, vol. 37, no. 1/2, pp. 31 .

Hair J.F., B. Black, B. Babib, A.R. Anderson and R.L. Tatham (2006), Multivariate Analysis, New York: Prentice Hall.

Haller M. (2003), 'Soziologische Theorie im systematisch-kritischen Vergleich' Wiesbaden: VS Verlag für Sozialwissenschaften (2. Auflage)

Haller M. (Ed.)(1990), 'Class Structure in Europe. New Findings from East-West Comparisons of Social Structure and Mobility' Armonk, N.Y./ London: Sharpe

Haller M. (Ed.)(2001), 'The Making of the European Union. Contributions of the Social Sciences' Berlin/Heidelberg/New York: Springer Verlag

Haller M. and Richter R. (Ed.)(1994), 'Toward a European Nation? Political Trends in Europe. East and West, Center and Periphery' Armonk, N.Y./London: M. E. Sharpe

Haller M. and Schachner-Blazizek P. (Ed.)(1999), 'Beschäftigung in Europa. Ergebnisse eines interdisziplinären Symposiums des Europaforums Steiermark' Graz: Leykam

Haller M. and Schachner-Blazizek P. (Eds.)(1994), 'Europa wohin? Wirtschaftliche Integration, soziale Gerechtigkeit und Demokratie' Graz: Leykam Verlag

Halliday F. (2000), 'Global governance: prospects and problems' Citizenship Studies, vol.4, n°1, February pp. 19-33.

Harris P. (2004), Social Inclusion, Globalisation and the Commonwealth. in C.J. Finer and P. Smyth (eds), Social Policy ad the Commonwealth. London: Palgrave.

Heidenreich M (1997), 'Wirtschaftsregionen im weltweiten Innovationswettbewerb'. In: Kölner Zeitschrift für Soziologie und Sozialpsychologie, Jg. 49, Nr. 3, S. 500-527. .

Heidenreich M (1998), 'The changing system of European cities and regions'. 'European Planning Studies'. Jg. 6, Nr. 3, S. 315-332. .

Heidenreich M. (2003), 'Territoriale Ungleichheiten im erweiterten Europa.' Kölner Zeitschrift für Soziolo-gie und Sozialpsychologie, Jg. 55, Heft 1, 2003, S. 1ff. .

Heidenreich M. (2004), 'Mittel- und Osteuropa nach der EU-Erweiterung. Eine Gratwanderung zwischen wirtschaftlicher Modernisierung und sozialer Integration' (Vortrag, Bamberg 2004), available at: http://www.uni-bamberg.de/sowi/europastudien/dokumente/modernisierung_mitteleuropa.pdf.

Henderson E. A. (1997), 'Culture or Contiguity: Ethnic Conflict, the Similarity of States, and the Onset of War, 1820-1989'. The Journal of Conflict Resolution, Vol. 41, No. 5 (Oct. 1997), pp. 649-668.

Herrmann P. (2005), Quality and Accessibility of Social Services for Inclusion. General Report: Brussels: Eurodiaconia, 2005.

Herrmann P. (2007a), European Social Model—Existence, Non-Existence or Biased Direction, Aghabullogue/Cork: William Thompson Working Papers, 1; http://wiliam-thompson.ucc.ie.

Herrmann P. (2007b), Person-Oriented Services and Social Services Providers in Comparative European Perspective, New York: Nova, 2007.

Herrmann P. (2007c), Social Professional Activities and the State; New York: Nova, 2007.

Herrmann P. (2008a), Social Quality and Challenges to Global Policy, [working title]; Hong Kong/Taipei: Casa Verde, forthcoming.

Herrmann P. [ed.] (2008b), Contemporary Trends in the Academic World – Between Social Commitment and Market Performance; New York: Nova Science, forthcoming.

Herrmann P. and D. Ryane (2005), Education – Just Another Commodity. Exposing the Rhetoric of «Human Capital» in the Light of Social Quality, in: Herrmann P. (ed.): Utopia between Corrupted Public Responsibility and Contested Modernity. Globalisation and Social Responsibility; New York: Nova Science, 2005: 43-60.

Herrmann P. and Tausch A. (Eds.)(2005), 'Dar al Islam--the Mediterranean, the world system and the wider Europe: the chain of peripheries and the new wider Europe' New York: Nova Science Publishers.

Herrmann P. and Tausch A. (Eds.)(2005), 'Dar al Islam--the Mediterranean, the world system, and the wider Europe: the 'cultural enlargement' of the EU and Europe's identity' New York: Nova Science.

Herrmann P., A. Brandstaetter and C. O'Connell (2007), Defining Social Services – between the particular and the general, Baden-Baden: Nomos.

Hertz E. et al. (1994), 'Social and Environmental Factors and Life Expectancy, Infant Mortality, and Maternal Mortality Rates: Results of a Cross-National Comparison.' Social Science and Medicine, 39:105-114.

Heshmati A. (2003), 'Measurement of a Multidimentional Index of Globalization and its Impact on Income Inequality' Helsinki: WIDER Discussion Paper 2003:69, 36 pages.

Heshmati A. (2003), 'Productivity Growth, Efficiency and Outsourcing in Manufacturing and Service Industries' Journal of Economic Surveys, Volume 17, Number 1, February 2003, pp. 79-112

Heshmati A. (2006), Measurement of a Multidimensional Index of Globalization, Global Economy Journal 6(2), Paper 1.

Heshmati A. (2006a), The World Distribution of Income and Income Inequality: A Review of the Economic Literature, Journal of World Systems Research 12(1), 60-107.

Heshmati A. (2006b), Measurement of a Multidimensional Index of Globalization, Global Economy Journal 6(2), Paper 1.

Heshmati A. (2007), Growth, Inequality and Poverty Relationships, in A. Heshmati and A. Tausch, "Roadmap to Bangalore? Globalization, the EU's Lisbon Process and the Structures of Global Inequality", Nova Science Publishers.

Heshmati A. and A. Tausch (2007), Eds. Roadmap to Bangalore? Globalization, the EU's Lisbon Process and the Structures of Global Inequality, Nova Science Publishers.

Heshmati A. and Addison T. (2003), 'The New Global Determinants of FDI Flows to Developing Countries The Importance of ICT and Democratization' Helsinki: Wider Discussion Paper Wdp, 2003, no. 45, (entire)

Heshmati A. and J-E. Oh (2006), Alternative Composite Lisbon Development Strategy Indices: A Comparison of EU, USA, Japan and Korea, The European Journal of Comparative Economics 3(2), 133-170.

Heshmati, A. (2003): "Measurement of a Multidimensional Globalization and its Impact on Inequality", WIDER Discussion Paper 2003/69, Helsinki 2003/69, Helsinki: UNU-WIDER.

Heshmati, A. (2006): "Measurement of a Multidimensional Index of Globalization", Global Economy Journal 6(2), Paper 1.

Hettne B. (1983), 'The Development of Development Theory' Acta Sociologica, 26, 3 - 4: 247 - 266.

Hettne B. (1989), 'Three Worlds of Crisis for the Nation State' in 'Crisis in Development' (Bablewski Z. and Hettne B. (Eds.)), pp. 45 - 77, Goeteborg: United Nations University: European Perspectives Project 1986 - 87, Peace and Development Research Institute, Gothenburg University, P.A.D.R.I.G.U Papers.

Hettne B. (1994), 'The Political Economy of Post - Communist Development' The European Journal of Development Research, 6, 1, June: 39 - 60.

Hettne B. (1995), 'Development theory and the three worlds: towards an international political economy of development' 2nd ed. Essex, England: Longman Scientific and Technical; New York, NY. Copublished in the United States by John Wiley.

Hettne B. (1995), 'International political economy: understanding global disorder.' Halifax, N.S.: Fernwood Pub.; Cape Town: SAPES SA; Dhaka: University Press Ltd.; London; Atlantic Highlands, N.J.: Zed Books.

Hettne B. (2004), 'In Search of World Order" in 'Global Governance in the 21st Century: Alternative Perspectives on World Order' (Hettne B. and Oden B. (Eds.)), pp. 6–25. Stockholm: Almkvist and Wiksell. Availabla also at: http://www.egdi.gov.se/pdf/study/study2002_2.pdf .

HM Treasury, Federal Ministry of Finance and Ministry of Finance, Sweden (2008), Social Brdges II. The importance of human capital for growth and social inclusion. A joint paper by the Swedish Ministry of Finance, German Ministry of Finance and HM Treasury, Stockholm, Berlin and London, March 2008.

Hofbauer H and Komlosy A. (1994), 'Eastern Europe: From 'Second World' to First or Third World.' Contention, 1994, vol. 3, no. 2, pp. 129 .

Hofbauer H and Komlosy A. (2000), 'Capital Accumulation and Catching-Up Development in Eastern Europe' Review, vol. 23, no. 4, pp. 459-502 .

Holzmann R. (2005), 'Old-age income support in the 21st century: an international perspective on pension systems and reform' Washington, D.C.: World Bank.

Holzmann R. (Ed.)(2001), 'New ideas about old age security: towards sustainable pension systems in the 21st Century' Washington, DC: World Bank, 2001. .

Holzmann R. (Ed.)(2002), 'Pension reform in Europe: process and progress / edited by Robert Holzmann, Mitchell Orenstein, and Michal Rutkowski'. Washington, DC: The World Bank.

Hotelling H. (1933), Analysis of a Complex of Statistical Variables into Principal Components, Journal of Educational Psychology 24, 417-441 and 24, 498-520.

Huang J. (1995), 'Structural Disarticulation and Third World Human Development' International Journal of Comparative Sociology, 36, 3 - 4: 164 - 183.

HUDSON Institute (Vidino L.) (2006), 'Aims and Methods of Europe's Muslim Brotherhood. Current Trends in Islamist Ideology vol. 4, available at: http://www.futureofmuslimworld.com/research/pubID.55/pub_detail.asp

Huntington S. P. (1991), 'The Third Wave: Democratization in the Late Twentieth Century' Norman, Oklahoma: University of Oklahoma Press.

Huntington S. P. (1993), 'The Clash of Civilizations?' Foreign Affairs, Summer: 22-49.

Huntington S. P. (1996), 'The clash of civilizations and the remaking of world order' New York: Simon and Schuster.

Huntington S. P. (2004), "Who are we?: the challenges to America's identity" New York: Simon and Schuster

ILO (2004): "Economic Security for Better World: ILO Socio-Economic Security Programme", Geneva.

Inglehart R. and Carballo M. (1997), 'Does Latin America Exist? (And is there a Confucian Culture?): A Global Analysis of Cross-Cultural Differences' PS: Political Science and Politics, 30, 1, March: 47 - 52.

Inglehart R. T. (1990), "Culture shift in advanced industrial societies" Princeton, N.J.: Princeton University Press

Inglehart R. T. (2007), "The Worldviews of Islamic Publics in Global Perspective" in "Values and Perceptions of the Islamic and Middle Eastern Publics" (Moaddel M. (Ed.)), pp. 25–46, Houndmills, Basingstoke, Hampshire: Palgrave Macmillan.

Inglehart R. T. and Norris P. (2003), 'Rising tide: gender equality and cultural change around the world' Cambridge, UK; New York: Cambridge University Press

Inglehart R. T. and Norris P. (2003), "Rising tide: gender equality and cultural change around the world". Cambridge, UK ; New York: Cambridge University Press, 2003

Inotai A. and Hettne B. (1999), 'Globalism and the new regionalism' New York: St. Martin's Press.

Inotai A. and Hettne B. (2000), 'The new regionalism and the future of security and development'. New York. St. Martin's Press

Intriligator, M. D (2004): "Globalization of the world economy: potential benefits and costs and a net assessment", Journal of Policy Modeling, Vol. 26, Issue 4, pp. 485-498.

Jabber P. (2001), 'Impact of the War on Terror on Certain Aspects of US Policy in the Middle East. A Medium-Term Assessment' Prepared for the United States National Intelligence Council. Available at: http://www.fas.org/irp/nic/jabber_paper.htm.

James, J. (2002): "Technology, Globalization and Poverty", Cheltenham: Edward Elgar.

Jayasuriya K. (2006), Statecraft, Welfare and the Politics of Inclusion, London Palgrave.

Jayasuriya K. (2008), Changing ideas of social policy from the welfare state to the enabling state, University of Western Australia, School of Social Work and Social Policy.

Jessop B. and N-L. Sum (2006), Beyond the Regulation Approach: Putting Capitalist Economies in their Place, Cheltenham/Northampton: Edward Elgar.

Johnson R. B. (1986), 'Income Inequality in the Third World: A Comparison of Three Theories.' International Review of Modern Sociology, 16, pps. 69-81.

Jorgenson A. K. and Rice J. (2005), 'Structural Dynamics of International Trade and Material Consumption: A Cross-National Study of the Ecological Foodprints of Less-Developed Countries' Journal of World-Systems Research, available at: http://jwsr.ucr.edu/index.phpXI, 1, July: 57-77.

Jourdon Ph. (2005), 'Wars on the Borders of Europe, and Socio-Economical Long Cycles' Université de Montpellier, I, UFR de Sciences Economiques, available at http://www.sceco.univ-montp1.fr/webenseignants/poudou/JourdonPhiPort.pdf .

Juchler J. (1992), 'The Socialist Societies: Rise and Fall of a Societal Formation' in 'Waves, Formations and Values in the World System' (Bornschier V. and Lengyel P. (Eds.)), pp. 145 - 174, New Brun-swick (USA), : Transaction Publishers.

Juchler J. (1994), 'Osteuropa im Umbruch: politische, wirtschaftliche und gesellschaftliche Entwicklungen 1989-1993: Totalueberblick und Fallstudien' Zuerich: Seismo Verlag.

Kalecki M. (1972), 'The Last Phase in the Transformation of Capitalism' New York: Monthly Review Press.

Kalecki M. (1979), 'Essays on Developing Economies. With an Introduction by Professor Joan Robinson' Hassocks, Sussex: The Harvester Press.

Kanbur R. (2001), 'Income Distribution and Development' World Development Report background paper at: http://www.worldbank.org/poverty/wdrpoverty/kanbur.htm.

Kanbur R. (2005), 'Growth, Inequality and Poverty: Some Hard Questions' Journal of International Affairs- Columbia University, vol. 58, no. 2, pp. 223-232 .

Kanbur R. and Squire L. (2001), 'The Evolution of Thinking about Poverty: Exploring the Interactions' World Development Report background paper at: http://www.worldbank.org/poverty/wdrpoverty/evolut.pdf.

Kang S.M. (2002), A Sensitivity Analysis of the Korean Composite Environmental Index. Ecological Economics 43, 159-174.

Karatnycky A. (1994), 'Freedom in Retreat' Freedom Review, 25, 1: 4 - 9.

Kasarda J.D. and Crenshaw E.M. (1991), 'Third - World Urbanization. Dimensions, Theories and Determinants' Annual Review of Sociology, 17: 467 - 501.

Katz S. (2006), Indicators for complex innovation systems, Research Policy 35(7), 893-909.

Katzenstein P. (1974), 'Corporatism and Change: Austria, Switzerland and the Politics of Industry" Ithaca, NY: Cornell University Press, 1984; paperback edition 1987.

Kay C. (1989), 'Latin American Theories of Development and Underdevelopment' London and New York: Routledge, Kegan and Paul.

Kay C. (1991), 'Reflections on the Latin American Contribution to Development Theory' Development and Change, 22, 1: 31-68.

Kearney, A. T., Inc., and the Carnegie Endowment for International Peace (2002): "Globalization's Last Hurrah?" Foreign Policy, January/February: 38-51.

Kearney, A. T., Inc., and the Carnegie Endowment for International Peace (2003): "Measuring Globalization: Who's up, who's down?", Foreign Policy, January/February: 60-72.

Kearny A.T. (2001), 'Measuring Globalization' Foreign Policy, at: http://www.foreignpolicy.com/issue_janfeb_2001/atkearney.html.

Kendall P. (2000), 'Interest Rates, Savings and Growth in Guyana' Economics and Programming Department, Carribean Development Bank, available at: http://www.caribank.org/Staff_Pa.nsf/Kendal-IntRates?OpenPage

Kennedy P. (1989), 'The Rise and Fall of the Great Powers. Economic Change and Military Conflict from 1500 to 2000' New York: Vintage Books, paperback edition.

Kennedy P. (1993), 'In Vorbereitung auf das 21. Jahrhundert' Frankfurt a.M.: S. Fischer TB.

Kent G. (1984), 'The political economy of hunger: the silent holocaust' New York: Praeger.

Kent G. (1991), 'The politics of children's survival' New York: Praeger. .

Kent G. (1995), 'Children in the international political economy' Houndmills, Basingstoke, Hampshire: Macmillan Press LTD, New York, N.Y.: St. Martin's Press.

Kentor J. D. (1998), 'The Long-Term Effects of Foreign Investment Dependence on Economic Growth, 1940-1990' American Journal of Sociology, 103, 4, January: 1024-46.

Kentor J. D. (2001), 'The Long Term Effects of Globalization on Income Inequality, Population Growth, and Economic Development' Social Problems, 48, no. 4 (2001): 435-455.

Kentor J. D. (2005), 'Transnational Corporate Power. Expansion, Spatial Distribution, and Concentration, 1962–1998' in 'The Future of World Society' (Herkenrath M. et al. (Eds.)) pp. 81–101; Sociological Institute, University of Zurich: Intelligent Book Production.

Kentor J. D. and Boswell T. (2003), 'Foreign Capital Dependence and Development: A New Direction' American sociological review. 68, no. 2, (2003): 301 ff.

Kentor J. D. and Jang J. S. (2004), 'Yes, There Is a (Growing) Transnational Business Community: A Study of Global Interlocking Directorates 1983-98' International Sociology 19, no. 3 (2004): 355-368.

Kentor J. D. and Woo J. (2000), 'Capital and Coercion: The Economic and Military Processes That Have Shaped the World Economy' New York: Garland Publishing.

Khan, A. R., and C. Riskin (2001): "Inequality and Poverty in China in the Age of Globalization". Oxford: Oxford University Press.

Khoury A. Th. (1980), ‚Toleranz im Islam' München: Kaiser und Grünwald.

Khoury A. Th. (1981), 'Gebete des Islams' Mainz: Matthias Grünewald Verlag, Topos TB.

Khoury A. Th. (1991), 'Was ist los in der islamischen Welt? Die Konflikte verstehen' Freiburg, Basel, Vienna: Herder.

Khoury A. Th. (1994), ‚Christen unterm Halbmond: religiöse Minderheiten unter der Herrschaft des Islam' Freiburg [im Breisgau]: Herder

Khoury A. Th. (2001), ‚Der Islam und die westliche Welt: religiöse und politische Grundfragen' Darmstadt: Primus, 2001

Khoury A. Th. (2002), ‚Mit Muslimen in Frieden leben: Friedenspotentiale des Islam' Würzburg: Echter, 2002.

Khoury A. Th. (2005), ‚Der Koran erschlossen und kommentiert' Patmos

Khoury A. Th. (2007), ‚Der Koran' Guetersloh: Guetersloher Verlagshaus

Khoury A. Th. (2007), ‚Lexikon religiöser Grundbegriffe, Judentum- Christentum – Islam'. Wiesbaden: Marix Verlag

Khoury A. Th. (2008), 'Der *Hadith*. Quelle der islamischen Tradition'. Guetersloher Verlagshaus

Khoury A. Th. (2008), ‚Muhammad, Der Prophet und seine Botschaft'. Freiburg: Herder Verlag

Khoury A. Th. et al. (2006), ‚Islam-Lexikon A-Z' Freiburg: Herder

Kick E. L. and Davis B. L. (2001), 'World-System Structure and Change: An Analysis of Global Networks and Economic Growth Across Two Time Periods' American Behavioral Scientist, vol. 44, no. 10, pp. 1561-1578.

Kick E. L. et al. (1990), 'Militarization and Infant Mortality in the Third World'. Journal of Political and Military Sociology, 18(2):285-305.

Kick E. L. et al. (1995), 'World-System and National Institutional Effects on Infant Mortality in Third World Countries'. International Third World Studies Journal and Review, 7:61-67.

Kick E. L., Davis B. L. and Burns T. J. (1998), 'A Cross-National Analysis of Militarization and Well-Being Relationships in Developing Countries.' Social Science Research, Volume 27, Number 4, December pp. 351 ff. .

Kick E. L., Davis B. L. and Burns T. J. (2000), 'World System Position, National Political Characteristics and Economic Development Outcomes.' Journal of Political and Military Sociology, vol. 28, no. 1, pp. 131 .

Kiljunen K. (1992), 'Finland and the new international division of labour. Foreword by Charles P. Kindleberger.' Houndmills, Basingstoke, Hampshire: Macmillan Press.

Kiljunen K. (2003), 'Global Governance' in 'Globalization: Critical Perspectives' (Kohler G. and Chaves E. Eds.)), pp. 55 – 92; Hauppauge, N.Y.: Nova Science Publishers.

Kinder H. and Hilgemann W. (1978) ‚The Penguin Atlas of World History' 2 volumes. London and Harmondsworth: Penguin Reference Books.

Kindleberger Ch. (1996), 'The World Economy and National Finance in Historical Perspectives' Ann Arbor: University of Michigan Press.

Kindleberger, C., 1996, Manias, panics, and crashes, Wiley, New York.

Kirby P. (2002), 'Celtic tiger in distress: growth with inequality in Ireland' Houndmills, Basingstoke, Hampshire; New York: Palgrave.

Kirby P. (2003), 'Introduction to Latin America: twenty-first century challenges' London; Thousand Oaks, Cal.: SAGE.

Kirby P. (2003), 'Macroeconomic success and social vulnerability: lessons for Latin America from the Celtic Tiger' Santiago, Chile: ECLAC, Special Studies Unit, Executive Secretariat Office.

Kirby P. (2006), 'Vulnerability and Violence. The Impact of Globalization' London and Ann Arbor, Michigan: Pluto Press.

Klein M. et al. (2001), 'Foreign Direct Investment and Poverty Reduction' Globalization Working Paper 2613, The World Bank, Washington D.C. at http://econ.worldbank.org/files/2205_wps2613.pdf .

Klein, L. (2004): "New Growth Centers in This Globalized Economy", Journal of Policy Modeling, Vol. 26.

Klitgaard R. and Fedderke J. (1995), 'Social Integration and Disintegration: An Exploratory Analysis of Cross - Country Data' World Development, 23, 3: 357 - 369.

Köhler G. (1998), 'The Structure of Global Money and World Tables of Unequal Exchange', Journal of World-Systems Research 4: 145:168; online: http://csf.colorado.edu/wsystems/jwsr.html .

Köhler G. (1998), 'Unequal Exchange 1965-1995: World Trend and World Tables', World-Systems Archive, Working Papers, online: http://csf.colorado.edu/wsystems/archive/papers/Köhlertoc.htm.

Köhler G. (1999), 'A Theory of World Income', World-Systems Archive, Working Papers, online: http://csf.colorado.edu/wsystems/archive/papers/Köhler.

Köhler G. (1999), 'Global Keynesianism and Beyond', Journal of World-Systems Research, 5: 225-241, online: http://csf.colorado.edu/wsystems/jwsr.html .

Köhler G. and Tausch A. (2000), 'Global Keynesianism: Unequal exchange and global exploitation'. Huntington NY, Nova Science. ISBN 1-59033-002-1.

Kohli A. et al. (1984), 'Inequality in the Third World: An Assessment of Competing Explanations.' Comparative Political Studies, 17, 3, October, pps. 283-318.

Kolar, V. and Soriano, G. (2000) Parenting in Australian Families. A Comparative Study of Anglo, Torres Strait, Islander and Vietnamese Communities. Australian Institute of Family Studies. Available at http://www.aifs.gov.au/institute/pubs/resrep5.pdf.

Korpi W. and Palme J. (2000), 'Distributive Conflict, Political Mobilization and the Welfare State: Comparative Patterns of Emergence and Retrenchment in Westernized Countries' Swedish Institute for Social Research, Stockholm University, available at: http://www.kub.nl/~fsw_2/home/worschot/rc19/papers/korpi.htm.

Korzeniewicz R. P. and Moran T. P. (1997), 'World Economic Trends in the Distribution of Income, 1965-1992'. American Journal of Sociology, 102, 4, January, pps. 1000-1039.

Krahn H. and Gartreil J. W. (1985), 'Effects of Foreign Trade, Government Spending, and World-System Status on Income Distribution.' Rural Sociology, 50, 2, pps. 181-192.

Kriz J. (1978), 'Statistik in den Sozialwissenschaften' Reinbek: rororo studium.

Krzysztofiak M. and Luszniewicz A. (1979), 'Statystyka' Warsaw: PWE.

Kunzmann P. et al. (1996), ,dtv Atlas zur Philosophie' München: Deutscher Taschenbuch-Verlag.

Kuznets S. (1955), 'Economic Growth and Income Inequality' The American Economic Review, 45, 1: 1 - 28.

Kuznets S. (1976), 'Modern Economic Growth: Rate, Structure and Spread' New Haven, CT: Yale U. Press.

Landesmann M. and Rosati D. (Eds.)(2004), 'Shaping the new Europe: economic policy challenges of European Union enlargement' Houndmills, Basingstoke, Hampshire; New York, N.Y.: Palgrave Macmillan.

Laxer G. (1993), 'Social Solidarity, Democracy and and Global Capitalism' The 1993 Porter Lecture, Canadian Sociology and Anthropology Association, available at: http://www.socsci.mcmaster.ca/soc/porterlectures/laxer.htm.

Lecaillon, J. et al. (1994), 'Income Distribution and Economic Development: An Analytical Survey'. Geneva, Switzerland: International Labor Office.

Lena H. F. and London B. (1993), 'The Political and Economic Determinants of Health Outcomes: A Cross-National Analysis.' International journal of health services, vol. 23, no. 3, pp. 585 .

Lewis - Beck M. S. (1980), 'Applied Regression. An Introduction' Beverly Hills: Sage University Paper.

Lewis B. (1993), ,Islam and the West' New York: Oxford University Press

Lewis B. (2002), 'What went wrong?: Western impact and Middle Eastern response' Oxford; New York: Oxford University Press, 2002

Lewis B. (2003), 'The crisis of Islam: holy war and unholy terror' New York: Modern Library

Lewis Sir W.A. (1978), 'The Evolution of the International Economic Order' Princeton N.J.: Princeton University Press.

Lindbeck A. (2006), Sustainable Social Spending, International Tax and Public Finance, 13(4), 303-324.

Lindert P. H, and Williamson J. G. (2001), 'Does Globalization Make World More Unequal?", National Bureau of Economic Research, Working Paper No. 8228, April.

Lipset S.M. (1994), 'The Social Requisites of Democracy Revisited. 1993 Presidential Address' American Sociological Review, 59, February: 1 - 22.

Lipton M. (1977), 'Why Poor People Stay Poor: Urban Bias in World Development' Cambrige, MA: Harvard University Press.

Lister, R. (2004), Poverty. Cambridge: Polity Press.

Lockwood B. (2001): "How Robust if the Foreign Policy/Kearney Index of globalization?", CSGR Working Paper 79/01.

Lockwood B. (2004), How Robust is the Foreign Policy-Kearney Globalization Index?, The World Economy 27, 507-523. .

Lockwood B. and M. Redoano (2005), 'The CSGR Globalization Index: An Introductory Guide' CSGR Working Paper 155/04.

London B. (1987), 'Structural Determinants of Third World Urban Change: An Ecological and Political Economic Analysis' American Sociological Review, 52: 28 - 43.

London B. (1988), 'Dependence, Distorted Development, and Fertility Trends in Non-Core Nations: A Structural Analysis of Cross-National Data.' American Sociological Review, 53, 4(August 1988):606-618.

London B. (1990), 'National Politics, International Dependency, and Basic Needs Provision: A Cross-National Analysis'. Social forces, 1990, vol. 69, no. 2, pp. 565 .

London B. and Robinson T. (1989), 'The Effects of International Dependence on Income Inequality and Political Violence.' American Sociological Review, 54, April, pps. 305-308.

London B. and Ross R. J. S. (1995), 'The Political Sociology of Foreign Direct Investment: Global Capitalism and Capital Mobility, 1965–1980' International Journal of Comparative Sociology, 36, 3 - 4: 198 - 218.

London B. and Smith D. A. (1988), 'Urban Bias, Dependence, and Economic Stagnation in Noncore Nations' American Sociological Review, 53: 454 - 463.

London B. and Williams B. A. (1988), 'Multinational Corporate Penetration, Protest, and Basic Needs Provision in Non - Core Nations: A Cross - National Analysis' Social Forces, 66, 3: 747 - 773.

London B. and Williams B. A. (1990), 'National Politics, International Investment, and Basic Needs Provisions: A Cross-National Analysis'. Social Forces, 69:565-584.

London B., Bradshaw Y. and Kim Y. J. (1993), 'Transnational Economic Linkages, the State, and Dependent Development in South Korea, 1966-1988: A Time-Series Analysis.' Social Forces, 72, 2(December 1993):315-345.

Lopez G. A. and Stohl M. (1989), 'Dependence, Development, and State Repression' Westport, CT: Greenwood Press.

Luttwak E. (1999), 'Turbo-Capitalism. Winners and Losers in the Global Economy' New York: Harper Perennial.

Maddison, A. (2001): "The World Economy: A Millennial Perspective". OECD Development Centre Studies. Paris: OECD.

Maddison, A.. (2000) The World Economy: A Millennial Perspective. Paris: Organisation for Economic Cooperation and Development (Development Centre Studies).

Mahler V.A. (2001), Economic Globalization, Domestic Politics and Income Inequality in the Developed Countries: A Cross-National Analysis, Luxembourg Income Study Working Paper 2001:273. Luxembourg.

Mandelbaum K. and Schneider K. (1945), "The industrialisation of backward areas" Oxford: B. Blackwell

Manning, S. (1999): "Introduction (to Special Issue on Globalization)". Journal of World-Systems Research, 5 (2): 137-41.

Martin W. and Wallerstein I. (Eds.)(1990), 'Semiperipheral States in the World-Economy' Westport, CT: Greenwood Press.

McCallum C. (1999), 'Globalisation, Developments and Trends in the New International Division of Labour' Centre for International Business Studies at South Bank University, London, available at: http://www.sbu.ac.uk/cibs/pdf/19-99.pdf.

McCarthy, I and A. Anagnostou (2004): "The impact of outsourcing on the transaction costs and boundaries of manufacturing", Int. J. Production Economics 88 (2004) 61–71.

McKinnon R. I. (1973), 'Money and Capital in Economic Development', Brookings Institution, Washington, D.C.

Meier G.M. and Seers D. (Eds.)(1984), 'Pioneers in Development' New York and Oxford: Oxford University Press.

Melchior A., Telle, K., and Wiig, H. (2000), 'Globalisation and Inequality: World Income Distribution and Living Standards, 1960-1998, Royal Norwegian Ministry of Foreign Affairs, Studies on Foreign Policy Issues, Report 6B: 2000. Available at: http://odin.dep.no/archive/udvedlegg/01/01/rev__016.pdf.

Metcalfe J. St. (1998), "Evolutionary Economics and Creative Destruction (Graz Schumpeter Lectures, 1)". London and New York: Routledge

Meyer W. H. (1996. 'Human Rights and MNCs: Theory versus Quantitative Analysis'. Human Rights Quarterly, 18: 368 – 397.

Microsoft Excel (1992), 'Microsoft Excel. Verzeichnis der Funktionen' Microsoft Corporation.

Midgal J. S. (2001), 'State in Society: Studying How States and Societies Transform and Constitute One Another ' Cambridge: Cambridge University Press.

Midlarsky M. I. (1982), 'Scarcity and Inequality: Prologue to the Onset of Mass Revolution. The Journal of Conflict Resolution, Vol. 26, No. 1 (Mar. 1982), pp. 3-38.

Midlarsky M. I. (1998), 'Democracy and Islam: Implications for Civilizational Conflict and the Democratic PeaceDemocracy and Islam: Implications for Civilizational Conflict and the Democratic Peace' International Studies Quarterly, Vol. 42, No. 3 (Sep., 1998), pp. 485-511.

Midlarsky M. I. (1998), 'Democracy and the Environment: An Empirical Assessment' Journal of Peace Research, Vol. 35, No. 3, Special Issue on Environmental Conflict (May, 1998), pp. 341-361.

Milanovic B. (2002), 'True World Income Distribution, 1988 and 1993: First Calculations Based on Household Surveys Alone' The Economic Journal, Volume 112, Number 476, January 2002, pp. 51-92 .

Milanovic B. (2003), 'Inequality in the World Economy-By the Numbers'. Multinational Monitor, 2003, vol. 24, no. 7/8, pp. 23-29.

Milanovic B. (2003), 'The Two Faces of Globalization: Against Globalization as We Know It' World Development, Volume 31, Number 4, April 2003, pp. 667-683 .

Milanovic B. (2005), 'Can We Discern the Effect of Globalization on Income Distribution? Evidence from Household Surveys' World Bank Economic Review, 2005, vol. 19, no. 1, pp. 21-44 .

Milanovic B. and Squire L. (2005), 'Does tariff liberalization increase wage inequality? Some empirical evidence' NBER Working Paper series, 2005, no. 11046, pp. (entire).

Miller C. D. (1999), 'Research note: How Did Economic Development and Trade Affect Women's Share of the Labor Force in the 1980s?' Journal of World-Systems Research, available at: http://jwsr.ucr.edu/index.phpV, 3: 463 – 473.

Miller M. A. L. (1995), 'The Third World in Global Environmental Politics ' Boulder, CO: Lynne Rienner.

Miller, T. C. (2001): "Impact of Globalization on US Wage Inequality: Implications or Policy", North American Journal of Economics and Finance, 12 (3): 219-42.

Mills J. (2002), 'A Critical History of Economics: Missed Opportunities' Basingstoke and London: Palgrave Macmillan.

Mirchandani D. (1999), Economic and social indicators of global competitiveness: an analysis of country rankings, 8th International Eastern Academy of Management Conference, (CD Rom version) Prague.

Mittelman J. (1994), 'The Globalization of Social Conflict' in 'Conflicts and New Departures in World Society' (Bornschier V. and Lengyel P. (Eds.)), pp. 317 - 337, New Brunswick (U.S.A.) and London: Transaction Publishers, World Society Studies, Volume 3.

Moaddel M. (1994), 'Political Conflict in the World Economy: A Cross - national Analysis of Modernization and World - System Theories' American Sociological Review, 59, April: 276 - 303.

Moaddel M. (1996), 'The Social Bases and Discursive Context of the Rise of Islamic Fundamentalism: The Cases of Iran and Syria'. Sociological inquiry, 1996, vol. 66, no. 3, pp. 330 .

Moaddel M. (1998), 'Religion and Women: Islamic Modernism versus Fundamentalism.' Journal for the scientific study of religion, vol. 37, no. 1, pp. 108 .

Moaddel M. (2002), 'The Study of Islamic Culture and Politics: An Overview and Assessment.' Annual Review of Sociology, Vol. 28, (2002), pp. 359-386.

Moaddel M. (2004), 'The future of Islam after 9/11' Futures, 2004, vol. 36, no. 9, pp. 961-977.

Moaddel M. (2005), 'Islamic modernism, nationalism, and fundamentalism: episode and discourse. Chicago: University of Chicago Press

Modelski G. (1996), 'Evolutionary Paradigm for Global Politics'. International studies quarterly, vol. 40, no. 3, pp. 321 ff.

Modelski G. and Perry, G (1991), 'Democratization in Long Perspective'. Technological forecasting and social change, vol. 39, no. 1/2, pp. 23 .

Modelski G. and Poznanski, K (1996), 'Evolutionary Paradigms in the Social Sciences'. International studies quarterly, vol. 40, no. 3, pp. 315 .

Modelski G. and Thompson W. R. (1996), 'Leading Sectors and World Powers: the Coevolution of Global Politics and World Economics' Columbia, SC: University of South Carolina Press.

Modelski G. and Thompson W. R. (1999), 'The Long and the Short of Global Politics in the Twenty-first Century: An Evolutionary Approach'. The International Studies Review, Volume 1, Number 2, 1999, pp. 109 .

Moeller St. et al. (2003), 'Determinants of Relative poverty in Advanced Capitalist Democracies' American Sociological Review, 68, 1, February: 22 – 51.

Moon B.E. and Dixon W.J. (1992), 'Basic Needs and Growth Welfare—Trade Offs' International Studies Quarterly, 36, 2: 191-212.

Moore M. (2003), 'A World Without Walls: Freedom, Development, Free Trade and Global Governance' Cambridge: Cambridge University Press.

Muenz R. (2006), "Population Change and the Impact of Demographic Aging: Consequences and Policy Options for Europe" International Conference on Cultural and Political Conditions for the Reform and Modernisation of Social Models in Europe and the U.S., Vienna, May 19-20, 2006, Institute for Human Sciences, Vienna

Müller Andreas et al. (2000), 'Global Capitalism, Liberation Theology, and the Social Sciences: An Analysis of the Contradictions of Modernity at the Turn of the Millenium' Nova Sciences: Huntington and Commack, New York.

Muller E. N. (1988), 'Democracy, Economic Development, and Income Inequality.' American Sociological Review, 54, pps. 868-871.

Muller E. N. (1993), 'Financial Dependence in the Capitalist World Economy and the Distribution of Income Within States.' in 'Development and Underdevelopment: The Political Economy of Inequality" (Seligson M. A. and Passe-Smith J. T. (Eds.)), pp. 267 – 293 – 39, Boulder CO: Lynne Rienner Publishers.

Muller E. N. (1995), 'Economic Determinants of Democracy.' American Sociological Review, 54, pps. 966-982.

Muller E. N. and and Seligson M. A. (1987), 'Inequality and Insurgency.' American Political Science Review, 81, pps. 425-449.

Munasinghe M., Miguel: de and Sunkel O. (2001), 'Sustainability of long-term growth: socioeconomic and ecological perspectives' Cheltenham, UK; Northampton, MA: Edward Elgar.

Myrdal G. (1984), 'International Inequality and Foreign Aid in Retrospect' in 'Pioneers in Development. A World Bank Publication' (Meier G.M. and Seers D. (Eds.)) pp. 151-165. New York and Oxford: Oxford University Press.

Nasierowksi W. (2007), Assessing Efficiency of Innovation: Some issues relevant to the European Innovation Scoreboard Index, University of New Brunswick, Faculty of Business Administration Working Paper series #2007-004.

Nielsen F. (1995), 'Income Inequality, Development and Dualism: Results from an Unbalanced Cross-National Panel.' American Sociological Review, 60, pps. 674-701.

Nielsen F. and Alderson A. (1997), 'The Kuznets Curve and the Great U-Turn: Income Inequality in U.S. Counties, 1970 to 1990.' American Sociological Review, 62, 1, February, pps. 12-33.

Nolan P. D. (1983), 'Status in the World System, Income Inequality and Economic Growth'; American Journal of Sociology, 89, 410-419.

Noland M. (2004), 'Religion and economic performance'. Washington D.C.: The Peterson Institute, available at: http://www.petersoninstitute.org/publications/wp/03-8.pdf

Noland M. (2005), 'Explaining Middle Eastern Authoritarianism'. Washington D.C., Institute for International Economics, Working Paper series 05-5 (entire), available at: http://www.iie.com/publications/wp/wp05-5.pdf

Noland M. and Pack H. (2004), 'Islam, Globalization, and Economic Performance in the Middle East'. International Economics Policy Briefs, Washington D.C., Institute for International Economics, PB 04-4, June (entire), available at: http://www.iie.com/publications/pb/pb04-4.pdf

Nollert M. (1990), 'Social Inequality in the World System: An Assessment' in 'World Society Studies. Volume 1' (Bornschier V. and Lengyel P. (Eds.)), pp. 17 - 54, Frankfurt and New York: Campus.

Nollert M. (1996), 'Verbandliche Interessenvertretung in der Europaeischen Union: Einflussressourcen und faktische Einflussnahme' Zeitschrift fuer Politikwissenschaft (vormals Jahrbuch fuer Politik), 6, 3: 647 - 667.

Nollert M. (2005), 'Transnational Corporate Networks. Theoretical Perspectives, Empirical Evidence, and Prospects' in 'The Future of World Society' (Herkenrath M. et al. (Eds.)) pp. 103 – 127; Sociological Institute, University of Zurich: Intelligent Book Production.

Nolte H. H. (1982), 'Die eine Welt. Abriss der Geschichte des internationalen Systems' Hannover: Fackeltraeger.

Nolte H. H. (1989), 'Tradition des Rueckstands. West - Ost - Technologietransfer in der Geschichte' Department of History, University of Hannover, FRG.

Noorbakhsh F. (1998), The Human Development Index: Some Technical Issues and Alternative Indices, Journal of International Development 10, 589-605.

O'Hara P. A. (2005), 'Growth and Development in the Global Political Economy. Social Structures of Accumulation and Modes of Regulation' Oxford and New York: Routledge, Taylor and Francis Group.

O'Loughlin J.; Ward M. D.; and Shin M. (1998), 'The Diffusion of Democracy, 1946-1994.' Annals of the Association of American Geographers, Volume 88, Number 4, December 1998, pp. 545 .

O'Neill H. (1997), 'Globalization, Competitiveness and Human Security: Challenges for Development Policy and Institutional Change' The European Journal of Development Research, 9, 1, June: 7-37.

O'Rourke, K. H. (2001): "Globalization and Inequality: Historical Trends". NBER Working Paper 8339. Cambridge, MA: National Bureau of Economic Research.

O'Rourke, K. H., and J. G. Williamson (2000): "Globalization and History: The Evolution of a Nineteenth-Century Atlantic Economy". Cambridge, MA: MIT Press (see Review Essay by A. G. Frank (2002). Journal of World-Systems Research, 8 (2): 276-90).

Obstfeld, M., Taylor A. M., (1998): "The Great Depression as a Watershed: International Capital Mobility over the Long Run" Published in Bordo, M. D., Goldin, C., and N. White, E. N., Eds. The Defining Moment: The Great Depression and the American Economy in the Twentieth Century. pp. 353-402 (Chicago: University of Chicago Press, 1998).

Oddone C. N. (2005), 'Globalización, Desigualdad y Pobreza'. (coautoría de Granato, L.). Encuentro Internacional sobre Pobreza, Desigualdad y Convergencia. Grupo EUMED, Universidad de Málaga, del 3 al 30 de marzo de 2005. (ISBN: 84-689-0637-9, incluido en el CD de EUMED).

Oden B. (2004), 'Alternatives Forms of International Governance and Development Cooperation" in in 'Global Governance in the 21st Century: Alternative Perspectives on World Order' (Hettne B. and Oden B. (Eds.)), pp. 184 - 202. Stockholm: Almkvist and Wiksell. Availabla also at: http://www.egdi.gov.se/pdf/study/study2002_2.pdf .

Olson M. (1982), 'The Rise and Decline of Nations' New Haven and London: Yale University Press.

Olson M. (1986), A Theory of the Incentives Facing Political Organizations. Neo-Corporatism and the Hegemonic State, International Political Science Review, 7, 2, April: 165 - 89.

Olson M. (1987), 'Ideology and Economic Growth' in 'The Legacy of Reaganomics. Prospects for Long - term Growth' (Hulten Ch.R. and Sawhill I.V. (Eds.)), pp. 229-251, Washington D.C.: The Urban Institute Press.

Opp K.D. and Schmidt P. (1976), 'Einfuehrung in die Mehrvariablenanalyse. Grundlagen der Formuiierung und Pruefung komplexer sozialwissenschaftlicher Aussagen' Reinbek: rororo studium.

Orenstein M. A. (2001), ‚Mapping the Diffusion of Pension Innivation' Paper presented to the IIASA Conference on the Political Economy of Pension Reform, available at: http://wbln0018.worldbank.org/HDNet/hddocs.nsf/2d5135ecbf351de6852566a90069b8b6/cc289fc4c077670285256a9c00666690/$FILE/Orenstein.pdf.

Papadopoulos, F. and Tsakloglou, P. (2003), Social Exclusion in the EU: A Capability- Based Approach, Unpublished paper, Athens, May 2003.

Paukert F. (1973), 'Income Distribution at Different Levels of Development: A Survey of the Evidence'. International Labor Review, 108, pps. 97-125.

Paul S. S. and Paul J. A. (1996), 'The World Bank and the Attack on Pensions in the Global South' Global Action on Aging, New York: http://www.globalaging.org/.

Pearson K. (1901), On Lines and Planes of Closest fit to Systems of Points in Space, Philosophical Magazine 6(2), 559-72.

Peters, H.E. and Mullis, N.C. (1997), The Role of Family Income and Sources of Income on Adolescent Achievement, in Duncan, G. and Brooks-Gunn, J. (eds), Consequences of Growing Up Poor. New York: Russell Sage Foundation, 340-81.

Pettersson Th. (2007), "Muslim Immigrants in Western Europe: Persisting Value Differences or Value Adaption" in "Values and Perceptions of the Islamic and Middle Eastern Publics" (Moaddel M. (Ed.)), pp. 71 - 104, Houndmills, Basingstoke, Hampshire: Palgrave Macmillan.

PEW Research Center for the People and the Press (2006), "The Great Divide: How Westerners and Muslims View Each Other. Europe's Muslims More Moderate" PEW, Washington D.C.: http://pewglobal.org/reports/display.php?ReportID=253 (June 22, 2006)

Pipes D. (2002), 'God and Mammon: Does Poverty Cause Militant Islam? The National Interest, Winter 2002, available at: http://www.danielpipes.org/article/104

Polany, K. (1979), 'Oekonomie und Gesellschaft' Frankfurt a.M.: suhrkamp taschenbuch wissenschaft.

Polanyi K. (1957), 'The Great Transformation' Boston: Beacon.

Polanyi K., Lewis J. Kitchin D. (1972), 'Christianity and the social revolution' Freeport, N.Y.: Books for Libraries Press..

Pollins B. M. (1996), 'Global Political Order, Economic Change, and Armed Conflict: Coevolving Systems and the Use of Force' American Political Science Review, 90, 1: 103-117.

Polychronious Ch. (1992), 'Perspectives and Issues in International Political Economy' New York: Frederic Praeger Publishers.

Popper Sir K. (1991), 'The Best World We Have Yet Had. George Urban Interviews Sir Karl Popper' Report on the USSR, 3, 22, May 31: 20 - 22.

Powell M. and A. Barrientos (2004), Welfare Regimes and Welfare Mix, in: European Journal of Political Research; Oxford: Blackwell, 2004 [43: 83-100].

Prebisch R. (1984), 'Five Stages in My Thinking on Development' in 'Pioneers in Development. A World Bank Publication' (Meier G.M. and Seers D. (Eds.)), pp. 175-191. New York and Oxford: Oxford University Press.

Prebisch R. (1988), 'Raúl Prebisch, pensamiento y obra' Fundación Raúl Prebisch. Buenos Aires, República Argentina: Editorial Tesis.

Prechel H. (1985), 'The Effects of Exports, Public Debt and Development on Income Inequality'. International Labor Review, 108, pps. 97-125.

Rabasa A. M. et al. (2006), "The Muslim World after 9/11. Prepared for the United States Air Force". Rand Corporation, Santa Monica, California, Rand Project Air Force, available at: http://www.rand.org/pubs/research_briefs/2005/RAND_RB151.pdf

Raffer K. (1987), 'Unequal Exchange and the Evolution of the World System Reconsidering the Impact of Trade on North-South Relations' London, Basingstoke and New York: Macmillan and Saint Martin's Press. .

Raffer K. and Murshed S. M. (1993), 'Trade, transfers, and development: problems and prospects for the twenty-first century' Aldershot, Hants, England; Brookfield, Vt., USA: E. Elgar Pub. Co.

Raffer K. and Salih M. A. M. (Ed.)(1992), 'Least developed and the oil-rich Arab countries: dependence, independence, or patronage?' New York, N.Y.: St. Martin's Press, 1992. .

Raffer K. and Singer H. W. (1996), 'The Foreign Aid Business, Economic Assistance and Development Co-operation, E.Elgar, Cheltenham [paperback: 1997].

Raffer K. and Singer H. W. (2001), 'Economic North-South divide: six decades of unequal development' Cheltenham, UK; Northampton, MA: Edward Elgar.

Ragin C. C. and Bradshaw Y. W. (1992), 'International Economic Dependence and Human Misery, 1938-1980: A Global Perspective'. Sociological perspectives, vol. 35, no. 2, pp. 217 .

Ram R. (1992), 'Intercountry Inequalities in Income and Basic-Needs Indicators: A Recent Perspective.' World Development, 20, 6, pps. 899-905.

Ramonet I. (1998), 'Die neuen Herren der Welt. Internationale Politik an der Jahrtausendwende' Zürich: Rotpunkt-Verlag.

RAND Corporation (Ch. Benard) (2005): „Civil Democratic Islam. Partners, Resources, and Strategies", freely available on the Internet at „Free downloadable PDF file(s) are available below. Full Document (File size 0.7 MB, 3 minutes modem, < 1 minute broadband)" at http://www.rand.org/pubs/monograph_reports/MR1716/

RAND Corporation (Rabasa A. M. et al.) (2006), "The Muslim World after 9/11. Prepared for the United States Air Force". Rand Corporation, Santa Monica, California, Rand Project Air Force, available at: http://www.rand.org/pubs/research_briefs/2005/RAND_RB151.pdf

Rao J. M. (1998), 'Development in the time of Globalization' UNDP Working Paper series, Social Development and Poverty Elimination Division, February 1998, available at http://www.undp.org/poverty/publications/wkpaper/wp2/RAO-Rf1.PDF

Ravallion M. (2005), On measuring aggregate "social efficiency", Economic Development and Cultural Change, 53(2), 273-92.

Ray J. L. (1983), 'The 'World System' and the Global Political System: A Crucial Relationship?' in 'Foreign Policy and the Modern World - System' (Mc Gowan P. and Kegley Ch.W. Jr. (Eds.)), pp. 13 - 34, Beverly Hills: Sage.

Rein M. (1970), Social Policy: Issues of Choice and Change. New York: Sharpe.

Rein M. (1976), Social Science and Public Policy. London: Penguin.

Rennstich K. J. (2002), 'The new economy, the leadership long cycle and the nineteenth K-wave.' Review of International Political Economy 9, no. 1 (2002): 150-182.

Rennstich K. J. (2003), 'The Future of Great Power Rivalries' Contributions in economics and economic history. 2, no. 230, (2003): 143-161.

Rennstich K. J. (2005), 'The Future of Hegemony and Global System Leadership' in 'The Future of World Society' (Herkenrath M. et al. (Eds.)) pp. 53 – 79; Sociological Institute, University of Zurich: Intelligent Book Production.

Reuveny R. and Thompson W. R. (2003), 'Growth, Trade, and Systemic Leadership' Ann Arbor: University of Michigan Press.

Ridge, T. (2002), Childhood Poverty and Social Exclusion, From a Child's Perspective'. Bristol: The Policy Press.

Roberts J. T., Grimes P. E. and Jodie L. Manale J. L. (2003), 'Social Roots of Global Environmental Change: A World-Systems Analysis of Carbon Dioxide Emissions.' Journal of World-Systems Research, available at: http://jwsr.ucr.edu/index.phpVol. 9, Num. 2 (Summer 2003): 277 – 315.

Robinson R. D. (1987), 'Direct Foreign Investment: Costs and Benefits' New York: Praeger Publishers.

Robinson T.D. and London B. (1991), 'Dependency, Inequality, and Political Violence. A Cross - National Analysis' Journal of Political and Military Sociology, 19, 1: 119 - 156.

Rodas-Martini P. (2001), 'Has income distribution really worsened in the South? And has income distribution really worsened between the North and the South?' Background paper for the Human Development Report 2001, available at: http://www.undp.org/hdr2001/.

Rodrik D. (1997), 'Globalization, Social Conflict and Economic Growth' Harvard University. Available at: http://ksghome.harvard.edu/~.drodrik.academic.ksg/global.PDF.

Rodrik D., A. Subramanian, and F. Trebbi (2002): "Institutional Rule: The Primacy of Institutions over Geography and Integration in Economic Development" Mimeo, IMF.

Roehrich W. (2006), 'Die Macht der Religionen im Spannungsfeld der Weltpolitik. München: Beck

Rogers R. (1992), 'The Politics of Migration in the Contemporary World' International Migration, 30, Special Issue: Migration and Health in the 1990s: 30 - 55.

Ross R. J. S. and Trachte K.C. (1990), 'Global Capitalism: The New Leviathan' Albany: State University of New York Press.

Rothgeb J. M. Jr. (1993), 'A Regional Analysis of the Relationship Between Foreign Investment and Political Conflict in Developing Countries.' Journal of Political and Military Sociology, 21, pps. 219-240.

Rothgeb J. M. Jr. (1996), 'Foreign Investment and Political Conflict in Developing Countries'. New York: F. Praeger.

Rothgeb J. M. Jr. (1996), 'War, Empire, and Democracy: Three New Examinations of Some Dominant Forces of the Twentieth Century.' The journal of politics, 1996, vol. 58, no. 2, pp. 551 .

Rothgeb J. M. Jr. (1999), 'Testing Mobilization Views of the Relationship Between International Interdependence and Political Conflict in Developing Countries'. The Social science journal, 1999, vol. 36, no. 3, pp. 469 .

Rothgeb J. M. Jr. (2002), 'Foreign Investments, Privatization, and Political Conflict in Developing Countries' Journal of Political and Military Sociology, vol. 30, no. 1, pp. 36-50 .

Rothgeb, J. M. Jr. (1995), 'Investment Penetration, Agrarian Change, and Political Conflict in Developing Countries' Studies in Comparative International Development, 30, 4: 46 - 62.

Rothschild K. W. (1944), 'The Small Nation and World Trade' The Economic Journal, April: 26 - 40.

Rothschild K. W. (1963), 'Kleinstaat und Integration' Weltwirtschaftliches Archiv, 90, 2: 239 - 275.

Rothschild K. W. (1966), 'Marktform, Loehne, Aussenhandel' Vienna: Europa - Verlag.

Rothschild K. W. (1993), 'Employment, wages, and income distribution: critical essays in economics' London; New York: Routledge.

Rothschild K. W. (1993), 'Ethics and economic theory: ideas, models, dilemmas' Aldershot, Hants., England; Brookfield, Vt.: E. Elgar.

Roubini N. and Sala-i-Martin X. (1992), 'Financial Repression and Economic Growth' Journal of Development Economics, Vol. 39: 5-30.

Rowntree, L et al. (2000): "Diversity amid globalization: World religion, environment and development", Prentice Hall.

Rubinson R. (1976), 'The World - Economy and the Distribution of Income within States: A Cross - National Study' American Sociological Review, 41: 638 - 659.

Ruggeri J. and Zou Y. (2007), "The fiscal burden of rising dependency ratios" Population Research and Policy Review, 26 (2): 185-201

Rummel R. R. (1994), 'Power, Genocide and Mass Murder' Journal of Peace Research, 31, 1: 1 - 10.

Rummel R. R. (1995), 'Democracy, Power, Genocide, and Mass Murder' The Journal of Conflict Resolution, 39, 1, March: 3 - 26.

Russell B. (1999), ‚Philosophie des Abendlandes. Ihr Zusammenhang mit der politischen und sozialen Entwicklung (A History of Western Philosophy)' Wien: Europa-Verlag.

Russett B. (1967), 'International Regions and the International System. A Study in Political Ecology' Westport, Con.: Greenwood Press.

Russett B. (1978), 'The marginal utility of income transfers to the Third World' International Organization, 32, 4: 913 - 928.

Russett B. (1983), 'International Interactions and Processes: The Internal versus External Debate Revisited' in 'Political Science: The State of the Discipline' (Finifter A. (Ed.)), pp. 541 - 68, Washington D.C.: American Political Science Association.

Russett B. (1983), 'The Peripheral Economies. Penetration and Economic Distortion, 1970 - 75' in 'Contending Approaches to World System Analysis' (Thompson W.R. (Ed.)), pp. 79 - 114, Beverly Hills: Sage.

Russett B. (1994), 'The Democratic Peace' in 'Conflicts and New Departures in World Society' (Bornschier V. and Lengyel P. (Eds.)), pp. 21 - 43, New Brunswick (U.S.A.) and London: Transaction Publishers, World Society Studies, Volume 3.

Russett B. M; Oneal J. R. and Cox M. (2000), 'Clash of Civilizations, or Realism and Liberalism Deja Vu? Some Evidence. Journal of Peace Research, vol. 37, no. 5, pp. 583.

Saisana M. and S. Tarantola (2002), State-of-the-art report on current methodologies and practices for composite indicator development, Joint Research Centre – European Commission, I-21020 Ispra (VA), Italy.

Samuelson P. (1964), Theoretical Notes on Trade Problems, The Review of Economics and Statistics, Vol. 46, No. 2, 145-154

Santos Pais, M. (1999) 'A Human Rights Conceptual Framework for UNICEF'. Innocenti Essay 9. Florence: UNICEF Innocenti Research Centre.

Sapir A. (2005), ‚Globalisation and the Reform of European Social Models'. Brussels, BRUEGEL Institute (Background document for the presentation at ECOFIN Informal Meeting in Manchester, 9 September 2005), available at: http://www.bruegel.org/ Repositories/Documents/publications/working_papers/SapirPaper080905.pdf .

Sapir A. (2005), ‚Globalisation and the Reform of European Social Models' Brussels, BRUEGEL Institute, bruegel policy brief, 01, November (restricted).

Sapir A. et al. (2004), "An agenda for a growing Europe. Making the EU economic system deliver" available at: http://www.euractiv.com/ndbtext/innovation/sapirreport.pdf

Sarma, A. (2002): "Prospects of trade and investment in India and China", International Studies, 39, 1, pp. 25-43.

Savage T. M. (2004), 'Europe and Islam: Crescent Waxing, Cultures Clashing' The Washington Quarterly, Summer, 27, 3: 25-50, available at: http://www.twq.com/ 04summer/docs/04summer_savage.pdfsearch=%22crescent%20waxing%20savage%22

Sawada Y. and Yotopoulos P. A. (1999), 'Currency Substitution, Speculation, and Financial Crisis: Theory and Empirical Analysis.' SIEPR Policy Paper series No. 99- 5.

Sawada Y. and Yotopoulos P. A. (2002), 'On the Missing Link between Currency Substitution and Crises' Zagreb International Review of Economics and Business, vol. 5, no. VOL 2, pp. 83-104.

Schmidinger T. and Larise D. (Eds.) (2008), "Zwischen Gottesstaat und Demokratie. Handbuch des politischen Islam" Vienna: Deuticke Zsolnay

Schmieding H. (2007), It's all about Real Estate.Newsweek – www.newsweek.com/id/84506.

Seers D. (Ed.)(1978), 'Underdeveloped Europe' Hassocks: Harvester Press.

Sen A. (1985) Commodities and Capabilities. Amsterdam: Elsevier.

Sen A. (1985), Commodities and Capabilities. Amsterdam: Elsevier.

Sen A. (1987), Equality for What?, in S.M. McMurrim (ed.), Tanner Lectures on Human Values, Vol. 1. Salt Lake City: University of Utah Press.

Sen A. (1992), Inequality Re-examined. Oxford: Clarendon.

Sen A. (1999) Development as Freedom. Oxford: Oxford University Press.

Sen A. (1999), Development as Freedom, Oxford: Oxford University Press.

Sen A. (2000) 'Social Exclusion: Concept, Application, and Scrutiny'. Social Development Papers. Office of Environment and Social Development.

Sen A. (2000), Social Exclusion: Concept, Application, and Scrutiny. Social Development Papers. Office of Environment and Social Development.

Senghaas D. (2002), 'Clash within civilizations: coming to terms with cultural conflicts' London; New York: Routledge.

Shafik N. and Bandyopadhyay S. (1992), 'Economic Growth and Environmental Quality. Time Series and Cross - Country Evidence' Policy Research Working Papers, WPS, 904, Washington D.C.: The World Bank.

Shandra J. M., London B. and Williamson J. B. (2003), 'Environmental Degradation, Environmental Sustainability, and Overurbanization in the Developing World: A Quantitative, Cross-National Analysis' Sociological Perspectives, vol. 46, no. 3, pp. 309-330

Shandra J. M., Nobles, J. E.; London B.; Williamson, J. B. (2005), 'Multinational Corporations, Democracy and Child Mortality: A Quantitative, Cross-National Analysis of Developing Countries' Social Indicators Research, vol. 73, no. 2, pp. 267-293 .

Shandra J. M., Ross R. J. S., London B. (2003), 'Global Capitalism and the Flow of Foreign Direct Investment to Non-Core Nations, 1980-1996: A Quantitative, Cross-National Analysis' International Journal of Comparative Sociology, Vol. 44, 199-238.

Shandra J. M.; London B.; Whooley O. P; Williamson J. B. (2004), 'International Nongovernmental Organizations and Carbon Dioxide Emissions in the Developing World: A Quantitative, Cross-National Analysis' Sociological Inquiry, Volume 74, Number 4, November, pp. 520-545 .

Shandra J. M.; London B.; Williamson J. B. (2003), 'Environmental Degradation, Environmental Sustainability, and Overurbanization in the Developing World: A Quantitative, Cross-National Analysis' Sociological Perspectives, 2003, vol. 46, no. 3, pp. 309-330 .

Shandra J. M.; Nobles J.; London B.; Williamson J. B. (2004), 'Dependency, democracy, and infant mortality: a quantitative, cross-national analysis of less developed countries.' Social Science and Medicine, vol. 59, no. 2, pp. 321-333 .

Sharpe A. (2001), 'Estimates of Relative and Absolute Poverty Rates for the Working Population in Developed Countries' Ottawa, Ontario, Canada: Centre for the Study of Living Standards, available at: http://www.csls.ca/events/cea01/sharpeilo.pdf

Shaw E. S. (1973), 'Financial Deepening in Economic Development'. Oxford University Press, 1973.

Shaw T. M. (1994), 'The South at the end of the twentieth century: rethinking the political economy of foreign policy in Africa, Asia, the Caribbean, and Latin America' New York: St. Martin's Press.

Shaw T. M. (1995), 'Globalization, Regionalisms and the South in the 1990s: Towards a New Political Economy of Development' The European Journal of Development Research, 7, 2, Dec.: 257 - 275.

Shen C. and Williamson J. B. (2001), 'Accounting for Cross-National Differences in Infant Mortality Decline (1965-1991) among less Developed Countries: Effects of Women's Status, Economic Dependency, and State Strength' Social Indicators Research, 53, no. 3 (2001): 257-288.

Shin M and Ward M. D. (1999), 'Lost in Space: Political Geography and the Defense-Growth Trade-Off.' The journal of conflict resolution, vol. 43, no. 6, pp. 793 .

Shin M. E. (1975), 'Economic and Social Correlations of Infant Mortality: A Cross-Sectional and Longitudinal Analysis of 63 Countries. Social Biology, 22: 315 – 25.

Shin M. E. (2002), 'Income inequality, democracy and health: A global portrait' University of California, Los Angeles, Department of Geography, available at: http://www.colorado.edu/IBS/PEC/gadconf/papers/shin.pdf.

Siegel J. J. (2005), "The future for investors: why the tried and true triumph over the bold and new" New York: Crown Business

Simpson M. (1990), 'Political Rights and Income Inequality: A Cross-National Test.' American Sociological Review, 55, pps. 682-693.

Singer P. I. (1971), 'Forca de trabalho e emprego no Brasil: 1920-1969. Com a assistencia de Frederico Mazzucchelli nos cálculos e na redacão do anexo metodológico'. São Paulo, CEBRAP.

Singer P. I. (1971), 'Dinámica de la población y desarrollo' Mexico D.F.: Ed. Siglo I.

Singer P. I. (1972), 'Milagre brasileiro': causas e consequencias'. Sao Paulo, CEBRAP.

Singer P. I. (1973), 'Economia política da urbanizacão; [ensaios, por] Paul Singer.' São Paulo: Editora Brasiliense, 1973. .

Singer P. I. (1974), 'Elementos para uma teoria do emprego aplicável a países não desenvolvidos' São Paulo: CEBRAP: Distributed by Editora Barsiliense.

Singer P. I. (1976), 'Crise do 'milagre': interpretacão crítica da economia brasileira' Rio de Janeiro: Paz e Terra, 1976. .

Singer P. I. (1977), 'Economia política do trabalho: elementos para uma análise histórico-estrutural do emprego e da forca de trabalho no desenvolvimento capitalista' São Paulo: Editora Hucitec.

Singer P. I. (1981), 'Dominacão e desigualdade: estrutura de classes e reparticão da renda no Brasil'. Rio de Janeiro, RJ: Paz e Terra.

Singer P. I. (1981), 'O feminino e o feminismo' in 'Sao Paulo: O povo em movimento' (Singer P.I. et al. (Eds.)), pp. 109 - 142, Petropolis, Rio de Janeiro: Editora Vozes.

Singer P. I. (1986), 'Reparticão da renda: pobres e ricos sob o regime militar' Rio de Janeiro: J. Zahar.

Singer P. I. (1987), 'Dia da lagarta: democratizacão e conflito distributivo no Brasil do cruzado' São Paulo, SP: Editora Brasiliense.

Singer P. I. (1988), 'Estado da transicão: política e economia na Nova República' São Paulo, SP, Brasil: Vértice.

Singer P. I. (1991), 'Formacão da classe operária' Campinas-SP: Editora da UNICAMP; São Paulo-SP: Atual Editora.

Singer P. I. (1998), 'Utopia militante: repensando o socialismo' Petrópolis: Editora Vozes.

Singer P. I. (1999), 'Brasil na crise: perigos e oportunidades' São Paulo: Editora Contexto.

Singer P. I. (1999), 'Globalizacão e desemprego: diagnóstico e alternativas' São Paulo, SP: Editora Contexto.

Singer P. I. et al. (1977), 'Multinacionais: internacionalizacão e crise'. São Paulo: Editora Brasiliense.

Smith D. A and London B. (1990), 'Convergence in World Urbanization?: A Quantitative Assessment'. Urban affairs quarterly, vol. 25, no. 4, pp. 574 .

Smith D. A. (1994), 'Uneven Development and the Environment: Toward a World-System Perspective. Humboldt Journal of Social Relations, 20(1):151-175.

Smith D. A. (1996), 'Third World Cities in Global Perspective: The Political Economy of Uneven Urbanization' Boulder, CO: Westview Press.

So A. Y. (1990), 'Social Change and Development. Modernization, Dependency, and World - System Theories' Newbury Park, CA.: Sage Library of Social Research, 178.

Soares R. R. (2005), "Mortality reductions, educational attainment, and fertility choice" American Economic Review, 95 (3): 580-601 JUN 2005

Sobolewski, J.M. and Amato, P.R. (2005), Economic Hardship in the Family of Origin and Children's Psychological Well-being in Adulthood. Journal of Marriage and Family 67, 141-56.

Soysa I. de (2002), 'Ecoviolence: Shrinking Pie, or Honey Pot?' Global Environmental Politics, 2, no. 4 (2002): 1-34.

Soysa I. de (2003), 'Foreign direct investment, democracy, and development: assessing contours, correlates, and concomitants of globalization' London, New York: Routledge.

Soysa I. de and Gleditsch N. P. (2002), 'The Liberal Globalist Case' in 'Global Governance in the 21st Century: Alternative Perspectives on World Order' (Hettne B. and Oden B. (Eds.)), pp. 26 – 23. Stockholm: Almkvist and Wiksell. Availabla also at: http://www.egdi.gov.se/pdf/study/study2002_2.pdf.

Soysa I. de and John R. Oneal, J. R. (2000), 'Boon or bane?. Reassessing the productivity of foreign direct investment.' Journal of Planning Literature, 14, no. 4 (2000).

Soysa I. de and Neumayer E. (2005), 'False Prophet, or Genuine Savior? Assessing the Effects of Economic Openness on Sustainable Development, 1980-99' International Organization, 59, no. 3 (2005): 731-772.

Soysa I. De and Nordas R. (2006), 'Islam's Bloody Innards? Religion and Political Terror, 1980 – 2000'. As yet unpublished Conference Paper, International Peace Research Institute, Oslo (PRIO), available at: http://www.prio.no/files/file48349_desoysa_nordas_wg3meeting.pdf

Soysa I. De and Nordas R. (2006), 'Islam's Bloody Innards? Religion and Political Terror, 1980–2000'. As yet unpublished Conference Paper, International Peace Research Institute, Oslo (PRIO), available at: http://www.prio.no/files/file48349_desoysa_nordas_wg3meeting.pdf

Spar D. (1999), 'Foreign Investment and Human Rights' Challenge, Vol. 42, 55 - 80.

SPSS (2007), Statistical Package for the Social Sciences, User Guide, Version 14, August 2007.

Stack St and Zimmerman D. (1982), 'The Effect of World Economy on Income Inequality: A Reassessment.' Sociological Quarterly, 23(Summer): 345-358. .

Stack St. (1978), 'The Effect of Direct Government Involvement in the Economy on the Degree of Income Inequality: A Cross-National Study.' American Sociological Review, 43 (December): 880-888. .

Stack St. (1980), 'The Political Economy of Income Inequality: A Comparative Analysis.' Canadian Journal of Political Science, 13, pps. 273-286.

Stack St. (1998), 'Marriage, Family, and Loneliness: A Cross-National Study.' Sociological Perspectives, 41(2): 415-432. .

Stalker P. (1994), 'The Work of Strangers: A Survey of international labor migration' Geneva: International Labor Office.

Stevens, K., Dickson, M., Poland, M. with Prasad, R. (2005), Focus on Families. Reinforcing the Importance of Family. Families with Dependent Children – Successful Outcomes Project'. Report on literature review and focus groups. Wellington: Families Commission. http://www.familiescommission.govt.nz/download/focus-on-families.pdf.

Stiglitz J. (1998), 'The Role of International Financial Institutions in the Current Global Economy' World Bank, Address to the Chicago Council on Foreign Relations, available at: http://www.gdnet.org/tm-frame.html?http://www.worldbank.org/html/extdr/extme/jssp022798.htm.

Stiglitz, J. (2004): "Globalization and growth in emerging markets", Journal of Policy Modeling, Vol. 26, Issue 4, pp. 465–484.

Stiglitz, Joseph. (2002): "Globalization and its discontents", New York: W. W. Norton.

Stilwell F. (2000), 'Globalization: How did we get to where we are? (and where can we go now?)' available at: http://www.phaa.net.au/conferences/stilwell.htm.

Stokes R. and Anderson A.. (1990), 'Disarticulation and Human Welfare in Less-Developed Countries'. American Sociological Review, 55, pps. 63-74.

Streissler E. (2002), 'Exchange Rates and International Finance Markets: An Asset-Theoretic Perspective with Schumpeterian Innovation' London and New York: Routledge.

Strom St. et al. (Eds)(1998), ‚Econometrics and Economic Theory in the 20th Century: The Ragnar Frisch Centennial Symposium' Cambridge, Cambridge University Press.

Sturgis, P. (2004) 'Analysing Complex Survey Data: Dimensioning, Stratification and Weights'. Social Research Update Issue 43. Downloaded at http://www.soc.surrey.ac.uk/sru/ SRU43.html, January 2006.

Sturgis, P. (2004), Analysing Complex Survey Data: Dimensioning, Stratification and Weights, Social Research Update Issue 43. Downloaded at http://www.soc.surrey.ac.uk/sru/ SRU43.html, January 2006.

Sunkel O. (1966), 'The Structural Background of Development Problems in Latin America' Weltwirtschaftliches Archiv, 97, 1: pp. 22 ff.

Sunkel O. (1973), 'El subdesarrollo latinoamericano y la teoria del desarrollo' Mexico: Siglo Veintiuno Editores, 6a edicion.

Sunkel O. (1973), 'Transnationale kapitalistische Integration und nationale Desintegration: der Fall Lateinamerika' in 'Imperialismus und strukturelle Gewalt. Analysen ueber abhaengige Reproduktion' (Senghaas D. (Ed.)), pp. 258 - 315, Frankfurt a.M.: suhrkamp. English version: 'Transnational capitalism and national disintegration in Latin America' Social and Economic Studies, 22, 1, March: 132 - 76.

Sunkel O. (1978), 'The Development of Development Thinking' in 'Transnational Capitalism and National Development. New Perspectives on Dependence' (Villamil J.J. (Ed.)), pp. 19 - 30, Hassocks, Sussex: Harvester Press.

Sunkel O. (1978), 'Transnationalization and its National Consequences' in 'Transnational Capitalism and National Development. New Perspectives on Dependence' (Villamil J.J. (Ed.)), pp. 67 - 94, Hassocks, Sussex: Harvester Press.

Sunkel O. (1980), 'Transnacionalizacion y dependencia' Madrid: Ediciones Cultura Hispanica del Instituto de Cooperacion Iberoamericana.

Sunkel O. (1984), 'Capitalismo transnacional y desintegracion nacional en America Latina' Buenos Aires, Rep. Argentina: Ediciones Nueva Vision.

Sunkel O. (1990), 'Dimension ambiental en la planificacion del desarrollo. English The environmental dimension in development planning ' 1st ed. Santiago, Chile: United Nations, Economic Commission for Latin America and the Caribbean.

Sunkel O. (1991), 'El Desarrollo desde dentro: un enfoque neoestructuralista para la America Latina' 1. ed. Mexico: Fondo de Cultura Economica.

Sunkel O. (1994), 'Rebuilding capitalism: alternative roads after socialism and dirigisme' Ann Arbor, Mich.: University of Michigan Press.

Suter Ch. (1992), 'Debt Cycles in the World-Economy: Foreign Loans, Financial Crises, and Debt Settlements, 1820-1990' Boulder, CO: Westview Press.

Suter Ch. (2005), 'Research on World Society and the Zurich School' in 'The Future of World Society' (Herkenrath M. et al. (Eds.)) pp. 377–383; Sociological Institute, University of Zurich: Intelligent Book Production.

Tamura R. (2006), "Human capital and economic development" Journal of Development Economics, 79 (1): 26-72 FEB 2006

Tanzi (2004): "Globalization and the need for fiscal reform in developing countries", Journal of Policy Modeling, 26 (2004) 525–542.

Tausch A. (1989), 'Armas socialistas, subdesarrollo y violencia estructural en el Tercer Mundo' Revista Internacional de Sociologia, CSIC, Madrid, 47, 4: 583-716

Tausch A. (1989), 'Stable Third World Democracy and the European Model. A Quantitative Essay' in 'Crisis in Development' (Z. BABLEWSKI and B. HETTNE (Eds.), The European Perspectives Project of the United Nations University, University of Gothenburg, PADRIGU-Papers: 131-161

Tausch A. (1990), 'Quantitative aspects of a socio-liberal theory of world development'. Economic Papers, Warsaw School of Economics, Research Institute for Developing Countries, 23: 64–167

Tausch A. (1993; in collaboration with Fred PRAGER), 'Towards a Socio-Liberal Theory of World Development'. Basingstoke and New York: Macmillan/St. Martin's Press

Tausch A. (1999, Editor, with Andreas Müller OFM and Paul Zulehner), "Global Capitalism, Liberation Theology and the Social Sciences. An analysis of the contradictions of modernity at the turn of the millennium" (with contributions by Samir Amin et. al), Huntington, New York: Nova Science. Paperback edition 2001

Tausch A. (2001, with Gernot Köhler), Global Keynesianism: Unequal exchange and global exploitation. Huntington NY, Nova Science. ISBN 1-59033-002-1. Paperback edition 2001

Tausch A. (2001, with Peter Herrmann), "Globalization and European Integration. Huntington NY, Nova Science. ISBN: 1-560729295.

Tausch A. (2002), 'Evropeiskii Sojus i budushaja mirovaja sistema" in Evropa, 2(3), 2002: 23–62, Warsaw, Polish Institute for International Affairs (in Russian language; translated from the English language manuscript by the Polish Institute for International Affairs),

Tausch A. (2002), 'The European Union and the World System'. in 'The European Union in the World System Perspective' (The Polish Institute for International Affairs, Ryszard Stemplowski (Ed.)), Warsaw: Collections PISM (Polish Institute for International Affairs): 45 – 93.

Tausch A. (2003), 'The European Union: Global Challenge or Global Governance? 14 World System Hypotheses and Two Scenarios on the Future of the Union' in 'Globalization: Critical Perspectives' (Gernot Kohler and Emilio José Chaves (Editors)), pp. 93–197, Hauppauge, New York: Nova Science Publishers

Tausch A. (2003), 'Jevropejskaja perspektiva: po puti k sosdaniju "obshtshevo srjedisemnomorskovo doma" i integrirovaniju polozytelnovo potencjala obshestvjennovo razvitija islamskich stran' in Evropa, 4 (9), 2003: 87 – 109, Warsaw, Polish Institute for International Affairs (in Russian language; translated from the English language manuscript by the Polish Institute for International Affairs)

Tausch A. (2003), „Social Cohesion, Sustainable Development and Turkey's Accession to the European Union". Alternatives: Turkish Journal of International Relations, 2, 1, Spring http://www.alternativesjournal.net/ and http://www.alternativesjournal.net/volume2/number1/tausch.htm (journal is available electronically)

Tausch A. (2003, Editor), 'The Three Pillars of Wisdom? A Reader on Globalization, World Bank Pension Models and Welfare Society'. Nova Science Hauppauge, New York, 2003

Tausch A. (2004), ‚Towards a European Perspective for the Common Mediterranean House and the Positive Development Capability of Islamic Countries' In ‚European Neighbourhood Policy: Political, Economic and Social Issues' (Fulvio Attina and Rosa Rossi (Eds.), pp. 145 – 168, Università degli Studi di Catania Facoltà di Scienze Politiche

Tausch A. (2005), ‚Did recent trends in world society make multinational corporations penetration irrelevant? Looking back on Volker Bornschier's development theory in the light of recent evidence'. Historia Actual On-Line, 6 Tausch A. (2005), [revista en línea, Universidad de Cadiz, Espana] Disponible desde Internet en: http://www.historia-actual.com/hao/Volumes/Volume1/Issue6/esp/v1i6c4.pdf (journal is available electronically)

Tausch A. (2005), ‚Europe, the Muslim Mediterranean and the End of the era of Global Confrontation'. Alternatives. Turkish Journal of International Relations, Volume 3, Number 4, Winter 2004, available at: http://www.alternativesjournal.net/volume3/number4/arno3.pdf (journal is available electronically)

Tausch A. (2005), ‚Tectonic shifts in the structure of international inequality'. Centro Argentino de Estudios Internacionales, Teoría de las Relaciones Internacionales Working Paper N° 11, Fecha de Publicación: 14/11/05, available at http://caei.com.ar/es/programas/teoria/working.htm

Tausch A. (2005), 'Is Islam really a development blockade? 12 predictors of development, including membership in the Organization of Islamic Conference, and their influence on 14 indicators of development in 109 countries of the world with completely available data'. Ankara Institute for Turkish Policy Studies, ANKAM, Insight Turkey, 7, 1, 2005: 124 - 135.

Tausch A. (2005, Editor, with Peter Herrmann), 'Dar al Islam. The Mediterranean, the World System and the Wider Europe. Vol. 1: The "Cultural Enlargement" of the EU and Europe's Identity; Vol. 2: The Chain of Peripheries and the New Wider Europe'. Hauppauge, New York: Nova Science Publishers. Abridged paperback editions, 2006, under the title: "The West, Europe and the Muslim World" (Vol. 1), and "Towards a Wider Europe" (Vol. 2)

Tausch A. (2005, with Russell A. Berman), „Yet Another reason They Dislike Us. „Europe is rich, but the United States is richer." Hoover Digest, 2005, 1: 69–73

Tausch A. (2006), 'On heroes, villains and statisticians'. The Vienna Institute for International Economic Studies Monthly Report, No. 7, July 2006: 20 - 23. Vienna: The Vienna Institute for International Economic Studies (wiiw)

Tausch A. (2006, with Almas Heshmati), 'Turkey and the Lisbon process. A short research note on the position of Turkey on a new "Lisbon Strategy Index" (LSI).' Ankara Institute for Turkish Policy Studies, ANKAM, Insight Turkey, 8, 2, 2006: 7 – 18.

Tausch A. (2007), 'Against Islamophobia. Quantitative analyses of global terrorism, world political cycles and center periphery structures' Hauppauge, N.Y.: Nova Science Publishers (for info: https://www.novapublishers.com/catalog/).

Tausch A. (2007), 'Jevropejskij sojuz: "Grad na Cholme" i lisabonskaja strategija.' Mirovaja ekonomika i meždunarodnyje otnošenija, RU(0131-2227), Vyp. 50, no. 3 Tausch A.

(2007), s. 65-72 (translated and shortened by Russian Academy of Science Member Professor Victor Krasilshchikov, IMEO, Moscow)

Tausch A. (2007), 'Some reflections on European regional development' In 'Stosunki ekonomiczne w rozszerzonej Unii Europejskiej. Economic relations in the EU enlarged' (Jaroslaw Kundera (Ed.)), pp. 399 – 408, Wroclaw: Kolonia Limited.

Tausch A. (2007), 'The City on a Hill? The Latin Americanization of Europe and the Lost Competition with the U.S.A.' Amsterdam: Rozenberg (for info: http://www.rozenbergps.com/).

Tausch A. (2007), 'World Bank Pension Reforms and Development Patterns in the World System and in "Wider Europe"' In 'Reforming European Pension Systems' (Arun Muralidhar and Serge Allegreza (Eds.)), pp. 167–222, Amsterdam, NL and West Lafayette, Indiana, USA: Dutch University Press, Rozenberg Publishers and Purdue University Press.

Tausch A. (2007), ,Quantitative World System Studies Contradict Current Islamophobia: World Political Cycles, Global Terrorism, and World Development'. Alternatives. Turkish Journal of International Relations, 6, 1and2, Spring and Summer 2007, p. 15 - 81. available at: http://www.alternativesjournal.net/ (journal is available electronically)

Tausch A. (2007), "Global Terrorism and World Political Cycles" in History and mathematics (special issue): Analyzing and Modeling Global Development (Moscow), Grinin L., Munck V. C. de, Korotayev A. (Ed.). Moscow: "Anthropology of the East" Center, Russian State University for the Humanities, 6 Miusskaya Ploshchad', Moscow 125267, Russia, pp. 99 - 126 [available from international book trade at: http://urss.ru/cgi-bin/db.pl?cp=andpage=Bookandid=53184andlang=enandLanguages=2andblang=enandlist=130]

Tausch A. (2007), "The world economy heading towards another depression? On the renewed international interest in Kondratiev waves" Social Evolution and History (Moscow), Vol. 6, No. 2, September 2007, pp. 39 – 74

Tausch A. (2007, Editor, with Almas Heshmati), 'Roadmap to Bangalore? Globalization, the EU's Lisbon Process and the Structures of Global Inequality' Hauppauge, N.Y.: Nova Science Publishers (for info: https://www.novapublishers.com/catalog/).

Tausch A. (2007, with a postface by Christian Ghymers), 'From the "Washington" towards a "Vienna Consensus"? A quantitative analysis on globalization, development and global governance'. Hauppauge, N.Y.: Nova Science Publishers (for info: https://www.novapublishers.com/catalog/).

Tausch A. (2007, with Almas Heshmati and Chemen S. J. Bajalan), "On the Multivariate Analysis of the "Lisbon Process", IZA Discussion Papers, (December 2007), No. 3198, available at http://www.iza.org/index_html?lang=enandmainframe=http%3A//www.iza.org/en/webcontent/publications/papers/papers%3Fyear%3D2007%26scroll%3DIIandtopSelect=publicationsandsubSelect=papers

Tausch A. (2007, with Almas Heshmati, and Chemen S. J. Bajalan), "Measurement and Analysis of Child Well-Being in Middle and High Income Countries", IZA Discussion Papers, (December 2007), No. 3203, available at http://www.iza.org/index_html?lang=enandmainframe=http%3A//www.iza.org/en/webcontent/publications/papers/papers%3Fyear%3D2007%26scroll%3DIIandtopSelect=publicationsandsubSelect=papers

Tausch A. (2007, with Christian Bischof and Karl Mueller), "Does Europe waste its human capital? First statistical estimates of the real situation of Europe's Muslims and the Lisbon process" available at: MPRA Paper No. 4982, available at: http://mpra.ub.uni-muenchen.de/4982/01/MPRA_paper_4982.pdf

Tausch A. (2007, with Christian Bischof, and Karl Mueller), '"Muslim Calvinism", internal security and the Lisbon process in Europe' Rozenberg Publishers, Amsterdam (for info: http://www.rozenbergps.com/).

Tausch A. (2007, with Christian Bischof, Tomaz Kastrun and Karl Mueller), 'Against Islamophobia: Muslim Communities, Social Exclusion and the Lisbon Process in Europe' Hauppauge, N.Y.: Nova Science Publishers (for info: https://www.novapublishers.com/catalog/).

Tausch A. (2008), 'Multicultural Europe: Effects of the Global Lisbon Process.' Hauppauge, N.Y.: Nova Science Publishers (for info: https://www.novapublishers.com/catalog/).

Tausch A. (2008), with Peter Herrmann, Almas Heshmati and Chemen S. J. Bajalan), "Efficiency and Effectiveness of Social Spending" IZA Discussion Paper No. 3482, available at: http://www.iza.org/index_html?lang=enandmainframe=http%3A//www.iza.org/en/webcontent/publications/papers/viewAbstract%3Fdp_id%3D3482andtopSelect=publicationsandsubSelect=papers

Tausch A. (2008, with Christian Bischof and Karl Mueller), 'Social Exclusion and Europe's Muslims'. The Vienna Institute for International Economic Studies Monthly Report, 2: 13 – 18. Vienna: The Vienna Institute for International Economic Studies (wiiw)

Taylor-Gooby P. (1996), The Response of Government: Fragile Convergence?, In: George, Vic/Taylor-Gooby P. [Eds.] European Welfare Policy. Squaring the Welfare Circle; Houndmills et al.: Macmillan Press Ltd., 199 ff.

Tellis A. J. et al. (2001), 'Measuring National Power in the Postindustrial Age' Santa Monica, California: The Rand Corporation.

Telo M. and Telr M. (2006), 'Europe: A Civilian Power? European Union, Global Governance, World Order'. Basingstoke: Palgrave.

The World Bank Group (2000), 'Flagship Course in Pension Reform' available at: http://www.worldbank.org/wbi/pensionflagship/.

Thompson W. R. (1999), 'Great Power Rivalries' Columbus: University of South Carolina Press.

Thompson W. R. (2001), 'Evolutionary Interpretations of World Politics' London and New York: Routledge.

Thompson W. R. and Modelski G. (1994), 'Long Cycle Critiques and Deja Vu All Over Again: A Rejoinder to Houweling and Siccama.' International interactions, 1994, vol. 20, no. 3, pp. 209 .

Tibi B. (1973), ‚Militär und Sozialismus in der Dritten Welt: allgemeine Theorien und Regionalstudien über arabische Länder'. Frankfurt am Main: Suhrkamp.

Tibi B. (1981), 'Arab nationalism: a critical enquiry. Edited and translated by Marion Farouk-Sluglett and Peter Sluglett' London: MacMillan Press, 1981..

Tibi B. (1985), 'Der Islam und das Problem der kulturellen Bewältigung sozialen Wandels' Frankfurt am Main: Suhrkamp, 1991.

Tibi B. (1990), 'Arab nationalism: a critical enquiry' New York, N.Y.: St. Martin's Press.

Tibi B. (1992), ‚Die fundamentalistische Herausforderung: der Islam und die Weltpolitik' München : C.H. Beck

Tibi B. (1992), 'Kreuzzug oder Dialog? Der Westen und die arabo - islamische Welt nach dem Golfkrieg' in 'Kreuzzug oder Dialog. Die Zukunft der Nord - Sued - Beziehungen' (Matthies V. (Ed.)), pp. 107-120, Bonn: J.H.W. Dietz Nachfolger.

Tibi B. (1995), ‚Krieg der Zivilisationen: Politik und Religion zwischen Vernunft und Fundamentalismus.' Hamburg: Hoffmann und Campe

Tibi B. (1996), ‚Der Wahre Imam: der Islam von Mohammed bis zur Gegenwart' München: Piper, 1996

Tibi B. (1997), 'Arab nationalism: between Islam and the nation-state' New York: St. Martin's Press.

Tibi B. (1997), 'Challenge of fundamentalism: political Islam and the new world disorder'. Berkeley: University of California Press.

Tibi B. (1997), 'Conflict and war in the Middle East, 1967-91: regional dynamic and the superpowers. Translated by Clare Krojzl'. Houndmills, Basingstoke, Hampshire: Macmillan in association with the Center for International Affairs, Harvard University.

Tibi B. (1997a), 'Arab nationalism: between Islam and the nation-state' New York: St. Martin's Press.

Tibi B. (1997b), 'Challenge of fundamentalism: political Islam and the new world disorder'. Berkeley: University of California Press.

Tibi B. (1998), 'Conflict and war in the Middle East: from interstate war to new security' New York: St. Martin's Press.

Tibi B. (1998), 'Crisis of modern Islam: a preindustrial culture in the scientific-technological age. Translated by Judith von Sivers; foreword by Peter von Sivers'. Salt Lake City: University of Utah Press.

Tibi B. (2000), ‚Fundamentalismus im Islam: eine Gefahr für den Weltfrieden?' Darmstadt: Primus

Tibi B. (2001), 'Islam between culture and politics'. New York: Palgrave, in association with the Weatherhead Center for International Affairs, Harvard University.

Tibi B. (2001), 'Kreuzzug und Djihad. Der Islam und die christliche Welt'. München: Goldmann Taschenbuchausgabe.

Tibi B. (2001), ‚Der Islam und Deutschland. Muslime in Deutschland' DVA

Tibi B. (2001a), 'Islam between culture and politics'. New York: Palgrave, in association with the Weatherhead Center for International Affairs, Harvard University.

Tibi B. (2001b), 'Kreuzzug und Djihad. Der Islam und die christliche Welt'. München: Goldmann Taschenbuchausgabe.

Tibi B. (2002), 'Islamische Zuwanderung: die gescheiterte Integration' München: Deutsche Verlags-Anstalt.

Tibi B. (2007), ‚The Totalitarianism of Jihadist Islamism and its Challenge to Europe and to Islam' Totalitarian Movements and Political Religions, 8, 1, March: 35 – 54.

Tilly Ch. (1992), 'Coercion, Capital, and European States, Ad 990 – 1992' Malden MA: Blackwell.

Timberlake M. and Kantor J. (1983), 'Economic Growth: A Study of the Less Developed Countries' Sociological Quarterly, 24: 489 - 507.

Timberlake M. and Williams K.R. (1984), 'Dependence, Political Exclusion, and Government Repression: Some Cross - National Evidence' American Sociological Review, 49: 141 - 46.

Timberlake M. and Williams K.R. (1987), 'Structural Position in the World - System, Inequality and Political Violence' Journal of Political and Military Sociology, 15: 1 - 15.

Titmuss R.M. (1974), Social Policy: An Introduction. London: Allen and Unwin.

Tovias A. (2002), 'The Political Economy of the Partnership in Comparative Perspective' The Hebrew University of Jerusalem, Department of International Relations, available at: http://ies.berkeley.edu/research/AlfredTovias.pdf.

Trezzini B. and Bornschier V. (2001), 'Social Stratification and Mobility in the World System: Different Approaches and Recent Research' Department of Sociology, University of Zurich, available at: http://www.suz.unizh.ch/bornschier/publikationen.pdf.

Troll S.J. Chr. (2001), "Muslime in Deutschland. Ziele, Strömungen, Ogranisationen/Strukturen" http://www.jesuiten.org/aktuell/jubilaeum/files/jahresthema_2001_troll_1.pdf

Troll S.J. Chr. W. (1978), 'Sayyid Ahmad Khan: a reinterpretation of Muslim theology' New Delhi: Vikas Publ. House

Troll S.J. Chr. W. (2001), ‚Der europäische Islam: eine reale Perspektive?' Berlin: Morus

Troll S.J. Chr. W. (2001), "Muslime in Deutschland. Ziele, Strömungen, Ogranisationen/Strukturen" http://www.jesuiten.org/aktuell/jubilaeum/files/jahresthema_2001_troll_1.pdf

Troll S.J. Chr. W. (2003), ‚Muslime fragen, Christen antworten' Dortmund: Topos Plus

Troll S.J. Chr. W. (2004), ‚Als Christ dem Islam begegnen' Würzburg: Echter

Troll S.J. Chr. W. (2007), "Progressives Denken im zeitgenössischen Islam" Friedrich Ebert Stiftung, Islam und Gesellschaft, 4 (entire)

Troll S.J. Chr. W. and Bsteh A. (Eds.) (1997), 'One world for all: foundations of a socio-political and cultural pluralism from Christian and Muslim perspectives' New Delhi: Vikas Pub. House

Troll S.J. Chr. W. and Donohue J. (1998), 'Faith, power, and violence: Muslims and Christians in a plural society, past and present' Roma: Pontificio Istituto orientale

Troll S.J. Chr. W. and Vahiduddin S. (1986), 'Islamic experience in contemporary thought' Delhi: Chanakya Publications

Tsai P-L. (1995), 'Foreign Direct Investment and Income Inequality: Further Evidence.' World Development, 23, 3, pps. 469-483.

Tusicisny A. (2004), 'Civilizational Conflicts: More Frequent, Longer, and Bloodier?' Journal of Peace Research, Vol. 41, No. 4 (Jul. 2004), pp. 485-498.

Twomey M. J. (1993), 'Multinational Corporations and the North American Free Trade Agreement' New York: Frederic Praeger Publishers.

United Nations (1995) International Trade Statistics Yearbook 1995, 2 Vols. .

United Nations Centre on Transnational Corporations (1983), 'Transnational Corporations in World Development' New York: United Nations.

United Nations Conference on Trade and Development (current issues), 'World Investment Report.' New York and Geneva: United Nations.

United Nations Development Programme (1998), 'Overcoming Human Poverty'. UN New York, UNDP.

United Nations Development Programme (1998), 'The Shrinking State' UN New York, UNDP.

United Nations Development Programme (2004), 'Reducing Disaster Risk. A Challenge for Development. A Global Report'. UNDP Bureau for Crisis Prevention and Recovery, available at: http://www.undp.org/bcpr/disred/documents/publications/rdr/english/rdr_english.pdf.

United Nations Development Programme (2005), 'Governance Indicators: A users' Guide'. Oslo and New York, United Nations Development Programme, Oslo Governance Centre, available at: http://www.undp.org/oslocentre/docs04/UserGuide.pdf .

United Nations Development Programme (2005), 'Overview Existing Framework of Governance Indicators' available at: Oslo and New York, United Nations Development Programme, Oslo Governance Centre, http://www.undp.org/oslocentre /docsjuly03 /Overview%20Existing%20Framework%20of%20Indicators.xls .

United Nations Development Programme (current issues), 'Human Development Report' New York and Oxford: Oxford University Press.

United Nations Development Programme, Arab Fund for Economic and Social Development (2002), 'Arab Human Development Report 2002. Creating Opportunities for Future Generations' Cairo and New York: United Nations Development Programme Regional Bureau for Arab States (RBAS).

United Nations Development Programme, Regional Bureau for Europe and the CIS (1999), 'Human Development Report for Central and Eastern Europe and the CIS' New York: UNDP.

United Nations Economic and Social Council (1993), 'International Migration Flows Among ECE Countries, 1991' New York: United Nations, CES/778, 27 May.

United Nations Economic Commission for Europe (1994), 'International Migration: Regional Processes and Responses' Geneva: United Nations Economic Commission for Europe Economic Studies, 7 (entire).

United Nations Economic Commission for Europe (1996), 'International Migration in Central and Eastern Europe and the Commonwealth of Independent States' Geneva: United Nations Economic Commission for Europe Economic Studies, 8 (entire).

United Nations Economic Commission for Europe (current issues), 'Economic Survey of Europe' New York: United Nations.

United Nations Economic Commission for Latin America, ECLAC/CEPAL, (2002), 'Globalización y desarrollo". available at: http://www.eclac.cl/cgi-bin/getProd.asp?xml=/publicaciones/xml/6/10026/P10026.xmlandxsl=/tpl/p9f.xslandbase=/MDG/tpl/top-bottom.xsl .

United States Arms Control and Disarmament Agency (current issues), 'World Military Expenditures and Arms Transfers' Washington DC.: US Government Printing Office.

United States Central Intelligence Agency, National Foreign Intelligence Board (2001), 'Growing Global Migration and Its Implications for the United States' Langley, Virginia, National Foreign Intelligence Board, NIE 2001-02D, March 2001, available at: http://www.cia.gov/nic/graphics/migration.pdf.

United States Department of State (curent issues), 'International Drug Control Strategy Report' Washington D.C.: US Government Printing Office.

United States Department of State (current issues), 'Country Reports on Human Rights Practices' Washington D.C.: US Government Printing Office.

United States Government (2002), 'The National Security Strategy of the United States of America". The White House, Washington D.C., available at: http://www.state.gov/ documents/organization/15538.pdf .

Vaeyrynen R. (1987), 'Global Power Dynamics and Collective Violence' in 'The Quest for Peace. Transcending Collective Violence and War among Societies, Cultures and States' (Vaerynen R. et al. (Eds.)), pp. 80 - 96, London: Sage.

Vaeyrynen R. (1997), 'Post-Hegemonic and Post-Socialist Regionalism: A Comparison of East Asia and Central Europe' University of Notre Dame, The Joan B. Kroc Institute Occasional Papers, Internet edition, http://www.nd.edu/.

Van Apeldoom B. (2002), 'Transnational Capitalism and the Struggle over European Integration' London and New York: Routledge.

Van Rossem R. (1996), 'The World System Paradigms General Theory of Development: A Cross - National Test' American Sociological Review, 61, June: 508 - 527.

Vedder R. K. and Gallaway L. E. (1999), 'Unemployment and Jobs in International Perspective' Joint Economic Committee Study, United States Congress, http://www.house.gov/jec/employ/intern.htm.

Veeramani, C. (2003): "Liberalisation, Industry-Specific Factors and Intra-Industry Trade in India", ICRIER Working Paper No. 97.

Vickrey W. (1996), 'Fifteen Fatal Fallacies of Financial Fundamentalism. A Disquisition on Demand Side Economics' New York: Columbia University, Website: http://www.columbia.edu/dlc/wp/econ/vickrey.htm.

Wagstaff A. and Watanabe N. (2002), 'Socioeconomic Inequalities in Child Malnutrition in the Developing World' World Bank Working Papers health and Population at: http://econ.worldbank.org/files/1189_wps2434.pdf.

Walker R. A. (1989), 'The Capitalist Imperative: Territory, Technology and Industrial Growth'. Oxford: Basil Blackwell.

Walker R. A. (1992), 'The New Social Economy: Reworking the Division of Labor.' Cambridge, MA: Basil Blackwell.

Walker R. A. (1995), 'Regulation and flexible specialization as theories of capitalist development. Challengers to Marx and Schumpeter?' in: 'Spatial Practices: Critical Explorations in Social/Spatial Theory.' (Liggett H. and Perry D. (Eds.)) pp. 167-208, London: Sage.

Walker R. A. (1996), 'California's collision of race and class' Representations, No. 55, 163-183, Summer. Reprinted: Robert Post and Michael Rogin (eds.), Race and Representation: Affirmative Action. New York: Zone Books, 1998, pp. 281-308.

Walker R. A. (1999), 'Capital's global turbulence'. Against the Current 78, January-February 1999: 29-35.

Walker R. A. (1999), 'Putting capital in its place: globalization and the prospects for labor'. Geoforum. 30/3: 263-84.

Walker R. A. (2004), 'The Conquest of Bread: 150 Years of California Agribusiness'. New York: The New Press.

Walker R. A. (2004), 'The Spectre of Marxism—The Return of The Limits to Capital'. Antipode (June) 36:3.

Wallerstein I. (1974), 'The Modern World-System 1: Capitalist Agriculture and the Origins of the European World-Economy in the Sixteenth Century'. New York and London: Academic Press.

Wallerstein I. (1976), 'Semi - Peripheral Countries and the Contemporary World Crisis' Theory and Society, 4: 461 - 483.

Wallerstein I. (1978), 'World-System Analysis: Theoretical and Interpretive Issues, ' in: Kaplan, B.H. (ed.), Social Change in the Capitalist World Economy. Beverly Hills, USA: SAGE Publishing, p. 219-235.

Wallerstein I. (1979), 'The Capitalist World Economy' Cambridge, England: Cambridge University Press.

Wallerstein I. (1979), 'Underdevelopment and Phase B: Effect of the Seventeenth - Century Stagnation on Core and Periphery of the European World - Economy' in 'The World - System of Capitalism: Past and Present' (Goldfrank W.L. (Ed.)), pp. 73 - 85, Beverly Hills: Sage.

Wallerstein I. (1980), 'The Modern World-System II: Mercantilism and the Consolidation of the European World-economy, 1600-1750'. New York and London: Academic Press.

Wallerstein I. (1982), 'Socialist States: Mercantilist Strategies and Revolutionary Objectives' in 'Ascent and Decline in the World - System' (Friedman E. (Ed.)), pp. 289 - 300, Beverly Hills: Sage.

Wallerstein I. (1983), 'Crises: The World Economy, the Movements, and the Ideologies' in 'Crises in the World - System' (Bergesen A. (Ed.)), pp. 21 - 36, Beverly Hills: Sage.

Wallerstein I. (1983), 'Historical Capitalism' London: Verso.

Wallerstein I. (1984), 'Der historische Kapitalismus. Uebersetzt von Uta Lehmann - Grube mit einem Nachwort herausgegeben von Hans Heinrich Nolte' Westberlin: Argument - Verlag.

Wallerstein I. (1986), "Krise als Uebergang' in 'Dynamik der globalen Krise' (Amin S. and associates), pp. 4 - 35, Opladen: Westdeutscher Verlag.

Wallerstein I. (1989), 'The Modern World-System III: The Second Era of Great Expansion of the Capitalist World-Economy, 1730-1840s'. New York and London: Academic Press.

Wallerstein I. (1989), 'The National and the Universal: Canada There Be Such a Thing as World Culture?'. Fernand Braudel Centre for the Study of Economies, Historical Systems, and Civilizations, Binghamton, New York: Suny Binghamton.

Wallerstein I. (1990), 'America and the World: Today, Yesterday, and Tomorrow' Fernand Braudel Centre for the Study of Economies, Historical Systems, and Civilizations, Binghamton, New York: Suny Binghamton.

Wallerstein I. (1991), 'The Concept of National Development, 1917 - 1989: Elegy and Requiem' Fernand Braudel Centre for the Study of Economies, Historical Systems, and Civilizations, Binghamton, New York: Suny Binghamton.

Wallerstein I. (1991), 'Who Excludes Whom? or The Collapse of Liberalism and the Dilemmas of Antisystemic Strategy' Fernand Braudel Centre for the Study of Economies, Historical Systems, and Civilizations, Binghamton, New York: Suny Binghamton.

Wallerstein I. (1997), 'The Rise of East Asia, or The World-System in the Twenty-First Century' SUNY Binghamton, http://fbc.binghamton.edu/iwrise-htm.

Wallerstein I. (1998), 'Is Japan Rising or Declining?' Commentary 3, 1, Fernand Braudel Center, Binghamton University.

Wallerstein I. (2000), 'The Essential Wallerstein' New York: The New Press.

Ward K. B. (1984), 'Women in the World-System: Its Impact on Status and Fertility'. New York: Frederic Praeger.

WCY (2006), World Competitiveness Yearbook, IMD, Lausanne, Switzerland.

Weede E. (1985), 'Entwicklungslaender in der Weltgesellschaft' Opladen: Westdeutscher Verlag.

Weede E. (1986), 'Catch - up, distributional coalitions and government as determinants of economic growth or decline in industrialized democracies' The British Journal of Sociology, 37, 2: 194 - 220.

Weede E. (1986), 'Verteilungskoalitionen, Staatstaetigkeit und Stagnation' Politische Vierteljahresschrift, 27, 2: 222 - 236.

Weede E. (1989), 'Democracy and Inequality Reconsidered.' American Sociological Review, 54, pps. 865-868.

Weede E. (1990), 'Wirtschaft, Staat und Gesellschaft' Tübingen: J.C.B. Mohr.

Weede E. (1992), 'Mensch und Gesellschaft. Soziologie aus der Perspektive des methodoligischen Individualismus' Tuebingen: J.C.B. Mohr.

Weede E. (1993), 'Development and underdevelopment: the political economy of inequality'. Boulder, Colo.: L. Rienner Publishers.

Weede E. (1993), 'The Impact of Democracy or Repressiveness on the Quality of Life, Income Distribution and Economic Growth Rates.' International Sociology, 8, pps. 177-195.

Weede E. (1994), 'Determinanten der Kriegsverhuetung waehrend des Kalten Krieges und danach: Nukleare Abschreckung, Demokratie und Freihandel' Politische Vierteljahresschrift, 35, 1: 62 - 84.

Weede E. (1996), 'Economic development, social order, and world politics with special emphasis on war, freedom, the rise and decline of the West, and the future of East Asia'. Boulder: L. Rienner Publishers.

Weede E. (1996), 'Political Regime Type and Variation in Economic Growth Rates' Constitutional Political Economy, 7, no. 3 (1996): 167 (10 pages).

Weede E. (1997), 'Income inequality, democracy and growth reconsidered.' European Journal of Political Economy, Volume 13, Number 4, December 1997, pp. 751 .

Weede E. (1999), 'Economic development, social order, and world politics'. Peace Research Abstracts, 36, no. 3.

Weede E. (1999), 'Future Hegemonic Rivalry between China and the West?' in 'The Future of Global Conflict' (Bornschier V. and Chase-Dunn Ch. K. (Eds.)), pp. 244 - 262, London, Thousand Oaks and New Delhi: Sage Publications.

Weede E. (2002), 'Impact of Intelligence and Institutional Improvements on Economic Growth'. Kyklos, 55, no. 3 (2002): 361-380.

Weede E. (2003), 'On the Rise and Decline of Two Nations' International Interactions, 29, no. 4 (2003): 343-364.

Weede E. (2004), 'Comparative Economic Development in China and Japan'. Japanese Journal of Political Science, 5, no. 1 (2004): 69-90.

Weede E. (2004), 'Does Human Capital Strongly Affect Economic Growth Rates? Yes, But Only If Assessed Properly' Comparative Sociology, 3, no. 2 (2004): 115-134.

Weede E. (2004), 'On Political Violence and its Avoidance' Acta Politica, 39, no. 2 (2004): 152-178.

Weede E. (2004), 'The Diffusion of Prosperity and Peace by Globalization' Independent Review, vol. 9, no. 2, pp. 165-186.

Weede E. (2006), 'Is there a contradiction between freedom and Islam? Paper, Department of Sociology, University of Bonn (FRG); available at: http://admin.fnst.o rg /uploads /896/Weede_engl.pdf

Weede E. and Muller E. N. (1998), 'Rebellion, Violence and Revolution: A Rational Choice Perspective.' Journal of peace research, vol. 35, no. 1, pp. 43 .

Weede E. and Tiefenbach H. (1981), 'Some Recent Explanations of Income Inequality: An Evaluation and Critique.' International Studies Quarterly, 25, 2, June, pps. 255-282.

Weil P. (2005), ‚A Flexible Framework for a Plural Europe' Paris: CNRS (Discussion paper prepared for the UK Presidency, available at http://www.eu2005.gov.uk/servlet/Front?pagename=OpenMarket/Xcelerate/ShowPageandc=Pageandcid=1107293391098anda=KArticleandaid=1119527321606).

Went R. (2002), 'The Enigma of Globalisation: A Journey to a New Stage of Capitalism' London and New York: Routledge.

Wheelwright T. (2001), 'Developments in the Global Economy and their Effects on Australia' available at: http://www.angelfire.com/ma/rank/tedw.html.

Wickrama K. A. S. and Mulford Ch. L. (1996), 'Political Democracy, Economic Development, Disarticulation, and Social Well - Being in Developing Countries' The Sociological Quarterly, 37, 3: 375 - 390.

Wilensky H.L. and C.N. Lebeaux (1976), Individual Society and Social Welfare. New York: Free Press.

Williamson J. G. (1991), 'Inequality, Poverty, and History'. Cambridge, MA.: Basil Blackwell.

Williamson J. G. (1996), 'Globalization, Convergence and History' The Journal of Economic History, 56, 2: 277 - 306.

Williamson J. G. (1997), 'Globalization and Inequalities, Past and Present' The World Bank Research Observer, 12, 2, August: 117-135.

Williamson J. G. (1998), 'Harvard Institute of Economic Research, Internet site (with link-up to the data base on wages in the world periphery 1820-1940): http://www.economics.harvard.edu/~jwilliam/.

Williamson J. G. (1998), 'Real Wages and Relative Factor Prices in the Third World 1820 - 1940: The Mediterranean Basin'. Discussion Paper 1842, Harvard Institute of Economic Research; http://www.economics.harvard.edu/faculty/jwilliam/papers/.

Williamson, J. G. (2002): "Winners and Losers over Two Centuries of Globalization". WIDER Annual Lecture 6. Helsinki: UNU-WIDER.

Wimberley D. W. (1990), 'Investment Dependence and Alternative Explanations of Third World Mortality: A Cross - National Study' American Sociological Review, 55: 75 - 91.

Wimberley D. W. (1991), 'Transnational Corporate Investment and Food Consumption in the Third World: A Cross-National Analysis.' Rural sociology, 1991, vol. 56, no. 3, pp. 406 ff.

Wimberley D. W. and Bello R. (1992), Effects of Foreign Investment, Exports, and Economic Growth on Third World Food Consumption. Social Forces, 70:895-921.

Wimmer A. (2002), 'Nationalist Exclusion and Ethnic Conflict: Shadows of Modernity' Cambridge: Cambridge University Press.

Winters, L. A. (2002): "Trade Policies for Poverty Alleviation", in B. Hoekman, A. Matto and P. English (eds.), Trade, Development and the WTO, Washington, DC, World Bank.

Woehlcke M. (1987), 'Umweltzerstoerung in der Dritten Welt' Munich: C.H. Beck.

Woehlcke M. (1993), 'Der oekologische Nord - Sued - Konflikt' Munich: C.H. Beck.

Wolf, R.; Weede, and E.; Snyder, J. (1996), 'Democratization and the Danger of War.' International security, vol. 20, no. 4, pp. 176 .

Wood A. (1994), 'Structural Unemployment in the North: Global Causes, Domestic Cures' Vienna: Kreisky Commission Symposion, 21 - 22 March.

Woods, N. (1998): "Editorial Introduction. Globalization: Definitions, Debates and Implications". Oxford Development Studies, 26 (1): 5-13.

Woodward A. and Kohli M. (2001), 'Inclusions and Exclusions in European Societies." London and New York: Routledge.

World Bank (2002): "Globalisation, Growth and Poverty: Building an Inclusive World Economy", Policy Research Report, Oxford University Press, New York.

World Bank (current issues), 'World Development Report' Washington D.C.: World Bank and Oxford University Press.

World Bank Middle East and North Africa Region (2002), 'Reducing Vulnerability and Inrceasing Opportunity. Social Protection in the Middle East and North Africa' Washington D.C.: ientations in Development Series.

World Development Report (2003): "FDI Policies for Development: national and International Perspectives".

World Resources Institute (in collaboration with the United Nations Environmental Programme and United Nations Development Programme), (1998), 'World Resources 1998-1999'. New York: Oxford University Press.

Yotopoulos P. A. (1966), 'Economic analysis and economic policy'. Edited by Pan A. Yotopoulos. Contributors: Arthur S. Goldberger [and others]. Athens [Center of Planning and Economic Research] (Center of Planning and Economic Research. Training seminar series, 6).

Yotopoulos P. A. (1967), 'Allocative efficiency in economic development; a cross section analysis of Epirus farming' Athens [Center of Planning and Economic Research] (Center of Planning and Economic Research. Research monograph series, 18).

Yotopoulos P. A. (1977), 'The population problem and the development solution' Stanford, Calif.: Food Research Institute, Stanford University, (Food Research Institute studies; v. 16, no. 1).

Yotopoulos P. A. (1984), 'Middle income classes and food crises' Athens: Centre of Planning and Economic Research, (Papers / Centre of Planning and Economic Research; 5).

Yotopoulos P. A. (1989), 'Distributions of real income: Within countries and by world income classes'. The Review of income and wealth, no. 4, pp. 357 ff. .

Yotopoulos P. A. (1989), 'The (Rip) Tide of Privatization: Lessons from Chile.' World development, vol. 17, no. 5, pp. 683 ff. .

Yotopoulos P. A. (1989), 'The meta-production function approach to technological change in world agriculture.' Journal of development economics, vol. 31, no. 2, pp. 241 ff.

Yotopoulos P. A. (1997), 'Financial crises and the benefits of mildly repressed exchange rates' Stockholm: Stockholm School of Economics, Economic Research Institute, (Working paper series in economics and finance; no. 202, October 1997).

Yotopoulos P. A. (1997), 'Food security, gender and population' New York, NY: United Nations Population Fund, 'E/850/1997'.

Yotopoulos P. A. (2004), 'The Success of the Euro, Globalization, and the EU Enlargement' University of Florence, available at: http://www.ceistorvergata.it/ conferenzeandcon vegni/mondragone/XVI_papers/paper-yotopoulos2.pdf .

Yotopoulos P. A. and Floro S. L. (1992), 'Income distribution, transaction costs and market fragmentation in informal credit markets.' Cambridge journal of economics, 1992, vol. 16, no. 3, pp. 303 ff.

Yotopoulos P. A. and Lin J. Y. (1993), 'Purchasing Power Parities for Taiwan: The Basic Data for 1985 and International Comparisons.' Journal of economic development, 1993, vol. 18, no. 1, pp. 7 ff.

Yotopoulos P. A., Nugent J. B. (1976), 'Economics of development: empirical investigations' New York: Harper and Row.

Yotopoulos P. and Sawada Y. (2005), 'Exchange Rate Misalignment: A New test of Long-Run PPP Based on Cross-Country Data' CIRJE Discussion Paper CIRJE-F-318, February 2005, Faculty of Economics, University of Tokyo, available at: http://www.e.u-tokyo.ac.jp/cirje/research/dp/2005/2005cf318.pdf .

Yunker J. A. (2000), 'Common Progress: The Case for a World Economic Equalization Program' New York: Frederic Praeger.

Zhang J. et al. (2001), "Mortality decline and long-run economic growth" Journal of Public Economics, 80 (2001), pp. 485–507

Zhang J. et al. (2003), "Rising longevity, education, savings, and growth" Journal of Development Economics, 70 (2003), pp. 83–101

ABOUT THE AUTHOR

Arno Tausch (born on February 11, 1951 in Salzburg, Austria) is an Austrian political scientist and one of the founders of quantitative world system and development research in Europe. His research program is focused on world systems theory, development studies and dependency theory, European studies in the framework of core-periphery relationships, and quantitative peace studies. Dr. Tausch, a liberal Catholic, is an active participant in the liberation theology movement and the ecumenical dialogue between the major world religions. He authored or co-authored 14 books in English, 5 books in German, and in all over 170 printed or electronic scholarly and current affairs publications in 6 languages (English, Finnish, French, German, Russian and Spanish) for well over 50 journals and/or publishing institutions around the globe. Among these publications there are 35 articles for 24 major peer-reviewed social science journals, and books and book chapters for such publishing houses as Dutch University Press, Nova Science Publishers, N.Y., Palgrave Macmillan, Rozenberg, Routledge, Saint Martin's Press, N.Y.. In all, Tausch already published in 24 countries around the globe: Argentina; Australia; Austria; Canada; China; Finland; France; Germany; Greece, India; Irish Republic; Israel; Italy; Luxembourg; the Netherlands; Pakistan; Poland; Russia; Slovenia; Spain; Sweden; Turkey, the United Kingdom and the United States of America.

INDEX

A

abortion, 11, 12, 51, 64, 86, 107, 112, 121, 215, 222, 249, 251, 253, 254, 276, 287, 290, 315, 372, 417, 428, 439, 450, 457, 462, 469, 522, 524, 526
academic, 90, 544, 560
acceleration, 191
achievement, 530
adult, 50, 246, 248, 385, 492
adult population, 50, 248
adultery, 86, 107, 113, 120, 215, 220, 249, 251, 255, 287, 319, 439, 450, 469, 491, 522, 524, 527
Afghanistan, ix
Africa, 36, 49, 71, 72, 74, 76, 92, 134, 149, 151, 157, 168, 175, 177, 206, 241, 243, 264, 265, 269, 272, 382, 387, 390, 392, 394, 397, 400, 402, 476, 479, 483, 486, 487, 488, 489, 496, 500, 505, 506, 563, 578
age, ix, 8, 25, 86, 88, 94, 97, 99, 100, 105, 107, 110, 113, 116, 118, 122, 125, 126, 148, 191, 220, 249, 252, 255, 263, 264, 287, 290, 300, 322, 420, 432, 440, 451, 469, 522, 525, 527, 537, 540, 547, 571, 574
agents, 155
aggregates, 207
aggregation, 66
aggression, 274
agricultural, 189
agricultural sector, 189
agriculture, 578
aid, 280, 301, 363, 413, 424, 437, 448, 467
AIDS, 148, 211, 219, 221, 223, 225, 250, 253, 254, 289, 329, 418, 429, 441, 452, 456, 457, 459, 461, 470, 524, 525, 528
Air Force, 559
Albania, 32, 35, 38, 59, 63, 73, 74, 77, 81, 133, 136, 144, 149, 152, 156, 157, 166, 170, 176, 184, 206, 263, 264, 268, 269, 383, 385, 388, 391, 394, 397, 400, 402, 474, 477, 481, 485, 486, 487, 488, 495, 497, 498, 500, 504, 506
alcohol, 24, 87, 88, 93, 109, 110, 114, 121, 249, 251, 255, 277, 283, 287, 317, 320, 417, 428, 439, 451, 469, 523, 525, 527
alcoholism, 283
Algeria, ix, 29, 34, 35, 36, 38, 44, 59, 63, 72, 74, 133, 136, 138, 149, 166, 169, 170, 176, 177, 184, 206, 228, 263, 264, 265, 383, 385, 388, 391, 394, 397, 400, 402, 474, 477, 481, 485, 486, 487, 488, 495, 498, 500, 504
ALL, 37, 177, 210, 213, 216, 225, 227, 251, 252, 253, 254, 255, 522, 524, 526
Allah, 5
allies, 3, 11, 62
alternative, 66, 566
Amsterdam, 148, 542, 562, 569, 570
anomalous, x
ANOVA, 405, 406, 407, 408, 410
Anti-Defamation League, 151
ants, 61, 191
anxiety, xi
apartheid, 274
APEC, 278
appendix, 22, 41, 59, 203, 205, 207, 210, 213, 216, 225, 227, 384
Arab countries, xi, 559
Arabia, 10, 60, 61, 63, 71, 74, 81, 134, 136, 149, 206, 264, 265, 269, 272, 382, 387, 390, 392, 476, 479, 483, 486, 487, 488, 489, 496
Arabs, 149, 289, 298
Argentina, 31, 36, 37, 73, 74, 76, 133, 143, 149, 151, 152, 156, 158, 166, 175, 177, 192, 206, 263, 264, 266, 268, 269, 382, 385, 388, 391, 395, 398, 401, 403, 474, 477, 481, 485, 486, 487, 488, 495, 497, 499, 503, 506, 559, 566, 581
argument, 188, 190, 191
armed forces, 23, 24, 26, 93, 105, 110, 116, 120, 123, 125, 305, 470, 523, 525, 527

Armed Forces, 85, 88, 98, 99, 102, 126, 220, 250, 252, 254, 277, 413, 423, 441, 452
Armenia, 30, 34, 36, 37, 71, 74, 77, 81, 133, 141, 143, 149, 166, 169, 176, 177, 206, 263, 264, 266, 383, 385, 388, 391, 474, 477, 481, 485, 486, 487, 488, 495, 500, 501, 505, 507
Army, 23, 24, 27, 84, 88, 93, 110, 116, 117, 122, 124, 190, 544
ASEAN, 278
Asia, 31, 32, 150, 153, 190, 530, 537, 563, 574, 575, 576
Asian, 12, 37, 64, 177, 278, 298, 542, 544
assassination, 25, 27, 51, 86, 94, 98, 99, 100, 104, 107, 114, 117, 122, 125, 126, 221, 249, 251, 255, 287, 323, 440, 451, 456, 461, 469, 523, 525, 527
assessment, 548
assets, 43, 227
assimiiation, 61
asylum, xiv
Athens, 558, 578
Atlantic, 190, 519, 547, 557
Atlas, 530, 551, 552
attacks, 57, 190
attitudes, ix, x, xi, 1, 10, 11, 43, 50, 55, 61, 62, 123, 133, 134, 155, 209, 211, 212, 214, 215, 218, 220, 221, 222, 227, 248, 249, 251, 255, 275, 295, 296, 348, 380, 444, 454, 456, 457, 459, 460, 462, 472, 524, 525, 527
Australia, 34, 59, 72, 74, 76, 133, 143, 149, 166, 169, 176, 191, 192, 206, 263, 264, 268, 269, 381, 385, 388, 391, 474, 477, 481, 485, 486, 487, 488, 495, 497, 502, 507, 537, 548, 577, 581
Austria, xiii, xiv, xv, 21, 34, 37, 61, 74, 79, 80, 81, 133, 149, 152, 157, 161, 163, 166, 170, 176, 178, 206, 246, 263, 264, 266, 268, 269, 382, 385, 388, 391, 395, 398, 401, 403, 474, 477, 481, 485, 486, 487, 488, 492, 493, 495, 499, 503, 506, 522, 533, 549, 581
authority, xiii, 11, 12, 64, 85, 106, 112, 119, 127, 217, 282, 342, 379, 380, 384, 391, 392, 414, 424, 433, 446, 465, 481, 482, 483
availability, 33, 39, 90, 166, 192
Azerbaijan, 11, 30, 34, 35, 59, 61, 63, 73, 74, 77, 81, 133, 136, 141, 143, 144, 149, 166, 169, 170, 176, 206, 263, 264, 268, 269, 383, 385, 388, 391, 474, 477, 481, 485, 486, 487, 488, 495, 499, 501, 505, 507

B

backwardness, xi, 187
Baltic States, 50, 243, 245
Bangladesh, 11, 29, 31, 34, 35, 36, 37, 38, 49, 59, 61, 63, 74, 77, 81, 133, 136, 138, 141, 143, 144, 149, 151, 166, 169, 170, 176, 177, 178, 184, 206, 243, 263, 264, 268, 269, 381, 385, 388, 391, 394, 397, 400, 402, 474, 477, 481, 485, 486, 487, 488, 495, 496, 501,□507, 540
barriers, 187, 189
basic needs, 284
behavior, ix, 50, 66, 155, 248, 251
Beijing, 531
Belarus, 28, 30, 31, 32, 33, 37, 50, 71, 72, 74, 77, 79, 130, 133, 141, 143, 149, 151, 152, 156, 157, 161, 162, 166, 175, 183, 206, 243, 245, 246, 247, 263, 264, 265, 268, 269, 383, 385, 388, 391, 395, 399, 401, 403, 474, 477, 481, 485, 486, 487, 488, 492, 493, 495, 501, 505, 507
Belgium, 21, 34, 50, 61, 73, 74, 79, 80, 133, 144, 149, 152, 157, 163, 166, 170, 176, 206, 246, 247, 263, 264, 268, 269, 270, 383, 385, 388, 391, 395, 398, 400, 402, 474, 477, 481, 485, 486, 487, 488, 492, 493, 494, 495, 499, 500, 501, 505, 522
beliefs, 27, 53, 85, 86, 94, 106, 107, 113, 114, 117, 118, 122, 222, 276, 285, 335, 372, 412, 415, 422, 426, 443, 445, 453, 455, 457, 462, 471, 473
benchmark, 66
beneficial effect, 51, 256
Bhagwati, 532
bias, 264
birth, 92, 99, 214, 218, 276, 286, 302, 416, 427, 439, 450, 459, 468
blame, 49, 241
blocks, 190
blogs, 59, 132
Bolivia, 192
boredom, 291
Bosnia, 31, 35, 60, 63, 72, 73, 74, 76, 133, 136, 149, 151, 158, 166, 170, 176, 206, 263, 264, 268, 270, 382, 385, 388, 391, 395, 398, 401, 403, 474, 477, 481, 485, 486, 487, 488, 495, 497, 498, 502, 507
Boston, 56, 558
Brazil, xvii, 1, 28, 30, 37, 71, 74, 77, 130, 133, 135, 136, 137, 141, 143, 145, 149, 166, 175, 183, 206, 261, 263, 264, 266, 268, 270, 383, 385, 388, 391, 474, 477, 481, 485, 486, 487, 488, 495, 500, 501, 505, 506
Bretton Woods, 40, 199
bribery, 28, 37, 50, 130, 183, 246, 247, 248, 496, 498, 500, 501, 502, 504, 506
bribes, 1, 25, 28, 29, 30, 31, 37, 97, 130, 131, 135, 136, 137, 140, 142, 145, 183, 379, 380
Britain, 74, 80, 149, 206, 263, 264, 486, 487, 488, 496
broadband, 559
Bronfenbrenner, 535
Brussels, 539, 541, 545, 562

Buddhism, 42, 203, 204, 208, 210, 213, 215, 216, 225, 226, 227, 421, 422, 423, 424, 425, 426, 427, 428, 429, 430, 431, 432, 433, 434, 435, 436, 437, 438, 440, 441, 442, 444, 445, 463
Buddhist, xiv, xv, 43, 70, 75, 78, 150, 156, 227, 261
budget surplus, 186
Buenos Aires, 559, 566
buffer, xi
buildings, 23, 26, 85, 88, 92, 98, 99, 102, 104, 110, 116, 121, 123, 124, 126, 292, 346, 418, 430, 445, 455, 473
Bulgaria, 10, 21, 33, 35, 36, 37, 61, 71, 74, 77, 78, 80, 103, 133, 149, 152, 157, 161, 162, 166, 170, 176, 177, 206, 246, 263, 264, 268, 270, 382, 385, 388, 391, 396, 399, 401, 403, 474, 477, 481, 485, 486, 487, 488, 492, 493, 495, 498, 499, 502, 522
bureaucracy, 26, 111, 190

C

Camp David, 155
Canada, 31, 33, 59, 72, 74, 133, 141, 143, 149, 151, 153, 156, 158, 166, 169, 175, 191, 206, 263, 264, 268, 270, 381, 385, 388, 391, 394, 397, 400, 402, 474, 477, 481, 485, 486, 487, 488, 495, 498, 502, 506, 532, 563, 575, 581
Cape Town, 547
capital intensive, 189
capitalism, 39, 55, 160, 186, 189, 192, 528, 566
Capitalism, 188, 529, 531, 534, 540, 549, 552, 553, 556, 560, 563, 566, 567, 574, 575, 577
capitalist, 188, 189, 190, 191, 540, 574
carbon, 560, 563
Caribbean, 563, 566
catalyst, 39, 186
category a, 112, 114, 116
Catholic, xiii, 12, 37, 40, 42, 43, 49, 50, 54, 64, 70, 75, 78, 80, 150, 156, 160, 177, 197, 213, 215, 226, 227, 243, 248, 261, 262, 268, 581
Catholics, 11, 32, 42, 43, 50, 51, 61, 153, 158, 205, 206, 213, 215, 218, 226, 227, 248, 249, 251, 256, 522
causality, 188
Census Bureau, 111
Central America, 298
Central Europe, xvii, 1, 41, 50, 135, 136, 137, 145, 200, 243, 245, 540, 574
Central Intelligence Agency, 573
CES, 573
Ceteris paribus, 40, 195
channels, 40, 199
charm, 280, 288
cheating, 1, 25, 28, 29, 30, 31, 37, 40, 50, 87, 94, 97, 98, 100, 105, 108, 113, 121, 123, 124, 125, 130, 131, 135, 136, 137, 140, 142, 145, 183, 199, 218, 220, 246, 247, 249, 251, 254, 277, 287, 313, 379, 380, 417, 428, 439, 451, 463, 469, 496, 498, 500, 501, 502, 504, 506, 523, 524, 526
child well-being, 65, 67
Chile, 31, 71, 74, 77, 133, 149, 151, 152, 156, 158, 166, 175, 192, 206, 263, 264, 266, 382, 385, 388, 391, 394, 397, 400, 402, 474, 477, 481, 485, 486, 488, 496, 498, 500, 505, 506, 551, 566, 578
China, 11, 31, 38, 62, 72, 74, 133, 141, 143, 149, 166, 175, 184, 206, 263, 264, 265, 268, 270, 381, 385, 388, 391, 394, 397, 400, 402, 474, 477, 481, 485, 486, 488, 496, 497, 499, 502, 507, 550, 562, 576, 581
Christianity, ix, 43, 49, 227, 242, 530, 533, 558
Christians, v, xi, 36, 148, 173, 227, 289, 535, 572
CIA, 97, 103
citizens, xi, xiii, 12, 27, 44, 56, 65, 91, 92, 106, 112, 114, 116, 117, 118, 120, 122, 123, 147, 204, 206, 231, 421, 422, 423, 424, 425, 426, 427, 428, 429, 430, 431, 432, 485, 486, 487, 495
citizenship, 53, 56, 60
Civil Rights, 538
civil service, 22, 24, 26, 93, 109, 115, 120, 125, 126, 307, 470, 523, 525, 526
civil society, 50, 248
classes, 300, 564, 578
classical, ix, 45, 47, 48, 207, 233, 237, 238
CO_2, 544
coalitions, 576
cohesion, x, xvii, 1, 2, 28, 39, 40, 130, 137, 144, 179, 186, 199, 541
Cold War, 544
collaboration, 567, 578
Colombia, 74, 76, 133, 143, 149, 192, 206, 263, 264, 266, 381, 385, 388, 391, 474, 477, 481, 485, 486, 488, 496, 498, 499, 503
colonialism, 44, 228
Colorado, 534, 537
Columbia, 28, 37, 55, 130, 183, 549, 555, 574
Columbia University, 28, 37, 55, 130, 183, 549, 574
commerce, 5
Common Market, 530
Commonwealth of Independent States, 573
Communism, 39, 190, 191, 536
communist countries, 40, 195
communities, x, xiii, xiv, xvii, 1, 32, 43, 125, 147, 151, 153, 206, 226, 264
community, ix, xiii, xiv, 25, 31, 40, 46, 56, 97, 103, 147, 197, 237, 294, 541
comparative research, 41, 188, 203

competition, 22, 43, 45, 46, 47, 81, 228, 233, 234, 237, 238, 250, 379, 380, 384, 385, 386, 387, 474, 475, 476, 523, 525, 527
competition policy, 45, 46, 47, 233, 234, 237
competitiveness, 555
compliance, 106
components, 65, 66, 67, 166, 208, 235, 236, 239, 240, 464, 493
computation, 65, 66, 67
computing, 66
concentration, 189
confession, 8, 54, 88, 110, 116, 122, 261, 263
confidence, 51, 124, 215, 220, 250, 252, 253, 254, 255, 259, 277, 278, 279, 441, 442, 452, 460, 463, 470, 522, 523, 524, 525, 526, 527, 528
confidence interval, 259
conflict, 23, 92, 155, 545, 563
conflict resolution, 23, 92, 563
confrontation, 79
Confucianism, 262
Congress, 545, 574
conjecture, 126
Connecticut, 529
consciousness, 50, 248
consensus, 26, 111, 112, 117
consent, 25, 86, 94, 97, 99, 100, 105, 107, 113, 118, 125, 126, 220, 249, 252, 255, 287, 322, 440, 451, 469, 522, 525, 527
conservation, 38, 184, 185, 209, 215, 218, 219, 221, 223, 247, 275, 300, 393, 397, 400, 412, 420, 422, 431, 434, 444, 447, 454, 455, 456, 458, 461, 465, 472
constraints, 190
construction, ix, 12, 65, 245
consumption, 189, 217, 280, 413, 424, 437, 448, 467
consumption patterns, 189
content analysis, 54
control, 5, 39, 191, 281, 283, 352, 414, 425, 440, 451, 469
convergence, 40, 189, 194, 195
conversion, xiv
conviction, 25, 97
corporations, 189
correlation, 28, 50, 67, 248, 251
correlations, 50, 51, 180, 248, 256
corruption, 5, 40, 50, 123, 124, 199, 248, 281, 413, 424, 445, 454, 472
costs, 548, 554, 579
country of origin, 148, 250, 253, 289, 332
credit, 58, 60, 62, 63, 132, 154, 159, 160, 161, 162, 189, 230, 579
credit market, 579
crime, 279, 543

criticism, 130
Croatia, 32, 49, 50, 61, 73, 74, 77, 78, 81, 133, 149, 152, 156, 157, 163, 192, 206, 243, 245, 246, 263, 264, 266, 268, 270, 382, 385, 388, 391, 395, 398, 401, 403, 474, 477, 481, 485, 486, 488, 492, 493, 496, 497, 499, 500, 503, 507
culture, ix, 10, 11, 25, 26, 28, 31, 36, 42, 43, 55, 56, 62, 97, 111, 127, 128, 141, 174, 188, 190, 226, 227, 281, 296, 297, 420, 431, 443, 453, 471, 571
current account, 188
current account balance, 188
cycles, 568
Czech Republic, 21, 33, 34, 72, 73, 74, 76, 79, 80, 133, 149, 151, 153, 157, 160, 163, 166, 170, 176, 206, 246, 263, 264, 266, 382, 385, 388, 391, 395, 398, 401, 403, 474, 477, 481, 485, 486, 488, 492, 493, 496, 498, 500, 504, 522

D

danger, 43, 50, 155, 227, 241, 248
data analysis, 259
data collection, xv, 53, 55
data set, 41, 54, 203
death, x, 214, 221, 275, 286, 297, 365, 412, 416, 422, 427, 434, 439, 441, 447, 450, 452, 456, 461, 463, 465, 469, 470
debates, ix, 55, 186, 187
decay, xvii, 1, 22, 31, 40, 50, 77, 135, 136, 137, 141, 145, 199, 246, 256
decision makers, 7, 37, 124, 177
decisions, 25, 51, 87, 94, 98, 99, 101, 104, 108, 115, 118, 292, 357, 419, 430, 434, 447, 465
defense, 249, 251, 287, 440, 451, 469
definition, 28, 135, 241
Denmark, 11, 21, 30, 33, 34, 36, 61, 64, 74, 79, 80, 81, 133, 138, 149, 151, 153, 157, 161, 163, 166, 169, 175, 177, 191, 192, 206, 246, 263, 264, 266, 268, 270, 383, 385, 388, 391, 395, 398, 401, 402, 474, 477, 481, 485, 486, 488, 492, 493, 496, 497, 498, 502, 522
Department of State, xiii, 150, 573
dependency ratio, 561
dependent variable, 39, 193, 406, 408
depressed, 209, 217, 220, 222, 281, 437, 448, 457, 462, 467
depression, 569
deprivation, 541
deregulation, 53, 536
destruction, 5, 49, 241, 494
developed countries, 188, 274, 411, 422, 563
developed nations, 35, 173
developing countries, 28, 37, 130, 183, 188, 189, 301, 567

developing nations, 188, 189
deviation, 100, 102
diminishing returns, 39, 191
direct investment, 187, 565
disability, 148
disabled, 277, 293
discipline, 186
discourse, 48, 55, 238, 555
discrimination, 8, 13, 31, 49, 53, 54, 148, 241, 242, 243, 276
disorder, 547, 571
dissatisfaction, 30, 31, 140, 142
distribution, 23, 86, 88, 188, 189, 292, 560, 561, 579
diversity, 53, 56
division, 187, 188, 189, 190, 551
division of labor, 188, 189
divorce, 11, 64, 85, 101, 106, 220, 222, 249, 251, 254, 287, 315, 417, 428, 439, 451, 457, 463, 469, 522, 524, 526
Dominican Republic, 10, 36, 49, 61, 73, 74, 76, 133, 143, 149, 167, 175, 177, 206, 243, 263, 264, 266, 381, 385, 388, 391, 474, 477, 481, 485, 487, 488, 496, 498, 499, 500, 503, 507
download, 89, 90, 91, 92, 210, 213, 216, 225, 227, 530, 536, 565
dream, 5, 51, 91, 256
drinking, 88, 110, 249, 251, 287, 317
drug addict, 330, 469, 524, 525, 527
drugs, 24, 87, 93, 109, 115, 120, 249, 252, 255, 277, 287, 318, 417, 428, 440, 451, 469, 523, 526, 527

E

earth, 10, 26, 27, 30, 61, 111, 122, 138, 234
East Asia, 190, 278, 530, 537, 544, 574, 575, 576
Eastern Europe, 49, 190, 241, 547, 573
ECOFIN, 562
ecological, 556
Ecological Economics, 549
ecology, 209, 215, 219, 221, 223, 275, 276, 300, 412, 422, 434, 447, 456, 458, 461, 465
Economic Commission for Latin America, 566, 573
economic development, 35, 173, 533, 567, 578, 579
economic growth, 35, 39, 40, 41, 55, 173, 186, 187, 188, 191, 193, 194, 195, 196, 199, 200, 297, 420, 431, 530, 531, 576, 579
economic growth rate, 40, 41, 187, 194, 195, 200
economic integration, 65
economic performance, 556
economic policy, 552, 578
economic reforms, 280
economic status, 13, 48, 238, 296, 419, 431, 440, 451, 469
economic theory, 561

economics, 35, 36, 173, 174, 191, 531, 540, 560, 561, 577, 578, 579
education, 25, 85, 88, 97, 98, 99, 101, 102, 104, 124, 250, 252, 254, 278, 280, 388, 389, 390, 413, 423, 424, 441, 452, 522, 546
educational attainment, 66, 532, 564
educational system, xi
EEA, viii, 59, 61, 80, 97, 100, 102, 103, 124, 125, 126, 264, 509
egalitarianism, 46, 48, 234, 238
Egypt, ix, 29, 31, 34, 35, 36, 49, 50, 55, 60, 63, 74, 81, 133, 136, 138, 141, 143, 144, 149, 152, 155, 167, 169, 170, 176, 177, 206, 243, 247, 263, 264, 268, 270, 381, 385, 388, 391, 474, 477, 481, 485, 487, 488, 496, 497, 502
El Salvador, 74, 77, 133, 149, 192, 206, 263, 264, 266, 382, 385, 388, 391, 474, 477, 481, 485, 487, 488, 496, 498, 500, 503, 506
elderly, 26, 29, 30, 38, 98, 99, 102, 104, 131, 135, 136, 137, 140, 141, 142, 145, 183, 185, 209, 212, 217, 219, 221, 222, 223, 224, 247, 275, 277, 293, 294, 300, 379, 380, 384, 388, 389, 390, 393, 394, 396, 400, 412, 420, 422, 432, 435, 445, 454, 456, 458, 460, 461, 465, 472, 477, 478, 479, 480
emancipation, 49, 241
embryos, 249, 251, 254, 287, 323, 523, 524, 527
emerging markets, 566
emotions, 288
employees, 290
employment, 53, 148, 188, 279
empowerment, 166, 168, 242
energy, 274
engagement, x, 65, 397
engines, 228
England, 533, 547, 559, 561, 575
enlargement, 53, 537, 540, 546, 552
Enlightenment, vii, viii, xv, 5, 11, 22, 25, 26, 32, 35, 41, 42, 44, 51, 62, 81, 98, 111, 112, 117, 147, 153, 155, 158, 173, 196, 200, 212, 228, 256, 405, 411
enrollment, 186
enrollment rates, 186
entertainment, 299, 420, 431, 444, 454, 472
environment, 1, 38, 65, 179, 184, 185, 186, 209, 212, 215, 217, 219, 220, 221, 223, 224, 247, 274, 275, 280, 281, 293, 301, 302, 393, 400, 412, 413, 419, 421, 422, 424, 430, 432, 434, 437, 442, 445, 447, 448, 452, 455, 456, 458, 459, 461, 465, 467, 470, 473, 561
environmental issues, 276
environmental protection, 11, 64, 93, 116, 118, 127, 309, 470, 523, 526, 527
EPC, 539

equality, 35, 44, 173, 233, 235, 236, 239, 240, 249, 251, 255, 282, 286, 347, 348, 414, 417, 424, 427, 433, 446, 465, 524, 525, 528
ERD, 39, 192, 194, 195, 406, 407, 408, 409, 410
erosion, 49, 50, 243, 245, 246, 248
espionage, 5, 155
EST, 111
Estonia, 21, 30, 34, 50, 72, 74, 76, 79, 80, 133, 141, 143, 149, 152, 157, 162, 167, 170, 175, 206, 243, 245, 246, 263, 264, 268, 270, 383, 385, 388, 391, 395, 398, 401, 403, 474, 478, 481, 485, 487, 488, 492, 493, 496, 500, 505, 522
ETA, 289
ethics, 3
ethnic background, 27, 86, 94, 107, 115, 117, 122, 285, 339
Euro, vii, ix, 12, 25, 40, 61, 97, 100, 103, 123, 124, 125, 126, 199, 264, 530, 578
European Commission, 31, 147, 536, 541, 562
European Community, 533, 536
European integration, 21, 55, 190
European Parliament, 53, 541
European policy, 32, 51, 52, 153, 158
European Union (EU), viii, xv, 8, 10, 11, 13, 24, 26, 31, 34, 36, 37, 39, 40, 41, 49, 51, 53, 59, 63, 87, 93, 98, 99, 101, 105, 108, 115, 119, 125, 126, 147, 190, 192, 193, 195, 200, 241, 250, 252, 255, 278, 310, 494, 509, 523, 525, 527, 530, 534, 540, 545, 552, 567, 570
Europeans, 25, 97, 103, 104, 105, 277, 298
Eurostat, 187, 192
euthanasia, 27, 87, 108, 112, 121, 123, 215, 222, 249, 251, 254, 276, 287, 316, 417, 428, 440, 451, 457, 462, 469, 522, 524, 526
evil, 5, 11, 28, 37, 62, 130, 183, 286, 297
exchange rate, 192, 578
exclusion, 31, 148
execution, xi
exercise, 166, 250
exploitation, 281, 551, 567
exposure, 281, 36
extraction, 208, 236, 240, 464
extremism, ix, x, xi, 297

F

factor analysis, 1, 2, 29, 45, 46, 47, 66, 128, 131, 133, 135, 136, 137, 140, 142, 145, 207, 210, 213, 216, 225, 227, 233, 237
failure, 179
faith, 40, 57, 148, 155, 192, 193, 211, 214, 217, 221, 284, 368, 415, 426, 438, 449, 450, 455, 459, 461, 468, 535

family, x, xiv, xvii, 1, 3, 10, 12, 22, 26, 43, 45, 46, 49, 50, 61, 63, 64, 65, 77, 79, 81, 111, 131, 214, 218, 220, 221, 226, 233, 234, 235, 236, 239, 240, 241, 243, 247, 276, 277, 281, 282, 283, 291, 293, 296, 298, 342, 412, 414, 423, 424, 425, 434, 435, 447, 456, 459, 461, 465, 466, 494, 530
family life, 214, 218, 220, 221, 276, 282, 342, 412, 414, 423, 425, 434, 435, 447, 456, 459, 461, 465, 466
family members, 49, 243
family relationships, 65
farming, 578
fatherhood, xv
fatwa, xi
FDI, 528, 546, 578
fear, 250
fears, 53
fertility, 564
finance, 531, 578
financial institution, 40, 199
financial institutions, 40, 199
financial markets, 187
financial resources, 5
financial support, xiii
financing, 191
Finland, 21, 30, 32, 34, 50, 72, 74, 77, 79, 80, 133, 139, 149, 152, 156, 157, 163, 167, 169, 175, 191, 206, 243, 245, 246, 263, 264, 266, 268, 270, 382, 385, 388, 391, 395, 398, 400, 402, 474, 478, 481, 485, 487, 488, 492, 493, 496, 498, 499, 500, 504, 507, 522, □551, 581
fire, 5, 229, 230
firms, 87, 108, 113, 121, 187, 281, 352
First World, 188
fluctuations, 188
focus group, 565
focus groups, 565
food, 51, 249, 251, 253, 254, 287, 297, 324, 523, 524, 527, 578
forecasting, 555
Foreign Direct Investment, 186, 543, 551, 553, 563, 565, 572
foreign investment, 187, 189
foreign policy, 563
foreigners, 127, 130
formal education, 282, 414, 425
Fox, 542
fragmentation, 579
France, xvii, 1, 11, 21, 30, 33, 34, 44, 49, 50, 54, 61, 64, 73, 74, 79, 132, 133, 135, 136, 137, 139, 141, 143, 145, 149, 152, 157, 163, 167, 169, 175, 186, 206, 228, 243, 245, 246, 247, 263, 264, 268, 270, 273, 383, 385, 388, 391, 395, 398, 401, 403, 474,

478, 481, 485, 487, 488, 492, 493, 494, 495, 496, 500, 505, 506, 522, 542, 581
fraud, 1, 28, 29, 31, 37, 50, 130, 131, 135, 136, 137, 140, 142, 145, 183, 246, 247, 248, 379, 380, 384, 388, 389, 390, 477, 478, 479, 480, 496, 498, 500, 501, 502, 504, 506
free trade, 11, 64
freedom, x, xiv, 11, 39, 62, 87, 108, 113, 121, 186, 190, 191, 192, 194, 195, 274, 280, 281, 282, 283, 302, 333, 347, 352, 373, 406, 407, 408, 409, 410, 413, 414, 424, 425, 440, 451, 469, 576
freedom of choice, 283, 414, 425, 440, 451, 469
freedoms, 11, 62
Friday, 43, 227
FTA, 61, 80, 100, 102, 124, 125, 126, 264
fuel, 48, 241
funds, 40, 191, 199

G

Gallup, 10, 22, 55, 57, 58, 59, 69, 303
Gallup Poll, 57
GDP, 39, 66, 186, 191, 192, 193, 194, 195, 406, 407, 408, 409, 410, 536
GDP per capita, 66
gender, ix, x, 8, 10, 12, 22, 36, 49, 55, 61, 64, 77, 79, 88, 110, 116, 122, 131, 148, 166, 168, 173, 190, 205, 206, 241, 242, 263, 264, 266, 269, 270, 271, 272, 548, 578
gender equality, ix, x, 12, 64, 190, 548
gender role, 12, 36, 64, 173, 242
generation, 10, 56
Geneva, 548, 552, 565, 572, 573
geography, 39, 191, 542
Georgia, 30, 72, 74, 77, 133, 141, 143, 149, 167, 176, 206, 263, 264, 268, 270, 383, 385, 388, 391, 475, 478, 481, 485, 487, 488, 496, 499, 500, 505, 506
Germany, x, 21, 30, 34, 50, 61, 73, 74, 77, 79, 80, 81, 133, 139, 149, 151, 152, 153, 157, 158, 159, 163, 167, 170, 176, 206, 243, 245, 246, 263, 264, 266, 268, 270, 383, 385, 389, 391, 395, 398, 401, 403, 475, 478, 481, 485, 487, 488, 492, 493, 496, 498, 499, 503, 506, 522, 581
global economy, 190
global terrorism, 11, 57, 61, 568
global village, 536, 542
GNP, 39, 192, 194, 195, 406, 407, 408, 409, 410
goals, 10, 61, 75, 76, 288, 291, 300, 302, 418, 420, 421, 429, 432, 436, 437, 445, 448, 454, 466, 467, 472
google, 228
governance, 545, 569
government intervention, 190

government policy, 276
graph, 192, 488
Great Britain, 21, 34, 71, 74, 79, 80, 81, 133, 149, 152, 158, 163, 167, 169, 176, 206, 246, 263, 264, 265, 268, 270, 382, 386, 389, 391, 394, 397, 400, 402, 475, 478, 481, 486, 487, 488, 492, 493, 496, 498, 499, 504, 522
Great Depression, 557
Greece, 21, 30, 34, 36, 37, 50, 61, 74, 78, 80, 81, 133, 141, 143, 149, 152, 157, 163, 167, 170, 176, 177, 206, 243, 245, 246, 263, 264, 266, 383, 386, 389, 391, 394, 397, 400, 402, 475, 478, 482, 486, 487, 488, 492, 493, 496, 500, 501, 505, 522, 581
Greenhouse, 538, 544
growth, 35, 39, 40, 41, 55, 173, 179, 186, 187, 188, 189, 191, 193, 194, 195, 196, 199, 200, 293, 297, 419, 420, 430, 431, 528, 530, 531, 538, 539, 540, 545, 547, 551, 556, 566, 576, 579
growth rate, 194
guest workers, 47, 237
guiding principles, 179
Guyana, 549
Gypsies, 148, 160, 162, 250, 253, 255, 289, 298, 332, 524, 526, 527

H

habitat, 299
Hamas, vii, 5, 32, 155
handicapped, 38, 183, 185, 209, 212, 215, 217, 221, 222, 223, 247, 273, 299, 300, 393, 394, 396, 400, 420, 432, 433, 445, 446, 454, 456, 457, 458, 460, 461, 462, 464, 472
handicapped people, 299
hands, 50, 246, 247, 294, 496, 498, 500, 502, 504, 506
happiness, 11, 63, 281, 414, 424
harm, 300, 343, 445, 454, 472
Harvard, 55, 531, 532, 535, 542, 544, 553, 560, 571, 577
health, 25, 27, 38, 65, 93, 108, 116, 117, 122, 184, 185, 186, 209, 211, 217, 219, 220, 221, 223, 224, 247, 273, 275, 297, 300, 310, 393, 397, 402, 412, 420, 422, 431, 433, 434, 444, 446, 447, 454, 455, 456, 458, 460, 461, 464, 465, 472, 523, 525, 527, 552, 563, 574
health care, 25, 27, 93, 108, 116, 117, 122, 310, 523, 525, 527
health care system, 25, 27, 93, 108, 116, 117, 122, 310, 523, 525, 527
health services, 552
heavy drinkers, 328, 469, 524, 526, 528
Hebrew, 572
height, 44, 228

higher education, 48, 238
HM Treasury, 547
homicide, 489
homicide rate, 489
homicide rates, 489
homosexuality, x, 11, 29, 63, 88, 100, 110, 131, 135, 136, 137, 138, 140, 142, 145, 212, 220, 222, 224, 249, 251, 254, 276, 287, 314, 379, 380, 384, 385, 386, 387, 417, 428, 440, 451, 457, 458, 460, 462, 469, 474, 475, 476, 523, 525, 526
homosexuals, 12, 45, 46, 47, 48, 64, 233, 237, 238, 330, 469, 524, 525, 528
honesty, 284
Hong Kong, 546
horizon, 32, 153, 158
hospitality, xiv
host, 187
hostilities, v, x
House, 282, 530, 535, 568, 572
household, 224, 243, 281, 285, 290, 295, 337, 416, 419, 427, 431, 443, 444, 453, 454, 459, 460, 471, 472
household composition, 243
housing, 285, 295, 336, 353, 415, 426, 442, 453, 471
human capital, 51, 547, 569
human condition, 188, 190
human development, 65, 66, 174, 530
human development index, 66, 174, 530
Human Development Report, 190, 560, 573
human resource development, 190
human rights, 38, 42, 184, 185, 209, 212, 213, 215, 217, 218, 219, 221, 223, 224, 247, 275, 295, 300, 301, 361, 393, 394, 396, 400, 412, 419, 420, 422, 430, 431, 434, 442, 444, 447, 453, 454, 455, 456, 458, 460, 461, 465, 471, 472
Human rights, 274
human values, 128
humane, xi
humanism, xvii, 1, 11, 62
humanitarian, 209, 212, 214, 222, 223, 224, 274, 411, 421, 433, 446, 457, 458, 463, 464
humanity, 50, 155, 248, 535
Hungarian, 188
Hungarians, 298
Hungary, 10, 21, 30, 39, 61, 71, 72, 74, 76, 79, 80, 81, 133, 141, 149, 163, 184, 192, 206, 246, 263, 264, 266, 268, 270, 383, 386, 389, 391, 395, 398, 401, 403, 475, 478, 482, 486, 487, 488, 492, 493, 496, 497, 498, 501, 504, 522
husband, 293, 419, 430, 436, 448, 466
hypothesis, 23, 36, 88, 173

I

ICT, 528, 546
identification, 207
identity, x, 1, 22, 28, 41, 53, 56, 84, 129, 200, 203, 205, 546, 548
ideology, 47, 55, 129, 237
ILO, 548
images, 44, 63, 132, 159, 161, 228, 229
imagination, 56, 215, 284, 415, 426, 438, 449, 450, 468
imbalances, 188
IMF, 538, 560
Immanuel Kant, 3
immigrants, 11, 22, 26, 27, 35, 45, 46, 47, 48, 52, 61, 69, 78, 80, 84, 86, 94, 98, 99, 101, 103, 105, 107, 115, 117, 122, 124, 125, 126, 130, 173, 233, 237, 238, 277, 286, 293, 294, 329, 417, 428, 469, 524, 526, 528
immigration, 59, 147
implementation, 63, 293
imprisonment, 297
in transition, 533, 538
inactive, 39, 40, 41, 140, 186, 193, 194, 199, 201, 344, 381, 382, 383, 408, 409
incentive, 40, 189, 199
incentives, 189, 348
incidence, 151
inclusion, 530, 547
income distribution, 188, 189, 560, 561
income inequality, 35, 36, 47, 173, 188, 189, 237, 536, 542
income support, 547
income transfers, 561
incomes, 295, 377, 419, 431, 444, 454, 472, 540
independence, 56, 215, 217, 284, 415, 426, 438, 449, 450, 468, 559
independent variable, 39, 192
index numbers, 66
India, xiv, 11, 32, 34, 38, 49, 64, 72, 73, 74, 77, 133, 149, 156, 167, 169, 176, 184, 206, 241, 263, 265, 268, 270, 271, 382, 386, 389, 391, 394, 397, 400, 402, 475, 478, 482, 486, 487, 488, 496, 498, 499, 500, 504, 507, 540, 562, 574, 581
Indian, xv, 298, 543
Indiana, 569
Indians, 148, 149, 289, 298, 299
indicators, 29, 42, 45, 50, 65, 66, 67, 137, 172, 174, 187, 190, 193, 207, 216, 217, 218, 220, 222, 223, 224, 233, 248, 568
indices, 2, 12, 65, 66, 67, 501, 502, 504, 506
indigenous, 189

Indonesia, 10, 29, 34, 35, 49, 60, 61, 63, 71, 74, 80, 133, 136, 138, 149, 167, 169, 170, 176, 206, 243, 263, 265, 268, 270, 271, 382, 386, 389, 391, 475, 478, 482, 486, 487, 488, 496, 497, 498, 501, 504
industrial, 543, 548
industrialisation, 554
industrialization, 189
industry, 282, 283, 286, 293, 414, 425
inequality, 36, 40, 50, 173, 186, 188, 189, 199, 248, 530, 543, 551, 555, 563, 568, 576
inequity, 189
infant mortality, 563
Information Age, 536
innocence, 124
innovation, 549, 562
Innovation, 556, 566
insertion, 187
inspection, 207
institutions, 9, 25, 53, 97, 124, 256, 257, 536, 581
insurance, 536
integration, 8, 13, 21, 22, 51, 52, 55, 59, 65, 69, 78, 80, 103, 104, 105, 190, 533, 537
interactions, 28, 128, 570
interest rates, 187
international division of labor, 187, 190
International Monetary Fund, 538
International Trade, 548, 572
Internet, 10, 44, 56, 65, 228, 229, 231, 232, 534, 536, 537, 559, 568, 574, 577
interrelations, 45, 233
interstate, 571
intervention, 190
interview, 8, 10, 56, 59, 88, 110, 116, 122, 263, 264, 266, 268, 269, 270, 271, 272, 277, 279, 287, 294, 295, 297, 419, 430
interviews, 10, 57, 59
inverted-U, 530
investment, 39, 186, 187, 188, 189, 193, 562, 565
investors, 189, 563
Iran, ix, xi, 10, 35, 37, 49, 55, 60, 61, 63, 71, 74, 80, 133, 136, 143, 144, 149, 167, 170, 175, 177, 178, 189, 206, 243, 263, 265, 268, 271, 381, 386, 389, 391, 475, 478, 482, 486, 487, 488, 496, 497, 500, 502, 555
Iraq, ix, 10, 31, 60, 61, 63, 71, 74, 133, 136, 143, 149, 151, 206, 263, 265, 268, 271, 382, 386, 389, 391, 475, 478, 482, 486, 487, 488, 496, 506
Ireland, 21, 34, 37, 50, 61, 73, 74, 78, 80, 133, 143, 149, 152, 158, 163, 167, 170, 176, 178, 191, 206, 243, 245, 246, 263, 264, 265, 266, 268, 271, 381, 386, 389, 391, 395, 398, 401, 403, 475, 478, 482, 486, 487, 488, 492, 493, 496, 498, 499, 503, 522, 551

Islamic, vii, ix, x, xi, xiii, xv, 3, 5, 11, 12, 28, 35, 37, 55, 60, 61, 63, 64, 71, 74, 80, 129, 133, 136, 143, 149, 155, 167, 170, 175, 178, 190, 196, 206, 229, 263, 265, 268, 271, 273, 286, 381, 386, 389, 391, 475, 478, 482, 486, 487, 488, 496, 497, 500, 502, 539, 548, 555, 558, 568, 572
Islamic movements, ix, 155
Islamism, 571
Israel, 32, 62, 63, 74, 133, 143, 149, 150, 155, 206, 263, 265, 268, 271, 284, 291, 382, 386, 389, 391, 475, 478, 482, 486, 487, 488, 496, 507, 581
Italy, x, 21, 33, 34, 36, 37, 50, 61, 73, 74, 78, 80, 133, 143, 149, 152, 157, 161, 162, 167, 170, 176, 177, 206, 243, 245, 246, 263, 264, 265, 266, 382, 386, 389, 391, 395, 398, 401, 403, 475, 478, 482, 486, 487, 488, 492, 493, 496, 498, 499, 503, 506, 522, 562, 581

J

Japan, 49, 73, 74, 77, 133, 143, 149, 191, 206, 243, 263, 265, 266, 267, 298, 299, 382, 386, 389, 391, 395, 398, 401, 403, 475, 478, 482, 486, 487, 488, 496, 497, 498, 502, 506, 547, 575, 576
Japanese, 299, 576
Jerusalem, 572
Jewry, 11, 61
Jews, ix, 10, 11, 32, 36, 45, 47, 48, 61, 62, 148, 149, 150, 151, 152, 153, 158, 173, 180, 206, 211, 216, 219, 221, 223, 225, 233, 235, 236, 237, 238, 239, 240, 250, 253, 254, 289, 299, 330, 418, 429, 441, 451, 455, 458, 459, 461, 469, 524, 526, 528
jihad, 3
job satisfaction, 286
jobs, 29, 86, 94, 107, 112, 119, 131, 135, 136, 137, 138, 140, 142, 145, 179, 286, 299, 379, 380, 384, 388, 389, 390, 433, 446, 464, 477, 478, 479, 480
joining, 100, 292, 345, 418, 430, 445, 455, 473
Jordan, 11, 29, 34, 35, 36, 37, 55, 60, 63, 64, 72, 74, 133, 136, 138, 149, 167, 169, 170, 176, 177, 178, 206, 263, 265, 268, 271, 382, 386, 389, 391, 475, 478, 482, 486, 487, 488, 496, 497, 502
Jordanian, 55, 149, 289
journalists, 28, 127
Judaism, 40, 42, 43, 199, 203, 204, 208, 210, 212, 213, 216, 225, 226, 227, 421, 422, 423, 424, 425, 426, 427, 428, 429, 430, 431, 432, 433, 434, 435, 436, 437, 438, 440, 441, 442, 444, 445, 463, 530
justice, v, 23, 24, 26, 51, 105, 110, 120, 125, 126, 282, 302, 310, 470, 523, 525, 527
justification, 32, 99, 153, 158

K

Kant, 3
Kazakhstan, 192
Keynesian, 190, 538
Keynesians, 190
killing, 249, 251, 283, 287, 327, 440, 451, 469
King, 539
knowledge-based economy, 179
Kondratiev waves, 569
Korea, 31, 32, 34, 36, 37, 73, 74, 134, 144, 149, 151, 156, 167, 169, 176, 177, 206, 263, 265, 267, 269, 271, 383, 387, 390, 392, 394, 397, 400, 402, 476, 479, 483, 486, 487, 488, 489, 496, 507, 547
Korean, 299, 549
Kurds, 149, 289
Kuznets Curve, 540, 556
Kyrgyzstan, 10, 30, 35, 37, 49, 60, 61, 63, 71, 74, 81, 133, 136, 141, 149, 151, 158, 167, 170, 175, 178, 206, 243, 263, 265, 268, 271, 383, 386, 389, 391, 395, 398, 401, 403, 475, 478, 482, 486, 487, 488, 496, 500, 505, 507

L

labor, 24, 25, 38, 93, 104, 120, 124, 183, 185, 189, 211, 212, 215, 217, 218, 219, 220, 221, 222, 223, 224, 247, 274, 275, 280, 300, 393, 394, 396, 400, 411, 412, 420, 421, 422, 431, 433, 434, 444, 446, 447, 454, 456, 457, 458, 459, 460, 461, 462, 463, 464, 465, 470, 472, 523, 525, 527, 565, 574
labor force, 189
labour, 306, 551
Lafayette, 569
land, 5, 189
landlocked countries, 39, 191
language, xiv, 23, 90, 129, 303, 567
large-scale, xvii, 1
Latin America, 12, 49, 64, 92, 241, 243, 299, 548, 549, 551, 563, 566, 569, 573
Latvia, 21, 30, 34, 39, 71, 72, 74, 77, 79, 80, 134, 141, 149, 153, 158, 163, 167, 170, 175, 184, 206, 246, 263, 264, 265, 268, 271, 382, 386, 389, 391, 395, 398, 401, 403, 475, 478, 482, 486, 487, 488, 492, 493, 496, 498, 499, 503, 522
law, ix, xiii, 25, 28, 37, 49, 59, 63, 97, 98, 103, 106, 128, 130, 135, 147, 183, 241, 283
laws, 8, 53, 63, 148, 189, 217, 243, 273, 285, 287, 291, 337, 374, 415, 426, 442, 453, 471
LDCs, 536
leadership, 284, 560
learning, 286
leisure, 296, 300, 302, 445, 455, 472
leisure time, 296, 300
Less Developed Countries, 535, 541, 543, 571
liberal, 3, 26, 43, 48, 49, 63, 111, 116, 186, 188, 190, 226, 238, 242, 567, 581
liberalism, 26, 46, 55, 116, 234
liberalization, 187, 538, 555
liberation, 155, 581
life cycle, 46, 234
life expectancy, 66, 536
lifestyle, 282, 343, 414, 424, 433, 446, 465
line graph, 136
linear, 35, 67, 173, 174, 191
linear function, 35, 173, 174, 191
linguistic, xv
Lisbon strategy, 179
Lisbon Strategy, 541, 568
Lithuania, 11, 21, 30, 32, 33, 35, 36, 37, 38, 61, 72, 74, 76, 79, 80, 134, 141, 143, 149, 151, 156, 161, 162, 167, 170, 176, 177, 178, 184, 206, 246, 263, 264, 265, 267, 268, 271, 383, 386, 389, 392, 396, 399, 401, 403, 475, 478, 482, 486, 487, 488, 492, 493, 496,☐499, 500, 501, 505, 506, 522
living conditions, 7
local authorities, 282, 343
local community, 294
London, ix, xiv, 63, 529, 530, 531, 532, 533, 534, 535, 536, 537, 540, 542, 544, 545, 547, 548, 549, 551, 552, 553, 554, 555, 557, 559, 560, 561, 562, 563, 564, 565, 566, 570, 572, 574, 575, 576, 577, 578
longevity, 579
Los Angeles, 563
love, xv, 5, 57, 280, 295, 301, 419, 430, 442, 452, 471
loyalty, 284
LSI, 568
LTD, 550
Luxembourg, 21, 30, 34, 61, 73, 74, 78, 80, 81, 134, 139, 149, 152, 158, 163, 167, 169, 176, 206, 246, 263, 264, 265, 268, 271, 383, 386, 389, 392, 395, 398, 400, 402, 475, 478, 482, 486, 487, 488, 492, 493, 494, 495, 496, 499, 500, 505, 506, 522, 553, 581
lying, 51, 86, 94, 107, 112, 121, 206, 249, 251, 255, 277, 287, 318, 417, 428, 440, 451, 469, 523, 525, 527

M

Macedonia, 30, 32, 71, 74, 76, 81, 134, 141, 144, 149, 152, 156, 157, 167, 175, 206, 263, 265, 268, 271, 383, 386, 389, 392, 395, 398, 400, 402, 475, 478, 482, 486, 487, 488, 496, 498, 499, 500, 504, 507

mainstream, 11, 63, 147
maintenance, 189
Malta, 21, 32, 34, 37, 61, 73, 74, 78, 80, 134, 149, 151, 156, 157, 163, 167, 170, 176, 178, 206, 246, 263, 264, 265, 267, 382, 386, 389, 392, 395, 398, 401, 403, 475, 479, 482, 486, 487, 488, 492, 493, 496, 497, 501, 522
manipulation, 51, 249, 251, 253, 254, 287, 324, 523, 524, 527
man-made, xv, 8
manners, 56, 284, 415, 426, 438, 449, 450, 468
manufactured goods, 189
manufacturing, 189, 554
mapping, 56
marginal utility, 561
maritime, 40, 41, 197, 200
market, 23, 26, 27, 40, 42, 46, 49, 50, 81, 87, 88, 94, 108, 111, 112, 117, 121, 123, 145, 186, 187, 197, 212, 228, 234, 242, 248, 280, 281, 286, 293, 362, 433, 446, 464, 579
market economy, 23, 26, 27, 42, 46, 49, 50, 81, 87, 88, 94, 108, 111, 112, 117, 121, 123, 145, 212, 234, 242, 248, 281, 362
market share, 228
markets, 189
marriage, 22, 23, 24, 27, 43, 49, 50, 63, 84, 85, 86, 87, 88, 93, 94, 106, 107, 109, 110, 113, 114, 115, 117, 120, 121, 122, 214, 217, 222, 226, 243, 245, 246, 248, 276, 284, 285, 286, 301, 334, 335, 336, 337, 338, 339, 415, 416, 426, 427, 439, 442, 443, 450, 453, □457, 459, 462, 463, 468, 469, 471, 494, 495
Marx, 534, 574
Marxism, 574
Marxist, 187, 188
material resources, 155
materialism, 379, 380, 384, 391, 392, 481, 482, 483
mathematics, 569
matrix, 67, 207
mature economies, 194
measurement, 65, 127, 530, 541
measures, 9, 53, 66, 86, 187, 292
media, ix, 5, 7, 53, 54, 58, 155, 159
medicine, xvii, 1, 41, 135, 136, 137, 145, 200
meditation, 85, 106, 113, 118, 211, 214, 219, 221, 288, 297, 370, 373, 417, 429, 440, 451, 456, 459, 461, 469
Mediterranean, 539, 540, 546, 568, 577
membership, 39, 40, 41, 190, 192, 193, 194, 197, 199, 200, 209, 212, 214, 215, 218, 220, 221, 222, 223, 224, 273, 274, 406, 407, 408, 409, 410, 411, 421, 422, 433, 446, 456, 457, 458, 459, 460, 461, 463, 464, 568

men, v, x, xv, 12, 25, 29, 51, 64, 98, 100, 103, 131, 135, 136, 137, 138, 140, 142, 145, 155, 286, 379, 380, 384, 388, 389, 390, 477, 478, 479, 480
Mexico, 31, 71, 74, 77, 81, 134, 149, 151, 157, 167, 175, 192, 206, 263, 265, 267, 268, 271, 382, 386, 389, 392, 394, 398, 400, 402, 475, 479, 482, 486, 487, 488, 496, 499, 500, 501, 505, 507, 536, 564, 566
Microsoft, 54, 204, 205, 489, 554
middle class, 376
Middle East, 49, 56, 241, 539, 548, 552, 556, 558, 571, 578
middle income, 35, 173
migrants, 47, 237
migration, 565, 573
militant, 148, 250, 253, 289, 331, 558
military, 229, 230, 273, 286
Millennium, 25, 97, 100, 103, 542
Minnesota, 530
minorities, ix, 7, 8, 10, 22, 59, 81, 124, 150, 153, 186
minority, 9, 11, 53, 54, 61, 148, 250, 253, 289, 331
mirror, 132
misconceptions, 53
misleading, 191
missions, 544
MIT, 531, 557
mobility, 189
models, 144, 191, 215, 561
moderates, 3
modernism, x, 55, 555
modernity, ix, x, 12, 31, 64, 135, 141, 567
modernization, xvii, 1, 11, 28, 29, 30, 37, 40, 64, 92, 130, 135, 136, 137, 138, 140, 143, 145, 183, 199
Moldova, 30, 31, 32, 37, 71, 74, 76, 81, 134, 141, 143, 149, 151, 156, 168, 175, 177, 206, 264, 265, 267, 269, 271, 383, 387, 390, 392, 394, 397, 400, 402, 476, 479, 483, 486, 487, 488, 496, 501, 506, 507
money, 5, 51, 57, 85, 86, 95, 106, 107, 112, 113, 118, 119, 211, 217, 218, 222, 249, 251, 255, 282, 283, 284, 287, 291, 325, 341, 376, 414, 415, 424, 425, 426, 434, 435, 438, 440, 446, 447, 450, 451, 456, 461, 465, 466, 468, 469, 523, 526, 527
Montenegro, 33, 73, 74, 77, 149, 157, 160, 161, 163, 206, 263, 265, 268, 271, 486, 487, 488, 496
Moon, 556
moral standards, 295, 296, 444, 454, 462, 472
morale, 1, 28, 37, 130, 183
morality, 26, 56, 111, 131, 541
Morocco, 11, 29, 35, 49, 50, 60, 63, 64, 73, 74, 81, 134, 136, 138, 149, 167, 170, 176, 189, 206, 243, 247, 263, 265, 268, 271, 382, 386, 389, 392, 475, 479, 482, 486, 487, 488, 496, 497, 501, 507

mortality, 563
Moscow, 569
mothers, 273, 290, 464
motivation, xvii, 1
movement, 24, 38, 47, 48, 93, 108, 115, 116, 118, 119, 184, 185, 209, 211, 215, 216, 217, 218, 219, 220, 223, 237, 238, 247, 274, 275, 300, 309, 393, 397, 402, 412, 420, 422, 432, 434, 445, 447, 454, 455, 458, 460, 465, 470, 472, 523, 525, 526, 527, 581
multicultural, ix, x, xv, 2, 30, 43, 46, 53, 54, 141, 227, 234
multiculturalism, 9, 45, 47, 53, 56, 233, 237
multidimensional, 65
multimedia, 153
multinational corporations, 568
multivariate, xvii, 1, 41, 67, 86, 190, 203, 210, 213, 216, 225, 227, 273. 274, 275, 276, 277, 279, 280, 281, 282, 283, 284, 285, 286, 287, 288, 290, 291, 292, 293, 294, 295, 296, 297, 299, 300, 301, 302
music, 38, 183, 185, 209, 211, 212, 215, 218, 219, 221, 222, 223, 224, 247, 274, 275, 299, 393, 394, 396, 400, 411, 412, 420, 421, 422, 431, 433, 434, 444, 446, 447, 454, 456, 457, 458, 459, 460, 461, 464, 465, 472
Myanmar, 11, 62

N

NAFTA, 278
nation, 188, 286, 288, 417, 428, 571
national identity, x, 1, 41, 200
national income, 189
National Security Service, xiv
National Security Strategy, 573
nationalism, 55, 129, 555, 570, 571
nationality, 12, 64, 148, 283, 415, 425
NATO, 24, 25, 87, 93, 98, 99, 101, 104, 108, 114, 120, 124, 126, 132, 250, 252, 254, 278, 311, 413, 423, 442, 452, 470, 523, 525, 527, 544
natural, 189, 191, 279, 282, 343, 414, 424, 433, 446, 465
natural resources, 189
Nazi Germany, 150
neglect, 191
negligence, 190
neoliberal, 160, 187
neo-liberal, 26, 111, 116
neo-liberal, 187
neo-liberal, 188
neo-liberal, 190
neo-liberalism, 26, 116
Netherlands, 11, 21, 30, 31, 33, 34, 36, 37, 61, 64, 74, 79, 81, 134, 138, 141, 143, 149, 151, 153, 158, 161, 163, 167, 169, 175, 177, 191, 192, 206, 246, 263, 264, 265, 267, 268, 271, 383, 386, 389, 392, 394, 397, 400, 402, 475, 479, 482, 486, 487, 488, 492, 493, 496, 500, 503, 522, 581
New England, 542
New World, 532
New York, 55, 56, 59, 529, 530, 532, 533, 534, 535, 536, 537, 538, 539, 540, 541, 542, 543, 544, 545, 546, 547, 548, 549, 550, 551, 552, 553, 554, 556, 557, 558, 559, 560, 561, 562, 563, 565, 566, 567, 568, 570, 571, 572, 573, 574, 575, 577, 578, 579
New Zealand, 34, 72, 74, 76, 134, 143, 149, 167, 169, 175, 206, 263, 265, 269, 271, 382, 386, 389, 392, 475, 479, 482, 486, 487, 488, 496, 498, 499, 503, 506
next generation, 3, 155
NIE, 573
Nielsen, 529, 556
Nigeria, 11, 34, 35, 36, 60, 61, 63, 71, 72, 74, 76, 80, 134, 136, 149, 157, 167, 169, 170, 176, 177, 206, 263, 265, 269, 271, 382, 386, 389, 392, 475, 479, 482, 486, 487, 488, 496, 498, 500, 503
Nile, 155
non-Muslims, x, 26, 56, 103, 111
non-violent, 10, 22, 61, 80
normalization, 65, 66
North Africa, 49, 241, 578
North America, 79, 540, 555, 572
North American Free Trade Agreement, 572
Northern Ireland, 21, 33, 73, 74, 79, 80, 149, 152, 157, 161, 162, 206, 263, 264, 265, 267, 486, 487, 488, 496, 522
Norway, 11, 21, 30, 59, 64, 73, 74, 77, 80, 81, 103, 134, 139, 149, 157, 167, 176, 206, 263, 264, 265, 269, 271, 382, 386, 389, 392, 475, 479, 482, 486, 487, 488, 496, 497, 500, 503, 507, 522
Notre Dame, 574
nuclear, 274
nuclear energy, 274

O

obedience, 11, 57, 64, 218, 219, 222, 284, 415, 426, 438, 449, 450, 456, 462, 468
obligation, 294
observations, 41, 67, 128, 150, 151, 152, 156, 157, 158, 160, 162, 203, 210, 213, 216, 225, 227
OECD, 59, 536, 537, 542, 553
offenders, 33, 34, 161, 169
oil, 230, 559
Oklahoma, 548
old age, 547
older people, 286, 302, 417, 428
old-fashioned, 190

omnibus, 205
online, 259, 537, 551
open markets, 186
openness, 53, 67, 186, 187, 190, 192
opposition, x, 189
optimism, 10, 61
optimists, 191
oral, 295, 444, 454, 462, 472
orientation, ix, 63
Osama bin Laden, 532
outrage, x
outsourcing, 554
ownership, xi, 44, 45, 46, 47, 48, 85, 102, 106, 112, 119, 189, 233, 234, 235, 236, 238, 239, 240, 249, 253, 255, 293, 349, 419, 430, 444, 454, 472, 524, 525, 528

P

pain, 31, 151
Pakistan, ix, 10, 29, 35, 37, 49, 60, 61, 63, 71, 74, 134, 136, 138, 149, 167, 170, 175, 177, 178, 206, 243, 263, 265, 267, 383, 386, 389, 392, 475, 479, 482, 486, 487, 488, 496, 497, 501, 581
Palestine, 155, 291
parents, 29, 127, 131, 135, 136, 137, 138, 140, 142, 145, 209, 211, 212, 214, 215, 218, 220, 221, 222, 243, 280, 283, 291, 294, 295, 296, 301, 379, 380, 384, 385, 386, 387, 418, 419, 420, 429, 430, 431, 436, 442, 443, 444, 448, 452, 453, 454, 456, 457, 459, 460, 462, 466, 471, 472, 477, 478, 479, 480
Paris, xiv, 230, 529, 532, 534, 540, 542, 553, 577
Parliament, 24, 26, 87, 93, 98, 99, 101, 105, 108, 115, 120, 123, 124, 125, 126, 250, 252, 254, 278, 307, 413, 423, 442, 452, 523, 525, 527, 541
partnership, 539
passive, 43, 226
passports, xiv
pathways, 30, 140
pay-as-you-go, 40, 197
PAYGO, 191
peacekeeping, 301
peer, 581
peers, 65
pension, 39, 40, 191, 192, 193, 194, 197, 199, 295, 353, 406, 407, 408, 409, 410, 542, 547
pension reforms, 40, 191, 197, 199
pension system, 191, 542, 547
pensions, 40, 87, 108, 191, 197, 295
per capita, 66, 192
perceptions, x, 1, 28, 37, 56, 130, 183, 258
performers, 28, 36, 37, 38, 130, 177, 183, 184
peripheral, 529, 561, 574
permit, 26, 44, 61, 105, 116, 228

perseverance, 57, 215, 284, 415, 426, 438, 449, 450, 468
personal goals, 302, 421, 432, 437, 448, 467
personal life, 205
personal values, 22, 77, 131
Peru, 10, 36, 37, 61, 72, 74, 76, 134, 149, 158, 167, 175, 177, 192, 206, 263, 265, 267, 382, 386, 389, 392, 395, 398, 400, 402, 475, 479, 482, 486, 487, 488, 496, 498, 499, 501, 504, 507
Philippines, 30, 32, 38, 71, 74, 76, 81, 134, 141, 143, 149, 156, 157, 167, 175, 184, 206, 262, 263, 265, 267, 383, 386, 390, 392, 394, 397, 400, 402, 475, 479, 482, 486, 487, 488, 489, 496, 500, 501, 505, 507
phobia, 33, 42, 43, 45, 46, 47, 63, 160, 161, 181, 182, 207, 208, 211, 226, 233, 234, 237, 464
planning, 5, 155, 566
play, 3, 41, 53, 155, 200, 230
pluralism, 56, 572
plurality, 55
Poland, 21, 31, 34, 38, 49, 50, 72, 74, 79, 80, 134, 149, 151, 157, 163, 167, 170, 176, 184, 192, 206, 243, 245, 246, 263, 264, 265, 267, 283, 382, 386, 390, 392, 396, 399, 401, 403, 475, 479, 482, 486, 487, 488, 492, 493, 496, 498, 499, 503, 522, 565, 581
polarization, 35, 173
police, 24, 26, 86, 93, 94, 104, 107, 109, 113, 115, 119, 123, 124, 125, 217, 249, 251, 287, 306, 325, 440, 451, 469, 470, 523, 524, 528
policy makers, 43, 227
politeness, 284
political leaders, 127, 288, 417, 429, 436, 448, 466
political parties, 38, 108, 114, 120, 183, 185, 209, 215, 218, 219, 221, 224, 225, 247, 275, 300, 308, 393, 394, 396, 400, 412, 420, 422, 432, 434, 445, 447, 454, 455, 459, 461, 465, 470, 472, 523, 525, 527
political power, 28
politicians, xi, 12, 28, 29, 64, 127, 131, 135, 136, 137, 138, 140, 142, 145, 160, 379, 380, 384, 385, 386, 387, 474, 475, 476
politics, ix, 1, 7, 27, 53, 55, 56, 85, 106, 113, 117, 122, 127, 276, 283, 285, 286, 336, 344, 375, 415, 417, 425, 426, 428, 441, 442, 452, 453, 470, 471, 533, 542, 545, 549, 560, 571, 576
pollution, 282, 286, 293, 414, 417, 425, 428, 438, 442, 449, 452, 468, 470
poor, 35, 40, 47, 51, 173, 186, 191, 197, 237, 249, 294, 297
population, 8, 10, 11, 12, 25, 31, 32, 33, 39, 40, 43, 50, 51, 52, 54, 61, 63, 64, 85, 88, 97, 100, 102, 103, 104, 105, 106, 110, 111, 112, 116, 119, 122,

151, 156, 160, 161, 166, 189, 192, 193, 194, 196, 197, 226, 246, 248, 263, 269, 270, 271, 272, 385, 394, 406, 407, 408, 409, 410, 492, 494, 495, 578
population group, 196
Population Growth Rate, 538
population size, 8, 88, 110, 116, 122, 263
Portugal, 21, 34, 38, 50, 73, 74, 79, 80, 134, 149, 152, 156, 158, 163, 167, 170, 175, 184, 206, 243, 245, 246, 263, 264, 265, 267, 382, 387, 390, 392, 396, 399, 401, 403, 476, 479, 483, 486, 487, 488, 492, 493, 496, 498, 499, 504, 522, 544
positive relation, 46, 47, 234, 238
positive relationship, 46, 47, 234, 238
poverty, 46, 47, 48, 50, 54, 85, 106, 112, 120, 187, 234, 237, 238, 239, 249, 276, 283, 364, 412, 414, 422, 425, 530, 537, 538, 549, 555, 559
power, 28, 188, 189, 282, 343, 364, 540, 572
powers, 148, 155
PPP, 39, 192, 194, 195, 406, 407, 408, 409, 410, 579
prayer, 43, 47, 85, 106, 113, 118, 211, 214, 219, 221, 227, 237, 283, 288, 297, 370, 373, 417, 429, 440, 451, 456, 459, 461, 469
predictors, 39, 190, 191, 568
preference, 86, 94, 107, 114, 118
prejudice, 31, 32, 130, 148, 151, 159, 257
press, 5, 24, 37, 40, 57, 93, 104, 109, 115, 119, 124, 177, 199, 306, 470, 523, 525, 526, 540
pressure, 217, 221, 285, 416, 427, 439, 450, 456, 461, 468
prices, 288
private, xiii, 46, 47, 85, 106, 112, 119, 191, 234, 237, 282, 293, 438, 444, 449, 454, 468, 472
private ownership, 46, 47, 85, 106, 112, 119, 234, 237, 293, 444, 454, 472
probability, 100, 102, 103, 106, 108, 110, 194
production, 46, 189, 234, 578
production function, 578
productive efficiency, 541
productivity, 530, 565
profit, 189
profits, 5, 189
program, xiii, 8, 88, 110, 116, 122, 263, 581
property, iv, x
prostitution, 27, 87, 100, 109, 113, 121, 123, 124, 125, 212, 222, 249, 252, 254, 287, 314, 417, 428, 440, 451, 457, 460, 462, 469, 490, 523, 524, 526
protection, 11, 64, 93, 116, 118, 127, 274, 301, 309, 470, 523, 526, 527
Protestants, 10, 11, 32, 43, 50, 51, 61, 148, 151, 153, 158, 205, 215, 224, 226, 227, 248, 249, 251, 256, 290
public expenditures, 186
public policy, 531

public schools, xiii
Puerto Rico, 72, 73, 74, 77, 149, 206, 263, 265, 267, 278, 486, 487, 488, 489, 496
pupil, 130

Q

questionnaire, 10, 56, 59, 106, 108, 110, 112, 114, 116, 117, 118, 120, 122, 207
questionnaires, 59
quotas, 187

R

race, 25, 27, 33, 35, 45, 47, 48, 51, 87, 94, 97, 98, 99, 101, 104, 108, 115, 117, 122, 123, 125, 126, 148, 166, 168, 172, 173, 174, 180, 196, 211, 217, 219, 221, 225, 233, 235, 236, 237, 238, 239, 240, 250, 253, 255, 289, 328, 418, 429, 441, 451, 455, 459, 461, 470, 524, 526, 528, 574
racism, 33, 42, 45, 46, 47, 48, 129, 147, 166, 168, 210, 233, 234, 237, 238, 239
radicalism, 57
radio, 162
range, 190, 241, 259
rationality, 11, 64
reading, 529
real income, 578
reality, 44, 103, 104, 105, 124, 125, 126, 130, 192, 228
reasoning, ix, 37, 40, 177, 195
recreation, 38, 184, 185, 209, 212, 222, 223, 224, 247, 274, 275, 300, 393, 397, 402, 411, 412, 420, 422, 432, 433, 435, 445, 446, 454, 456, 457, 458, 460, 461, 464, 465, 472
redistribution, 46, 47, 189, 234, 237
reforms, 40, 90, 197, 286, 293, 348, 433, 446, 464
refugees, 301
regional, 541, 569, 571
regionalism, 548
regression, 28, 39, 135, 193
regression equation, 39, 193
regular, 43, 210, 213, 216, 225, 226, 227
regulations, 187
reincarnation, 367
rejection, xv, 10, 43, 45, 46, 47, 49, 54, 61, 63, 78, 90, 151, 226, 233, 237, 243, 245, 256
relationship, x, 24, 27, 35, 36, 40, 41, 46, 47, 88, 93, 110, 114, 121, 123, 130, 173, 174, 188, 189, 197, 200, 234, 238, 280, 285, 288, 294, 296, 297, 334, 337, 415, 426, 443, 453, 471, 530
relationships, 55, 65, 67, 282, 414, 425, 581
relatives, 279, 292, 296, 420, 431, 441, 443, 452, 453, 470, 471

reliability, 269, 270, 271, 272, 539
religions, xiii, xv, 3, 41, 43, 44, 53, 55, 63, 154, 203, 206, 226, 227, 228, 256, 581
religious belief, 27, 40, 85, 86, 94, 106, 107, 113, 114, 117, 118, 122, 199, 206, 276, 335, 372, 412, 422, 445, 455, 471, 473
religious beliefs, 27, 85, 86, 94, 106, 107, 113, 114, 117, 118, 122, 276, 335, 372, 412, 422, 445, 455, 471, 473
religious freedom, x, 11, 62
religious groups, 41, 50, 51, 203, 207, 210, 213, 216, 225, 227, 248, 255
religious traditions, 297, 368
repatriation, 189
repression, 11, 62
research design, 44, 45, 50, 191, 205, 206, 207, 231, 233, 248
residuals, 1, 28, 36, 67, 135, 136, 137, 143, 145, 175, 406, 408, 410
resistance, 31, 40, 141, 197
resolution, 23, 92, 563
resources, 5, 155, 189, 281
responsibilities, xiii, 291, 418, 429, 443, 453, 471
retention, 56
returns, 186
rewards, x
risk, 65, 273, 433, 446, 464
Robert Mundell, 191
Roman Catholics, 10, 61, 81, 151
Romania, 10, 11, 21, 30, 32, 33, 35, 37, 38, 50, 61, 71, 72, 74, 76, 78, 80, 81, 134, 141, 143, 149, 151, 156, 157, 161, 162, 168, 170, 176, 178, 184, 206, 243, 245, 246, 264, 265, 267, 269, 271, 383, 387, 390, 392, 396, 399, 401, 403, 476, 479, 483, 486, 487, 488, 492, 493, 496, 497, 498, 500, 503, 507, 522
Rumania, 103
rural, 40, 41, 199, 200
Russia, 31, 37, 49, 50, 151, 177, 243, 245, 543, 569, 581
Russian, xiv, 23, 30, 38, 71, 74, 77, 79, 80, 90, 134, 141, 143, 149, 152, 158, 162, 168, 175, 184, 206, 246, 264, 265, 267, 269, 271, 272, 383, 387, 390, 392, 396, 399, 401, 403, 476, 479, 483, 486, 487, 488, 492, 493, 496, 499, 500, 504, 507, 567, 569, 581

S

sabotage, 5, 155
safety, 65
sample, 8, 10, 31, 44, 45, 47, 50, 59, 80, 88, 100, 102, 106, 108, 110, 116, 122, 150, 151, 152, 153, 156, 157, 158, 160, 162, 192, 204, 206, 216, 228, 233, 238, 248, 263, 264, 266, 269, 270, 271, 272, 411, 412, 413, 414, 415, 416, 417, 418, 419, 420, 421
sampling, 10, 56, 59
satisfaction, 87, 93, 119, 281, 286, 294, 295, 379, 380, 384, 388, 389, 390, 438, 449, 450, 468, 477, 478, 479, 480
Saudi Arabia, 10, 60, 61, 63, 71, 74, 81, 134, 136, 149, 206, 264, 265, 269, 272, 382, 387, 390, 392, 476, 479, 483, 486, 487, 488, 489, 496
savings, 40, 45, 46, 187, 195, 233, 234, 235, 236, 239, 240, 281, 376, 414, 424, 579
Scandinavia, 190
school, xiii, xv, 3, 29, 85, 92, 106, 113, 118, 127, 137, 155, 186, 188, 293, 297, 373, 436, 448, 466
school enrollment, 186
scientific method, x
scores, 1, 67, 135, 136, 137, 145, 192, 207, 209, 210, 211, 214, 381
search, xv, 23, 44, 90, 147, 228, 529
search engine, 44, 228
searches, 228
Second World, 547
secret, 5, 532
secular, ix, x, 1, 3, 11, 26, 28, 29, 30, 37, 40, 43, 45, 46, 47, 48, 51, 64, 111, 128, 130, 133, 134, 135, 136, 137, 138, 139, 140, 145, 151, 154, 183, 199, 226, 233, 234, 237, 238, 239, 256, 287, 380
secular Muslims, 40, 43, 46, 47, 51, 151, 154, 199, 226, 237, 238, 256
secularism, 1, 3, 26, 45, 46, 47, 111, 135, 136, 137, 144, 145, 234, 238, 239, 254, 256, 257, 258
secularization, 2, 22, 26, 28, 29, 30, 50, 51, 77, 111, 135, 138, 140, 143, 248, 250, 253, 255, 256, 379, 380, 384, 385, 386, 387, 474, 475, 476
security, 22, 24, 26, 40, 93, 109, 116, 118, 123, 125, 126, 127, 197, 222, 285, 295, 307, 416, 427, 439, 450, 456, 462, 468, 470, 523, 525, 527, 547, 548, 570, 571, 577, 578
Security Council, 5
self, 12, 51, 64, 250, 253, 255, 263, 295, 347, 524, 526, 528
self-control, 284
self-expression, 11, 12, 28, 37, 63, 64, 128, 130, 183
self-improvement, 3
Sensitivity Analysis, 549
sentences, 51
September 11 (9/11), 57, 190, 529, 555, 559
Serbia, 33, 38, 72, 74, 76, 134, 149, 158, 160, 161, 163, 168, 184, 206, 264, 265, 269, 272, 382, 387, 390, 392, 396, 399, 401, 403, 476, 479, 483, 486, 487, 488, 496, 497, 498, 499, 502, 506
series, 39, 53, 148, 192, 531, 555, 556, 559, 562, 578

services, xvii, 2, 5, 41, 45, 46, 47, 102, 143, 203, 212, 215, 220, 222, 233, 234, 235, 236, 237, 239, 240, 250, 274, 283, 293, 307, 370, 371, 385, 386, 387, 415, 419, 425, 430, 441, 452, 457, 460, 462, 470, 495, 523, 525, 526, 552
sex, 25, 50, 86, 87, 94, 97, 99, 100, 105, 107, 108, 113, 118, 125, 126, 220, 243, 245, 246, 249, 251, 252, 254, 255, 277, 287, 321, 322, 440, 451, 469, 491, 492, 493, 522, 525, 526, 527
sexual orientation, 8, 49, 63, 148, 241
sexuality, 10, 22, 26, 61, 77, 117
Shahid, 153
shape, 23, 88, 530
shares, 40, 46, 196, 197, 237
sharing, 26, 49, 91, 111, 209, 212, 215, 218, 220, 222, 242, 295, 296, 337, 444, 454, 457, 460, 462, 471, 472
short-term, 188, 189
sign, 11, 62, 154, 190
significance level, 206, 264, 269, 270, 271, 272
signs, 140
similarity, 130
Singapore, 36, 74, 134, 149, 168, 176, 177, 192, 206, 264, 265, 269, 272, 382, 387, 390, 392, 395, 398, 401, 403, 476, 479, 483, 486, 487, 488, 489, 496, 498, 499, 504, 507
skills, 294
slavery, ix
Slovakia, 21, 28, 30, 33, 34, 36, 37, 71, 72, 74, 76, 79, 80, 130, 134, 141, 149, 152, 157, 161, 162, 168, 170, 176, 177, 178, 183, 206, 246, 264, 265, 267, 383, 387, 390, 392, 394, 397, 400, 402, 476, 479, 483, 486, 487, 488, 492, 493, 496, 498, 500, 501, 505, 522
Slovenia, 21, 30, 34, 37, 50, 72, 74, 76, 79, 80, 134, 141, 149, 152, 157, 163, 168, 170, 176, 178, 206, 243, 245, 246, 264, 265, 269, 272, 383, 387, 390, 392, 395, 398, 401, 403, 476, 479, 483, 486, 487, 488, 492, 493, 496, 499, 500, 504, 507, 522, 581
smoking, 86, 94, 107, 112, 121, 123, 249, 252, 254, 287, 321, 523, 525, 526
social attitudes, 218, 296, 444, 454, 462, 472
social benefits, 103
social change, 555
social cohesion, xvii, 1, 2, 28, 39, 40, 130, 137, 144, 179, 186, 199, 541
social development, 188
social exclusion, xv
social indicator, 555
social institutions, x, 17
social order, 576
social organization, 40, 197
social policy, 243, 536, 548

social problems, 214, 217, 220, 221, 276, 412, 423, 435, 456, 461, 466
social security, 22, 24, 26, 40, 93, 109, 116, 118, 123, 125, 126, 197, 307, 470, 523, 525, 527
Social Security, 84, 87, 98, 99, 101, 103, 104, 124, 250, 252, 254, 278, 413, 423, 442, 452, 536, 542
social services, xvii, 2
Social Services, 545, 546
social situations, 269, 270, 271, 272
social systems, 187
social welfare, 29, 30, 38, 102, 131, 135, 136, 137, 138, 140, 141, 142, 145, 183, 185, 209, 212, 217, 219, 221, 222, 223, 224, 247, 275, 300, 379, 380, 384, 388, 389, 390, 393, 400, 412, 420, 422, 432, 435, 445, 454, 456, 458, 460, 461, 465, 472, 477, 478, 479, 480
social work, 40, 194, 197
socialism, 46, 47, 48, 234, 238, 566
socialist, 42, 188, 190, 210
socioeconomic, 556
sociological, 28, 42, 56, 127, 128, 129, 130, 187, 191, 226, 534, 538, 550
sociologist, 28, 37, 130, 183
sociology, xiv, 47, 50, 56, 60, 237, 238, 249, 535, 539, 545, 577
soil, ix, 129
solidarity, x
South Africa, 36, 49, 71, 72, 74, 76, 134, 149, 151, 157, 168, 175, 177, 206, 243, 264, 265, 269, 272, 298, 299, 382, 387, 390, 392, 394, 397, 400, 402, 476, 479, 483, 486, 487, 488, 489, 496, 500, 505, 506
South Asia, 12, 64
South Carolina, 555, 570
South Korea, 553
Soviet Union, 299
Spain, xiv, 10, 21, 31, 32, 34, 39, 50, 61, 73, 74, 76, 79, 80, 134, 149, 151, 152, 154, 156, 157, 158, 163, 168, 169, 176, 184, 206, 243, 245, 246, 264, 265, 267, 269, 272, 382, 387, 390, 392, 396, 399, 401, 403, 476, 479, 483, 486, 487, 488, 492, 493, 496, 498, 499, 503, 506, 522, 581
specialization, 574
spectrum, 48, 92, 112, 114, 116, 117, 118, 120, 122, 241
spiritual, xv, xvii, 1, 3, 214, 276, 412, 423, 435, 459, 466
spirituality, 51, 256
sports, 38, 184, 185, 209, 212, 222, 223, 224, 247, 275, 300, 393, 397, 402, 412, 420, 422, 432, 435, 445, 454, 456, 458, 460, 461, 465, 472
spouse, 280
stability, 10, 61, 293

stages, 35, 36, 40, 41, 173, 174, 199, 200
standard error, 408, 410
Standard error, 194, 405, 406, 407, 408, 409, 410
standards, 143, 295, 296, 444, 454, 462, 472, 554, 563
stars, 30, 141
state intervention, 39, 40, 46, 47, 191, 192, 193, 194, 195, 234, 238
state-owned, 46, 234
Statistical Package for the Social Sciences (SPSS), viii, 8, 41, 45, 47, 51, 88, 89, 90, 91, 92, 110, 116, 122, 194, 196, 197, 198, 199, 200, 203, 204, 205, 207, 208, 209, 210, 212, 213, 215, 216, 225, 227, 233, 236, 237, 240, 248, 249, 253, 255, 256, 257, 258, 263, 303, 565
statistics, 8, 9, 37, 53, 88, 110, 116, 122, 174, 176, 178, 179, 180, 181, 242, 263
stereotype, 45, 46, 233, 237
stereotypical, ix
stock, 39, 193
strategies, 47, 187, 189, 237
stratification, 189
strength, 81, 100, 103, 105, 211, 214, 220, 221, 282, 370, 414, 425, 438, 449, 456, 459, 461, 467
stress, xv, 187, 189
strikes, 23, 26, 51, 85, 88, 92, 98, 99, 102, 104, 110, 116, 121, 123, 124, 126, 292, 345, 418, 430, 445, 455, 473
students, 300
subjective, 88, 110, 115, 119, 228, 296, 297, 376, 419, 420, 431, 440, 444, 451, 454, 469, 472
suicide, x, 88, 110, 211, 222, 249, 252, 254, 287, 316, 417, 428, 440, 451, 457, 460, 462, 469, 523, 524, 526
suicide bombers, x
Sunday, 40, 42, 199, 213
Sunni, ix, 149, 261, 265, 268, 290
supernatural, 275
surplus, 186, 189
surprise, 10, 61
survival, 12, 28, 37, 64, 127, 128, 130, 183, 549
sustainable economic growth, 179
Switzerland, 21, 30, 59, 73, 74, 77, 80, 103, 134, 139, 149, 157, 168, 176, 191, 192, 206, 264, 265, 267, 269, 272, 382, 387, 390, 392, 476, 480, 483, 486, 487, 488, 496, 498, 500, 504, 506, 522, 549, 552, 575
symbolic, xv
symbols, 189
synthesis, 131
Syria, xi, 56, 555
systems, 42, 49, 187, 188, 191, 206, 207, 241, 537, 542, 547, 549, 581

T

Taiwan, 71, 74, 77, 150, 157, 206, 261, 264, 265, 267, 486, 487, 488, 496, 579
Tanzania, 29, 31, 38, 49, 72, 74, 134, 138, 141, 143, 150, 158, 168, 175, 184, 206, 243, 264, 265, 269, 272, 381, 387, 390, 392, 394, 397, 400, 402, 476, 480, 483, 486, 487, 488, 489, 496, 497, 502, 507
Taoism, 261
targets, 530
tariffs, 187, 555
tau, 150
tax evasion, 50, 248
tax rates, 186
taxation, 530
taxes, 1, 25, 28, 29, 30, 31, 37, 50, 87, 94, 97, 98, 100, 105, 108, 113, 121, 123, 124, 125, 130, 131, 135, 136, 137, 140, 142, 145, 183, 218, 220, 246, 247, 249, 251, 254, 277, 279, 286, 287, 296, 313, 379, 380, 417, 428, 439, 442, 451, 452, 463, 469, 470, 495, 496, 498, 500, 501, 502, 504, 506, 523, 524, 526
teaching, xv, 3
technological change, 578
technology, x, 22, 65, 81, 84, 85, 106, 282, 341, 414, 425, 434, 447, 465, 530
television, 23, 24, 93, 110, 116, 119, 278, 308, 470, 523, 525, 527
territory, 155
terrorism, ix, x, xi, 11, 57, 61, 63, 153, 273, 281, 286, 291, 295, 568
terrorist, 62, 190
terrorist attack, 62, 190
terrorists, ix, 289
testimony, 242
TGV, 522
theology, 572, 581
thinking, ix, 40, 41, 46, 47, 48, 49, 57, 197, 203, 234, 237, 238, 243, 281, 297, 441, 452, 463, 470
Third World, 47, 238, 535, 545, 547, 548, 550, 551, 552, 553, 555, 561, 564, 567, 577
threatened, x, 144
threatening, 27, 44, 86, 107, 114, 117, 123, 221, 229, 250, 252, 287, 326, 440, 451, 456, 461, 469
threats, 32, 158
tiger, 551
time periods, 57
TIPS, 534
title, 32, 155, 546, 568
TNC, 189
TOC, 161
Tokyo, 528, 579
Topos, 550, 572

traction, 3
trade, 11, 36, 37, 40, 42, 47, 50, 51, 64, 67, 168, 174, 177, 178, 179, 186, 190, 195, 210, 237, 246, 249, 536, 562, 569
trade union, 47, 237
trade-off, 36, 37, 40, 50, 51, 168, 174, 177, 178, 179, 190, 195, 246, 249
tradition, x, 28, 32, 40, 43, 128, 130, 135, 153, 158, 189, 197, 215, 227
traditionalism, x
trajectory, 35, 126, 128, 173
transaction costs, 554, 579
transfer, 39, 187, 188, 192
transformation, 26, 28, 37, 48, 111, 130, 135, 183, 190, 241
transition, 23, 39, 40, 41, 90, 127, 191, 192, 193, 194, 195, 199, 200, 406, 407, 408, 409, 410
transition countries, 41, 200
transitional economies, 538
translation, 90
transnational, 26, 39, 111, 189, 192, 193, 195
transnational corporations, 189
transparency, 40, 143, 199, 381, 382, 383
transparent, 29, 138, 140
transport, 25, 86, 94, 97, 98, 100, 105, 108, 113, 120, 123, 124, 125, 209, 220, 249, 251, 254, 276, 277, 287, 312, 417, 428, 439, 451, 469, 523, 525, 527
transportation, ix
transpose, 48, 238
Treasury, 530, 547
treaties, 187
Treaty of Amsterdam, 148
trust, 51, 59, 256, 283, 290, 302
turbulence, 574

U

Uganda, 38, 73, 74, 134, 150, 151, 158, 168, 176, 184, 206, 264, 265, 269, 272, 382, 387, 390, 392, 394, 397, 400, 402, 476, 480, 483, 486, 487, 488, 489, 496, 498, 500, 505, 506
Ukraine, 28, 30, 33, 37, 38, 50, 71, 74, 76, 79, 130, 134, 141, 143, 150, 152, 157, 161, 162, 168, 175, 183, 184, 206, 243, 245, 246, 264, 265, 269, 272, 383, 387, 390, 392, 396, 399, 401, 403, 476, 480, 483, 486, 487, 488, 492, 493, 496, 500, 505, 507
unemployment, 189, 191, 276
unhappiness, 281, 438, 449, 467
UNICEF, 537, 538, 562
uniform, 10, 61, 187
unionism, 42, 210
unions, 24, 25, 38, 93, 104, 120, 124, 183, 185, 211, 212, 215, 217, 218, 219, 220, 221, 222, 223, 224, 247, 274, 275, 300, 306, 393, 394, 396, 400, 411, 412, 420, 421, 422, 431, 433, 434, 444, 446, 447, 454, 456, 457, 458, 459, 460, 461, 462, 463, 464, 465, 470, 472, 523, 525, 527
United Kingdom (UK) 10, 11. 50, 55, 56, 61, 64, 176, 191, 192, 243, 245, 532, 544, 548, 556, 559, 543, 577, 581
United Nations (UN), 5, 66, 87, 94, 108, 115, 117, 250, 252, 254, 279, 311, 413, 423, 442, 452, 470, 519, 523, 525, 527, 528, 538, 547, 566, 567, 572, 573, 578
United Nations Development Program (UNDP), 35, 38, 39, 49, 50, 172, 173, 174, 176, 179, 180, 181, 183, 185, 190, 192, 242, 243, 245, 246, 247, 393, 400, 402, 489, 501, 502, 504, 506, 559, 572, 573
United Nations Environmental Programme, 578
university students, 300
urbanisation, 191, 193
urbanization, 39, 40, 195
urbanized, 40, 197
Uruguay, 74, 76, 81, 134, 143, 150, 152, 168, 176, 192, 206, 264, 265, 267, 382, 387, 390, 392, 476, 480, 483, 486, 487, 488, 489, 496, 497, 502, 506
USSR, xvii, 1, 49, 135, 136, 137, 145, 241, 558
Utah, 535, 562, 571

V

variables, 28, 29, 37, 38, 39, 40, 41, 44, 45, 47, 50, 51, 65, 66, 67, 103, 127, 130, 138, 140, 183, 185, 191, 192, 195, 203, 207, 208, 210, 213, 216, 225, 227, 228, 232, 233, 234, 237, 245, 246, 247, 249, 255, 384, 393, 405, 406, 407, 408, 410
variance, 35, 37, 42, 44, 45, 46, 47, 51, 67, 173, 180, 207, 208, 228, 233, 234, 236, 237, 240, 256, 380, 464
Venezuela, 10, 31, 37, 61, 72, 73, 74, 76, 134, 150, 151, 168, 175, 177, 206, 264, 265, 267, 382, 387, 390, 392, 476, 480, 483, 486, 487, 488, 489, 496, 497, 499, 500, 504, 507
Vietnamese, 552
violence, ix, x, xi, 3, 10, 11, 44, 57, 61, 75, 76, 83, 229, 292, 300, 346, 420, 432, 445, 454, 472, 572
violent, 8, 10, 22, 26, 61, 76, 80, 111, 280
vision, 28, 49, 135, 242
voice, 191
voluntary organizations, x
volunteer work, 66, 394
vulnerability, 551

W

wages, 561, 577
Wall Street Journal, 39, 192, 532
war, xiv, 2, 3, 5, 155, 301, 340, 532, 552, 571, 576

War on Terror, 548
Warsaw, 41, 200, 543, 552, 567
Washington Consensus, 26, 111, 186, 187
watches, 220, 229, 230, 282, 414, 424, 438, 449, 467
water, 217, 241, 280, 413, 424, 437, 448, 467
wealth, 189, 578
welfare, 29, 55, 131, 135, 136, 137, 140, 142, 145, 279, 296, 379, 380, 384, 388, 389, 390, 394, 396, 477, 478, 479, 480, 531, 541, 548
welfare state, 531, 548
well-being, 65, 67
western countries, 10, 59
Western countries, 11, 26, 62, 111, 264, 281, 297
Western Europe, 55, 59, 533, 558
White House, 573
wind, 444, 454, 472
windows, 292, 346
witnesses, 70, 75, 156, 261
wives, 276
work environment, 209, 215, 218, 219, 221, 300, 420, 431, 444, 454, 455, 461, 472
working conditions, 285

World Bank, 39, 40, 187, 190, 191, 192, 193, 197, 199, 406, 407, 408, 409, 410, 528, 533, 539, 540, 547, 551, 554, 556, 558, 559, 562, 565, 568, 569, 570, 574, 577, 578
World Development Report, 549, 578
World Resources Institute, 578
World War, 5, 188, 537, 538
World War I, 5, 538
World War II, 5, 538
World Wide Web, 537
WTO, 187, 577

X

xenophobia, 11, 33, 42, 45, 47, 63, 166, 210, 234, 237

Z

Zimbabwe, 11, 29, 37, 64, 72, 74, 134, 138, 150, 152, 157, 168, 175, 177, 206, 264, 265, 269, 272, 382, 387, 390, 392, 394, 397, 400, 402, 476, 480, 483, 486, 487, 488, 489, 496, 497, 502, 506